READINGS IN FINANCIAL
MARKETS AND
INSTITUTIONS

READINGS IN FINANCIAL MARKETS AND INSTITUTIONS

J. VAN FENSTERMAKER

University of Mississippi

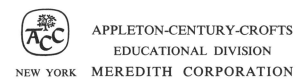

APPLETON-CENTURY-CROFTS
EDUCATIONAL DIVISION
NEW YORK   MEREDITH CORPORATION

To Joan, Van, and JoAnn

Preface

The number of college courses focusing on the institutions and markets that make up the nation's financial system has expanded more rapidly than any other area of finance during the postwar period. This changing emphasis has resulted from the increasing attention being given to the role of the financial system in influencing the national levels of output, employment, and income. Although historically primary attention has been given to the function of commercial banks in the financial system, scholars and policy makers alike are now recognizing the impact of nonbank financial institutions on financial markets. The growing importance of this nonbank area has resulted in numerous recent studies of both new and old institutions (S.E.C., Commission on Money and Credit, etc.).

The continuing expansion of knowledge about our financial system makes it impossible for a single textbook to definitively treat all areas in the field. Consequently, outside reading assignments are typically made to round out courses. The purpose of this readings book is to provide collateral reading material for undergraduate and graduate courses in financial institutions, money and capital markets, and commercial banking.

The articles, which range from the theoretical to the empirical and the descriptive, cover a variety of topics dealing with money and capital markets, interest rates, financial institutions, and international capital markets. They can provide a new depth to a number of areas treated lightly in textbooks and can reinforce major concepts presented in the formal texts. The readings provide more flexibility and realism in financial courses by permitting and encouraging the student to explore beyond the basic course material.

My appreciation is extended to the authors and publishers who generously granted permission to use the articles in the book.

University, Mississippi   J.V.F.

Contents

READINGS IN FINANCIAL MARKETS AND INSTITUTIONS

I

MONEY MARKETS

The money market is a sector of the financial market where the demand for and the supply of short-term funds meet. Rather than one specific location, the term money market, refers to the machinery that is used in the lending and borrowing of money for short periods of time. While the center of the machinery is located in New York, communication networks connect that city to smaller financial centers throughout the nation and the world.

The lenders in the money market consist primarily of the federal reserve banks, nonfinancial corporations, state and local governments, United States Government trust funds, mutual savings banks, savings and loan associations, insurance companies, and pension funds. The largest borrowers of money market funds are the United States Treasury, state and local governments, business corporations, and Federal agencies.

The transfer of money takes place through a variety of instruments that mature within one year and are highly liquid. The first article in Part I examines money markets in general, while the remaining ones analyze particular segments of the market: U.S. Government securities, negotiable time certificates of deposit, bankers' acceptances, commercial paper, federal funds, repurchase agreements, and call loans. Short-term Federal agency securities, state securities, and local securities that mature in less than a year are also traded in the money market; however, they are treated separately in Part II.

1.

The Money Market

JAMES PARTHEMOS

Economic units, such as banks, other business firms, governmental units, or even individuals, find, as a rule, that their inflow of cash receipts does not coincide exactly with their cash disbursements. The typical economic unit finds that on some days its cash holdings build up because receipts exceed outlays. On other days, it might experience a sharp reduction in cash balances because spending outstrips cash inflow.

One of the most important reasons for holding cash reserves is to bridge the gap between receipts and outlays and to insure that a planned stream of expenditures can be maintained somewhat independently of cash inflow. There are, of course, other reasons for holding reserves. In particular, commercial banks and certain other financial institutions must conform with legal reserve requirements.

Maintenance of cash reserves involves cost, either in the form of interest paid on borrowed balances, or in the form of interest foregone on nonborrowed balances which have not been lent out. For many economic units, especially large firms, these costs can assume significant proportions. To minimize such costs, economic units usually seek to keep their cash holdings at a minimum consistent with their working needs and their legal requirements. This may be done by holding almost riskless and highly marketable income-bearing assets instead of cash and by establishing and preserving their ability to borrow, at very short term, at favorable interest rates. The institution of the "money market" has evolved to meet the needs of such economic units.

Reprinted from *Instruments of the Money Market,* 1968, pp. 5–12, by permission of the publisher, the Federal Reserve Bank of Richmond, and the author.

[3]

THE MONEY MARKET

The term "money market" occurs frequently in financial literature and in financial parlance but is seldom defined. In general, the term applies not to one but rather to a group of markets. In early periods of United States financial history, the term was frequently used in a narrow sense to denote the market for call loans to securities brokers and dealers. At other times in the past, it has been employed broadly to embrace some long-term as well as short-term markets. In current usage, it generally refers to the markets for short-term credit instruments such as Treasury bills, commercial paper, bankers' acceptances, negotiable certificates of deposit, loans to or repurchase agreements with securities dealers, and Federal funds.

In general, money market instruments are issued by obligors of the highest credit rating, and are characterized by a high degree of safety of principal. Maturities may be as long as one year but usually are of 90 days or less, and as a practical matter can be arranged to span only a few days or even one day. These instruments accordingly involve small risk of loss due to changes in interest rates. Moreover, the market for these instruments is extremely broad and on a given day can absorb a large volume of transactions with relatively little effect on yields. The market also features highly efficient machinery which allows quick and convenient trading in virtually any volume. Unlike organized securities or commodities markets, the money market has no specific location. Like other important financial and non-financial markets in this country, it centers in New York, but it is primarily a "telephone" market and is easily accessible from all parts of the nation as well as from foreign financial centers. No economic unit is ever more than a telephone call away from the money market.

The heart of the money market's machinery is composed of approximately 45 "money market banks," including the large banks in New York and other important financial centers; about 20 Government securities dealers, some of whom are large banks; a dozen-odd commercial paper dealers; a few bankers' acceptance dealers; and a number of money brokers who specialize in finding short-term funds for money market borrowers and placing such funds for money market lenders. The most important of the last-mentioned group are three major Federal funds brokers in New York.

MARKET PARTICIPANTS

Apart from the groups that provide the basic trading machinery, money market participants usually enter the market either to raise funds or to convert temporary cash surpluses into highly liquid interest-bearing investments. Funds may be raised either by borrowing outright, or through selling existing holdings of money market instruments, or through issuing new instruments. The issue and sale of new money market instruments is, of course, a form of borrowing.

Generally, money market rates are below rates on bank loans even for prime borrowers, and the ability to borrow funds on the open market is correspondingly advantageous. The U. S. Treasury, many commercial banks, large sales finance companies, and well-known nonfinancial corporations of the highest credit standing borrow regularly in the money market by issuing their own short-term debt obligations, which comprise the standard money market instruments. Short-term loans to Government securities dealers, loans of reserves among commercial banks, and Federal Reserve loans to commercial banks are also money market instruments although they do not give rise to negotiable paper.

Suppliers of funds in the market are those who buy money market instruments or make very short-term loans. Potentially, these include all those economic units that can realize a significant gain through arranging to meet future cash requirements by holding interest-bearing liquid assets in place of nonearning cash balances. The major participants on this side of the market are commercial banks, state and local governments, large non-financial businesses, and nonbank financial institutions such as insurance companies and pension funds. Foreign bank and nonbank businesses are increasingly important suppliers of funds.

BY FAR THE MOST IMPORTANT MARKET participant is the Federal Reserve System. Through the Open Market Trading Desk at the New York Federal Reserve Bank, which executes the directives of the Federal Open Market Committee, the System is in the market on a virtually continuous basis, either as a buyer or as a seller, depending on financial conditions and monetary policy objectives. The System's purpose in entering the market is quite different from that of other participants. As noted in greater detail below, the Federal Reserve buys and sells in certain parts of the money market not to manage its own cash position more efficiently but rather to supply or to withdraw bank reserves. The point of this is to provide appropriate monetary and credit conditions for the country at large. In addition, the Federal Reserve enters the market as an agent, sometimes as a buyer and sometimes as a seller, for the accounts of foreign official institutions and for the U.S. Treasury. Overall, the operations of the Federal Reserve dwarf those of any other money market participant.

INTERRELATION AND SIZE OF THE VARIOUS MARKET SECTORS

While the various money market instruments have their individual differences, they are close substitutes for each other in many investment portfolios. For this reason the rates of return on the various instruments tend to fluctuate closely together. For short periods of time, the rate of return on a particular instrument may diverge from the rest or "get out of line," but this sets in motion forces which tend to pull the rates back together. For example, particular circumstances in the market for commercial paper may produce a rapid run-up of commercial paper rates, resulting in a relatively large spread between these rates and rates on Treasury bills. Sophisticated traders note the abnormal differential and shift funds from bills into commercial paper, causing bill rates to rise and commercial paper rates to fall. In this way, a more "normal" or usual rate relation is restored. This process, known as interest arbitrage, insures conformity of all the money market rates to major interest rate movements. This is illustrated in Chart 1–1 which shows a period of generally falling rates and a period of generally rising rates.

A measure of the relative dimensions of the various money market sectors may be obtained from data on amounts outstanding and/or volume of trading. Table 1–1 suggests that in terms of volume outstanding, short-term Treasury issues constitute the backbone of the money market's stock in trade. Moreover, the characteristics of these instruments make them appropriate for inclusion in a wide variety of portfolios and the daily average volume of trading is very large, exceeded only by daily average transactions in Federal funds. Because of their versatility and huge volume, these short-

CHART 1–1

Money Market Rates

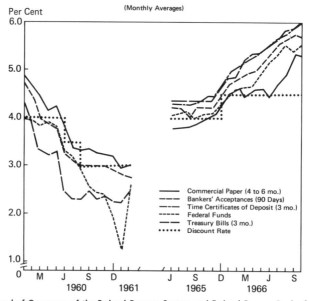

Source: Board of Governors of the Federal Reserve System and Federal Reserve Bank of New York.

TABLE 1–1

Selected Money Market Instruments: Volume Outstanding and Volume of Trading, December, 1966

($ millions)

	Volume Outstanding	Volume of Transactions (Monthly average of daily figures)
U. S. Government securities:		
Treasury bills	64,684	1,868
Other under 1 year	40,534	129
Federal Agencies, within 1 year (including certificates of participation)	12,957	193
Negotiable certificates of deposit	15,642	31
Bankers' acceptances	3,603	265
Commercial paper place through dealers	3,089	
Finance company paper	10,190	
Dealer loans and repurchase agreements	4,314[1]	
Federal funds		5,200[2]

[1]Covers financing only for Government securities and CD's.
[2]Reported through the New York market.

term Governments can safely be accorded the number one position in the hierarchy of money market instruments. Further ranking becomes highly speculative and will not be attempted.

THE MARKET'S SIGNIFICANCE

For individual economic units, the money market provides an important source of short-term borrowing on advantageous terms. Since there is a continuous flow of loan funds through the market, it is possible for borrowers, through successive "roll-overs," or renewals of loans, to raise funds on a more or less continuous basis and in this fashion to finance not only their immediate cash requirements but also their working capital and some of their other capital needs. By bringing together quickly, conveniently, and to their mutual advantage those units with cash surpluses and those with cash deficits, the market promotes a more intensive use of the cash balances held in the economy and perhaps facilitates real capital formation.

The market is especially important to commercial banks in managing their money positions. To this end, banks in the aggregate are large-scale buyers and sellers of most money market instruments, especially Federal funds. In general, the money market mechanism makes for a more intensive use of bank reserves and enhances the ability of the commercial banking system to allocate funds efficiently. By allowing banks to operate with lower margins of excess reserves, it also makes the banking system more sensitive to central bank policy actions.

Finally, conditions in the money market provide an important guide for monetary policy. The money market is an eminently free and competitive market, and the yields on money market instruments react instantaneously to changes in supply and demand. As a result, the behavior of the market provides perhaps the most immediately available indication of the current relationship between credit supplies and credit demands. Changes in rates on money market instruments, in flows of funds through strategic sectors of the market, in the ability of Government securities dealers to finance their inventories, and other objective money market indicators usually figure importantly in assessments of current credit conditions.

THE FEDERAL RESERVE AND THE MONEY MARKET

The Federal Reserve System influences the money market not only through open market operations conducted at the New York Bank but also through the discount windows of the 12 Federal Reserve Banks. Commercial banks that are members of the Federal Reserve System borrow temporarily from the Federal Reserve as an alternative to selling money market securities or borrowing Federal funds to cover cash and reserve deficiencies. Similarly, banks with cash or reserve surpluses can repay outstanding borrowings at the Federal Reserve rather than invest the surpluses in money market instruments. Thus, for member banks the Federal Reserve discount window is an operational part of the market mechanism for matching surpluses and deficiencies. For this reason, the Federal Reserve's discount facilities should be considered part of the money market.

Use of the discount window by banks as an alternative to other money market facilities may have important implications for credit conditions. When banks, on balance, add to their borrowings from the Federal Reserve, new bank reserves are created. By contrast, when banks raise money elsewhere in the money market, existing reserves are simply shifted about in the banking system. Thus, in making reserve adjustments, the choice by bankers between the discount window and other parts of the money market can affect the total volume of reserves in the banking system and may alter overall credit conditions in the economy. The relationship between the discount rate, which bankers pay on Federal Reserve borrowings, and other money market rates influences bankers' choices in this regard. Thus, money market developments that affect this relationship can also affect the outstanding volume of bank reserves.

In adjusting their reserve positions, member banks are free, within limits, to move between the discount window and other parts of the money market as suits their advantage. Their shifts between these two sources of funds tend to bring money market rates into line with the discount rate. For this reason, among others, changes in the Federal Reserve discount rate have important implications for the money market. The year 1966, especially the last half, constituted something of an exception to the general rule that money market rates tend to move closely with the discount rate. Money market rates during this period rose substantially higher than the discount rate, and the differential was maintained because of stringent administration of the discount window.

Of even greater significance for the money market are the daily operations of the Federal Open Market Trading Desk. For many years the Desk has conducted transactions in U.S. Government securities and in bankers' acceptances, and in December 1966 was authorized to conduct operations in Federal Agency issues also. Generally, the Federal Reserve enters the market daily, either to provide new bank reserves through purchases or to withdraw bank reserves through sales. To a large extent, Federal Reserve operations are undertaken to compensate for the movement of other factors, such as float, the Treasury balance, currency in circulation, etc., which affect the volume of reserves held in the banking system. Such operations are undertaken primarily to insure the smooth technical functioning of the market mechanism. But the operations of the greatest importance from the standpoint of the economy are those undertaken to change basic money and credit conditions in the country as a whole. Thus, in addition to its other functions, the money market serves as the mechanism through which the Federal Reserve undertakes to influence basic money and credit conditions.

2.

Floating Debt —
An Instrument
of Financial Policy

FEDERAL RESERVE BANK OF CLEVELAND

Although it is a relatively small segment of gross Federal debt, floating debt performs an important function as an instrument of fiscal and credit policy in the United States. As used here, the term "floating debt" is actually a shorthand expression referring to the outstanding volume of marketable U.S. Government securities that mature within one year. Such issues include Treasury bills and certificates of indebtedness as well as Treasury notes and bonds having only a year remaining until final maturity.[1]

DESCRIPTION OF FLOATING DEBT

The chief characteristic of floating debt is that it is highly liquid, i.e., very close to cash. Because of the nearness to maturity of such securities, changes in market yields result in relatively small price changes. Thus,

Reprinted from *Money Market Instruments*, 1964, pp. 31–40, by permission of the publisher, the Federal Reserve Bank of Cleveland.

[1] Nonmarketable debt such as Savings Bonds has been excluded from the definition of floating debt. Although they represent a potential source of liquidity, the issues themselves are not liquid because they are not marketable and because they are usually held as long-term savings.

TABLE 2–1

Maximum Price Change During Year

Type of Issue*	Issues Due Within:		
	One Year	1-2 Years	2-3 Years
Treasury Bonds			
1961 (through September)	$ .20	$ .41	$ .99
1960	1.52	2.73	4.51
1959 (May through October)	——	1.22	2.03
1958 (through May)	.32	.55	2.03
1½% Treasury Notes			
1961	.44	1.32	1.75
1960	1.34	2.87	5.13
1959	1.13	2.94	3.37
1958	.91	2.69	3.94
All Other Treasury Notes			
1961	.35	.89	1.54
1960	.82	2.71	5.02
1959	.57	1.50	2.62
1958 (August through December)	.97	.39	.98

* Based on an average price derived from prices of all issues outstanding in each of three maturity groups on the last trading day of each month. Prices used were closing bid quotations in the New York market, as published in the monthly *Treasury Bulletin.*

holders of the floating debt have less risk of capital loss in the market than do the holders of longer-length securities. Table 2–1 illustrates the declining amount of price fluctuation in intermediate and long-term Government debt as maturities shorten, using 1958 through 1961 as a sample period.

Size of Debt

At the end of 1945 the floating debt had equaled $70.5 billion, an amount that represented a sharp increase from the prewar levels of $5 billion or less.[2] By way of comparison, at the end of 1963 the outstanding amount of the floating debt reached a near-record high of $89.4 billion. The all-time high of $93.7 billion was reported in August 1962.

Since the end of World War II, the size of the floating debt has been influenced primarily by fiscal policy and debt management, which in turn have reflected the general course of economic activity. The postwar period has been characterized by more deficits than surpluses in the Federal budget, with the result that the total Federal debt on balance has increased. Net new debt frequently has been financed in the form of short-term securities.

[2] The gross Federal debt outstanding today is chiefly a product of World War II. Huge sums of money were required by the war, and the Federal debt subsequently climbed rapidly. The floating debt participated in the general rise, partly for the reason that interest rates on short-term Treasury securities were pegged at extremely low levels during the war, thus providing a relatively inexpensive source of Government borrowing.

Concurrently, some of the long-term Government bonds issued in World War II have been moving closer to final maturity, becoming part of the floating debt. Until the last few years only a relatively small amount of long- and short-term maturing debt was refinanced with longer-term issues. The trend of shortening maturities is reflected quite clearly in the fact that the average maturity of the Federal debt shrank from 107 months at the end of 1945 to a low of just over 50 months in 1960.

In recent years, additional factors have occasionally led to a heavy dependence by the Treasury on short-term issues. Limitations have been set by Congressional action on both the total size of the gross Federal debt and the maximum interest rate that can be carried by Government bonds. Because of the latter limitation, the Treasury at times has been unable to compete for long-term investment funds in the market and has had to depend on short-term borrowing instead. In addition, the debt-size limit occasionally has forced the nation's debt managers to borrow in amounts as small as $100 million, a quantity that is best satisfied by short-term issues such as weekly Treasury bills. Still another factor influencing recent debt management has been the changing ownership of the Federal debt, which is discussed later.

Against this background of postwar developments, the floating debt rose to a year-end peak of $89.4 billion at the close of 1963. Of this amount, Treasury bills accounted for 58 percent of the total, certificates of indebtedness for 12 percent, and Treasury notes and bonds within one year of final maturity for 30 percent. The composition "mix" of the floating debt is not constant. Usually the mix reflects the Treasury's current vehicle for short-term borrowing. In 1961 and late 1963, for example, the Treasury placed increased reliance on short-term notes at the expense of the outstanding volume of certificates.[3] In contrast, in 1958 certificates made up about half of the floating debt.

Ownership of Debt

When the Federal debt was increasing by giant steps in World War II, the debt managers tried to tap excess savings as a chief source of borrowed funds. Thus, individuals and companies bought Government securities in larger amounts than ever before. At the same time, a significant portion of the public debt became lodged in banks and other financial institutions. Although the wartime pattern of debt ownership proved somewhat temporary, it did serve to acquaint various sectors of the economy with an investment in the form of a top-quality, highly marketable debt instrument that

[3] In May 1964, Treasury certificates disappeared completely from the debt structure, at least temporarily.

could be converted into cash at any time.[4] It was soon recognized that short-term Treasury instruments were liquid enough to be considered as virtually cash.

Ownership of the Federal debt has shifted substantially in the postwar period because holders such as corporations have needed funds for expansion of plant and equipment, and other holders have seen an advantage in moving into securities paying a higher return. As a case in point, much interest has been shown in moving temporarily idle funds into liquid securities guaranteeing a short-run return. Short-term Treasury issues have become a likely candidate. The result of the shifting ownership has been that on balance the total demand for long-term Government securities has shown a relative decline, while the demand for short- or intermediate-term issues has increased. Looking at it another way, it is likely that the floating debt has grown partly as a result of the increased demand for such securities.

As of the end of December 1963, the largest proportion of the floating debt, nearly two-fifths of the total, was held by a miscellaneous group of investors including securities dealers and brokers, pension funds, foreign accounts, non-profit institutions, and individuals. Another large segment (over one-fourth) was held by the Federal Reserve banks and U.S. Government agencies and trust funds. About 19 percent of the floating debt was owned by commercial banks, while nonfinancial corporations and state and local governments each held somewhat smaller shares. The remaining volume of this type of Federal debt was spread among insurance companies, savings and loan associations, and mutual savings banks.

FUNCTIONS OF THE FLOATING DEBT

It is important to remember that the floating debt represents both a liability of the Treasury and a source of borrowed funds for the use of the Federal government. Both the funds and the liability have a short life until maturity and will be either perpetuated by refinancing or eliminated by funds becoming available to retire the maturing issues. From the information on the size of the floating debt, it is obvious that a large amount of debt is constantly being rolled over. In some instances the Treasury has taken advantage of the short life of floating debt by issuing securities in regular cycles, with maturities scheduled to be of advantage to potential purchasers and to avoid unnecessary market interference by the Treasury. Important examples would be tax anticipation bills, which are particularly useful for corporations in meeting tax payment obligations, and the regular monthly Treasury bills instituted in August 1963.

[4] This was the consequence of the Treasury-Federal Reserve policy prior to 1959 of "pegging" the interest rates of Government securities at a constant level.

In this article, however, we are chiefly interested in the floating debt as a mass of liquid assets and as a group of extremely important money market instruments. As suggested earlier, such debt is often acquired as an outlet for temporarily idle funds—funds that are frequently earmarked for a future expense. Short-term investors choose floating debt issues because they (1) are close to cash, (2) represent liquidity in investment portfolios, or (3) are an investment that can be used readily to adjust overall liquidity positions. In addition, such issues provide an interest return on funds that otherwise would be idle and non-interest earning. Another advantage to holders of floating debt is the fact that the total quantity outstanding does not decline in times of business difficulties, unlike the supply of private debt forms such as the old call loans. In short, emphasis on efficient use of cash balances and investment reserves has led to a rising demand for liquid assets in the form of the floating debt issues.

The floating debt is also important as a factor in the money market. It undoubtedly helps to link the various financial markets because it is widely held by a diverse group of owners. (The wide ownership and the large size of the floating debt help to explain why such debt constitutes more than half of the trading in the Government securities market.) Shifts of funds in and out of these short-term investments in turn may result in changing flows of funds in the medium- and long-term markets. As a result of inter-relationships of this type, the floating debt can be used as a tool to affect demands for credit and interest rate levels. For example, in 1961–63 the Treasury increased the outstanding volume of Treasury bills in order to hold short-term interest yields at a level that would help discourage short-term capital from leaving the United States and thus help protect our balance of payments position.

The outstanding volume of the floating debt (and the changes in that volume) also can be related to changes in general credit demands. It is unlikely than an increase in the supply of floating debt would absorb capital funds on a permanent basis; such funds might be invested temporarily until a more opportune time for spending, but probably not for periods of more than a year. On the contrary, a number of analysts have suggested that increased investments in the floating debt do not absorb any spending power but only shift it into a near-money substitute, i.e., as a sort of delayed action. However, increased holdings of floating debt do tend to reduce the demand for money and credit, while in most cases causing the velocity (or use) of money that remains in circulation to rise. The acquisition of floating debt may have an additional effect that would actually increase spending. This is the so-called wealth effect, which indicates that additions to liquidity tend to be reflected in increased spending by the holders of liquid assets. The wealth effect is pertinent when an increase in holdings of floating debt is made possible through a reduction in holdings of long-term or fixed assets, for example.

With these functions of the floating debt in mind, the purposes for which various groups hold floating debt may become more clear. Nonfinancial corporations use such debt as a highly liquid but temporary investment outlet for earmarked funds, for example, tax payments. Commercial banks invest in floating debt to provide secondary reserves, the amount of which can be adjusted quickly, easily, and with little risk of capital loss. Most of the miscellaneous owners of floating debt share these or similar investment motives.

The Federal Reserve System, another large holder, buys floating debt issues for another reason, namely, to influence the reserve base of the banking system, and thus, bank credit and the money supply. The Federal Reserve System conducts open market operations mainly in short-term Government securities—the floating debt—because such issues are outstanding in large amounts, are widely held, and can be bought and sold in large quantities without undue effect on prices; in addition, the short-term market gradually transmits these operations to other financial markets.

ASSET MANAGEMENT AND THE FLOATING DEBT

In the past few years, another economic development has had effect on the floating debt, namely, changes in the management of assets. It was mentioned earlier that the outstanding volume of Treasury bills was increased in this period in order to prevent market yields on these issues from declining substantially. The floating debt has been faced with increased "competition" recently in its role as a short-term investment outlet. The volume of funds available for such investment has been expanding rapidly due to rising depreciation allowances for businesses and to the growth in efficiency and sophistication of cash management. Whereas the larger volume of funds formerly might have been channeled into floating debt issues, other earning assets such as time certificates of deposit became attractive because of interest yields that compared favorably with market yields on the floating debt. Moreover, some of the larger short-term investors began to place their funds abroad, frequently in the form of a higher-yielding time deposit in a Canadian bank or in the purchase of instalment paper in Great Britain or Mexico. Outflows of short-term funds to foreign countries of course affected the U.S. balance of payments adversely.

To discourage these outflows, debt management and monetary policy have been directed toward the support of short-term interest rates, particularly on Treasury bills. In addition, other debt management steps have been taken to increase the attractiveness of the floating debt. The outstanding volume of Treasury certificates has declined, as previously noted, because of the diminished usefulness of the issues to many short-term investors. Instead, there has been a noticeable shift to the issuance of more Treasury bills, some offered at regular monthly intervals or in anticipation of corporate tax payments. Finally, the debt managers have worked to offset the shortening of maturities of Government notes and bonds, primarily through advance refundings. These operations have the concurrent results of lengthening the average maturity of the Federal debt while allowing the sale of increased amounts of the more-in-demand Treasury bills. Perhaps as a consequence of these actions, the amount of the floating debt held by insurance companies and nonfinancial owners increased by $5.6 billion from 1961–63, in comparison with a net increase of $3.8 billion in the preceding three years.

A contrasting trend is apparent in commercial bank ownership of the floating debt. Because of the influx of funds into high-cost time and savings deposits, the banking system has sought to cover added expenses partly by obtaining more income from investment portfolios. This, in turn, has meant a shift of bank assets into higher-yielding, less liquid securities. Bank holdings of floating debt issues hit a recent peak of $24 billion in August 1962; by the end of 1963 such holdings had dropped to $17 billion. This development has important implications for the purported inflationary effect of the floating debt.

CYCLICAL IMPORTANCE OF THE FLOATING DEBT

An important question that is perennially raised regarding the floating debt is whether or not it is potentially inflationary. Many observers feel that the inherent liquidity of the floating debt tends to increase the amount of spending in the economy because of the wealth effect mentioned earlier and the fact that such assets can be quickly and easily converted into cash. The floating debt, it is also argued, is said to have an expansionary effect in the economy (1) when it activates the idle cash balances of its purchasers, (2) when its purchase increases the velocity of the remaining money in circulation, or (3) when the Federal Reserve System creates additional bank reserves in order to ensure that a new issue of short-term Government issues will be sold successfully. Finally, many analysts carry the argument further and point out that substantial bank ownership of floating debt tends to insulate the banks from Federal Reserve attempts to restrict the supply of credit in the nation if such a course of monetary policy were deemed desirable. (Banks can easily liquidate or run off floating debt to raise cash. It is also possible that banks may not be too concerned about capital losses that might result from the sale of such assets if loan demands are very heavy.) It would seem that a basic issue regarding the floating debt in this context is that there exists a large volume of assets with many of the characteristics of money, but which cannot be adjusted over the course of the business cycle as can the money supply.

types of liquidity instruments thus seem to have moved in concert in the past decade.

In business declines, if a decline in the floating debt were the result of cash retirements of such debt, both liquidity and the money supply would be increased counter-cyclically. To have the greatest expansionary effect, the cash payments would have to come from the Treasury's cash balance. Any other method of raising the cash—new Treasury borrowing through short- or long-term securities, for example—would offset the injection of cash into the economy. But it has not always happened this way. For example, between July 1953 and August 1955, $16 billion in floating debt was repaid in cash, but three-quarters of this debt was rolled over, or refinanced. Between August 1957 and April 1959, cash retirements amounted to $9 billion, but much more than this was absorbed in new cash borrowing. In 1960 and 1961, cash retirements were very large ($27 billion) but all of the maturing debt was either rolled over or refinanced within a short time of the due date. In all of these cases the net impact of retiring floating debt was at best minimal in terms of expansionary effects.

An examination of the floating debt in a period of inflation results in similar findings. In 1956–57, the wholesale price index rose 6½ percent and the consumer price index rose 6 percent. Within the same period, the floating debt increased by $13.7 billion, or 22½ percent. The last five months of 1957 fell in a recession (as defined by the National Bureau of Economic Research) but the increase in the floating debt during these months was less than one percent.

This leads to the conclusion that until the most recent business downturn the floating debt had not been used, in the past decade, as a counter-cyclical tool. Some of the relative lack of use was no doubt due to the Treasury's burdensome task of handling the ever-present volume of maturing debt, both long- and short-term, while at the same time providing funds for expanding Government programs and operations. Because of this situation, it frequently has been difficult to issue new securities in just the right proportions of various maturity lengths. Instead, there has been a tendency to sell those Treasury issues that gained the quickest market acceptance in the largest dollar amounts.

With the foregoing in mind, it can be seen that any solution to the cyclical adjustment of the volume of the floating debt must be undertaken with the cooperation of fiscal policy, monetary policy, and debt management. Economic logic seems to dictate that in a period of decline in business activity the Federal budget should be in deficit; that this deficit should be financed by an increase in the outstanding volume of short-term Government securities, and that monetary policy should be conducted so as not to absorb other liquidity (such as demand and time deposits) from the economy. Conversely, during inflationary periods, if the Federal budget is in surplus, the nation's debt managers may use the "breathing space" to shift short-term debt into longer-term issues. The resulting decline in the floating debt might make easier the Federal Reserve System's task of controlling the supply of money and credit in that bank reserves would not have to be adjusted in order to offset the liquidity of the floating debt.

Coordination within financial public policy is essential when it is realized that the floating debt has a financial impact at different points of time on different sides of the ownership "fence." The advantages of coordination were well revealed during the 1960–61 recession. During that period the Federal budget posted a deficit, the Federal Reserve System supplied large amounts of reserves to the banking system, and the Treasury refinanced a large amount of debt in short-term issues that appealed to the banks. This coordination was perhaps an important factor in both the shallowness of the recession and the relatively early recovery. In short, the floating debt seems to have performed as an important and effective counter-cyclical weapon from May 1960 through 1961.

3.

Negotiable Certificates
of Deposit

JANE F. NELSON

In February 1961 the First National City Bank of New York announced that it would issue negotiable certificates of deposit in large denominations, and that a major Government securities dealer had agreed to make a market in them. Other money market banks and dealers quickly followed suit, thus preparing the way for the spectacular growth of this new money market instrument.

A negotiable certificate of deposit, or CD, is a marketable receipt for funds deposited in a bank for a specified period at a specified rate of interest. The owner of the CD at the time of its maturity receives both principal and interest, while its readily salable feature enables the original purchaser to retrieve his funds before maturity by selling the instrument to another holder. Time certificates did not originate in 1961, but prior to that time they represented primarily savings-type deposits and were generally not negotiable due either to explicit or tacit agreement or to the absence of a secondary market. Before 1961 about $2.7 billion of these instruments issued to individuals, partnerships, and corporations were outstanding at all member banks, with only about $29 million representing obligations of New York banks. In contrast, today's CD market is dominated by the nation's largest banks, particularly those in New York, and by their corporate customers.

Reprinted from *Instruments of the Money Market*, 1968, pp. 51–58, by permission of the publisher, the Federal Reserve Bank of Richmond.

BACKGROUND

Although traditionally loath to accept corporate time deposits, New York banks were forced by converging postwar economic and financial developments to reconsider their policy. The competitive position of these banks deteriorated during this period, partly because of the slower rate of population growth in the Northeast than elsewhere and partly because of the trend toward industrial decentralization. Of still greater significance was the loss of demand deposits which resulted from the increasing sophistication of corporate treasurers in managing their cash balances. As short-term interest rates rose, the accumulation of temporarily excess cash in demand accounts become more and more costly. Consequently, corporations began economizing cash balances and seeking liquidity through investments in such money market instruments as Treasury bills, commercial and finance paper, and repurchase agreements with dealers. This caused New York banks, which are the principal depositaries of large corporations, to experience a further reduction in their share of total member bank deposits, which fell from 31 percent to under 17 percent between 1940 and 1960.

The negotiable CD was designed specifically to attract corporate deposits and to enable banks to compete more effectively for short-term funds. This explains its immediate popularity with the New York and other money market banks. The volume of all negotiable CD's outstanding at weekly reporting banks was less than $1.0 billion at the end of 1960. By the close of 1966, even after a huge run-off of large denomination CD's in the second half of the year, the volume outstanding amounted to $15.6 billion, larger than the combined volume of bankers' acceptances and prime commercial paper, and second only to Treasury bills among money market instruments (see Table 3–1). As interest rate relationships became more favorable to the issuance of CD's in the first half of 1967, the volume outstanding rebounded sharply and reached a total of over $20 billion in August.

CD CHARACTERISTICS

CD's may be in registered or bearer form, although the latter is more convenient for secondary market trading. Denominations range from $25,000 to $10 million, depending on the size of the issuing bank and the type of CD customer it is trying to attract. Large New York banks seldom issue a CD of less than $1.0 million. By setting a high minimum they hope to attract only those funds which are already destined for the money market. Smaller denominations could encourage the conversion of normal corporate demand balances to CD's, with no resulting benefit to the issuing bank. The CD maturity date is chosen by the purchaser to fit his cash needs and

TABLE 3–1

Volume of Selected Money Market Instruments Outstanding at Yearend

($ millions)

Date	Negotiable Certificates of Deposit* ($100,000 and over)	Prime Commercial Paper	Bankers' Acceptances	Treasury Bills
1960	796	4,497	2,027	39,446
1961	2,782	4,686	2,683	43,444
1962	5,442**	6,000	2,650	48,250
1963	9,579	6,747	2,890	51,539
1964	12,291	8,361	3,385	56,476
1965	16,251	9,058	3,392	60,177
1966	15,642	13,279	3,603	64,684
Percentage Increase	1,865%	195%	78%	64%

* Data covers all weekly reporting member banks.

** December 5 data.

Sources: Board of Governors of the Federal Reserve System, Federal Reserve Bank of New York, and U. S. Treasury Department.

may range from 1 to about 18 months. A survey taken in December 1966 showed that over 75 percent of total CD's outstanding at weekly reporting member banks matured within four months.

Interest is paid on the certificate's par value and accrues on a 360-day basis. The actual rate is, of course, determined by current money market conditions and is competitive with yields on other short-term instruments, within the limitations of legally imposed ceilings. In general, a CD must yield about 25 basis points more than Treasury bills of comparable maturity to attract investors. Certificates bearing popular maturity dates, such as tax and dividend dates, may yield as little as 10 basis points more, however. The size of the issuing bank and the denomination of the certificate also influence the rate. CD's smaller than $1.0 million, for instance, will usually carry a higher rate than larger CD's of comparable maturity. The 20 or so largest "prime-name" banks can ordinarily issue CD's bearing lower rates than those of smaller banks which are not widely known. The latter must usually pay ⅛ to ½ of 1 percent above the prime CD rate to attract funds.

REGULATION Q

The Federal Reserve's Regulation Q, which sets the maximum rates payable on time and savings deposits, is a fundamental consideration in the market for CD's. When short-term open market rates rise above, or even approach, the prescribed ceiling, CD's cease to be competitive. Bankers find it increasingly difficult to replace maturing certificates and are likely to experience large deposit losses as investors turn to higher yielding instruments. As a rule, since "lesser-prime" banks in the regional financial centers must pay a premium over prime CD rates to attract funds, they are the first to be constrained by Regulation Q during a period of rising market rates. Loss of funds may compel banks to make compensating reserve and portfolio adjustments which may be especially costly in the face of rising interest rates.

A situation of this nature occurred in 1966 when the Board of Governors of the Federal Reserve System chose not to revise the Regulation Q ceiling as the general pattern of interest rates rose. This decision was a departure from previous policy. From January 1957 through December 1965 the Regulation Q ceilings were raised four times to allow CD rates to keep pace with yields on other short-term instruments. The latest upward revision, which was concurrent with the discount rate hike in December 1965, increased the maximum rate on all maturities beyond 30 days to 5½ percent. While the new ceiling was substantially higher than rates prevailing at that time, banks increased their rates steadily as they aggressively sought to attract time deposits. The competition for time deposits, in turn, derived from booming economic conditions and a strong demand for bank loans. By mid-1966 many banks were paying the ceiling rate on the shortest maturities, and by August this was common practice. As short-term rates continued to rise, the System allowed CD's to become increasingly noncompetitive. This policy reflected a desire by the System to curtail the expansion of bank loans by restricting the ability of aggressive banks to secure the necessary reserves by attracting new deposits. Between mid-August and November, major U.S. banks lost over $3.0 billion of deposits evidenced by CD's. To compensate for this, banks stepped up the liquidation of investments, thus aggravating the steep climb in money and capital market rates. A change in climate occurred in September, and by the end of the year rates had eased considerably, enabling CD's again to compete effectively with other instruments.

PRIMARY MARKET SUPPLY

Many factors figure in bank decisions regarding the issuance of CD's. Among them are: (1) the profitability of investment outlets for the new funds, and (2) the outlook for renewals at maturity. Most banks establish a flexible limit on total CD's issued. This limit may be expressed in dollars or, more likely, as a percent of total deposits.

Although a bank often will negotiate with a large or important lender, it usually has a set of "base rates," expressed in eighths, for various maturities. The bank adjusts these rates according to its eagerness for new deposits, and a very small change often results in appreciable increases or decreases in deposits. Most large money market banks will issue CD's to any corporation, bank, or organization, other than brokers and dealers, without having had any previous relationship with the depositor. Indeed, CD sales may afford the bank the opportunity to acquire new customers. A bank may refuse to issue a CD if the deposit consists of funds which otherwise would constitute the corporation's normal demand account.

Although CD's are issued by banks of all sizes throughout the country, 58 percent of the total outstanding at the end of 1966 originated in the New York and Chicago Federal Reserve Districts, which contain the majority of prime-name banks. New York City alone accounted for almost 40 percent. Federal Reserve surveys indicate that the CD's of New York and Chicago banks are widely held by corporations for tax and dividend reserve purposes.

PRIMARY MARKET DEMAND

Nonfinancial corporations dominate the demand side of the CD market. On December 5, 1962, for example, they owned an estimated 70 percent of the outstanding volume of CD's. States and political subdivisions held about 16 percent, and foreign governments, central banks, individuals, and others owned the rest. This distribution reflects the appeal of the CD to corporate treasurers who are interested in maximizing returns on their liquid balances.

Like banks, corporations usually set flexible ceilings on their CD holdings, often limiting them to a percent—commonly 25 percent to 33 percent—of their Government security holdings. In addition, a corporation may set a limit on total holdings of a particular bank's CD's. Some corporations prefer the certificates of banks with which they maintain other important accounts or credit lines. Others seek a more impersonal approach and limit themselves largely to prime CD's. Purchasers try to avoid maturity dates falling on a weekend or holiday so that income will not be sacrificed before the funds can be reinvested. If a corporation is reasonably sure it will not need its funds prior to maturity, it may purchase CD's from a smaller regional bank and thereby obtain a higher rate. As a rule, corporations use Treasury bills in adjusting their cash positions, with certificates providing second-line liquidity.

SECONDARY MARKET

Although most original purchasers hold their CD's to maturity, the existence of an organized secondary market is of vital importance to prime-name banks in attracting corporate funds. Participants in this market show a marked preference for prime CD's, chiefly because of their greater marketability. Corporations may enter the market at any time: on the selling side when they wish to raise cash or to realize a profit, or on the buying side when they want maturities shorter than can be acquired in new issues.

Activity in the secondary market expanded rapidly from 1961 through 1964. During that period dealer positions and transactions increased, in part because banks were forbidden by Regulation Q to pay more than 1 percent for time deposits of 30 to 89 days. This forced a downward sloping yield curve on the market, and, of course, provided market participants, including dealers with the opportunity to profit from riding the curve. Under these circumstances, dealers were willing to hold fairly large inventories and the volume of trading increased.

Conditions changed when the Federal Reserve amended Regulation Q in November 1964 to permit banks to pay as much as 4 percent on maturities of 30 to 89 days. The volume of trading slackened noticeably and dealers ceased to add to their inventories. Activity declined further when uniform rates on all CD's were established by another amendment to Regulation Q in December of 1965. This permitted issuing banks to undercut dealer positions by extending maximum rates to shorter and shorter maturities. Flattening of the yield curve eliminated an important source of profit. Daily average dealer positions declined sharply in 1966 to about $103 million from an average of about $230 million in 1964 and 1965, while daily average transactions dropped to $33 million from about $58 million. As short-term market rates dropped below the Regulation Q ceilings in late 1966, dealers became more willing to hold inventories. Daily average positions in the first eight months of 1967 expanded to 307 million and daily average transactions rebounded to $52 million.

The heart of the secondary market is located in New York City. Since many of the largest corporations have accounts at New York banks, transactions between dealers and customers can be conducted with ease. CD's of out-of-town banks are frequently issued and redeemed through their New York correspondents. This saves the investor the trouble and expense of presenting them in another city and thus enhances their marketability. New York City money market banks will lend funds to dealers against CD's at the same rate as for call loans secured by Government securities. Regulation Q permits a bank to extend a loan against its own CD, but only at a rate 2 percent in excess of the rate on the instrument. In no case, however, may a bank purchase its own CD in the secondary market.

Dealers rarely trade in "non-prime" CD's or in those in smaller denominations than $1.0 million. Rates fluctuate in response to money market conditions. Transactions may be either for immediate or regular delivery, but the former predominates since payment is usually in Federal funds. A dealer will bid more aggressively for CD's if he thinks rates will fall and this helps to narrow the spread between bid and asked quotations.

It seems unlikely that the CD market can achieve the smooth functioning of the Treasury bill market at any time in the near future. A main reason for this is the large degree of heterogeneity among CD's as compared with bills. While large blocs of Treasury bills represent a homogeneous asset type with common rates, maturities, denominations, etc., the CD is likely to come in a greater variety of contractual terms. Thus, the feature that makes the CD an effective fund-raising device for bankers also impedes large-scale secondary trading. Issuing banks will rarely split or consolidate certificates to aid secondary market transactions.

EFFECT OF CD'S ON LONG-TERM RATES

The 75 percent increase in time deposits of all insured commercial banks between 1961 and 1965, compared with a 44 percent increase in the four preceding years, can be attributed in large part to the use of CD's. As the volume of CD deposits rose, banks seeking higher yielding investments lengthened the average maturity of their portfolios of Government securities and stepped up purchases of mortgages and tax-exempts. This, in turn, contributed for a time to the maintenance of relatively stable long-term rates in the face of a concurrent rise in short rates.

By the same token, a loss of CD's or even a reduction in their rate of growth tends to put upward pressure on long rates as banks withdraw from the long end of the markets. This pattern was especially noticeable in the tax-exempt market in 1966 when banks in the aggregate ceased to add to their portfolios of municipal securities.

CD'S AND RESERVE ADJUSTMENT

The growth and development of the CD market has provided banks with another means of reserve adjustment. In addition to borrowing from the Federal Reserve, buying Federal funds, or liquidating short-term assets, a bank may now acquire additional funds by simply raising its rate payable on CD's provided, of course, that there is room under the ceiling set by Regulation Q. Thus far, this technique has been used primarily by money market banks. Since owners of short-term funds are responsive to interest rate differentials, banks have been known to acquire millions of dollars of new deposits in a single day by this method. Normally this approach would be used to adjust only those reserve imbalances which do not seem to be of a strictly temporary nature. Banks also make use of the secondary market in adjusting reserve positions, by trading in CD's of other banks in much the same fashion as they trade in the markets for other secondary reserve assets.

4.

Bankers' Acceptances

ROBERT L. COOPER

The volume of short-term credit extended through bankers' dollar acceptances has grown very substantially since the end of World War II. This growth has reflected the unique character of the bankers' acceptance as an instrument for financing the expanding volume of international commerce, as well as the high quality attributed to bankers' acceptances by investors of short-term funds. This article describes the nature of bankers' acceptances and the market for them as it has existed in recent years.

Bankers' dollar acceptances outstanding increased almost steadily from a level of $104 million at the end of May 1945 to a record high of $3,467 million at the end of May 1965; a total of $3,464 million was outstanding at the end of April 1966. The postwar revival in the use of acceptance credit followed a long period of virtual extinction during the depression and war years. After reaching a peak of $1,732 million at the end of 1929, the volume of acceptances outstanding declined steadily with the shrinkage of international and domestic trade in the 1930's. During the four years of United States involvement in World War II, the month-end volume outstanding ranged roughly between $100 million and $200 million. After the war, the renaissance of normal international commerce, the reestablishment of currency convertibility, the new role of the dollar as a free world reserve currency, and the vast capacity of the United States credit market all combined to generate a burgeoning worldwide demand for dollar acceptance financing. As a result, the market for bankers' acceptances has

Reprinted from *Monthly Review*, June 1966, pp. 127–135, by permission of the publisher, the Federal Reserve Bank of New York. This article represents a thorough revision and updating of the article of the same title in the June 1961 issue of this *Review*.

become significantly broader and more active, although it is by no means as important a segment of the total money market as it was in the 1920's, when the volume of other high-grade short-term paper outstanding was much smaller.

BANKERS' ACCEPTANCES AS A FINANCING DEVICE

A bankers' acceptance usually comes into being in connection with a commercial transaction in which a buyer of goods is obligated to make payment to the seller. In most cases the buyers and sellers are importers and exporters who are located in different countries. Consequently, the credit standing of each may well be unknown to the other. Dollar acceptance financing provides a means whereby an internationally known American bank assumes the obligation to pay the amount involved at a given time in the future.

In order to establish the bank's obligation, the importer or the exporter, or an agent of either, draws a time draft on the American bank. The draft is a written order for the American bank to pay a certain amount of money in dollars (the amount involved in the commercial transaction) to a designated recipient (usually the party who draws the draft) on a specified date in the future, say ninety days after the date the draft is drawn or after the date it is presented to the paying bank. Upon presentation, if the draft has been authorized by the bank and is found to be in order as described below, it will be stamped "Accepted" and signed by an officer of the bank. By this action, the bank unconditionally assumes liability for payment of the obligation when it matures (in this case in ninety days) even if the party for whom it was created fails to reimburse the bank. A bankers' acceptance is therefore a time draft drawn on and accepted by a bank.

The process of acceptance financing may be traced through by means of a characteristic example, such as the importation of goods into the United States from abroad. One way of handling such a transaction would be for the United States importer to approach his bank with a request for acceptance credit. If the bank agrees to finance the importer, it would send a letter to the foreign exporter (or to the exporter's bank) advising him that the credit has been established. The letter, generally known as a commercial letter of credit, would authorize the exporter to draw a time draft (described earlier) on the American bank. The bank would agree—for a fee—to accept the draft when it is presented, provided it is accompanied by certain documents related to the underlying commercial transaction, as specified by the importer. Documents most usually required are an invoice describing the goods shipped and the terms of sale, a bill of lading giving evidence of the shipment and conveying title to the goods, and evidence that the goods are insured. When arrangements for the shipment have been completed, the foreign exporter draws the time draft on the American bank and delivers it to his local bank, together with the required documents. At this point, the exporter may receive cash immediately by, in effect, selling the draft to his bank. However, the amount paid for the draft would be less than its face value, in order to compensate the bank for handling costs and risks and to allow a return to the bank on the money advanced on an obligation that does not become payable until sometime in the future. The difference between the face amount of the draft and the amount paid to the exporter by his bank is known as a discount, and the draft is then said to have been discounted.

The exporter's bank then forwards the draft to the American bank, which examines the accompanying documents. If it finds them to be in order, the bank accepts the draft as described above, thereby making it a bankers' acceptance. Once the draft is accepted, the obligation to pay it at maturity is irrevocably assumed by the bank, although the importer is, of course, obligated to reimburse the bank at, or prior to, the maturity of the acceptance.

The acceptance thus created is then ordinarily discounted for the foreign bank by the accepting bank, i.e., the accepting bank pays the face amount less its discount charge to the foreign bank. Even after the deduction of this amount, the foreign bank receives enough to reimburse it for the amount originally paid to the exporter since, as will be recalled, the exporter was paid less than the face amount of the acceptance.

The accepting bank may now retain the discounted instrument in its own portfolio, in which case it is similar to a loan by the bank, and the amount of the discount charged to the exporter's bank becomes an earning to the accepting bank. More commonly, the acceptance would be sold by the accepting bank to an acceptance dealer or directly to a customer of the bank at the prevailing rate of discount for prime bankers' acceptances. In the latter case, the bank would recoup the money paid to the foreign bank and would therefore have "lent" only its name and credit standing to the importer. The ultimate buyer of the acceptance, a domestic or foreign investor, would actually provide the funds to finance the importation of the goods.

There may be variations in this pattern. For example, the terms of the import transaction might call for immediate payment by the United States importer. Instead of drawing a time draft on the importer's bank as above, the exporter might draw a sight draft on the importer. This draft would be a written order for the importer to pay the amount involved as soon as the draft is presented to him. If the importer's bank agreed to extend acceptance credit to him, the importer would draw a time draft on the bank, ordering it to pay the importer the amount involved at a future date, say in ninety days. The bank would accept this draft upon presentation and would discount the resulting acceptance by paying the importer the face amount less the bank's discount charge. The funds would be used by the importer to pay the exporter's sight draft on him, while deferring any drain on the importer's cash until the maturity of the acceptance. By that time, the importer would presumably have received and sold the goods and would be in a position to reimburse the bank in time for it to pay the maturing acceptance.

Under still another variation, if the import transaction calls for payment by the United States importer at a future date, the foreign exporter rather than the importer might make arrangements for the acceptance credit. In this case, the exporter's local bank would request its American correspondent bank to accept a time draft drawn upon the American bank by either the exporter or his bank. The resulting draft would be accepted and discounted by the American bank, as above, and the funds would be paid to the exporter through his own bank. The eventual payment for the goods by the importer, under the terms of the commercial transaction, would enable the exporter to repay his bank, which in turn would repay the American bank in time for it to meet the acceptance at maturity.

A primary function of the acceptance is to enable the seller or exporter of goods to obtain cash as soon as possible (by discounting the acceptance) while permitting the buyer or importer to defer payment, at least until the goods have been received and sold. Acceptance credit may also finance the accumulation of goods by an exporter who has contracted to ship them abroad within a reasonable time (a pre-export acceptance). A foreign exporter, for example, having contracted to sell goods abroad, might arrange through his local bank to have an American bank extend acceptance credit. The proceeds of the credit would be used by the exporter to purchase and ship the goods. Acceptances may also be used to finance an importer until he can distribute the goods into the channels of trade (a post-import acceptance). In this case, an importer may arrange for a bank to finance the temporary carrying of imported goods which are expected to move within a relatively short time.

Dollar acceptances have been used to an increasing extent in recent years to refinance other credit arrangements previously made between buyers and sellers. For example, Japanese trading companies in the United States export goods to Japan and draw either sight or time drafts on the United States agency of a Japanese bank. The agency finances the shipment by discounting the draft for the trading company and then forwards the draft to its home office in Japan, together with the accompanying documents that will be needed by the Japanese importer. The home office of the Japanese bank refinances the shipment, or a number of shipments, by drawing a time draft on an American bank, which accepts and discounts the draft, thereby creating a dollar acceptance. The proceeds of the discounted acceptance reimburse the Japanese bank and/or its agency in the United States for the money it had paid to the Japanese trading company in the United States.

Only about 115 institutions in the United States—those that emphasize international transactions—currently engage in any significant volume of acceptance financing. These institutions include commercial banks and Edge Act Corporations,[1] two private banks, foreign banking corporations, and United States agencies and branches of foreign banks. The bulk of acceptances is created by institutions in New York City and in the San Francisco Federal Reserve District, reflecting the importance of these strategically located banks in the financing of international trade.

A prime bankers' acceptance, i.e., an acceptance of a bank whose name has gained recognition in the marketplace as one that is experienced and active in creating acceptances, is considered an investment of top quality by holders of short-term funds. This quality depends mainly upon the unconditional obligation of the acceptor, which is a widely known and respected, although not necessarily a large, financial institution. Virtually all acceptances trade at the prime rate—not to be confused with the prime rate on direct loans—and rates are not publicly quoted for paper that is not prime. In addition, the drawer of the bank draft and any unqualified endorsers are contingently liable to pay the instrument in the event that it is not paid by the acceptor. The sale of the goods involved in the underlying transaction is expected to generate funds that, directly or indirectly, will enable the borrower to liquidate his indebtedness to the accepting bank. Moreover, the liquidity and attractiveness of prime bankers' acceptances are enhanced by their eligibility for discount or purchase by Federal Reserve Banks if the paper conforms to certain conditions set forth in Regulations A, B, and C of the Board of Governors of the Federal Reserve System. Regulation C describes such commercial drafts or bills as those growing out of any of the following transactions:

(1) the importation or exportation of goods,
(2) the shipment of goods between foreign countries,
(3) the storage of readily marketable staples in the United States or in any foreign country, and
(4) the shipment of goods within the United States.

Acceptances, to be eligible, must mature within six months of the date of acceptance and should bear evidence of the nature of the underlying transaction in a form satisfactory to the Federal Reserve Bank.[2]

---

[1] For a description of the organization and operations of Edge Act Corporations, see the article "Edge Act and Agreement Corporations in International Banking and Finance," this *Review*, May 1964, pages 88–92.

[2] A member bank may not extend acceptance credit of more than 10 percent of its paid-up and unimpaired capital and surplus to any one borrower unless the bank is secured for that portion in excess of 10 percent by documents or other security arising out of the transaction. In addition, the total amount of drafts accepted by a member bank may not amount to more than 50 percent of its paid-up and unimpaired capital stock and surplus except with the special permission of the Board of Governors of the Federal Reserve System, which may allow a maximum of 100 percent of capital stock and surplus; domestic acceptances, however, are limited to 50 percent of capital and surplus in any event. There are no restrictions on the amount a member bank may invest in eligible acceptances of other banks.

TYPES OF ACCEPTANCE FINANCING

International Trade

The bankers' acceptance is especially adaptable to the financing of international trade, and such acceptances constitute the bulk of total acceptances outstanding (see table). Chief among United States imports typically financed by acceptances are coffee, sugar, iron and steel products, wool, and textile products. United States exports most frequently financed by acceptances are grains, machinery and parts, cotton, ores, oil, and iron and steel (including scrap). In connection with trade between foreign countries, acceptances drawn on banks in the United States most frequently finance transactions in oil, ores and metals (chiefly iron), wool, cotton, grains, sugar, and rubber. The volume of dollar acceptances financing international trade has more than doubled since the end of 1960. A major portion of the

CHART 4–1

Estimated Volume of Outstanding Dollar Acceptances Drawn to Finance International Trade Transactions

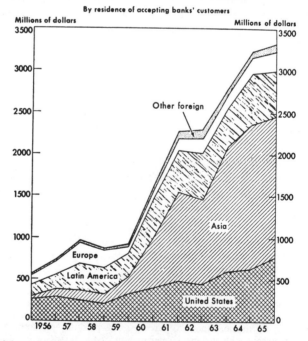

Source: United States Treasury Department report, "Claims on Foreigners." Prior to May 1963 drafts accepted by American banks for foreign customers were shown in this report under "all other short-term dollar claims" (claims other than collections and loans) but are believed to represent nearly all the amounts reported. Since May 1963 acceptances made for the account of foreigners are reported separately.

growth has been in acceptances covering trade between foreign countries (known as third-country trade), which about tripled during the same period. Acceptances against United States imports have also grown steadily, although at a much slower pace, while the year-end volume of export acceptances has been relatively stable since 1961.

As indicated in Chart 4–1, borrowing by foreigners has been primarily responsible for the growth of dollar acceptances during the 1960's, while acceptance borrowing by firms domiciled in the United States has increased much more slowly. The rise in foreign borrowing has been mainly by the Japanese, who have accounted for most of the Asian borrowing shown on the chart. As already indicated, acceptance credit is especially tailored to the financing of international trade, and such trade is of vital importance to the Japanese economy. Moreover, with interest rates in Japan generally at a very high level, Japanese merchants and bankers have intensively utilized the comparatively cheaper credit available in the United States to finance their expanding world trade. To a lesser extent, there has been an increase in the extension of acceptance credit to Latin American borrowers, mainly to finance exports to the United States and a growing volume of trade among Latin American countries. In contrast, the volume of dollar acceptances used by Europeans has been relatively small and reflects the more active utilization by Europeans of financing alternatives, including the Euro-dollar market. European credit has been more readily available and somewhat more competitive with United States credit than Japanese and Latin American credit facilities.

Domestic Trade

Bankers' acceptances have long ceased to be used in significant volume to finance domestic trade. At the close of April 1966, there were only $20 million of acceptances outstanding for this purpose, of which $11 million were created to finance the shipment of goods within the United States and $9 million were to finance the storage of certain types of goods pending their further movement into trade. Business practice in the United States has never encouraged the use of bankers' acceptances to finance domestic shipments of goods since most such transactions customarily involve the direct extension of credit by the seller to the buyer, without any formal written obligation. Furthermore, in order for domestic shipment acceptances to be eligible for Federal Reserve discount or purchase, they must bear a certification that, at the time of acceptance, shipping documents conveying or securing title were attached or were in the physical possession of the accepting bank or its agent. Because of inconveniences related to this requirement and the availability of other means of financing, banks have not encouraged the use of acceptances for the financing of domestic shipments.

TABLE 4–1

Federal Reserve Bank of New York: Dollar Acceptance Outstanding, Classified by Type of Acceptances

In millions of dollars

Type of transaction	1929	1939	1945	1950	1955	1960	1961	1962	1963	1964	1965	April 1966
International trade	1,348	163	128	364	562	1,596	2,273	2,293	2,792	3,321	3,330	3,410
Imports into the United States	*383*	*102*	*103*	*245*	*252*	*403*	*485*	*541*	*567*	*667*	*792*	*829*
Exports from the United States	*524*	*39*	*18*	*87*	*210*	*669*	*969*	*778*	*908*	*999*	*974*	*875*
Goods stored in or shipped between foreign countries	*441*	*22*	*7*	*32*	*100*	*524*	*819*	*974*	*1,317*	*1,565*	*1,564*	*1,706*
Domestic trade	308	54	26	28	63	308	293	171	41	43	35	20
Shipments	*23*	*10*	*12*	*10*	*9*	*13*	*18*	*12*	*9*	*12*	*11*	*11*
Storage	*285*	*44*	*15*	*18*	*54*	*295*	*275*	*159*	*32*	*31*	*24*	*9*
Dollar exchange	76	16	*	2	17	122	117	186	56	111	27	34
Total	1,732	233	154	394	642	2,027	2,683	2,650	2,890	3,385	3,392	3,464

Note: Data refer to end of period. Because of rounding, figures do not necessarily add to totals.
* Less than $500,000.

In the past, most domestic acceptances financed the storage of readily marketable staples such as cotton, grain, rice, wool, or tobacco. To be eligible for Federal Reserve discount or purchase, storage acceptances must be secured by a warehouse receipt or other such document conveying or securing title to the stored goods. Control of the warehouse involved must be completely independent of the borrower, and the goods should be stored pending a reasonably prompt sale, shipment, or distribution into the process of manufacture. Domestic storage acceptances have not been created in any significant volume in recent years (see Table 4–1), partly because direct bank loans, even after allowing for compensating balances, have been cheaper to the borrowers involved, many of whom are able to borrow at the "prime rate." At no time since late 1961 has the cost of acceptance financing (including both the accepting bank's commission and the cost of discounting) been lower than the commercial bank prime lending rate on direct loans. Also, since 1958, the Commodity Credit Corporation has been financing most domestic storage of cotton, thereby minimizing the need for private financing for this purpose. Prior to that time, the seasonal financing needs of cotton merchants generated a large volume of storage acceptances whenever relative costs favored acceptance financing over other sources of credit.

Dollar Exchange Acceptances

Dollar exchange acceptances are time drafts drawn by banks (usually the central bank) in certain foreign countries and accepted by banks in the United States, for the purpose of creating dollar exchange.[3] Thus, dollar exchange acceptances do not arise from specific merchandise transactions but are designed to alleviate seasonal shortages of dollar exchange for certain countries, when it can be reasonably expected that the credit will be subsequently liquidated from funds acquired in the normal course of trade. Most frequently, dollar exchange acceptances have been drawn by Latin American banks. To be eligible for Federal Reserve discount or purchase, dollar exchange acceptances may not have an initial maturity exceeding three months and may only originate in a limited number of countries designated by the Board of Governors.

The volume of dollar exchange acceptances has fluctuated widely (see table), and a total of only $34 million was outstanding at the end of April 1966. Political and economic unsettlement in some Latin American countries has limited the use of dollar exchange acceptances. However, the expanded use of pre-export acceptances in some countries tends to furnish dollar exchange in a less direct manner. In contrast to dollar exchange acceptances, the eligibility of pre-export acceptances for Federal Reserve discount or purchase depends on the existence at the time the acceptance is created of an actual contract to ship specific merchandise. Such a contract gives pre-export acceptances a larger element of self-liquidity.

THE COST OF ACCEPTANCE FINANCING

The cost of acceptance financing consists of a commission charged by the accepting bank plus all charges involved in the handling and discounting of the accepted draft. For prime customers, a much broader group than in the case of direct loans, the commission charge of United States banks is usually 1½ percent, but higher rates may be charged for others. The rate of discount charged is normally the current market bid rate of acceptance dealers for the appropriate maturity. At the end of April 1966 this rate was 5⅛ percent for three-month acceptances. The combined commission and discount charge for three-month acceptance financing for a prime borrower was, therefore, 6⅝ percent. Whether the acceptance commission, the cost of discounting, and charges of intermediary banks are to be paid by the

---

[3] The total amount of dollar exchange acceptances that a member bank has outstanding may not exceed 50 percent of its paid-up and unimpaired capital and surplus, with a maximum of 10 percent for any one drawer (unless fully secured). This limitation is separate and distinct from, and in addition to, the limitations prescribed with respect to the acceptance of commercial drafts (see footnote 2, page 33).

exporter or importer depends upon which party arranged for the credit and on the terms agreed upon in the underlying commercial transaction. In the case of pre-export and post-import financing, however, the exporter or importer, respectively, being in each case both the borrower and drawer of the related drafts, would normally pay the entire cost of financing.

The cost of alternative financing opportunities, particularly direct bank loans, exerts a significant influence on a borrower's willingness to finance his transactions by acceptance credit. Thus, the volume of acceptances would be expected to increase if their cost is low relative to direct loans and to contract when acceptance financing is relatively costly. However, when banks are under reserve pressure, they may actively encourage borrowers to use acceptances rather than direct loans, since the banks can then sell the acceptances in the open market and conserve their cash resources. A comparison of the relative costs of borrowing on acceptances versus direct loans must take into account the indirect cost of maintaining compensating balances in the case of direct loans (where these balances exceed the borrower's normal transactions balance needs). Also, as noted above, the minimum acceptance commission of 1½ percent applies to many borrowers that would not be able to obtain direct loans at the prime rate.

The cost of borrowing in foreign countries may exert some influence on the volume of dollar acceptances. For example, large active borrowers might shift their demand for credit to London if the cost of sterling acceptances dropped significantly below that on dollar acceptances, assuming there were no British governmental restrictions on the financing of foreigners. The borrower would have to repay in sterling and would normally hedge the exchange risk by buying sterling for future delivery. He would therefore have to consider the premium or discount on forward sterling in arriving at the net cost of sterling acceptance financing.

BANKERS' ACCEPTANCES AS AN INVESTMENT

The tested safety and high degree of liquidity of prime bankers' acceptances make them a useful vehicle for the investment of short-term funds. Over the years, market rates for bankers' acceptances have usually been only slightly higher than those for United States Treasury bills (see Chart 4–2), and at times the Government's bills have actually sold at the higher of the two rates. It should be noted that the prime character of an accepting bank's name does not necessarily depend on the size or location of the bank but rather upon the bank's reputation for knowledge and skill in the field of international lending. Thus the acceptances of well-known smaller banks with proven experience in the financing of international commerce are traded in the market at the same rate of discount as those of the largest accepting banks. This is quite different from the situation in the

CHART 4-2

Yields on Treasury Bills and Bankers' Acceptances

Note: Data are monthly averages of daily market yields.

Source: Board of Governors of the Federal Reserve System.

market for negotiable time certificates of deposit, where a substantial concession may be required to induce investors to buy the paper of a smaller bank despite a long history of prudent and successful management. As noted above, the liability of endorsers and drawers, the presumption (except in the case of dollar exchange acceptances) of the existence of a self-liquidating commercial transaction underlying each credit, and eligibility for Federal Reserve discount and purchase all contribute to the quality of prime bankers' acceptances, although the importance attached to each of these considerations varies among different types of investors. Corporate buyers of acceptances, for example, reportedly rely almost solely on the obligation of the accepting bank.

THE MARKET FOR BANKERS' ACCEPTANCES

Bankers' acceptances are negotiable and marketable short-term obligations. As such, they may be bought or sold in the market, competing with other short-term obligations such as Treasury bills, commercial paper, and negotiable certificates of deposit for the attention of investors. Participants in the market are acceptance dealers, accepting banks, foreign and domestic investors, and the Federal Reserve System.

Dealers

Six dealers regularly conduct operations in bankers' acceptances. All are located in New York City and all but one actively deal in other money market obligations. These dealers stand ready to buy and sell various maturities of prime bankers' acceptances at publicly posted prices which are quoted in terms of a rate of discount from the face value of an acceptance. Rates of discount are higher for longer than for shorter maturities because of the increased risk of a rise in interest rates over the longer period and because of the need to provide increased compensation to the ultimate investor for committing his funds for a longer period of time. The rate of discount at which dealers will sell acceptances is normally ⅛ percent lower than the rate at which they will buy acceptances of the same maturity. This spread is the principal source of the dealers' income. Although the spread is currently larger than dealers' spreads for some other short-term obligations, acceptances are relatively costly to handle because of the number of individual acceptances usually involved in a single transaction and because of the need for careful examination to establish the eligibility and negotiability of the instruments. For example, a dealer buying $1 million of acceptances might have to process thirty or forty individual instruments while a similar transaction in Treasury bills might involve only one piece of paper.

Dealers' bid quotations also provide the basis for the discounting of acceptances by accepting banks, as described above, and any changes in dealers' posted rates are immediately communicated by the banks to their customers and correspondents around the world. Dealers' quotations are usually not subject to very frequent changes since the cost of discounting acceptances is an important consideration in the negotiations constantly under way between international buyers and sellers of goods. Subject in varying degree to these considerations, dealers' rates for bankers' acceptances fluctuate in response to persistent movements in other short-term money rates and to marked changes in the level of dealers' portfolios. During 1965, there were only nine occasions when a majority of the dealers changed their rates.

Prior to November 1963, dealers conducted their operations in bankers' acceptances with very small portfolios in relation to turnover. During the years 1955 through 1962, the annual average position of all dealers combined ranged from about $5 million to $35 million and dealers frequently found it impossible to satisfy the demand of investors. More recently, however, dealers have been carrying much larger portfolios, aver-

CHART 4–3

Dealers' Portfolios of Bankers' Acceptances, 1962-65

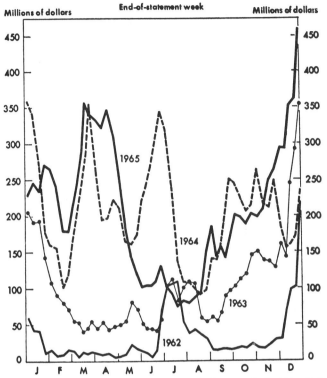

Source: Reports of acceptance dealers to the Federal Reserve Bank of New York.

aging around $210 million in 1964 and 1965 (see Chart 4–3). Portfolios have been particularly heavy over most quarterly statement dates, reaching a record level of $461 million on December 31, 1965, as banks relied heavily on sales of acceptances to help meet seasonal reserve needs. Dealer portfolios are usually financed by call loans from commercial banks in New York City. The Federal Reserve Bank of New York also makes funds available to dealers under repurchase agreements at times when the reserve effect of such accommodation is consistent with the System's general monetary objectives.

Accepting Banks

Investors who buy acceptances do not normally resell them but hold them until maturity so that, once placed with investors, relatively few acceptances find their way back into the market. Therefore, dealers are dependent upon sales by accepting banks as the major source of supply. The willingness of banks to sell their acceptances varies significantly with changes in general money market conditions. Accepting banks tend to hold a large proportion of their own acceptances in their portfolios in the absence of pressure on bank reserves. On the other hand, when banks are under pressure they may sell newly created acceptances or those that they had been holding. This enables them to recoup the funds paid out when they discounted the paper and to transfer the extension of credit from themselves to the ultimate buyers of the acceptances. Thus, between the end of 1964 and the end of 1965, when banks came under gradually increasing pressure, the percentage of outstanding acceptances held by accepting banks (including acceptances of other banks) dropped from 49.4 percent to 36.1 percent. This meant that acceptances were more readily available to other investors than in 1964. Many banks sell some portion of their acceptances directly to their customers, bypassing the dealer market, although the banks depend upon the dealers to absorb their bills at times of money market strain and lagging investor demand. Both accepting and nonaccepting banks are also important buyers of other banks' acceptances as an investment when rates on acceptances are relatively attractive vis-à-vis other short-term obligations.

Foreign Investors

Investors abroad have long recognized the highly safe and liquid character of bankers' acceptances and consider them attractive assets for the placement of short-term funds. Consequently, foreign central and commercial banks and, to some extent, nonbank foreign investors, are important holders of bankers' dollar acceptances. Accepting banks have among their foreign bank customers many who require acceptances with two bank names. These acceptances are obtained predominantly through swapping operations with the dealers. The accepting bank sells its own acceptances to the dealer at his buying rate, say 5¼ percent, and buys back the acceptances of other banks at the dealer's selling rate (5⅛ percent). When selling these acceptances to a foreign bank, the selling bank generally adds its own endorsement, charging ⅛ of 1 percent commission for assuming the related risk. The net rate of discount to the foreign bank, based on the above example, would be 5 percent. Foreign demand for endorsed bills have reportedly been declining somewhat in recent years as nonbank investors, and even some banks, have been satisfied with only one bank name, so that swapping operations presently constitute a smaller proportion of total dealer activity than they did in the late 1950's.

Domestic Investors

Domestic investors in acceptances, other than commercial banks, include savings banks, insurance companies, and a variety of nonfinancial corporations. Corporations have shown increasing interest in acceptances in recent years whenever acceptance rates become sufficiently attractive relative to rates on Treasury bills, commercial paper, and negotiable time certificates of deposit. Some disadvantages of acceptances as an investment, such as their comparatively small and oddly denominated amounts, lack of convenient maturities, and uncertainty of adequate supply, are being overcome to some extent. The large-scale refinancing of Japanese trade through dollar acceptances, for example, has produced larger acceptances in round amounts (most frequently $100,000) and with attractive maturity dates, covering not one but many individual shipments of goods. These multiple-type acceptances are purchased by the Federal Reserve Bank of New York, provided the underlying transactions are adequately described on each acceptance or on an attachment thereto. Also, the larger positions regularly carried by dealers since late 1963 have increased the possibility that an investor can obtain sufficient bills of a desired maturity at a given time to satisfy his requirements. Domestic investors buy unendorsed acceptances almost exclusively, depending upon the obligation of the accepting bank to provide sufficient safety.

Federal Reserve Bank Operations

The Federal Reserve Bank of New York purchases a substantial volume of acceptances in the dealer market for its foreign correspondents and for its own account. Acceptance holdings for foreign accounts amounted to $144 million as of December 31, 1965. The Federal Reserve Bank (whether for its own account or for foreign accounts) buys only endorsed bills, i.e., acceptances bearing three names—those of the acceptor, of the drawer, and in most instances, of an endorsing dealer. The rate of discount to the buyer of endorsed bills is $\frac{1}{16}$ percent less than that for two-name paper (unendorsed bills). In addition, the Federal Reserve Banks guarantee payment of acceptances purchased for the account of foreign correspondents, charging $\frac{1}{8}$ of 1 percent for the guarantee. Therefore, if endorsed bills were offered by dealers at $5\frac{1}{16}$ percent discount, the net return to foreign correspondents on acceptances purchased for them by the Federal Reserve Bank of New York would be $4\frac{15}{16}$ percent. The contingent liability arising from the guarantees is participated among the twelve Reserve Banks —as are the proceeds of the guarantee fees.

In 1955, the Federal Open Market Committee authorized the Federal Reserve Bank of New York to purchase acceptances from the dealers for its own account and to make repurchase agreements with nonbank dealers against bankers' acceptances, as part of its open market operations for the Federal Reserve System. The purpose was to encourage the postwar redevelopment of the bankers' acceptance market and to demonstrate official recognition of the high quality and usefulness of these instruments in international finance. This participation in the market also affords the Reserve Bank added opportunities to examine the quality of the paper flowing through the market as an aid to the fulfillment of the System's traditional supervisory function in this area. In recognition of the increasing importance of bankers' acceptances, a separate Acceptance Department was created at this Bank in January 1964.

Outright holdings of acceptances by this Reserve Bank for its own account have been deliberately limited to marginal amounts. At the close of 1965, the peak of year-end seasonal pressures on the money market, these holdings amounted to $75 million, only 2 percent of total acceptances outstanding.

CONCLUSION

Bankers' dollar acceptances have become increasingly important in the financing of international trade during the postwar era, and particularly since the mid-1950's, as acceptances have proved their usefulness to borrowers, banks, and investors. The market for these instruments has also grown and acceptances have been competing with other short-term investment media. Much of the growth has reflected the intensive use of the instrument by the Japanese. The prospects for further growth in the use of acceptances seem good, particularly if they should come to be utilized more intensively by the developing countries of South America, Africa, and Southeast Asia.

5.

Prime Commercial Paper

JOY S. JOINES

Commercial paper, defined to include what the *Federal Reserve Bulletin* calls "commercial and finance company paper," means short-term promissory notes which some large businesses sell at a discount to dealers or institutional investors to raise cash. Since the notes are usually unsecured and bear only the name of the borrower, only large corporations with impeccable credit ratings are able to obtain funds in this way. Notes are issued in multiples of $1,000, ranging upward from $5,000 to $5.0 million or more. Maturities commonly vary from four to six months on paper placed through dealers and from 3 to 270 days or longer on paper placed directly with investors.

Since about 1920, when the General Motors Acceptance Corporation pioneered in the placing of paper directly, commercial paper has been distinguished as either dealer paper or directly placed paper. The first type is sold by borrowers to dealers, who in turn sell it to investors in the market. Directly placed paper, on the other hand, is sold by the borrower to the lender directly, by-passing the dealer. Due to the necessity of maintaining a trained staff and a complex network of contacts, only about 17 large finance companies placed paper directly in 1964.

Reprinted from *Instruments of the Money Market*, 1968, pp. 56–66, by permission of the publisher, the Federal Reserve Bank of Richmond. This article relies heavily on the following excellent work: Richard T. Selden, *Trends and Cycles in the Commercial Paper Market*, National Bureau of Economic Research, 1963.

HISTORY OF COMMERCIAL PAPER

The history and development of commercial paper have been almost exclusively American. In its early use, commercial paper was issued by a buyer to a manufacturer or seller in payment for a specific shipment of goods. The recipient usually endorsed the note and sold it either to his own bank or to a dealer specializing in such paper. Early notes carried the names of both maker and payee and were issued in odd denominations, according to the value of the transactions.

In the 1920's, borrowers included manufacturers, wholesalers, and retailers in a wide variety of product lines. Virtually all paper was handled by dealers, and banks held by far the largest portion of the amount outstanding. In our system composed of thousands of banks, and especially before the Federal Reserve System was established in 1914, the commercial paper market allowed banks, in effect, to make loans outside their local market areas. Thus, commercial paper provided a means whereby idle bank funds could be shifted from one part of the country to another.

Although no secondary market existed, banks regarded commercial paper as highly liquid because the impersonal nature of the loan usually meant there would be no requests for extensions or renewals. Moreover, this paper provided banks with an opportunity to diversify their portfolios with instruments whose rates of interest compared favorably with yields on alternative investments. Since borrowers were subjected to thorough credit investigations and were required by dealers to maintain open credit lines with banks equal to the amount of paper outstanding at all times, commercial paper proved a relatively safe investment. After 1914 paper defined as "eligible" by the Federal Reserve had the additional advantage of being rediscountable when banks needed temporary funds.

Although the volume of directly placed paper increased during the 1920's, the total volume of commercial paper outstanding declined. One factor contributing to this decline was the great bull market in stocks in that period. Rising stock prices apparently induced many borrowers to meet their needs for working capital by floating new stock issues. Furthermore, between 1929 and 1933, when the demand for short-term business credit was drastically curtailed as the economy plunged into depression, the outstanding volume of commercial paper fell off precipitously.

From 1933 to the outbreak of World War II, the amount outstanding increased rapidly, reflecting general economic improvement, the growing role of consumer credit in financing consumer durables, and the rapid rise of finance companies. The dearth of consumer goods during World War II produced a decline in outstandings from 1940 through 1945. In the postwar period, however, the amount outstanding rose from 178 million in January 1946 to $13,279 million in December 1966. The first half of 1967 witnessed an unusually rapid increase, particularly of paper placed through dealers. A number of corporations apparently began to sell commercial paper for the first time. After the experience of late 1966 when bank credit became very tight, several corporate treasurers apparently decided to reduce their reliance on banks by opening up alternative sources of financing.

DIRECT PLACEMENTS

The rapid growth of directly placed paper justifies separate treatment of this sector of the commercial paper market. General Motors Acceptance Corporation began placing paper directly in 1920, and in 1934 several other large finance companies adopted the practice. From the beginning, the amount of direct paper outstanding grew impressively. There was a sharp, though temporary, decline during the Great Depression, but by 1935 direct paper outstanding equaled the volume of dealer paper. During World War II direct placement ceased entirely but was resumed shortly after the end of hostilities. The volume of directly placed paper grew rapidly and has exceeded by a substantial margin the volume placed through dealers in recent years.

Before World War II commercial banks were reluctant to hold directly placed finance paper, partly because bankers tended to look askance at paper which arose mainly out of financing consumption rather than production. This reluctance has continued down to the present time but for a substantially different reason. In the postwar period bankers themselves have entered the consumer credit field, and some have hesitated to finance competitors in this area. The large growth in alternative secondary reserve assets, such as Treasury bills, has also been a factor. As a result, the great bulk of direct paper is held outside the banking system and chiefly by non-financial corporations.

MARKET CHANGES

Practices in the commercial paper market today differ significantly from those in the 1920's. For one thing, the number of both dealers and borrowers has declined sharply. This has been due mainly to the emergence of large finance companies which rely almost exclusively on the commercial paper market for their working capital. Many of these companies place their paper directly, but those which borrow chiefly through dealers tend to dominate the dealer market. Unlike industrial and commercial companies, finance companies that borrow through dealers are in the market for large amounts on a more or less continuous basis. Dealers have, therefore, found it more profitable to work with these and have tended to neglect borrowers who seek funds only intermittently. As the number of borrowers has declined, competition among dealers has become more intense and attrition has taken its toll.

The growth of finance companies has contributed to improving the quality and liquidity of commercial paper, broadening the range of maturities, and lowering the cost of borrowing. The quality of dealer paper has improved because the fewer borrowers per dealer permit closer scrutiny of the financial condition of borrowers. Moreover, the borrowers themselves are larger, better-known firms with higher credit ratings. Liquidity has improved because direct borrowers frequently agree to repurchase their notes in case lenders should suddenly need cash. Maturities have become better suited to investor purposes as direct borrowers have tailored terms to coincide with investors' needs for cash. For instance, maturities of less than 30 days are becoming increasingly common on directly placed paper, and it has been estimated that about half of the volume of this type paper falls within this maturity range. Large corporations and insurance companies, seeking to economize cash balances, are the most frequent purchasers of this so-called "week-end paper." To some extent this practice has also been adopted by finance companies which place their paper through dealers.

The cost of borrowing has been lowered as a result of increased competition among dealers and also as a result of declining interest rates during the Great Depression. In the 1920's, dealer commissions were usually a flat ¼ of 1 percent, regardless of maturity. This amounted to an annual cost of 1 percent on three-month paper. When short-term interest rates dropped below 1 percent in the 1930's, the commission comprised more than half of the total borrowing cost. In the face of this movement dealers abandoned the flat commission and began to derive their compensation from the varying spread between buying and selling prices. For some years now the minimum spread for the best paper has been ¼ of 1 percent per annum, which, on three-month paper, is only one-fourth of a flat ¼ of 1 percent commission applied to that maturity.

BORROWERS

The number of manufacturers, wholesalers, and retailers borrowing in the commercial paper market decreased from about 2,250 in 1922 to about 241 in 1964. Firms in these lines tend to rely heavily on bank credit for working capital and turn to the commercial paper market for supplementary funds only in times of heavy seasonal or cyclical demand. Most of their paper is placed through dealers. Figures are not available, but probably the number of such borrowers has increased since the credit stringency of 1966.

By contrast, the number of finance companies borrowing in the commercial paper market increased from 9 in 1920 to 137 in 1964. Although

This will acknowledge the receipt of

Fenstermaker: READINGS IN FINANCIAL MARKETS AND
                           INSTITUTIONS

My comment is:

Name: ....

Institution: ....

City and State: .... *Zip* ....

━━━━━━━━ **APPLETON-CENTURY-CROFTS** ━━━━━━━━

It is our pleasure to send for your consideration a copy of

Fenstermaker: READINGS IN FINANCIAL MARKETS AND
                           INSTITUTIONS $ 5.95

which we have just published. We hope you will examine it soon and
will send us your comments on the attached card.

List prices are given for your convenience.

APPLETON-CENTURY-CROFTS,

Division of Meredith Corporation

these companies represented only 32 percent of all borrowers in the market, they accounted for about 87 percent of outstanding commercial paper at the end of 1960. Today, there are three major types of finance companies— sales finance, personal loan, and business finance companies. From the standpoint of both the number that borrow and the amount of paper outstanding, sales finance companies are the most important. In 1964, 74 such companies borrowed in the commercial paper market. The 17 large firms which placed paper directly accounted for 72 percent of all commercial paper outstanding in 1964.

Personal loan companies, business finance companies, and the smaller sales finance companies rely primarily on bank credit to meet their short-term needs and use the dealer paper market as a supplementary source. Nevertheless, they probably account for the bulk of dealer paper outstanding. The large sales finance companies, on the other hand, rely primarily on directly placed commercial paper for short-term funds and use banks as a sort of backstop.

ADVANTAGES TO BORROWERS

The principal advantage of commercial paper over bank credit is its lower cost. Its total cost is generally below the prime rate on bank loans, even after allowing for the dealer commission charge (or the administrative cost of direct placement) and the cost of maintaining open credit lines as insurance. From 1960 through 1962, the cost advantage of commercial paper was particularly pronounced and explained in large part the sharp increase in commercial paper outstanding which occurred during that interval. The recurrence of an enlarged cost advantage in the first half of 1967 is perhaps a significant factor behind the sharp increase in outstandings during that period.

Evidence of borrower sensitivity to cost differentials is provided in Chart 5–1 which shows the behavior of outstanding dealer paper over the course of several business cycles. Dealer paper normally declines during the expansion phase of a cycle and expands sharply during the recession phase. This is due mainly to the fact that bank rates are sticky while commercial paper rates are flexible, closely paralleling the fluctuations in Treasury bill rates. As rates fall during recession periods, borrowing through the commercial paper market becomes relatively cheaper and borrowers shift from bank loans to paper. The converse tends to occur during expansion periods.

In 1966, however, a somewhat different situation occurred. While the spread between the prime rate and the dealer paper rate narrowed, as in past expansions, the volume of paper outstanding increased. This reflected the booming economy and tremendous demand for funds by corporations, which supplemented bank loans with sales of paper.

CHART 5–1

Rate Differences and Commercial Paper Outstanding

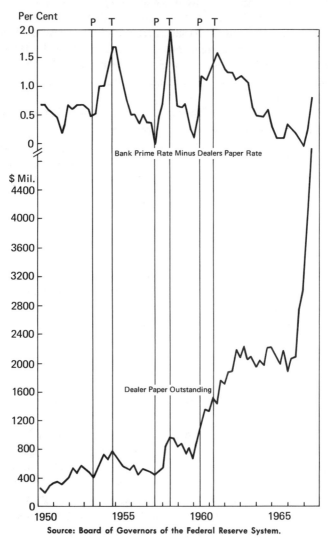

Source: Board of Governors of the Federal Reserve System.

A factor on the supply side is also important in explaining the cyclical behavior of dealer paper. Banks still hold a sizable fraction of dealer paper, and during recessions, when customer loan demand slackens, they become more willing to supply funds to the dealer paper market. In the expansion phase, on the other hand, banks prefer to extend customer loans and, therefore, buy less dealer paper than during recessions.

LENDERS

The most striking change in the lender side of the commercial paper market since the 1920's has been a substantial increase in the number of nonbank investors and an accompanying decline in the role of banks. This trend has been especially pronounced in the postwar period. Although banks hold more paper now than ever before, their share of the total market has been drastically reduced.

The most important new lenders in the market are the nonfinancial corporations, which have gone heavily into commercial paper for several reasons. In the 1930's they were greatly attracted to commercial paper when banking legislation forbade the payment of interest on demand deposits. Corporations found a ready substitute for demand deposits in direct paper which finance companies would tailor to mature on dates corresponding with corporate cash needs. Directly placed paper may be "tailor-made" in regard to amount and maturity, and dealer paper can usually be obtained with the desired characteristics. In addition, most direct placers of paper now have a "gentleman's agreement" with the investor to buy back the paper should the latter experience a sudden need for funds. In recent years, rising interest rates have induced corporate treasurers to look intensively for appropriate short-term investments. While short-term Government securities, especially Treasury bills, are the most popular means of employing temporary cash funds, commercial paper offers a greater yield for only a small additional risk. Corporations are increasing their commercial paper holdings and presently hold over half of the paper that is directly placed.

In addition to banks and nonfinancial corporations, trust funds, college endowment funds, and insurance companies also find commercial paper an attractive investment.

6.

Federal Funds

JIMMIE R. MONHOLLON

One of the most important money market developments in the post-war period has been the growth of trading in Federal funds, or deposit balances held with Federal Reserve Banks. While the intricacies of this market are familiar only to those who use it in the course of conducting day-to-day business, a general knowledge of the market is necessary to a proper understanding of our financial system.

WHAT ARE FEDERAL FUNDS?

Arriving at a workable definition is not easy. There are a number of rather closely related transactions involving the use of immediately available funds which might conceivably be classified as Federal funds transactions.

After several years of intensive study, the Federal Reserve System brought out a "New Series on Federal Funds" in its August 1964 *Bulletin*. In this series, which is published regularly in the *Bulletin* and made available each week in a statistical release (H.5), a useful distinction has been made between interbank Federal funds transactions and related transactions with Government securities dealers. This article will deal only with interbank transactions.

For present purposes, a Federal funds transaction is defined as any transaction between banks involving the purchase (borrowing) or sale (lending) of member bank deposits at Federal Reserve Banks for one busi-

Reprinted from *Instruments of the Money Market*, 1968, pp. 27–34, by permission of the publisher, the Federal Reserve Bank of Richmond.

ness day at a specified rate of interest. A supply of Federal funds arises because some member banks have reserves on a given day in excess of reserve requirements. Demand arises because other member banks on the same day run reserve deficits. Since excess reserves yield no income, many bankers try to convert them into earning assets, if they are large enough to be significant. This may be done in a variety of ways, but if the excess is expected to be only temporary, a practical approach is to sell Federal funds. If the bank then suddenly loses reserves, it may need to take no further action since the reserves it has sold will be returned automatically the next day; or if the reserve loss has been very large, it may enter the market as a buyer.

Thus, the Federal funds market affords the banker a maximum degree of flexibility in adjusting his reserve position so as to come out with a minimum of average daily excess reserves over the course of the reserve averaging period—one week for reserve city banks and two weeks for country banks.

PARTICIPANTS IN THE MARKET

Historically, most of the trading in Federal funds has been conducted by relatively large member banks. This is natural since participation in the market requires a very close and almost constant scrutiny of the bank's money position, and only the larger banks have found it economical to employ full-time money position managers. Another factor has been the market practice of trading funds only in very large blocks, typically in units of $1.0 million. In recent years, however, trading in smaller units has become increasingly common as smaller banks have become more active in the market. Their greater participation has been due, in part, to the increasing cost of holding idle funds as interest rates have risen. Also important has been the growing readiness of large banks to trade funds in smaller blocks as an accommodation to their correspondents.

LOCATION OF THE MARKET

In a sense, the Federal funds market is nationwide inasmuch as excess reserves may arise anywhere in the country. Since funds in even multiples of $1,000 may be transferred instantaneously and without cost over the Federal Reserve's wire transfer facilities, any member bank is potentially a part of the nationwide network.

Although funds may originate anywhere and be dispatched anywhere, the focal point of the market is New York City. Because of its prominence as a commercial, industrial, and financial center, a system of communications has developed which makes it convenient to channel a majority of transactions through New York. In the first place, the money market banks in New York are generally net buyers of Federal funds, and out-of-town banks have come to look on New York as a place where funds can readily be sold. Second, these New York banks serve as correspondents for banks all over the country and are therefore in a position to know where Federal funds can be found and where they are needed. Third, some of these banks stand ready to accommodate their out-of-town correspondents by absorbing or supplying funds regardless of their own reserve positions. Fourth, two stock exchange firms and one large bank in New York City serve as brokers, receiving reports on sources of and demands for funds, and bringing buyers and sellers together.

DEVELOPMENT OF THE MARKET

The practice of trading in balances at the Federal Reserve originated in New York City in the early 1920's. Soon local markets developed in other Federal Reserve cities and financial centers. Trading between Federal Reserve Districts, however, remained quite small during the market's early years. Federal funds trading of all types died out almost completely in the 1930's when banks were laden with excess reserves and remained dull in the 1940's when the Federal Reserve System helped finance the war by standing ready to buy Government securities at fixed prices. Banks preferred to make reserve adjustments in the latter period by purchasing and selling Government securities, since Federal Reserve practices eliminated the risk of market loss.

It was not until the resumption of flexible monetary policy in the early 1950's that the market in Federal funds began to revive. With the unpegging of bond prices and increased borrowing from the Federal Reserve, banks began to seek alternative means of adjusting reserve positions. The secular rise in interest rates also encouraged them to manage their reserve positions more carefully.

Although the basic function of the market has not changed much since the 1920's, the breadth of the market has expanded greatly. This has been largely due to the rise of accommodating banks and to their willingness to trade in relatively small blocks of funds.

TYPES OF TRANSACTIONS

Federal funds transactions are of three basic types. The most common is the so-called "straight" transaction which involves a purchase and sale of Federal funds on an unsecured, overnight basis. Closely akin to the straight transaction is that in which the overnight borrower (buyer) of Federal funds pledges appropriate collateral to secure the loan.

Repurchase agreements, the third type, are sometimes, though not frequently, used in interbank transactions. As a rule, banks dislike the extra bookkeeping, trouble, and expense that is involved. Under the terms of the repurchase contract, the borrowing bank obtains Federal funds by selling securities to the lending bank. The borrower then repays the "loan" the following day by repurchasing the securities generally at the same price plus interest at a rate specified in the contract. Some repurchase agreements are made for more than one business day, but these are generally made with Government securities dealers and are therefore outside the scope of this article.

MARKET MECHANICS

The mechanics of market transactions vary, of course, with the type of transaction and the location of the buyers and sellers. Since straight transactions constitute the bulk of trading, the mechanics of this type of operation are of primary interest.

Trading between banks in New York City is customarily accomplished by a simultaneous exchange of checks. The selling bank gives the buying bank a check drawn on its balance at the Federal Reserve and receives in exchange a check which the buying bank writes on itself. The draft on the Federal Reserve Bank is paid immediately, but the check which the buying bank writes on itself is collected through the clearing house and is not paid until the following day. Thus, the buying bank has use of the selling bank's excess reserves for one day and for this pays the agreed rate on Federal funds. The interest on the loan is normally included in the clearing house check which the buyer gives the seller.

Exchange of checks is confined largely to New York City. Procedures differ somewhat in other areas, but, in general, trading within a single Federal Reserve District may be described as follows: After arranging the terms of the transaction by phone, the seller notifies the Federal Reserve Bank to transfer the agreed-upon amount from his account to that of the buyer. The notification may be made by letter, by wire, or by telephone followed by written confirmation. The following day the procedure is reversed. The interest on the loan may be paid with the principal in the return transfer, or it may be remitted separately either by debiting or crediting a correspondent balance, or if no correspondent relationship exists, by cashier's check.

When the transaction is between banks in different Federal Reserve Districts, the actual transfer is made over the leased-wire facilities which connect all Federal Reserve Banks and branches. After arranging the details of the transaction by telegraph or telephone, the selling bank orders the Federal Reserve Bank in its District to debit its reserve account and to wire instructions to the buyer's Federal Reserve Bank to credit a like amount to its account. Repayment is made the following day by reversing the procedure. Normally, the interest on the loan is not included in the return wire because the Federal Reserve levies a charge on wires involving amounts not in multiples of $1,000. Interest, therefore, is generally paid by separate check or by debiting or crediting a correspondent balance.

These procedures apply also to secured transactions, with only one additional step. The borrowing (buying) bank offers collateral by pledging securities which will be held in custody for the account of the selling bank until the transaction is reversed.

IMPORTANCE OF THE FEDERAL FUNDS MARKET

The Federal funds market is important to bankers because of its prominent role in the process of reserve adjustment. As already mentioned, many member banks try to hit their required reserve targets as accurately as possible because deficiencies may be charged at the discount rate plus 2 percent and the existence of excess reserves means loss of income.

The Federal funds market, of course, is not the only means of reserve adjustment. A bank needing additional reserves may sell Treasury bills or other marketable paper, borrow from the Federal Reserve, call a loan with a Government securities dealer, or raise dealer loan rates to encourage the dealers to refinance elsewhere. To a large extent a bank's choice depends on relative costs and also on the length of time the additional reserves will be needed. If funds are needed for only a very brief time, the bank may buy Federal funds or borrow from the Federal Reserve to avoid the cost involved in selling short-term assets one day and buying them back the next.

The Federal funds market is also important to the monetary authorities because it speeds up the transmission of changes in monetary policy. This is true because the shifting of reserves from banks with excesses to those with deficits permits banks in the aggregate to stay more fully invested. In other words, a given volume of banking business can be conducted with a smaller volume of excess reserves. This minimizing of excess reserves results in less slippage between a change in monetary policy and the resulting response.

The market also supplies useful information to policy-makers, since it is highly sensitive to changes in the demand for and supply of funds. The Federal Reserve personnel who manage the System's Open Market account watch closely the rate and the volume of transactions because these are excellent barometers of ease and tightness in the central money market.

RATE DETERMINATION

As with other free market rates, the rate on Federal funds depends on supply and demand conditions in the market. To a greater extent than other rates, however, it is influenced by special considerations which cause it to fluctuate more widely than other money market rates. One of the special factors is the Federal Reserve's system of reserve requirements. Reserve requirements must be met on a daily average basis over a reserve averaging period of one week for reserve city banks and two weeks for country banks. Since excess reserves cannot be carried over from one reserve averaging period to the next, banks tend to dispose of their excess reserves for whatever price they can get as the reserve averaging period draws to a close. Country banks tend to hold on to excess reserves during the first part of their reserve period and release them to the market only when it becomes clear that they will not be needed. Consequently, the Federal funds rate tends to break sharply every other Wednesday as country banks close out their reserve settlement period. This pattern is not invariant, but is nonetheless quite common and helps explain some of the sharp day-to-day movements in the Federal funds rate.

Broader movements of the Federal funds rate are determined by the same factors influencing other money market rates. Consequently, the Federal funds rate is closely related to other money market rates. The rate with which it is most closely related has differed over time, however. As

CHART 6–1

Selected Money Market Rates

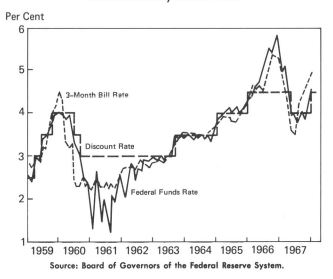

Source: Board of Governors of the Federal Reserve System.

CHART 6–2

Federal Funds Rate and Bank Reserve Position

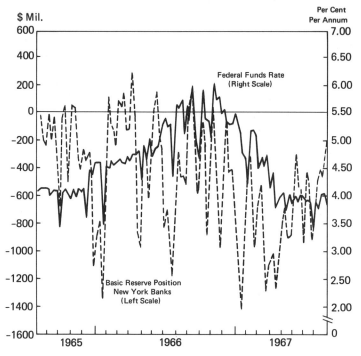

Source: Board of Governors of the Federal Reserve System.

Chart 6–1 shows, the Federal funds rate stayed very close to the discount rate during the tight money period of 1959. Bankers used the Federal funds market primarily as a means of reserve adjustment and switched back and forth between the discount window and the Federal funds market. Strong demand for reserves pushed the Federal funds up to the discount rate, which acted as a ceiling because bankers refused to pay more than the discount rate for Federal funds. As money market conditions began to ease in 1960, the three-month Treasury bill rate fell sharply below the discount rate. But the Federal funds rate continued to be more closely associated with the discount rate than the bill rate, since bankers had few bills to liquidate and continued to buy heavily of Federal funds in order to reduce their borrowing from the System. Once bank liquidity was restored, banks could use the bill market to a greater extent as a means of reserve adjustment. With the bill rate well below the discount rate during 1961 and early 1962, the Federal funds rate fluctuated more closely around the bill rate.

A basic change in rate relationships occurred in 1965. For the first time since the 1920's, Federal funds began to trade at rates consistently above the discount rate. As Chart 6–2 shows, this development was closely associated with a tightening of monetary policy as evidenced by a shift from free reserves to net borrowed reserves. The new rate relationship apparently reflected the emergence of a more expanded role of the Federal funds market. In addition to serving as a means of reserve adjustments, banks apparently began to rely to a greater extent on the Federal funds market as a permanent source of reserves to support an aggressive program of asset expansion. When monetary policy became increasingly tight in 1966, the Federal funds rate followed the bill rate and the differential between the discount rate and the Federal funds rate reached as much as 1¾ percent.

The influences on the Federal funds rate and its relationships with other money market rates are intricate and complex. For this reason it is difficult, if not impossible, to identify rigorously the factors affecting the demand and supply of Federal funds. A useful approach, however, is to focus on the concept of the "basic reserve position," which takes into account both the volume and distribution of reserves in the banking system. Weekly data on the basic reserve positions of the large money market banks are now published in the *Federal Reserve Bulletin*. The basic reserve is defined as excess reserves minus borrowings from the Federal Reserve System and net Federal funds purchases. It attempts to measure how large a surplus or deficit in reserves would have been had it not been for these two forms of corrective action. As a rule, a large basic reserve deficit for an important group of banks will be associated with heavy demand for Federal funds and vice versa. The above chart suggests that the rate on Federal funds tends to vary directly with the basic reserve deficit of the money market banks in New York.

7.

Dealer Loans
and Repurchase
Agreements

JIMMIE R. MONHOLLON

Loans made at very short term to large Government securities dealers constitute an integral part of today's money market mechanism. These loans resemble closely brokers' call loans, which for many years were the chief money market instrument of interest to banks. In this type of loan, the dealer retains title to the securities but transfers them to the lender or his agent as collateral for the duration of the loan. Although a sizable fraction of dealer loans are demand obligations, some have specific maturities ranging from one day to several months. The loans with stated maturities are often extended under a contract involving the actual sale of securities to the lender by the borrowing dealer, with a commitment on the part of the latter to repurchase the securities within a specified time at the same price plus a stipulated interest charge. Such contracts are termed repurchase agreements, or simply RP's.

Banks and other money market lenders frequently use dealer loans and repurchase agreements as a convenient means of making short-run adjustments in their liquid assets positions. Thus, these loans compete with other

Reprinted from *Instruments of the Money Market*, 1968, pp. 35–42, by permission of the publisher, the Federal Reserve Bank of Richmond.

money market instruments that are widely used for the same purposes, i.e., Treasury bills, Federal funds, negotiable certificates of deposit, bankers' acceptances, prime commercial paper, and discounts and advances at the Federal Reserve. Like these other instruments, dealer loans possess unique characteristics which assure them a special niche in the money market.

ROLE OF GOVERNMENT SECURITIES DEALERS

The tremendous growth of the Federal debt over the past few decades has been accompanied by the development of a highly organized U.S. Government securities market in which a huge volume of business is transacted daily. The smooth and orderly operation of this market requires a vast network of machinery communications which focuses on a core of about 20 specialized Government securities dealers who operate principally in New York City. Dealers include a few large banks with their own dealer departments as well as nonbank dealers. A number of brokers, commercial banks, and other intermediaries handle transactions for customers, but most of these institutions turn ultimately to the specialized dealers to execute their orders. Dealer banks, of course, transact such business through their own dealer departments.

The market for U.S. Government securities is not an organized exchange but rather an over-the-counter market in which dealers buy and sell from their own inventories or positions at their own risk. This feature greatly increases the liquidity of Government securities, since the brokerage function of matching buyers and sellers in multimillion-dollar transactions would prove difficult, if not impossible, at least in some maturities.

A broad and active market in Government securities is extremely important to the U.S. Treasury, which faces heavy competition from many other borrowers in today's money and capital markets. Dealers play an important role in the Treasury's multi-faceted financing operations. During Treasury cash and exchange financings, dealers usually take substantial amounts of the new issues into position, hoping to place them with investors as demand develops. Without dealer participation these periodic deluges of new issues would be quite difficult for the market to absorb and would tend to depress prices temporarily to unrealistic levels.

Government securities dealers also occupy a strategic position in the machinery through which the monetary authorities influence the availability and cost of money and credit. Through them the Federal Reserve conducts its open market purchases and sales of Government securities to influence member bank reserves. The effects of Federal Reserve operations thus impinge first on Government securities dealers and spread from them to all financial markets.

DEALER FINANCING

Dealers finance the major portion of their sizable positions or inventories with borrowed funds, and consequently total positions and total financing fluctuate closely together, as may be seen in Chart 7–1. Data on dealer financing include nonbank dealer borrowing and dealer bank use of "own bank funds," or funds allocated by the bank to its own dealer depart-

CHART 7–1

Dealer Positions and Financing

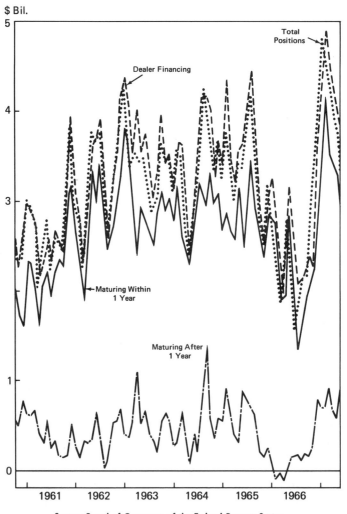

Source: Board of Governors of the Federal Reserve System.

ment. Discrepancies between the two series result primarily because data on positions are reported on a commitment basis while data on financing are reported on a delivery basis. The lag between the commitment to buy or sell and actual delivery is sufficient to account for significant discrepancies, even when monthly averages of daily figures are used.

LENDERS

Dealer financing requirements are ordinarily quite large. Their daily average needs in 1966, for example, were $2.7 billion, varying from a low of $2.0 billion in March to a high of $4.2 billion in December. Since borrowing is such an important part of dealers' activities, one of their prime concerns each day is to secure loans to meet their requirements at the lowest possible cost. Competition forces them to search the country for new sources of funds at low interest rates and to fashion attractive loan arrangements adapted to the needs of each different type lender.

Suppliers of dealer loans include nonfinancial corporations, commercial banks, and miscellaneous lenders such as state and local governments, foreign institutions, insurance companies, and—when necessary to implement monetary policy—the Federal Reserve Bank of New York. Chart 7–2 shows that from September 1960, when the Federal Reserve began collecting statistics from all primary dealers, through 1966, corporations have supplied on the average about 41 percent of dealer financing. Banks in New York City supplied about 25 percent, banks elsewhere about 22 percent, and other lenders about 12 percent. Because rates charged by out-of-town lenders are generally lower than those charged by New York City banks, dealers usually try to tap out-of-town sources early in the morning and turn to the New York banks for their residual needs later in the day.

Many lenders, especially corporations, prefer repurchase agreements to the more conventional type loan. From the corporate standpoint, repurchase agreements afford good rates of return as well as convenient maturities, which range from one day to several months and are easily tailored to coincide with corporate needs for cash. Another attractive feature is the absence of market risk; the borrowing dealers carry the risk by contracting to repurchase the securities at a specified price.

Commercial banks outside New York City are another important source of funds. In contrast to New York banks, most of these banks will not lend to dealers when their reserve positions are so low that they may subsequently be forced to borrow in the Federal funds market. However, in regional centers for Federal funds, such as Cleveland, Indianapolis, Boston, Philadelphia, and San Francisco, there are banks which will make RP's and deliberately take a short reserve position which they will plan to cover with funds from correspondents. Banks make both collateral loans and repur-

CHART 7–2

Sources of Dealer Financing

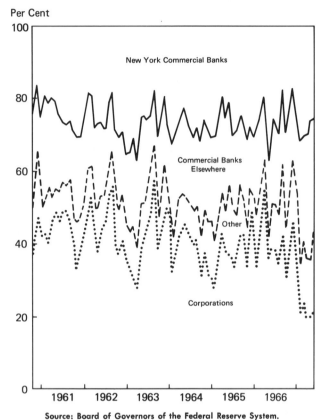

Source: Board of Governors of the Federal Reserve System.

chase agreements with dealers, and often prefer these alternatives to selling Federal funds because the rate of return is frequently higher. Repurchase agreements, however, may involve considerable trouble and expense because title to the securities must be transferred, and many banks regard RP's as unprofitable unless they run for three days or more. If excess reserves are expected for several days running, a repurchase agreement will avoid the expense of arranging a new Federal funds sale each day.

NEW YORK BANK LENDERS

If dealers cannot find financing elsewhere, they turn to the banks in New York. Rates charged by New York banks are generally higher than those charged by out-of-town lenders, even after the cost of clearing out-of-town loans through New York banks is taken into account. Nevertheless, most dealers do part of their daily borrowing at these banks. Their proximity is convenient for late-in-the-day transactions and for cash transactions which require payment and delivery on the same day the transaction is negotiated.

New York banks regard collateral loans to dealers as a very important means of adjusting reserve balances to desired levels. Their preference will generally hinge on relative costs, the availability of alternative instruments, and the length of time reserve surpluses (or deficiencies) are expected to last. The rate of return on dealer loans is generally higher than on other reserve adjustment media.

Each morning the major money market banks in New York post dealer lending rates for both new loans and renewals. Depending on their reserve positions and conditions in the money market, they encourage or discourage dealer loans by varying the rates they charge. Consequently, on a given day the posted rate may vary somewhat from bank to bank. There are five major banks that stand ready to make loans to dealers at their posted rates even if such transactions force them to purchase Federal funds to replace their reserve losses. Thus, at some price dealers are always able to finance their positions.

If the money market is particularly tight and the Federal Reserve needs to supply reserves to the banking system, the Federal Reserve Bank of New York may agree to enter into repurchase contracts with dealers. These agreements are made only at the initiative of the Federal Reserve and are an important complement to regular purchases and sales of Government securities in the open market. They are particularly useful when reserves are currently needed but reserve projections indicate that the need will not last for more than a few days. In such a case the Federal Reserve may make repurchase agreements scheduled to mature when reserves will probably be more readily available. This procedure makes it unnecessary to buy outright a large block of securities one day and sell them the next or in the very near future. Repurchase agreements have also been used in the Federal Reserve's effort to keep short-term rates up for balance of payments reasons. Their use avoids the direct downward pressure exerted on bill rates when the System buys short-term Government securities outright.

In July 1966 the System initiated the practice of using "reverse" repurchase agreements to withdraw reserves on a temporary basis. A reverse RP is nothing more than a sale of a block of securities to a Government securities dealer with the understanding that the Federal Reserve will repurchase the securities at an agreed upon time in the future. A massive airlines strike, which caused a sharp rise in float and hence reserves, was the occasion for the first use of the reverse RP. Since then, this technique has continued to be used from time to time.

CONCLUSION

Dealer loans and repurchase agreements are important money market instruments. Nonbank participants in the money market frequently adjust their liquidity positions by making RP's with dealers or by allowing maturing RP's to run off; and banks, under certain circumstances, like to adjust reserve positions by use of dealer loans instead of through such alternatives as Federal funds, Government securities, bankers' acceptances, or certificates of deposit.

Since dealer loans are fairly close substitutes for other money market instruments, it is logical to expect a fairly close relationship between rates on dealer loans and other money market rates. This is evident from the accompanying chart. Because dealer positions are financed primarily with borrowed money, a rise in dealer loan rates, for example, may induce dealers to lighten inventories by marking down prices, which raises the effective return to investors. Although the relationship between various short-term rates is not fixed or rigid, a rise in one tends to be transmitted fairly soon to several of the others.

8.

Call Loans

FEDERAL RESERVE BANK OF CLEVELAND

The call loan is one of the oldest money market instruments; it was first introduced in the United States in the mid-1800's. Although the call loan is not currently one of the more important money market instruments, it was at one time not only the most important instrument, but was the chief source of secondary reserves for commercial banks.

The call loan represents short-term funds loaned by banks to securities brokers and dealers for the purpose of financing their customers' purchases of common stock. The securities purchased with the proceeds of the loan, in turn, become the principal collateral. The call provision allows termination of the loan by either lender or borrower on one-day notice. While customer borrowings from brokers are also on a call basis, they are excluded from the usual definition of the call loan.[1]

The bulk of call loan activity occurs in New York City because securities trading is concentrated there. For example, at the end of 1963 about one-half of the 5.4 billion in commercial bank loans to brokers and dealers

Reprinted from *Money Market Instruments*, 1964, pp. 55–61, by permission of the publisher, the Federal Reserve Bank of Cleveland.

[1] Although call loans represent only a portion of total security credit, the two terms are often, and incorrectly, used interchangeably. Other sources of security credit are customer net free credit balances (funds left on deposit with brokers) and bank loans made to others than brokers and dealers for the purpose of carrying or purchasing securities. While bank loans to "others" are extensive, the call loan rate refers specifically to collateralized broker borrowings. Occasionally, security collateral loans are made on a time basis, but because of the dominance of the call provision, all brokers' loans are generally designated as the call money market. In addition, security credit often is extended to facilitate underwriting and distribution of new issues, overall operations of security dealers, and for a variety of reasons not necessarily related to the money market.

CHART 8–1

Call Loan Rates and Yields on 91-Day Treasury Bills, 1952-1963

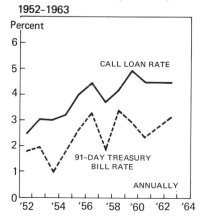

Note: Call load rate refers to loans secured by
customers' stock exchange collateral at
N.Y. City banks. Yields on 91-day
Treasury Bills refer to new issues.

Source: Board of Governors of the Federal Reserve System.

was carried by New York City banks.[2] The relative deemphasis of call loans in bank portfolios is reflected in the change in the percentage of total earning assets accounted for by call loans between 1929 and 1963. At the end of 1929 call loans represented 45 percent of earning assets ($8.1 billion) of New York City banks; at the end of 1963 the comparable figures were 8 percent of $34.8 billion.

Although the call rate displays a secular relationship with other money market rates, it is not a particularly sensitive indicator of money market conditions. The behavior of the call loan rate during 1952–63 is plotted in Chart 8–1, where it is compared with the market yield on 91-day Treasury bills, which is the pivotal money market rate. As the chart shows, the bill rate fluctuates much more widely in response to changes in both economic and money market conditions. Moreover, the call loan rate usually exceeds the bill rate by approximately one percentage point.

A clear indication of the relative insensitivity of the call loan rate has been demonstrated during the current economic recovery that began in 1961. The chart shows that the call rate has remained unchanged despite variation in other money market rates. This is shown quite clearly in Chart 8–2 where the range of yields on various interest rates during 1961–64 is presented.

[2] These and other data included in this article, unless otherwise indicated, are from various issues of the *Federal Reserve Bulletin*.

CHART 8-2

Range of Selected Interest Rates, 1961-1964

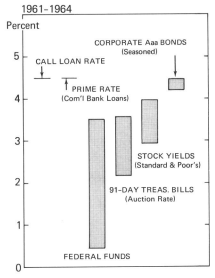

Note: 1964 rates as of July 10, 1964.

Source: Board of Governors of the Federal Reserve System.

The experience of the 1920's, however, would indicate that the demand for call loans is not closely related to the cost of this form of credit. As shown in Chart 8-3, despite the fact that the call loan rate rose dramatically between January 1927 and September 1929, there was an increase in the absolute amount of security loans outstanding as well as an increase in the ratio of security loans to total commercial bank loans. This experience indicates that restraint in the use of call loans would have to be achieved through a curtailment of demand for this form of credit rather than through an increase in cost.

HISTORICAL BACKGROUND

The call loan market developed in New York City around 1830. Call loans served as secondary reserves of large city banks partly because the United States did not have the developed Treasury bill or commercial bill markets such as existed in London.

After the termination of the Second Bank of the United States in 1836, country banks began to use banks in New York City and Chicago as reserve depositories. In turn the large city banks began to compete for the reserve balance of country banks by offering competitive interest rates.

CHART 8–3

Indexes of Selected Rates and Call Loans, 1927-1929

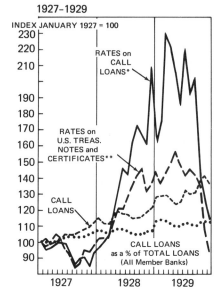

1927–1929

INDEX JANUARY 1927 = 100

*daily average rate.

**daily average rate; 6-9 month maturities used in some cases, 3-6 month maturities in most cases.

Source: Board of Governors of the Federal Reserve System.

Because such deposits were subject to immediate withdrawal, city banks employed them primarily in the call loan market. Call loans were regarded as highly liquid because the collateral behind such loans could be sold quickly to obtain funds. By the end of the 19th century, approximately 50 percent of New York City bank loan portfolios were represented by call loans.

The relative liquidity of call loans was subjected to wide fluctuations primarily because of seasonal swings in rural economic activity. For example, farmers needing funds to facilitate harvesting or planting usually withdrew deposits and requested loans at country banks. These institutions, in turn, frequently found it necessary to draw on their correspondent balances in New York City and Chicago banks to meet the deposit drain and demands for credit. Since call loans constituted the secondary reserves of large banks, the call privilege was widely exercised in order to meet the withdrawals of banks. However, brokers and dealers were frequently unable to meet the calls on their loans and were forced to request that their customers, for whom the funds had been borrowed, repay the amount due on the securities purchased on margin. Because many customers were unable to meet the payments, the securities were sold to meet the call. Since calls were concentrated in short periods of time mass liquidations of securities and sharp declines in securities prices usually occurred. As a result, the financial system underwent severe pressures as the demands for credit far outstripped the amount of credit available, and the value of securities declined sharply under repeated forced liquidations. In addition, the lack of liquidity and decline in security prices frequently resulted in bank failures, which further aggravated financial conditions. At times these pressures were so intense that financial panics resulted, e.g., in 1884, 1893, 1903 and 1907.

The Federal Reserve Act in 1913 provided facilities to member banks for alternative sources of liquidity to meet temporary deposit drains. This was done through the rediscounting of short-term business loans. However, call loans were not rediscounted by the Federal Reserve System, and the denial of rediscounting facilities for call loans resulted in a temporary demise of call loans as secondary reserves of banks. A surge in equity financing after World War I brought about a widespread return to using call loans. Portfolios of commercial banks thus began to include larger amounts of call loans during the 1920's. For example, between 1922 and 1929, brokers' loans held by commercial banks rose from $1.5 billion to $8.5 billion. By September 1929 brokers' loans accounted for 44 percent of all member bank loans and 50 percent of New York City bank loans.

When stock values collapsed in late 1929, however, call loans were once again relegated to limbo. In many instances, call loans could not be repaid and the collapse of the market reduced the demand for such credit. In less than three years after October 1929, the volume of call loans dropped from $8.5 billion to only $335 million.

CALL LOAN REGULATION

It was clear in the early 1930's that the previous marked rise in the volume of call loans was closely related to the speculative rise in stock values. Consequently, following the collapse of the stock market in 1929, steps were taken to control the use of such credit. In 1931, the New York Clearing House Association prohibited its members from acting as call market agents for non-bank lenders. This was formalized by the Banking Act of 1933, which also permitted the Federal Reserve System to limit the percentage of a bank's capital that could be utilized for security loans.

The Securities Exchange Act of 1934 gave the Federal Reserve Board of Governors the authority to set margin requirements. In setting these requirements the Board of Governors specifically states what proportion of the purchase price of securities the buyer must provide at the time of purchase. The balance, of course, may be borrowed. Margin requirements cover only the initial purchase and are not affected by changes in market value that occur later.

EFFECTIVENESS OF MARGIN REGULATION

Attempts to evaluate the effectiveness of margin regulation have resulted in varying interpretations. Most of the differences seem to center on the issues of (1) determining the aspects of security credit that should be considered most important and (2) determining the appropriate time lags. Analysis is further complicated by the inability to isolate the significance of margin changes from other factors within the context of a changing economy. In addition, the Federal Reserve System does not specify quantitative goals whenever it makes a change in margin requirements.

The following analysis attempts to relate margin changes to various aspects of stock market activity, customer credit, and broker credit. These aspects are examined at one-, three-, and six-month intervals before and after changes in margin requirements to determine individual performance and response. Individual totals were computed for each concept for each time period and for all 18 margin changes that occurred from 1934 to 1963; the figures were then put on an index basis. To lessen the influence of disproportionate changes that appear immediately before and after a margin change, the six-month period prior to the change was used as an index base (see Chart 8–4). Margin increases and decreases were examined separately to determine whether direction of change in margin requirements exerted significant influence on stock market activity. It should be remembered, however, that the following analysis cannot fully reflect all of the factors that may have influenced the selected variables.

Generally, reductions in margin requirements have tended to reverse prechange patterns more than have increases in margin requirements. As shown in Chart 8–4, six months after margin reductions, all six series had turned up, while in the case of margin increases, two series had declined, one remained virtually the same, and three maintained an upward movement.

In both increases and decreases, net customer debit balances (C on Chart 8–4) appear to have been most responsive, with the index returning to the level of twelve months earlier (100) six months after margin decreases, and remaining virtually unchanged after margin increases. The other component of customer credit, bank loans to others than brokers and dealers, showed a similar pattern after margin reductions, but continued upward following margin increases. Broker credit (E and F on Chart 8–4) behaved approximately the same as bank loans to "others" although not in the same magnitudes.

Stock market activity, expressed both as volume and prices on the New York Stock Exchange, displayed perhaps the most volatile behavior of the six series. In the case of margin decreases, stock volume increased markedly from six months to three months prior to margin changes, then declined until one month after changes, rising markedly thereafter.

CHART 8-4

Indexes of Stock Market Activity, Customer Credit, and Broker Credit

SPECIFIC MONTHLY PERIODS PRIOR AND SUBSEQUENT TO STOCK MARGIN CHANGES, 1934-1963

INCREASES

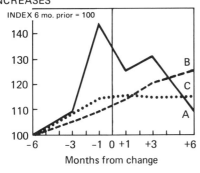 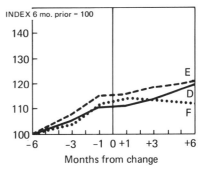

DECREASES

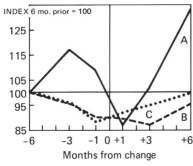 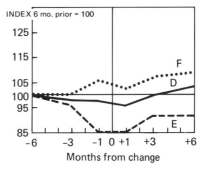

A = Volume on the New York Stock Exchange, daily average for the month in which the log fell.

B = Standard and Poor's Index of Stock Prices. Original 90-stock index changed to 500-stock indexes in 1957.

C = Net customer debit balances.

D = Bank loans to others than brokers and dealers for the purpose of purchasing or carrying securities. Average of weekly Wednesday figures from weekly reporting banks. No data prior to the 1945 margin change.

E = Money borrowed on total collateral (includes U.S. securities) from banks and trust companies and other lenders for the purpose of purchasing and carrying securities. No data available prior to August, 1935. 1950, category changed to only commercial banks and in 1954, changed to weekly reporting member banks.

F = Customer net free credit balances.

Sources: Barron's; Board of Governors of the Federal Reserve System.

Prior to margin increases, stock volume rose appreciably, declined one month after changes, rose slightly at three months, and dropped substantially at six months. Stock prices showed a tendency to reverse trend after margin reductions, but usually maintained upward movement following margin increases.

Net customer debit balances are the most important factor in determining the adequacy of existing margin requirements. As Chart 8-4 shows, these balances have displayed much sensitivity to changes in margin requirements. This reflects one of the purposes of the Securities Exchange Act, which was to influence the amount of credit utilized for stock purchases rather than the level of stock prices or the volume of trading.

The past 30 years have witnessed an almost continuous rise in stock prices and investor participation. The Securities Exchange Act provides that margin regulation generally applies to stocks traded on organized exchanges, e.g., the New York Stock Exchange. Thus, the existence of a large over-the-counter market, where a larger number of issues are traded, provides a possible means of circumventing margin requirements.

SUMMARY

The call loan in terms of dollar volume is quite clearly one of the least important money market instruments. However, in addition to its uniqueness as one of the oldest of existing instruments, the call loan continues to play an important role in the daily operations of organized securities markets. As such, its chief contribution is in the form of the liquidity it provides for securities transactions.

II

CAPITAL MARKETS

The capital market can be defined as that sector of the financial market that deals with the supply of and demand for intermediate and long-term funds (loans and instruments that have maturities greater than one year). This market contains specialized markets for mortgages, corporate bonds, common and preferred stocks, state and local securities, Federal obligations, term loans, and consumer credit.

The capital market can also be classified in a number of ways for study. Primary and secondary markets distinguish between new credit instruments and the resale of "second hand" instruments. The primary market is used for new capital formation and refunding old debt that is maturing. The secondary market facilitates formation by making primary security issues easier to resale, and it provides a place where the conservative lenders can buy proven securities and thus release funds to be used for new venture capital.

Another distinction can be made in the capital market, between open and negotiated markets. Open markets deal in standardized instruments that can be purchased and transferred by anyone through established channels. These would include stocks, bonds, government securities, etc. Negotiated markets involve instruments that are designed to meet the needs of specific lenders and borrowers. These would involve bank loans and directly placed securities. Capital markets can be analyzed in terms of the degree of contact between buyer and seller. Instruments negotiated through other parties comprise the indirect markets while instruments negotiated directly between seller and buyer comprise the direct market.

The readings in Part II describe and analyze the changes in various capital markets during the postwar period and examine some specific problems related to recent developments.

9.

Techniques of Treasury Financing

TILFORD C. GAINES

The economics of Treasury debt management discussed in the May issue stressed the important influence that debt management decisions may have upon the health of the economy and, as a consequence, the need that these decisions be intelligently coordinated with the monetary policies of the Federal Reserve System. In a very real sense, the success of debt management policies in achieving their intended purpose depends upon the technical financing procedures used to carry them out. Sound policy intentions may be entirely frustrated if the techniques employed to effectuate them have not been imaginatively developed to do the job.

WHY POLICIES FAILED

The history of the management of the public debt in the United States contains many instances of good policies failing because of inadequate financing techniques. Most recently, the failure of the Treasury debt managers during most of the 1950's to prevent the steady shortening of the debt,

Reprinted from *Banking*, Journal of the American Bankers Association, Vol. LVII, No. 3, September 1964, pp. 59–60, by permission of the publisher.

although this was an objective of policy, probably added to the inflationary pressures of the decade. It was only with the development of the advance refunding technique in 1960 that the Treasury finally was able to stabilize and control the maturity structure of the public debt.

The amount of financing the Treasury must undertake each year is enormous. In addition to the amounts shown in Table 9–1, the Treasury also refunds about $2 billion of bills each week, or some $100 billion over a full year. While the weekly auction of 3-month and 6-month bills is routine, it does require that the Treasury be almost continuously in the market. And in any given week there is the danger, however small, that a set of circumstances might emerge that would cause the auction to "fail" by not generating enough tenders to cover the offering. The Treasury must be alert even in the routine part of its market financing. Much greater alertness and careful planning is, of course, necessary in refunding coupon securities and in scheduling necessary new borrowing. The size of Treasury financing requirements is an advantage in that it provides the leverage through which economic policy objectives may be realized. But it also is a burden in that it imposes the need for frequent, unpostponable trips to the market without regard for market conditions at the moment.

TYPES OF FINANCING

There are three principal types of Treasury financing operations: Refunding of maturing securities; advance refunding of securities that have not reached maturity; and cash financing to raise new money. The actual securities employed in each of the three types of operations may be identical, but different technical procedures are used in each type of financing and different considerations are involved in determining the timing and the securities to be used. The following discussion describes Treasury financing techniques and the determinants of financing decisions.

TABLE 9–1

Treasury Financing, 1957-1963*

(billions of dollars)

| Year | Total | Refunding | | | Cash |
		Cash	Exchange	Advance	Financing
1957	$64.2	$—	$45.6	$—	$18.7
1958	66.9	—	49.8	—	17.1
1959	63.9	—	38.6	—	25.3
1960	62.7	9.6	33.2	2.3	11.7
1961	64.0	16.8	25.0	9.8	12.4
1962	71.7	13.8	36.7	13.1	8.2
1963	66.3	10.6	29.0	14.7	12.0

* Excludes regular weekly Treasury bills.

Source: U.S. Treasury Department, *Treasury Bulletin*.

The largest part of the Treasury's financing task is refunding the securities that mature each year. At times when the budget is in surplus it is possible to retire some part of the issues scheduled to mature, but this has not been an important consideration in most recent years. For all practical purposes, it may be assumed that maturing debt is to be replaced with new debt.

During the last several years, the Treasury in its offerings of new coupon securities has scheduled all new issues to mature at mid-month in either February, May, August, or October. These are, therefore, the principal refunding dates, even though a number of older issues that are still outstanding carry maturities at other times in the year. The maturing securities may originally have been certificates of indebtedness (one year or shorter), notes (one to five years), or bonds (over five years). But the original term of the maturing issues ordinarily does not have much bearing upon the selection of the new issues to replace them. Even if they originally were longer-term bonds, the bulk of the issue will have shifted into the hands of short-term investors as it approached maturity, and it may not be assumed that there will automatically be demand for a new long-term security in the refunding.

METHODS OF REFUNDING

The Treasury in refunding maturing debt may either sell its new securities for cash settlement and use the proceeds to retire the old issues, or it may offer holders of the maturing securities the right to exchange for the new issues. Usually the Treasury offers exchange "rights." The principal advantage of a "rights" exchange is that it permits more equitable treatment for investors in the maturing issues, particularly smaller banks and similar institutions. A cash offering usually is heavily oversubscribed, and securities are allotted on a percentage of subscriptions, with some minimum amount (often $50,000) allotted in full. Institutions that either are unwilling or unable to pad their subscriptions so as to get allotment of the total they want are forced to turn to the secondary market to "round out" their holdings. Right to exchange for the new securities automatically eliminates this problem.

ADVANTAGES OF CASH

On the other hand, a cash refunding has certain advantages that sometimes dictates its use. It avoids the cash outflow or "attrition" that results when maturing securities are not presented for exchange. When the ownership distribution of the issues being refunded suggests that attrition might be large (as is the case in the 5% notes maturing in August 1964), this can be an important consideration. Also, the threat that maturing securities *might* be refunded in a cash operation holds down speculation in the "rights." Such speculation has at times created unfortunate financing results, the best known case being the June 1958 refunding. And finally, refunding for cash eliminates the constraint upon the selection of the new issues that may be imposed by the pattern of ownership of the maturing securities. For example, if the Treasury wishes to include an intermediate bond in its offering, it may prefer not to use a "rights" exchange if most of the maturing securities are owned by institutions that typically invest only in short-term securities.

The detailed procedures followed by the Treasury in its regular refunding are uniform from one operation to the next. On Tuesday and Wednesday in the third week prior to the maturity date, the Treasury debt officials meet and consult with committees of The American Bankers Association and the Investment Bankers Association on the terms to be employed in the refunding. Federal Reserve officials also are consulted and, in those instances when thought is being given to a long-term bond, representatives of the insurance and savings bank industry may be brought in for consultation. Then, on Wednesday afternoon, the terms of the offering are announced, with exchange or cash subscription books scheduled to open the following Monday and settlement on the maturity date of the old securities. Subscription books typically are held open for three days on an exchange and only one day on a cash refunding.

WHEN TRADING STARTS

The new securities begin to trade "when issued" in the secondary market immediately after the announcement of terms in the case of an exchange, but not until after subscription books have closed in the case of a cash offering. It is necessary that trading begin promptly in an exchange operation in order to provide for transfer of ownership of "rights" from those owners not interested in the new securities to others who find the new issues attractive. The price of the "rights" adjusts promptly to reflect the value of the when-issued securities.

Typically the Treasury will attempt to offer a rate of return on its new securities that will cause them to trade at ⅛ to ¼ point premium against the current market. Naturally this premium is reflected in the price investors are willing to pay to obtain "rights" to the exchange, and the resulting "rights" premium provides inducement to sell for owners not planning to exchange, thus limiting attrition on the operation. Barring unexpected developments, the Government securities dealers are able to maintain a flat, steady market during the refunding so as to facilitate orderly placement of the billions of dollars of new securities that ordinarily are involved.

SHORT VS. LONG TERMS

As mentioned earlier, the Treasury encountered serious difficulty through the 1950's in its efforts to sell enough longer-term bonds to prevent steady shortening of the maturity structure of the outstanding debt. Whatever the original maturity of an issue, by the time it approached maturity it had become a short-term investment and its ownership tended to shift to holders interested only in shorter securities. When it was refunded, therefore, the Treasury's choice was either to refund at fairly short term or, by including a longer obligation in its offering, to pre-empt *new* long-term funds. Sometimes such an offering was ruled out because the Treasury did not wish to compete at that time with other users of capital funds; at other times it was effectively ruled out by the limited available supply of long-term funds. As one Treasury official remarked, there was no good time for the Treasury to finance at longer term.

One solution to the problem appeared to be to offer investors in longer-term U.S. Government securities an attractive opportunity to extend into new bonds *before* the outstanding issue they owned had moved into a shorter maturity bracket. In this way, long-term funds committed to Governments could be prevented from leaking away. To this end, the Treasury since 1960 has engaged in nine advance refunding operations. In these operations, an impressive total of some $14.5-billion bonds of more than 10-year maturity has been issued.

ADVANCE REFUNDING

The technical procedures employed in an advance refunding are almost identical to those in a regular exchange refunding. Owners of the securities selected for advance refunding are offered optional exchange into one or more new issues of longer maturity at an effective rate of interest calculated to make such exchange attractive. The key measure used to determine attractiveness is the "reinvestment rate." That is the rate of interest the investor would have to receive upon reinvestment at maturity, were he to hold to maturity rather than exchanging, that would give him a net return as favorable as that offered by the Treasury in the advance refunding. The "reinvestment rate" offered by the Treasury customarily has been about ¼ point higher than the current market rate for a comparable maturity, a spread that has provided strong inducement for investors to exchange.

Development of the advance refunding technique has significantly improved the Treasury's ability to regulate its debt structure, not only by making it possible for the Treasury to issue the necessary volume of long bonds but also in the management of its short and intermediate maturities. Large blocks of securities that might create unwieldy refunding problems at maturity are "pre-refunded" a year or so before maturity. The size of the blocks may thus be whittled down and replaced by smaller issues at carefully selected niches throughout the intermediate range.

Some dealers have complained that advance refunding permits investors to make most of their portfolio adjustments at times of Treasury offerings, thus reducing the extent to which they use the secondary market. And there has been the more important criticism that the attractive reinvestment rates necessary to attract voluntary exchange in an advance refunding probably have added to the interest cost of the public debt. But the benefits of improved debt management made possible by advance refunding no doubt outweigh whatever disadvantages or cost it has entailed.

In addition to the cash offerings of new securities that are made from time to time to refund maturing debt, the Treasury must also come to market several times each year to borrow new money. Such cash financing is necessary even when the budget is in balance, to replace attrition incurred in exchange refundings and to adjust for seasonal swings in the Treasury's cash flow. Much the largest part of the Treasury's cash financing in most years, in fact, is to meet seasonal needs. For example, the Treasury currently estimates that it will have to borrow about $9 billion in the last half of calendar 1964, of which perhaps $7 billion will be intra-fiscal year financing and will be retired out of surplus revenues in the first half of 1965.

RECENT FINANCING

Except in those occasional years of large deficits, therefore, the typically seasonal nature of much of the new borrowing minimizes the problem for the Treasury. Excluding securities sold for cash to refund maturing debt, the Treasury issued approximately $48.5 billion of new securities for cash settlement in the three years 1961–1963 inclusive. Of this total, nearly $17 billion represented tax anticipation bills that were redeemed at maturity and another $24.6 billion was in the form of additions to the regular weekly bills or to the cycle of 1-year bills. Only $7.1 billion of new coupon securities were sold for cash.

Procedures for selling coupon securities for cash are similar to those used in refunding. The Treasury announces its offering terms on a Wednesday or Thursday afternoon and subscription books open the following Monday. Books usually are open for only one day, however, and trading in the when-issued securities does not begin until subscription books have closed. Payment may be to the Treasury's account with the Federal Reserve banks or, if the new money is not immediately needed, all or a fraction of the proceeds may be credited to Treasury tax and loan balances with commercial banks.

The Treasury has introduced several successful innovations in its

Treasury bill program in recent years, resulting in a better arranged, more orderly short-term debt. As late as 1958 the Treasury sold only 3-month bills and occasional tax anticipation bills. Today, in addition, there are full cycles of 6-month and 1-year bills. The issuance of 1-year bills maturing at the end of each month through the year has been particularly helpful. These bills not only provide investors a larger selection of short maturities but, since they have replaced most of the regular short-term coupon securities, they have simplified the management of the short-term debt.

NEW TECHNIQUE

Each week new issues of 3- and 6-month bills are auctioned and each month a new 1-year bill is sold at auction. The auctions are usually very routine. Placing the major part of the short-term debt on this orderly roll-over arrangement has helped to free the Treasury's hands to deal more flexibly with its quarterly financing in coupon securities.

In 1963 the Treasury introduced a new and rather controversial technique for selling long-term bonds for cash. In January and again in April of last year the Treasury offered new issues of long-term bonds for subscription by underwriting syndicates organized to bid for the issues. The purpose was to see if the Treasury could not raise reasonably small amounts of new long-term money at periodic intervals through a technique similar to the standard underwriting arrangements employed by corporations and state and local governments to raise new money.

Even though the amount raised might be only a billion dollars or so each year, it would supplement the long bonds placed through more traditional Treasury financing methods and might contribute importantly to the maintenance of a well-spaced maturity structure. Market professionals who had to assume the responsibility of bidding on and underwriting the new bonds have taken a very dim view of the whole procedure, and as this is written it is uncertain whether or not the Treasury will attempt further use of it in the future.

Each time the Treasury approaches a financing, whether to refund debt or to raise new money, a set of decisions must be made as to timing, securities to be offered, rates of interest, and other terms of the offering. These decisions are shaped by the basic Treasury policies being pursued and by the limitations imposed by market circumstances at the time. Sometimes the decisions are simple. With respect to the type of securities offered in new cash borrowings, the Treasury may be guided heavily by the length of time for which funds are being raised. If, for example, the Treasury needs cash to cover a seasonal deficit in the fall and if there is every reason to believe that there will be a surplus to retire the borrowing during the last half of the fiscal year, the indicated decision would be to sell March or June tax anticipation bills.

With respect to the timing of refunding offers, Treasury financing tends to be governed by the schedule of maturing issues. For example, if securities are scheduled to mature within a few weeks and the money is not available to retire them, the Treasury will have very little latitude in setting the timing of the refunding. In most areas of decision making, however, the Treasury has considerable latitude.

The policy objectives of public debt management were outlined in the first article of this series. Briefly, the overriding objective is to manage the debt in coordination with Federal Reserve monetary policy so as to create a unified set of policies intended to promote economic stability and growth. In keeping with this objective, the Treasury should avoid pre-empting long-term funds in periods of recession or underemployment and should avoid permitting the debt to become more liquid in periods of strong business activity or boom.

Another objective is to use Treasury financing to affect the shape of the yield curve as a defense against unwanted outflows of short-term "hot money" to foreign markets. Still another objective, of course, is to finance in such a way as to hold the interest cost on the debt to a minimum, so long as this is consistent with other objectives.

NEED FOR LONG TERM

As a practical matter, the working out of these objectives in the past usually has resulted in the Treasury offering securities at every opportunity that were designed to achieve maximum debt lengthening. The Treasury's financing experience most of the time since the end of the Second World War has been that it must seize every opportunity to *lengthen* debt if it is to prevent the debt from *shortening*. The sheer size of the outstanding debt and its inexorable movement toward shorter maturities ordinarily has left the Treasury little room for decision other than to offer the longest maturity the market will take.

It now appears, however, that the success of the advance refunding operations in recent years has given the Treasury a bit more latitude. Outstanding maturities are better spaced than they have been for many years, so that if economic or international conditions should arise which dictated that the Treasury confine itself to the shorter market, such a policy might be feasible for a period of several months without serious piling up of debt in the short sector.

Perhaps the most important constraint on the Treasury's selection of terms and conditions for its financing operations is the state of the securities markets. Experience has shown that disregard of market conditions and bull-headed insistence upon pursuit of broad policy objectives whatever the circumstances can do more harm than good. There are times, for example, when there simply is no demand for any security of more than short or short-to-intermediate maturity—at least at rates of interest close to the current market. Such conditions might arise in badly glutted markets or at times of deep uncertainty about the outlook for interest rates and bond prices. The Treasury must necessarily bow to the market's wishes at these times.

THE RATE LIMIT

Another limiting influence on the decision process is the arbitrary 4¼% interest rate limit on Treasury bonds—a limit that is still in the law more by accident than by design. At times of high interest rates, the Treasury must confine its financing to maturities of no more than five years as a result of this provision of the law. In a 1961 opinion, Attorney General Kennedy informed Secretary Dillon that the law would permit the Treasury to sell bonds at a discount to give an effective rate of return greater than 4¼%. The Treasury has never tested this interpretation, however, and it should be assumed that the 4¼% limit will continue to impede Treasury financing decisions until Congress acts to remove it.

WISE MANAGEMENT

Our huge public debt exists as an inescapable fact; whether its existence is to be harmful or useful to the performance of the economy depends, finally, upon the wisdom with which it is managed. The first requirement for wise management is understanding of the influence that management of the debt may have and conscious policy planning to make that influence beneficial. The second requirement is the development of financing techniques designed to achieve policy objectives with minimum disturbance to the market and minimum interest cost to the public.

Public debt management under the last two Treasury administrations has been excellent with respect both to policy planning and technical execution.

10.

Federal Agency Securities

JANE F. NELSON

The securities of certain Federal Government agencies have long occupied a small corner of the nation's money and capital markets. For many years the volume of these securities outstanding was relatively small, but recently it has grown rapidly, rising from $1.5 billion in 1950 to more than $19 billion in 1966, excluding participation certificates. Behind this rapid growth are a number of innovations in Federal budgetary and agency financing practices that have added new dimensions to both primary and secondary markets for agency securities. This article examines briefly the chief characteristics of agency securities, the markets for these securities, and recent developments affecting the relative importance of these markets.

THE ISSUING AGENCIES

Certain Federal Government corporations and agencies, established by law to implement the Federal Government's various lending programs, issue securities to finance their activities. Federal Land Banks, Federal Intermediate Credit Banks, Banks for Cooperatives, Federal Home Loan Banks, and the Federal National Mortgage Association ("Fannie Mae") constitute the major source of agency securities. A number of other Federal agencies

Reprinted from *Instruments of the Money Market*, 1968, pp. 75–82, by permission of the publisher, the Federal Reserve Bank of Richmond.

come to the market from time to time to offer their own debentures, to sell participations in their loan portfolios, or to sell some of their loans outright. These include the Tennessee Valley Authority, the Federal Housing Administration, the Farmers Home Administration, the Commodity Credit Corporation, the Export-Import Bank, and the Small Business Administration.

The "big five" agencies were originally financed by the Treasury; that is, the Treasury subscribed most of their capital stock. In most cases, however, their stock either has been or is being retired and ownership is passing to member organizations. For instance, member institutions, mostly savings and loan associations, have owned all the capital stock of the Federal Home Loan Banks since 1951.

INVESTMENT CHARACTERISTICS

The interest and principal of most Federal agency issues are guaranteed only by the issuing agency, not by the Federal Government. Such issues are sometimes referred to as "nonguaranteed" debt. Exceptions include obligations of various agencies such as the Federal Housing Administration and the Farmers Home Administration, which are directly guaranteed by the Federal Government. Under recent legislation passed by Congress, certificates of participation are, in effect, guaranteed. The Export-Import Bank and the Commodity Credit Corporation sell their own certificates. Those of a number of other agencies are sold under Fannie Mae's supervision and are serviced by a pool of loans of the several agencies. The law authorizes the selling agency to make "indefinite and unlimited" drawings on the Treasury, if needed, to service the certificates. Because of this provision, the Attorney General of the United States has designated all participation certificates as obligations of the United States.

The eligibility of agency issues as investments of regulated financial institutions and as collateral for public deposits depends, to some extent, on the guaranteed or nonguaranteed status of the agency, and the maturity and marketability of the individual issue. Most agency issues are eligible as collateral for Treasury Tax and Loan Accounts and other public deposits. A few are acceptable collateral for all types of accounts which require a specific pledge of Treasury securities. Some, although not all, are eligible as collateral for Federal Reserve advances, and there are some which qualify as legal reserve requirements of savings and loan associations.

Virtually all agency securities bear a fixed rate of interest, and interest on the longer obligations is usually paid semiannually. Exceptions include the Farmers Home Administration which pays interest only once a year, and three other agencies which pay only at maturity. The Tennessee Valley Authority, the Commodity Credit Corporation, and Fannie Mae have sold

CHART 10–1

Maturity Distribution of Federal Agency Securities, December 31, 1966

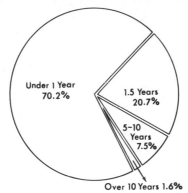

Source: Board of Governors of the Federal Reserve System.

short-term notes at a discount, where the interest is the difference between the discount price and par.

The broad maturity range of agency securities, as shown in Chart 10–1, enables them to compete with money market instruments as well as with intermediate and long-term instruments. Maturity patterns vary widely among individual agencies. For instance, the Federal Intermediate Credit Banks and the Banks for Cooperatives usually sell six- to nine-month paper, while the Federal Home Loan Banks, the Federal Land Banks, and Fannie Mae offer both short-term paper and long-term securities.

Call features also vary; some agency issues are noncallable while others are callable by the issuing agency after a specified period of time. Export-Import Bank notes offer the investor the option of reselling the notes to the agency under certain terms. Holders of Farmers Home Administration notes may extend the maturity of the notes or redeem them, after the initial fixed maturity of the Government's insurance endorsement has been reached.

Interest income and principal on most agency issues are subject to all Federal taxes but are usually exempt from all state and local taxes except inheritance and gift taxes. Some issues, however, are not exempt from any taxes. This is true of obligations of the Farmers Home Administration and any securities issued directly or indirectly by Fannie Mae.

CERTIFICATES OF PARTICIPATION

A certificate of participation represents a beneficial interest in a pool of agency loans or mortgages. It is a formal credit instrument carrying a contractual interest obligation on a specified principal amount. In contrast to an outright sale of assets in which the title to the asset actually is transferred to the investor, the investor does not acquire title to any of the pooled assets at any time. Rather, the issuing agency continues to hold the pooled loans and to receive interest and principal payments on them. These payments, in turn, are used to service the certificates. The Commodity Credit Corporation initiated sales of certificates of participation in a pool of crop loans in 1953, and the Export-Import Bank began selling participations in its loan portfolio in 1962. But the first sale of certificates by Fannie Mae in November 1964 probably marked their beginning as a significant new instrument of agency financing.

With the passage of the Sales Participation Act of 1966, this method of financing was broadened significantly to include the pooling of assets of at least ten governmental departments and agencies. The eligible loans include credit extended to farmers, small businesses, veterans, colleges, and numerous types of building projects. By the end of 1966, about $39 billion of loans were eligible for pooling.

The certificate sales are not designated as debt in governmental bookkeeping procedures. Proceeds from these sales are returned to the Treasury to be credited proportionately to the lending authorizations of the agencies represented in the pool. In fiscal 1966, direct sales of Federal loans and participation certificate sales totaled about $3.0 billion; in fiscal 1967, the estimated total of such sales amounts to about $4.1 billion. For budgetary purposes, proceeds from the sales are counted as negative expenditures and the budget deficit is reduced correspondingly.

Many loans eligible for pooling originally were made at lower interest rates than would be required currently to attract private investors to participation certificates. To meet this situation, the new legislation stipulated that the Appropriations Committee of the Congress will be required to approve each package of pooled assets, and such approval will automatically assure Congressional appropriation of funds needed to bridge any gaps between the two rates.

PRIMARY MARKET

To facilitate primary market sales, most agencies have under contract a Fiscal Agent in New York City. One or more agencies may use the same Agent. When an offering is to be made, the Fiscal Agent assembles his selling group of securities dealers, brokerage houses, and dealer banks. Unlike syndicates formed for the sale of a specific stock or bond issue, the Agent's selling group does not dissolve after the issue is sold, and the selling groups do not bid against each other. Rather, each agency offering is made through only one selling group. To establish the price or price range of the new issues, the Fiscal Agent consults with the members of the selling group, the

Treasury, the Federal Reserve Bank of New York Trading Desk, and the issuing agency regarding maturity, amount, coupon, and price. When the sale date arrives, the price is telegraphed by the Agent to the members of the group who then communicate subscriptions to the Agent. The latter determines the allotments, which are usually a fraction of investor subscriptions.

This method of sale is used primarily by the five large agencies which account for the bulk of agency financing. Other agencies often use other methods. Certificates of participation, for example, have been sold generally through syndicates headed by large brokerage houses and dealer banks. The Farmers Home Administration sells notes, which represent long-term, insured loans to farmers, directly to investors, primarily commercial banks. The Farmers Home Administration acts as a middleman between farmers and investors, servicing the loan and collecting interest and principal payments which are forwarded to the owner of the note. The Export-Import Bank used to sell participations in its loan pool directly to commercial banks on an allotment basis, but in February 1967 it marketed a large issue through a syndicate for the first time. The Commodity Credit Corporation and the Tennessee Valley Authority have employed the auction method of selling short-term paper.

SECONDARY MARKET

Some agency issues have an active secondary market while others do not. Obligations of the Federal Land Banks, the Federal Intermediate Credit Banks, the Banks for Cooperatives, the Federal Home Loan Banks, and the Federal National Mortgage Association have well-established secondary markets. Dealers' inventories usually include large amounts of these securities. The spread between the bid and offered prices is narrow on short-term issues of these agencies, and trades of $1.0 to $5.0 million can be made without upsetting the market.

The secondary market for issues due in five years and over is a different story. Long-term maturities are usually available in comparatively small amounts, and the spread between bid and offered prices is often as large as ten dollars. Consequently, when new issues have been placed with investors, the secondary market has been able to give only a rough indication of the issues' current value. Actual trades, particularly of large amounts, are often negotiated on an individual basis.

In December 1966 the Federal Open Market Committee, pursuant to a recent act of Congress, authorized the use of repurchase agreements involving agency obligations. These agreements are similar to those involving direct obligations of the United States insofar as terms and conditions are concerned. This development not only increases the means available to the

System for supplying and absorbing reserves, but it also tends to strengthen and broaden the secondary market for agencies.

Among smaller agencies, secondary sales are arranged in various ways. In the case of Farmers Home Administration notes, at least one dealer has made a special effort to provide a secondary market by "packaging" notes of small denominations into larger units for large investors. Commodity Credit Corporation notes had no secondary market until the Comptroller's recent ruling that national banks can underwrite and deal in these securities. Formerly, these notes were held only by banks and could be resold only to the Commodity Credit Corporation.

In 1966, a year of heavy financing activity in the Federal agency market, dealers' daily positions in Federal agency securities averaged $436 million, of which about 80 percent was accounted for by issues due within one year. Dealers' positions were about 47 percent larger than in 1965. Overall dealer transactions in agencies of all maturities averaged $204 million daily in year 1966, almost double the 1965 level.

DEMAND

Agency issues contain many desirable investment features and it is not surprising that the demand for them has become more broadly based. During much of the past decade, commercial banks constituted the only important buyers of agency issues. In December 1950, according to the Treasury survey of ownership, they held 79 percent of the total outstanding, but in 1960 their share of the total had fallen to about 16 percent. By the end of 1965, bank ownership had moved up to 21 percent, due in part to bank efforts to find higher yielding assets as they attracted increasingly costly time deposits. By the end of 1966, banks' share had again declined to about 16 percent, reflecting the strong loan demand that year which forced banks to curtail or reduce other investments.

U.S. Government investment accounts and the general funds of state and local governments are probably the next largest owners of agency issues, holding between 6 and 7 percent each at the end of 1966.

Federal trust fund holdings, which had formerly been quite limited, increased significantly during the tight money conditions in 1966. Heavy agency financing in the January-June period had contributed to congestion in the capital market and the rapid rise in interest rates. Over $5.0 billion in new money was raised during these six months, more than double the total for all fiscal 1965. Early in September the situation reached a crisis, as investment money dried up despite the high yields. The Treasury announced that sales of participation certificates would be suspended temporarily to help alleviate the pressure on the market, and that where financings could not be postponed, Government trust funds would purchase a substantial portion of the new offerings, by-passing the private market.

Individuals and trust funds have recently become increasingly important buyers, particularly of the new participation certificates. Other owners include fire and casualty companies, mutual savings banks, savings and loan associations, and state and local government pension funds.

RECENT TRENDS

The sharp increase in agency financing will undoubtedly promote a more active and flexible secondary market. Hitherto, agency offerings have retailed successfully only at yields above those on comparable instruments. In March 1966, for instance, a Fannie Mae offering of noncallable participation certificates with maturities out to 15 years was priced to yield from 5.25 to 5.50 percent. A few days later, a large, 34-year, Aaa-rated corporate issue, noncallable for five years, sold out at a 5.11 percent yield. This disparity in yields has been due partly to the novelty of the new participation certificates, and partly to investor disappointment in their marketability. The heavy volume offered in 1966 also tended to widen the spread. With a broader range of maturities and a steady expanding supply, however, marketability should improve in the long run. Also, the Attorney General's decision that participation certificates are direct Governmental obligations should contribute to relatively lower yields. Moreover, the sale of participation certificates as larger individual term issues, instead of serial bonds, and the introduction of the bearer form should enhance their marketability. The wide spread in 1966 between short-term agency issues and Treasury bills of comparable maturity was due both to the deluge of agency offerings and to the limited marketability of certain types, notably the Export-Import Bank notes.

11.

Some Postwar Trends
in Muncipal
Bond Financing

JOHN L. O'DONNELL

1. THE BASIC FRAMEWORK

Any review of postwar trends in municipals must take into account several basic factors that influence all aspects of state and local government financing. The first is the increase and relocation of our population and shift in its age composition. Between 1950 and 1960, for example, total population grew by 18.5 percent, the five- to nineteen-year age group increased by nearly 40 percent, while people over sixty-five years of age increased by approximately 35 percent. The number of residents in the urban fringe areas jumped by 81.5 percent. This type of change has generated a big demand for all kinds of public improvements, like new schools, sewer and water facilities, and all the other utility services required by a modern society.

Second, income distribution has been altering in favor of the middle-income groups. More families than ever before now own such capital assets

Reprinted from *Journal of Finance*, Vol. XVII, No. 2, May 1962, pp. 259–268, by permission of the author and the publisher.

as houses and cars. Possession of these assets, in turn, generates a demand for highways, parking lots, and related public capital investments. Some idea of what is involved can be gained from a study conducted in California, which claims that each new family moving into a particular area requires around $13,000 in public improvements.[1] The dollar figures have become progressively more startling when compared with 1939 or 1945, because inflation, combined with the wartime backlog of deferred construction, has contributed a third factor to the problems facing municipal finance officers.

A fourth factor is the peculiar legal status of municipals, which greatly complicates their relationship with other sectors of the capital markets. Traditionally, the bulk of public construction undertaken at the local level is financed by borrowing. Each state has developed constitutional and statutory provisions intended to insure fiscal responsibility. All bond issues are surrounded by a tangle of laws that, in one way or another, impose limits on the freedom of local communities to incur debt. In addition, the interest income from municipals is exempt from federal taxes.

This special legal status was arrived at many years ago before current conditions could be imagined. As a result, the inflated demand pressures already noted have forced local debt to balloon within a constricting legal corset. It is this set of circumstances that provides the basic framework for consideration of postwar trends in state and municipal bond financing.

II. TYPES OF FINANCING

With these general forces at work, it is hardly surprising that the volume of new long-term borrowing rose from $1.2 billion in 1946 to $7.1 billion in 1960 and promises to exceed $8 billion in 1961. It has been estimated that this constitutes one-seventh to one-ninth of the gross volume of long-term funds raised through the capital markets.[2] In general terms, over 90 percent of this borrowing represented new money required to finance capital projects. Around 20 percent of the money went to build schools, 17 percent for highways, and 11 percent for sewer and water facilities. The remainder was scattered among a fairly wide variety of improvements, the largest single category being residential building, which accounted for approximately 7.5 percent of the total.

At the same time, there was a steady increase in the proportion of revenue-type financing as opposed to bonds enjoying the full faith and credit of issuing authorities. Since 1945, the proportion has risen irregularly from 17 percent to nearly 30 percent of total new offerings. Better than one-third

---

[1] Southern California Research Council, *The Cost of Metropolitan Growth* (1958).
[2] Roland I. Robinson, *Postwar Market for State and Local Government Securities* (Princeton: Princeton University Press for the National Bureau of Economic Research, 1960). I have drawn liberally on this excellent study throughout this paper.

of the net increase in tax-exempt debt since 1946 has been raised by unguaranteed securities that took on varied legal forms. Indeed, it has become
extremely difficult to classify many of these issues under the familiar head-
ing of revenue bonds.

In part, the trend toward unguaranteed revenue financing may reflect
a desire to place the burden of costs on the immediate beneficiaries of public improvements. However, the main reason seems to be that many communities found themselves pressing hard against constitutional and other
legal ceilings that limit tax rates and permissible debt levels. In Michigan,
for example, local governments are prohibited from levying taxes in excess
of 15 mills of assessed valuation.[3] If any project calls for financing that vio-
lates this limit, it must first be approved by a special local election. Many
other states have much tighter restrictions, so that the methods of escape
and degree to which they can be used differ widely between the states.

An obvious solution to this problem would be to relax the legal restraints. Unfortunately, in most instances this could be achieved only by
surmounting virtually impossible political road blocks. Thus local governments have tended to find relief by resorting to revenue types of financing
under enabling legislation which does not conflict with existing statutes.
One interesting development in this direction is a form of lease financing
extended to the municipal area.

Lease Financing

The detailed mechanics of lease financing as used by local governments differ between the states, but the central idea remains much the same:
a general law is passed permitting the formation of non-profit authorities or
instrumentalities for the express purpose of constructing facilities that are
then leased to the local political subdivision or municipality. Each such
lessor is empowered to issue tax-exempt bonds that will be serviced and eventually retired out of contractual lease payments made by the leasing governmental unit(s). Where these arrangements are in force, state supreme courts
have usually held that neither the payments called for by the lease contracts
nor the bonds issued by such non-profit bodies violate any debt or taxing
limits in force in the state.

The concept of leasing as broadly outlined is not new, and there is
some evidence that it originated in Pennsylvania before World War II. Today, the Commonwealth of Pennsylvania has over one thousand special
authorities, most of which have floated bond issues. The sum of the issues
now amounts to more than 358 million. Another profuse issuer is the
Florida Development Commission, which is currently the "obligor" of more
than $150 million of road and bridge construction bonds secured by, and

[3] *Constitution of the State of Michigan*, Art. X, Sec. 23.

payable from, a portion of the state's gasoline excise tax. Georgia has a multiplicity of instrumentalities, such as the Bridge Building Authority, the Farmers Market Authority, and the Hospital Authority. The Georgia Rural Roads Authority has about $100 million of bonds outstanding for the purpose of building and leasing highways.

In the Midwest the leasing technique has been employed most frequently to secure the payment of revenue bonds issued to build schools and government offices. Michigan is using this approach to construct governmental office buildings, although, so far, relatively few issues have been made under a law passed in 1948.[4] On the other hand, Indiana provides an excellent example for detailed study because, until very recently, municipal lease-rental arrangements were confined to building schools, and the volume of underwritings is sufficiently large to establish some fairly clear characteristics for this kind of financing.

Indiana School-building Corporations

In Indiana, local governments are confined to a 2 percent debt limit coupled with very low property valuations. Together, these constitute one of the tightest restrictions on local financing in the United States. By 1947, the demand for new school buildings became so desperate that a law was passed allowing the creation of school-building corporations.[5]

Once the preliminaries are completed, these corporations may issue first-mortgage bonds in an amount necessary to cover all expenses of building the structure on a site usually contributed by the future lessee at a nominal cost. A yearly rental charge for a period not exceeding 30 years is fixed at a level sufficient to service the bonds, pay any taxes and assessments levied on the property, and meet necessary fire and extended insurance coverage. All additional expenses, like occupancy insurance, maintenance, repairs, renewals, and the like, must be met by the local government lessee(s) from other funds.

The annual rentals specified in the lease are obtained from an ad valorem tax levy made against all taxable property in the area covered by the contracting local government(s). However, the law also specifies that no local government can be held directly responsible for the indebtedness of any school-holding corporation, nor can any local government be bound to purchase the buildings on termination of the lease for any reason whatsoever. On the other hand, all contracts must give local governments an option to renew the lease on the same terms or to purchase the property at a price

---

[4] Act 31, *Public Acts of Michigan, 1948* (First Extra Session) as amended.
[5] *Burns Indiana Statutes Annotated*, Vol. VI, Part 2, Sec. 28–3221, 1961 Cum. Supp.

just sufficient to enable the corporation to liquidate all indebtedness.

The first issue under the above law came to market in December, 1949, and in the following ten years 190 issues were floated, totaling approximately $147.5 million. Nearly half of all underwritings were less than $500 thousand, 44 exceeded $1 million, and only 10 exceeded $2 million. Since the rating agencies treat rental revenue issues like revenue bonds, most issues go unrated because they are either too small or do not have a sufficiently long earnings record.

Given the above conditions, large out-of-state investment bankers usually were uninterested in school-building corporation bonds unless they already had an established clientele in Indiana or were associated in bidding groups with local houses intimately familiar with the market characteristics of each situation. However, by 1956, outside competition became vigorous to a point which school-holding corporation bonds are now actively sought after by quite large syndicates.

Three principal reasons seem to explain this change in attitude. First, underwriters have been successful in educating a widening circle of investors to the basic merits of school-building corporation bonds. Second, because these securities were essentially a new type of investment medium, their yields could be scaled at high enough levels to be attractive at the short end to commercial banks and at the long end to insurance companies. Third, profit margins on these issues are sufficiently larger than those obtained on other issues to attract attention from underwriters and compensate them for the time and trouble of making a bid. For example, the gross margins realized on reofferings of these issues ranged from $16 to $17.50 a bond. From the underwriter's point of view, a spread of this order compares most favorably with the usual average of around $14 a bond for most unlisted issues or $9–$10 a bond for Aaa rated issues having more than a 15-year maturity.

Whatever legal theory may imply, imposing a non-profit entity cannot alter the basic economics of a taxing situation. When legal veils are torn aside, it becomes evident that the burden of both servicing and retiring rental revenue bonds still remains in the form of taxes imposed by the leasing body upon its taxpayers. Any appraisal of rental revenue issues must take this into account, along with the special legal provisions surrounding each issue.

Investors have recognized the revenue characteristics of these issues and demanded a differentially higher yield than that paid on general obligations. An analysis of Indiana School Holding Corporation bonds shows that this yield differential amounts to about 0.50 percent in the first 10 years and rises in a linear manner to around 1.25 percent in the remaining time to maturity. In a very real sense, this is the cost of state politics which prevent altering the law, and, as already indicated, variations of this trend occurred in many other states.

III. TAX EXEMPTION AND YIELDS

Common sense suggests that revenue issues will carry higher yields than general obligation bonds. However, the surprising thing to most observers is that the differential is as wide as it has been during most of the postwar period. This fact is in sharp contrast to the noticeable shrinkage in yield differentials that has taken place between grades of corporate securities.

From 1946 to 1956 Aaa and Baa municipals had yields that differed by an average of nearly one percentage point. This kind of risk premium is more than sufficient to provide a reserve fund adequate to cover the worst loss experiences ever noted in the municipal market. Roland I. Robinson notes that in 1955 the prevailing yield margin of Baa bonds over Aaa bonds fluctuated between 90 and 100 basis points. This would accumulate a fund of about $260 for each $1,000 bond having a 20-year maturity.

An excellent example of this overestimation of risk is provided by Public Housing Authority (PHA) obligations. These bonds are issued by local housing authorities and are protected by a contract with the PHA guaranteeing service of the bonds. In effect, the bonds have a tax-exempt credit, guaranteed by the federal government. Even so, small highly rated municipal issues sold in the same month as a batch of new PHA contract housing authority bonds will frequently bring a better price than that obtained for the housing bonds. These apparent illogical investor preferences pervade the municipal market, giving rise to odd yield relationships between the various kinds of municipals and municipals in general when compared with the rest of the capital markets.

Comparatively little research has been done to explore and explain the maturity-yield patterns for tax-exempt securities. The most recent inquiries in this area are contained in the *Statistical Bulletin* published by the Investment Bankers Association.[6] Among other things, it has been discovered that the wide yield differentials noted earlier have begun to decline. An analysis of Aaa and Baa municipals covering 1956–61 revealed that the yield spread declined by more than 40 percent. The differentials are still too great to be explained in purely actuarial terms, but it seems that the spread may continue to narrow.

The exemption of interest payments from federal income tax largely accounts for the lower yields on municipals as compared with the yields of comparable fully taxed securities. In theory, investors will put money in tax-exempt issues only at yields at least equal to, or greater than, the net yield on comparable fully taxed securities. In turn, this implies that the yield differential between comparable tax-exempt and fully taxable bonds should not be a greater fraction of the fully taxable yields than the tax rate apply-

---

[6] See, for example, the *IBA Bulletins* for June and September, 1961.

ing to the investor's marginal income. But, for a variety of reasons, most investors do not act so rationally and simply demand some margin of protection against unexpected changes in income and tax rates.

Tax exemption also means a loss of revenue for the federal government that may be regarded as a subsidy extended to state and local authorities. It is an interesting, but rather frustrating, exercise to try tracing the size and division of this subsidy between the issuing authorities and investing public. How the subsidy is shared will depend on the relative market power of the two contending groups. If in any period it is found that investors get most of the subsidy, then it seems reasonable to assume that demand for tax-exempt securities is weak relative to the supply. Conversely, if most of the subsidy is retained by local authorities, then this would indicate that the supply of securities is small relative to the demand.

For many years there has been a running debate concerning the advisability of continuing to exempt municipals from federal taxes. The debate tends to be the hottest at two critical points. In the first place, any attempt to measure tax revenues lost by the federal government usually entails the assumption that, without tax exemption, yields on all comparable securities would be equal.[7] Having made this assumption, it is then possible to use existing yield differentials between municipals and fully taxed securities to estimate the extra tax revenue that would accrue if the exemption was rescinded. Apart from a host of subsidiary assumptions that these calculations involve, there is also the question whether or not it is reasonable to expect that fully taxable municipals will in fact sell at the same price as corporate bonds of similar quality. Historically, this is not true, as evidenced by yield relationships prior to the enactment of the federal income tax law.

The second most contentious area of the debate centers upon the extent to which tax exemption lowers the cost of financing for local authorities. Advocates of tax exemption claim that local authorities are able to keep most of the benefit for themselves, while opponents demonstrate that investors are the main beneficiaries. The issue remains unresolved, and estimates of the dollar magnitudes involved differ by wide margins. In relative terms, the smaller communities seem to benefit least from tax exemption. Moreover, most communities have been obliged to bargain away the benefits of tax exemption as the volume of new issues has risen.

The division and size of the tax-exemption benefit has also been influenced by the pronounced rise in municipal yields over the period. In 1946, 20-year Aaa municipals sold to yield less than 1 percent. They rose irregularly and now stand around 3.50 percent. In the same period, long-term United States governments rose from 2.25 to 4 percent, and Aaa corporate

---

[7] For example, see Henry J. Frank, "Federal Revenues from Taxing Municipals," *Journal of Finance*, September, 1961, pp. 387–408.

bonds from 2.60 to 4.50 percent.[8] Many explanations can be advanced to explain the absolute and differentially greater rise in municipal yields. The "accord" of 1951, for example, reactivated monetary policy and introduced a potent force that some argue has had an unusually big impact on municipals. Another rather persuasive explanation has to do with the nature of demand for tax-exempts. It is pointed out that tax-exempt securities are, at best, a second-order preference for most important investors and that the market for such securities has failed to expand in anything like the same proportions as the supply of securities. As a result, yields have been forced up.

IV. DEMAND FOR MUNICIPALS

Municipals have little attraction for investors who do not place a high value on tax exemption. As a result, tax-exempt institutions or organizations that can obtain partial tax relief display only casual interest in municipals. By far the greatest demand comes from high-income individuals, commercial banks, and fire and casualty insurance companies.

These three important types of investor have entered the market with varying degrees of enthusiasm since 1945. It has been estimated that, in that year, private individuals owned about 60 percent of outstanding tax-exempt securities, commercial banks 25 percent, while fire and casualty insurance companies owned approximately 2 percent.[9] By 1956 the estimated proportions were as follows: private individuals, 46 percent; commercial banks, 30 percent; and fire and casualty insurance companies, 11 percent.[9] It will be noted that, according to these estimates, private individuals have tended to account for a smaller share of all outstanding municipals, while casualty companies and commercial banks have made advances.

The most recently published estimates made in June, 1960, by the United States Treasury Department show the $66.4 billion of state and local government securities owned as follows: private individuals, 41 percent; commercial banks, 25 percent; insurance companies, 16 percent, while 17 percent was owned by a wide variety of other investors.[10] The latter estimates are not strictly comparable with those made by R. I. Robinson, but the similarities of ownership distribution are sufficiently alike to be significant.

V. OTHER DEVELOPMENTS

All the changes noted so far have been of sufficient statistical importance to catch the eye of most analysts. Inevitably, many smaller trends are in motion, but it is extremely difficult to predict which of them will blossom

[8] Board of Governors of the Federal Reserve System, *Historical Chart Book* (1961).
[9] Robinson, *op. cit.*
[10] U.S. Secretary of the Treasury, *Annual Report for the Fiscal Year Ended June 30, 1960.*

into major market forces. At least two currently minor factors are worthy of note on the ground that they may well evolve into something quite big.

The first is the growing popularity of industrial aid bonds used to supplement industrial development programs. These securities are issued by a municipality or other local authority under much the same conditions as all other municipals. The new money raised by such bonds can then be used to construct factory buildings for sale or lease to an incoming firm. Since the capital is raised on advantageous terms, the savings can be passed on to the private firm using the facilities and serve as a special incentive for moving into the area. In effect, of course, the local government is directly or indirectly using its credit standing and legal status for the benefit of a private company.

The recent popularity in the use of municipal credit for private firms began in 1936, when Mississippi initiated industrial aid bonds as part of a program called "Balance Industry with Agriculture." By March, 1961, nine states had issued an estimated 334 separate industrial bond issues having a par value of around $173.5 million. There is growing opposition to this trend, and many experts point out that, historically, lending public credit to private businesses has always resulted in calamity. Nevertheless, the urge on the part of local communities to attract new industries may well produce a boom in industrial aid bonds during the next few years.

A second event that may eventually become significant is an application of mutual-fund techniques for the purpose of selling tax-exempts. Two nationally known municipal bond houses now offer investors the opportunity to own certificates in registered investment companies. The assets of these funds are invested in a diversified group of state and local government securities. In this way, the promoters hope to attract investors interested in the familiar advantages offered by a mutual fund with the added attraction that interest income will be exempt from federal taxation.

As already noted, most municipal bond financing is undertaken to create badly needed public improvements. This stands in sharp contrast with federal spending, a large proportion of which goes into armaments. It seems reasonable to suppose that the demands for public capital expenditures will continue to rise. If this proves correct, then we are almost bound to see some sweeping adaptations and innovations in the municipal bond field during the coming decade. Few people doubt our basic economic ability to pay for the amenities of civilized living. Unfortunately, overlapping local jurisdictions and a jungle of related problems present special difficulties. It will be fascinating to see how our traditional inventiveness meets the tremendous challenge of providing for the public sector of the economy.

12.

State and Local Debt

JANE F. NELSON

For many years state and local governments have relied on sales of bond issues to finance about one half to three quarters of their capital expenditures. In 1965 these governments borrowed almost $11.1 billion for such purposes as the construction of schools, water systems, and highways. This article will focus on the principal investment characteristics of state and local government securities, how they are sold, who buys them, and recent developments affecting them as capital market instruments.

INVESTMENT CHARACTERISTICS

One of the most important features of state and local government securities, or "municipals" as they are commonly called, is the exemption of their interest from Federal income taxes. The exemption applies to interest only, and any gain resulting from a rise in the price of the bond is taxed as a capital gain. If a bond is originally *issued* at a discount, that portion of a realized gain between the discount and par is regarded as interest, because the discount is part of the cost which the issuing authority had to incur to sell its bonds. As such, the gain is tax exempt.

The tax exemption becomes increasingly valuable as the tax rate paid by an individual or corporation rises. An individual earning $50,000, or a

Reprinted from *Monthly Review*, November 1966, pp. 2–5, by permission of the publisher, the Federal Reserve Bank of Richmond. Not reprinted here is part I of the same article which appeared in June, 1966.

couple earning $100,000 and filing a joint return, both of which are in a 62% bracket, would have to realize a taxable yield of 10% to equal a yield of 3.80% on a tax exempt municipal. A corporation in the 48% tax bracket would have to receive a taxable equivalent yield of 7.31% to equal the 3.80% tax exempt return.

The quality of a bond is generally of great interest to investors. Rating agencies such as Moody's and Standard and Poor's assign quality ratings to many municipal issues, as well as to corporate bonds. These ratings are based on such factors as the past payment performance of the issuer, the amount of debt outstanding measured per capita or as a percentage of assessed property valuation, appraisals of economic prospects and, in regard to revenue bonds, estimates of the new asset's earning power. These ratings range from Aaa, signifying top quality in terms of earnings and risk, to C, the lowest quality and most speculative. Moody's Investors Service rates bonds of issuers which have over $600,000 of debt, but excludes bonds of all educational institutions, projects already under construction, enterprises without established earning records, or where necessary financial data are lacking. A bond may be of superior quality although unrated. Ratings are given for both general obligations, which are backed by the full faith and credit of the issuing government, and revenue or other nonguaranteed bonds. Ratings have become important as the criteria for determining which bonds are eligible for purchase by regulated institutions. Banks, for example, may purchase only bonds in the top four categories—Aaa through Baa —or unrated bonds of equivalent quality. Ratings are also the basis for determining which bonds are acceptable as collateral for various types of loans and deposits.

Most municipal bonds are "serial," which means that a portion of the total offering matures each year, starting after the issue date. Some bonds are "term" bonds, with the entire issue maturing on one date. Prices of serial bonds are usually quoted in terms of the interest which will be obtained if the bond is held to maturity. This is known as a "yield basis." Prices of some municipals, including most revenue bonds, are quoted in dollars, and are known as "dollar bonds."

UNDERWRITING AND DISTRIBUTING

New issues of municipal bonds are purchased through bidding or negotiation from the issuer by securities dealers and dealer banks who buy them outright and then reoffer them to the public. This process is known as underwriting, and the difference, or spread, between the price the underwriter pays the issuing government and the price at which the bonds are reoffered to the public, is the underwriter's profit, after deducting his costs. Small offerings may be purchased, either through bidding or negotiation, and sold to investors by a single underwriter, but larger issues are usually marketed by syndicates. A syndicate consists of a number of security firms temporarily associated for the purpose of selling a particular bond issue. Each firm is assigned a percentage participation by the syndicate's managing firm, but syndicate agreements vary in regard to the extent of the member's liability for any losses incurred. In an undivided, or Eastern account, the percentage indicates the extent of the member firm's liability for any residual unsold bonds or losses regardless of how many bonds the firm succeeded in selling. If a firm with 15% participation succeeds in selling 15% of all the bonds, it is still liable for 15% of the bonds which are not sold. In a divided, or Western account, the percentage signifies the amount of bonds allotted to the member firm to sell, and the firm's liability ceases when it has sold its total allotment. If a firm sells more than its allotment in a Western account, it is helping another firm reduce its liability. Both Eastern and Western accounts are undivided as to selling, that is, the bonds remain with the syndicate manager and member firms confirm their sales with the manager. The chief advantages to the underwriter of retailing bonds through a syndicate lie in being able to reach a much broader market than would otherwise be possible, and in sharing the liability if the issue does poorly.

Most syndicate agreements are in effect for a 30-day period. During that time the bonds may not be sold by members of the syndicate at any price, or range of prices, other than that established by the syndicate. When the bonds are all sold, the syndicate dissolves. If the issue is not all sold at the end of 30 days, the syndicate may be renewed if a majority of the members consent. If the syndicate is not renewed, the unsold bonds are distributed among the syndicate members according to the terms of the agreement, and the members are released from all trading restrictions. Syndicate restrictions may be lifted at any time, however, upon agreement of the majority interests in the account, and in times of declining prices a slowly selling issue may be released within a few days of the original offering in order to avoid or to minimize losses to the participating members.

THE SECONDARY MARKET

There is no organized exchange for trading in municipals. The secondary market consists of over-the-counter transactions arranged by dealers for other dealers, institutions, and individual investors. Dealers advertise their inventories in the *Blue List,* a daily publication which lists the current offerings and the price the dealer is asking that day for each particular issue. Since the start of 1966, the par value of issues included in the *Blue List* has ranged between $260 million and $636 million. The *Blue List* represents the largest part, but not the total, of the floating supply. Dealer banks, for instance, may sell bonds out of their portfolios in addition to the issues listed on their offering sheets. Also, dealers may withdraw issues from the *Blue List* if they believe that prices are going to rise, and relist them later at higher levels. Finally, issues which do not have a fairly wide market are generally not listed. The over-the-counter market is primarily a telephone market. Millions of dollars worth of bonds are sold every day over the telephone. A price quoted over the telephone is considered absolutely firm, and, if the bid is accepted, a dealer will not renege under any circumstances.

PREPARATIONS FOR A BOND OFFERING

Once a government or authority has decided to raise funds through a bond flotation it must follow a lengthy and complicated procedure in order to insure that the sale meets all legal requirements and is concluded on the most favorable terms possible. All phases of the planning are normally supervised by an attorney who specializes in municipal law, and the lawyer's opinion regarding the legality of the sale and the tax exempt status of the bonds is usually made available to all dealers and prospective investors. The issuer should also prepare a prospectus containing comprehensive data on its financial situation and estimates of reputable engineers or analysts regarding the cost of the capital improvement and, where appropriate, the income it will generate. Complete information should be submitted to a rating agency to assure the best possible rating and therefore the lowest possible interest cost.

Virtually all state and local governments are required by their own laws to market general obligation bonds publicly, through the solicitation of sealed competitive bids. Bonds which are not backed by the full faith and credit of the issuing government, such as toll road and industrial aid bonds, may be sold competitively but are more often priced through direct negotiation with the underwriter.

It is in the best interest of the issuing authority to publicize the approaching sale by advertising in local and perhaps national newspapers. The object of such publicity is to receive as many bids as possible and to sell the bonds at the lowest possible interest cost. Sizable offerings are usually advertised with all pertinent information in the *Daily* or *Weekly Bond Buyer*, which is received by practically every firm concerned with tax exempt financing. If none of the bids received is satisfactory to the issuer, all may be rejected and the offering postponed or cancelled.

For most states and large municipal borrowers the procedures involved in bond sales do not pose significant difficulties. Large borrowers are usually familiar with the necessary steps and also maintain close contact with capital market developments. Small towns, counties, school districts, and other special districts, however, are often relatively unfamiliar with the correct procedures and market conditions. Mistakes may cause them to pay too high a price for borrowed funds, perhaps saddle the community with too heavy a financial burden, or even prevent the sale from occurring at all due to legal complications or lack of sufficient advertising. At least four states, Virginia, North Carolina, Michigan, and Louisiana, have created commissions which assist and oversee the borrowing operations of small governmental units. The Virginia Commission does not offer aid or advice unless requested by the locality, but in North Carolina localities are required by law to receive the Commission's approval before soliciting bids unless the issuing unit, by a referendum vote, decides to proceed with the issue despite the Commission's disapproval. The North Carolina Commission takes an active part in many phases of the bond flotation, including advertising, receiving the bids, and printing and delivering the bonds. The Commission's supervision assures investors that the correct procedures have been followed and that data on the community's finances will be readily available. The community benefits from the wider market and lower interest costs which result from dealers' and investors' knowledge of the Commission's standards and the uniformity of the offering procedures.

THE PRINCIPAL INVESTORS

Individuals have been the largest holders of tax exempts in the postwar period except for 1965 when commercial banks moved into first place. From 1955 through 1960 individuals held roughly 40% of the total out-

CHART 12–1

Ownership of State and Local Government Securities

Percentage Distribution

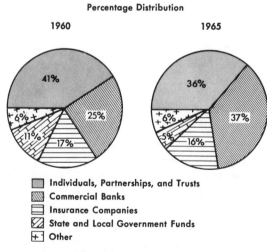

Source: Office of the Secretary of the Treasury.

standing. During the past six years, however, individuals' holdings of municipals have declined by about 5 percentage points, as shown in Chart 12–1. As a result of recent developments, it seems likely that individuals again hold the largest block of outstanding tax exempts. During this same period state and local governments have also become less important holders of tax exempts as public officials have become increasingly aware of more profitable alternatives, and as laws governing the investment of public funds have been liberalized.

Commercial banks more than doubled their holdings of tax exempts between 1960 and 1965, from $16.8 billion to $36.6 billion. The latter figure represented about 37% of the total volume outstanding in 1965. The nation's one hundred largest commercial banks hold about one half of all municipals owned by banks, and about 19% of the total outstanding. Municipals averaged almost 10.5% of the total assets of these banks in June 1966, compared to about 6% in June 1961. In 1962 and 1963 the net increase in total bank holdings accounted for over three fourths of the net increase in total state and local securities outstanding, while in 1964 and 1965 bank acquisitions came to over 60% of the net addition to tax exempts.

The surge in commercial bank buying of municipals can be traced in part to changes in ceilings on the interest rates which commercial banks are permitted to pay on time and savings deposits. The Board of Governors of the Federal Reserve System has raised these ceilings four times since the end of 1961, most recently in December 1965. As banks paid progressively higher rates on their time deposits, and attracted a large volume of new high cost deposits, they sought higher yielding investments.

Insurance companies rank third in importance as holders of municipals. Fire and casualty companies are the principal holders as life insurance companies receive little benefit from the tax exempt feature. Nonfinancial corporations have been stepping up their purchases, although their total holdings are still relatively small. Other holders include mutual savings banks, savings and loan associations, corporate pension trust funds, dealers and brokers, and foreign investors.

13.

The Development
of an Effective Secondary
Mortgage Market

OLIVER JONES

I. INTRODUCTION

For over forty years the secondary market for mortgages on one- to four-family non-farm residences has been attacked with regularity.[1] Encouraged by the Federal Land Bank and the Federal Reserve System innovations, proponents of a credit system for residential mortgages repeatedly introduced legislation into the Congress. However, it was not until the collapse of mortgage financing in the early 1930's that the federal

---

Reprinted from *Journal of Finance*, Vol. XVII, No. 2, May 1962, pp. 358–370, by permission of the author, Executive Vice-President, Mortgage Bankers Association of America, and the publisher.

[1] This analysis is confined to federally underwritten and conventional mortgages on one- to four-family non-farm residences, hereafter referred to as "residential mortgages." Such mortgages are reasonably homogeneous in type of securing property, type of risk, and method of financing. They are the most frequently traded and the most promising area for the development of an effective secondary mortgage market. For a comprehensive study of the secondary mortgage market see Oliver Jones and Leo Grebler, *The Secondary Mortgage Market—Its Purpose, Performance, and Potential* (Berkeley and Los Angeles: University of California Press, 1961).

government took steps to seek improvement in both the primary and the secondary segments of the market.

In 1934 the Federal Home Loan Bank System was created to provide a mortgage credit system, and the Federal Housing Administration was created to insure residential mortgages. In 1938 the Federal National Mortgage Association began buying and selling federally insured mortgages. The VA-guaranteed mortgage appeared on the scene in 1944 and was added to FNMA's stock in trade four years later. In the postwar years, mortgage lenders still found the secondary market inadequate for their needs and developed substitute market arrangements.

The controversy over the secondary market's inability to perform effectively continues to this day. In the last two years, every major institutional group with an interest in mortgage finance or housing construction has formulated a plan for market reform. Indeed, it is likely that Congress will again be dealing with the inadequacies of the secondary market for mortgages in its next session.

II. EFFECTIVENESS OF THE EXISTING SECONDARY MARKET

The Complaint

What do the market's critics expect of an effective secondary market? Despite differences in the details of their proposals to revise the secondary mortgage market, they agree that it has performed inadequately in four major areas: (1) it has provided only a limited degree of marketability for mortgages; (2) it has failed to stabilize the flow of funds into mortgage investment; (3) while contributing to the movement of funds from capital-surplus to capital-deficit areas, it has not fully met the needs of growth areas; and (4) the secondary market has had little success in tapping pools of savings that are apparently cut off from mortgage investments.

One can find little argument with these goals. Increased marketability and liquidity for mortgages, greater stability, and improved resource allocation—these are clearly desirable objectives. It can also be agreed that such goals are not being achieved by the existing secondary mortgage market. However, it is not the purpose of this paper to seek agreement but to show why the mortgage market as it is now organized cannot achieve the objectives credited to the secondary market and to outline the steps that must be taken if an effective secondary market is to be developed.

To a large extent, measures that have been designed to develop an effective secondary market have failed because of a predisposition to circumvent, rather than deal directly with, the causes of its shortcomings. The use of roundabout means has, in turn, been encouraged by the failure to identify the economic role of a secondary market. According to common usage, the secondary mortgage market encompasses the sale of mortgages, while the primary market includes the original extension of credit. By this definition, the secondary market for residential mortgages is a substantial segment of the mortgage market. In 1960, for example, transfers of FHA home mortgages equaled $4,565 million, or nearly 15 percent of the total outstanding debt represented by such mortgages. Although comparable data are not available for VA-guaranteed and conventional mortgages, the organization of market processes and available statistics on originations and holdings by type of lender indicate that a large share of the outstanding volume of VA mortgages and a relatively small but significant share of outstanding conventional mortgages have been acquired by present holders in the resale market. However large, the economic role of this secondary market is quite limited, and it does not appear to be capable of overcoming the failures in performance attributed to it by the market's critics.

The Evidence

Under prevailing operating methods, the bulk of the "sales" that take place in the secondary market is made to buyers who have agreed to purchase the mortgages in advance of origination, often in advance of construction. Thus the seller is, in fact if not in law, an agent of the buyer.

In the typical market arrangement, a mortgage company sells mortgages to a life insurance company that has previously committed itself to buy the mortgages. The insurance company makes the decision that brings about the origination of the mortgage, and it accepts the risks involved. The mortgage company contributes little more to the marketing process than a branch office of an insurance company. Its market function is little more than a mirrored image of the insurance company. The process is simply one of the methods by which certain lenders originate mortgage loans. Thus the existing secondary market, despite its size and postwar growth, can offer the primary mortgage market no more than it can do for itself.

The lack of an independent market for existing mortgages has caused the federal government and portfolio lenders to devise a variety of substitute arrangements for making adjustments in mortgage holdings. Although they have gained some measure of marketability and liquidity, the devices used have also contributed to the existing degree of instability and distorted the allocation of resources.

Consider, first, the practice of varying holdings of liquid assets as a substitute for a ready market for mortgages. Portfolio lenders have long relied on holdings of government securities as a cushion to fall back on when commitments to purchase mortgages exceeded the anticipated inflow of savings. Indeed, reduction of the highly liquid positions in government securities of the early postwar years accounted for an important part of the expansion in mortgage lending activity of the period. This procedure slowed sharply when the government securities market was unpegged in 1950 and shifts to mortgages began to involve losses.

While holdings of liquid assets continue to provide a means for adjusting mortgage portfolios, there are now narrow limits to the use of this device. If government securities are sold to cover an overcommitted position in mortgages, the ratio of mortgage holdings to liquid assets that the lender desires to maintain will be exceeded. In order to redress the portfolio's balance, the lender will temporarily withdraw from the mortgage market. This type of response to changing market conditions accentuates instability in the mortgage market. In addition, portfolio lenders, who might have been potential mortgage buyers had mortgages been sold instead of government securities, are excluded from the adjustment process. If the secondary market were able to purchase the mortgages at discounts equal to capital losses taken on government securities and sell them later to other investors, the transactions would improve the allocation of mortgage funds, enable both groups of lenders to maintain their liquidity position, and avoid disturbing the market for government securities.

Commercial bank credit has also served as a substitute for a secondary market for mortgages when portfolio adjustments were in order. While commercial bank loans can strengthen the ability of mortgage companies to provide a market for mortgages, bank loans to portfolio lenders in lieu of adjustment of their mortgage assets short-circuits the discipline of the market place and makes it impossible for lenders seeking adjustment in the opposite direction to participate. Borrowing from the Federal Home Loan Banks has similar shortcomings. In addition, it is available only to savings and loan associations and, thereby, largely for conventional mortgages.

It would appear that the Federal National Mortgage Association (FNMA) is the ideal substitute for a private secondary mortgage market. Mortgages could be sold to FNMA to alleviate unforeseen pressures, thereby focusing activity on a central point and giving potential buyers an opportunity to participate. Conversely, mortgages might be purchased from FNMA when prices were attractive and savings inflows exceeded expectations.

The secondary market operation established late in 1954 was apparently designed for such purposes. By limiting advance commitments to below-par prices and by purchasing within the range of market prices, the abuses of FNMA's earlier period were to be abolished and a true secondary market facility created. However, the association has limited its purchases to relatively new mortgages—most often to mortgages no older than four months. The time that elapses between mortgage origination and completion of processing for delivery to FNMA takes from two to three months. Thus the decision to sell to FNMA must be made shortly after the mortgage is originated. Such an arrangement is hardly conducive to the use of the association as an adjustment device. Instead, it has become an outlet for mortgages originated by mortgage companies when their regular clients are out of the market.

On the other side of the secondary market, FNMA has been unable to sell mortgages at a loss or to sell during periods when the availability of funds from other sources was putting pressure on the housing market's resources. Thus the association continues to be in large measure a primary lender and an inadequate substitute for an effective secondary market, despite the safeguards provided. Moreover, the association's activities have only a limited indirect influence on a large segment of mortgage financing because it does not deal in conventional mortgages.

In general, there are numerous flaws in the arrangements devised to substitute for a ready market for mortgages. They are incapable of producing the consequences attributed to an effective secondary market and, indeed, aggravate instability in the flow of funds into mortgages and further distort resource allocation. All the substitutes are not available to all lenders, and, at times, none are available to some lenders. By their very variety, substitute arrangements disperse the impact of changes in supply and demand conditions in such a way that the equilibrating focus essential to an effective secondary market cannot be obtained.

The Verdict

What, then, is needed? The successful achievement of the goals attributed to the secondary market turns on its ability to provide a market for existing mortgages by always standing ready to buy and sell mortgages at prevailing prices. It is an obvious tautology to argue that marketability can be achieved only by making a market for mortgages. Nevertheless, this is a vital facet in the development of an effective secondary market that has been consistently ignored. And yet, greater stability and improved resource allocation cannot be attained by a secondary market where some participants only sell and others only buy mortgages, nor can they be attained by a federal agency that only buys mortgages.

To gain these expected ends, the secondary market must provide a reliable barometer of the value of existing mortgages and bring buyers and sellers together by providing a ready market for the purchase or sale of existing mortgages. It must be two-sided and focused on a single center or a highly integrated group of centers, where the bulk of the transactions can take place and where the net balance of supply and demand can be ultimately reflected in price. Only then can changes in supply and demand conditions in the markets for non-mortgage as well as mortgage investments be accurately reflected in price. Accordingly, resource allocation can be guided by going market prices and not be distorted by the destabilizing shifts to and from mortgages that have typified the postwar mortgage market. The much desired marketable mortgage is therefore a necessary, but not a sufficient, condition of effective performance by the secondary market for mortgages.

III. CONSEQUENCES OF AN EFFECTIVE SECONDARY MARKET

Only an entrepreneur making decisions and taking risks independent of the primary lender—a market maker—can offer marketability and market-pricing. By taking a position in mortgages without benefit of an advance commitment, by always standing ready to buy and sell mortgages, the market maker can provide a market for existing mortgages and thereby achieve the consequences so often sought in proposals to reform today's secondary market.

Providing a market for existing mortgages will, for example, increase the appetite of portfolio lenders for mortgage investments. A more liquid mortgage would reduce the likelihood of their being frozen into a mortgage position. Thus the volume of highly liquid, non-mortgage assets held for portfolio adjustment purposes could be reduced in favor of higher-yielding mortgages. However, no secondary market can guarantee that mortgages could always be liquidated without loss. The current value of a mortgage or, for that matter, of any long-term investment changes during its lifetime, and no secondary market could provide a continuing market for such investments at par prices. Attempts to do just that through the Federal National Mortgage Association have resulted in its becoming, in effect, a primary lender. In short, the secondary market can provide a degree of liquidity at a cost that will depend on prevailing market conditions.

To the extent that the residential mortgage can be endowed with marketability, the conversion of mortgages into debentures to tap pension and trust funds, which now shun mortgage investment, would be less necessary. Still, pension-fund managers may prefer the convenience of debentures over servicing monthly amortized mortgages. Several organizations have already experienced some success in meeting this need by performing the home-office functions of managing a mortgage portfolio and selling debentures or collateral trust notes to pension and similar funds. Once the market maker is sufficiently large and capitalized, he could participate in similar arrangements. However, converting mortgages to debentures is not distinctly a secondary market function. It can be performed equally well in the primary market.

While marketability may encourage some expansion in the flow of funds into mortgage investments, the same goal could be reached by a federal facility that would always be prepared to buy mortgages. This appears to be the objective of some of the current proposals for market reform. All too often it is assumed that a federal facility can generate the economic consequences attributed to the secondary market for mortgages, by acting as a lender of last resort. But such a facility would only make the purchase side of the market and, in effect, perform functions similar to those of a large portfolio lender. It would, indeed, become a portfolio lender whose size would be determined only by its authority to draw on the Treasury. Still, it would fail to generate the consequences attributed to an effective secondary mortgage market, because the equilibrating focal points represented by participants who are willing and able to make both sides of the market would still be missing.

This distinction is crucial to the development of an adequate secondary mortgage market, for it is through effective price determination in a two-sided market for mortgages that improvements in resource allocation and in the stability of the flow of mortgage funds can be attained. Although market makers would not hold mortgages as long-term investments, the net balance between sales and purchases would influence their mortgage positions and therefore their pricing policies. Purchases of mortgages in excess of sales would increase their inventories, depress prices, and increase yields; conversely, sales of mortgages in excess of purchases would reduce their inventories, increase prices, and depress yields. Thus the marginal operation of the secondary market would provide the essential focal points—an accomplishment that is not possible in today's "one-way" market.

Price and yield determination in an effective secondary market would vary between federally underwritten and conventional mortgages, between areas of capital surplus and areas of capital deficit, and between high- and low-risk loans. Primary lenders could readily compare the yield on residential mortgages with the yield on alternative investments. Funds would be allocated within the mortgage market and between housing and other uses according to investor-borrower judgments of alternative returns, alternative costs, and expected risks.

The debilitating effect of sudden withdrawals from mortgage investments and equally sudden floods of funds seeking mortgage investments would be alleviated by the market maker's ability to take long and short positions as warranted by his judgment of market conditions. In today's market, when portfolio lenders withdraw en masse, yields tend to rise and prices fall. When they return with large demands for mortgages, the situation is reversed. Under these conditions, it would be in the market maker's own self-interest to supply the shock-absorbing capacity that the market now lacks. In so doing, he would improve the stability of the flow of mortgage funds and the allocation of resources over time.

Stability would also be enhanced by the market maker's self-interest in the collection and dissemination of information on prices and yields. To be informed on prevailing conditions, he would have to become closely linked with other market makers to communicate information on changing conditions. The changing facts would, in turn, be available to his potential clients and improve their decision-making processes.

While an effective secondary market can enhance the stability of the flow of funds into mortgage investments, it does not offer a panacea for avoiding cyclical swings. The secondary market can smooth the adjustment to changing supply and demand conditions, but it cannot remove them. If such adjustments prove to be socially undesirable, other means outside of the market framework should be used to offset their effects.

In summary, then, the requirements of an effective secondary market include the provision of a two-way market for existing mortgages and the capacity to work out the net balance of supply and demand in the form of a going price for mortgages. Such a market can provide a degree of liquidity that is appropriate for long-term investments in mortgages, contribute to the stabilization of the flow of funds into mortgage investments, and improve the allocation of the nation's financial resources between mortgage and non-mortgage uses, among different types of mortgages, and among geographic areas.

IV. BARRIERS TO THE DEVELOPMENT OF AN EFFECTIVE SECONDARY MARKET

In the foregoing discussion, the market maker emerges as the indispensable means of unlocking the mortgage market's potential ability to generate an effective secondary market for residential mortgages. The need for his services is evident in the instability that has characterized the flow of mortgage funds in the postwar years, in strivings for suitable alternatives, and, indeed, in the repeated criticism of the market's performance.

The most likely candidate—the mortgage company—holds tenaciously to the advance-commitment device that relegates risk-taking and decision-making to the primary lender. Mortgage companies have, of course, been hampered by lack of capital, credit resources, and experience with a flexible market for money and credit. Still, these would not be insuperable obstacles if they chose to become market makers. What, then, are the barriers to making a market for mortgages?

Willingness to make a market for any commodity is predicated on reliable sources of supply, as well as sufficient breadth and scope in market outlets to warrant the expectation that the commodity can be resold at a price that will produce a profit. If the market's outlets are thin, the risks may be too great to attract market makers. If the lack of outlets is inherent in the nature of the commodity—a mortgage on a $50,000, uniquely styled, and remotely located residence—resale markets cannot be developed. Many mortgages are so differentiated from the "average" that they will never be traded in an organized secondary market. To some observers, the lack of homogeneity in the properties securing residential mortgages and in the borrowers' credit positions is the major barrier to the development of an effective secondary mortgage market. However, homogeneity per se cannot be the stumbling block. If it were, mortgage lending would be strictly limited to local markets, and this is clearly refuted by the large annual volume of precommitted transfers of conventional, as well as federally underwritten, mortgages in the existing secondary market.

On the other hand, differentiation that results from man-made statutes and regulations does restrict the scope of the market maker's outlets and discourages his development. For example, the would-be market maker is greatly limited when offered a conventional mortgage. The variety of underwriting standards results in an endless spectrum of mortgage quality that is not matched by a spectrum of willing buyers. Mortgages are classified, but there are too many systems of classification. With the exception of life insurance companies, the market maker cannot find customers for a conventional mortgage beyond the relatively narrow geographic area that circumscribes the lending operations of other institutional lenders. Even life insurance companies, in most cases, are excluded from his market if the loan exceeds two-thirds of the property's value.

The situation is only somewhat better for trading in federally underwritten mortgages. Not all lenders can reach across state lines to acquire federally underwritten mortgages; those who can, will not purchase mortgages on properties in states where foreclosure costs are high, redemption periods are long, and doing-business requirements represent a formidable barrier. Besides, an important segment of the primary market is largely wedded to the conventional mortgage. Most importantly, federal interference through price fixing and sporadic support programs exaggerate the influence of monetary policy and changes in economic conditions on the price of FHA and VA mortgages, often creating a degree of uncertainty that the entrepreneur is unable to cope with.

Thus markedly different restrictions on the investment powers of primary lenders divide potential outlets into narrow segments and discourage the entrepreneur from venturing into the business of making a market for mortgages. Fearful of unpredictable changes in the prices of mortgages that result from discretionary decisions of the federal government, market middlemen in the existing market seek the shelter of the advance commitment.

V. OUTLINE OF REFORMS

Thus the development of an effective secondary market for residential mortgages will make it necessary to clear the primary market of its man-made imperfections.

First, the contract rate on newly originated FHA and VA mortgages should be market-determined. Discounts and premiums should be permitted in the secondary market to provide for adjustment to prevailing yields. However, this would not single-handedly generate an effective secondary mortgage market. If the contract rates on FHA and VA mortgages were market-oriented, a number of secondary markets specializing in meeting the needs of the several compartments of the primary market might develop. However, the ability of such a group of satellite secondary markets to improve the efficiency of the market mechanism would still be quite limited. The essential ingredient—the equilibrating focal points—would still be missing, and barriers that unnecessarily splinter the mortgage market would remain.

Thus a number of other steps should be initiated to break down the compartmentalization now prevalent in the primary market. These include (1) standardization of statutory restrictions on terms that may be offered on conventional mortgages; (2) removal of geographic restrictions on lending operations; (3) adoption of a uniform mortgage code to reduce area differentiation generated by variations in foreclosure costs, redemption periods, and doing-business requirements; and (4) revision of statutes that particularly circumscribe mortgage lending by commercial banks. In addition, competition between mortgage and non-mortgage investments should be increased by more nearly equalizing the ability of mortgage lenders to attract savings and to invest in non-mortgage assets; for the powers of the secondary market to improve the allocation of resources can be no more extensive than the powers of its clients to consider alternatives.

Besides making changes in the primary market, changes must be made in the secondary market. The market maker would be divorced from the advance commitment, and this alteration would require the establishment of a relationship among participants that is now foreign to the mortgage market. In the existing secondary market, confidence between participants has been built upon a long-standing relationship, periodically buttressed by an audit of the mortgage company's books by institutional investors dealing with the company. Even then, the buyer conducts an on-the-site inspection of the property; some lenders are required by law to do so. In an effective secondary market, however, the market maker must do business with a large number of originators as well as primary lenders. Like his customers, he would find it cumbersome and expensive to check the property. This would tend to reduce the number of his potential customers and increase his risks by extending the time he must hold the mortgage. Thus a new basis for establishing and creating confidence among originators, market makers, and portfolio lenders must be found.

For this purpose, market makers and mortgage companies should be allowed to obtain federal charters, which would place them under federal supervision, and statutes that require on-the-site inspections should be revised. Transactions in the secondary market would also be facilitated by seeking a greater degree of homogeneity through the development of a classification system for conventional mortgages, simplification of the legal and administrative red tape that surrounds the transfer of mortgages, and simplification of the complex and often changed regulations of the federal underwriting agencies.

It is believed that the foregoing proposals alone would encourage the development of a secondary market where mortgages would be traded without the protection of an advance commitment. Indeed, most of the recommendations are worth pursuing, even if they made no contribution to the secondary market. Nevertheless, the period of transition would be one of great uncertainty, experimentation, and even turmoil. The secondary market would not be transformed overnight from a thin and erratic specter into a full-blown, efficient mechanism. It is at this point that the need for a federal facility to ease the transition from the current to the prospective market structure emerges.

The objectives of such a facility can be divided into three groups. First, it would provide an orderly environment during the period of transition and act as an adjustment device for market makers. To this end, the facility should be empowered to buy and sell mortgages. The principal distinctions between this function and its application by FNMA would be the inclusion of conventional mortgages in its activities and permitting the facility to make the decision to buy or sell at its own volition.

The facility should also be permitted to make short-term adjustment loans to market makers. Care would have to be exercised to avoid creating a "Commodity Credit Corporation" for mortgages, but the loan device is necessary to encourage entrepreneurs to make a market for mortgages. Of course, when commercial banks become more willing to lend to market makers without the assurance of an advance commitment, this function should be allowed to dwindle to a vestigial operation. Short-term loans to portfolio lenders, for emergency purposes only, would strengthen the facility's hand in maintaining an orderly market and should therefore be permitted.

The second objective would be to supplement other reforms. The federal facility should be empowered to charter and supervise market makers and mortgage companies, conduct studies necessary to develop a workable system for classifying conventional as well as federally underwritten mortgages, and take appropriate actions to encourage state governments and state supervisory authorities to co-operate with the program of reform.

Finally, the facility could accelerate the evolutionary process by collecting and disseminating current information on prices and activity and providing the centralizing focus necessary to bring the net balance of supply and demand forces to bear on the price of mortgages. Until the market middlemen are of such size and proved capability that they can issue debentures tailored to the needs of pension funds and similar untapped pools of savings, the federal facility could also perform this function.

The reforms proposed here are extensive and almost forbidding in scope. However, there can be little hope for the development of an effective secondary market without such a comprehensive program. The choice is between tolerating the present imperfections and failures of the market to perform efficiently and a bold move to reduce, if not remove, existing impediments to competition.

14.

Major Developments
in the Market for Consumer Credit
Since the End of World War II

ROBERT P. SHAY

INTRODUCTION

Ten years ago, I addressed this association's member-
ship on the subject of postwar developments in the consumer credit market.
My conclusion, then as now, was that this market which was born in the
early 1900's, grew up in the 1920's, and matured in the 1930's, was a
sturdy enough adult to handle the postwar growth of credit without basic
structural changes. In the past decade we have seen many innovations come
into the consumer credit market. Credit cards, charge account banking, and
check credit plans have become commonplace among commercial banks
which are offering diversified plans to meet their customers' entire credit
needs. Savings institutions now make some consumer loans and look long-
ingly upon further extension of their activities now denied them under many
state laws. If one disregarded the current statistics and measured the market
by criteria other than the amount of credit outstanding, there would be a
stronger impression of structural changes than the data imply.

Yet changes have occurred in the last decade which put us closer to a
day when consumers will carry debit, rather than credit balances in their

Reprinted from *Journal of Finance*, Vol. XXI, No. 2, May 1966, pp. 361–381, by permission of the author and the publisher.

checking accounts with commercial banks. We are certainly closer to the day when savings institutions will be able to make the mortgage an all purpose credit instrument. We may come to find finance companies making direct loans from offices selling credit together with diversified services of an insurance, legal, or financial nature. When these changes occur, I will readily admit that basic structural changes have occurred in the consumer credit market.

The most important developments during the postwar period are the sharply increasing size of the consumer instalment credit market, the easing of credit terms and the closer competitive relations among consumer credit institutions. Consumer instalment credit outstanding has continued to rise at a rapid rate in the postwar period. The easing of credit terms has fostered this growth ever since the early 1900's with few interruptions. Finally, the increased competitiveness among financing institutions accompanied a rise in incomes which qualified more borrowers to obtain credit in larger amounts from virtually all types of consumer credit agencies. Up to the present, consumer instalment credit has continued to grow more rapidly than income, as has total private debt.

Once consumer instalment credit is recognized as important, the degree of instability which is reflected in its movements and their timing must be appraised with respect to the stability of the economy. We shall see that the pronounced cyclical patterns of instalment credit are not markedly different from those in the prewar years. It is mainly the size that has changed. Finally, there are differences in the competitive positions of institutions participating in the credit market. If these had occurred to an important degree, one would have found structural changes in the market. From reviewing the data I can only detect signs that future changes may occur. But today, I shall aver that there are two basic reasons why the structure of the instalment credit market has changed little since the prewar days. First, there have been compelling legal barriers restraining competitive forces among institutions on the instalment credit market. Second, borrowers have chosen to seek out competition in credit terms, rather than price, in expanding credit use.

I shall not say much about the deterioration in credit quality which has occurred with the easing of terms in the postwar period. Measured by higher loan to value ratios and longer maturities, there is a prima facie quality decline. Yet, this may also be viewed as a relaxation of lender constraints upon borrowers who are now better qualified to obtain credit as well as to repay it. If economic events are adverse, there may be greater defaults and losses than would have been the case with more stringent terms. But, the pricing policy should reflect the risks assumed, including the possible adverse consequences from recession. Credit quality is an elusive strand to capture. Its decline is a facet of postwar experience but the overall probability of repayment may not be substantially lower.

I shall review changes in the consumer credit market since 1939 and 1952 as a means of evaluating major postwar developments. The continued growth in size, cyclical behavior, and changing market shares among competing credit sources, lead me to believe that the automobile credit market is the harbinger of competitive changes which may spread to the other markets. Much will depend upon current proposals for reform to improve the functioning of the market.

INSTALMENT CREDIT AND HOUSEHOLD CAPITAL FORMATION

The last two decades have provided evidence that consumer instalment credit has assumed significant proportions in relation to economic activity. The durable goods which consumer instalment credit helps to finance are now collectively dignified by the title, "household capital formation." Household capital formation results from a flow of saving encouraged by the availability of credit to purchase goods. The equity originally acquired through down-payment plus (or minus) the excess (deficiency) of repayments in relation to depreciation represent sources of saving through credit use. F. Thomas Juster's work at the National Bureau has indicated that household gross capital formation has grown relative to enterprise investment both in respect to cyclical variability and as a fraction of gross national product.[1] Indeed, in the postwar decades consumer capital expenditures on residential construction and consumer durable goods have exceeded producer capital expenditures in virtually every year since 1950.[2] Both consumer and producer capital formation fluctuate cyclically and fill the traditional role of investment as a source of growth and instability.

One observation about consumer capital formation in the postwar period is that much of its growth has depended upon consumer financing. Consumers have increased their borrowing to undertake capital expenditures. Both short-term and long-term (owner-occupied mortgage) consumer credit have shown rapid rates of growth in the postwar period. Consumer instalment credit outstanding, exclusive of mortgages, has grown at a considerably faster rate than the growth in Gross National Product and Disposable Personal Income. Yet this was true of the prewar period as well. Between 1950 and 1964, using current dollar figures, consumer instalment credit grew at an annual 10.5% rate while GNP and DPI grew at 5.8%

---

[1] For illustrations of the rate of growth of household capital and indebtedness as well as the changing shares of household and enterprise investment in gross national product since 1897, see "Consumer Credit Markets, a Progress Report," Forty-fifth Annual Report of the National Bureau of Economic Research, Inc., June, 1965, pp. 26–28.

[2] See *Flow of Funds Accounts*, 1945–62, 1963 supplement, Board of Governors of the Federal Reserve System, and subsequent *Federal Reserve Bulletins*.

CHART 14-1

Quarterly Flows of Consumer Durable Goods Outlays and Instalment Credit, 1952-64

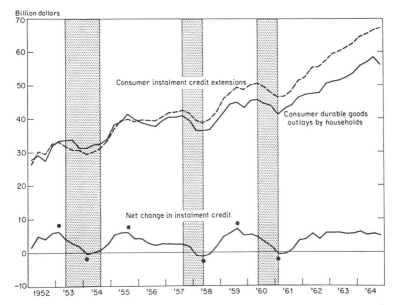

Shaded areas represent business cycle contractions. Dots identify peaks and troughs of specific cycles.

Source: Consumer durable goods outlays exclude residential construction, see Table 4, pp. 109-114, and instalment credit data from Table 29, pp. 189-190, Flow of Funds Accounts, 1945-62, 1963 Supplement, Federal Reserve Board. The quarterly data are seasonally adjusted and expressed at annual rates. The 1963 and 1964 instalment credit estimates differ slightly from those obtained directly from the flow of funds accounts in other years.

and 5.5% respectively. Between 1929 and 1941, the corresponding growth rates were 4.7%, 1.6%, and .9%, respectively. Thus, credit use has grown relative to income since 1929 at least, and will probably continue to do so as long as credit use continues to maintain its present growth rate.

The enlarged magnitude of consumer capital expenditure has been accompanied by an even sharper growth in extensions of consumer instalment credit. The top two lines of Chart 14-1 reveal the close conformity between total instalment credit extensions and consumer durable goods outlays since 1952. Although some portion of the credit extensions is used to finance the purchase of nondurables and services, and often to consolidate non-instalment debts, it is clear that the durable goods financing must be responsible for the closeness of movements in the two series. The bottom line, net change in instalment credit, is also closely related to changes in both credit extensions and durable goods outlays. It shows no apparent trend because it re-

TABLE 14-1

Specific Turning Points in the Quarterly Net Change of Consumer Instalment Credit Outstanding in Relation to NBER Reference Cycle Turning Points

1929-41						1953-64					
NBER Reference Cycle Dates		Change in CIC Outstanding Dates		Lead (—) or Coincidence (0)		NBER Reference Cycle Dates		Change in CIC Outstanding		Lead (—) or Coincidence (0)	
T	P	T	P	T	P	T	P	T	P	T	P
	3—29		2—29		—1		2—53		—2		—2
1—33	2—37	2—32	1—36	—3	—5	3—54	3—57	—2	—9	—2	—9
2—38		1—38		—1		2—58	2—60	0	—3	0	—3
						1—61		0		0	
		Average						**Average**			
		—2 1/2						**—2 2/3**			

Source: 1929-41, McCracken, Mao, and Fricke, Table 11; 1953-64, Flow-of-Funds Accounts, 1945-62, Board of Governors of the FRS.

flects the net difference between extensions and repayments, which both contain a similar rising trend over these years. The net change series tends to reflect the extensions series and offers perhaps the best measure of the net contribution of instalment credit to expenditure.[3]

McCracken, Mao, and Fricke have analyzed the change in instalment debt and other measures in relation to the change in disposable personal income, personal consumption expenditure and to gross national product.[4] On the basis of any of their measures they conclude that changes in instalment credit outstanding have become substantially more important in the postwar period than in the prewar period.

The cyclical variability of instalment credit is apparent in the net change in instalment credit, shown in the lower part of Chart 14-1. So also is the marked lead of the peak in the net change series before the business cycle peak in contrast to the coincidence of net change with business cycle troughs in two of three turning points. McCracken, Mao and Fricke found that turning points in consumer credit showed a pattern of timing in the prewar period similar to that shown in the postwar period.[5] The data in

[3] As long as net change is positive it adds to total expenditure, under the assumption that extensions add and repayments subtract (dollar for dollar) from expenditure. When the change in net change declines although net change remains positive, it adds less and less to expenditure. Because of the indirect (multiplier and accelerator) effects of credit and expenditures upon business activity, movements in the change in net change probably indicate better the cyclical contributions of credit to income changes. On the latter point, see Paul F. Smith, "Multiplier Effects of Hire Purchase," *Economica*, May, 1964.

[4] *Consumer Instalment Credit and Public Policy*, Bureau of Business Research, University of Michigan, 1965, Table 16, pp. 65–66.

[5] Ibid., p. 54.

Table 14–1 reveal that the net change in instalment credit led four National Bureau Reference cycle turning points by an average of two and one-half quarters in the prewar period and by two and two-thirds quarters in the six postwar turning points. The average lead at peaks over the entire period was four quarters while at trough it was less than two quarters. The greater lead before reference cycle peaks suggests that dampening effects of a slower rate of credit increase took longer to become general than the reverse movement before troughs.

CYCLICAL BEHAVIOR OF THE MAJOR COMPONENTS OF INSTALMENT CREDIT OUTSTANDING

The three major components of instalment credit are automobile credit, other consumer durable goods credit and personal loans. The first two categories include only durable goods financing, as the credit must be secured by the type of good purchased. Personal loans, on the other hand, are largely unsecured. Together, the three represented about ninty-four percent of instalment credit outstanding during the period, the remainder being repair and modernization credit. Chart 14–2 shows monthly net changes in each of the three components. Automobile credit, ranging in importance from 40 to 46 percent of instalment credit over the period, clearly dominates the cyclical movements of the change in total instalment credit shown previously in Chart 14–1. Yet there are other interesting aspects to be noted. First, except for the divergent peaks in other consumer durable goods credit in 1952 and 1956, the timing of movements in the three series have been markedly similar. Second, the growth in personal loan net change has been stronger since 1958 and its movements indicate greater cyclical variability than in the earlier years. It is likely that personal loans have been used more frequently as a substitute for the other consumer durable goods credit as well as to finance an increasing flow of services, such as vacation, education, and travel. The share of total instalment credit gained by personal loans between 1952 and 1964 has been almost exactly offset by the declining share of "other consumer durable goods credit."

On balance, the main inference to be drawn from the movements of automobile credit, other consumer durable goods credit and personal loans is that all three show substantial leads at reference cycle peaks and shorter leads (or lags) at reference cycle throughs. Thus, even though automobile credit is predominant in size, the timing of instalment credit movements exclusive of automobile credit, would probably not have been markedly different except for the 1955 peak, relative to cyclical movements in the economy over the period shown.

Total instalment credit since 1950 has grown from $19 billion to over

CHART 14–2

Net Change in Major Types of Consumer Instalment Credit Outstanding Monthly, 1952-65

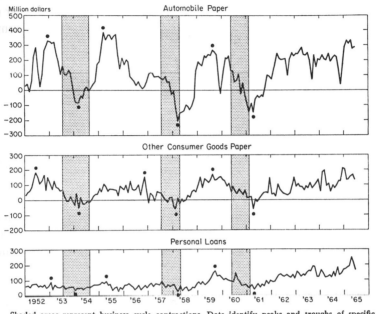

Shaded areas represent business cycle contractions. Dots identify peaks and troughs of specific cycles.

Source: Consumer Credits Statistics, seasonally adjusted data, Board of Governors, Federal Reserve System.

$60 billion at mid-1965. The annual rate of growth between 1960 and 1964 (end of year) in current dollars, was about 9 percent in contrast to the 11 percent rate of the 1950–60 decade. The rapid expansion in credit use has changed competitive relationships among financing agencies, especially during the past decade. The manner in which market shares have changed among institutions competing for consumer borrowers strongly suggests that price competition has become an important factor in the market for automobile credit and to a lesser extent in personal loans. Since these two markets encompass over two-thirds of instalment credit outstanding at the end of 1964, it may be reasonable to suggest that the secular growth of consumer credit is reaching a stage where the influence of price, the rate of charge, has begun to make itself felt in the allocation of borrowers among institutions. Unfortunately, the empirical basis for this generalization is not firm, since it depends upon pieces of evidence derived from either borrowers or lenders with respect to particular credit markets. Yet it is an encouraging development after many years of structural growth and continued change in the competitive relationships among credit agencies.

THE AUTOMOBILE CREDIT MARKET

Changes in shares of the automobile credit market have represented continuing gains for commercial banks since 1939, with minor interruptions (Table 14–2). Between 1955 and 1964 the share of "credit union and others" doubled, from 5% to 10%, reflecting the growing interest of credit unions in automobile financing, often at rates below the 1 percent per month traditional charge. Sales finance companies, although showing absolute gains, have borne the brunt of the decline in market shares, dropping from 59% of the market at the end of 1939 to 51% in 1955, and finally to 36% at the end of 1964. The total commercial bank share passed that of the sales finance group in 1959 and represented more than one-half of total automobile credit outstanding at the end of 1964.

The share of the market going to direct loans from commercial banks, credit unions, consumer finance companies and others has increased relative to paper purchased from dealers by sales finance companies and commercial banks. The direct loan segment of the market is usually conducted with advertised rates of charge, albeit on an add-on or discount basis in terms of dollars per hundred of the amount borrowed, but nevertheless provides a means of calling the attention of borrowers to rates of charge. While direct auto credit has gained in its share of the market, it remains only 31% of the 1964 end of year automobile instalment credit outstanding. Paper purchased from dealers, called indirect financing, has represented the bulk of com-

TABLE 14–2

Amount and Distribution of Automobile Instalment Credit Outstanding by
Method of Finance and Holder, Selected Years

Year	End of Year Outstanding Amount ($ bil)	(%)	Indirect Finance		Direct Finance			
			Sales Finance	Commercial Bank Purchased Paper	Commercial Bank Direct Loans	Credit Unions and Others†	Auto Dealers	Consumer Finance Companies
			Percentage Shares					
1939	1.5	100	58.7	15.8	11.9		13.6	
1954	9.8	100	49.7	23.1	17.0		10.2	
1955	13.5	100	51.3	24.1	15.3	4.6	3.6	1.1
1959	16.4	100	43.8	29.4	15.4	7.7	2.9	.8
1964	24.5	100	35.5	33.8	18.2	10.3	1.5	.7

† Includes industrial loan companies, mutual savings banks, savings and loan associations and others.

Source: Board of Governors of the Federal Reserve System.

mercial bank inroads into the sales finance segment of the market. Although the sales finance share of the purchased paper market remained above that of the commercial bank share at the end of 1964, the latter share became predominant in May, 1965. There is reason to believe that rate competition has played a significant part in the increasing gains of the commercial bank and credit union categories. First, rates of charge on direct lending are typically below customer rates of charge on dealer paper.[6] Second, since 1958, changes in rates charged borrowers and buying rates for paper held by four large sales finance companies have declined, suggesting that these rates have been under pressure for a good portion of the period.[7] Commercial bank and credit union competition for direct loans to automobile borrowers are focused primarily upon rates because credit terms on direct financing are customarily more restrictive than those on indirect financing. Meanwhile, within indirect financing, the nature of commercial bank competition for dealer paper is primarily upon buying rates relative to the quality of paper accepted, as terms are relatively standard at the limits of acceptability.

The automobile credit market has undergone considerable adjustment during the postwar period. There has been a marked shift from sales finance companies to commercial banks and credit unions. Were these shifts an indication of rate sensitivity among borrowers in the market? To some extent, I believe they were, particularly since customer new-auto finance rates from large sales finance companies have declined with only minor interruptions since early 1961. While the evidence is fragmentary, the gains by lower rate institutions suggest that rate sensitivity may have increased in importance relative to the effects exerted by other terms of credit.

THE PERSONAL LOAN MARKET

The rapidly growing personal loan market is a more heterogeneous market than the automobile loan market. The direct loan market has produced a wide variety of plans and arrangements packaged to suit particular groups of borrowers. Further, the market category is mixed in the sense it includes loans to finance non-durable goods and services as well as to finance the purchase of durable goods. Different types of institutions offer different kinds of loan services, cater to different credit risk categories, and charge different finance rates. Yet competition among lenders for borrowers is keen and the price of credit is used in advertising, albeit in dissimilar

[6] For evidence from 1954 and 1955, see my New Auto Finance Rates, 1924–62, NBER Op. #86, 1963, p. 10. Casual observation supports the supposition that the relation remains typical.

[7] See my "The Price of New Automobile Financing." *Journal of Finance*, May, 1964, p. 216.

forms often difficult to compare among alternative credit sources.

Sales finance companies, credit unions and others have shown the major gains in market shares of the personal loan market (Table 14–3). The share of banks fell and rose again from 1952 to 1964, ending at a level similar to their share in 1939. Consumer finance companies show the only decline, but much of this cannot be construed as a drop in the consumer finance business because the corresponding sales finance companies gains represent their increased activity in licensed consumer finance operations. The remainder of the drop in the consumer finance company market share occurred in 1959, the year in which Alaska and Hawaii were added to the statistics, suggesting that the loss may not have been attributable to market competition but rather to the lower market shares in these states. Yet there has been considerable churning about outside of the market shares of total personal loans outstanding. Diversification of activities has become much more characteristic of the large consumer finance companies in the past decade, especially in recent years. To some extent this reflects an expectation that there may be only a limited market for high cost consumer loan services under competitive conditions in the years to come. In another view, there is profit in growth through the provision of diversified but related products and services. It should be recognized that consumer finance companies are relatively late to follow the example of sales finance companies and banks in the search for diversified activities.

TABLE 14–3

Amount and Distribution of Personal Loans Outstanding by Holder,
Selected Years

Year	End of Year Outstanding ($ billions)	Financial Institutions	Commercial Banks	Sales Finance Companies	Consumer Finance Companies	Credit Unions and Others‡
			Percentage Shares			
1929	569	100	21	†	79	
1939	1,088	100	33	5	61	
1952	4,111	100	33	8	36	22
1954	5,392	100	31	7	35	26
1955	6,112	100	31	8	35	26
1959	9,386	100	34	10	30	25
1964	16,071	100	34	13	27	26

‡ Includes industrial loan companies, mutual savings banks, savings and loan associations and other lenders.
† Less than .5%.
Source: Board of Governors of the Federal Reserve System.

Commercial banks have developed a wide variety of new plans in the postwar period to attract borrowers. While rate competition has been evident in the traditional instalment loan business, the newer plans stress convenience and differentiated services to justify rates of charge typically higher than charges on regular instalment loans. While there are no regularly published series on rates of charge on personal loans by commercial banks, Paul F. Smith noted a rise in gross finance charges on personal loans in his sample of nine banks from 9.54 to 10.94 dollars per hundred and outstanding credit between 1955 and 1959.[8] Rates of charge within this range keep commercial banks as a low-cost credit source for borrowers. Rates of charge for all types of consumer credit held by the nine banks rose from 8.6 to 10.0 dollars per hundred in the same period. Recent cost studies for larger samples of commercial banks show average charges about 9 dollars per hundred in 1963 and 1964.[9] Credit union charges are competitive with commercial bank charges while sales finance and consumer finance company charges tend to be considerably higher despite the narrowing differentials as the larger loans being made by finance companies typically carry lower rates. Thus, rate competition in the personal loan market does not appear to have appreciably affected market shares since 1952 between the combined sales and consumer finance higher-cost group and the commercial bank and credit union lower-cost group. The changed share between sales finance companies and consumer finance companies probably results from the impetus to diversified activities given sales finance companies by their declining share of the automobile credit business. Finally, it is important to note that the personal loan market has been the most rapidly growing component of instalment credit and all segments of the market have shown absolute gains.

OTHER CONSUMER GOODS PAPER

The market for other consumer goods paper has declined in its relative share of total instalment credit since 1952, as well as since 1939. Financial institutions gained in their holdings of this paper at the expense of retailers, increasing their market share from 44 to 54 percent of the market while sales finance companies became the dominant institutional holders, rising from 11 to 25 percent of the market. The shares of other institutional holders remained relatively constant during the period. The sales finance company gains undoubtedly reflect the activities of wholly owned subsidiaries of manufacturers who have competed successfully for paper from dealers.

---

[8] *Consumer Credit Costs, 1949–59*, NBER, 1963.

[9] *Functional Cost Analysis, Comparative Study, 146 Banks, 1964–63;* Federal Reserve Banks of New York, Boston, and Philadelphia, 1964 p. A 11. Banks furnishing data were in the $315 million to $50.0 million deposit size range.

Rate competition is not apparent in this field, and no reliable data exist as to the level of rates charged borrowers.

Among retailers, only department stores and mail order houses have gained in their share of the other consumers goods paper market, which rose from 18 to 26 percent of total credit outstanding between 1952 and 1964. Furniture, appliance and other retail stores all declined in relative importance in a growing market.

REPAIR AND MODERNIZATION LOANS

Repair and modernization loans have remained relatively constant in their share of total instalment credit outstanding since 1939 and since 1952. Within components, however, commercial banks' share declined sharply from 82 to 69%. The major development in this market has been the increased market share gained by the financial institutions other than commercial banks, sales and consumer finance companies. It is savings institutions such as mutual savings banks and savings and loan associations which have made the major inroads.

IMPLICATIONS OF POSTWAR EXPERIENCE

Developments in the market for consumer instalment credit have become strategic to the continued growth of output and employment because it finances durable consumer investment which is quantitatively important and highly variable. The absolute size of consumer durable goods expenditure is more than double that of residential construction expenditures by consumers, and the total of the two has been characteristically larger than all producer investment, including the farm sector, in the postwar period. We must recognize that the volume of consumer investment is the outcome of the interplay of borrowing costs and consumer decisions to undertake investment, as in traditional investment theories. We are beginning to learn more about the demand for household capital, particularly with respect to housing and automobiles. In both cases, credit is a factor affecting demand along with income, the stock of capital, prices, and other factors. F. Thomas Juster and I have argued elsewhere, that most consumer borrowers are insensitive to the price of credit because they are rationed by lenders under imperfect market conditions.[10] If, as implied, consumers want more credit than they can get at market finance rates they will be more sensitive to a given percentage increase in maturity than to a corresponding percentage

[10] *Consumer Sensitivity to Finance Rates: An Empirical and Analytical Investigation*, NBER, Occasional Paper 88, 1964.

drop in finance rate because of the greater lowering of the monthly payment. If borrowers were offered a continuous range of credit alternatives with finance rates graduated upward with longer maturities and risk, then there would be less credit rationing and a larger group of marginal borrowers to respond to finance rate changes. As matters stand, there appear to be relatively few borrowers willing and able to curtail credit use in response to increases in credit cost. Thus, if monetary policy is to affect consumer investment under current conditions it must do so primarily through credit rationing by lenders, rather than through the effects of higher finance rates upon borrowers. Yet interest rate sensitivity may increase when credit use becomes marginal to a wider range of borrowers because of rising levels of incomes and financial assets.

Competition among credit agencies has become a major force working to break down market imperfections and it has been operative during the postwar period. The period has been favorable to the growth of large companies through mergers as well as through other means of expansion. The identities of sales and consumer finance companies are less distinct today than they were in the prewar period. Wholly-owned finance subsidiaries have spread within the sales finance group. Up to now these developments have probably accompanied a decline in market power among credit agencies operating within regional and local markets.

Competition for sources of funds has also affected operations and costs of extending credit to consumers. As it has caused commercial banks to increase the scale of their consumer credit operations it may have made credit more inexpensive to borrowers, at least in the automobile credit market. More costly funds have also caused finance companies to trade more heavily on equity to offset lower profit margins. There has been little or no tightening of credit terms in response to more costly sources of funds, except that automobile finance rates have been observed to rise, with a lag, during periods of tight money.

CONCLUSIONS AND FUTURE PROSPECTS

The three major conclusions drawn from reviewing developments in the consumer instalment credit market since World War II were that (1) the market has grown markedly in size and importance in the economy with its structure substantially unchanged, (2) the easing of credit terms has continued to foster credit use throughout the period, and (3) the closer competitive relations within the existing market structure suggest that borrowers are responding more to differences in finance rates among alternative credit opportunities, at least in the automobile credit market. Each of these conclusions has implications for future developments in the consumer installment credit market.

First, the increase in size and relative importance indicates that, because of the cyclical volatility of instalment credit and durable goods expenditures, its continued expansion may not be consistent with an overall stable growth of total investment expenditures. If there is continued success with combined fiscal and monetary measures in stabilizing total investment, cyclical fluctuations in consumer instalment credit may be offset by fluctuations in housing or producer credit sectors. If, on the other hand, plans for total investment either exceed or fall short of levels needed to maintain a stable economic growth at high employment levels, there will be renewed interest in selective credit regulation either to restrain or accelerate credit spending when political or economic considerations preclude effective monetary and fiscal policies.

Second, the continued easing of credit terms up to the present raises questions as to whether further easing will continue to enlarge the demand for credit as it has in the past. Because maximum maturities have tended to become standard in the past, I believe that there remains a substantial amount of additional borrowing which would be undertaken at the lower monthly payments associated with longer maturities even at higher rates of charge. If credit quality considerations prevent longer term credit from being extended by lenders within the existing market structure, there will be pressure to alter the present structure by borrowers who reopen first mortgages at savings institutions or who add second mortgages to finance household capital expenditures.

Third, the closer competitive relations among consumer credit agencies, now including savings institutions, has increased pressure on legislatures and regulatory authorities to change the rules to enhance competition among borrowers as well as among financial institutions. Two proposals have been offered to improve the functioning of this market through legislative reform. One, the federal Truth in Lending Bill, would legislate uniform disclosure of finance rates and dollar charges. The second, a proposal for uniform state legislation by the National Conference of Commissioners on Uniform State laws, envisions comprehensive legislation to simplify the regulations governing consumer credit operations among the states. The second approach, the model bill, would include provision for disclosure, price ceilings, creditors' remedies, and other aspects now covered in state legislation. The functioning of consumer credit markets would undoubtedly benefit from some uniform method of disclosing rates of charge, especially for those borrowers who are in a position to curtail credit use. More fundamental, however, is the proposal for greater uniformity in state laws governing credit use. Much of the segmentation which exists comes from the fact that some classes of lenders fall under one law, others come under separate laws, and some must operate under several laws. Different legal restrictions among the states affect the use of capital by national companies which operate within many states. While uniformity of state legislation and uniform methods of disclosure will improve the functioning of consumer credit markets, many imperfections will remain. But these proposals have come about largely because postwar developments have demonstrated that the effective functioning of consumer credit markets is vital to our national welfare while further competition, within limits, will provide added benefits.

15.

The Impact of Consumer Knowledge
On Instalment Credit

J. VAN FENSTERMAKER
and KEITH K. COX

"Truth in lending" bills have been introduced in Congress each year since 1961. The bills typically require all firms which extend instalment credit to state the total cost of credit in some uniform manner. For example, H.R. 155 requires the lenders to disclose "the percentage that the finance charge bears to the total amount to be financed expressed as a simple annual rate on the average outstanding unpaid balance of the obligation."[1] A finance charge in this paper is defined as the total cost of deferring a payment, rather than paying cash for a purchase.[2]

Two of the underlying assumptions of the "Truth in Lending" bills are
(a) that the statement of instalment credit terms used by lenders today differs so greatly that consumers find it hard to compare the cost of credit from various sources, and
(b) that given a knowledge of alternative credit charges, consumers will tend to choose the lowest cost credit.

The first assumption appears to be valid. Wallace P. Mors, in a definitive study for the National Bureau of Economic Research on consumer

Reprinted from *Business Perspectives*, Vol. II, No. 4, Summer 1966, pp. 14–17, by permission of the publisher.

[1] U.S. Congress, House 89 Congress, 1st Sess., H.R. 155.

[2] The authors wish to avoid in this paper the controversy over what is the true rate of interest, or whether a finance or service charge is comparable with interest. Many articles have been written in this area. This paper is concerned with the "Finance charge" as defined in H.R. 155.

TABLE 15-1

Finance Cost of a 12 Month Loan from Various Lenders in a Simple Annual Percent*

(paid in equal monthly payments)

| Amount of Loan | FINANCIAL INSTITUTIONS | | | | RETAIL OUTLETS | | | |
| | Credit Unions | Commercial Banks | Sales Finance Companies | Consumer Finance Companies | Department Stores | | Appliance Stores | Furniture Stores |
					Instalment	Revolving		
$ 250	9–12%	12–13.04%	19.3%	28.5%	15.4–16.9%	18–22.8%	14–28.6%	15.4–17.4%
500	9–12	12–13.04	16.4	27.8	14.5–17.2	18–19.2	14–27.8	15.4–17.4
1,000	9–12	12–13.04	14.4	22.1	14.5–17.2	15.6	14–22.1	14.1–17.4

* Computed with the constant ratio formula.

Source: Survey by authors of lending institutions in a major Ohio city, 1965.

TABLE 15-2

Dollar Cost of a 12 Month Loan from Various Lenders

| Amount of Loan | FINANCIAL INSTITUTIONS | | | | RETAIL OUTLETS | | | |
| | Credit Unions | Commercial Banks | Sales Finance Companies | Consumer Finance Companies | Department Stores | | Appliance Stores | Furniture Stores |
					Instalment	Revolving		
$ 250	$12.19–16.25	$16.25–17.66	$26.14	$ 38.73	$20.85–22.89	$24.37–30.88	$18.96–38.73	$20.85–23.56
500	24.37–32.50	32.50–35.32	44.42	75.29	38.27–46.58	48.75–52.00	37.92–75.29	41.70–47.12
$1,000	48.65–65.00	65.00–70.64	78.00	119.71	78.55–93.16	84.50	75.84–119.71	76.38–94.25

Source: Survey by authors of lending institutions in a major Ohio city, 1965.

finance charges, concludes that "consumers do not receive easily comparable information from alternative suppliers of credit."[3] A study of suppliers of instalment credit in a major Ohio city, made by the authors in 1965, found that, indeed, finance charges stated in various ways, such as a percent per month, "dollars per hundred," and size of monthly payments, are difficult to compare.

The survey included (a) all commercial banks, (b) all credit unions, (c) all consumer finance companies, (d) two sales finance companies, (e) all department stores, (f) five furniture stores, and (g) five appliance stores. Each lender was asked to state the total finance cost of borrowing $250, $500, and $1,000 for a 12-month period. The costs of insurance, where included in the finance charge as an optional charge, were deducted to make the data more comparable. In order to compare the finance costs, the authors reduced all costs to a single annual rate and a total dollar cost on the average unpaid balance. The following formula was used.[4]

$$R = \frac{2Ni}{P(n+1)}$$

R = effective finance rate
N = number of payment periods in a year
i = actual interest charges (dollars)
P = net amount of loan
n = number of payments to be made

Tables 15–1 and 15–2 present the finance charges as an annual rate on the unpaid balance and in dollar amounts for the sums of $250, $500, and $1,000 from the lenders surveyed. For computational purposes, the unpaid balance of revolving credit was assumed to have been reduced in twelve equal instalments. Otherwise, it would be impossible to obtain the dollar amount of finance charge for revolving credit except on an individual consumer basis, and then only after the borrowing is repaid.

The purpose of this paper is to examine the second assumption from the points of view of both the consumer and the lender. That is, if they are given a "Truth in Lending" Law, consumers will tend to choose the lowest cost credit.

For purposes of analysis, this study assumes that the influence of changes in finance rates on the level of consumer borrowing is negligible

[3] Wallace P. Mors, *Consumer Credit Finance Charges* (New York: National Bureau of Economic Research, 1965), pp. 4–5.

[4] Example: A man borrows $518 to be repaid in 12 monthly instalments at $50 each. (12 × $50 = $600—$518 = $82 finance charge)

$$R = \frac{2 \times 12 \times 82}{518(12+1)} = \frac{1968}{6734} = 29.2 \text{ percent finance rate.}$$

Examples of lender use of this formula can be found in Ralph R. Botts, "Interest and the Truth-in-Lending Bill," *The Accounting Review*, (October, 1963), pp. 789–795.

(although this assumption may not be valid for all consumers), and it concentrates on the distribution of instalment debt rather than changes in the total level of instalment debt.[5]

CONSUMER BEHAVIOR

Given the assumption of a "Truth in Lending" Law, the major question is how the consumer will react when the cost of borrowing from various sources is available to him and stated in both simple annual finance rates on the average outstanding balance of the obligation and in total dollar amounts. Tables 15–1 and 15–2 show the finance rates and dollar charges for loans in a major Ohio city.[6] In most cities there is a wide variety of credit charges.

The solution is simple for many economists. They think of the average consumer as a rational individual who tries to get the most satisfaction or utility out of his limited money income. Herbert Simon describes the economic man as "that omniscient paragon of rationality who spends his time maximizing the satisfactions of a limited budget while he slips back and forth on a set of indifference curves and otherwise gets the most for his money."[7] Under this behavior model, familiar to all of us, one would expect the consumer automatically to seek out the lowest cost credit. However, experts in marketing, psychology, and social psychology have a different image of consumer behavior. According to George Katona,

> Modern psychology . . . does not conceive of people as automata and does not post a fixed one-to-one relation between simuli and responses. Stimuli elicit responses; they present occasions for responses rather than fully determining them. It is not possible to predict the response by knowing the stimulus alone. Two persons may react differently to the same stimulus, and the same person may react differently to it on successive occasions.[8]

Many factors influence consumer choices of instalment lenders. They include the level of consumer information, habit, convenience, promotion of product differentiation, expectations, stock of liquid assets, age, family size, and emotion, to mention only a few. Therefore, one should not assume, *a priori*, that consumers will necessarily choose the lowest cost credit. Con-

---

[5] F. Thomas Juster discusses consumer elasticities in, "Consumer Sensitivity to the Price of Credit," *American Economic Review*, (May, 1964), pp. 222–223.

[6] Much controversy exists over whether or not finance charges can be stated in a uniform manner. However, this is not the concern of this paper.

[7] James G. March and Herbert A. Simon, *Organizations*, (New York: John Wiley & Sons, 1958), pp. 9–11.

[8] George Katona, *The Powerful Consumer: Psychological Studies of the American Economy*, (New York: McGraw-Hill, 1960), pp. 54–56.

sumer behavior may take many directions. The authors believe that the three following responses will describe much of the behavior.

(a) Some consumers are not responsive to the various costs of credit.

(b) Some consumers may be responsive to the differences in simple annual finance rates.

(c) Some consumers may be responsive to the differences in the absolute dollar costs of instalment loans.

Consumers in the first group are indifferent to the cost of a loan for a variety of reasons. No matter how finance charges are stated, some tend to ignore credit costs in making purchase decisions. One empirical study found that some consumers surveyed did not know the current dollar costs or even the nominal finance rates on their most recent instalment debt.[9] A knowledge of cost differentials is of little help to consumers with poor credit ratings, for only certain high cost lenders will grant them loans. It is possible that some consumers have a preconceived notion that most credit cost differences are minor; therefore, they will not be responsive to cost differentials. If consumer car purchases may be used as an analogy, Professor Feldman cites a Ford Motor Company survey of new automobile purchases which revealed that 44 percent bought cars at the first dealer they visited and 84 percent visited no more than three dealers.[10] Such a lack of shopping can be due to the fact that consumers believe price differentials are minor. Other consumers, although aware of cost differentials, believe that time spent in searching for the lowest rate outweighs potential cost savings.

For example, again from the Feldman study, 75 percent of the purchases of Chevrolets and Fords were from dealers located within 15 minutes driving time from the buyers' homes. The fact that the cost of credit is stated in a uniform way does not guarantee that consumers will shop and compare costs. Finally, some consumers have little or no purchase planning horizon. Therefore, knowledge of alternative costs may not change their behavior. This occurs particularly for small purchases; the impulse buyer is a case in point.[11]

But if the consumer has any sort of planning horizon (and a limited income), one would expect that the cost of borrowing should at some point influence his choice of lending institutions. Studies by Robert Ferber indicate that consumers often formulate purchase plans in advance, and in

[9] Jean Due, "Consumer Knowledge of Instalment Credit Charges," *Journal of Marketing*, (October, 1955), pp. 162–166.

[10] Laurence P. Feldman, "The Location of Franchised Retail Automobile Dealerships, in the Twin Cities Metropolitan Area," (Ph.D. Dissertation, unpublished), University of Minnesota, 1965, p. 82.

[11] George Katona, *Psychological Analysis of Economic Behavior*, (New York, McGraw-Hill, 1951), p. 66. In reference to a consumer survey, he said, "In general, it was found that the less expensive the item, the larger the proportion of unplanned purchases."

general, the larger the purchase, the longer the planning period.[12] Planned purchases are especially common for large household appliances and automobiles.[13] The fact that many consumers plan in advance provides an opportunity to shop for lower cost credit. With uniform methods of stating finance charges, the consumer should be able, if he is willing to shop around, to find the various charges and to compare them. The following sets of consumers compare credit costs.

The second set of consumers tend to be responsive to differences in the simple annual finance rates.[14] Whenever a large spread in the finance rate structure exists, this group will tend to choose the lowest rate. For example, in Table 15–1, this consumer will seek the lowest rate whether the sum borrowed is $250 or $1,000. Thus, he would borrow from credit unions or commercial banks. However, when several rates cluster close around the low point, such things as habit and convenience may affect the final rate chosen.

The third set of consumers may be responsive to the actual dollar cost differential among lenders. These consumers have little preference among lenders when the actual dollar difference is small even though the simple annual finance rate differential is large. In Table 15–2, the dollar difference between a $250 loan at a commercial bank and an appliance store is small. However, as the range in dollar costs increases, in particular with larger loans, this group of consumers will tend to choose the lowest cost loan. For a $1,000 loan there is an $11 difference between a commercial bank and an appliance store. If the dollar costs tend to cluster at the lowest end of the range, the factors of convenience and habit may affect the final consumer choice.

In reality, consumers are not divided neatly into various sets, for elements of each type of response are likely to be present in any group of consumers and any one consumer may respond differently at different times.

The consumer may well be a creature of habit; that is, he may continue past patterns of behavior without considering alternative courses of action, and a knowledge of relative costs of instalment credit may not affect the behavior of some consumers. However, if a large enough body of consumers is responsive to simple annual finance rates and to dollar costs of instalment credit, the net effect of a knowledge of credit costs would be a

[12] Robert Ferber, "The Role of Planning in Consumer Purchases of Durable Goods," *American Economic Review*, (December, 1954), p. 858.

[13] Katona, "Among all kinds of purchases, there are some that are planned in advance (as the term is used in the surveys); for purchases of more than $1,000, planning is relatively frequent; for purchases of several dollars, somewhat less frequent, and for purchases of less than $100, quite infrequent", p. 67.

[14] The evidence of this behavior appears common among consumers with liquid assets. See F. Thomas Juster and Robert P. Shay, *Consumer Sensitivity to Finance Rates: An Empirical and Analytical Investigation*, (New York: National Bureau of Economic Research, 1964).

shift of borrowers to lower cost credit. The final effect of a "Truth in Lending" Law rests upon the relative strengths of the foregoing three sets of consumer responses.

LENDER BEHAVIOR

If there is a shift of many credit worthy consumers to less expensive credit, then a redistribution of instalment debt holdings would take place. Credit unions and commercial banks, the lowest cost lenders, currently hold about 51.1 percent of the outstanding instalment debt.[15] Assuming no change in existing finance charges, the passage of a "Truth in Lending" bill should result in a larger share of new instalment credit going to credit unions and commercial banks.

But other lenders may not be content to see a greater share of their credit business erode. At least three avenues of recourse appear feasible. The most obvious action would be to lower finance rates. The degree to which rates could be lowered would depend upon the lenders' cost structure and the total demand for credit.

A second course of action would be to make loans to fewer credit worthy individuals. This would be profitable if the incremental revenue generated by this decision is greater than the incremental cost of extending credit, which would include a bad debt loss. A third alternative would be for these lenders to intensify competition on a non-price basis with the credit unions and commercial banks. Appropriate non-price policies might include emphasizing the convenience factor and using larger amounts of advertising and other forms of promotion. In the case of retail institutions, lenders might absorb some of the credit cost in the price of goods sold.

SUMMARY AND IMPLICATIONS

Current methods of stating finance charges throughout the nation make comparisons of the cost of credit difficult for the consumer. The assumption that consumers cannot easily compare alternative sources of instalment credit appears to be substantiated. Yet when stated in a uniform manner the rates currently charged by lenders vary widely.

Undoubtedly some consumers would not change their borrowing practices. But given a "Truth in Lending" Law which necessitates the lender stating the total dollar costs and the finance charges as a simple annual rate on the average outstanding upaid balance of the obligation, a significant proportion of consumers may tend to choose lower cost loans. If this occurs,

---

[15] *Federal Reserve Bulletin*, (November, 1965), p. 1592.

then the net result should be a reduction in the total cost of instalment debt and an increase in total consumer welfare.

An increased demand for loans from lower cost lenders would cause a redistribution of the instalment debt and force a re-examination by suppliers of lending practices. Both commercial banks and credit unions would probably stress their lower cost credit. Other types of lenders might reduce finance charges but they would certainly make additional effort to de-emphasize credit cost comparisons and emphasize such factors as convenience, habit, and different forms of promotion.

This article has explored several possible actions of both consumers and lenders deductively, and it is far from clear that consumers as a group will more actively seek lower cost credit through a "Truth in Lending" Law than they currently do. This paper suggests that it would be fruitful to explore the responses of consumers and lenders carefully through empirical studies.

16.

Direct Placement
of Corporate Debt

FEDERAL RESERVE BANK OF CLEVELAND

Two basic sources of capital funds are available to corporations. Capital funds may be (1) generated internally, or (2) acquired from outside sources. When capital is generated internally, a portion of a corporation's cash flow (net profits and depreciation charges) must be retained. When capital is acquired from external sources, a corporation may choose among alternatives. Thus, funds can be obtained through (1) the sale of equity issues, or (2) by borrowing. In either case, there is the further option of making (1) a public offering, or (2) a direct placement of securities with large institutional investors.

The raising of long-term external capital by means of a public offering of securities (debt or equity) is a familiar method used by corporations. The offering is handled by an underwriting syndicate which, either by competitive bidding or through negotiation, purchases securities from a borrowing company, and in turn sells the securities to individual and institutional investors. Underwriters assume all of the marketing risk in return for a profit, which is represented by the spread between the price paid *to* the borrowing corporation and the price paid *by* the investor minus underwriting expenses.

The alternative to a public offering is the direct placement of securities

Reprinted from *Economic Review*, March 1965, pp. 3–12, by permission of the publisher, the Federal Reserve Bank of Cleveland.

CHART 16-1

Net Funds Raised in Capital Markets

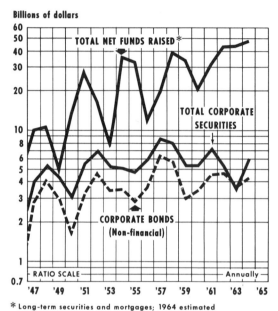

* Long-term securities and mortgages; 1964 estimated

Source: Board of Governors of the Federal Reserve System.

with large institutional investors, a method that has assumed growing importance in recent years. Direct placement involves direct negotiation between borrower and lender and eliminates the underwriting function. In direct placement, a prospective borrower investigates, often with the aid of an agent, the possible sale of securities to one or a small group of institutional investors.[1] Terms and conditions of the offering are negotiated by borrower and lender, with the exchange of funds and securities taking place directly.

In recent years corporate demands for external capital have increased only moderately. As shown in Chart 16-1, corporate demands have accounted for a progressively smaller share of increasing total net demands for funds in capital markets.[2] In the early part of the period shown (through 1953) corporate demands accounted, on an annual average basis, for about

---

[1] An agent (usually a securities underwriter) will often bring borrower and lender together and assist in negotiating terms and conditions of the offering. The agent receives a fee for these services (usually paid by the borrower).

[2] Net funds raised in capital markets include net long-term borrowing by the U.S. Government, state and local governments, nonfinancial corporations, foreigners, and net new mortgage debt.

47 percent of total net funds raised. Since 1954, the annual average has been reduced to 22 percent. During the entire 1946–64 period, the ratio of corporate demands to total capital funds raised ranged from a high of 87.5 percent in 1949 to a low of only 8 percent in 1963.

In contrast, corporate bond offerings have represented a consistently large proportion of total corporate demands for external capital funds, averaging 68 percent per year during the 1946–64 period, and accounting in most years for the swings in total corporate demands. Interestingly in 1963, as the chart shows, the increase in the volume of corporate bonds actually exceeded that of total corporate funds raised, indicating a net retirement of corporate stock in 1963.

Corporate preference for borrowed funds (as contrasted to equity funds) when raising external capital has principally reflected the availability of larger amounts of corporate funds generated internally. That is to say, the increased availability of internally generated funds—arising from larger depreciation allowances, investment tax credits, and the reduction in corporate tax rates—has contributed importantly to the smaller need for external equity capital. It should also be noted that the internal generation of funds through retained earnings improves the capital base and encourages the use of borrowing to satisfy external financing requirements. In addition, as compared with the cost of equity capital, borrowed funds often provide a less costly source of corporate working capital, since interest payments on bor-

TABLE 16–1

New Issues of Corporate Securities, 1953-64

	Public Offerings and Direct Placements			Direct Placements of Debt Issues		
	Equity and Debt	Debt Issues*			As % of	
Year	Volume (millions of $'s)	Volume (millions of $'s)	As % of Equity and Debt (Col. 1)	Volume (millions of $'s)	All Debt Issues (Col. 2)	As % of Equity and Debt (Col. 1)
1953	$ 8,898	$ 7,083	79.6%	$3,228	45.6%	36.3%
1954	9,516	7,488	78.7	3,484	46.5	36.6
1955	10,240	7,420	72.5	3,301	44.5	32.7
1956	10,939	8,002	73.2	3,777	47.2	34.5
1957	12,884	9,957	77.3	3,839	38.6	30.0
1958	11,558	9,653	83.5	3,320	34.4	28.7
1959	9,748	7,190	73.8	3,632	50.5	37.3
1960	10,154	8,081	79.6	3,275	40.5	32.3
1961	13,165	9,420	71.6	4,720	50.1	35.9
1962	10,705	8,969	83.8	4,529	50.5	42.1
1963	12,237	10,872	88.8	6,158	56.6	50.3
1964	13,381	10,300	77.0	6,900	67.0	51.6
Average 1953-64	—	—	78.3%	—	47.7%	37.4%

*Debt issues include mortgage bonds, unsecured notes and debentures and convertible bonds, notes and debentures.

Source: U. S. Securities and Exchange Commission.

rowings are a tax-deductible expense. Moreover, a higher proportion of borrowed funds may exert favorable leverage on a corporation's net income.

Growth in the volume of direct placements of debt issues has been impressive, even though corporate reliance on external funds has not increased very much in recent years. Table 16–1 points up the growing importance of direct placements. A somewhat dramatic comparison is found in the fact that the volume of direct placements (debt issues) in 1964 was 114 percent larger than in 1953. Less dramatic but nevertheless clearly reflecting the trend toward increased emphasis on direct placement of debt issues is the fact that the annual average for 1961–64 is substantially greater than for any other 4-year period shown in the table. Although not shown in Table 16–1, it is noteworthy that direct placement of debt issues accounted for nearly 96 percent of all direct placements (equity and debt) in the 1953–64 period.

For 1953–64 as a whole, of all debt issues, direct placements accounted for an average of nearly 48 percent, with the proportion ranging higher in recent years, and reaching 67 percent in 1964. For 1953–64 as a whole, direct placements of debt issues accounted for 37 percent of all corporate securities sold, with this proportion also ranging higher in recent years, and reaching an all-time high in 1964 (see Table 16–1).

REASONS FOR GROWTH OF DIRECT PLACEMENTS

Why have direct placements of corporate debt increased in importance in recent years? What have been the characteristics of such placements? In the pages that follow we attempt to answer these questions.

Initial Costs

The cost saving to borrowers is perhaps the most frequently mentioned reason for the growing use of direct placements. While supporting data are admittedly fragmentary, there is evidence that costs involved in negotiating direct placements are significantly less than the costs of floating a registered public offering.

Table 16–2 presents some earlier cost comparisons of public offerings and direct placements.[3] For the time period studied, the data indicate that

[3] The data for 1951, 1953 and 1955 are from *Cost of Flotation of Corporate Securities 1951–55*, U.S. Securities and Exchange Commission, U.S. Government Printing Office, Washington, D.C., June 1957. Total costs of public offerings include underwriters' compensation and all other fees and expenses incident to the offering, e.g., legal, printing, accounting and engineering expenses. Total costs of direct offerings include the fees paid agents or finders and other expenses of the offering. Data for 1963 on public offerings are from a special study of underwriting spreads on 123 issues of debt securities. See *Statistical Bulletin*, Investment Bankers Association of America, Washington, D.C., June 1964.

TABLE 16–2

Comparative Costs of Public Offerings and Direct Placements of Corporate Debt Securities

Size of Issue (millions of $'s)	1951-53-55							1963
	Public Offerings			Direct Placements			Cost Differential	Underwriting Spread on Public Offerings
	Underwriting Spread	Other Expenses	Total	Fees	Expenses	Total		
	(as a % of proceeds)			(as a % of proceeds)				(as a % of proceeds)
Under 0.3	—	—	—	1.86	1.49	3.35	—	—
0.3—0.4	—	—	—	1.60	1.06	2.66	—	—
0.5—0.9	7.53	3.96	11.49	1.31	0.83	2.14	9.35	4.73
1.0—1.9	5.80	2.37	8.17	0.97	0.59	1.56	6.61	7.89
2.0—4.9	2.37	1.41	3.78	0.69	0.43	1.12	2.66	3.87
5.0—9.9	1.01	0.82	1.83	0.49	0.34	0.83	1.00	1.61
10.0—19.9	0.88	0.64	1.52	0.31	0.32	0.63	0.89	0.89
20.0—49.9	0.85	0.48	1.33	0.22*	0.22	0.44	0.89	0.80
50.0 & Over	0.88	0.32	1.19	—	—	—	—	0.79

*20.0 million dollars and over.

Source: U. S. Securities and Exchange Commission and Investment Bankers Association of America.

in all comparable size classes the cost of negotiating a direct placement is significantly less than for floating a public offering. The cost differential (column 8) is particularly large for smaller issues, diminishing gradually as the size of issue increases. A major part of the wide differential is accounted for by the relatively high underwriting cost of public offerings (column 2). Nearly all costs of distribution are avoided in direct placements, with the exception of modest fees paid to agents or "finders." The differential is even wider when the services of an agent are not required.

Lack of data prohibits a more up-to-date comparison of costs of public offerings and direct placements, but available evidence indicates that the latter continue to be less costly to arrange. A tabulation of underwriting spreads on public offerings of debt issues in 1963 (last column in Table 16–2) shows that there have been only minor changes in this expense since the earlier U.S. Securities and Exchange Commission survey. In four of the seven size classes, spreads were higher in 1963 than in the earlier period, while in three size classes some reduction occurred. If expenses of direct placements and other expenses of public offerings have been essentially unchanged, cost comparisons would continue to favor direct sales, particularly for smaller issues.

Total Costs

While direct sales seem to involve lower initial costs to the borrower, the lack of data on costs of public offerings and direct placements over their life span makes it difficult, if not impossible, to compare total costs of capital raised through the alternative methods. A comparison of this type is important because differential costs of borrowing due to interest costs could appreciably reduce initial advantages.

Some light has been shed on the matter by a study that compared offering yields on public offerings and direct placements of Industrial-Financial-Service (IFS) borrowers, and which showed that yields on direct placements were consistently above yields on public offerings in the 1952–58 period.[4] In that period, the annual spread between yields on public offerings and direct placements of IFS debt of $1 million and over averaged 51 basis points, with a high spread of 86 basis points and a low of 30 basis points. While this comparison represents only approximate average yields—due to lack of data on such determinants of yield as quality, maturity, size, and time of offering—it does indicate the magnitude of yield differentials that may exist. To whatever extent a yield differential exists, it will at least partly offset the advantage of lower initial costs of negotiating direct placements.

Flexibility

A second important reason cited for the growth of direct placements is the convenience and flexibility provided to both borrower and lender. Because a direct placement involves a limited number of investors (lenders), borrower and lender are closely associated in negotiating terms and conditions of the offering. As a result, terms and conditions can be more precisely tailored to the requirements of both parties.

By paying a small commitment fee, a borrowing corporation can arrange in advance for future capital requirements. An advance commitment provides the issuer some insurance against market uncertainties, while granting the option of canceling the issue if the need for funds does not materialize. An investor is able to earmark funds for future investment and receive an immediate return from the commitment fee. Final negotiations to formulate terms and conditions that best suit the needs of both parties take place at the time of actual takedown.

After an issue has been placed, it is possible to renegotiate terms such as rate and maturity in light of changing requirements of either borrower or lender. Similar flexibility is not possible in widely distributed public offerings.

Institutional Demand

Another frequently mentioned reason for growth in direct placements is increased demand for corporate debt securities by institutional investors, which has not been matched by a corresponding increase in supply. As indi-

---

[4] See Avery B. Cohan, *Private Placements and Public Offerings: Market Shares Since 1935* (University of North Carolina, 1961), pp. 16–17.

CHART 16–2

Financial Assets of Selected Financial Institutions and Corporate Bond
Outstandings

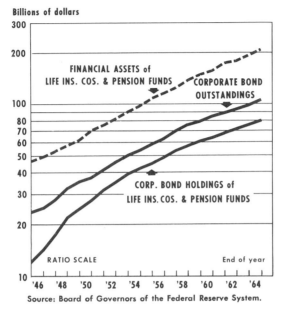

Source: Board of Governors of the Federal Reserve System.

cated in Chart 16–2, institutional holdings of corporate bonds more than
doubled in the 1945–50 period, while the volume of corporate debt outstanding rose by only 58 percent. Since 1950, the rate of growth in institutional holdings has moderated somewhat, but the increase has more than
kept pace with growth in outstanding corporate debt. In the 1945–50 period, corporate bond holdings of life insurance companies and pension funds
on average amounted annually to about three-fifths of total corporate bonds
outstanding; since 1950, the proportion has averaged about three-fourths,
on an annual basis.

As total assets of life insurance companies and pension funds have
mounted in the post-war period, these institutions have faced the continuing
task of employing funds in suitable investments until needed to meet claims.
Since 1950, growth of total assets of these institutions has outstripped the
growth of corporate bonds, as the stream of premium payments has added
considerably more to reserves than is required to meet current claims. Since
most claims are long-term in nature, investment policy is designed to maxi-
mize income, with less emphasis on liquidity and marketability. Corporate
debt securities generally are well suited to this purpose, offering acceptable
quality and a yield advantage over some other forms of long-term investment.

Institutional preference for corporate bonds is evidenced by the fact that holdings of these securities have constituted a relatively large proportion of the financial assets of life insurance companies and pension funds. For example, corporate bond holdings of life insurance companies and pension funds amounted, on average, to about 41 percent of total assets during 1950–64. Reflecting the slowdown in the rate of growth of corporate bonds outstanding, however, the proportion has declined in each year (with one exception) since 1957. In the way of comparison, the assets of these institutions rose by 67 percent from 1957 through 1964, while the volume of corporate bonds outstanding increased by only 50 percent. Hence, although corporate bond holdings of life insurance companies and pension funds increased at a faster rate than outstandings, the ratio of holdings to total financial assets declined from 43 percent in 1957 to 39 percent in 1964.

Simplicity

Another factor that may have stimulated the increased use of direct placements is the burden of registration and disclosure requirements imposed on public offerings by the Securities Act of 1933. Direct placements were exempted from the provisions of the Act, thus providing a way by which borrowers could avoid the expense and inconvenience of compliance. While this factor may have been important initially, it is likely that other reasons cited above have been more important to the sustained increase in direct placements.

CORPORATE DEBT ISSUES AND ECONOMIC ACTIVITY

The pattern of growth in the volume of direct placements (debt issues) in the post-war period has been associated to a large extent with the nation's business and monetary cycles. As indicated in the top panel of Chart 16–3, direct placements have usually accelerated during periods of business expansion, and leveled off or declined prior to cyclical peaks. This pattern is explained to a large extent by the behavior of debt placements of manufacturing firms, which have historically accounted for a large proportion of direct placements—nearly two-fifths of the total during the 1948–64 period.

As indicated in Chart 16–3, the volume of direct placements of manufacturing firms has increased during the early stages of business expansion, a period usually characterized by interest rates that were either declining or below previous highs (as measured by the rate on Aaa new corporate issues). As the economy has changed direction, with accompanying changes in interest rates, direct placements of manufacturing firms have tended to level off or decline, with the pattern often extending beyond a subsequent reversal in business activity as well as in interest rates. Some of this behavior is of

CHART 16–3

New Corporate Debt Issues and Related Economic Variables

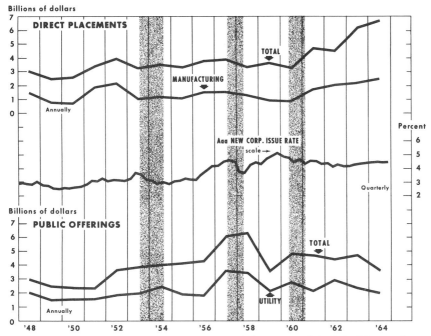

Source: U. S. Securities and Exchange Commission; Board of Governors of the Federal Reserve System.

course associated with traditionally early peaks in corporate profits during business expansions, in subsequent cutbacks in capital spending, and in correspondingly smaller needs for borrowed capital.

The importance of direct placements of manufacturers is suggested by the fact that in the years when the total volume of direct placements (debt issues) was rising—1951–52, 1956–57, and 1961–64—the former accounted for a larger percentage of the total (44 percent) than in years when volume was declining—33 percent in 1949–50, 1953, and 1958–59.

While placements of manufacturing firms have continued to be a major component in the total volume of direct placements, the relative influence has been moderated somewhat in recent years by the growing importance of other types of borrowers (especially real estate and finance firms). For example, while the volume of direct sales by finance and real estate firms accounted for 21 percent of all direct placements in the entire 1948–64 period, the percentage has been on the higher side in each year since 1958, accounting for nearly 29 percent of total placements in 1958–64. Such placements have been particularly significant in the sharp rise in the total volume of direct placements since 1960.

TABLE 16-3

Comparative Costs and Public Offerings and Direct Placements of Corporate
Debt Securities: Classified by Size of Issue and Industry of Issuer, 1951-53-55

Size of Issue (millions of $'s)	MANUFACTURING			UTILITYa		
	Public	Direct	Cost	Public	Direct	Cost
	(as % of proceeds)		Differential	(as % of proceeds)		Differential
Under 0.3	—	2.36	—	—	3.46	—
0.3—0.4	—	2.37	—	—	3.01	—
0.5—0.9	12.12	2.07	10.05	—	2.30	—
1.0—1.9	9.03	1.48	7.55	5.00	1.72	3.28
2.0—4.9	6.16	1.08	5.08	2.23	1.43	0.80
5.0—9.9	3.47	0.71	2.76	1.52	0.93	0.59
10.0—19.9	2.34	0.55	1.79	1.28	0.82	0.46
20.0—49.9	1.71	b0.46	1.25	1.20	b0.61	0.59
50.0 & Over	1.30	—		1.15		—

aIncludes electric, gas, and water companies.
b20.0 million dollars and over.

Source: U. S. Securities and Exchange Commission.

Public offerings of corporate debt securities have shown a somewhat
different relationship to monetary and business cycles than have direct
placements. As indicated in the lower portion of Chart 16–3, the volume
of public offerings has usually risen markedly in the later stages of business
expansion, often continuing at high levels through subsequent recessions.

The pattern of public offerings mainly reflects the behavior of public
utility borrowers (gas, electric, water, and communications companies). The
volume of offerings of these companies, which accounted for nearly 58
percent of all public offerings in the 1948–64 period, has often expanded
during periods when the economy was depressed, in other words, following
a peak in business activity. Such periods are usually characterized by improving availability of funds and declining interest rates. The fact that
utilities often borrow heavily during periods of depressed economic activity
also reflects the stability associated with the demand for utility services as
well as the near-guarantee of a target rate of return on investment from
public utility regulation.[5] An exception to the usual pattern of public utility
offerings occurred in 1957, reflecting in large part the capital spending

[5] In most instances, public utilities are not permitted to enter into direct placement
agreements. The Public Utility Holding Company Act of 1935 prohibits such agreements by stipulating that specific security issues must be issued via competitive bidding.
In addition, many state laws also require public issuance of public utilities securities.

boom which reached a peak in that year. At that time, public offerings (including utility offerings) increased sharply, despite a rapid rise in the level of interest rates.

The predominance of public utility issues among public offerings, as indicated earlier, reflects in part restrictions that require many companies to offer securities at competitive bidding. Moreover, costs of flotation in an underwritten offering of utility debt may be considerably smaller than flotation costs for other types of public offerings. This was clearly evident in the 1951–55 period, for example, according to results of the U.S. Securities and Exchange Commission study of flotation costs (see Table 16–3). The relatively lower flotation costs of public offerings of utility issues reflects the generally higher quality of such offerings and the benefit of smaller underwriting spreads.

As indicated in the table, public offerings of manufacturing companies involved higher flotation costs than utility offerings, although the differential narrowed as the size of issue increased. In contrast, costs of direct placements of manufacturers were generally lower than those of direct placements of utility issues. As a result, the differential cost advantage in the use of direct placements was quite sizable for manufacturing issues, although the differential diminished as the size of issue increased.

EXPERIENCE IN 1963

Since the most recent complete data available on the volume of directly placed corporate debt issues are for 1963, a review of the experience during that year is presented here to highlight the major characteristics of direct placements. The volume of direct placements of debt securities of domestic corporations acounted to $6,421 million during 1963, representing a total of 1,217 individual issues.[6] Table 16–4 summarizes offerings in 1963, and presents a distribution of direct placements by type of borrower, type of issue, and size of issue.

In terms of both number of issues and dollar volume, manufacturing industries accounted for the largest share of direct placements in 1963, while companies in the finance and real estate field were second most important. These two categories of borrowers accounted for more than two-

[6] See "Corporate Financing Directory," *Investment Dealers' Digest*, Section II, July 29, 1963 and February 3, 1964. While totals reported are amounts contracted for in 1963, the latter are taken down over a period of time. For this reason, the total derived for domestic corporate debt issues does not correspond to that reported by the Securities and Exchange Commission. Despite an overstatement of volume, reported characteristics of the issues are revealing. The volume of foreign borrowing is not included.

TABLE 16–4

Direct Placement of Corporate Debt Securities: Distribution by Type of Borrower, Type of Security, and Size of Issue, 1963

Type of Borrower	Number of Issues	Percentage Distribution	Volume of Issues (millions of $'s)	Percentage Distribution
Manufacturing a	453	37.3%	$2,973	46.3%
Public utility b	128	10.5	604	9.4
Finance and real estate	397	32.6	1,787	27.8
All other c	239	19.6	1,057	16.5
TOTAL	1,217	100.0%	$6,421	100.0%
Type of Security				
Mortgage bonds	46	3.8%	$ 194	3.0%
Other notes and debentures d	1,137	93.4	6,125	95.4
Convertible bonds, notes & debentures	34	2.8	102	1.6
TOTAL	1,217	100.0%	$6,421	100.0%
Size of Issue (in millions of $'s)				
Under 0.5	244	20.0%	$ 62	0.9%
0.5—0.9	182	15.0	120	1.9
1.0—2.9	357	29.3	594	9.2
3.0—4.9	124	10.2	455	7.1
5.0—9.9	139	11.4	883	13.8
10.0—24.9	114	9.4	1,603	25.0
25.0 and Over	57	4.7	2,704	42.1
TOTAL	1,217	100.0%	$6,421	100.0%

aIncludes mining and extractive companies.

bIncludes electric, gas, water, and communication companies.

cIncludes railroads, other transportation companies, commercial, and other businesses.

dIncludes some issues secured by various kinds of collateral other than real estate.
Source: Investment Dealers' Digest.

thirds of the number and nearly three-fourths of the dollar volume of direct placements during 1963. Public utilities accounted for only about 10 percent of both the number and volume of issues, while all other borrowers accounted for less than one-fifth of the number of issues and only one-sixth of the volume.

The pattern of direct placements is in marked contrast to public offerings in 1963, where public utility issues accounted for slightly more than one-half of the dollar volume and manufacturing firms for only one-fifth. Offerings by finance and real estate firms and all other borrowers accounted for the remainder of the volume of public offerings.

The summary of direct placement of corporate debt by type of security in Table 16–4 shows that in 1963 the bulk of both the number and dollar volume took the form of unsecured borrowing (principally notes and debentures). The relatively small remainder was accounted for by mortgage bonds and debt obligations with some form of conversion privilege.

While relatively small issues accounted for the bulk of the number of placements, dollar volume was centered in a small number of large placements. Placements of more than $10 million constituted about two-thirds of the dollar volume but only 14 percent of the number, while placements of less than $3 million accounted for nearly two-thirds of the number but only 12 percent of the dollar volume.

Analysis of the size distribution of placements by type of borrower indicates there is no uniform pattern among industry classes (see Table 16–5). Compared with other industry groups, a larger proportion of the placements of manufacturers was centered in large issues. Large issues (over $10 million) accounted for nearly three-fourths of the total dollar volume of placements by manufacturers, compared with an average of about three-fifths for the other industry groups. A similar situation existed with respect to number of issues sold.

The dollar volume of issues in the intermediate size class ($3 million to $10 million) represented a fairly uniform proportion of placements of each industry group except manufacturers, where the degree of concentration was somewhat lower. The use of small issues was most prevalent among finance and real estate concerns.

Using maturities and coupon rates as criteria, Table 16–6 presents a summary distribution of direct placements during 1963 (maturity and/or coupon rate were not reported for all offerings). As shown by the table, a large number of issues were uniformly distributed among the three longest maturity classes, with nearly 85 percent of all issues due to mature in more

TABLE 16–5

Direct Placements of Corporate Debt Securities: Percentage Distribution of Number and Dollar Volume by Size of Issue and Type of Borrower, 1963

Size of Issue (in millions of $'s)	Type of Borrower							
	Manufacturing		Finance and Real Estate		Public Utility		All Other	
	Number	Volume	Number	Volume	Number	Volume	Number	Volume
Under 0.5	17.9%	0.8%	20.2%	1.1%	24.2%	1.0%	21.8%	1.2%
0.5—0.9	13.9	1.4	16.6	2.4	10.2	1.3	16.7	2.6
1.0—2.9	30.9	7.8	31.2	11.6	27.3	9.1	24.3	9.4
3.0—4.9	9.0	5.2	9.6	7.7	10.9	8.4	13.0	10.6
5.0—9.9	11.0	11.1	11.3	15.6	14.1	17.7	10.9	16.0
10.0—24.9	11.3	25.7	6.0	16.8	10.2	31.0	10.9	33.1
25.0 and Over	6.0	48.0	5.1	44.8	3.1	31.5	2.4	27.1
TOTAL	100.0%	100.0%	100.0%	100.0%	100.0%	100.0%	100.0%	100.0%
Total Number	453	—	397	—	128	—	239	—
Total Volume (millions of $'s)	—	$2,973	—	$1,787	—	$ 604	—	$1,057

Source: Investment Dealers' Digest.

TABLE 16–6

Direct Placements of Corporate Debt Securities: Distribution by Maturity and Coupon Rate, 1963

Maturity Class	Number of Issues	Percentage Distribution	Volume of Issues (in millions of $'s)	Percentage Distribution
No maturity reported	77	6.3%	$ 307	4.8%
Under 5 years	36	3.0	141	2.2
5 to less than 10 years	73	6.0	233	3.6
10 to less than 15 years	348	28.6	688	10.7
15 to less than 20 years	348	28.6	1,844	28.7
20 years and Over	335	27.5	3,208	50.0
TOTAL	1,217	100.0%	$6,421	100.0%
Coupon Rates				
No coupon reported	116	9.5%	$ 524	8.2%
Under 4.00%	2	0.2	10	0.2
4.00—4.49%	31	2.5	619	9.6
4.50—4.99%	175	14.4	1,846	28.7
5.00—5.49%	231	19.0	1,480	23.0
5.50—5.99%	315	25.9	1,378	21.5
6.00—6.49%	242	19.9	354	5.5
6.50% and Over	105	8.6	210	3.3
TOTAL	1,217	100.0%	$6,421	100.0%

Source: Investment Dealers' Digest.

TABLE 16–7

Direct Placements of Corporate Debt Securities: Percentage Distribution of Number and Dollar Volume by Maturity and Coupon Rate and by Type of Borrower, 1963

	Type of Borrower							
	Manufacturing		Finance and Real Estate		Public Utility		All Other	
Maturity Class	Number	Volume	Number	Volume	Number	Volume	Number	Volume
No Maturity Reported	6.6%	4.2%	5.8%	1.9%	3.9%	1.0%	7.9%	12.6%
Under 5 years	1.4	0.7	4.7	3.5	2.3	0.2	3.4	5.5
5 to less than 10 years	7.5	2.4	5.8	4.0	—	—	6.7	8.5
10 to less than 15 years	26.0	10.4	40.8	15.7	3.1	0.5	26.8	8.9
15 to less than 20 years	38.6	37.6	22.7	23.0	9.4	6.1	29.7	27.2
20 years and Over	19.9	44.7	20.2	51.9	81.3	92.2	25.5	37.3
TOTAL	100.0%	100.0%	100.0%	100.0%	100.0%	100.0%	100.0%	100.0%
Coupon Rates								
No Coupon Reported	9.3%	6.1%	11.8%	8.2%	0.8%	0.1%	10.9%	18.6%
Under 4.00%	0.3	0.1	0.3	0.6	—	—	—	—
4.00—4.49%	1.3	7.5	1.3	3.8	9.4	44.7	3.3	5.4
4.50—4.99%	9.7	24.5	11.8	38.3	45.3	41.2	10.9	17.6
5.00—5.49%	19.2	26.8	19.9	16.9	21.1	7.8	15.9	31.4
5.50—5.99%	29.8	29.8	24.4	15.9	17.2	2.2	25.5	18.3
6.00—6.49%	24.7	4.7	16.9	7.7	3.9	0.5	24.3	7.1
6.50% and Over	5.7	0.5	13.6	8.6	2.3	3.5	9.2	1.6
TOTAL	100.0%	100.0%	100.0%	100.0%	100.0%	100.0%	100.0%	100.0%
Total Number	453	—	397	—	128	—	239	—
Total Volume (in millions of $'s)	—	$2,973	—	$1,787	—	$ 604	—	$1,057

Source: Investment Dealers' Digest.

than 10 years from date of issue. The dollar volume of placements was also heavily concentrated in over-10-year maturities, and the bulk of the total dollar volume (one-half in 1963) was accounted for by issues maturing in 20 years or longer.

While net interest costs of direct placements cannot be evaluated because of lack of data, the distribution of reported coupon rates does provide an approximation of the range of borrowing costs in 1963 (see Table 16–6). Nearly three-fifths of the number and three-quarters of the dollar volume of placements carried coupon rates ranging from 4½ to 6 percent. Placements carrying rates of 4½–5 percent accounted for the largest single share of total dollar volume (nearly 29 percent), while the heaviest concentration in number of issues was in the 5½–6 percent range (nearly 26 percent). Issues carrying rates in excess of 6 percent accounted for a large share of the number of placements but a small part of the dollar volume.

Data on maturity and coupon rates by type of borrower reveal considerable variation in the distribution of direct placements among several industry groups (see Table 16–7). For example, public utility borrowing was heavily concentrated in long maturities and relatively low interest rates; the latter reflects the generally high quality of public utility obligations.

While not as heavily concentrated as those of public utilities, placements of manufacturers and finance and real estate firms were also centered largely in longer-term maturities. In contrast, offerings of borrowers in the all-other category were noticeably shorter in maturity than those of other industry groups (possibly due to the relatively high proportion of such placements for which maturity was not reported).

For a relatively high proportion of non-utility placements the coupon rates were not available. Incomplete information indicates, however, that such placements generally carried higher rates than those of public utilities. For example, only 14 percent of the volume of public utility placements car-

TABLE 16–8

Corporate Bond Authorizations, Direct Placements: Reporting Life Insurance Companies

Year	Total Authorizations (millions of $'s)	First Quality		Second Quality		Third Quality		Fourth Quality		Unclassified	
		millions of $'s	% of Total	millions of $'s	% of Total	millions of $'s	% of Total	millions of $'s	% of Total	millions of $'s	% of Total
1960	$2,271	$16	0.7%	$110	4.8%	$593	26.1%	$ 973	42.9%	$579	25.5%
1961	2,702	30	1.1	160	5.9	676	25.0	1,260	46.7	576	21.3
1962	3,360	7	0.2	201	6.0	610	18.2	1,762	52.4	780	23.2
1963	3,408	18	0.5	223	6.6	676	19.8	1,713	50.3	778	22.8
1964	3,995	60	1.5	255	6.4	650	16.3	2,122	53.1	908	22.7

Source: Life Insurance Association of America.

CHART 16-4

Corporate Bond Authorizations, Direct Placments: Reporting Life
Insurance Companies

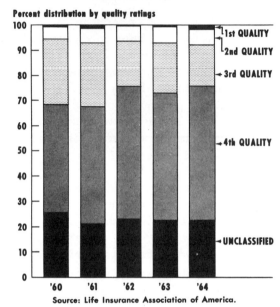

Percent distribution by quality ratings

Source: Life Insurance Association of America.

ried rates of more than 5 percent, compared with an average of 56 percent
of the volume for other industry groups.

YIELD AND QUALITY CHARACTERISTICS

Additional insight into selected characteristics of direct placements of
corporate debt is provided in data from the monthly reports of the Life Insurance Association of America. These reports present information on
direct placement authorizations of life insurance companies, and are available beginning in 1960.[7] As indicated in Table 16–8, reporting insurance
companies have committed increasing amounts of funds each year to the

---

[7] Data are from reports of "Average Yields on Directly Placed Corporate Bond
Authorizations," published monthly by the Life Insurance Association of America since
January 1960. The report is a tabulation of statistics on direct placements of corporate
dept obligations for which commitments were made during each month by life insurance companies holding approximately two-thirds of the assets of all United States life
insurance companies. The data cover bonds contracted for but not actually taken down
during the months. The data are used here with permission of the Life Insurance Association of America.

CHART 16–5

Corporate Bond Yields, Direct Placements and Public Offerings

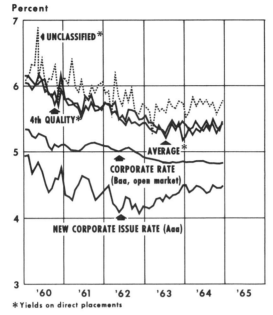

Percent

* Yields on direct placements

Sources: Life Insurance Association of America; Board of Governors of the Federal Reserve System.

purchase of corporate bonds that are direct placements. During 1964, commitments totaled nearly $4 billion, or 76 percent more than in 1960. In addition, the table shows that a smaller proportion of recent commitments has been made in direct placements that are in the higher quality grades.[8] The quality distribution of authorizations of direct placements is depicted in Chart 16–4.

The reduced proportion of commitments in higher quality obligations is at least in part a reflection of the less attractive yields available on these obligations, compared with other issues. It may also reflect the relative shortage of higher quality bond issues. As indicated in Chart 16–5, average yields on direct placement commitments of life insurance companies were consistently higher than those on both newly offered Aaa corporate bond offerings and outstanding issues of Baa rated bonds in 1960–64. The differ-

[8] Monthly volume and yield are reported on the basis of first, second, third, and fourth quality issues (corresponding to Moody ratings), and issues unclassified as to quality, including those with quality lower than fourth grade, convertible obligations, foreign corporates, oil production loans, and issues with which stocks or warrants are received. Higher quality issues, as used above, refer to those in the first through third quality grades.

ential between the Aaa corporate new issue rate and that on direct placements averaged 1.16 percent during the period. The weighted average yield on direct placements also exceeded the average market yield on Baa rated corporate bonds (the differential averaged .58 percent in the 1960–64 period). In addition, yields on first, second, and third quality direct placements (not shown in chart) were consistently above the Aaa new corporate issue rate, although the yield differential was considerably smaller.

Although yield comparisons show that yields on direct placements have exceeded rates on public offerings, the differential narrowed considerably in the 1960–64 period. For example, the differential between the average rate on direct placements and the average rate on Aaa new corporate offerings declined from a high of 1.30 percent in 1962 to .92 percent in 1964. Compared with yields on Baa rated corporates, the spread also narrowed, from a high of .77 percent in 1960 to .53 percent in 1964. A narrowing differential reflects in part increased demand for direct placements, which in turn has exerted downward pressure on interest rates. In addition, increasing institutional acceptance of this type of financing, coupled with ready availability of funds, has resulted in a downward adjustment in the historical relationship between yields on direct placements and on public offerings. The average yield on direct placements of life insurance companies has been in a declining trend throughout the period under review, while the volume of such issues has risen in each year. The yield on direct placements in 1964 averaged 60 basis points less than the average yield in 1960. In contrast, the rate on marketable Aaa new corporate offerings in 1964 was only 24 basis points less than the average yield in 1960.

17.

Pricing a Corporate Bond Issue:
A Look Behind the Scenes

ERNEST BLOCH

Making markets for securities means setting prices. This is a demanding job, for it requires a continuous evaluation of the various factors acting and reacting in the markets. Securities dealers must make day-to-day, hour-to-hour, and sometimes minute-to-minute adjustments, and the dealer who falls asleep, even briefly, may find his snooze a costly one.

Underwriters engaged in competitive bidding for new corporate bonds have a special pricing problem in that each flotation involves the distribution of a relatively large supply of securities in the shortest time feasible. While the market for outstanding securities does provide some guidance to the pricing process, it is a rough guide at best. A new bond issue will be similar to, but rarely identical with, any securities being traded in the secondary market. Furthermore, the relatively large amount involved in many new offerings increases the difficulty of gauging the market. Finally, pricing decisions on new securities are not made at the actual time of sale to the ultimate investors but must be made a short time before the bonds are released for trading, while the distribution itself may stretch over a number of days during which market rates may be in motion. The pricing of a new issue even under the best conditions thus takes place at the edge of the unknown.

The specialized job of buying, selling, and pricing new corporate se-

Reprinted from *Essays in Money and Credit*, 1964, pp. 72–76, by permission of the publisher, the Federal Reserve Bank of New York.

curities is primarily the province of investment bankers.[1] Not all issues are priced through a competitive bidding process, however, and the pricing of some flotations is negotiated directly between borrower and underwriter. But in all successful flotations, investment bankers function as quick intermediaries for new securities between borrowers and ultimate investors. This involves two distinct, although closely related, objectives. In cases of competitive bidding—formal or informal—the first objective is to "win" the right to offer the security to the public by paying the borrower more for it than any other underwriter. The second is to "reoffer" the security to investors at a price higher than that paid the borrower. If a number of underwriting groups are competing against each other for an issue, each must strike a balance between (1) pressing hard to win the issue by paying a relatively high price to the borrower and (2) increasing the risk that the issue cannot be sold to the public at a price to yield a profit.[2]

This article is concerned with the pricing problem in a competitive underwriting process, the resolution of which boils down to setting the bid price to the borrower. It illustrates how this price is set by following through the process for an actual issue of corporate bonds. Nonessential details that might serve to identify the borrower or the investment banking houses that underwrote the issue have been slightly altered.

Because the offering discussed below was quite sizable, the pricing problem involved an added dimension. The pricing decision was made not by a single underwriter, but by a large underwriting group acting jointly as a syndicate. The pricing decision thus was to be hammered out among the members of the underwriting group, each of which had been tentatively assigned a share of the new issue. And this pricing decision, if successful, had to better that of the strong rival syndicate.

---

[1] These firms have traditionally been called "investment bankers" although they are now bankers in name only. As is well-known, the Banking Act of 1933 specifically prohibits commercial banks that accept deposits and make loans from underwriting corporate securities. Under the act, commercial banks are permitted to continue some "investment banking"-type activities, such as underwriting direct obligations of the United States and general obligations of States and political subdivisions. At present, underwriters for corporate issues perform none of the basic functions of commercial banks, but the term "investment bankers" continues in use, and this usage will be followed in this article.

[2] In a negotiated flotation, the problem of reaching an optimum bid between (1) and (2) would appear to be less than it is under the competitive bidding process. And a negotiated deal clearly offers the short-run advantage to the underwriter that he cannot "lose" the issue to another syndicate. A negotiated underwriting will not necessarily carry a higher borrowing cost, however, for many large borrowers have some degree of choice between competitive and negotiated flotations. If borrowing costs in, say, negotiated deals were to rise out of line with costs on competitively priced flotations, the cheaper method of raising funds would be used to a greater extent.

PREPARATION FOR A LARGE ISSUE

When a corporation plans a large financing, it customarily gives fair warning as a means of preparing the capital market. In line with this practice, the firm to be called Large Company, Inc., had announced its intention to borrow $100 million *several months* before the date of actual issue. The early announcement gave potential investors, such as insurance companies, pension funds, and bank trust accounts the opportunity to adjust their financial commitments so as to make room, if they wished, for sizable chunks of the Large Company issue. At the same time, other potential corporate borrowers were made aware that the Large Company underwriting would bring special pressures on the market, making it unwise to schedule other sizable flotations around that period.

A light calendar of flotations makes possible a more eager participation in the underwriting by syndicate members because their over-all market commitments during the flotation period will be less. And the better the demand for bonds among syndicate members, the stronger their bid will be, and the lower the borrowing cost to the borrowing firm. As noted, in the underwriting of the Large Company issue two competing syndicates were formed. One of the groups, managed by X Investment Bank, consisted of more than 100 investment firms, and the competing syndicate, led by Y Investment Bank, was about as sizable.

Managing such large syndicates has become the business of about a half dozen large investment banking houses. Only the largest among them have the capital, the manpower, and the market contacts necessary to propose the proper price for a large offering. If a given house, acting as syndicate manager, wins what the market considers a fair share of the bidding competitions in which it participates, it gains in a number of ways. Not only is its prestige enhanced—which helps in managing future syndicates—but the house that is continuously proving the high quality of its market judgment may be more successful in attracting *negotiated* financings. This concern for the future tends to intensify present competition among managing underwriters.

But while the half dozen syndicate leaders are rivals, they are also potential allies because a grouping of underwriters exists only for a given flotation, and the next offering on the market will involve a different group. Indeed, during the preparation for the Large Company issue, two of the major firms in the rival syndicate led by Y Investment Bank knew that they would be associated with X Investment Bank in a large secondary stock offering within two weeks. As a consequence of the shifting associations and combinations of firms from syndicate to syndicate, the current associate in an underwriting insists on conserving his own independence of action, and this has an important bearing on the pricing process, as we shall see below.

The first informal "price meeting" on the forthcoming issue took place at X Investment Bank two days before the actual bidding date set for the issue. Fifteen senior officers of X Investment Bank actively engaged in trading and underwriting met at this point to discuss pricing recommendations that would win the issue and at the same time find ready acceptance in the market. The terms of the new issue were discussed in the light of current market factors, and each pricing suggestion was, in effect, an answer to a double-barreled question: first, how attractive was the issue in terms of quality, maturity, call provisions, and other features; and, secondly, how receptive was the market at this time? Among the factors discussed as leading to a lower yield was the new bonds' Aaa rating, while factors leading to a higher yield included the lack of call protection and the large size of the issue.

The preliminary discussion of the offering price then shifted to the "feel of the market." Even the proponents of a relatively high yield recognized that the final bid should be close to current market yields on similar securities, owing to the relatively light calendar of forthcoming new corporate flotations. Another sign pointing to aggressive bidding was a relatively light dealer inventory of corporate securities. The discussion of competitive demands for funds was not confined to the corporate securities market, however, but extended to the markets for municipal and Treasury issues as well. Here the picture was mixed. The light calendar of forthcoming municipal issues was cited by proponents of a lower yield, while those in favor of a higher yield pointed to expectations of a relatively heavy volume of Treasury financing. Finally, the discussion moved on to assess the possibility of changes in significant market rates such as the prime loan rate and Federal Reserve Bank discount rates during the flotation period. It was agreed that the likelihood of such changes during the financing period was small. Each of the officers of X Investment Bank then independently set down his opinion of the proper pricing of the issue (i.e., the combination of coupon rate and price offered the borrower) and the reoffering "spread" (i.e., the difference between the bid price and the reoffering price to the public).

The majority of the fifteen members of the group agreed that the new bonds should carry a rate of 4¼ percent to the borrower with the bonds priced at par, and with a reoffering spread of about $7 per $1,000 bond.[3] One member of the group thought that a lower yield might be needed to win the bid, and two or three others indicated yields higher than 4¼ percent. The aggressiveness of X Investment Bank's price ideas can be judged from the fact that newspaper comment on the likely level for the winning bid on the day of this meeting indicated a yield in the neighborhood of 4.30 percent.

---

[3] It should be noted once again that these rates have been changed from those placed on the actual bond issue.

MARKETING STRATEGY

Simultaneously, assessments of the market for the purpose of establishing a proper bid for the issue were under way in the offices of the allied syndicate members. The comparison of various opinions of the "best" bid of the syndicate members took place a day later, the day before the actual opening of the bids by the borrower. This was the "preliminary price meeting," to which each firm in the syndicate was invited. At the meeting each participant firm named the price it was willing to pay for the number of bonds tentatively assigned in the underwriting.[4] The poll of the 100-odd allied syndicate members revealed far less aggressiveness (i.e., willingness to accept a low yield) by the smaller firms than was shown by the syndicate manager. Relatively few ideas were at 4¼ percent, while one of the "major underwriters" (i.e., a firm tentatively assigned $3 million of bonds or more) put his offering yield at 4.35 percent, and a small firm went as high as 4.40 percent.

In this particular underwriting, X Investment Bank seemed quite eager to win the bid, partly because of its optimistic appraisals of the state of the bond market and partly because it is the syndicate manager's responsibility to push for a winning bid and to exercise the proper persuasion to carry his syndicate along. Prestige is peculiarly the concern of the syndicate manager because, right or wrongly, the market apparently does not attach nearly so much significance to membership as to leadership in a losing syndicate.

This factor explains the paradox that the followers, rather than the manager, may be more responsible for the failure to win a bid for lack of aggressiveness, even though the market tends to place the blame on the manager. But smaller syndicate members may be reluctant participants at lower yields because their commitment of funds for even a relatively small portion of a large underwriting may represent a larger call (or contingent liability) against the small firm's capital than it does for a bigger firm. Even though the larger firm's capital may be as fully employed as that of the smaller firm in its *total* underwriting business, the commitment of a large portion of capital for a single underwriting may make the smaller firm more hesitant to take that particular marketing risk.

In preparing for the final price meeting, the syndicate manager held the first of a number of behind-the-scenes strategy sessions. At these meetings, some basic decisions were made about ways and means of holding the syndicate together. During the final price meeting, any firm believing that the market risk of the proposed group bid was too great (i.e., that the yield was too low to sell well) had the right to drop out of the syndicate. Conversely, if the syndicate member liked the group bid, he could raise the

---

[4] In this meeting, as in the final price meeting, a number of security measures were taken to prevent a leak of information to the competing syndicate.

extent of his participation. Of course, if many syndicate members drop out, particularly major underwriters, too much of a burden is placed on the remaining members, and the result is, in effect, to veto the proposed bid. The aggressive manager thus is placed squarely in the middle of a tug of war: if his bid is too aggressive, and carries a relatively low yield, the syndicate may refuse to take down the bonds; if the bid is too cautious and carries too high a yield, the syndicate may lose the bidding competition to the rival group. This conflict was resolved at the final price meeting.

SYNDICATE TACTICS

On the morning of the day on which the final bids were made to the borrower, the officers of the syndicate manager held their final conference at which decisions were reached regarding their willingness to raise their own share of the underwriting. In effect, a manager who believes in an aggressive bid puts up or shuts up by expressing his willingness to absorb a greater or a lesser share of the total underwriting as firms drop out of the syndicate at lower yields. A strong offer to take more bonds by the manager may induce a number of potential dropouts to stay at a lower yield, partly because their share of the flotation won't be raised by a given number of dropouts since the manager is picking up the pieces. But beyond the arithmetic effect, a strong offer may have a psychological impact, and some reluctant participants may decide that the manager knows more than they do, and that his willingness to raise his share at a given yield is his way of backing the strength of his judgment.

This "psychological" downward push on yields may be small, but sometimes even a tiny difference between two competing bids can spell the difference between success and failure. For example, in late 1959, the winning syndicate for a $30 million utility issue bid $1/100$ of a *cent* more per $1,000 bond than the loser; the borrower received exactly $3 more from the winning syndicate for the $30 million issue than was offered by the loser.[5]

Another important factor in holding the syndicate together is the strength of the "book" for the new issue. The "book" is a compilation of investor interest in the new bonds. This interest may have been solicited or unsolicited, and may have gone directly to X Investment Bank from, say, institutional investors or to other members of the syndicate. Thus the book is a sample of market strength. All the interest in the book is tentative since no lender would commit funds for an issue of unknown yield. Nevertheless,

[5] At times, tie bids are received. On September 12, 1961, two underwriters bid identical amounts, down to the last $1/100$ of a penny per $1,000 bond, for a $3 million issue of municipal bonds. Such tie bids are as rare as a golfer's hole in one, however.

it is impossible to exaggerate the importance of a large book to an aggressive syndicate manager in holding his group together at the lowest possible yield. Because reluctant participants in an underwriting are particularly concerned about the selling risk, the larger the book the more reassured they will feel at any given rate. Put another way, the better the book, the more bonds a firm will take at a given rate, thus absorbing more dropouts. Indeed, the size of the book was considered so important that the final price meeting on the Large Company underwriting was interrupted a number of times by the latest indications of interest in the issue.

THE FINAL PRICE MEETING

As a means of preventing information leaks, representatives of the firms attending the final price meeting were locked in a room. The meeting was opened by a vice president of X Investment Bank with a brief review of the good state of the "book"—about half the issue had been spoken for, tentatively. He derived further encouragement for an aggressive bid from the healthy state of the bond market. Thus he proposed to make his bid at the 4¼ percent rate agreed upon at the X Investment Bank preliminary meeting two days earlier.

The immediate reaction to this statement was a chorus of moans. Apparently, the book was not sufficiently broad to carry the doubters along with the first bid, nor did the manager indicate any other action that would have made his proposal more acceptable. When the group was polled, large and small dropouts cut the $100 million underwriting by about a third. The failure to carry the syndicate at the first go-round was later attributed by some X Investment Bank people to the fact that three dropouts occurred among the first set of major underwriters polled (i.e., the eight largest firms, each of which had been tentatively assigned $3 million of bonds). And in the second set ($2 million assigned to each firm) another few had fallen by the wayside.

Thus a new bid proposal had to be presented to the group. Following another behind-the-scenes consultation of the senior officers of the managing underwriter, a 4⅜ percent coupon was proposed with a big yield of 4.27 percent. Amid continued grumbling of the majority of the members of the meeting, this was readily accepted by nearly every firm.

Judging that they might have leaned over too far in the direction of their reluctant followers, the officers of the syndicate manager consulted once again, and decided to present a somewhat more aggressive bid to the syndicate. In the third proposal, the bid price on the 4⅜ coupon was upped by 20 cents per $1,000 bond. The underwriters, still grumbling, were polled again and, following a few minor dropouts, approved the new price. The final allocation of the bonds differed relatively little from the tentative original allocation except that the manager picked up the allotments of the dropouts by adding about $3 million to his own commitment. By this time only a few minutes were left until the formal opening of the competitive bids by Large Company, Inc. The final coupon and price decisions were telephoned to the syndicate's representative at the bidding, who formally submitted the bid to Large Company.

Promptly at 11:30 a.m. the doors of the price committee meeting were thrown open, and within thirty seconds of that time the news was shouted from the trading room that the X Investment Bank bid had lost. The difference in the bid prices between the two syndicates came to little more than $1 per $1,000 bond.

The bonds were released for trading by the Securities and Exchange Commission at around 4 p.m. and were quickly snapped up by market investors. At X Investment Bank the feeling of gloom hung heavy, particularly since the first bid offered to the price meeting would have won the issue.

Would a better X Investment Bank book have carried the defecting major underwriters along on the first bid? Should the manager have been willing to take more bonds to carry the group along in the first recommendation which would have won the issue? And would market acceptance of that bid have been as good as that accorded the actual winning bid of Y syndicate? These post mortems were bound to be inconclusive, and the unremitting pressures of the underwriting business soon cut them short. Within the next several days a number of other securities were scheduled to come to market. Tomorrow was another day, and another price meeting.

18.

Term Loans—

Big Business for Big Banks

DOROTHY M. NICHOLS

How far commercial banking practice has departed from the old idea of short-term self-liquidating loans is demonstrated by information now available on the amount of "term" loans outstanding at banks.[1]

Reports from about 150 of the nation's largest banks indicate that more than 45 percent of their outstanding commercial and industrial loans were made under agreements that provide the borrower with credit for more than a year—up to seven or eight years in many cases. Such loans account for almost two-thirds of the net increase in business loans of these banks since a year ago.

The trend toward longer loan maturities has been underway since the mid-1950's. But the recent upsurge in term loans coupled with moderate net growth in total business loans, suggests that corporations have been seeking firm credit commitments from their banks, possibly in anticipation of tighter credit.

Reprinted from *Business Conditions*, May 1968, pp. 2–6, by permission of the publisher, the Federal Reserve Bank of Chicago.

[1] A new statistical series on commercial and industrial term loans at the large banks in major cities. The series, which reports loans by industry, is available from the Board of Governors of the Federal Reserve System as a supplement to its weekly H.12 release. Data begins on January 25, 1967.

WHAT ARE "TERM" LOANS?

Several types of borrowing arrangements are called term loans, their common characteristic being a contractual agreement that the bank will supply credit for longer than a year. The type of arrangement (ordinary term loans, revolving credits, and standby credits) usually reflects the purpose of borrowing and the timing of the customer's financing needs. Such arrangements are made only for "qualified" customers—those with well established relations with the bank and with financial conditions and prospects that meet rigid standards.

An ordinary term loan is a business loan with an original maturity of more than one year. It may be repayable in a lump sum or in periodic instalments—a serial term loan. (Loans collateralized by real estate are excluded from the definition used here.) The terms of the loan agreement are tailored to the specific needs of the borrower and vary greatly. Repayment schedules can range from monthly to annually, and the amounts to be repaid can vary over the life of the loan.

Revolving credit agreements normally allow the borrower access to a specified amount of credit for up to two or three years. Individual notes written under such agreements are short-term—often with 90-day maturities. But the notes can be renewed at maturity, and the borrower can pay down and reborrow to suit his needs for the duration of the agreement. Thus, the credit used is in effect long term, even though the outstanding amount often varies with seasonal needs.

Standby credit is another arrangement that allows the borrower to draw funds from time to time up to a maximum amount until the expiration date. There is no provision, however, for paying down and reborrowing as there is with revolving credit. Under either arrangement, the borrower normally pays a small commitment fee on the unused portion of credit and may never take down the entire amount available to him.

A variation that appears to have gained popularity in recent years is a revolving or standby credit that can be converted into a term loan after a certain length of time. Under this arrangement, the borrower can be assured of credit for seven or eight years. The arrangement is appropriate where a borrower needs flexible bank financing during initial stages of plant construction and expects to arrange for permanent financing from another source but wants protection from the need to do so under adverse circumstances.

Both ordinary term loan and revolving credit agreements usually specify definite conditions regarding the use of the funds and standards of performance in the maintenance of the borrower's business and financial position. In a sense, the bank and its customer become working partners in the accomplishment of specific corporate objectives.

As long as he complies with the conditions of the agreement, the borrower is assured of bank financing up to the limits stated. For this privilege, he pays interest on the outstanding balance and often a commitment fee on the unused credit—usually ¼ percent. He may also be required to maintain a compensating balance.

The bank, in turn, assumes the risks involved in making a commitment to supply a certain amount of funds as required by the customer. Sufficient funds to meet loan demands when they arise may be difficult or costly to obtain. To minimize this risk, the bank may maintain fairly high liquidity, thereby reducing current income without any assurance that the customer will actually use the funds. Moreover, while his contract with the bank usually provides the customer some protection against rising interest rates, the bank normally comes under great pressure to renegotiate the contract if rates fall.

WHY TERM LOANS?

Term lending on a large scale by commercial banks is a fairly recent development. Traditionally, prudent commercial bankers were expected to hold assets with short maturities in keeping with their liabilities—mainly demand deposits. Long-term credit needs were served largely by capital markets.

Banks began to venture into the intermediate area in the 1930's, when funds were plentiful and the need for such credit was widespread. Longer maturities were encouraged both by experience with Reconstruction Finance Corporation loans and a shift in emphasis of supervisory authorities from liquidity to soundness of assets. In recent years, it has been recognized that both the increased ability of banks to manage their liabilities and the cash flows resulting from serial repayment schedules provide substantial liquidity—more perhaps than when most business loans were 90-day notes that might have to be renewed several times. At the same time, intermediate-term bank credit has considerable appeal to many businesses as a flexible means of financing.

Term loans are well suited to financing of capital expenditures that can be recouped from the borrow's earnings and depreciation allowances in five to eight years. Also, credits with one to two-year maturities can be used to provide interim financing in the early stages of plant construction or equipment purchases that will eventually be funded through security issues. Or, term loans may be preferred over sales of securities at times when capital market rates are believed high.

Another factor affecting the demand for term loans and revolving credit is business expectations regarding the future availability of bank loans. When monetary policy is restrictive, or is expected to become restrictive, some companies that normally borrow under established lines of credit prefer more formal credit agreements with their banks and are willing to pay a fee for a firm commitment.

WHO BORROWS?

Typically, term loans have been extended primarily to large companies in extractive industries and transportation utilities, such as railroads, airlines, and trucking concerns, where operating units are large and financing needs are not purely seasonal. The funds are often used to finance equipment purchases.

Term loans are most important in New York and Chicago, where many of the largest business companies do their banking. Of all banks reporting term loans, those in the New York Federal Reserve District accounted for 54 percent of the term loans reported at the end of February, compared with 38 percent of total commercial and industrial loans. As a proportion of the commercial and industrial loans in each district, term loans ranged from 61 percent in the New York district to 20 percent in the San Francisco district. Slightly more than half the business loans on the books of the 15 large reporting banks in the Chicago district were term loans, but ratios for individual banks in the district ranged from 10 to 65 percent.

Differences in the importance of term loans at large banks in the Seventh District partly reflect the industrial mix of the banks' business customers. Term loans are made most often to large companies in industries with large capital expenditures. Of outstanding credits at large Seventh District banks to companies engaged in mining or petroleum refining, almost 90 percent had more than one-year maturities. The ratio was about 80 percent for transportation utilities and 70 percent for producers of primary metals.

But the willingness of banks to extend term loans may be influenced by the amount of funds they have employed in other long-term earning assets. Thus on the West Coast, where, in contrast to New York, banks have very large investments in mortgages, business term loans are relatively small.

HOW MUCH "INSURANCE"?

Outstanding commercial and industrial loans to domestic borrowers at reporting banks expanded $4 billion over the year ended in late February. Of that, nearly $2.8 billion was in term loans. There was only modest expansion in term loans before December. But since then, term loans have risen sharply while short-term loans have declined. At Seventh District banks, term loans accounted for more than 80 percent of the net gain in total business loans.

Both the industrial distribution of the expansion in term loans and its timing suggest a considerable substitution of term loans for short-term borrowings. Many loan officers have said corporate borrowers want "insurance" that they can obtain bank credit as needed under tightened credit conditions and are willing to pay the commitment fee as a "premium."

Much of the recent growth, especially for Seventh District banks, can be attributed to borrowings by companies engaged in metal manufacturing. A fourth of the increase at district banks went to producers of primary metals, who a year ago accounted for only 2 percent of the outstanding term loans. Borrowings of these companies, which include steel companies, probably reflects the financing needed to carry stocks built up to meet customer demands in case of a strike this fall. Mining companies, which are normally the largest term-loan borrowers, account for almost none of the expansion in the period ended in late February.

Part of the recent upsurge in term loans undoubtedly represents the financing of long-term capital needs. With yields on high-grade corporate securities well above 6 percent, businesses eligible to borrow at the prime rate—which was 6 percent until mid-April—found bank credit attractive. However, much of the funds currently taken down under long-term loan agreements is apparently of the revolving credit type.

Clearly, the recent shift to term loans cannot be related to any particular type of business expenditure. A number of factors have combined to enhance the appeal of these loans to borrowers in the current financial environment. But in the long run, the growth of term loans as a proportion of bank assets must also be attributed to their appeal to the lending banks. The comparatively high yields on these loans, coupled with increased confidence that a significant degree of liquidity can be provided through the management of bank liabilities, help explain this trend.

Many smaller businesses borrow under serial term-loan contracts. The evidence suggests, however, that this type of accommodation is provided mainly to large well-established companies with the demonstrated ability to make repayments out of earnings.

19.

Commercial Banks
as Suppliers
of Capital Funds to Business

GEORGE BUDZEIKA

Commercial banks are an important source of the funds business requires for financing expansion or modernization of plant and equipment and for other long-term needs. To be sure, commercial banks have not been permitted since 1934 to engage in underwriting new corporate securities issues. This function is performed by investment banking houses. Many smaller businesses, however, do not have access to the securities market; and larger businesses sometimes prefer to borrow capital funds for shorter periods than are typical of the bond, stock, or mortgage markets. These financing needs can be, and often are, met by banks through the offer of medium-term credits of up to eight years' maturity. Thus, commercial banks and the securities market are in many cases viewed as alternative sources of capital funds by the business borrower, who can draw on one or the other according to convenience and cost. After describing how banks participate in the provision of capital funds to business, this article examines secular and cyclical trends in the relative use of these alternatives.

Reprinted from *Essays in Money and Credit*, pp. 67–71, by permission of the publisher, the Federal Reserve Bank of New York.

NATURE AND MAGNITUDE OF COMMERCIAL BANK PARTICIPATION

Commercial banks participate in supplying capital funds to business through term loans in two different, although interrelated, ways. First, they extend intermediate-term loans that are repaid from the borrower's earnings or from other internal sources; second, they extent interim credits of one- to two-year maturity, which are repaid from the proceeds of new bond or stock issues in the securities market.

For the first type of credit, commercial banks are very attractive sources to many businesses. Many small firms that do not have ready access to the long-term securities market find bank credit the only practicable source of new capital funds. And for large businesses, borrowing from banks is often a quicker, cheaper, and more convenient method of raising long-term funds—particularly for loans with maturities of five to eight years —than the public offering of bonds or the flotation of equities in the securities market. Also, bank loans can be tailored to individual borrower needs through direct negotiations with the lending bank, thus giving the borrower more leeway in determining repayment schedules and frequently permitting more efficient use of loan proceeds.[1]

Since these bank loans are generally used by borrowers to finance capital expenditures and are repaid from internal cash flows—current earnings or depreciation allowances—they are akin to long-term credits extended by life insurance companies, pension funds, and other financial institutions and by individual investors in the bond, stock, and mortgage markets. However, the original maturity of new corporate bonds publicly offered during 1950–61 averaged about twenty-five years, whereas that of term loans outstanding at member banks is estimated to have averaged about five years recently. Consequently, commercial banks are provided each year with a relatively larger flow of repayments for relending to other customers than nonbank holders of corporate bonds, equities, and mortgages. To be sure, the funds repaid to, and relent by, banks reflect only shifts of existing credits from one business firm to another. But these shifts represent a redirection of resources—from firms that are no longer in need of them to firms seeking to increase their resources through external financing. In thus shifting existing credits among various businesses in the economy, commercial banks contribute a great deal of flexibility to the financing of capital formation.

Banks offer a second type of capital financing assistance to business by providing interim credits for financing the initial stages of new plant construction. This type of bank activity tends to come about in the following

---

[1] The nature of term loans and their trends at large New York City banks during 1955–60 were discussed in "Term Lending by New York City Banks," this *Review*, February 1961, pp. 27–31.

way. The need for funds in heavy capital investment projects arises only gradually as work proceeds. Some business firms, therefore, may be reluctant to borrow the full amount in the securities market at the outset, preferring to borrow temporarily from banks—in the form of either a formalized revolving credit agreement or a short-term line of credit—with such credits remaining on the books for one to two years.[2] These arrangements enable firms to borrow only the amount needed at each stage of construction, which economizes on borrowing costs. At or near the time of completion of the project—when exact long-term credit needs are finally known—the borrower normally repays the interim bank debt from the proceeds of a new bank loan carrying a longer maturity or, more typically, from the proceeds of sales of new securities in the capital market.

This role of bank term credit as an interim substitute for securities market credit is most pronounced in the financing of capital expenditures by electric, gas, and water public utilities. On the basis of data provided by the Securities and Exchange Commission, it is estimated that during 1959–62 commercial banks initially financed nearly half of the total capital expenditures of public utilities that were ultimately financed in the securities market. In manufacturing industries, the interim financing by banks covered about one quarter of the capital expenditures eventually financed in the securities market.

The gross flow of capital funds from banks to business is sizable. During 1959–62, for instance, extensions of intermediate-term loans by banks to nonfinancial, nonfarm corporate and noncorporate businesses are estimated to have averaged nearly $7 billion annually,[3] while extensions of interim credits—granted under both revolving credit agreements and line-of-credit arrangements—are estimated at $2 billion or more per year. (Routine renewals of loans are excluded from these figures.) It happens that, over the same period, the volume of new bond issues sold by non-

---

[2] The revolving credit agreement permits the borrower to draw short-term notes on the bank from time to time up to the maximum amount of the commitment, with the privilege of repaying and reborrowing during the life of the agreement. The bank's promise to extend credit is a firm commitment. The line-of-credit arrangement is similar, differing mainly in the lack of a formal agreement and of a legally binding obligation to extend credit.

[3] The figures on extensions of term loans by banks were pieced together from a number of sources, including the Commercial Loan Surveys of 1946, 1955, and 1957, conducted by the Federal Reserve System; the *Quarterly Financial Report for Manufacturing Corporations*, compiled jointly by the Federal Trade Commission and the Securities and Exchange Commission; weekly reports on term loans by large New York City banks; statistics on bank loan refundings in the securities markets, provided by the Securities and Exchange Commission; and statistical material on New York City banks, developed from bank examination sources. The estimates thus derived refer to banks' commercial and industrial loans, mortgage-secured loans to business, and single-payment loans to individuals for business purposes, all with an original maturity of more than one year. Though the estimates are rough, they are considered workable approximations for an analysis of cyclical and secular trends.

financial corporations to investors also averaged nearly $7 billion, and the volume of new stock issues about $2 billion. Although these data are on a gross basis, the comparison provides some notion of the place of commercial banks in satisfying the demands of American business for external capital financing.

TRENDS IN THE USE OF COMMERCIAL BANK AND BOND MARKET CREDITS

Over the business cycle as well as over longer periods, the role of banks in supplying capital funds to business is significantly affected by the over-all demand and supply conditions for such funds. In the last five years,

CHART 19–1

Capital Expenditures and Gross Financing of Nonfinancial Business

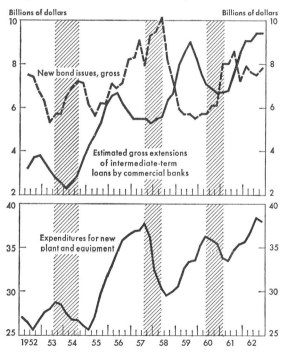

Note: All series are shown at seasonally adjusted annual rates, with bond issues and bank lending on a three-quarter moving average. Shaded areas represent recession periods, according to National Bureau of Economic Research chronology.

Sources: Board of Governors of the Federal Reserve System, Federal Reserve Bank of New York, Securities and Exchange Commission, and United States Department of Commerce (for details of derivation of estimates, see text footnotes 3 and 4).

the most important factor affecting business demand for capital funds has been a sharp rise in corporations' internal cash flows (comprising retained earnings and depreciation allowances) relative to their capital expenditures. According to the flow-of-funds tabulations prepared by the Board of Governors of the Federal Reserve System, internal cash flows of nonfinancial corporations were $2.6 billion a year lower in 1952–57 than corporate expenditures for fixed investment, but exceeded fixed capital expenditures by $1.9 billion per year during 1958–62.

The effects of this relative increase in the internal cash flows of corporations were a reduction in the corporate demand for bond market credit, little change in the demand for equity funds, and increased demand for intermediate-term bank credit. Chart 19–1 presents the figures given above on these major types of credit for a longer period and in a slightly different form. As this chart shows, the dollar volume of gross new bond issues by nonfinancial corporations declined sharply after 1957 to an average of about $7 billion per year during 1960–62, only slightly more than the 1952–54 average. Gross new stock issues increased slightly, from $1.7 billion to $2.0 billion per year. In contrast, gross extensions of intermediate-term loans and interim credits by banks during 1960–62,[4] at about $8 billion per year, were around 2½ times their $3 billion annual average for the years 1952–54. The relative importance of bank financing has also increased in terms of amounts outstanding; bank loans of the types indicated have grown faster than outstanding corporate bonds[5]—the primary alternative to such bank credits.

There is good reason to believe that the rise in the internal cash flows of corporations may actually have contributed in some degree to the augmented demand for bank funds. Expecting an increased flow of cash from internal sources, some companies have become able to repay borrowings in a shorter period than twenty-odd years, the typical maturity for publicly offered bonds, and bank term loans therefore have emerged as a feasible alternative.

Shifts between banks and the bond market by borrowers are also a feature of business cycles. As can be seen in Chart 19–1, bank lending and

---

[4] The figures on bank lending, as plotted in Chart 19–1, combine intermediate-term loans and interim credits, because their separation for years prior to 1959 was not possible. But extensions of interim credits under line-of-credit arrangements were not included in the combined figures because of the difficulty of statistically measuring their trends. This omission understates actual bank lending to business by perhaps as much as $1 billion per year on the average.

[5] According to estimates prepared for this study, the volume of commercial banks' outstanding term loans to nonfinancial business rose between 1952–54 and 1960–62 by about 130 percent (from an average of $12 billion to $28 billion), while in the same period the volume of outstanding bonds of nonfinancial business, according to statistics compiled by the Board of Governors of the Federal Reserve System, rose by only 70 percent (from an average of $47 billion to $79 billion).

bond financing have moved inversely over the last three cycles. Bank extensions of intermediate-term loans rose sharply in the early part of business expansions, reached a peak around the mid-points, and thereafter declined through mid-recessions; bond financing generally reached its peak around recessions, and its trough during business expansions. However, these inverse cyclical movements of the two sources of credit are not necessarily attributable entirely to direct shifts of borrower demand from one to the other. In fact, there are numerous institutional and cyclical factors that induce business firms to borrow less in one credit market and to borrow more in another during a given stage of a business cycle. Some of these factors may be described briefly.

In the first half of a business expansion, when bank funds are in ample supply, business borrowers show a strong preference for bank rather than bond market credit. One explanation is probably the relative ease of obtaining bank credit, for at that time it is simpler to borrow from banks than to go through the relatively time-consuming procedures required by the bond market. In addition, many businesses are then embarking on new capital expenditures, and there is thus an increased desire for interim bank credits, to be repaid at the completion of construction from the proceeds of new bond issues.

During recessions, the long-term borrowing undertaken by business occurs mainly in the bond market. Many businesses have by that time completed their new construction projects and turn to the long-term bond market to refund their interim bank indebtedness. Furthermore, borrowers find that during recessions the cost of borrowing in the bond market is declining, and some of them decide to refund part of their outstanding high-coupon bond debt with low-rate new issues, as happened on a relatively large scale during the 1954 recession.[6] Still other borrowers may tend to substitute bond credit for stock market financing during recessions, because stock prices are ordinarily depressed during such periods.

The role played by the alternating uses of bank credit and bond financing during a business cycle can be examined in more detail only for the most recent years. Pertinent bank loan refunding figures are available since mid-1958. These figures, which are shown in Chart 19–2, cover repayments of bank credits from the proceeds of new corporate bond and stock issues sold in the securities market by nonfinancial corporations, as recorded in the registration files of the Securities and Exchange Commission. In bank loan refundings, as in the case of new borrowing to meet capital financing needs, bond rather than stock issues have been the main alternative in recent years.

Although the period covered by loan refunding statistics is relatively short, the figures are suggestive of the behavior of bank loan refundings

---

[6] The effect of such refunding is not evident in Chart 19–1, since its figures on bond credit cover all new issues, regardless of purpose.

during recessions. Refundings rose sharply during the second quarter of 1961, after the trough of the 1960–61 recession. As has been suggested above, such a rise is to be expected during, rather than after, recessions. To be sure, the 1961 increase in bank loan refundings lagged into the early post-recession period; but this may to some extent have been a reflection of the relatively short duration of the preceding expansion in capital expenditures. As Chart 19–1 shows, the expansion in expenditures for new plant and equipment lasted only 1¾ years in the 1958–61 cycle, compared with 2½ and 3¾ years during the 1954–58 and 1949–54 cycles. At the end of relatively short expansions many construction projects may remain uncompleted. Therefore, the upturn in refinancing may be delayed beyond the end of the recession.

The timing of bank loan refundings in the bond market is also related to the level of interest rates in the bond market, and to the anticipations of businessmen with respect to future rate changes. If borrowers expect bond rates to decline in the near future, they have little incentive to borrow in the bond market. If they anticipate a rise in interest rates, however, they may

CHART 19–2

Bank Loan Refundings and Interest Rates in Securities Markets

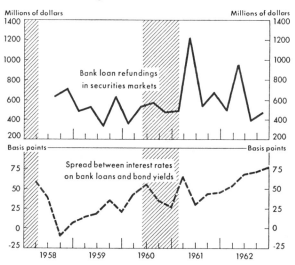

Note: Bank loan interest rates are rates on short-term business loans at selected commercial banks in nineteen cities, as reported in the Quarterly Interest Rate Survey published regularly in the Federal Reserve Bulletin. Bond yields refer to FHA-compiled average yields of recently issued Aaa-rated corporate bonds. The spread equals interest rates on bank loans minus bond yields. Shaded areas represent recession periods, according to National Bureau of Economic Research chronology.

Sources: Board of Governors of the Federal Reserve System, Federal Housing Administration, and Securities and Exchange Commission.

wish to borrow in the bond market before the rise takes place. Such considerations may have contributed to the sharp rise in refundings during the second quarter of 1961. By then it was clear that an upward trend in the economy had started. Judging from historical experience, this trend could be expected to bring about a rise in interest rates on bonds.

Changes in the relative costs of bank and bond market borrowing also help explain the timing of bank loan refundings. When relative costs move in favor of bond financing, firms that have to refinance their interim bank debt have an incentive to do so through bond borrowing. And, conversely, if the cost of bond market credit becomes relatively high, business borrowers have reason to postpone their loan refundings until a more favorable situation arises.

During the 1960–61 recession and the short periods preceding and following it, bank loan refundings rose—with a lag of about a quarter of a year—after increases in the spread between bank and bond market rates in favor of the latter (see Chart 19-2). The lag may represent the time needed by borrowers to reach their decisions and to complete the procedures necessary for a new flotation in the securities market. This two-year performance suggests that bank loan refundings are sensitive to interest rate spreads during recessionary or near-recessionary periods, when business firms have completed the construction projects financed with interim bank credits and have an option about the timing of their refunding. On the other hand, during the nonrecessionary periods covered by the data—late 1958, early 1959, and 1962—when such an option did not exist, no direct relationship could be discerned between bank loan refundings and the relative cost of bank and bond market credits. The response of business borrowers to changing relative costs of bank and bond borrowing clearly requires further analysis once figures for longer periods are available.

CONCLUSIONS

Commercial banks now play an important role as a source of capital finance. They act as buffers for the capital market, absorbing a significant proportion of the initial pressures for capital funds by medium-sized and large corporations. Thus they contribute to the relative stability of the market for business capital finance within a business cycle, and to more efficient financial planning by borrowers and ultimate lenders of long-term funds.

Possibly even more important, commercial banks act as significant lenders to businesses that seek intermediate-term funds. These may be borrowers who do not have ready access to the securities market and do not generate sufficient amounts of funds from internal sources to finance their new plant expansion or their more permanent working-capital needs. Or they may be firms whose internal cash flows allow them to contract for capital credits of shorter maturity than are typical in the bond market. Particularly for those borrowers who do not have access to the securities market, the possibility of borrowing from commercial banks may be the decisive factor in going ahead with expansion plans.

These activities are evidence of a changing function of commercial banks. In addition to supplying short-term funds to business—the traditional function of commercial banks—they are now also providing substantial amounts of medium-term funds and thus are emerging as an important financial intermediary in the savings-investment process. This service helps generate capital formation and is another instance of the evolutionary adaptation of the country's financial mechanisms to the economy's needs.

20.

The Third Market—

The Nature of Competition

in the Market for Listed Securities

Traded Off-Board

M. E. POLAKOFF
and A. W. SAMETZ

I. INTRODUCTION

In order to evaluate the performance of the market in securities listed on an organized exchange but traded off the exchange, it is essential that guideposts be established. Accordingly, criteria are developed to distinguish between perfect and imperfect markets; such standards are then applied to auction markets in general and specifically to the over-the-counter market in listed securities, that is, to the so-called "Third Market."

II. COMPETITIVE MARKETS AS A NORM

It is standard practice in economic discussions to illustrate competitive markets by reference to security markets and, in particular, to the auction

Reprinted from *The Antitrust Bulletin*, Vol. XI, Nos. 1 and 2, January and February 1966, pp. 191–207, by permission of the publisher.

market of the New York Stock Exchange.[1] Consider the general structural characteristics of competitive markets and their application to the organized security markets.

(1) There are a large number of buyers and sellers each of whom has little or no effect on the price of the commodity—there are over one million owners of AT&T stock each of whom has by himself little influence on the price at which the stock is traded.

(2) All such buyers and sellers are engaged in the purchase and sale of identically similar commodities—one share of AT&T is like any other share.

(3) Buyers and sellers are in close contact with each other and are perfectly informed with respect to current prices of the commodity—the stock market tape and the financial pages of the better daily newspapers and the Wall Street Journal help perform this function.

(4) Buyers and sellers trade freely among themselves—the analogy here to one aspect of free entry is the ability of the ultimate customer to call his broker and instruct him vis-à-vis buy and sell orders.

Given the above structure, one may reasonably expect competitive markets to perform in certain clearly defined ways. An equilibrium price will be achieved, i.e., one which clears the market, so that there is neither excess demand nor supply at that price. Markets in which such clearing prices are traditional are attractive to potential customers because in such markets sales can be made readily at prices close to the last clearing price, the concept of liquidity; and in some volume, the concept of depth. Easy transferability of claims is thus a prime attribute of such competitive markets; this characteristic is perhaps the chief explanation of the success of mass equity finance or the raising of corporate capital in general.

But equilibrium prices in other than the instantaneous or market period are also ideal from the viewpoint of costs. In the short run, it is a least-cost price in the sense that it just covers marginal costs of transferring securities and risk. Such a price may yield above (or below) normal profits because the short run is defined as that period during which there is insufficient time for new firms or resources to be made operational. In the long run, however, free entry or exit assures that price is also least cost in the sense that it just covers all costs including a rate of return on capital just sufficient to keep the firm in the industry.[2]

---

[1] K. E. Boulding, *Economic Analysis* (3d ed.; Harper, 1955), p. 47.

[2] The long run equilibrium price of equities not only assures ideal allocation of resources within the securities industry but also in the allocation of real capital to the security-issuing firms, i.e., in the long run, equity prices in equilibrium will reflect discounted expected returns. Thus new equity issues will be encouraged or discouraged in accordance with management's demonstrated success or failure in using past funds.

III. IMPERFECTLY COMPETITIVE MARKETS

The essence of imperfect markets is that individual sellers (or buyers) can and do influence market price. The seller's ability to be a price-maker, rather than simply the price-taker of purely competitive markets, may stem from the fact that he is one of but a few sellers (dealers) for the particular product (securities), or that the security package he is selling is not quite the same as that offered by his competitors, or that the buyers are ill-informed or irrational. Under any of these conditions, market price will be higher than under purely competitive circumstances because the seller is aware that his activities, say, a change in his offers, will affect price. In perfect competition, no single seller is sufficiently large or unique to affect price, no matter how he varies the quantities he offers at various prices. Even when entry of firms competes profits away, if the firms are still too few in number to act perfectly competitively or if the product is differentiated, resources will continue to be inefficiently utilized though no one is the gainer and all of society is the loser.

In contradistinction to traditional opinion, auction markets are necessarily imperfect markets. (1) Although there are numerous buyers and sellers in such markets they do not meet directly but have their orders taken by a much smaller number of brokerage commission houses who, in turn, channel these orders to the floor of the exchange where they are executed by a relatively small number of broker members or specialists, the latter not only matching buy and sell orders but also taking a position in such stocks. Such pyramiding effectively reduces the number of direct participants in the market and may lead to certain abuses which arise whenever the number of those engaged in buying and selling are relatively few.

(2) The product bought and sold, i.e., seasoned securities, is not homogeneous because the customer purchases a package of services and not merely a share of stock. Lack of perfect knowledge on the part of the investor calls for research and other investment advice from the professional brokerage firm; lack of finance (or the desire to purchase equities whose value are in excess of the customer's resources) necessitates the financing of such purchases, in part, by the securities firm handling the client's business; and the desire for custodial services in the form of holding the customer's equities, posting of his position, etc. all may be at least as important as the simple brokerage function of executing a trade. Further, the cluster of such services performed by brokerage commission houses for their clients varies from one house to another with the result that the final product is highly differentiated or non-homogeneous.

(3) Closely allied to the above is the fact that information necessary for effectuating a trade is highly variable in terms of quantity and quality. Furthermore, investors may be arrayed in terms of varying degrees of rationality from those institutional investors who have their own research and

trading departments to the small investor who relies heavily on the research and other advice of his broker. And yet information is not a free good but has cost, for example, in the form of the tape and prospectuses.

(4) Entry to the auction market is not free. This is a highly regulated industry involving self-regulation by the Exchanges which, in turn, are supervised by the Securities and Exchange Commission. The Exchanges themselves determine the maximum number of members who can trade on the floor and set minimal standards via written and other examinations for registered representatives and specialists. As a consequence of all these deviations from the ideal conditions to be found in the competitive market model, perfectly competitive performance on the organized exchanges cannot and should not be expected.

However, the SEC's special study concludes that, although the specialist is not merely a price-taker, for "There are not enough public participants at any one time to assure, in a continuous auction market, that buy and sell orders will be so neatly matched as to provide a true reflection of value in the classic market sense . . . , the existing specialist system results, in most cases, in a reasonable approximation of what a true continuous auction market would be if there were sufficient participants at one time."[3] In other words, the specialist-administered price approximates market-clearing equilibrium price but the spread (price of service) probably slightly exceeds the cost of the service. (We say "slightly" for third market or so-called "competitive" spreads are at least as great as those on the New York Stock Exchange.)

While there are sufficient numbers of competing brokers, they are not allowed to compete in price, only in services. But despite service proliferation, the institutional customer is driven to special or *ad hoc* arrangements anyway if he requires unusual services. And if a customer wants no services, he is necessarily driven off-board in the search for a price that will not charge him for services he does not want. In this sense, but in this sense only, is the third market "competitive"—it offers basic brokerage services at prices closer to the cost of those (stripped-down) services than is available in the auction markets. However, as shown in the next section, third market pricing is oligopolistic: the price is lower because the cost is lower, but price is not lowered proportionally with cost-savings, and oligopolistic profits arise.

IV. THE THIRD MARKET AS AN IMPERFECT MARKET

The Third Market engages in the trading of listed securities off the floor of the organized exchanges, including the New York Stock Exchange.

---

[3] Report of Special Study of Securities Markets of the Securities and Exchange Commission (88th Congress, 1st Session, House Document No. 95), U.S. Government Printing Office, part 2, p. 79.

The firms in this market exist largely to service the needs of institutional investors, investors whose wants are basically different from those of individuals who need research and other services to make intelligent decisions about stocks. According to the Securities and Exchange Commission, this market has developed only by dint of its ability to perform a useful function for investors in listed securities and it has recommended that there be no arbitrary impairment of the operations of this market since it offers the advantages of competition with the auction markets, especially the New York Stock Exchange, and is thus in the public interest. The SEC has taken this position even though it understands that such activity might impair the depth and liquidity of the primary or auction market.[4] The purpose of this paper is to analyze the term "competition" as it applies to the performance of the firms comprising the Third Market and to the internal structure of that market.

A. Structure

The first thing to note about the Third Market is that it is *not* competitive but oligopolistic in structure. Entry as a market-maker, i.e., as a firm positioning inventories, is not free but is limited by specialized abilities and the need for sizable capital, or ready access to bank credit, to finance the positioning of such inventories. This helps, in part, to account for the fact that in 1962 there were only 17 market makers.[5] A year earlier there were 13 market makers, but only seven of these did over 95% of the third market business.[6] This high degree of concentration also is reflected in the fact that of the 270 listed stocks traded in the Third Market at this time, ⅓ or 90 stocks had markets made by one firm; over one-half of the stocks had markets made by two firms, and three-firm markets applied to approximately ¾ of the 270 listed securities.[7]

Similarly, while there were some 400 off-board broker-dealers who did not make a market in listed securities but who dealt with the market-makers on behalf of their customers, only 20 of these did the bulk of the broker-dealer business on the Third Market.[8] Moreover, the fact that their home offices or branches are scattered throughout the country implies that, at best, only a handful can be found in each medium-sized American city. Thus, we find that lack of large numbers and a high degree of concentration exists in this segment of the Third Market as well. The only difference in classifying the market structure of the market-makers and those broker-dealers in the Third Market who fail to make a market in listed securities would appear to be that the latter perform under conditions of differentiated

---

[4] Special Study, Pt. 2, pp. 908, 910.
[5] *Ibid.*, p. 872.
[6] *Loc. cit.*
[7] *Ibid.*, table VIII–45, p. 1063.
[8] *Ibid.*, p. 872.

as contrasted with homogeneous oligopoly since their product includes not only the basic brokerage function but also some research and other services while such services are basically dispensed with by the market-makers who conduct their business almost exclusively with professional investors.

B. Performance

In spite of general misunderstandings brought about by the *Special Study* of the SEC, it can safely be said that the oligopolistic nature of the Third Market is reflected in its pricing policies. Like their counterparts, the specialists on the Exchange, but unlike them in the sense that their activities are unregulated, the Third Marketeers are price-makers rather than price-takers except in those individual cases where very large block orders are matched by them. No one has maintained that their spreads are lower nor that the level of their prices *net of commissions* are systematically below those to be found for the same stocks on the Exchange. Their prices are "competitive" only in the sense that they do not include charges for services that their customers do not need or want, such customers being primarily composed of institutional investors and non-member broker dealers who are interested only in the basic brokerage function of execution and transfer.[9] However, pricing is still oligopolistic: the price is lower because the cost is lower, but the price is not lowered proportionally with cost-savings, and oligopolistic profits arise. This is reflected in the fact that, despite the absence of volume discounts and its rigid commission structure, average customer costs of block trades on the Board were either equal or only somewhat higher than in the Third Market.[10]

As for the non-member broker-dealer, the total price he charges his individual customer certainly is no less, and in many instances is greater, than that charged by the member brokerage firm. Yet a competitive price structure would find him charging a lower price since his costs are less, based as they are on fewer services than those provided by member firms. That prices, on the average, are higher in the Third Market than on the Exchange may be seen from 1952 data which show that, aside from block trades, over-the-counter average costs to customers in listed securities exceeded the average cost when transacted on the New York Stock Exchange by 2½ % of security price. Actually, the over-the-counter price was 3½ %

---

[9] The large institutional investors who trade with the market-makers in many instances have their own specialized research and trading departments and so the cost to them of security purchases and sales must include not only basic brokerage costs provided by others but also the additional costs charged to their own specialized departments.

[10] I. Friend, G. W. Hoffman, and W. J. Winn, *The Over-The-Counter Securities Markets* (McGraw-Hill, 1958), p. 403. So narrow a margin of advantage to the over-the-counter market in block trades no doubt could be reversed if minimal brokerage charges or volume discounts were allowed on the New York Stock Exchange.

higher than the tape but, after allowance for the New York Stock Exchange commission, the net difference came to 2½%.[11]

To the extent that the Third Market sets prices "competitive" with the Exchange, it is basically due to its non-service lower-cost price and to the external economies provided by the Exchange for which the Exchange receives no recompense. Third Market firms depend heavily on access to the tape and quotation system of the Exchange in setting *nominal* prices competitive with those on the Exchange; Third Market-makers subscribe to the New York Stock Exchange ticker service and have direct wires to member firms. One can view this process as a system of administered pricing in which price leadership is exercised by the Exchange. Furthermore, the risk inherent in a large inventory position with a consequent widening of spreads is materially reduced by the option which the market-maker has to unload inventories on the Exchange specialist when he feels the need to do so. This option is not open to the specialist. As has been pointed out by the manager of a large mutual fund, "the NYSE is standby equipment" for the Third Market.[12]

In sum, the Third Market is an oligopolistic market which is not truly cheaper nor more competitive than the organized exchanges; it is simply different inasmuch as it permits serviceless transactions to large institutional investors who have their own research and trading departments and so have no need for the essentially individual-oriented services offered by member firms.[13] Likewise, the non-member broker-dealer who takes a full Exchange commission for his services and sells the stock to or for his customer at a price "competitive" with that offered by a member firm actually is charging his customer more than the latter.[14]

---

[11] Friend, *et al.*, *op. cit.*, p. 400.

[12] F. E. Brown, Duke University, School of Law, *Conference on Securities Regulation*, ed. R. H. Mundheim, Commerce Clearing House: Chicago, 1965, p. 182. The Third Market's narrow price advantage in block trades could also be whittled away if somehow they were charged for their use of the tape, the specialists' market-making for them, and other New York Stock Exchange facilities which service them and for which they do not pay. In effect, the New York Stock Exchange is subsidizing its own competition!

[13] That the large Third Market-maker is well aware of the differentiated nature of his market and welcomes it may be seen from the following statement by one of them: "I would be reluctant to see this type of business expand beyond professional customers to individual investors. When you cater to individuals you get into a different type of business. Our present customers trade on their own responsibility. I cannot conceive of very many individual customers availing themselves of the Third Market in order to secure a better price and then not demanding a little handholding and a little advice." F. Weeden, Duke conference, *op. cit.*, p. 173.

[14] Even if it were true that transactions costs on the New York Stock Exchange were greater than on the Third Market, does the value of *information* flowing from the organized exchange (e.g., the tape) and the *continuity* or depth of specialists' markets compensate for that compulsory higher cost? What is it worth to keep the public knowledgeable about stock markets and to safeguard the public from unusually large spreads (short-run fluctuations) in stock price-making?

C. Role in Block Trades

In the post-war period, financial intermediaries have grown at a very rapid rate and as their assets have grown so have their stock holdings increased greatly. At the end of 1963, intermediaries held approximately 20% of all New York Stock Exchange listed stock as compared with 12.7% in 1949. It is expected that such intermediaries will hold about 24% of such stock in 1970 and 30% in 1980.[15] Given the increasing importance of institutional equity ownership, it is significant to note that while the Third Market's share of all transactions in listed securities on the New York Stock Exchange came to some 4% in 1962, 10% of institutional transactions in listed securities took place in the Third Market in that year.[16] Since then it is estimated that the Third Market's share has grown to 5% although there are no statistics currently available on the increase in institutional transactions in that market. The increased volume of institutional trading in equities off the auction market has given rise to fears that eventually the weaknesses of an auction market in handling large transactions will result in extending the exempt list beyond governments, corporate bonds and preferred stocks to utility stocks and other stocks of less than average activity on the principal exchange. In the process, the off-Board market might become the dominant market in the trading of these stocks in addition to capturing a substantial share of stocks now traded actively on the Board with a resulting loss of depth and liquidity in the auction market.

Even if the Exchanges were to introduce a non-service minimal charge to institutional investors in the form of volume discounts or varying fee schedules, it has been argued that this might not arrest the trend since large institutional investors are also attracted to large off-Board market-makers because the latter are able and willing to quote firm bids for relatively large blocks. As has been stated by one keen observer, "It is the rare portfolio manager who does not appreciate the convenience of being able to launch a sizable transaction with but one phone call!"[17] On the other hand, the specialist must first be consulted on his backlog of buy and sell orders so that the broker can determine whether the specialist can and will handle the transaction and whether it will be handled at one or several prices. Presumably the financial capacity of the large Third Market-maker is greater than that of the average specialist in absorbing the block into his inventory.

However, if one divides the capital position of the market-makers by the number of stocks in which they make a market, there is no evidence that their financial capacity is any greater, or even as great, as most of the specialists on the New York Stock Exchange. This is attested to by the fact

---

[15] New York Stock Exchange, *Institutional Shareownership* (June, 1964), p. 8.
[16] Special Study, *op. cit.*, p. 875 and p. 895.
[17] Lee Silberman, "Critical Examination of SEC Proposals," *Harvard Business Review* (November–December, 1964), p. 126.

that the recent increase in capital requirements laid down by the New York Stock Exchange for the specialist (from 400 to 1,200 shares for each stock he takes a position in) has affected only some 5% of all specialists on the Exchange. If the specialist falls short of the Third Market-maker, it is more likely due to unwillingness rather than to inability to accept the risks of a *large* inventory position in the face of supply-demand imbalances in the auction market. While the specialist must assume a neutral role in terms of market orders, the Third Market-maker is analogous to the commission house in actively seeking out institutional customers on both sides of the market. In part, the differences in market structures rather than financial capacity explain the differences in attitudes of the market-maker and the specialist.[18] The inventorying of relatively large blocks by the specialist is analogous to taking a position in stocks with a thin market. Interim price fluctuations may result in sizable losses, forcing the specialist to hedge by widening his spread in the stock. Given the market power of specialists, it makes more sense to extract oligopolistic profits from the "jobbers turn" rather than to widen spreads to a point which adequately covers risk but which can lead to accusations by the New York Stock Exchange that they are not maintaining an orderly market in their stocks. It is extremely doubtful that SEC proposals to establish an Exchange-administered capital fund from which specialists could borrow to finance large block transactions would alter this situation. But the New York Stock Exchange does have methods currently available whereby institutional investors in large blocks seeking single block transactions at an assured market price could negotiate these trades.[19] And the New York Stock Exchange could extend these special arrangement techniques should this prove necessary. If these were negotiated on the Exchange at a minimal service charge, moreover, much of the Third Market business transacted by institutional investors for reasons of assured price could be diverted back to the Exchange.

D. Segmented Markets and Competition

Crucial to the notion of equilibrium price and market depth and liquidity is a large number of transactions in the *same* market. In fact, a characteristic of perfect competition is the extent of *the* market in a particular commodity (security). The SEC would seem to be in error in its notion that the Third Market as compared with the New York Stock Ex-

---

[18] However, should blocks be offered on the Third Market well in excess of 5000 shares, market-makers find themselves in the same dilemma as the specialist and react by performing an agency rather than a principal role.

[19] That these special methods of handling large block transactions have proven quite effective may be seen from the fact that shares offered in this manner increased from 2.7 millions in 1942 to 18.5 millions in 1963. New York Stock Exchange, *op. cit.*, p. 39.

change "provides the public customer with overall markets of greater depth."[20] Such a notion assumes a fluidity between the two markets that is not warranted by the facts.[21] The auction and Third Markets basically are *segmented* inasmuch as they tend to satisfy different wants and needs. The auction market through its tape and full disclosure of information assures a basis for rational buying and selling decisions and provides other services desired by individuals; the Third Market is shrouded in a cloak of semi-secrecy and primarily serves as a discount market for those institutional investors who already have the information and techniques necessary for intelligent trading.[22] Furthermore, by segmenting the market into at least 270 listed stocks, the Third Market tends to widen the spread in these stocks on the New York Stock Exchange without, at the same time, narrowing it over-the-counter. The auction market suffers because the specialist is left with a larger proportion of trades in less active issues and, consequently, may have to widen the spread on these to offset the risks of lesser diversification. Thus, while only some 5% of total listed stocks on the New York Stock Exchange are traded over the counter, perhaps 15% of trading in the 270 listed stocks takes place in the Third Market while some 10% of all institutional trade in listed securities is off-board.[23]

The upshot of all this is less depth and continuity on the New York Stock Exchange auction market which leaves the smaller security holder more at the mercy of short-run price instability though least able to bear it. Thus the lack of depth on the New York Stock Exchange requires greater specialist risk and participation.[24] However, if such erosion continues, there may be no alternative but delisting. In the long run, the disruption of the auction market cannot help but remove the current gauge of the tape and, with it, the discipline invoked on the prices charged customers by firms in the Third Market. As has been pointed out by an eminent financial economist: "Lifting the large block business off the exchange yet trying to main-

[20] Special Study, *op. cit.*, p. 903.

[21] If the two markets were not highly differentiated they would, in effect, constitute one market.

[22] The SEC goes on to qualify the above statement by applying it solely to the institutional customer with orders too large to be transacted on the auction market without price effects or too large to be handled entirely by the specialist. Consequently, it argues, that trading in large block transactions with the market-makers as well as with the specialist adds depth to the markets available to the institutional trader. (*Ibid.*, p. 963.) To the extent that such business is diverted from the Board, however, it leads not only to a thinner market for the majority of institutional investors still trading on the Exchange but for the overwhelming majority of individuals who have their business conducted on the Board.

[23] Special study, *op. cit.*, Table VIII–44, p. 1063; Table VIII–52, p. 1068; and Table VIII–60, p. 1072.

[24] Unlike his counterpart on the Exchange, an important Third Market-maker has stated that his function is not to provide for price continuity. Thus he states: ". . . if conditions change very rapidly, the market ought to drop right down instead of going down quarter by quarter." F. Weeden, Duke Conference, *op. cit.*, p. 182.

tain exchange trading as a guidepost of price is, of course, hazardous."[25] Moreover, it must be recalled that, unlike the specialist on the organized exchange, each market-maker is free to make or discontinue a market in a listed security at will. Consequently, as has been pointed out by a spokesman for a large financial institution concerned with the problem of liquidity: "When adversity comes, there are a great many dealers in the over-the-counter market who simply disappear. Prices don't decline. Markets just fade away."[26]

Segmenting of the market for listed securities would also raise costs for reasons unconnected with risk-taking. Insofar as the extent of any one market for a security is reduced, economies of scale in trading will be lost.[27] Basic transactions costs will rise in the organized markets with no offsetting fall in the Third Market.

In sum, the segmentation of markets does not add to competitiveness in any true sense and it does tend to make the primary market less deep and liquid. Market depth and liquidity are a function of many buyers and sellers in *one* market rather than in *many* markets, each of which is highly differentiated.

V. PERFECTING THE IMPERFECT MARKET FOR LISTED SECURITIES

In the sense that off-Board trading allows customers to buy listed securities at low cost-low service prices, it offers an alternative way of transacting business not available on organized exchanges where fixed (minimum) commission schedules are the rule. However, the Third Market does not offer these minimal service transactions at competitive (i.e., cost) prices. Over-the-counter prices in listed securities must more than make up in added spread for the absence of *basic* brokerage fees; but over-the-counter trading does allow for prices in which the spread is greater by *less* than the *full* service brokerage fee on the exchange. In short, the Third Market offers less service and lower costs but the price charged is lower by *less* than the cut in costs. If the Exchange were to allow for service-less brokerage, cost-saving prices could be more easily achieved on- than off-Board.

The New York Stock Exchange has been considering the grant of volume or block discounts to institutions and rebates to non-member firms

---

[25] Friend, *et al., op. cit.,* p. 439.

[26] F. E. Brown, Duke Conference, *op. cit.,* p. 181.

[27] "The costs of search are so great . . . that there is powerful inducement to localize transactions. . . . The *medieval markets* commonly *increased their efficiency* by prohibiting the purchase or sales of the designated commodities within a given radius or on non-market days." (Market tolls are signs of the value of access to localized markets.) G. J. Stigler, "The Economics of Information," *Journal of Political Economy* (June, 1961), p. 216.

as tools to recapture some of the business lost to the Third Market.[28] A commission schedule permitting customers not to buy ancillary services if not wanted would obviate the need for such discounts and rebates. In either case increased flexibility and competitive uses of *commission* (brokerage) pricing would also increase the competitiveness of *dealer-specialist* pricing. Insofar as the revised commission schedules bring back to the floor of the New York Stock Exchange the trades now lost to the Third Market, a thickening of the organized markets would result. It is precisely in thick markets that the dealer-specialist's price-making discretion is most limited. Moreover, to add to the tape the price and volume transactions handled off-Board will move us closer to the perfect information requirement of perfectly competitive markets. Furthermore, the opportunity to offer (enter) or not to offer (exit from) specific services would be increased if the brokerage firm were allowed to price its wares variably. In sum, a cost-oriented or variable commission schedule would not only eliminate the waste of differentiated products with undifferentiated prices, it would also reduce the mild market power of the specialist. It would add significantly to the ability of firms in effect to enter and leave subsectors of the industry thus adding a natural competitive restraint on profit-making in the industry.

At the same time, the efficiency of the dealer-specialist will be improved through economies of scale. With added volume on-Board the specialist will experience economies in carrying securities. First, inventory theory tells us that when sales double, the economic order quantity for inventory less than doubles. Second, specialist risk will be reduced because the thicker the trading, the thinner the spread. Third, since many Exchange fees are fixed charges, the dealer's average total costs should fall with added volume. Note that all these economies of scale accrue without conferring monopoly power in the process because the heavier the volume of trading in any security on the Exchange, the less is the need for specialist synchronizing behavior and the smaller is the range within which price-making powers can be exercised.

Of course, non-cost directed pressures to go off-Board would remain but the volume of transactions involved is not likely to be great. For example, large blocks seeking secrecy or assured market prices would still seek negotiated trades—but these might well be handled by Exchange personnel as in New York Stock Exchange extends its special arrangements techniques. And, in the future, more private placements of blocks, i.e., exchanges of blocks of securities between two institutions with a broker-dealer serving as mere finder, is likely—this might well be called the Fourth

---

[28] Exchange members cannot go off-Board in pursuit of such business because Rule 394 of the New York Stock Exchange states that, except with the special permission of the Exchange, member firms cannot trade in listed securities off-Board.

Market—but here too there is reason to expect that finders *on* the Exchange will be more informed and thus more efficient at the job.

Just as it is possible to reduce the thinning effect of the Third Market without removing the competitive alternative invented by the Third Marketeers, so it is possible to deepen and to extend the continuity of the organized auction market without adding to the market power of the specialists.

III

MONEY,
INTEREST RATES,
AND ECONOMIC ACTIVITY

Money serves two basic functions in an advanced economy. As a medium of exchange it makes possible the division of labor, specialization, and roundabout methods of production that characterize our economy. The second major role is to promote capital accumulation and, through it, greater output. In a dynamic society, consumers and businesses save part of their income. These savings are then channeled either directly or indirectly into investment in real capital. Most savings are placed into financial institutions, which then invest in capital or instruments representing capital investments. The transformation from savings to investment takes place through financial markets, which allocate money among many current uses, and between present and future uses.

The price paid for the use of loanable funds is interest. The first article in Part III discusses the interrelationship of money, interest rates, and economic activity in a market economy. Professor Woodworth analyzes the loanable funds theory, which provides one explanation of the interest rate structure of financial markets. The third article explores the current theories concerning the forces that determine the relationship between short- and long-term interest rates in the money and capital markets.

21.

Money, Interest Rates, and Economic Activity: Their Interrelationship in a Market Economy

PAUL A. SAMUELSON

REAL AND MONETARY DETERMINANTS OF THE INTEREST RATE STRUCTURE

Classical Real Theory: Statics

Although interest appears superficially as a percentage yield on money values, to the classical economist it represents at the deeper level the real productivity of roundabout, time-consuming production embodied in machines, industrial plants, and unfinished goods in process. Capital goods are limited in amount, and their scarcity can be relieved only by sacrificing current consumption—transferring resources from them to enhanced capital formation. More roundabout processes may be more productive, but it takes *waiting* by consumers to get them going. The disutility of labor was thought to keep labor scarce and its productive wage high, and thus the wage can in a sense be called the reward for sweat. In the same way, the disutility of *abstaining* from current consumption and of engaging in further waiting is what keeps capital instruments scarce and productive. Thus, interest can be regarded as the reward for abstinence or waiting, the

Reprinted from *Proceedings of a Symposium on Money, Interest Rates and Economic Activity*, 1967, pp. 45–60, by permission of the sponsor and publisher, the American Bankers Association.

price needed to overcome this natural human impatience to consume now and not in the future.

The classical view regards interest as determined by demand and supply—the productivity of capital goods providing the main elements of demand (albeit reinforced by consumer-loans demand on the part of especially needy and impatient borrowers), and the supply of capital being limited by the reluctance to abstain from current consumption and do more saving, resulting in cumulative capital formation.

What follows from this classical model of interest as being determined solely by real factors? Here are some consequences.

1. Though interest is paid in money terms on money loans and assets, *the level of interest has nought to do with the level of money and with the price level.* If metal coins form the currency, and if their supply is much augmented by, say, past mining discoveries of precious metals, the only effect is to raise the level of *all* prices proportionately. Thus, if money M doubles, so will be doubled the prices of tea, cloth, lumber, machinery, and land. The dividends of stocks and the coupons of bonds will, in the new equilibrium, be exactly doubled, but so too will the principal values of these assets be exactly doubled—with the result that the percentage ratio of money yield to money principal will work out to exactly the same interest rate. (David Ricardo and Knut Wicksell were nineteenth-century writers who clearly insisted on this classical fact.)

2. Commercial banks are mere *conduits* for the more efficient channelling of savings into the best investment outlets. Except for transitional states in which the system moves from one long-run equilibrium to another, the banks do not affect the level of interest rates.

3. Suppose banks can issue currency in the form of bank notes or checkable bank deposits which the people treat as the equivalent to holding currency. Then laissez faire in banking can *not* be counted on to lead to equilibrium with stable price levels. In particular, a basic notion underlying the founding of the Federal Reserve System in 1913 is quite false; providing for an "elastic" total supply of money and credit by enabling banks to create new money whenever they can lend to manufacturers, merchants, and farmers on genuine productive assets (to finance inventories, permit production maintenance and expansion, et cetera), will *not* be conducive to stability of the price level and of general business activity.

At what levels of interest are the "legitimate" demands of production and trade to be met? If market interest rates prevail below the real equilibrium levels set by the classical quasi-barter model, the total money supply will grow, thus creating demand-pull inflation. Lending against real goods (the so-called real-bills doctrine) is *not* guaranteed to produce an enhanced supply of goods that will quench (at unchanged prices) the manufactured increase of new M (and the resulting increased flow of its MV spending).

Although the level of the money supply and prices cannot affect the interest rate in the crudest classical system, classical writers are correct to insist that there must be some limitation on the total supply of money set by the Government if the price level is to be determinate. And if there can be expected to be a steady growth of population and productivity, leading to a steady growth of real output—and if there can be expected to emerge a generally constant level of interest rates, as the result of cancelling out innovations of a capital-saving- and labor-saving-type in comparison with any capital accumulation relative to labor supply—then a desire for a generally stable level of prices can only be achieved if the Government contrives that there be a rise in the supply of money commensurate with the changes in real output.

Dynamic Modifications of the Crude Classical System

The above real system abstracts from innumerable factors known to be of importance in any economy that actually exists, whether it be the Victorian model of England in the nineteenth century or the mixed economies of the present. Thus, its postulates leave no room for a Great Depression with mass unemployment on a lasting basis; its postulates throw no light on the fluctuations of business conditions as they have been studied by the National Bureau of Economic Research for this country and for the major industrial nations. The classical model that I have caricatured above operates upon the premise of quixotic flexibility of prices. The 25 percent rate of unemployment that prevailed both in the United States and in Germany in the 1930's could not have happened if downward flexibility of prices and wages existed. So, at a low enough wage level all the unemployed could find willing employers (whose effective demand had not, because of the "Pigou effect," been undetermined by the hyperdeflation itself). On the inflationary side, the classical model has no room within its postulates for cost-push inflation, such as many observers claim to have observed in many mixed economies of the post-World War II generation.

However, within the classical system itself, we can discern some systematic theorizing about dynamic transitional states between states of stable equilibrium. Since the time of David Hume, two centuries ago, classicists noted that unforeseen inflation could be expected to favor debtors at the expense of creditors, to favor entrepreneurial profit-seekers at the expense of *rentiers* and contractual wage earners, and to favor vigorous high-employment conditions at the expense of more stagnant conditions.

After the 1890's Wicksell, the great Swedish neoclassical economist, kept insisting that practical men were right to think that lowering the market rate in the short run, by having the banks create and lend out money, would indeed raise prices and expand business activity. Wicksell insisted, however, that once the system was at full employment such expansion of money would lead only to an increase in price tags; and each impulse of new-money creation by the banks would be followed by a tendency for all prices to rise, including those of the rents from capital goods and the market values of those goods—so, ultimately, the interest rate would tend to move back to its real classical level. Indeed, once the market rate of interest was set by the central bank back at that classical real level, there would cease to be an increase in the money supply and in the price level. But, if the central bank persisted in keeping the market rate of interest below the true real rate, it would thereby give rise to a more or less permanent rate of money creation and price inflation (adding to the real interest rate a percentage price-increase allowance).

We may summarize thus: *The independence of the interest rate from the behavior of money and banks that is posited in the statical classical theory disappears in considerable part once dynamic assumptions are made about the creation of money growth as a result of mines, banks, or governments.*

By the early 1930's there had grown up the so-called neo-Wicksellian view[1] that the real supply-and-demand curves determining interest rates should have added to them a component of the supply of savings which is associated with the creation of new money, or M. According to this view banks have a great deal to do in the short run with increasing the flow of capital formation and reducing the market rates of interest. If banks are able to create new M, which they lend out to would-be investors in new construction, inventory, and equipment, they change the mix of gross national product toward capital formation and away from current consumption; and they are able to "force" this money on the system only by lowering the explicit interest rate, or diminishing the effective stringency of rationing, and thereby implicitly lowering the interest costs of borrowing. The rest of the community, even if it wants to save the same fraction of its incomes as before, undergoes "forced saving" in consequence of the fact that the banks have created inflation of the price level; and by the time the community comes to spend its incomes, it buys less in the way of real goods.

Moreover, in our day when the Government is committed to following a militant fiscal policy of its own, involving budget surpluses and deficits at different levels of total taxation and spending, we recognize that fiscal policy interacts with monetary policy in shaping the behavior of interest rates, capital supplies, price levels, and intensity of unemployment.

For example, if fiscal policy is chronically expansionary—in the sense of involving high levels of public expenditure with low levels of tax receipts so that large budget deficits continuously take place—and if monetary

---

[1] See Gottfried Von Haberler, *Prosperity and Depression; A Theoretical Analysis of Cyclical Movements* (originally published by the League of Nations in 1937; later postwar editions available), Chapter 3, for an exposition of the writings of F. Hayek and other similar writers.

policy is chronically tight—so that interest rates are kept high enough and the rate of growth of M slow enough to hold down investment and consumer-durable spending to a level low enough to wipe out demand-pull inflationary gaps—then the community will evolve with less capital formation than would otherwise have taken place. It will evolve with higher short-term and higher long-term interest rates than would otherwise be the case.

The last two cases involved maintenance of full employment and assumed no cost-push inflation problem. If we consider mixed economies that are characterized by price-wage inflexibilities and which display chronically different degrees of unemployment and underemployment, different policies by the Fed can lead to different levels of achieved employment and production. Expansionary monetary policies that keep investment spending higher than would otherwise be the case lead initially to lower money rates of interest and ultimately to lower real-productivity yields on the enhanced stock of physical capital equipment. But they achieve this not at all at the expense of current consumption, for consumption too is higher than would otherwise be the case. Both capital formation and consumption can be increased by utilizing resources that would otherwise be dissipated in mass unemployment and industrial excess capacity.

The Extreme Keynesian Case

A few years after J. M. Keynes wrote his 1936 *General Theory of Employment, Interest and Money*, there grew up the strong notion that the interest rate is purely a monetary phenomenon. Passages can be found in the *General Theory* claiming that interest is merely the difference between the yield on safe money and risk-involving securities, and therefore interest is merely the price for giving up the liquidity of holding money. Statements like these can be harmless if nothing is read into them. They can be misleading if we read into them the view that the real productivity of capital has nought to do with the short- or long-run levels of interest, or infer that current thrift has nought to do with interest rates, or that shifts in the marginal efficiency of capital cannot affect the rate of interest as it can in the classical system. And if we look critically at the actual properties of the system of relations in the *General Theory*, we find they are usually in agreement with the results previously mentioned.

For example, if banks are given extra reserves and use them to bid down the yields of loans and bonds, that increase in M leads, in the Keynesian system, to lower interest rates, more investment, and greater total dollar spending. If employment was not previously full and still falls short of full employment, there is no reason why the increase in M should cause a proportional increase in prices generally.

If businessmen discover new investment opportunities, that will, with total M fixed, raise interest rates and the level of dollar GNP. If people save less out of current incomes, that will depress money GNP and interest rates. In short, if one reads the *General Theory* rigorously, one ends up with conclusions not too different from those of an eclectic neoclassical monetary theorist.

Nevertheless, in times like those which prevailed in, say 1938 when most disciples were just mastering the *General Theory*, banks held considerable excess reserves and short-term interest rates on Treasury Bills were often down to ⅜ of ⅜ of 1 percent.[2] Hence, massive changes in M have little effect even on short-term interest rates, and, a fortiori, little changes in employment, production, or capital formation. Moreover, in times of deep depression, such as in 1932 when existing plants were operating at losses and idle capacity was everywhere, even if one could contrive by monetary policy a substantial change in short- and long-term interest rates, little new investment could be coaxed out by such monetary policies. And, since we are discussing conventional central bank operations which merely involve buying existing assets with M (old bonds and Treasury Bills), there is no significant change in the *net worth* of the public generally. Investors have no incentive to spend more on capital formation, and consumers have no new incentive to spend more on consumption. In consequence, Federal Reserve operations of N billion dollars then involve less than their normal potency.[3]

The Neoclassical Synthesis

As I have insisted upon in the recent editions of my *Economics*, once we introduce systematically into a post-Keynesian system treatment of stocks of assets, monetary and real, and take into account fluctuation levels of real unemployment, there remain no inconsistencies between the classical system and the Keynesian system. The synthesis of common content emerges with an eclectic position on the interplay of real and monetary factors in determining the structure and levels of interest rates.

In the short run, changes in the money supply contrived by conventional Federal Reserve open-market operations produce opposite effects upon the level of interest rates. Within limits, changes in the composition of Fed purchases as between short bills and long bonds can slightly influence the shape of the yield differentials between long- and short-term assets. But apparently only within narrow limits unless massive "twists" are indulged in.

---

[2] On occasions the yield was zero or even negative, a fact to be accounted for presumably in terms of personal property tax exemptions and subscription rights. Often, Treasury Bills were not cashed in at maturity. When I then asked a Government official why, he said to me, "Do you know a better way to hold a million dollars?"

[3] In this model we have one of those rare cases in which a contrived increase in M can be predictably expected to induce an opposing change in velocity of circulation V, with the product MV little increased.

In the longer run, if expanded credit achieves a restoration of full employment and beyond, there tends to be a permanent bidding up of all prices, and there reemerges a strong tendency for interest rates to revert to their real level. This is the continuing kernel of truth in the classical crude "quantity theory."

Fiscal policy changes can produce substantial changes in total GNP or MV magnitudes. if M is not changed concommitantly, this can be expected to produce changes in the interest rate (and opposing changes in V).[4]

HOW MONETARY POLICY AFFECTS THE LEVEL OF ECONOMIC ACTIVITY

Scope of Monetary Policy

By monetary policy we mean primarily Federal Reserve actions designed to affect the tightness and easiness of credit conditions, and the behavior of the total supply of money and money substitutes (that is, the supply of currency, checkable bank deposits, various categories of time deposits, and other liquid instruments).

The chief weapon of the Federal Reserve in doing all this is its *open-market purchases and sales of Government securities*. But intermittently, as last month, changes in the *legal reserve requirement ratios* that must be held against various categories of demand and time deposits have effects like those of open-market operations. Furthermore, *raising or lowering the dis-*

---

[4] The valid core of the "quantity theory" that is implied by neoclassical reasoning does not require constancy of the velocity of circulation, V. It requires only that a balanced change in *all* prices should itself have no effect on V. Moreover, it is only a quirk of law that keeps banks from paying interest on demand deposits. In eras when the market would determine a high, short-term interest rate, free competition would permit us to use as our circulating medium interest-bearing bank deposits. When fiats prevent banks from paying interest on checkable accounts, nature ordains that competitive substitutes will flourish, time deposits will in fact require no notice, they will pay daily interest, they will become negotiable, and institutional arrangements will be made so that they can serve as a close money substitute for most exchange purposes. As soon as the liquid assets that we use to perform the function of money begin to pay interest, an entirely new pattern of velocity is to be expected from a rational man. That is why I should not expect V to be constant in the future, even if it had been more constant in the past than it actually has been.

Furthermore, along with the noninterest-bearing public debt that we call money, there is the interest-bearing public debt. This too acts like an "outside asset" making the community feel richer than it really is. As soon as we realize this, we see not that there is substantive difference between an increase in M resulting from *past* gold mining or greenback financed war expenditure and an equal increase in M resulting from an open-market purchase. The gold and greenbacks result in a permanent increase in the net worth as envisaged by the typical person. The M created by open-market purchase takes from people some of their net worth embodied in bonds, and in return gives them some net worth in the form of M.

count rate at which banks can borrow from the Federal Reserve can reinforce or offset the effects of open-market operations. And aside from the quoted rate at which discount borrowing is permitted to take place, *the manner in which access to the discount window is administered* can have powerful effects upon the actual volume of such borrowing and hence on the reserves of the banking system.

Moral suasion, by which I mean the whole atmosphere in which banking is carried on—including letters to the banks like that of last year which urged them to go easy in making loans, and including voluntary programs of foreign lending by the banks—is constantly being pooh-poohed by many economists as a factor of any quantitative importance for monetary policy. But in my judgement, it is often a significant variable and, as in so many countries abroad, it will become an increasingly important variable in the future.

Although I have mentioned these five weapons of the Federal Reserve, the first is by all odds the most important. And in principle, by more vigorous use of open-market operations alone in both the downward and upward direction, we could achieve most of the same goals that can be achieved by all five weapons. (This is only approximately true and is not meant as a recommendation for a monistic reform.)

I am purposely defining monetary policy broadly to include attention to credit conditions as well as to the supply of money. I am thus explicitly rejecting the view that it should be concerned only with achieving some desired pattern of behavior in some defined magnitude of "money," such as currency plus demand deposits or the latter plus certain categories of time deposits. Like fiscal and other macroeconomic policies, monetary policy is concerned with achieving the desired total of gross national product spending; and if one writes GNP as the product of some defined M and its implicitly defined V, then the neoclassical position which I have already expounded militates against considering the factor M independently of the V in MV. Moreover, one cannot stipulate in advance that a modern mixed economy will be indifferent to the composition of the GNP, as for example between residential construction and other forms of investment. And hence the central bank, as an important and indispensable arm of the modern state, has a responsibility in conducting overall macroeconomic activities to take into account alternative effects upon sectors. Ours is a pluralistic society, and properly so. In a pluralistic society it makes no sense to set up institutions with a monistic function and then have to set up new superagencies to coordinate them.

Hence, although it is the principal function of the Federal Reserve to deal with overall credit conditions, it must also perform many selective functions. The Board and the System are not now so overworked that this will negate accomplishment of their principal function, and if the System were to shrink back from these duties, that would only create a political vacuum into which other agencies would rush. I do not think it would be a good thing to have competing central banks in this country, one dealing primarily with residential real estate, one with farm problems, and so forth.

From the broad way in which I have defined monetary policy, it will be evident that the Federal Reserve is merely the chief instrument of such policies, not the exclusive instrument. In particular, the United States Treasury, in connection with the way that it floats and refunds debt—using at one time long-term and at other times short-term instruments, selling at one time to its Trust Funds and at another to the open market—is also powerfully affecting monetary and credit conditions. And within the sector of finance, commercial banks which are outside of the Federal Reserve are of some importance in just the way that mutual savings and savings and loan institutions are important in affecting the overall pattern of monetary conditions and GNP aggregates. Because financial intermediaries both initiate and reinforce changes in credit conditions, they too come within the province of my broad definition of monetary policy.[5]

How Federal Reserve Policy Affects GNP

We may concentrate upon the open-market purchases and sales of the Federal Reserve. If the Fed were to print bank notes or write checks in order to provide free current services for the people (weather forecasting, national defense, research and development) or to give people transfer incomes every month (Social Security payments, relief, et cetera), that would be quite another thing from what it actually does. Instead, it buys and sells existing assets—not used cars or factories, but Government securities of all durations. Like any bidder or seller of Government bonds, it has a direct effect on the market price of those bonds and an opposite effect upon the bonds' yields. Indeed, only by bidding up or down the yields of existing bonds can the Fed persuade people and banks to let it consummate its open-market operations. It has no powers of eminent domain or fiat.

DIRECT EFFECTS ON INTEREST RATES AND CREDIT AVAILABILITY. Whenever anybody bids up or down the yields on Government bonds, that automatically has an effect upon the supply-and-demand bids that determine the pattern of yields on corporate bonds and other securities that are alternatives to Government bonds. There is, thus, a direct effect upon the struc-

---

[5] Fiscal policy questions, such as whether there should be an increase in personal income tax rates, affect directly the flow of income and would be distinguishable from monetary policy actions. But policies that call for earlier payments of accruing tax obligations are definitely akin to monetary policies. Some authorities would even try to draw the line between monetary and fiscal policy actions by means of the functional criterion: Does the policy act primarily upon a *stock* (the stock of money, of outstanding bonds, of liquid money substitutes, of less-liquid housing assets, et cetera); or does it act primarily upon a *flow* (as in the case of a reduced tax rate on current incomes or increased expenditure on current public services)?

ture of interest rates from open-market purchases by the Fed. Such purchases directly lower the yields on the issues bought and (with attenuation) tend to lower the yields on Governments of other maturities and the yield of corporate bonds. Since bonds are substitutes, albeit not terribly close ones, for other forms of investment such as mortgage loans, the lowering of bond yield tends to channel funds into mortgages and to lower their yield, at the same time making mortgage loans somewhat more available, and more available with lower down payments and longer amortization periods.

INDIRECT EFFECTS ON INTEREST AND CREDIT CONDITIONS. What has been already described would be the whole story if ours was not a fractional reserve banking system. Because the Fed's purchase has increased the cash of someone in the system, and because that someone is likely to hold most of that cash in some bank, there is now an increase in the investable reserves of the banking system. These will generally not be left in the form of excess reserves, but instead will encourage the banks to make new loans or acquire other securities. We thus have a repetition and reinforcement of the bidding down of the yields of the whole spectrum of assets in the community, and concomitantly this increases the availability of loans to borrowers at the same time that costs of borrowing are being bid down. There is nothing mechanical about the process; it takes place at each stage of the game in terms of people being motivated to make new supply-and-demand bids. It rests on the multilateral willingness of people to leave their money in banks, of banks to make loans or buy bonds, and of the rest of the community to borrow money and to issue new securities or give up old ones in favor of holding demand or time deposits. Although not mechanical, the process is in normal times highly predictable. A certain fraction of the Fed's created reserves will go into currency holdings, a certain fraction into repayment of discounts, a certain fraction into holding of deposits, a certain (normally very small) fraction into extra excess reserves; and in consequence we can predict that there has been created somewhere in the system several times as much of new bank deposits for each dollar of open-market purchase.[6]

DIRECT AND INDIRECT EFFECTS ON NET WORTHS. When Federal Reserve open-market purchases achieve some lowering of interest yields, they produce some increase in the capitalized value of assets people own. My 20-year bonds now sell for $103 instead of $100, and I may somewhat increase my consumption spending on food, travel, TV sets. My home may

---

[6] In deep depression when short-term yields had already been bid down to a fraction of a percent, and when everybody was pessimistic about the marginal profitability of additions to inventory, plant, and equipment, the predictable results would be quite different from that in normal times. Conceivably, the only effect would be to exchange near-M for M and to bid up slightly the existing value of long-term securities. Existing excess reserves would be added to in such times.

sell for a bit more, and it may be regarded by me as more easily sellable and hence a bit more liquid. This may increase my consumption and depress my current saving rate. The same is true of business enterprises— their balance-sheet assets may be bid up in price and be of increased liquidity, and this could be one of the determinants of their spending more on new investments.

In sum, open-market purchase creation of M has some upward effects on total community net worth, and therefore some direct effects upon increasing current consumption and investment spending. But this is not a strong effect by itself. The new M is not burning a hole in someone's pocket and aching to be spent at the old velocity of circulation. On the contrary, we have got hold of this new M in exchange for selling liquid securities; if they were not burning a hole in our pockets, neither will the new M, particularly since our securities have been bid up just enough by this process to make us content to forego them and instead hold cash as an asset.

I do not wish to be misunderstood. In a moment I shall trace through how the direct and indirect lowering of interest rates coaxes out more spending on investment goods and creates an increased flow of current income and employment. That has a powerful effect on total spending. But it is the much smaller effects on saving through the channel of increased net worths that I am now trying to evaluate.

To make my point, imagine an unrealistic experiment. Suppose rationing on capital formation kept the Fed's open-market purchase from inducing any increased inventory spending or plant and equipment spending. Suppose that consumers' durable finance was already copiously available at rates that could be brought down very little, even if the Treasury Bill rate were negligible. Then where would a substantial increase in the current flow of spending come from? The M itself does not represent any increase in net worth for the banks and public; it is only the rise in securities prices that it created in coming into existence (that is, in coming out of the Fed in exchange for bonds that go into the Fed) that raises net worth. Undoubtedly, under my bizarre rationing of investment, the resulting drop in interest rate from the open-market purchase would be all the larger; prices for existing bonds would be bid up a lot before people would be content to hold the zero-earning new M. Only if you have what I regard as an unrealistic theory for the functional relationship between velocity and interest rates will you conclude that net worths in the community will be bid up to whatever gigantic levels are needed to get all the new-M spending on consumption at the old rate of turnover.[7]

In any case when we trace through realistically the *modus operandi* of an expansion of credit, we find that it works only slightly through direct

---

[7] See the equation on page 212.

increases in net worth; instead it works primarily through inducing new investment spending (including in the term "investment spending," spending on consumers' durables in excess of their being used up). It is to this vital link that I now turn.

INCREASE IN INVESTMENT SPENDING INDUCED BY LOWER-COST AND MORE AVAILABLE CREDIT. Now comes the most important step in the process by which monetary policy works to affect business activity. When banks and lenders generally have more funds to lend, and when the interest yields of investments have been bid down, the result will tend to be an increase in lending and borrowing activity. It does not matter in the first instance whether the increase in business spending on inventory, plant, or equipment comes from a lowered interest cost of finance which makes projects pay that previously did not pay; or whether the increased investment spending comes because the investor is able to arrange for financing that was previously just not available to him. In either case, there follows an increase in investment spending which gives jobs to someone and which directly increases production in the form of capital formation or investment. The incomes received in these new lines of activity are spent by their recipients in considerable measure by the familiar propensity-to-consume mechanisms. Hence, the primary expansion in investment, induced by credit-easing, results in a secondary chain of consumption respending in accordance with familiar multiplier sequence.

Nor is this all. With production higher, the profitability of existing capital goods is enhanced; there is both an extra desire for additions to capacity and also an extra cash and income flow available to would-be investors to finance such activity. So, along with secondary consumption respending, the multiplier chain sets off a tertiary flow of acceleration-principle investment spending. This in turn begins another multiplier-accelerator chain. I do not imply that the process leads to perpetual expansion. Far from it; in most circumstances any particular once-and-for-all open-market purchase leads to a subsequent increment of spending that is finite in total amount, and which reaches a maximum effect within a finite time (perhaps one or two quarters) and then tails off to insignificance.

It should be understood that this induced investment leads to the creation of real capital and adds to the lasting net worths of people and businesses. While it is generating the higher flow of incomes, it also leads to a desire for the holding of more cash for transaction purposes, and thus transiently to a higher velocity of circulation than would be the case without the income increase; and it thus leads transiently to less of a fall in the interest rate than will ultimately take place after the induced expansion production subsides.

All the above is premised upon the postulate that the open-market purchase impinged upon a system which was at underemployment and which was capable of increase in production and employment. If industry is already operating at capacity, and if the labor market is already so tight as to be nonexpandable, the induced increase in investment demand will serve merely to produce an inflationary gap. At preexisting prices, there will be a demand-pull gap and there will tend to result a bidding up of commodity prices generally, and through derived demand, a bidding up of wages. Although money wages will be observed to be growing faster than the growth in physical productivity, there is no need to conclude that any cost-push inflation is going on. It could be—and as I am describing it, would be—all demand-pull inflation. As long as this is going on, there is being generated an enhanced need for cash balances for purely transactional purposes.

If the price level ultimately rises by as great a percentage as the increase in the M created by the open-market purchase, there can emerge a new equilibrium with the interest rate back to where it was in the beginning. In this particular case, the effect of the open-market purchase has been to raise prices and nothing else. Only in the transitional stages have there been real effects. Here we have a case, often envisaged by economists like Marshall, where an initial decrease in the interest rate leads ultimately to a restoration of the old interest rate at a higher price level. And indeed if we envisage a dynamic system with some momentum in it which generates psychological and other self-reinforcing mechanisms, we should not be surprised to meet a model in which an initial lowering of interest rates by open-market M creation leads penultimately to raising the interest rates above the *ex ante* level. If the system is ultimately stable, this penultimate state would, in its turn, subside.

For the specialist, symbolism may clarify. Let *net worth* equal the sum of *money* plus *Government bonds* (mostly short-term) plus *value of capital goods*.

$$NW = M + B + K$$
$$= M + \pi (i) (b + k)$$
$$= NW (a_1 \mid a_2 \mid a_3)$$

where $\pi (i)$ represents the capitalization factor that depicts a bidding up of prices of existing machines or face-value bonds when the interest rate drops; and where (a_i) represents the respective fractions of NW represented by the three kinds of assets. An open-market purchase represents an increase in M matched by a decrease in b; except that this would involve a lowering of i and a (slight) increase in $\pi (i)$, the drop in b would equal the rise in M. Writing Y for money income and assuming for expositional simplicity that the price level of consumption, C, and investment goods, I, remains constant until full employment is reached, our simplest system becomes—

$$(1) \quad Py = P\,C\left(\frac{Y}{P}, \frac{NW}{P}; a_2, a_3\right) + P\,I\left(i, \frac{Y}{P}, k\right)$$

$$(2) \quad \frac{M}{Y} = L\left(i, \frac{\pi\,(i)\,b + \pi\,(i)\,k}{P}, \frac{Y}{P}\right),$$

with the usual properties—

$$\frac{\partial C}{\partial y} > 0, \frac{\partial C}{\partial (NW/P)} > 0, \frac{\partial I}{\partial i} < 0, \frac{\partial I}{\partial y} > 0, \frac{\partial I}{\partial k} < 0$$

$$\frac{\partial L}{\partial i} < 0, \frac{\partial L}{\partial (\pi b)} > 0, \frac{\partial L}{\partial y} > 0$$

The first row above is noncontroversial. The second row relations would be challenged by those who believe that L is a constant, a view that I respect but differ with. Particularly at a low i, such constancy seems doubtful to me. In (1), an increase in a_2 *and* a_3, at the expense of M's share of net worth, I judge to be, at most, a mild depressant on C; that is, $\partial\,C/\partial a_i < 0$, but small in magnitude.

For this model, an increase in M through an open-market operation that lowers b will slightly decrease i, slightly raise NW, significantly raise I, and thereby Y and C. After full employment is reached (and assuming no cost-push Phillips-curve problem), increases in M will tend to result ultimately in rises in P with small ultimate further changes in i or y. If k/y is increased in the transition by the positive M, k and y will be permanently higher and i lower.

AVAILABILITY OF CREDIT AS A FACTOR DIFFERENT FROM THE COST OF CREDIT

My argument thus far can be briefly summarized: Central bank open-market operations produce their primary effects on the economic system *by lowering or raising the spectrum of interest rates,* thereby increasing or decreasing the flow of investment and durable-goods spending, which leads in turn to expansion or contraction in the aggregate of GNP flow. How the change in dollar spending is divided into real output or price-level changes depends upon the amount of slack in the system and upon the institutional factors that make for price-wage inflexibility or for cost-push rises in prices and wages.

In using the expression "spectrum of interest rates," I wish to make room explicitly for various intensities of rationing of credit. Loans are not auctioned off in perfect markets so that the scarcity of funds can be accurately measured by a quoted market rate of interest. Loans and securities are negotiated in a great variety of retail and wholesale markets. Often interest rates are like administered prices—the rates quoted are changed, but infrequently. However, the unavailability of funds at these rates changes markedly and in sympathy with the movement of market interest rates.

Thus, when the Treasury Bill rate is rising from 4 to 5 percent, when the long-term bond yields on corporate and Government securities are rising from 5 to 5½ percent, and when the discounts are growing on mortgages quoted in the secondary markets, you will find your friendly banker less friendly. No longer will he press funds on you. If you ask for a $50,000 loan for six months, he may agree only to $30,000 for four months. And although he may stick by the 6 percent rate he has long been charging you, there may now be an insistence that you maintain at least 30 percent in the form of compensating balances instead of the usual 10 percent (a shift which already raises 6 percent effectively to almost 8 percent). Moreover, many people who have been relying on such 6 percent bank loans will now be turned down and will have to go to a finance company and pay 7 percent or more. Hence, even though each posted interest rate may seem to change little, the effective interest rates at which people really borrow will have gone up much by virtue of the concomitant changes in the severity of rationing of credit.

How important is this factor of rationing? And (since it seems to operate in the same direction as changes in market interest rates) does the subject matter? I think that practical men exaggerate the importance of the rationing factor, and academic men underestimate its short-run effectiveness. Aside from those who deny that rationing plays any important role, there exist two schools. Both agree it is important, but one insists that this is a dreadful phenomenon which is in fact responsible for giving bankers such a bad name and which leads to serious distorions and inequities as between small and large business, new and old businesses, and different sectors of the economy. The other school congratulates monetary policy on its potency and effectiveness that stems from the alleged importance of induced credit availability conditions.

Lending and borrowing and evaluation of securities must from their nature involve uncertainties and different degrees of imperfection of knowledge and information. From its nature, therefore, we must expect the banking and investment business to be peculiarly vulnerable to Chamberlinian imperfections of competition. In such markets we expect to encounter somewhat inflexible administered prices with hidden or open departures from those quoted rates. And even in a steady state where there are no changes in overall money supply or market rates of interest, the lenders must always be forming judgements about credit-worthiness so that a decision process involving rationing of credit is inevitable. Nevertheless, the longer changed credit conditions prevail, the more will differences in degree of rationing tend to be replaced by differences in stated rates. If funds are scarce, the efficient way of allocating them is to change their market prices; and it is increasingly to the self-interest of parties on both sides of the market to push in that direction. Why should the banks throw a gift in the direction of those firms lucky enough to qualify for loans in terms of credit stringency? And why penalize the refused firms? Moreover, what good are low rates to a firm that can not get a loan? The excluded firms will, one way or another, try to bribe the providers of funds into meeting their needs; that is, meeting them at a price.

Some might say that we live in the best of all possible worlds. It is precisely in the short run that economists would expect the demands for investable funds to be inelastic, thereby reducing the dollar-for-dollar potency of central bank operations. And it is in this short run that highly effective (if inequitable and distorting) elements of rationing prevail. Then in the longer run, just when rationing is dissipating its effects and spreading into differences in the cost rather than mere availability of credit, we can expect lowering of interest rates to coax out new long-term projects, and raising of interest rates to discourage such projects.

Before leaving the subject of credit rationing, I ought to mention some transitional frictions that also help to increase the short-run potency of Federal Reserve credit policy.

NEW-ISSUE BOTTLENECKS. When interest rates are hardening, new securities issues often go to a discount in the period when the underwriters are bringing them out. Since underwriters are subject to the tremendous risks involved in their extreme leveraging, one or two debacles of this type can discourage them from bidding and can dry up the effective supplying of any new issues.[8]

BOTTLENECKS FROM INHERITED NOTIONS OF NORMAL RATES. If long-term interest rates have been at one level for some time, and if the Federal Reserve engineers a tightening of them, many localities and states will drop out of the new-issue market completely. By law or custom they may be restricted from borrowing at the higher rate. By psychological belief that they can do better if they wait until rates are not so high, they may desist from borrowing. Often such phenomena have been observed. Of course, in the longer run, should the high-rate trend continue, many borrowers will be forced to come into the market willy-nilly later on, paying a penalty for their mistaken delay. And, to the degree that some canny borrowers correctly appraise the beginning of a rising trend of interest rates, they may overborrow in the early stages of a period of credit contraction.

---

[8] Analytically, a high level of i discourages new investment, but so does a transitional large negative value of di/dt.

This can lead to a frictional weakening, rather than enhancing, of the short-term potency of monetary policy.[9]

EFFECTS OF MAXIMUM-RATE REGULATIONS ON INTEREST

The Bible, Aristotle, and the medieval Schoolmen have generally mirrored the everpresent disapproval of interest and usury. After the Reformation, antipathy toward interest diminished, but we still have laws and regulations that put limits on interest rates. Indeed, in many countries and in some states ceilings on interest rates did no harm only because market rates happened to fall well below the ceilings. But the recent rise in interest rates has resulted in collisions with such ceilings and created important economic problems. I shall here discuss only those most important for recent American monetary policy.

Government-insured mortgages by FHA and VA played an important role in the postwar period. Ceilings on their rates could be circumvented only by devices that involved some inconvenience. In consequence, whenever interest rates tended to harden above the ceiling rates, mortgage money for these sources tended to dry up completely. Contrariwise, when the Fed wished to ease credit, there resulted a powerful stimulus to residential construction from the coming back to life of these guaranteed mortgages.

Thus, almost by inadvertence, ceiling interest rates on insured mortgages worked out to be powerful stabilizers in the first postwar decades when such mortgages were quantitatively important. Upward shifts in demand were kept from evoking a higher supply response to higher yields; control of maximum rates automatically tended to lead to self-control of supply by suppliers. By the 1960's insured mortgages became of much less importance.

More important for recent monetary policy have been interest ceilings on deposits. As already mentioned, prohibiting interest on demand deposits is bound, in a time of high and safe short-term interest rates, to lead to a shrinkage of those deposits in favor of time deposits, and is bound to lead to all kinds of subterfuges and substitutes for the paying and receiving of interest on checkable balances. The negotiable certificate of deposit, if it had not been invented in the last decade by the First National City Bank, would have had to be invented by somebody else.

Regulation Q, which puts ceilings on time deposit interest rates, cre-

---

[9] When the Federal Reserve is trying to ease credit conditions, correct anticipation by speculators can speed up and amplify the decline in market interest rates; although di/dt is negative, juicy capital gains are to be earned from buying bonds (but, unfortunately, this could lead to a high level of yield inclusive of capital gains and thus temporarily raise the attractiveness of alternative to real investment in new brick and cogs).

ated the same difficulties once Treasury Bill rates began to exceed these ceilings. It was for this reason that ceiling rates had been repeatedly raised in the 1960's. Although raising Regulation Q ceilings improved the competitive position of the commercial banks, by the same token it undermined the competitive advantage that the savings and loan associations had previously been enjoying. They began to run into informal ceilings imposed by their regulatory authorities and by prudence as to what their actual earnings from mortgages could stand.

This not only depressed the flow of funds available for housing, thereby depressing starts, but in addition it began to impair the liquidity and solvency of the savings and loans. Something of a crisis was thus precipitated by tight money; actually what the crisis did was to unveil a situation already existing that has within it certain disturbing properties.

Time deposits are nominally liquid within 30 days of some similar brief period, but S&Ls invest such funds in mortgages that have a duration which runs into decades. Moreover, the interest rate payable on such mortgages is set at the beginning of the period at a frozen level. Consequently, even with Government insurance of such time deposits, it is easy for the whole system to become technically insolvent, having short-term liabilities that require a higher interest rate to hold them than can be earned on long-term assets. For short periods of time, there is no reason why the S&Ls should not pay quite high rates to hold deposits; yet such a solution could not meet the long-term problem if it should persist.

The importance of all this for monetary policy is twofold: (1) Disorderly markets inhibit the authorities from using monetary policy strongly (this same point holds for disorderly security markets, a phenomenon whose importance is, in my view, often exaggerated); and (2) relaxing of Regulation Q tends to make the impact of tight money particularly harsh on residential construction and on the smaller banks outside the great urban centers.

Last year's reimposition of Regulation Q ceilings gave us but temporary relief from this long-term structural problem. By accident, the fact that the need for tight money ended in the fall of 1966 put off the longer-run consequences of these stopgap measures.

Without further research I am not able to make an unequivocal diagnosis as to whether the potency of monetary policy is helped or hindered by Government regulation of interest rates. There are crosscurrents in each direction; numerical estimation is needed to appraise the final effect.

BRIEF REVIEWS OF CONFLICTING VIEWS OF THE EXPERTS

My earlier discussion touched upon the issues raised by the mix of stabilization and growth policy as between monetary and fiscal measures.

Because this paper is already long, and because so much has been written about the international balance of payments, I shall merely state that our international deficit severely limits the scope of independent domestic monetary policy. Only within limits, and only by concomitant use of selective controls on the capital accounts, can we contrive monetary ease at home in order to offset deflation and to promote capital formation. Conventional central banking measures would have to be supplemented (as, for example, by increased investment tax credits for domestic investment) if domestic credit ease were to be relied on in the face of international deficits.

Let me conclude by stating the view that the position taken here is a modern middle-of-the-road position. It reflects what some people would contemptuously, and others admiringly, call the "conventional wisdom." It differs in degree and in kind from the following various viewpoints.

1. Some economists (such as J. K. Galbraith) are against the use of restrictive monetary policy. They believe the only good interest rate is a low one, and rates should be kept low. Some of this persuasion think monetary policy has little or no potency; others think it has too much potency and will have bad social effects. This school of thought is important in populist politics, but of decreasing importance among American academic economists.

2. Some economists (for example, Milton Friedman) think that control of the supply of money is the important goal of monetary policy. They believe that steady trends in the supply of M should be contrived by the Federal Reserve and that preoccupation with interest rates or net free reserves will only serve to distract the Fed from its legitimate goals. Variants of this school abound. Some think that tracing the impact as I have done through effects on interest rates and credit availability, as these impinge on investment and durable-goods spending, is unnecessary; and some think it is wrong.

3. Associated with one-time New York Federal Reserve economists such as John H. Williams, Robert Sproul, and Robert Roosa, is the view that monetary policy has very great potency indeed because of the importance of credit rationing, the contriving uncertainty by the monetary authorities, and the dominance of lenders' supply attitudes over borrowers' demand elasticities. In the last dozen years the market quotation in the bourse of academic opinion has perhaps gone down, just as that of the supply-of-M school has perhaps gone up.

Personally, I prefer to stick to the middle-road of good, strong value.

22.

Forces Governing

The Rate of Interest

G. WALTER WOODWORTH

Aside from wage rates, interest rates are the most significant and pervasive prices in the economy. To business firms they represent one of the costs of operation and of new investment. Hence, low rates encourage business expansion, and high rates discourage it. Similarly, low rates encourage consumers to purchase houses and other durable goods with borrowed money, while high rates provide an obstacle to such outlays. On the supply side, interest rates significantly influence the flow of savings at any given level of income. High rates constitute a greater inducement to save rather than to spend on consumption, while low rates discourage saving. Thus, interest rates have a substantial influence on both the overall level of economic activity and the allocation of scarce resources among competing uses, including consumption.

The purpose of this chapter is to summarize the theoretical background of the forces governing the level of interest rates as a basis for subsequent analysis of the money market. For the sake of simplification it is assumed that there is only one rate of interest, representative of the entire market. This is, of course, an abstraction, since in fact the rate structure is highly complex, with many separate rates which cover a wide range because of varying risks, maturities, and degrees of liquidity. But the main forces governing the level of rates have a pervasive influence throughout the

Reprinted from *The Money Market and Monetary Management* by G. Walter Woodworth, Ch. II, pp. 18–29, by permission of Harper and Row, Publishers, and the author. Copyright © 1965 by G. Walter Woodworth.

structure. Most individual rates increase and decrease along with the general level despite differences in timing and in degree. Hence the assumption of a single rate can be made without seriously departing from realities.

The theory of interest has understandably occupied a large place in the literature of economics since the seventeenth century. Due to the great complexity of the phenomenon, many different theories have been developed. Before the 1930's nonmonetary theories prevailed, with emphasis on real savings and real investment—productivity theories, use theories, abstinence theories, labor theories, time preference theories, and others. Since the late 1930's, however, the monetary aspects of the problem have received greater emphasis. This had led to classification of the two most widely accepted explanations as "monetary theories" of the rate of interest: (1) the liquidity preference theory, and (2) the loanable funds theory. Both are partial equilibrium theories which are valid only under the assumption of no change in gross national product or in the general price level. Despite the use of different concepts and emphasis on different variables, the two theories are reconcilable and arrive at the same destination. For the present purpose the loanable funds theory has definite advantages, mainly because it explicitly recognizes more of the forces determining rates, and because the concepts utilized are more commonly used in money-market parlance. Space does not permit an exposition of the liquidity preference theory,[1] but only an abbreviated version of the loanable funds approach.

The analytical method employed is the familiar one of the interaction of a demand schedule and a supply schedule for loanable funds which results in the emergence of a market rate of interest. Thus, price determination follows the same procedure as in competitive commodity markets. However, special consideration must be given to the meaning of these schedules in order to attain reasonable precision, and to avoid inconsistent interpretations. This becomes evident as one ponders the following questions: (1) Should demand and supply be defined broadly to include direct investment of savings by consumers and by businesses? (2) Should the schedules embrace all transactions in existing securities, or only those that pertain to new securities offered during the period? (3) Should investment, savings, and hoarding of money be treated as gross or net concepts? Specific answers to these questions can best be given as part of the discussion which follows. But, in general, the approach utilizes gross rather than net concepts. In this way one is better able to understand the significance of all possible transactions in claims, and to see how certain transactions cancel out on opposite sides of the equation.

---

[1] For an exposition of the liquidity preference theory, see John Maynard Keynes, *The General Theory of Employment, Interest and Money* (New York: Harcourt, Brace & World, 1936), chaps. 13, 14; Alvin H. Hansen, *A Guide to Keynes* (New York: McGraw-Hill, 1953), chap. 6.

DEMAND FOR LOANABLE FUNDS

The aggregate demand schedule of loanable funds shows the amounts which seekers of money capital will take at each of a series of interest rates. The time period to which the schedule applies is a short one, say a week, during which it is assumed that there is no change in expectations with respect to future income. In general more will be demanded as the rate of interest declines, and less will be taken as the rate rises. However, as we shall see, there are considerable differences in the interest-elasticity of demand for money capital among industries and under different economic conditions. (See Chart 22–1 for a graphic presentation of the demand schedule of loanable funds, *D*.) It is desirable to divide the users of funds into three groups: (1) businesses, (2) consumers, and (3) governments. The funds are employed by these groups mainly for purposes of investment and consumption. Also, funds are demanded in some circumstances to increase money balances, i.e., for hoarding (*H*).

1. The business sector is by far the most important source of demand for funds in peacetime. Net corporate debt increased $48 billion during

CHART 22–1

Determination of the Interest Rate

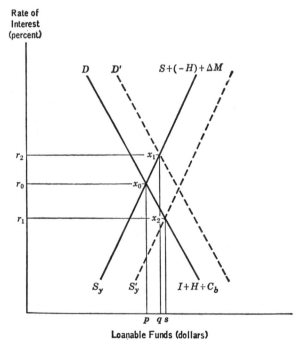

Loanable Funds (dollars)

1962, and the amount outstanding at the end of the year was $672 billion.[2] Business firms use loanable funds principally to finance investment in plant, equipment, and inventories. Decisions to invest depend heavily on the prospect for profits, and on the availability and cost of investible funds. The demand schedule is interest-elastic since at high rates only the more promising investment opportunities may economically be exploited. However, as the costs of borrowed funds decline, more and more projects come into the range of profitability. That is, the series of expected net returns from the new investment, allowing for risks and uncertainties, more than covers all costs, including those of borrowing. Business firms may also borrow in some cases to increase the size of their bank balances; in other cases they may hold all or part of the proceeds of borrowing as deposits prior to subsequent investment expenditures. Such borrowing is prompted by the so-called *finance* motive, and may be regarded as part of the increase in demand for money to hoard (*H*).

2. The growth of demand for consumer credit constitutes one of the outstanding financial developments since World War I. Largely liquidated during World War II, consumer credit rose from $5.7 billion at the end of 1945 to nearly $65 billion at midyear 1963. Over three-fourths of the total was composed of instalment credit to finance the purchase of automobiles and other consumer durable goods; the remainder was noninstalment credit in the forms of single-payment loans, charge accounts, and service credit.[3] Expenditures financed by the foregoing categories of consumer credit are classified as consumption expenditures in the national income accounts, and it is usual to treat a net increase in such credit as dissaving, and a net decrease as personal saving. The demand schedule for consumer credit is rather inelastic to the interest rate, at least within the range of actual rate changes. Most consumers who buy on credit are said to be influenced more by the size of monthly instalment payments than by the rate of interest which is only one of several elements determining instalments. Nevertheless, there is doubtless some degree of interest-elasticity; that is, consumers will borrow somewhat more as the interest cost declines.

Like businesses, consumers may also desire to hold larger money balances in relation to expected expenditures; if so, this becomes part of the hoarding demand for money (*H*). To some extent consumers may borrow money for this purpose, but they may also express their desires by holding back on the spending of income, and by selling assets to build up money balances.

Consumer outlays for residential construction are classified in the national income accounts as a component of private investment. They give rise to large amounts of mortgage borrowing. For example mortgage debt

[2] *Economic Report of the President*, January, 1963, p. 234.
[3] *Federal Reserve Bulletin*, September, 1963, p. 1300.

on 1- to 4-family houses rose from $18.6 billion at the end of 1945 to $171.6 billion in the first quarter of 1963—an annual increase on the average of $9 billion. Most of these loans are payable in instalments over long periods of between 10 and 30 years. Consequently, changes in the rate of interest materially affect the total cost of the property, and also make an appreciable difference in the size of instalment payments. The demand schedule of borrowers is, therefore, considerably more interest-elastic than that of borrowers of short-term consumer credit.

3. Since the early 1930's governments—federal, state, and local—have greatly expanded their services and have assumed a much more important position in the market for loanable funds. When government purchases of goods and services (G) exceeds tax receipts less transfer payments, or net receipts (T_n), a budgetary deficit exists, and borrowing is necessary to cover the deficit. This has happened in 22 of the 32 years during the period 1930–1962. During World War II huge deficits were incurred, ranging from $31 billion to $52 billion. However, since the war there has been an approximate balance in government budgets as measured in the national income accounts, with eight deficit years and nine surplus years.[4] As additional evidence, it may be noted that the marketable federal debt at midyear 1963 amounted to $204 billion, and that the average annual increase of federal debt during the period 1950–1963 was $4.5 billion.[5] State and local securities were outstanding in the amount of $72 billion at the end of 1962, and increased on the average by $4.3 billion annually—almost as much federal securities.

The demand schedule of the federal government for loanable funds is inelastic to changes in the rate of interest. The amount of the federal deficit arises out of broad policies with respect to expenditure programs and revenue programs on which the interest rate has little bearing. This is particularly true of wartime deficits, but it is almost equally so in peacetime when, for example, a deficit may be planned to spur business recovery or to encourage economic growth. However, the demand schedule of state and local governments for loanable funds is generally held to be moderately interest-elastic. Like business firms, these governments postpone some construction projects if borrowing costs are high, and tend to move forward with certain projects when borrowing costs are low.

Looking back it may be noted that all components of the demand schedule, with the exception of the federal government, are interest-elastic in varying degrees. Therefore the aggregate demand schedule may reasonably be drawn with a moderate downward slope as in Figure 2–1.

For those who prefer to think in mathematical terms it may be helpful

[4] *Economy Report of the President, op. cit.,* p. 181.
[5] *Treasury Bulletin,* August, 1963, pp. 1, 70.

to summarize the components of the demand schedule for loanable funds as follows:

$D = I_b + I_c + H + C_b$, or $(-S_p) + (G - T_n)$ or $(-S_g)$, where I_b represents both new and replacement investment by businesses;

I_c refers to new and replacement investment by consumers in houses and other consumer durable goods;

H represents the demands by businesses and consumers for additional money to hold, i.e., hoarding;

C_b represents demands for consumer credit, usually classified as personal dissaving $(-S_p)$;

$(G - T_n)$ represents government deficits which must be covered by borrowing when $G > T_n$; this factor may also be designated as government dissaving $(-S_g)$.

SUPPLY OF LOANABLE FUNDS

The aggregate supply schedule of loanable funds indicates the amounts which lenders and investors will offer at each of a series of interest rates. Again the time period assumed is very short, say one week, during which expectations with respect to incomes and prices remain unchanged. In general they will offer more in the market as the interest rate rises, and will offer decreasing amounts as the interest rate declines. (See Chart 22–1, p. 220, for a graphic presentation of the supply schedule, S_y.) The various components of supply are: (1) savings (S) which divides into (a) personal savings (S_p), (b) business savings (S_b) and (c) government savings (S_g); (2) dishoarding ($-H$); and (3) changes in the amount of money ($\triangle M$).

Personal Savings

As defined in the national income accounts personal saving is measured by the difference between disposable personal income and personal consumption expenditures. In 1962 these amounts were $384.4 and $355.4 billion, respectively, so that net personal savings (S'_p) were $29 billion. This should be interpreted as the amount of realized savings on the supply schedule at the rate of interest prevailing in 1962. In relative terms 92.5 percent of disposable income was spent on consumption and 7.5 percent was saved. It should be noted here that this concept of personal savings is net rather than gross. Some people borrow to buy consumers' goods, a fact which we have explicitly recognized on the demand side of the equation as C_b. Other consumers are assisted by welfare payments of governments. If gross personal saving is designated S_p, and dissaving is represented by $(-S_p)$ then net personal saving, $S'_p = S_p - (-S_p)$. Part of personal saving is invested directly in capital goods such as houses, part is invested directly in securities by individual savers, but the largest part enters the capital markets indirectly through intermediary financial institutions—banks, savings and loan associations, insurance companies, investment companies, and others.

The exact relation between personal savings and the rate of interest at a given level of income is unknown, but most economists believe that it is a positive one. That is, savings will rise at least moderately as the reward in the form of interest increases, and will fall as the interest rate declines. However, people respond differently to changes in the rate of interest. Most individuals are doubtless disposed to save more of their incomes as the rate rises, since they are motivated to build up larger future incomes and larger estates. The savings decisions of others are probably not appreciably affected by changes of the rate within the range of market fluctuations. But a third group tends to react in opposite fashion; that is, to save more as interest rates decline, and to save less as rates rise. They do not wish to curtail current consumption in order to build up future income and wealth beyond certain rather limited amounts. Since these goals can be achieved more quickly at high rates of interest, they will save less and consume more when rates are high; in opposite fashion, they will save more and consume less when rates are low. This group, however, is believed to be much less important than the first one, with the net result that personal savings at given income levels are positively related to the interest rate.

Business Savings

Gross business savings (S_b) are made up of undistributed corporate profits and depreciation allowances. In 1962 they amounted to $8.1 billion and $49.4 billion, respectively and aggregated $57.5 billion.[6] These amounts should be viewed as business savings realized at the prevailing rate of interest. The supply schedule of business savings has a moderately positive relation to the interest rate. Corporations tend to retain a larger proportion of net profits as the interest rate (cost of outside funds) rises, and to retain a smaller proportion as the rate declines. But the size of depreciation allowances has little or no relation to the interest rate. Instead, such allowances are based on the estimated economic life of each type of capital asset, adjusted to conform with federal income tax regulations.

It should be noted that gross business savings is consistent with the concept of gross business investment (I_b) included on the demand side of the equation. Depreciation allowances are largely used to finance the replacement category of investment while undistributed corporate profits are more closely associated with financing new business investment. While gross

[6] *Federal Reserve Bulletin, op. cit.*, pp. 1316–1317.

business savings are large, they are mainly invested directly in capital assets, and they are not generally offered in the loan market. In fact nonfinancial businesses as a whole borrow in much greater amounts than they lend. Corporate lending takes place chiefly in connection with administration of liquid assets which are invested in short-term federal securities, finance company paper, certificates of deposit, and other near-moneys.

Government Savings

Just as government deficits give rise to borrowing to cover them when government purchases (G) exceed net receipts (T_n), so governments may save and repay indebtedness when net receipts exceed purchases of goods and services. The amounts of savings (S_g) is then represented by aggregate government budget surpluses $(T_n - G)$. In fact net savings by governments have occurred in only 10 of the 32 years during the period 1930–1962. However, the postwar record exhibits a rather surprising degree of equality in this respect. Surpluses were recorded in nine years, aggregating $54.2 billion; and deficits in eight years, totaling $40 billion.[7] The schedule of supply of government saving doubtless shows a moderate degree of positive interest-elasticity. This is attributable to state and local governments which are inclined to defer construction projects when costs of borrowing are high, and to proceed with programs more freely when borrowing costs are low. The state of the federal budget, however, bears little relation to the interest rate level.

Dishoarding of Money

The disposition of businesses and consumers to hold a greater part of their incomes, wealth, or expenditures in the form of money is known as hoarding. This factor was included as one of the components (H) of the demand schedule of loanable funds. Dishoarding $(-H)$ is the antithesis of hoarding, i.e., the disposition of spending units to hold a smaller part of income, wealth, or expenditures in the form of money. By treating these concepts in the gross sense, H can be entered for emphasis on the demand side of the equation and $(-H)$ can be included on the supply side. This is the procedure followed here. The alternative is to treat hoarding and dishoarding on a net basis, and to choose one side or the other of the equation more or less arbitrarily as its home.

When people wish to dishoard they will offer to lend and invest the undesired part of their bank balances; in other words, they will increase the supply of loanable funds, and thereby tend to reduce the interest rate. The schedule of dishoarding is positively interest-elastic, although there is

[7] *Economic Report of the President, op. cit.*, p. 181.

no way of knowing the amount of increase in dishoarding as the interest rate rises. The entire schedule of dishoarding moves upward in the short run in response to expectations of businesses and consumers that prices of commodities, real estate, and common stocks will rise, and that incomes will increase. Thus, dishoarding increases with the developing optimism of a period of prosperity. It will be recognized that dishoarding is only another name for a rise in velocity of money, and that hoarding is identical with a decline in velocity of money.

Change in the Amount of Money

The remaining component in the supply schedule of loanable funds is change in the stock of money, designated $\triangle M$. The appropriate concept of money is the active money stock (M), consisting of currency outside banks and adjusted demand deposits of commercial banks. At midyear 1963 the aggregate stock of money in the United States was about $150 billion, composed of $31.6 billion of currency and $118.2 billion of demand deposits.[8] Changes in the amount of money are governed principally by the policies of the monetary authorities, operating through the legal reserve position of member (commercial) banks. An additional dollar of reserve money released to the commercial-banking system by Federal Reserve Banks provides the basis for a several-fold expansion of bank loans and investments, and thereby of deposits. Under the spur of the profit motive banks usually put excess reserves to work. If acceptable loans are not available, they purchase United States, municipal, and other securities in the open market.

When a new increment is added to the money stock the supply schedule of loanable funds is correspondingly increased, and the interest rate tends to decline. Conversely, when the money stock declines, the supply of loanable funds decreases, and the interest rate tends to rise. Economists usually treat changes in the stock of money as an autonomous supply factor which is inelastic to the interest rate. This is a logical procedure since monetary policies are largely designed to achieve broad economic goals, such as full employment, growth, and a stable dollar. Implementation of these policies is likely to exert a strong, and often dominant, influence on the interest rate. For example high rates of interest—as in 1959—may reflect a restrictive monetary policy, and low rates—as in 1958—may be in large part the result of an expansionary monetary policy. Under these conditions changes in money govern the interest rate instead of rate changes governing money. In the short run, however, there is some tendency for money to increase and decrease directly with changes in the interest rate. This arises from the fact that commercial banks have a greater profit incentive to keep ex-

[8] *Federal Reserve Bulletin, op. cit.*, p. 1270.

cess reserves at work when rates are high than when they are low. But this tendency is too weak to be given emphasis since within the range of rates which usually prevails, the banks systematically strive to avoid holding excess reserves. Hence the assumption that changes in the stock of money are typically autonomous and interest-in-elastic appears to be justified.

Having identified the various components of the supply schedule of loanable funds, we are now in position to summarize, as follows:

$$S_y = S_p + S_b + S_g, \text{ or } (T_n - G) + (-H) + \triangle M, \text{ where}$$

S_p represents gross personal saving;

S_b refers to gross business savings, which is the sum of undistributed corporate profits and depreciation allowances;

S_g represents aggregate budget surpluses of governments; that is, $(T_n - G)$;

$(-H)$ indicates the amount of dishoarding by consumers, businesses, governments, and other holders of money;

$\triangle M$ represents changes in the stock of active money.

EQUATION OF DEMAND AND SUPPLY OF LOANABLE FUNDS

We are now in position to bring together the demand and supply sides of the equation:

Demand for loanable funds = Supply of loanable funds
$$I_b + I_c + H + C_b, \text{ or } (-S_p) + G_b, \text{ or } (G - T_n) =$$
$$S_p + S_b + S_g, \text{ or } (T_n - G) + (-H) + \triangle M$$

By disregarding the government sector and adding the components of investment and saving, we may now simplify this equation to read:

$$I + H + C_b = S + (-H) + \triangle M$$

This equation, for purposes of emphasis, presents investment, saving, and hoarding on a gross basis, rather than on a net basis. A rise of consumer borrowing on the demand side is considered to be the measure of dissaving.[9] The interaction of the demand and supply schedules produces an interest rate at which the realized demand equals the realized supply of loanable funds.

Attention should be called to an additional aspect of the loanable funds market. While the equation presented above utilizes gross concepts, they are gross in the national product sense, but not in an over-all transactions sense. That is, the schedules of demand and supply do not include the huge

---

[9] If investment saving, and hoarding are treated on a net basis, the equation may be further simplified to a form which is rather generally used: $I + H = S + \triangle M$.

volume of trading in existing securities. The seller of United States securities may be thought of as a borrower of loanable funds, and when he re-invests in other securities he becomes a lender of loanable funds. But since sellers and buyers are always on opposite sides of such transactions, their influence cancels out, and they may be disregarded in the determination of the interest rate level. However, purchases and sales of existing securities greatly influence the relationships of the many separate rates which are quoted in the money and capital market. For example a material decrease in corporate and personal income tax rates would doubtless lead to a significant shift of investment funds out of tax-exempt municipal securities and into federal and corporate issues. In this event yields on municipals would tend to rise and yields on federal and corporate obligations would tend to decline.

THE LOANABLE FUNDS THEORY

Despite the fact that the degree of interest-elasticity of the demand and supply schedules for loanable funds is unknown, it may be helpful to present them schematically in graphic form, as in Chart 22–1. As previously developed, and as shown on the demand schedule (D), the amount of loanable funds demanded increases as the interest rate declines. Schedule (D) is the aggregate of the separate schedules for investment (I), hoarding (H), and consumer borrowing (C_b). Also, as indicated on the supply schedule (S_y), the amount of loanable funds offered increases as the interest rate rises. Schedule (S_y) is the aggregate of the separate schedules for saving (S), dishoarding $(-H)$, and changes in the stock of money $(\triangle M)$. The interaction of schedules D and S_y result in equality of the amount of loanable funds demanded and offered (O_p) at the interest rate r_o. At any higher rate supply exceeds demand, and at any lower rate demand exceeds supply. Thus, r_o is the only equilibrium rate for schedules D and S_y. If the schedule of supply increases to S'_y while demand remains at D, the equilibrium amount of loanable funds become O_s and the rate drops to r_1. Again, if the schedule of demand rises to D' while supply remains at S_y, the equilibrium amount is O_q and the rate rises to r_2.

The loanable funds theory is usually known as a partial equilibrium theory. While for succeeding short-planning periods the market for loanable funds may be in equilibrium, it is unlikely that equilibrium will also exist in the economy as a whole. For this to be the case planned saving would have to be equal to planned investment at the market rate of interest. Since it would be a coincidence if all these conditions were realized at the same time, it is likely that the seeds of change in income, savings, investment, and interest rates are sprouting in the current period even though equilibrium exists in the loanable funds market.

REFERENCES

Bain, Joe, *Pricing, Distribution and Employment* (New York: Holt, Rinehart and Winston, 1953), pp. 626–691.

Board of Governors of the Federal Reserve System, *The Federal Reserve System: Purposes and Functions*, 4th ed. (Washington, D.C.: 1961), chaps. V and VI.

Conard, Josph W., *An Introduction to the Theory of Interest* (Berkeley: University of California Press, 1959), 375 pp.

Fisher, Irving, *The Theory of Interest* (New York: Macmillan, 1930), 566 pp.

Homer, Sidney, *A History of Interest Rates* (New Brunswick, N.J.: Rutgers University Press, 1963), 617 pp.

Keynes, J. M., *The General Theory of Employment, Interest and Money* (New York: Harcourt, Brace & World, 1936), chaps. 13 and 14.

Leigh, A. H., "Supply and Demand Analysis of Interest Rates," *American Economic Review*, XLI (September, 1951), pp. 579–602.

Mao, James C. T., *National Income and Monetary Policy* (Ann Arbor, Mich.: Braun and Brunfield, Inc., 1958), chap. 3.

Robertson, D. H., "Alternative Theories of the Rate of Interest," *Economic Journal*, 47 (1937), pp. 428 ff.

Shaw, Edward S., *Money, Income, and Monetary Policy* (Chicago: Irwin, 1950), chaps. 12–14.

Tsiang, S. C., "Liquidity Preference and Loanable Funds Theories, Multiplier and Velocity Analysis: A Synthesis," *American Economic Review*, XLVI (September, 1956), pp. 539–564.

23.

Current Debate on the

Term Structure of Interest Rates

FREDERICK M. STRUBLE

Can the monetary authorities—the Federal Reserve System and the U.S. Treasury—alter the relationship among maturity yields on Government securities by changing the maturity composition of Government securities outstanding? For many years, two different theories— the expectations theory and the segmented markets theory—have been used as a basis for answering this question.

The expectations theory contends that a change in relative supplies of securities with different maturities will not affect maturity yield relationships unless, in the process, it brings about a change in market expectations of future interest rates. On the other hand, the segmented markets theory argues that maturity yield differentials are caused by an imbalance between the maturity composition of debt demanded by lenders and supplied by borrowers. From this it follows that a shift in the maturity composition of supply will affect relative yields. The segmented markets theory acknowledges that market expectations of future interest rates may be changed as relative supplies in the various maturity sectors are altered, thus augmenting the change in yield differentials brought about by this operation. In general, however, most discussions of the segmented markets theory have emphasized the direct effects that changes in relative supplies will have on relative yields apart from any possible changes which might occur in expectations of future interest rates. Discussions of the expectations theory

Reprinted from *Monthly Review*, January-February 1966, pp. 10–16, by permission of the publisher, the Federal Reserve Bank of Kansas City.

similarly have played down the possible effects that changes in the maturity composition of debt might have on interest rate expectations. As a result, the theoretical controversy has been clearly defined.

Although each of these theoretical positions has a long history, it seems a safe judgment that the segmented markets theory has been and continues to be the theory most generally accepted by market analysts. However, the degree of consensus on this question has been reduced considerably as a result of recent research. Older statements of the expectations theory have been reinterpreted incorporating more plausible behavioral assumptions and the more rigorous modern formulations have added clarity to the meaning of the expectations hypothesis. On an empirical plane, several of the more sophisticated tests have provided strong support for the expectations theory.

This article reviews the current state of this controversy. To simplify the discussion, references to specific studies have been avoided. The reader interested in pursuing the topic further is referred to the brief bibliography of the major works on this question at the end of this article.

THE SEGMENTED MARKETS THEORY

Although the term, segmented markets, is used here to identify one theory of the term structure of interest rates, in other discussions this theory has been identified by several other terms, including institutional, imperfect substitutes, and hedging. Each refers to a type of balance sheet decision-making complicated by legal restrictions and traditional practices such as the matching of the maturity structure of one's assets with the maturity structure of one's liabilities—presumably in order to avoid risk. It is argued that because major groups of borrowers and lenders prefer to match assets and liabilities in this way, the market for credit instruments is partly compartmentalized, or segmented, according to the maturity of debt instruments. As a result, loans with different maturities are imperfect substitutes in the aggregate as well as for individual investor and borrower groups in the sense that different rates of return are required to hold securities with different maturities, and also, the size of the difference in rates of return varies with changes in the maturity composition of asset portfolios. This means that maturity yield differentials are determined by an imbalance between the maturity structure of debt demanded by investors and the maturity structure of debt supplied by borrowers.

Since the alternative theoretical position to be discussed in the next section of this article stresses the importance of interest rate expectations, it is worthwhile to note that discussions of the segmented markets theory generally have limited the influence of interest rate expectations to possible effects that *changes* in expectations of future interest rates can have on *current* interest rate relationships. This is quite different from the primary role assigned to expectations in the expectations theory. For, briefly, the expectations theory asserts that *current* differences in the maturity yields exist because the market expects interest rates to change over future periods of time. Moreover, it contends that it is possible to determine from a given yield relationship the pattern of future interest rates predicted by the market. Discussions of the segmented markets theory have either ignored this issue or have asserted that a current yield structure is not affected by interest rate expectations in this manner.

Several facts appear to provide strong support for the segmented markets theory. In particular, the behavior of many institutional lenders accords with the assumptions about investor behavior made by this theory. For example, commercial bank portfolios are heavily weighted with assets of short maturity while assets held in the portfolios of insurance companies and savings and loan institutions are predominantly long term. Many examples of borrower behavior also may be cited which conform to the assumptions underlying the segmented markets theory. Consumers usually finance purchases of houses with long-term mortgages and purchases of less durable consumer goods with shorter-term debt agreements. In a similar manner, business firms generally attempt to match the maturity of their liabilities with the durability of their assets—inventories are financed by short-term loans while plant and equipment investments are financed by longer-term loans. These examples clearly are far from exhaustive. Presumably, it is the pervasiveness of such practices that makes the segmented markets theory so compelling to many analysts, particularly those involved in the day-to-day operations of credit markets.

Against this evidence supporting the segmented markets theory, the results of recent empirical studies have been surprising. One study after another designed to measure the effects of the maturity composition of debt on maturity yield differentials was unable to discern a substantial relationship between these variables. Consequently, these findings have cast doubt on the segmented markets theory.

These empirical studies have not been entirely convincing, however. In attempting to estimate the implications of changing supply conditions, all but one study ignored the possible consequences of simultaneous shifts in demand. Most studies assumed that the demand for loans with different maturities remains relatively stable over time. If this is the case, then changes in maturity yield differentials can be attributed to changes in relative supply. If, however, conditions of demand change concurrently with changes in relative supplies, this would reduce the correlation between relative supplies and relative yields. The failure of most studies to consider this problem reduces their significance. The fact that the one study which did consider this problem came to essentially the same conclusions as the others, however, suggests that failure to consider this contingency may not have been an important deficiency. In addition, on an *a priori* basis, it seems unlikely that changes in demand would vary inversely with changes in supply so consistently that an actual relationship between relative supplies and relative yields would be entirely obscured.

THE EXPECTATIONS THEORY

The consistent findings that changes in relative supplies of securities with different maturities have only small effects on maturity yield differentials not only cast doubt on the segmented markets theory, they also provide indirect support for an alternative theoretical explanation of the term structure of interest rates. Both the pure expectations theory and the version of this theory which contends that liquidity preference is partly responsible for the establishment of maturity yield differentials, agree on one vital point: that the maturity structure of outstanding debt does not affect the maturity structure of yields.

The basic assertion of the pure expectations theory is that loans with different maturities, that are similar in all other respects, are perfect substitutes to investors in the aggregate. This means that the relationship among current prices and yields on securities with differing maturities are adjusted so that the rates of return on this debt—calculated to include capital gains and losses where applicable—are expected to be equal for any given period of time; and that the maturity composition of outstanding debt does not affect maturity yield differentials. From these assertions it follows that maturity yield differentials exist because the market is expecting interest rates to change over the future—to change in such a way that apparent differences in return which might be inferred from yield differentials are wiped out in the process—rather than because it expects the rates of return on loans with different maturities to differ. Moreover, any process which alters the maturity composition of investor portfolios, but does not change expectations of future interest rates, will not affect the existing structure of yields on loans with different maturities.

It should be emphasized that loans with different maturities may be perfect substitutes in the aggregate even though not every investor views them as such. Credit markets may be dominated by a relatively small but well-financed group of traders who treat loans of different maturities as perfect substitutes. If this is the case, the investors, whose actions are offset by these traders, would have no influence on security prices and yields. Security prices and yields would be established by traders willing to adjust their holdings of securities with different maturities until they expect the realized rates of return on the securities to be equal over any given period.

Still another possibility exists for rationalizing that certain securities in the aggregate are perfect substitutes. The preferences of different investor groups may overlap so that all securities within one maturity range may be perfect substitutes for one investor group, while securities in another maturity range may be perfect substitutes for another investor group. For example, banks may consider debt instruments over a certain range of short-term securities to be perfect substitutes while savings and loan associations, insurance companies, and other investors may view longer maturity dates as perfect substitutes. If the maturity ranges of different investor groups overlap sufficiently, the structure of yields would be adjusted as if each investor believed all securities to be perfect substitutes.

However one views the process which leads to loans with differing maturities being perfect substitutes in the aggregate, the essential point is that the yields and prices are determined by investors who expect the rates of return on these securities to be the same over any given period of time. It is necessary to qualify this statement moderately, since most presentations of the expectations theory do recognize that such factors as market impediments and transactions costs may result in some inequality in expected rates of return and may cause some distortion between actually established yield structures and those which would be established if these factors did not exist. In general analysis, however, it seems a valid practice to ignore these factors, for yield differentials change rather substantially over time, and it is highly unlikely that this behavior could be attributed in any significant way to changes in transactions costs or other market impediments.

There are two compatible ways to look at the equality of expected rates of return. An existing long-term rate can be considered equal, roughly speaking, to an average of a current short-term rate and the short-term rates which are expected to be established over time until the long-term loan matures. On the other hand, a current long-term rate can be viewed as standing in a specific relationship to a current short-term rate such that its price is expected to change just sufficiently so that its rate of return will equal the short-term rate over the period required for the short-term loan to mature.

In either case, any yield differential represents a market prediction that interest rates will change over the future. For example, consider two loans with 1 and 2 years to maturity that are selling to yield 2 percent and 3 percent, respectively. According to the pure expectations theory, this interest rate relationship indicates a market prediction that the price of the 2-year loan will fall by roughly 1 percent over the year. Or, it indicates that the market is expecting the yield on a 1-year loan to be roughly 4 percent 1 year in the future. This prediction is implied because the average of the current 1-year yield of 2 percent and the expected 1-year yield of 4 percent is roughly equal to the current 2-year maturity yield of 3 percent. In short, the expectations theory contends that differences in yields on loans with different maturities are established not because the market expects to receive a higher return on one security than on another, but instead, because the market expects the rates of return on the two securities to be the same over an equal period of time.

To view this conception from a broader perspective, consider the relationship among a whole range of yields on loans with differing maturities. This relationship is usually depicted by a yield curve, a curve which provides a general picture of the relationship among all maturity yields on a particular date. Three prevalent types of yield curves have been established during this century. The first is an upsloping curve with yields rising as maturity lengthens and then generally becoming flat in the range of longest maturity dates. The second is a downsloping curve with yields declining as maturity lengthens and then generally becoming flat in the range of longest maturity dates. The third is a flat yield curve with all maturity yields equal.

According to the expectations theory, the upsloping curve indicates that the market is expecting all yields to rise over future periods of time, with the greatest increases expected among short-term yields. The downsloping curve reflects market expectations that all yields will fall over future periods of time, with the greatest declines expected in shorter-term yields. The flat curve reflects market expectations that all yields will remain unchanged.

As might be expected, yield curves tend to vary over the business cycle and the types associated with the various phases of the business cycle lend plausibility to the expectations theory. For example, upsloping yield curves are usually observed during recessions and throughout the early part of a business expansion. It seems quite plausible that borrowers and lenders would be expecting interest rates to increase at such times. Conversely, downsloping yield curves generally have been established at or near the peaks of business expansion. With interest rates generally high historically, it is at least plausible that investors would be expecting to see yields decline in the future.

THE LIQUIDITY PREFERENCE VERSION
OF THE EXPECTATIONS THEORY

Several discussions of the expectations theory have concluded that expected changes in yield relationships provide only part of the explanation for the existence of yield differentials. They have argued that lenders generally prefer to hold short-term loans as assets because the price of these assets tends to vary minimally. This preference is reflected in the willingness of investors to forego some expected return in order to hold short-term assets. As a result, longer-term assets generally provide a liquidity premium and their expected rate of return tends to be higher. To put this another way, it is asserted that the level of longer-term yields is always higher than it would be if the structure of yields was determined solely by market expectations. The fact that yield curves have sloped upward considerably more often than they have sloped downward since World War II often is cited as evidence of the existence of a liquidity premium on longer-term securities. It should be noted, however, that the predominance of upsloping yield curves is not necessarily inconsistent with the pure expectations theory. If the market generally had expected yields to rise over this period—and yields did rise—the larger proportion of yield curves would have had an upward slope. It will be remembered that at the outset of the postwar period interest rates were at historically low levels.

Although the liquidity preference variant of the expectations theory contends that rates of return on loans with different maturities are expected to differ, it does not view credit markets as being segmented. Instead, the size of the presumed liquidity premium is held to be unrelated, or essentially unrelated, to the maturity composition of outstanding debt. Thus, the position of the liquidity preference approach is the same as the pure expectations approach on this vital point. In addition, the liquidity preference theory asserts that, in general, changes in yield differentials imply that the market has changed its expectations about the future course of interest rates. Here, again, the liquidity preference approach is in accord with the pure expectations approach and in conflict with the segmented markets approach. For these reasons, it is possible to consider this position as a variant of the expectations theory.

IMPLICATIONS OF EMPIRICAL EVIDENCE

The expectations theory has never been widely accepted outside of academic circles. Until recently, one reason was the inability of analysts to develop a test which supported this theory. In fact, early studies which purported to test this theory concluded that it had no empirical validity. This conclusion was based upon the demonstration that yield predictions derived from a structure of yields in accordance with logic of the expectations theory were usually wrong. Recent presentations of this theory have made it clear, however, that this is not a valid test. A test of the market's ability to form accurate forecasts of future interest rates does not constitute a test of whether an existing yield structure depends upon market expectations of future interest rates. All that is asserted by the expectations theory is that yield differentials exist because the market expects interest rates to change. It is not claimed that the predictions of the market necessarily will be accurate. In addition to this clarification, recent studies have generated new evidence in support of the expectations approach. And, although these findings taken individually are not overwhelmingly compelling, as a group they do serve to increase the degree of acceptance of the expectations theory.

It is impossible in the short space available to describe these tests in detail, but their general approach may be outlined. First, hypotheses about how interest rate expectations are formulated at one point in time or how they are altered with the passage of time are developed. Maturity yield relationships established at various points in time and the subsequent changes in these relationships with the passage of time are then compared with this independent evidence of market expectations. A high degree of correlation has been found between these variables.

Another approach has been to draw inferences about the validity of the expectations approach by comparing actual interest rates established over a certain period of time with forecasted interest rates as implied by yield structures established in the past. The criterion used for judging the results was not whether market predictions always turned out to be correct, however, as it was in earlier tests of this kind. Rather, it was one of determining whether actual rates turned out *on the average* to be above or below forecasted rates. The presumption has been that if, on the average, actual rates were equal to forecasted rates, this suggested that the pure expectations theory was correct. The findings in several studies that forecasted rates generally exceeded actual rates has been the principal source of support for the assertion that a liquidity premium on long-term debt must be recognized as a factor in determining maturity yield relationships.

Although most recent empirical studies of the expectations theory have proceeded along the lines described above, it should be noted that some investigations have approached the problem from a different perspective and have found evidence which casts doubt on this theory. One piece of evidence of this kind has been the inability to identify a group of balance sheet units that behave like the hypothetical speculators assumed in some presentations of the expectations theory. Moreover, objections have been raised as to the possibility of the type of speculative activity ascribed to traders because of technical deficiencies in the market with regard to short-selling. Additional evidence, which would appear to be particularly damaging to the overlapping markets version of this theory, was the finding in one recent study that interest rate expectations were not uniform among different market observers. This conflicts with one of the assumptions usually made in presenting the expectations theory which is that interest rate expectations of all investors tend to be uniform.

SUMMARY AND CONCLUSIONS

The problem of explaining maturity yield relationships remains unresolved. The implications of recent empirical findings, although far from being one-sided, have shifted opinion away from the segmented markets theory and toward either the pure expectations theory or this theory modified to include the existence of a liquidity premium on long-term debt. Perhaps the most compelling evidence produced by these studies was the consistent finding that changes in the maturity composition of debt have little, if any, effect on the maturity structure of yields. This, of course, constitutes not only a direct challenge to the segmented markets approach but, in addition, provide indirect support for the alternative theory. Other direct tests of the expectations hypothesis have added further support for this theory. In fact, on the basis of the results of these two groups of tests, a strong argument has been made for rejecting the segmented markets theory and accepting the expectations theory. However, all the evidence does not point in one direction. The generally acknowledged fact that major groups of borrowers and lenders are constrained either by legal restrictions or personal preferences from viewing securities with different maturities as perfect substitutes, the inability to identify economic units performing as speculators, and the evidence of diverse interest rate expectations all serve to temper any inclination to discard the segmented markets approach and accept the expectations theory. Perhaps the best appraisal at this time is that, as a result of recent research, the expectations approach has won an important skirmish, but the outcome of the war remains in doubt.

REFERENCES

CONARD, JOSEPH W. *An Introduction to the Theory of Interest.* Berkeley and Los Angeles: University of California Press, 1959.

COOTNER, PAUL H. "Speculation in the Government Securities Market," *Fiscal and Debt Management Policies,* a series of research studies prepared for the Commission on Money and Credit. Englewood Cliffs, N. J.: Prentice-Hall, 1963, 267–310.

CULBERTSON, J. M. "The Term Structure of Interest Rates," *Quarterly Journal of Economics,* LXXI (November 1957), 485–517.

DE LEEUW, FRANK. "A Model of Financial Behavior," *The Brookings Quarterly Econometric Model of the United States,* ed. J. S. Duesenberry *et al.* Chicago: Rand McNally & Company, 1965, 465–530.

KESSEL, REUBEN A. *The Cyclical Behavior of the Term Structure of Interest Rates.* (Occasional Paper 91, National Bureau of Economic Research.) New York: Columbia University Press, 1965.

MALKIEL, BURTON G. "The Term Structure of Interest Rates," *American Economic Review,* LIV (May 1964), 532–543.

MEISELMAN, DAVID. *The Term Structure of Interest Rates.* Englewood Cliffs, N. J.: Prentice-Hall, 1962.

OKUN, ARTHUR M. "Monetary Policy, Debt Management and Interest Rates: A Quantitative Appraisal," *Stabilization Policies,* a series of research studies prepared for the Commission on Money and Credit. Englewood Cliffs, N. J.: Prentice-Hall, 1963, 331–380.

SCOTT, ROBERT H. "Liquidity and the Term Structure of Interest Rates," *Quarterly Journal of Economics,* LXXIX (February 1965), 135–145.

IV

THE DEVELOPMENT
OF PRIVATE FINANCIAL
INSTITUTIONS

American financial institutions evolved to meet the needs of the economy, and new institutions developed whenever the demands were not being met by existing institutions. Together they have played a major role in American economic development by bringing together the supply and demand for loanable funds.

The first article in Part IV explores the evolution of American financial intermediaries in an effort to understand the development of today's financial system and to draw implications from its historical development.

The second article examines the changing structure of American financial institutions in an effort to see how they are now affecting economic growth, to see if the shift in relative importance necessitates new economic controls, and to see if the impact of various regulations creates inequities among the institutions.

The third article evaluates the recommendations of the Report of the Commission on Money and Credit as they will affect the future operations of private financial institutions.

24.

The Development
of American Financial
Intermediaries

EDWARD C. ETTIN

In the last few years renewed theoretical interest in financial intermediaries[1] and the studies of the Commission on Money and Credit have led to a searching investigation of the American financial system. The emphasis of these investigations has centered on two areas: (1) the influence of the growth of non-bank financial intermediaries on central

Reprinted from the *Quarterly Review of Economics and Business*, Vol. 3, No. 2, Summer 1963, pp. 51–69, by permission of the publisher, the Bureau of Economic and Business Research, University of Illinois, Urbana, Illinois. This article grew out of the study *Portfolio Regulations and Policies of Financial Intermediaries*, a monograph for the Commission on Money and Credit (to be published in the near future by Prentice-Hall in the volume *Private Financial Institutions*). I should like to thank my co-authors on this monograph, Professors Thomas G. Gies of the University of Michigan and Thomas Mayer of the University of California (Davis), for helping me to better understand the financial system of the United States. I should also like to thank my colleagues, Professors William Yohe, David George Davies, and Louis De Alessi, as well as Mrs. Marie Saylor, for their comments and suggestions. I, of course, take full responsibility for this paper. Gratitude is also expressed for the support of a departmental grant from Ford Foundation funds and a grant for typing from the Duke University Research Council.

[1] By financial intermediary is meant "An institution [that] has financial or monetary relations on each side of its balance sheet." Roland I. Robinson (ed.), *Financial Institutions* (Homewood: Irwin, 1960), p. 12.

bank policy,[2] and (2) the influence of intermediary portfolio and claim regulations, as well as intermediary policies themselves, on both financial markets and the composition and efficiency of the financial system.[3]

The objective of this paper is to take a broad overview of the evolution of American financial intermediaries in order that it may be better
understood how the present financial system developed, and then to draw
some implications from this record of historical development. The major
conclusion that emerges from this study is that the financial *system* has successfully avoided regulation-enforced and policy-induced ossification and
inflexibility by the simple expedient of financial mutation.[4]

EVOLUTION OF INTERMEDIARIES

Financial development does not take place in an economic vacuum but
reflects and has its counterpart in real development. Therefore, it can be
expected that a developing economy will find itself reflected in an evolving
financial system. The American experience clearly demonstrates such an
evolution.

Pre-Banking Finance

Participants in the economy are always seeking ways out of the financial confines in which they find themselves—always seeking to lower the
financial barrier. Thus, an economy without a developed financial system
improvises methods of performing the finance function. The American
colonial and early post-revolutionary economic history gives numerous
examples of such expedients. Gurley and Shaw suggest several of these:

---

[2] See, for example, J. G. Gurley and E. S. Shaw, "Financial Aspects of Economic
Development," *American Economic Review*, Vol. 45, No. 4 (September, 1955), pp.
515–38, and their *Money in a Theory of Finance* (Washington: Brookings, 1960). See
also D. A. Alhadeff, "Credit Controls and Financial Intermediaries," *American Economic Review*, Vol. 50, No. 4 (September, 1960), pp. 655–71; J. M. Henderson, "Monetary Reserves and Credit Growth," *American Economic Review*, Vol. 50, No. 3 (June,
1960), pp. 348–69; D. Shelby, "Some Implications of the Growth of Financial Intermediaries," *Journal of Finance*, Vol. 13, No. 4 (December, 1958), pp. 527–41; and
W. L. Smith, "Financial Intermediaries and Monetary Controls," *Quarterly Journal of
Economics*, Vol. 73, No. 4 (November, 1959), pp. 533–53.

[3] See C. H. Kreps, Jr., and D. T. Lapkin, "Public Regulation and Operating Con-
ventions Affecting Sources of Funds of Commerical Banks and Thrift Institutions,"
Journal of Finance, Vol. 17, No. 2 (May, 1962), pp. 289–301; T. G. Gies, "Portfolio
Regulations of Selected Financial Intermediaries: Some Proposals for Change," *ibid.*,
pp. 302–10; T. Mayer, "Is the Portfolio Control of Financial Institutions Justified?"
ibid., pp. 311–17; and the Commission on Money and Credit studies from which these
papers are drawn, listed in the footnotes to these articles.

[4] Cf. Hyman P. Minsky, "Central Banking and Money Market Changes," *Quarterly Journal of Economics*, Vol. 71, No. 2 (May, 1957), pp. 171–87.

partnerships formed to combine and mobilize savings; lotteries in which the prize was worth less than the sum of the price of the tickets, the difference being available for investment; government taxation and money issue in order to have funds available for various purposes; and tangible assets used as "barter" finance, e.g., land grants to canals and railroad companies.[5] Each of these methods attempts to perform the same function as would be performed by a financial system, but all are clearly imperfect and inefficient substitutes for such a system.

The Rise of Commercial Banks

In the late 18th and early 19th centuries, the immediate financial obstacles were limited sources of short-term finance and an inadequate stock of money. Both of these problems were met by the rapid growth of commercial banks.[6]

Economic, social, and political conditions during the era fostered a rapid expansion of an atomistic commercial banking system. Economic growth due to new land brought under cultivation and large immigration added to the demand for banks. The failure of privileged banking groups to develop, as they did on the Continent, made it easier for individuals to open banks. Finally, the tradition of Jacksonian democracy and the end of the First and Second Banks of the United States reinforced the tendency of the development of autonomous unit banks pursuing independent policies. Laissez-faire policies in general, and uneven state regulation in particular, also made bank formation easy.

The resultant rapid increase in banking in America was not without real costs. Prior to the Civil War, the bank-created currency stock was heterogeneous (with all the inefficiency that this implies) and banks, because of poor management and supervision, were prone to a high incidence of failure. Moreover, bank policies and failures tended to be cycle intensifying by fostering overexpansion during booms and contraction during economic declines. Banks, on the other hand, were the victims as often as the villains, for many of these failures were due to the highly unstable economic conditions of the period.

The point that still remains, however, is that regardless of efficiency, shortcomings, and by-products, the rapid increase in banking helped and fostered the real economic expansion that took place by increasing the supply of credit and augmenting the money stock. In so doing, commercial

[5] *Money in a Theory of Finance*, pp. 50–52.

[6] In 1800 there were 28 commercial banks with assets of $40 million. By 1850 there were over 700 banks with assets of $500 million and dealing exclusively in short-term finance. Raymond W. Goldsmith, *Financial Intermediaries in the American Economy Since 1900* (Princeton: Princeton University Press, for National Bureau of Economic Research, 1958), pp. 57 n and 58.

banks maintained their dominant financial position in the first half of the 19th century. As Appendix Table 1 shows, by 1850 they were ten times as large as their nearest competitor, insurance companies (mainly fire insurance companies).

The Rise and Fall of Savings Banks

Mutual savings banks, one of the earliest mutations of the American financial system,[7] developed to fill a competitive gap as a savings depository; indeed, until 1880 they had virtually no competition as a savings outlet for the great majority of the growing urban population.[8] Eastern commercial banks during most of the 19th century considered themselves "gentlemen's institutions" interested only in serving businessmen and the wealthier citizens, and hence, were not particularly interested in serving the small, urban saver.[9] This policy was reinforced by the National Bank Acts of 1863–64, which raised some question about the legality of the payment of interest on savings accounts by commercial banks—a subject not cleared up until 1912. However, prior to 1912 some national banks did pay interest on savings accounts and most state banks were not restricted in this regard.

In the capital markets, savings banks also found little competition from commercial banks. Mid-19th century commercial banks dealt almost exclusively in short-term finance *as part of their traditional policy*, even though one-half of their resources came from equity funds.[10] This policy, too, was strengthened by the National Bank Acts' prohibition of real estate loans—a legislative provision growing out of the unfavorable experience of some earlier commercial banks in speculative financing of real estate loans.[11] It must be remembered, however, that state banks were generally permitted to make mortgage loans during this period but did not take very much advantage of their greater freedom. At first, savings banks were also blocked in this market. Early 19th century charters limited savings bank

[7] None existed in 1800, but by 1850 there were about 100 such institutions with deposits of $43 million, placing them fairly close in size to insurance companies (Appendix Table 1). In the third quarter of the 19th century they exhibited extremely rapid growth, and by 1875 (their relative peak) there were 674 such institutions with deposits of $850 million—second only to commercial banks. *Ibid.*, p. 21.

[8] John Lintner, *Mutual Savings Banks in the Savings and Mortgage Markets* (Cambridge: Harvard University Press, 1948), p. 29.

[9] *Ibid.*, p. 45. Indeed, the first savings banks ". . . originated largely as a philanthropy sponsored by wealthy business and professional men with the paternalistic object of managing 'the savings of mechanics, laborers, servants, and others.'" C. F. Distelhorst, "Savings and Loan Associations and Mutual Savings Banks," in H. V. Prochnow (ed.), *American Financial Institutions* (New York: Prentice-Hall, 1951), p. 154.

[10] Goldsmith, *op. cit.*, p. 58.

[11] The original acts completely prohibited national banks from making real estate loans. In 1913, the law was amended so that such banks could make one-year mortgage loans and in 1927 national banks were allowed to buy mortgages with a five-year maturity. Today they may make amortized mortgage loans of a 20-year maturity.

portfolios to government bonds.[12] However, by 1875 mortgage provisions were the norm in savings bank charters[13] and since that time over one-half of the portfolios of these institutions have been placed in mortgages (Appendix Table 2). The higher yields earned on this type of asset, and consequent higher interest paid on deposits, tended to reinforce the attractiveness of savings banks as a savings depository.

The failure of commercial banks to compete in both the savings and the mortgage markets led directly to the rise of both the savings bank and, as will be discussed later, the savings and loan associations. The reasons for this behavior were regulatory and managerial: the commercial banks' self-image, lower asset yields, and the provisions of the National Bank Acts were all instrumental in blocking their entry into the growing savings and mortgage markets. Both explanations complement each other but one is left with the impression that banks brought competition on themselves by failing to perceive and act upon profitable markets because of their preoccupation with "business" and short-term finance. Regulations, to be sure, hampered any competitive reaction by commercial banks but regulation is not the full explanation. Not only did commercial banks prior to the National Bank Acts not enter these markets, but state banks, generally without contrary regulations during this period, also did not aggressively seek savings or mortgages. Moreover, Western commercial banks, as will be discussed hereafter, were later able to pre-empt the savings market and block the growth of savings banks.

In filling these competitive voids, savings banks succeeded by 1880 in attracting 60 percent of savings in all private savings depositories and life insurance companies in the United States.[14] Since that time, however, their share of savings has dropped each year except in the early 1920's and again in the early 1930's. It seems that as soon as there were acceptable alternatives for savings outlets, the mutual savings banks began to lose ground. Why?

Most importantly, savings banks never left the confines of the New England and Middle Atlantic States.[15] In the early days of the Western frontier, as there was little or no *financial* saving, there was little demand for financial savings outlets in the area. Savings in the West were immedi-

---

[12] Weldon Welfling, *Savings Banking in New York State* (Durham: Duke University Press, 1939), p. 11.

[13] Franklin J. Sherman, *Modern Story of Mutual Savings Banks* (New York: J. J. Little and Ives Co., 1934), p. 71.

[14] Goldsmith, *op. cit.*, p. 32.

[15] Professor Yohe suggested to me that this phenomenon is not unrelated to the "puritanical version of the so-called 'Protestant Ethic,' " which emphasized thrift and was heavily represented along the eastern seaboard—especially in New England. This is probably a partial explanation but it is impossible to test if (a) propensities to save were, in fact, higher in these areas and (b) if so, whether or not such propensities were due to different geographic stages of economic development or ethnic characteristics.

ately put into real capital formation by the savers themselves. The mutual savings bank was unable to supplement such local savings with deposits from distant areas. The commercial bank, moreover, was adapted to doing just that. The creation of credit via the loan-note expansion process "forced" a movement of savings to the frontier areas, for the newly created purchasing power was usable for acquiring capital goods in Eastern markets. The net effect of bank credit expansion was the lending of savings from the East to agricultural borrowers in the Middle West.

By the time financial savings became available in the West, commercial banks, which had located there early for short-term lending purposes, were willing to care for the small savers. In addition, by this time savings and loan associations also were growing in the West. "Under such circumstances new mutual savings banks . . . found themselves in the position of newcomers trying to make inroads on an established position in the savings market instead of themselves having the prior position they held in the East.[16] A few Western states erected entry barriers for savings banks— probably under pressure from already existing commercial banks and savings and loan associations—but the savings banks never took a real foothold in most Western states. This inability "to make inroads on an established position" is indicative of a basic lack of competitive aggressiveness by savings banks.[17] Savings banks remain the dominant savings depository in the East, having held their entrenched position against competition, but other institutions dominate the West and Midwest.[18]

Savings and Loan Associations

Just about the time that savings banks were reaching their relative zenith in the last quarter of the 19th century, savings and loan associations began to increase in importance (Table 24–1). Aside from certain technical differences on the source side,[19] savings and loan associations look like

---

16 Lintner, *op. cit.*, p. 55.

17 Ross Robertson suggests that a partial explanation for this lack of aggressiveness is the fact that savings bank managers are selected by a self-perpetuating group of incorporators. "It is hard to imagine a less likely device for electing officers who will be aggressively competitive with 'new' institutions." *Memorandum on the Growth of Financial Intermediaries*, privately circulated study for the Commission on Money and Credit, June 10, 1960, p. 24 n.

18 In 1960, 88 percent of savings bank deposits were in 4 eastern states, and all deposits were located in only 17 states. G. Brooke Willis, "Gross Flows of Funds Through Mutual Savings Banks," *Journal of Finance*, Vol. 15, No. 2 (May, 1960), p. 170.

19 Mutual savings banks accept deposits, and the depositors become creditors of the bank, even though there are no owners or capital stock accounts. Most savings and loan associations (and all those chartered by the federal government) do not accept deposit accounts, but sell "shares" to savers who legally become owners of the association. Technically, therefore, the former needs more liquidity than the latter. Actually, for competitive reasons, both will allow liquidation of deposits without or on short notice.

TABLE 24-1

Assets of Selected American Financial Institutions Various Dates, 1800 to 1960

(Millions of dollars)

Institution	1800	1850	1875	1900	1929	1945	1952	1960
Commercial banks	$40	$500	n.a.	$10,011	$65,621	$160,263	$188,603	$257,552
Private life insurance companies	10	50	n.a.	1,742	17,482	44,797	73,375	119,576
Fire, property, casualty, and miscellaneous insurance companies			n.a.	484	4,388	7,781	15,860	30,000[a]
Savings and loan associations	..b	..c	...c	490	7,411	8,608	22,505	71,476
Mutual savings banks	..b	43	$850	2,430	9,873	17,021	25,233	40,574
Private, self-administered pension funds (book value)	..b	..b	..b	...c	500	2,900	9,000	28,700
Investment companies (open- and closed-end)	..b	..b	..b	...c	7,000	3,350	7,260	23,000[a]
Consumer finance companies	..b	..b	..b	...b	410	580	1,990	4,100[a]
Sales finance companies	..b	..b	..b	...c	2,070	1,130	7,700	12,500[a]
Credit unions	..b	..b	..b	...c	n.a.	435	1,516	5,653

[a] Estimate; all estimates made by author based on partial data and past relationship between asset components for that institution.
[b] Nonexistent.
[c] Negligible.
n.a. Not available.

Sources: Bankers Trust Company, The Investment Outlook, various issues; Board of Governors of the Federal Reserve System, Federal Reserve Bulletin, various issues; Board of Governors of the Federal Reserve System, Flow of Funds/Savings Accounts, 1946-60, Supplement 5 (1961); Commission on Money and Credit, unpublished data; Credit Union Year Book, 1962; Thomas Mayer, and Edward Ettin, Portfolio Regulations and Policies of Financial Intermediaries, to be published by the Commission on Money and Credit; Raymond W. Goldsmith, Financial Intermediaries in the American Economy Since 1900 (Princeton: Princeton University Press, for National Bureau of Economic Research, 1958); Life Insurance Fact Book, 1961; Harold Oberg, Managed Investment Companies, to be published by the Commission on Money and Credit; Ross Robertson, Memorandum on the Growth of Financial Intermediaries, privately circulated study for the Commission on Money and Credit, June 10, 1960; Saving and Loan Fact Book, 1961; U. S. Securities and Exchange Commission, Statistical Series, Release 1750, May 31, 1961.

savings banks, tapping the same savings stream and lending in the same major area of the capital market—mortgages. Indeed, the public treats both savings media as very close substitutes.[20] If these two institutions look like the same animal, why, then, did savings and loan associations prosper relatively more than mutual savings banks?

Although both institutions operate in the same markets, the savings and loan associations brought the two, mortgages and savings, directly together, investing over 80 percent of their funds in home mortgages. Indeed, one of the major reasons why the savings and loan associations invest so heavily in mortgages is that many of the associations were started by builders, real estate agents, and insurance agents who were looking for a way to provide mortgage money to improve their business. Historically, it was the demand for money to put into mortgages that made the savings and loan associations savings institutions, whereas it was being an outlet for savings that made mutual savings banks mortgage buyers. Moreover, the latter originally did not buy mortgages of wage earners, but took their savings, whereas the former did both. In this endeavor, savings and loan associations pioneered the low down-payment, long-term, monthly amortized mortgage, thus increasing the effective demand for home mortgages and establishing a customer loyalty in the process. This loyalty was no doubt improved by the greater return savings and loan associations could offer on shares, relative to savings bank accounts, as a result of their greater mortgage concentration. Mutual savings banks, with their more diversified portfolios, could not match the return generated by a portfolio with an 80 percent mortgages composition (Table 24–2).

The pioneering of amortized mortgages by the savings and loan associations is indicative of their basic aggressiveness. In addition, new offices were opened and advertised, savings and loan shares were promoted, and higher yields were merchandised to the public. The management remained not only aggressive but flexible (within the confines of mortgage portfolio concentration), making GI loans, for example, when they were new and untried, and then using their successful experience to move into conventional mortgages on liberal terms.

Public acceptance of savings and loan associations was also greatly enhanced by New Deal legislation. In an attempt to foster residential expenditures in the 1930's, the Administration encouraged the savings and loan associations, not only by creating the Federal Home Loan Bank System to give liquidity and added safety to the associations, but also by creating an insurance program for savings and loan shares and by starting to offer federal charters to these institutions. The fact that savings and loan associations were interested in mortgages at the time that the federal gov-

TABLE 24-2

Various Assets as a Proportion of Total Assets of Selected Financial Institutions, Year-end, 1960

(Percentages)

Asset	Commercial banks	Life insurance companies	Other insurance companies	Savings and loan associations	Mutual savings banks	Private pension funds (self-administered)[a]	Investment companies (open-end)	Consumer finance companies	Sales finance companies	Credit unions
State and local government bonds	0.7	3.0	29.2[b]	....	1.7	....	....	....	....	....
Publicly held U.S. government and agency bonds	23.7	5.4	22.6[b]	7.5	17.0	6.2	3.5	n.a.	n.a.	n.a.
Corporate securities	0.1	44.2	23.2[b]	....	11.3	86.6	94.1	....	....	....
Bonds	0.1	40.0	6.2[b]	....	9.3	41.0	7.1	....	....	....
Stocks (excluding investment companies)[c]	....	4.2	17.0[b]	....	2.0	45.6	87.0	....	....	....
Mortgages	11.2	34.8	n.a.	84.0	67.0	2.5	....	....	....	....
Consumer instalment credit	6.5	....	....	....	....	....	....	90.0[b]	90.0[b]	69.0

a All assets at market value.
b Estimate; all estimates made by author based on partial data and past relationships between asset components for that institution.
c Market value
n.a. Not available

Sources: Tables 24-1 and 24-3 and sources cited there.

ernment wanted to encourage the construction market made the two obvious candidates for a marriage.[21]

Favorable legislation was not the only fortunate event in the history of savings and loan associations. Government-sponsored public acceptance, promotion, and aggressiveness put the associations in a good position to exploit post-World War II population and income growth. As Robertson observed: "There is indeed such a thing as being at the mouth of the river when the salmon start to run."[22]

Thus, by fulfilling the mutual savings bank savings outlet function more competitively, adding a few changes of their own, and getting some favorable breaks, savings and loan associations were able to become major mortgage lenders and joined commercial banks in usurping the major savings *depository* function from savings banks.[23] In addition, like savings banks, they were able originally to capitalize on the growing demands of the mortgage market because of commercial bank tradition and legal restrictions. They were never, however, able to get very far in those states where savings banks were already successfully established and, of course, are strongest themselves in states where mutual savings banks are outlawed. In most other states, where no legal restrictions were in force, savings and loan associations developed first and *competitively* blocked the savings banks.

[21] Federal legislation also tended to reinforce savings and loan policy by tending to confine their activities to local markets and their portfolios mainly to mortgages.

[22] *Op. Cit.*, p. 26.

[23] In 1960, savings and loan associations accounted for 36.4 percent of savings deposits; the commercial banks, 39.2 percent; the mutual savings banks, 21.2 percent; credit unions, 2.8 percent; and postal savings accounts, 0.4 percent. *Credit Union Year Book*, 1962.

Insurance Companies

Although not an obvious intermediary from a depository point of view, life insurance companies have generated savings more rapidly than all other savings media combined.[24] While it is doubted that people buy life insurance merely in order to save, the mechanical results of the level premium plan produce a sizable savings element (legal reserves).

In the mid-19th century, most of the insurance assets of $50 million were accounted for by property, fire, and casualty insurance companies. Life insurance was little understood and even considered "sinful speculation in human life" by some legal and religious authorities.[25] Moreover, the general level of income was probably not sufficient at the time to create a very large market for life insurance, but this obstacle did not remain for long.

A major factor in the growth of life insurance companies has been their efficiency in explaining and aggressively promoting their product. The agency system or commissioned selling staff, which the mutual companies pioneered in the last half of the 19th century, provided an excellent marketing scheme to "push" the product. Even though their marketing scheme was well tailored for effective selling, the life insurance companies had to have something to sell. Here, too, they were efficient in constantly bettering their product. They altered old contracts and introduced new ones in order to tap latent demand better. With little exaggeration, one may say that life insurance companies in the 20th century have been willing to sell the public insurance plans to meet any objectives, combining any characteristics desired of insurance, savings, maturity, and coverage.

In addition, life insurance provides a good substitute for savings with certain motivations, namely, security and accumulation of funds for retirement. Moreover, the insurance loss for missing a premium is of such relative magnitude that it is one of the last discretionary payments to be eliminated if income declines. Even in the depths of the Great Depression, life insurance cash income exceeded cash outgo in every year. Parenthetically, it may be added that for all these reasons, the introduction, development, and extension of insurance has reduced the demand for savings via other media. Savings depositories ceased to be the most efficient method for serving *all* thrift objectives.

Finally, life insurance companies have shown rapid growth by becoming efficient, aggressive, and astute investors in both the mortgage and cor-

---

[24] The savings element of life insurance has increased from $650 million in 1890 to $93.2 billion in 1960. Derived from *Life Insurance Fact Book*, 1961, pp. 62, 66, and 91. (Policy reserves less policy loans.) This savings element is essential to the concept of the level premium; it is not just grafted on. This savings element increases over the life of the policy, hence reducing the insurance element. It is at its minimum when the policy is started. The savings may be withdrawn (cash value), less charges, at any time by the policyholder and the policy terminated.

[25] J. B. MacLean, *Life Insurance* (New York: McGraw-Hill, 1939), p. 522.

porate markets, and hence, have been able to pay high rates on funds left with them. For example, they pioneered the private placement of corporate securities and compete with most other financial intermediaries in the capital and money markets (Tables 24–2 through 24–4).

Fire, property, and casualty insurance company assets exceeded life company assets in 1850, but by 1900 the situation was reversed. Fire, casualty, and property insurance assets of slightly less than $500 million in 1900 were about one-fourth of life assets (Table 24–1). Since that time, the assets of fire, casualty, and property insurance companies have continued to grow much less fast than the assets of life insurance firms.

Fire, casualty, and property insurance companies do not directly fulfill the functions of any of the financial intermediaries discussed so far. They create no liquid assets (unless one thinks of "prepaid insurance" as a liquid asset), and they do not act as savings depositories or attempt to fulfill any savings functions. They are in the business of attempting to protect the spending unit, by use of insurance principles, against losses from certain contingencies. However, as these companies receive insurance premiums in advance, a savings element is derived as a by-product of their method of doing business. These funds plus capital contributions (about 40 percent of total sources) are invested mainly in corporate and government securities (Table 24–2).

Finance Companies[26]

Sales finance companies grew up in the 20th century to finance consumer durable goods on an instalment credit basis. Although instalment credit was not unknown prior to 1900—it was used by durable goods retailers to a limited degree in the 19th century—the advent of the automobile and home appliance industries gave great impetus to consumer finance in general. Once the possibility of tapping a mass market was clearly apparent, the need for an organized system of financing such purchases became evident, and a close alliance between automobile manufacturing and automobile finance was formed.[27] Thus, "sales finance companies were an outgrowth

---

[26] Finance companies look even less like standard intermediaries than do insurance companies—probably because they do not have depositors. Their funds come from capital investment by owners and creditors as well as from short-term borrowing and then are re-lent to the public. In 1955, for example, 78 sales finance companies received 54 percent of their funds from short-term debt, 35 percent from long-term debt, and 11 percent from equity. In the same year, 47 consumer finance companies received 37 percent of their funds from short-term debt, an equal amount from long-term debt, and 26 percent from equity capital. These figures vary with the size of the institution. Board of Governors of the Federal Reserve System, *Consumer Instalment Credit* (1957), Part I, Vol. 2, pp. 36 and 38.

[27] The three largest sales finance companies today—General Motors Acceptance Corporation, C.I.T. Financial Corporation, and Commercial Credit Company—were all originally affiliated with automobile manufacturing firms.

of the selling of goods rather than of money lending."[28]

The demand for vastly greater quantities of consumer credit, however, does not explain the origin and rapid growth of sales finance companies, for it is conceivable that commercial banks and other institutions already in existence could have absorbed this new demand. There seem to be a number of reasons for the failure of these existing institutions to occupy the emerging market for instalment credit on a more extensive scale in the early decades of this century. First, the extension of credit for consumer durables was outside the commercial banks' traditional area of short-term business credit. Just as the vacuum left by commercial banks in the savings and mortgage markets provided a major impetus to savings banks and savings and loan associations, so the failure of commercial banks to enter the consumer credit field helped foster the rise of finance companies.

Although the apparent lack of desire on the part of commercial banks to jump the wall of tradition was the basic force that kept them from this market, other factors also played a part. Costs of investigation, collection, and administration on consumer loans were high, and lack of trained personnel for such operations was also an obstacle to entry. The consequent need for higher rates and uncertainty regarding application of usury laws also deterred banks from this market. Sales finance companies exempted themselves from the usury laws by lending direct to retailers and skipping the consumer—a route that banks and other institutions could have used. Banks also felt that consumer credit was too risky for their institutions, which had to stand ready to meet withdrawals on demand by depositors. Finance companies, with their more permanent capital sources, did not have this problem.

Although a few sales finance firms had already been organized and were in successful operation before World War I, the decade of the twenties, when they were almost without competition, saw a rapid growth in their number (Table 24–1). Between 1921 and 1925, the number of such organizations increased from a handful to an estimated 1,600 to 1,700.[29]

Consumer finance companies, or small loan companies as they are known more traditionally, also developed in the 20th century to service the consumer finance market—but in a different subsector from the sales finance company. They are the outgrowth of efforts around the turn of the century to eliminate the "loan shark" evil and establish a system of lenders able to meet the needs of the urban family for credit in small amounts. Apart from the *sub rosa* operations of illegal lenders and nominal amounts of credit provided by miscellaneous institutions such as pawnbrokers, remedial loan societies, and other businesses and individuals only incidentally

[28] *Consumer Instalment Credit*, Part I, Vol. 1, p. 38.
[29] E. R. A. Seligman, *The Economics of Installment Selling* (New York: Harper, 1927), Vol. I, pp. 48–50.

and occasionally making loans, there was no source of small loans to the necessitous consumer-borrower. This deficiency existed because the majority of states had legislated small loans out of the financial markets by means of statutory interest ceilings on loans to consumers of 6 to 8 percent —an economically unacceptable rate for this type of credit.[30] As the nature of the American economy altered progressively toward an industrial, urbanized society, the old usury statutes stood in the way of the development of lending institutions able to serve this particularly costly type of credit. The maximum rates permitted under general usury statutes were inadequate to pay the costs of making, holding, and collecting small loans; hence, capital could not be attracted on a commercial basis and early efforts to accommodate needful borrowers through charitable societies proved entirely insufficient.

In the first two decades of this century, when the need for new legislation was finally recognized—and when it was finally recognized that a 6 to 8 percent interest ceiling had no special inherent sanctity—new statutes were drawn up which permitted consumer credit agencies to supply funds in small amounts under conditions vigorously supervised to protect the borrowers from exploitation. That basic legislation is still in force and exempts licensed small loan companies from the usury law in return for state control of the maximum rate (usually 2½ to 3 percent a month) and maximum loan size (originally about $300 and still generally under $1,000).

Thus, consumer finance companies could not develop until legislation was enacted to permit them to escape usury laws. It is also possible to hypothesize that, even if this rate limit had not originally blocked small consumer loans, separate institutions would still have grown up to meet the demand. The history of financial institutions suggests that existing institutions would probably not have filled the void because of conservatism, tradition, and uncertainty. This seems especially true of commercial banks.

Indeed, it can be argued that the failure of commercial banks to enter the consumer finance field, for both regulatory and policy reasons, spawned the consumer and sales finance companies. However, commercial banks have vigorously entered this field they once avoided. Entering slowly in the 1920's, circumstances of the 1930's accelerated their activities in consumer finance. Earnings were down, and excess reserves were high. Finance com-

[30] Morris Plan Banks (Industrial Banks) prior to World War I exempted themselves from the usury laws by the simple expedient of charging the maximum allowable rate on their loans, and then having the debtor make monthly "deposits" which would be used to make one single "repayment" at maturity. In effect, the debtor had only one-half of the loan outstanding for the period, which doubled the interest charge. At the present, Morris Plan Banks are indistinguishable from commercial banks, but in 1929 they were the second largest instalment credit lender. See E. E. Edwards, "Consumer Credit Institutions Other Than Commercial Banks," *American Financial Institutions*, pp. 718 and 733; and *Consumer Instalment Credit*, Part I, Vol. 1, pp. 37–38.

TABLE 24-3

Ownership of Various Assets, Year-end, 1960

Asset	Total securities outstanding	Owned by									
		Commercial banks	Life insurance companies	Other insurance companies	Savings and loan associations	Mutual savings banks	Private pension funds (self-administered)	Investment companies (open-end)	Consumer finance companies	Sales finance companies	Credit unions
(Billions of dollars)											
State and local government bonds	67.9	17.6	3.6	8.8	...	0.7	...	...	...	...	...
Publicly held U.S. government and agency bonds	194.8	61.0	6.5[a]	6.8	5.4	6.7	2.6	0.6	n.a.	n.a.	n.a.
Corporate securities	532.2	1.0	53.1[a]	7.0[a]	...	4.6	29.5	16.0	...	...	...
Bonds	90.2	1.0	48.1	1.9	...	3.8	14.9	1.2	...	...	...
Stocks (excluding investment companies)[b]	442.0	...	5.0[a]	5.1[a]	...	0.8	14.6	14.8	...	...	...
Mortgages	206.8	28.7	41.8	n.a.	60.1	27.2	0.8	...	...	...	0.3
Consumer instalment credit	42.6	16.7	...	...	...	...	...	...	3.7	11.2	3.9
(Percentage distribution)											
State and local government bonds	100.0	26.0	5.3	13.0	...	1.0	...	...	...	...	...
Publicly held U.S. government and agency bonds	100.0	31.4	3.3	3.5	2.8	3.4	1.3	0.3	n.a.	n.a.	n.a.
Corporate securities	100.0	[c]	10.0[a]	1.3[a]	...	0.9	5.5	3.0	...	...	...
Bonds	100.0	1.2	53.5	2.1	...	4.2	16.5	1.3	...	...	...
Stocks (excluding investment companies)[b]	100.0	...	1.1[a]	1.1[a]	...	0.2	3.3	3.3	...	...	...
Mortgages	100.0	13.9	20.2	n.a.	29.2	13.4	0.4	...	...	...	0.1
Consumer instalment credit	100.0	39.2	...	...	...	...	...	...	8.7	26.0	9.2

a Estimate: all estimates made by author based on partial data and past relationship between asset components for that institution.
b Market value
c Less than 0.1 percent
n.a. Not available

Sources: Bankers Trust Company, *The Investment Outlook, 1962*; Board of Governors of the Federal Reserve System, *Flow of Funds/Savings Accounts, 1946-1960, Supplement 5* (1961); *Federal Reserve Bulletin*, various issues; U. S. Securities and Exchange Commission, *Statistical Series, Release 1750*, May 3, 1961.

pany experience offered convincing evidence to banks that consumer finance was not only safe but highly profitable. Moreover, in 1934, many banks were introduced to consumer lending under Title I of the National Housing Act, and experience was so good that banks began to make such loans without FHA insurance. The experiences of unexpected levels of profits from and safety of consumer finance, the high levels of bank liquidity, and the increased competition in bank loan markets by other institutions all combined in the post-World War II period to accelerate bank consumer instalment lending.

As a result, commercial banks have succeeded in wresting the original position of dominant consumer lender from finance companies. Indeed, while sales finance companies are now of larger size, today there are the same number of firms as in 1925. By 1960, banks held almost two-fifths of all consumer instalment paper, sales finance companies held one-fourth, and consumer finance companies less than one-tenth (Table 24–3). Bank participation in consumer finance is even higher than these figures indicate as banks lend to sales finance companies, other lenders, and retail dealers.[31] Parenthetically, it might be added that, although the markets of commercial banks and finance companies overlap, the institutions are not directly competitive on all grounds because of different charges and quality criteria. Banks *tend* to take the "cream" of the consumer business.

Consumer finance companies have been taking a smaller share of the market not only because of bank competition but also because of anachronistic legal loan limits and the growth of credit unions. Credit unions have almost tripled their share of the market in the postwar period and are now larger in aggregate size than consumer finance companies (Table 24–1). These co-ops have lower costs because of the donation of office space and clerical help by employers and the contribution of time and service by credit union members. Credit investigation costs are also lower because of the closely knit group in which they operate.[32] However, it is probably the old loan-size limit, originally set up to "protect" consumers when incomes were lower, that has severely hampered the consumer loan companies' ability to compete in the consumer finance market.[33] It is interesting that regulations which originally created these institutions now serve to limit their growth.

[31] The Federal Reserve Board in 1957 estimated that in recent years commercial banks probably have supported either directly or indirectly more than one-half of total consumer credit. *Consumer Instalment Credit*, Part I, Vol. 2, p. 26 n. This dependence has also tended to put commercial bank rivals—especially sales finance companies—at a competitive disadvantage. During periods of rising loan demand, the banks cut back or fail to increase loans to sales finance companies. They consider finance companies as competitive, and hence, "alien" borrowers, and in any event, find the use of funds for consumer lending is more profitable. *Ibid.*, pp. 73–92.

[32] *Ibid.*, Part I, Vol. 1, p. 42.

[33] See Gies, *loc. cit.*, pp. 308–10, and for a detailed discussion of the problem in one state, Thomas G. Gies and others, *Consumer Finance Companies in Michigan* (Ann Arbor: University of Michigan, Bureau of Business Research, 1961).

Investment Companies[34]

Investment companies are different from most financial intermediaries in that holders of the secondary securities are not creditors.[35] Moreover, these institutions are directly selling their asset portfolio, per se, rather than assuming responsibilities and risks which they intend to meet by investing, as most other intermediaries do. Holders of secondary securities pool their funds and share pro rata in the portfolio, with the "fund" giving the investor management and diversification.

Investment companies in the United States grew up in the interwar period. Prior to the 1920's, the prerequisite for the growth of such institutions did not prevail: the general public was not familiar with financial investment in negotiable securities; common stocks were not generally accepted investment media; and the level of income was not sufficiently high to open up a wide market for investment company shares. After World War I, incomes were higher, and the war loans had educated large segments of the American population about the nature of securities. Moreover, growing public interest in stocks and the new-era philosophy and psychology widened the market for investment company shares. Promoters saw a demand for a product that was cheap to manufacture—investment company shares—and many of the new companies that were formed were watered, over-levered, over-complicated, and over-priced. In short, fraud was rampant. In spite of this—or because of it—funds increased in size from $15 million in 1923 to $700 million in 1927, $1.2 billion in the middle of 1928, and over $7 billion at the end of 1929.[36] However, by the middle of 1932, investment companies' assets had declined by 75 percent to $2 billion.[37] The stock market crash, fraud, poor management, high leverage, disgust with the investment company media, and the Depression itself were all to blame for the sharp drop.

Remedial legislation dealing with investment companies was overlooked during the period of the 1930's. It was not until 1940 that the In-

---

[34] "Investment companies" are technically "close-end" companies, i.e., do not continuously buy and sell their own shares; "mutual funds" are technically "open-end" companies, i.e., they continuously buy and sell their own shares. Unless otherwise stated, "investment companies" will cover both types of institutions in this study. Today 90 percent of the "funds" are open-end.

[35] Holders of bonds are, of course, creditors, but such holdings are small. Open-end companies may not have bonds outstanding unless they were issued prior to 1940. In other financial intermediaries, such as federally chartered savings and loan associations, depositors are not legally creditors, but in a pragmatic sense, they may be considered creditors.

[36] Harold Oberg, *Managed Investment Companies*, a monograph for the Commission on Money and Credit by the National Association of Investment Companies (preliminary draft, 1960), p. 16. Actually only $4 billion of the 1929 figure was truly in investment companies, the remainder being in holding companies. Hugh Bullock, *The Story of Investment Companies* (New York: Columbia University Press, 1959), p. 46.

[37] Bullock, *op. cit.*, p. 46.

TABLE 24-4

Net Increase in Various Types of Assets by Selected Financial Intermediaries, 1947-60

Asset	Net total securities issued	Purchased by									
		Commercial banks	Life insurance companies	Other insurance companies	Savings and loan associations	Mutual savings banks	Private pension funds (self-administered)	Investment companies (open-end)	Consumer finance companies	Sales finance companies	Credit unions
(Billions of dollars)											
State and local government bonds	47.5	13.6	2.9	8.2	....	0.6	....	....	....	....	....
Publicly held U.S. government and agency bonds	10.7	-13.5	-15.1	3.0	3.2	-5.1	1.1	n.a.	n.a.	n.a.	n.a.
Corporate securities	102.5	-1.2	37.2	3.7	....	3.3	23.9	7.6[a]	....	....	....
Bonds	62.8	-1.2	35.0	1.8	....	2.7	14.0	1.0[a]	....	....	....
Stocks (excluding investment companies)	39.7	....	2.2	1.9	....	0.6	9.9	6.6	....	....	....
Mortgages	165.5	21.4	34.6	n.a.	53.0	22.9	0.8	....	....	....	0.3
Consumer instalment credit	38.4	15.1	....	....	....	....	....	....	3.1	10.5	3.8
(Percentage distribution)											
State and local government bonds	100.0	28.6	6.1	17.5	....	1.3	....	....	....	....	....
Publicly held U.S. government and agency bonds	100.0	....[b]	....[b]	28.0	30.0	....[b]	10.3	n.a.	n.a.	n.a.	n.a.
Corporate securities	100.0	....[b]	36.2	3.6	....	3.2	23.2	7.4[a]	....	....	....
Bonds	100.0	....[b]	55.7	2.9	....	4.3	22.6	1.6[a]	....	....	....
Stocks (excluding investment companies)	100.0	....	5.5	4.8	....	1.5	24.7	16.6	....	....	....
Mortgages	100.0	12.9	20.8	n.a.	32.0	13.8	0.5	....	....	....	0.2
Consumer instalment credit	100.0	39.4	....	....	....	....	....	....	8.1	27.4	9.9

[a] Estimate; all estimates made by author based on partial data and past relationships between asset components for that institution.

[b] Liquidation securities

n.a. Not available

Sources: Bankers Trust Company, *The Investment Outlook, 1962;* Board of Governors of the Federal Reserve System, *Flow of Funds/ Savings Accounts, 1946-1960,* Supplement 5 (1961); *Federal Reserve Bulletin,* various issues; Thomas Gies, Thomas Mayer, and Edward Ettin, *Portfolio Regulations and Policies of Financial Intermediaries,* to be published by the Commission on Money and Credit.

vestment Company Act was passed. The 10-year lag and the industry's cooperation and house cleaning joined forces to make the act a relatively mild one. Except for limiting concentration in portfolios and requiring "full disclosure," this legislation allows investment companies to select and supervise their portfolio without qualification. Moreover, just as the creation of federally chartered savings and loan associations aided that industry, the Investment Company Act of 1940 has greatly benefited the managed investment companies by restoring their respectability. This factor, plus growing incomes and renewed interest in the stock market, made for rapid growth in investment company assets in the post-World War II period (Table 24–1). In 1960, over 85 percent of investment company assets were placed in common stocks (Table 24–2). These funds have thus become important suppliers of equity capital to the financial markets (Table 24–4), but mainly to blue-chip firms. Evidence seems to indicate that buyers of investment company shares prefer this quality concentration.[38]

Pension Funds

Although some private, self-administered pension funds existed during the interwar period, these institutions reached importance only after World War II, when the necessary socioeconomic forces existed. Political economy, rather than economic theory, better explains the growth of pension funds. From 1950 to 1960 pension funds more than quadrupled and now stand at over $28 billion in assets.[39]

Several factors have combined to foster this rapid growth of pension funds in the postwar era. Perhaps the largest of these is the growing "security consciousness" of Americans. In addition, the whole area of pension funds was determined by the courts to be within the sphere of collective bargaining and companies were less prone to fight these funds, since they could be designed to bind employees to them and reduce costly turnover. The special tax treatment (employer contributions are tax deductible, fund income is tax free, and benefits are not taxed until received by employees) also contributed to the growth of these funds.

Regulations of pension funds place no legal prescription on investment of funds. Fund investment policies are guided, instead, by an awareness that the rapid growth of cash inflows under present contracts reduces liquidity needs and by a desire of employers to cut pension costs by increasing fund yields.[40] Thus, pension funds tend to keep most of their assets in corporate securities with a sharply growing proportion of these funds in equities

[38] See Gies, Mayer, and Ettin, *op. cit.*

[39] U.S. Securities and Exchange Commission, *Statistical Series*, Release 1750, May 3, 1961.

[40] Funding is not required to have a pension plan. The fund is only a method of helping the company pay benefits and benefits may not be limited to this source. Indeed, most plans are of a fixed benefit type so that if the fund is not sufficient to pay benefits, the employer must pay the difference.

(Tables 24–2 through 24–4). In 1960, at book value, slightly over 30 percent of fund assets were in common stocks (44 percent of assets at market value) and 50 percent of fund inflows were used to acquire common stocks.[41] Indeed, pension funds are now the largest single institutional investor in common stocks, and since 1958 have bought more stock than any other investor group.[42]

IMPLICATIONS OF HISTORICAL DEVELOPMENTS

Several important factors seem to be evident from this sketch of historical developments:

Most American financial intermediaries developed to meet a demand not being adequately fulfilled by other intermediaries because of regulations, policies, institutional influences on the source-of-funds side, or simple lack of business acumen by other institutions. Finance companies and mutual savings banks, for example, grew up for a combination of all these reasons. Other intermediaries, such as savings and loan associations, grew up to service an area already being served, but did so more efficiently or aggressively. Indeed, demand taken alone cannot completely explain the relative positions of several intermediaries. Life insurance companies, savings and loan associations, and investment companies worked aggressively to develop latent demands. Institutions such as pension funds, on the other hand, had to await the proper sociopolitical, as well as economic, developments before they could grow to importance.

Although demand factors are, of course, a necessary prerequisite for the growth—relative and absolute—of financial intermediaries, it seems that entrepreneurial aggressiveness in spotting gaps of both a qualitative and quantitative nature has played a crucial role in the development of intermediaries. Mutual savings banks, for example, lost out in the competitive race to commercial banks and savings and loan associations owing to a lack of aggressiveness and, as a result, decreased in relative importance. Similarly, commercial banks tended to become conservative with success and failed to take advantage of opportunities—for example, in the mortgage, savings depository, and consumer credit fields. Legal restrictions played a part here, but management policies seemed to keep bankers away from anything that was not in their traditional bailiwick. "Traditional" policies of banks were *probably* as important as disadvantageous regulations in the competitive battle with other financial institutions. Evidence is available that many times commercial banks just did not *try* to compete. Thus, if economic forces and legal prohibitions were the parents of savings banks, savings and loan associations, and finance companies, commercial banks were surely the midwife. It is also interesting to note that the commercial

[41] U.S. Securities and Exchange Commission, *op. cit.*
[42] *Ibid.* In 1960, they purchased 52 percent of new equity issues.

bank midwife became jealous with the growth of these offspring and has done its best to contain them. For example, banks are now the major grantor of consumer instalment credit and are a not-insignificant factor in the mortgage and savings depository markets (see Tables 24–3 and 24–4). Imitation is the sincerest form of flattery, and bank observations of profit and safety in these markets led them into areas that they once ignored.

Thus, the present financial system is not a child of caprice but grew up to meet the needs of the economy. Indeed, the financial system has been fairly responsive to long-run real demands. While the financial system's short-run flexibility and sensitivity to changing patterns of demand is much less than perfect, the degree to which legal regulations have hampered the creation of an optimal financial system is not known. Surely they have hampered flexibility, but the record is here interpreted to mean that the American financial system has met the real demands of the economy—often by the development of new institutions when regulations, as well as policies, stood in the way of existing intermediaries. While it is not possible to ignore the influence of regulations and operating policies on fund allocation via financial intermediaries, it is more important to realize that such factors have, in some cases, been *overcome* by the financial system. Regulations have been and are unfair and discriminatory and do, without question, negatively influence the reaction of the financial system to real forces—not only by prohibiting or limiting certain asset purchases, but also by helping to "sponsor" certain institutions (e.g., federally chartered savings and loan associations and the inception of regulated small loan companies). The point is that these problems are not as serious as they look at first. Regulations may be noneconomic but the system has bridged gaps and jumped barriers and as a result has worked fairly well as individuals and institutions seek ways out of the financial confines in which they find themselves. The record seems to indicate that if this basic dynamism by economic participants continues, then—from the point of view of an efficient allocation of resources—there is little to fear from "poor" regulations and conservative and inflexible operating policies.

Another point that is indicated by this historical review is that financial intermediaries, taken as a whole, form a financial system straining to take funds from surplus units and put them to use in deficit units. In fulfilling this function they are in competition with each other on both the source-of-funds side and on the use-of-funds side. Even though the historical evolution of financial intermediaries has produced a substantial differentiation in the products available for the portfolio of surplus units, competition in a rivalry sense still exists. The ability of each intermediary to merchandise its product in competition with all the rest determines which intermediary has funds to invest, but this ability is intimately conditioned by the earnings the intermediaries are able to get on these funds.

On the use-of-funds side, intermediaries are overlappingly competitive in most markets (Tables 24–3 and 24–4). However, there also tends to be specialization by American financial institutions—fostered by regulation, policy, or the nature of the source of funds. For example, as Tables 24–3 and 24–4 indicate, among financial institutions commercial banks are the largest investors in state and local as well as federal government securities; life insurance companies in corporate bonds; pension funds and investment companies in corporate equities; and, while savings banks, savings and loan associations, life insurance companies, and commercial banks are all major investors in mortgages, savings and loan associations dominate in the acquisition of new mortgages. Of course, these generalizations ignore submarket concentrations and qualitative specializations. Examples of these are the differences in credit risks accepted in consumer paper between finance companies and banks, and emphasis on VA and FHA mortgages by life insurance companies while savings and loan associations emphasize conventional mortgages.

Even with these tendencies toward specialization, there is no one financial market in which an intermediary faces no competition from at least one other intermediary (Tables 24–3 and 24–4). However, four intermediaries tend to limit their portfolio accumulations to one major type of asset: finance companies to consumer instalment paper, savings and loan associations to mortgages, investment companies to corporates, and pension funds also to corporates (Table 24–2). Of these, however, the suppliers of funds to finance companies and investment companies choose this concentration and it is probable that one of the major reasons for growth in savings and loan associations is their mortgage concentration.

Several possibilities follow from this specialization in portfolio composition, some good and others bad from the point of view of efficient allocation of resources. On the positive side, such specialization may make intermediaries more safe by making them expert buyers in one narrow area —an economy of scale that should improve resource allocation. On the negative side, it may make the specializing institution vulnerable to shifts in the market in which it concentrates its lending; it may foster misallocation of resources by the intermediaries that aggressively gather savings and then specialize in their use of funds; and it may make it more difficult for the new firm, industry, or market to obtain adequate financing.

I do not believe, from the point of view of an efficient allocation of resources, that intermediary asset specialization is a real problem. If an institution continues specialization in a particular market that is of declining importance, it will tend to decline in importance itself. In addition, if its lending market can no longer meet the market test for funds, and the institution stays with that market, it simply cannot continue for long to attract new funds. Moreover, and most important, there is ample evidence that if new, real, profitable demands for resources develop, a new institution will grow up to service this demand if old ones do not do so.

25.

The Changing Structure
of Financial Institutions

MARVIN E. ROZEN

Recent changes in the structure of our financial institutions raise issues of considerable interest. Heightened concern with problems of economic growth has led to a reappraisal of the process whereby financial institutions are affecting, and being affected by, the development of the economy. Shifts in the relative importance of financial institutions have raised new problems for economic control policies. Difficult issues of equity emerge in connection with the impact of various kinds of regulation on the circumstances of the different financial institutions. A broad reconsideration of the causes of change in our financial structure should help place these complex issues in proper perspective.

In brief, I shall argue as follows: large and significant changes, involving great shifts in the relative importance of the different kinds of financial institutions, have occurred in. our financial structure. For the most part, these changes reflect the powerful real forces of variation in patterns of expenditure and in the acquisition of financial assets by households and businesses. At the same time, however, environmental constraints of an organizational, asset-liability, and regulatory nature, through their effect

Reprinted from the *Quarterly Review of Economics and Business*, Vol. II, No. 4, November 1962, pp. 69–80, by permission of the publisher, the Bureau of Economic and Business Research, University of Illinois, Urbana, Illinois.

on the competitive responses of financial institutions, contribute to shaping our financial structure. The evolution of the structure of such institutions is thus marked by continuous interaction between the forces of economic change and the reactive capabilities of the various institutions. In a sense, change in financial structure is an index of accommodation to processes of economic transformation.

CHANGES IN THE RELATIVE IMPORTANCE OF FINANCIAL INSTITUTIONS

Table 25–1 reveals the extent of postwar change in the financial structure in terms of the share of total assets held by each kind of financial institution; Table 25–2 provides some historical perspective. The explanation of these broad movements will be deferred to the next section. Relative positions based on asset rankings are something less than a complete indicator of importance and power. Assets are, of course, not the same thing as net worth, and there are substantial differences in the nature of the liabilities offsetting the assets of the various financial institutions. Moreover, measurement of importance in terms of assets overlooks the impact of those types of institutions having small asset holdings but nonetheless great influence over the flow of financial investment. Investment and mortgage bankers, brokers, and financial counselors have a disproportionate weight in financial markets relative to their size as measured by assets. Partly this is because of their position in advising actual holders of financial assets and,

TABLE 25–1

Percentage Shares of Total Financial Assets Held by Private Financial Institutions, 1945-60[a]

Institution	1945	1946	1947	1948	1949	1950	1951	1952	1953	1954	1955	1956	1957	1958	1959	1960
Commercial banks	61.20	57.79	56.70	54.71	52.73	51.65	51.16	50.00	48.25	46.73	44.60	43.45	42.58	41.97	40.34	39.35
Mutual savings banks	7.30	8.10	8.11	8.19	8.14	7.87	7.64	7.61	7.69	7.63	7.56	7.63	7.66	7.55	7.30	7.13
Savings and loan associations	3.59	4.29	4.70	5.07	5.38	5.76	6.13	6.73	7.47	8.13	9.00	9.71	10.34	10.87	11.76	12.42
Credit unions	0.17	0.22	0.25	0.28	0.30	0.35	0.39	0.45	0.51	0.58	0.66	0.74	0.81	0.85	0.93	0.96
Life insurance	18.75	20.30	20.72	21.25	21.63	21.42	21.27	21.06	21.21	20.95	20.77	20.85	20.90	20.32	20.11	19.85
Other insurance	3.89	4.20	4.49	4.79	5.19	5.30	5.38	5.48	5.59	5.82	5.89	5.77	5.56	5.67	5.80	5.69
Private pension funds	0.99	1.22	1.37	1.56	1.70	2.07	2.39	2.67	3.02	3.30	3.62	3.97	4.39	4.63	4.97	5.46
Finance companies	0.86	1.40	1.79	2.28	2.61	3.13	3.15	3.45	3.74	3.59	4.50	4.54	4.61	4.19	4.57	4.86
Investment companies	0.56	0.57	0.58	0.60	0.72	0.84	0.98	1.18	1.17	1.60	1.90	2.08	1.91	2.66	2.99	3.02
Security brokers and dealers	2.67	1.92	1.29	1.28	1.60	1.62	1.51	1.36	1.34	1.65	1.51	1.27	1.23	1.31	1.23	1.24

[a] Totals will not add to 100 percent because of rounding.

Source: Federal Reserve Board, flow-of-funds data.

TABLE 25–2

Percentage Distribution of Assets of Private Financial Institutions, 1900, 1929, 1945, and 1958[a]

Institution	1900	1929	1945	1958
Commercial banks	52.9	41.8	56.5	39.5
Demand deposit business[b]	47.3	29.5	45.8	28.7
Savings and time deposit business[b]	5.6	12.3	10.7	10.8
Mutual savings banks	12.7	6.2	6.0	6.2
Savings and loan associations	2.6	4.7	3.1	9.1
Credit unions			0.1	0.7
Finance, mortgage, and loan companies	1.1	2.1	0.7	3.4
Life insurance companies	9.0	11.0	15.8	17.8
Other insurance companies	2.6	3.5	3.3	5.0
Private pension funds		0.3	0.8	4.1
Investment companies[c]		4.7	1.3	3.3
Personal trust departments[d]	15.9	18.9	10.2	9.3
Security brokers and dealers	3.2	6.7	2.1	1.6

[a] Details may not add to totals because of rounding.
[b] Allocated in proportion of deposit liabilities.
[c] Includes investment holding companies.
[d] Includes common trust funds.

Source: The Report of the Commission on Money and Credit, *Money and Credit: Their Influence on Jobs, Prices, and Growth,* © 1961, p. 155. By permission of Prentice-Hall, Inc., Englewood Cliffs, N.J.

in general, in widening and broadening participation of others in financial markets so as to reduce the share of financial institutions; in this role they may be termed "knowledge intermediaries." Partly it is due to the importance of turnover—financial institutions differ greatly in their activity and those whose portfolios are constantly changing are bound to have a greater effect.

Another deficiency of any table of shares of total assets held by different types of financial institutions is the neglect of intra-institutional financial change. First, there are likely to be, over time, significant variations in the internal interrelationships within any particular kind of financial institutions, e.g., changes in the number and size distribution of firms. Thus a commercial banking system dominated by large branch systems and giant unit banks would behave differently from one composed of small unit banks. (Changes in internal structure, moreover, are likely to coincide with shifts in relative importance because the accelerated, or decelerated, industry growth such shifts imply also creates the most favorable environment for rearranging interfirm relationships.) Second, although names remain the same, the operational behavior of financial institutions is likely to show considerable flexibility. Indeed, one of the most significant changes in financial structure is the extent to which financial institutions are capable of internal regeneration—taking on new functions and sloughing off old. With these qualifications in mind, let us turn to the explanation of the changing financial structure.

DETERMINANTS OF FINANCIAL STRUCTURE

Changes in the financial structure can be explained in terms of three factors: (1) the basic supply-demand dispositions underlying the various financial markets and the real forces (preference shifts, resource availabilities, technological changes) producing them, (2) the specific environmental conditions surrounding particular markets and financial institutions, and (3) the competitive responses of financial institutions themselves.

Supply-Demand Forces

Fundamental supply-demand factors determine the kinds of claims economic units are prepared to issue and the kinds they wish to hold. This is highly relevant to the position of the different financial institutions because it affects directly the growth rates in different financial markets and indirectly how these markets are shared. If the public wants more housing, the supply of residential mortgages will rise relative to other financial assets; yields on mortgages will increase relative to other yields; institutions specializing in mortgages will be able to attract more funds because of their ability to pay more for their use; and thus they will tend to grow faster. Similarly, if the public becomes more thrifty, thrift institutions will expand at a more rapid rate and those markets in which they employ most of their funds will also grow faster.

Thus the growth and diffusion of real income has led, on the one hand, to the large increase in thrift, thereby benefiting savings institutions, and on the other hand and more recently, to the rise of the small investor via mutual fund participation. The increasing concern for security has sustained the position of insurance companies, and aided by other factors, has contributed to the rapid expansion of pension funds. The greater importance of consumer "investment" in housing and durables combined with changing public attitudes toward personal indebtedness has led to the growth of consumer credit institutions. Private placement, increasing reliance on internal sources of funds, lease-back arrangements, and trade credit extensions have changed the pattern of corporate finance. The expanded role of the federal government in deposit insurance, mortgage guarantees, monetary control, and the maintenance of full employment has greatly influenced the behavior of economic units in their financial asset and liability choices. All of these changes and more have left a heavy imprint on the structure of our financial institutions. The long-run effect of these broad economic forces should be emphasized; at the same time, their secular nature permits institutional flexibility and adaptiveness to offset adverse trends. To what extent, however, the different financial institutions will possess these needed qualities depends to a considerable degree on precisely those organizational, asset-liability, and regulatory changes which are now to be discussed.

Institutional Differences

There is a clear line of influence leading from specific institutional traits to the reactive capabilities of the various types of financial institutions. This section will focus on three distinct but related kinds of institutional differences: organizational, asset-liability, and regulatory.

ORGANIZATIONAL STRUCTURE

(1) The legal form of enterprise will vary both within any single type of financial institution and between different types. The distinction between the corporate and mutual form is perhaps the most obvious and, because of the taxation controversy, has been commented upon most extensively. Mutual savings institutions were allowed to accumulate out of current earnings a reserve fund of up to 12 percent of their deposits without such earnings being liable for income tax. Because mutual savings institutions have experienced rapid growth in their liabilities (deposits) relative to earnings, their tax liability has been exceedingly small. As a result, commercial banks, which are treated differently in this respect, assert that they are at a competitive disadvantage because of the more favorable tax treatment of mutual institutions.[1] If mutual institutions were taxed as heavily as commercial banks, it is argued, they could not afford to pay higher rates on savings, and thus they would grow appreciably slower and commercial banks appreciably faster. Likewise the impact of tax considerations on portfolio choice, by inducing institutions having large tax liabilities to look for tax-exempt securities and capital gains, also affect the growth possibilities and patterns of market participation of the several financial institutions.

Other distinctions of legal form also affect business decisions. The

---

[1] Briefly, the justification for differential tax treatment lies in the theory that the reserve fund accumulated by mutual institutions provides a cushion, analogous to the role played by capital and surplus in a corporate organization, to protect the depositors against asset depreciation. In practice the distinction has evolved from the desire to aid mutual institutions because of their origins as self-help and cooperative undertakings. The differential treatment has been a serious bone of contention and perhaps the best safeguards might be in a prepay insurance premium scheme which takes care of losses after they occur instead of attempting to protect against possible loss by building up a fund before the event. Recent legislation, however, has produced a compromise formula which will increase somewhat the tax liabilities of mutual thrift institutions.

persistence of closely held corporations and family- and/or individual-dominated firms in many financial markets reflects the influence of personal service and personal contacts in highly localized markets. Recent gains by financial holding companies and captive finance companies are likewise reminders that new forms of legal organization can confer distinct advantages on their users, and thus can be vehicles for increasing one's market share.

(2) Spatial and locational differences are important in determining the ability of financial institutions to react flexibly.[2] Some intermediaries are organized along nationwide lines with numerous offices; others are local one-office institutions limited to and serving a single market; still others may be limited in their physical location but nevertheless function in a geographically dispersed market. Some draw funds locally and lend nationally; others draw funds nationally and lend locally. The changing character of local markets and the restrictions on the mobility of some financial institutions tend to work to the disadvantage of those dependent on local conditions.

Differing rates of regional growth and the resultant patterns of regional savings surpluses and deficits magnify these basic spatial differences. Financial institutions in areas of surplus depend for their expansion on their ability to overcome the immobility of capital; thus mutual savings banks in eastern states have welcomed the development of nationally acceptable mortgage instruments. Financial institutions in deficit areas are handicapped by persistent shortages of funds, and their growth depends on successfully finding external sources of funds. Accordingly, savings and loan associations in California advertise nationally and employ brokers to turn up funds.

(3) Closely allied to locational differences are entry conditions. Here, too, regulation is all-important. For instance, a restrictive chartering policy coupled with an easier branching policy can lead to preemptive branching, thereby making entry much more difficult for outsiders as compared with expansion by existing firms. Another important distinction may be found in the ability of financial institutions which depend on salesmen to enter new markets by expanding their selling operations easily and quickly as, for example, mutual funds and insurance companies have done. In this connection, the low incremental cost of loading additional kinds of financial services on to an existing sales force creates considerable pressure for also expanding into related fields. Finally, as a result of high short-term interest rates and vigorous activity by "knowledge intermediaries," material changes have occurred in the market for large, short-term balances. Wherever non-holding intermediaries are most active, they will be a force widening mar-

---

[2] As is true of many other organizational differences, in part they reflect the impact of regulatory control. Differences in regulatory treatment, however, are sufficiently important and distinctive to merit separate discussion in a later section.

kets and pushing forward the entry of outsiders, since their earnings are very sensitive to the volume of operations.[3]

(4) There are significant relative and absolute size differences. Absolute size matters because, on the one hand, substantial economies of scale are attainable for financial institutions, and on the other hand, participation in many financial submarkets is a function of size alone. For the latter reason, relative size within a single kind of financial institution is also a determinant of submarket participation, and contributes thereby to the establishment of a more finely drawn division of labor. The combination of size differences and economies of scale is very conducive to mergers, as is quite apparent, for instance, in commercial banking. Size disparities raise some especially acute problems in regulated industries because of the difficulties of framing rules of conduct for a nonhomogeneous population. Likewise, great size differences, as in commercial banking, make it very difficult for industry-wide organizations to speak with one voice; the internal conflicts spill over into public disagreement on issues affecting the industry.[4] Again this is much more significant for a regulated industry because of its great dependence upon the actions of legislative and public bodies.

(5) Still another important difference has to do with whether financial institutions are engaged primarily in providing financial services or in pure intermediation. The public's demand for financial assets is of a dual nature. In some cases, for example, checking accounts, insurance-security protection, and, partly, thrift, a service is purchased and considerations of yield are either absent or distinctly secondary. In pure intermediation, yield dominates all else. Financial assets in which yield dominates are likely to be more sensitive reflectors of market pressures, whereas financial assets acquired through service transactions will be partly insulated from market forces and will reflect, to a greater extent, slowly changing public attitudes toward the particular service provided. There is a mechanism operating, it seems, as follows: pure intermediaries tend to specialize in areas of most rapid growth (mortgages, consumer credit) and obtain their funds by offering a yield inducement to potential suppliers. The rising demand for the

---

[3] The expansion of brokerage activity always confronts asset-holding intermediaries with a difficult choice; in many cases they can also engage in brokerage, but only at the expense of infringing on their more normal activities. Thus if they react, they may jeopardize their usual role; if they remain passive, they find their market share being nibbled away. Another layer of complexity is added when it is realized that many broker-type activities perforce have large inventory requirements (either because the brokers are traders too or because of industry practice) and therefore have large demands for short-term finance. Thus it is not unusual to find a situation where, say, money brokers are competing with commercial banks, and at the same time are dependent on banks for carrying their inventories. In such cases, brokers appreciate the diversity in commercial banking.

[4] I submit that savings and loan associations lobby much more effectively than commercial banks precisely because less glaring size disparities lead to a much greater degree of internal unity.

commodity to be financed causes a widening spread between rates paid and yields that can be obtained and thereby provides pure intermediaries with both the means and the incentive to compete successfully for funds by raising the price they are willing to pay. They pass on, as it were, the public's increased desire for particular commodities in the form of increased demand and higher rates for money to accommodate this primary market shift. Service-oriented intermediaries, on the other hand, possess more steady and assured sources of funds, obtained by providing their primary service. They seek to place this reliable stream wherever yields appear most attractive, subject of course to statutory restraints and (slowly changing) customary portfolio practices. Thus some financial institutions have money to invest, and within given operating constraints they search for the most profitable outlets. Others have found or specialize in growing and favorable markets and seek funds to employ therein by offering yield inducements based on the profitability of the ultimate outlet.

This distinction has an important implication for the growth rates of the two types of intermediaries. In times of excess demand for money, the advantage lies with those who stimulate and induce rather than those who passively accept, unless, as with pension funds, the passive type of intermediary has struck a new and rich vein of consumer demand. In times when demand slacks off, the passive intermediaries, one expects, gain at the expense of the active ones. The explanation for this lies in the preference structure of the public with respect to financial assets. The passive intermediaries cater to some fairly basic demands of the public for security, insurance, checking services, and the like. The flow of money to these intermediaries, therefore, is not likely to be as income-sensitive as is the flow to specialist and risk-bearing intermediaries. Nor, likewise, is there much scope for yield blandishments as a means of increasing the flow of the public's savings into their hands. As a consequence, when yields rise, the more volatile and spread-sensitive intermediaries are activated and start positively bidding for funds. The rise in rates deflects funds to them, and other financial institutions must await the day when the return they offer will once again appear attractive.

(6) Another difference to be found among financial institutions lies in the character of the other side of their market. Some financial intermediaries predominantly serve consumers; others deal mostly with nonfinancial enterprises; and some deal in large part with other financial intermediaries. Some financial institutions of course deal with all three, either obtaining money from households and supplying it to business and government, or obtaining funds from, and providing funds for, whomever they can. Transactions in consumer markets are likely to be smaller in size, more diffuse, and less organized; transactions with business and government are of larger magnitudes, and on the whole the bargaining parties are more evenly matched. One important development is the captive consumer market—the tendency

to deal with ultimate consumers with respect to the financing of durables and housing through the selling agent of the particular commodity. This will affect relative growth by enabling some financial institutions to have access to rapidly growing consumer credit markets which would otherwise be excluded from such markets because of lack of direct contact with consumers.

This catalogue of organizational differences should not be considered exhaustive; for some purposes a much finer breakdown is necessary. For instance, variations exist in willingness to bear risk, engage in extensive selling effort, and innovate. Enough has been said, however, to make the general point that organizational dissimilarities do have a strong influence in determining the reaction of the various financial institutions to changing economic conditions.

ASSET-LIABILITY DIFFERENCES

The financial structure of the institutions themselves is of obvious importance, defining as it does the nature of intermediary activity. Intermediaries exhibit great differences in their sources of funds. Some have predominantly quick liabilities; others can predict with actuarial certainty the long-range translation of their liabilities into actual claims. Some rely on highly predictable and regular sources; others attract funds in extremely irregular movements, and their efforts to smooth the flow are conspicuously unsuccessful. Intermediaries differ greatly in ability to control the inflow of funds by their own actions; some can be very adept at matching flow to opportunity for use; others are more prone to feast or famine, and not always at appropriate times. Some rely predominantly on the general public as a source; others have specialized and fewer sources; still others depend on other financial intermediaries to a significant extent. Some, as we have seen, obtain their funds on a strictly yield basis; others receive funds in connection with the provision of financial services.

Likewise, there is great variation in the asset holdings of financial institutions—owing in no small measure to the need for matching assets with their pattern of liabilities. Some intermediaries must prize liquidity very highly; for others, this is not an important consideration. Portfolios differ widely in maturity structure and in riskiness. Some intermediates confine their holdings to a single major type; others hold a wide variety of financial assets. Readiness to shift from one kind of asset to another varies greatly among intermediaries. There are correspondingly great differences in unit size of transactions. Thus, on both sides of the balance sheet, financial institutions will be subject to differential constraints arising out of dissimilarities in the structure of their assets and liabilites.

REGULATORY TREATMENT

The third, and final, factor affecting the responses of financial institutions is differences in degree and kind of regulation and in the ability to influence such regulation. As indicated in the discussion of organizational structure, regulation is significant and pervasive in establishing what financial institutions will and will not do. Now, however, the focus is on the general problems associated with regulation rather than on its specific incidence. In part, the impact of regulation is due to its inability to keep pace with a rapidly changing economy. Moreover, the regulation of financial institutions has been exceedingly detailed. No doubt the fiduciary responsibilities of financial institutions have motivated such extreme care, but nevertheless it has made for rigidity and thereby has greatly circumscribed intermediary freedom of action. Economic change erodes specific regulation at a much faster rate than regulation framed along more general lines and allowing more supervisory discretion. The diversity of regulatory authority is another factor which produces large variations in the scope and freedom of intermediary action. The same type of financial institutions can be, and different kinds of financial institutions are, subject to different regulatory authorities. Some intermediaries may be regulated strictly; others may be subject to merely nominal and perfunctory regulation, or to none at all. Enforcement can be sporadic or continuous. The aims of regulation vary from maintaining fiduciary integrity to achieving credit control objectives. Thus differences are found in regulatory treatment as well as in the statutory framework of regulation.

Equally important is the ability to influence regulation and regulators, for not only existing regulation and its interpretation are relevant, but also the possibilities for changing regulations and for getting sympathetic treatment from regulatory authority. The preceding discussion has suggested that the erosion of regulation by economic change makes revision imperative. In this connection, the power structure within the financial community plays a large and significant role. The size and quality of legal and lobbying staffs, the importance and geographical representation of the particular intermediary, and its relative size will determine what kind of hearing legislators and regulators will give to requests from the several financial institutions. I do not mean to imply that the large and the powerful will always have their way; even less do I wish to suggest that any hint of wrongdoing or improper influence is involved. I simply mean that, all things considered, any regulated industry operating within some basic statutory framework will continually run up against complex problems arising out of this special status; and the more resources available for pleading its case before regulatory and legislative bodies, the better. For similar reasons, a class of financial institution with a high degree of internal cohesion among its constituent firms will be better placed to achieve legislative or regulatory reform than one which has great internal divisions.

Reactive Capabilities

Differences in organizational and financial structure and in regulatory treatment thus determine the nature and scope of market participation, and when set in the context of rapid and uneven economic change, play a large role in shaping the responses of the several financial institutions. Not all financial institutions are equally well placed in their ability to adapt and alter their mode of operation consequent to unfavorable change, and naturally, any particular economic change is unlikely to have an equal and uniform impact on all financial institutions. Where economic change has an adverse effect, an attempt is of course made to eliminate those factors responsible for the competitive disability. Such a response is made more difficult for some than for others, however, because rigidities and immobilities of organizational and financial structure and lags in regulatory change are also not distributed uniformly.

In this way nonuniformities, both in the incidence of economic change on financial institutions and in their ability to respond, affect relative positions; variation in ability to react, within broad limits laid down by the direction of economic change, thus determines the relative situations of the different financial institutions. True, all firms find it difficult to make structural adjustments and are subject to economic change; in these respects, financial institutions are not different. Luck is always pleasant, change hard, and resiliency, flexibility, and adaptability are the guarantors of competitive success. Regulatory restraint, however, places financial institutions in a different category; to the extent that regulation impairs the maneuverability of intermediaries in a nonuniform way, economic change provides opportunities for some but harms others. For this reason, regulation must be conscious of the equity issues it raises.

SPECIFIC EXAMPLES

Having asserted that organizational, asset-liability, and regulatory differences affect the ability of financial institutions to react to economic change, perhaps it may prove fruitful to trace some of the ways in which our financial structure has evolved and the specific reasons which account for this pattern of development. Institutions which have experienced enormous growth in the postwar period include such different types as mortgage companies, pension funds, mutual funds, and credit unions. The explanations for the rise of these institutions are correspondingly diverse.

Mortgage companies have mushroomed as a joint result of the housing boom and the impact of federal intervention upon the nature of the mortgage instrument. Federal underwriting and standardization have produced a security which can attract funds from afar, and the crucial role of originating and servicing mortgages has been the necessary complement to increasing the mobility of capital of institutional lenders. Mortgage companies were ideally suited to perform these functions. Other possible developments were for traditional, local mortgage lenders to expand their originating and servicing departments and for large institutional lenders to integrate forward instead of relying on local contacts. Although some progress was made in each of these directions, it was not on the scale that attended the growth of mortgage companies. There are several reasons for this: mortgage holders face potential conflict-of-interest problems if they also act, in effect, as brokers of mortgages; local mortgage holders may be reluctant to send mortgages outside the locality because of the consequences for positions of local market power if they contribute to the extension of the market; commercial bank holders of mortgages are also the chief sources of finance of mortgage companies themselves, and therefore may feel constrained not to compete with their customers or may believe that the arrangements reflect an agreeable division of labor; local mortgage holders traditionally prefer low-risk conventional mortgages, whereas servicing and origination are largely in government-underwritten mortgages; finally, custom plays a role —local mortgage holders conceive of their job as getting and holding mortgages, not servicing them. Forward integration, on the other hand, has been deterred largely by the legal complexities of doing business in the different states and the complex and nonuniform legal environment surrounding the mortgage contract. In addition, relationships with mortgage companies have simplified the problem of portfolio shifts and irregular savings flows with respect to regular sustained mortgage lending. In essence, the problem of reconciling the desire for mortgages with the flow of mortgage money has been shifted, for a price, onto the backs of the specialized institution.

The evolution of the mortgage company, however, is a continuing process, and it is still too early to see where it will end. As Goldsmith has written:

> Will mortgage companies remain essentially an ancillary institution, an originating and service organization for institutional investors in government-insured and -guaranteed home mortgages, using short-term bank credit to carry a temporary inventory of mortgages already spoken for by institutional clients? Or will they, by adding operations characteristic of some companies prior to the days of mortgage insurance, broaden into a more diversified and independent type of institution—a sort of general mortgage dealer and underwriter—handling mortgages of all types, placing them with individual as well as institutional investors, and carrying a general

inventory of uncommitted mortgages for sale? Are they likely, as well, by expansion or amalgamation, to increase their general real estate operations blurring further the distinction between mortgage companies and real estate investment, brokerage, and development companies? Finally, will they remain within their generally local spheres of operation, or will many of them develop, as a few have, into organizations working to a considerable extent through branch offices on a regional or even a nationwide scale?[5]

The growth of the other financial institutions mentioned can also be explained by specific circumstances surrounding each. Pension fund growth reflects, basically, the desire for security among industrial workers and the ability to achieve this end through collective bargaining. Mutual fund growth is based on the spread of income and wealth, the consequent diversification of relatively small savers into more risky fields, and vigorous selling activities. In both cases growth was largely a response to and implementation of strong underlying real trends which demanded a novel kind of financial institution rather than outright extension or adaptation of existing ones. But though new financial institutions took root and grew, at the same time the management of pension funds and the creation of mutual funds, and the provision of investment advisory services to both, became grounds on which existing kinds of financial institutions actively competed. The growth of credit unions reflects a somewhat different emphasis. Although consumer credit too has undergone a rapid increase, the improvement of the position of credit unions is due, on the one hand, to the ability to take advantage of and undercut the relatively high consumer credit rates prevailing, and on the other hand, to the natural associational ties on which the movement was founded. Competitive opportunities plus unique natural advantages were important factors in the more rapid expansion of credit unions. In all four cases, the growth of the financial institution reflected the strong real trends at work. On the whole, regulation was minimal and exercised little constraint.

Another institution which has shown a rapid advance in the postwar period has been the savings and loan association. In this case, growth has been influenced to a greater extent by very favorable regulatory action. Savings and loan associations have successfully striven, in recent years, for regulatory action on participation mortgages, permission to engage in site-development finance, controls over premiums and giveaways, restriction of funds obtained through brokers, and 90 percent loan-to-value ratios for mortgages. Regulatory authorities can thus be sensitive to, as well as obstacles in the way of, the need for change. Favorable regulatory treatment is, however, still only part of the story. The housing boom and the pull of

[5] Raymond W. Goldsmith, in the Foreword of Saul B. Klaman, *The Postwar Rise of Mortgage Companies*, Occasional Paper No. 60 (New York: National Bureau of Economic Research, 1959), p. vii.

favorable interest rate differentials supply the rest. The former emphasizes our dependence on real trends; the latter reflects aggressive competition and the imposition of interest-rate ceilings on their chief competitors.

The evolution of commercial banking over a generation of bankers is another piece of substantial evidence showing adaptability and flexibility on the part of financial intermediaries. The growth of and emphasis on consumer banking, both in searching for deposits and in consumer loan activity, the rise of interim real estate financing, the refinement of time-deposit certificates, the spread of term-lending, and the expansion of bank services in general add up to an extraordinary amount of change compressed within a short period of time. Here, too, regulatory authority has been both permissive and restrictive. For instance, under the press of wartime circumstance and postwar expansion, supervisory authorities have allowed risk asset-capital ratios to rise. On the other hand, the requirements of monetary control have undoubtedly damped the growth of demand deposits, and ceilings on savings deposit rates have weakened the competitive position of banks in relation to other thrift institutions. The share of financial assets held by banks would have fallen much further if banks had not adjusted their activities to such a great extent.

Finally, consideration of various proposals for changes in the legal and regulatory framework of financial institutions provides some insights into the forces working to produce structural variation. Insurance company pressure for the variable annuity, changes in the legal and tax status of real estate syndicates, central mortgage banking facilities, the packaging of mortgages for the pension fund market, the federal chartering of mutual savings banks, and the question of the tax-exempt status for state and local securities have been and are live issues and portents of change to come. Such healthy ferment is hardly a sign of ossification; yet it can also be seen to what extent change depends upon the ability to persuade regulatory authority of its desirability. As indicated earlier, the importance of this factor makes the evolution of financial structure distinctive.

CONCLUSIONS

In its broad dimensions the changing structure of financial institutions reveals a familiar picture. Within the general constraints of institutional and regulatory differences, the force of economic change shapes the pattern of development. The organizational, asset-liability, and regulatory differences among financial institutions provide the basis for their varied responses. Thus the impact of exogenous economic change is reflected mainly in intra-financial institution rivalry and shifts in relative importance. Our financial institutions tend to have a small impact on economic growth itself precisely because they can be so flexible and accommodating in the aggregate. In the

process, however, the shape of this aggregate undergoes recognizable transformation as the direction of real change and institutional adaptability
jointly determine its structural evolution. This result is not as startling as
might appear at first glance. After all, it is supremely important to emphasize, as Warren L. Smith has done, that "the basic function of financial
institutions is the mobilization of the financial resources of the economy in
support of economic activity." But the implications of this process for the
changing shape of our financial institutions have not been adequately realized. The extent to which our financial structure changes form is a measure
of both the capabilities and resourcefulness of our financial institutions
when faced with challenges to institutional survival and growth and their
limited power to affect significantly the real growth path of our economy.

Two important corollaries derive from this argument. The first is that
to the extent that our financial control measures are predicated on a restricted and limited view of the proper area for their exercise, that part of
our financial machinery not covered will be sure to work against the purposes of control. Furthermore, the very changes in the structure of our financial institutions will undermine our ability to control because these
changes are themselves an offset to our control measures. The second
corollary is an issue of equity: differences in regulatory treatment, as we
have seen, affect the competitive position of financial institutions. Thus it is
necessary to review our regulatory procedures with a view to deciding between the conflicting considerations of equity and effective control. Both
equity and efficiency are likely to be served by more comprehensive (but
less detailed) regulation applied more consistently to all financial institutions.

26.

Prospects for Private
Financial Institutions

HARRY G. GUTHMANN

No group of private institutions has a more pervasive influence on the stability and growth potential of our economy than do our private financial institutions, which affect not only the affairs of companies to whom they supply funds, but also the vigor, the competitiveness, and the stability of the economy as a whole. Thus, their activities are important to all businessmen. An excessive willingness on the part of these financial institutions to assume risks can stimulate business but may lead to instability. Institutional inadequacies, on the other hand, can encourage greater government activity and may lead to the uneconomic allocation of resources which is so frequently associated with government lending and overregulation of financial activities.

MAJOR OBJECTIVES

Against this background, what general objectives did the Commission on Money and Credit[1] adhere to in probing into possible weaknesses within our private financial institutions.

Reprinted from *Harvard Business Review*, March–April 1962, pp. 151–164 and 168–169, by permission of the publisher. © 1962 by the President and Fellows of Harvard College; all rights reserved.

[1] *Money and Credit, Their Influence on Jobs, Prices, and Growth: The Report of the Commission on Money and Credit* (Englewood Cliffs, New Jersey, Prentice-Hall, Inc., 1961).

Perhaps the most succinct statement of the general objectives in this area is the one made by Gaylord Freeman that the recommendations in Chapter 6 aim at "greater equality of chartering, investment, branching, supervision and taxation," to the end of achieving competition on a more equal basis.

How well the Commission implemented this objective is illustrated by its recommendations:

- New entrants should be allowed in the chartering of banks "even if their business must be partially bid away from existing competitors."
- Applications for new branches should be given equal treatment with new unit bank applications.
- Applications for new branches of nonlocal banks should be treated equally with those from local banks.
- Savings and loan associations, mutual savings banks, and commercial banks should be given freedom to invest their time and savings accounts in similar long-term debt instruments.
- In making equity investments, they should all enjoy the least burdensome restriction commonly placed on any one of them.
- As for the branching privilege, national banks and federally chartered mutual savings banks and savings and loan associations should be permitted to branch freely and for this state laws should be liberalized to conform.
- Commercial banks, mutual savings banks, and savings and loan associations should be so treated under corporate income tax law as to contribute to capital and reserve adequacy and ensure competitive equality.

This willingness to allow freer expansion by our larger financial institutions is of special interest in view of the increasingly critical attitude taken by the Department of Justice and by the Congress toward concentration in commercial banking. It would seem to run counter to the country's historic policy of preserving competition through favoring local, grass-roots financial institutions. Some, however, will regard the Commission's position as merely an extension of a developing trend toward bigness, of which branch and holding company banking is but one facet. The Commission favors carrying this trend one step further by permitting expansion beyond state boundaries so that a commercial bank or other financial institution can serve a "trading area," which might extend over two or more states. The question of how far these proposals are supported by evidence of need for change to provide adequate banking service, to reduce its costs, and to increase competition will be considered in this article.

The other major idea is an apparent endorsement of more government activities in finance (Chapter 7). Here, government guarantees or loan insurance for credits to be extended by private institutions are favored over direct lending by federal agencies. The Commission seems to believe that only by the intervention of such federal aid, even in normal times, will private financial institutions be able to extend sufficient credit to achieve the full employment and growth that are given as our major economic goals.

EFFECT ON PRIVATE INSTITUTIONS

In this section of the article, a review is given of the recommendations offered by the Report as they apply to these private financial institutions:

1. Life insurance companies.
2. Pension funds.
3. Credit unions.
4. Mutual savings banks.
5. Savings and loan associations.
6. Commercial banks.

We shall deal first with those institutions for which the Commission has suggested the fewest changes and then take up those for which changes are most numerous or far-reaching.

Two questions will particularly concern us: (1) Is there a demonstrated economic need for these changes, and (2) have the disadvantages of these proposals been fully weighed? Questions will also be raised as to whether there are potential weaknesses that have gone unprobed.

Life Insurance Companies

The life insurance companies (which occupy as prominent a place in the capital market as commercial banks do in the money market) escape with only two specific recommendations. The reason is apparent from what has just been said: they are already spread across the country wherever they are willing to conform to local regulations and tax requirements, and they have comparative freedom to invest in a wide variety of forms. (The Commission looks with disfavor upon state laws which require that any legal reserves on local policies be invested within that state.)

The first recommendation offered by the Report is that federal chartering and regulation be made available to avoid the complications of multiple state jurisdictions and to encourage uniformity of high standards. Whether such a change would achieve progress will doubtless be bitterly debated. No note is made of how much life insurance business is now concentrated in companies chartered in states with the strictest standards. If federal chartering did raise standards, it would chiefly influence the more free-wheeling states. In the absence of compulsion, it is difficult to see how new insurance companies formed in the more easygoing states could be induced to elect a federal rather than a state charter. Any restrictions that would improve safety would be likely to reduce the kind of risk assumption which the Commission favors elsewhere in its Report for the purpose of promoting growth and full employment.

The second recommendation grows out of this philosophy of encouraging risk assumption to stimulate economic growth. The regulatory device of a "leeway" or "basket" clause, already found in some states, is recommended by the Commission to give greater investment flexibility. This arrangement permits a company to invest a percentage of its assets or surplus in types of assets not otherwise permitted, but not specifically prohibited. Loans to small businesses and investments in state development corporations are mentioned as examples. More will be said about this matter of risk assumption later because it is of such importance for all financial institutions.

Since a great amount of the funds held by financial institutions is derived from fixed dollar obligations, and their equity cushion is so small, a policy of fixed-value investment has become traditional. A variety of relaxations in recent years, e.g., common stock investment, suggests careful consideration of this trend, which is favored by the Report.

Private Pension Funds

The rise of private pension plans to supplement Social Security is largely a post-World War II development. Many businesses, particularly smaller ones, take care of this matter through group annuity policies with a life insurance company. But some large corporations have elected to use pension trust funds, many of which are administered by large commercial banks. Such noninsured plans have accumulated approximately $31 billion in assets as compared with $19 billion of reserves behind insured plans.[2]

Therefore, the Commission recommends that an appropriate regulatory body be created to develop and enforce standards of prudent investment for these private pension funds to assure periodic disclosure and to bring suit against any malfeasors. But the need for such regulation for all of these funds (except for a small fringe) may be questioned in view of the sophisticated and responsible character of the trustees and their client corporations. Also, the individual corporations are financially responsible for their noninsured pension obligations and bear the risk of investment losses should their particular funds fail to accumulate according to actuarial assumptions.

Because so many of these funds were set up in recent years when interest rates were low and dividend yields high, they were invested heavily in common stocks in a way not permitted for life insurance companies. In the bull markets that have characterized the past decade, these securities have enjoyed spectacular appreciation while rising interest rates have lowered bond values.

[2] *Life Insurance Fact Book* (New York, Institute of Life Insurance, 1961), pp. 35, 37.

Today, however, bond yields, which sometimes ran only half as much as stock yields in the late 1940's, are now around one and one-half times as much. This tremendous reversal of position raises a fundamental question of market risk, especially since appreciation is a much more hazardous basis for long-term actuarial accumulation than is interest or even dividend return. Because the pension obligations of the corporation are relatively fixed in value, the wisdom of fluctuating value investments under present conditions needs careful consideration. Pension liabilities are often very large, relative to corporate net worth. What really are "appropriate" standards of "prudence"? Does the present arrangement not constitute a huge speculation in common stocks for the stockholders of those corporations liable for these pension obligations?

On the other hand, if the motivation for common stock investment is to hedge against inflation, should the benefits of such commitments not be funneled through to the pensioner? (The beneficiaries are typically protected against deflation by their federal old-age, survivors, and disability insurance benefits.) In profit-sharing funds and variable annuities both the risk and the benefits are funneled through to ultimate beneficiaries. With the change in the New Jersey law permitting variable annuities, a landmark has been set which suggests a need for some new thinking throughout the nation.

A few guideposts have been set by the pioneering College Retirement Equities Fund (CREF), founded in 1952, which offers variable annuity retirement benefits from a common stock fund, coupled firmly with a conventional fixed-value deferred annuity administered by its companion institution, the Teachers Insurance and Annuity Association (TIAA). Those familiar with the huge sums required to fund pension benefits will appreciate the importance of what lies ahead for a system of funded pension benefits. The TIAA, which serves, comparatively, only a handful of college teachers (112,000), has accumulated annuity reserves of $613 million and the relatively new, affiliated CREF already has approximately $161 million in assets. Thus, some corporations may in time find that their pension fund investments are approaching their own invested capital per employee.

Credit Unions

The Commission makes no specific recommendations with regard to credit unions "because of their specialized characteristics and the basic voluntary self-help feature." It does suggest, however, that if their shares are made eligible for deposit insurance, the Federal Savings and Loan Insurance Corporation would be an appropriate body with which to do business. In view of the marked difference between the small personal loans, often unsecured, made by credit unions and the larger long-term loans secured by home mortgages, made by the savings and loan associations, separate insuring institutions would seem to be more appropriate. This separation would provide better risk allocation and specialized supervision for a field which is rapidly growing.

The Commission concludes that "as credit unions grow in size and gradually change their characteristics so that they resemble commercial institutions, their tax exemption should be reconsidered."

Mutual Savings Banks

Inasmuch as mutual savings banks can now be chartered in approximately one third of the states (18 including Alaska), the Commission recommends that their extension into other states be made possible by federal chartering. Designed as thrift institutions to serve the small saver, these banks have been limited in:

- Their investments, which have been concentrated on high-grade bonds and first mortgages (until the recent exception of limited common stock holdings).

- Their management, which is committed to trustees required to observe fiduciary standards.

- Their funds, in terms of the savings that they are permitted to accept from any one person.

The vigorous expansion of the savings and loan association, together with the promotion of savings accounts by commercial banks, makes it doubtful as to how far the lack of mutual savings banks in many states has been felt. Originally, the savings and loan association raised all of its funds through shares sold on an instalment plan. Today, it accepts any amount at the convenience of the saver and allows withdrawals so that it operates much like the savings bank. If these associations were allowed to invest in bonds, as recommended by the Commission, the resemblance between the two institutions would be even closer than it is now.

Some individuals will feel that the historic orientation of the savings bank toward the interests of the saver is important and will point out its exceptional record of safety during the Great Depression of the 1930's. (Their deposits actually increased between 1930 and 1935, although savings accounts with both commercial banks and savings and loan associations suffered a large shrinkage.) Thus, friends of the savings bank believe that the traditional emphasis of the savings and loan association on the promotion of home ownership may not always serve the best interests of the saver. They look with doubt on new developments and their attendant risks, which permit the association to invest outside of the home mortgage field, and on the changeover of a growing number of associations from the mutual to the stock form of organization.

Savings & Loan Associations

The most important of the Commission's proposals for the savings and loan associations is probably that of broadening their investment powers. A "wider range of suitable long-term debt instruments" would presumably imply permission to invest in corporation and municipal bonds and in long-term loans to industrial and other business concerns on a private-placement basis. As far as borrower needs are concerned, it is hard to believe that any of these areas has been starved for funds, particularly when compared with the home mortgage field. Borrowers have been well served by life insurance companies, savings banks, pension funds, and to some extent commercial banks.

Furthermore, the question arises as to whether most savings and loan associations are suitable lenders for these fields. Although the largest associations are now comparable in size to some of the biggest commercial banks, the industry has been primarily made up of many small associations. The local home mortgage is a particularly suitable investment for an unsophisticated management. Thus, mortgage security and instalment repayment can offset minor errors of judgment. Also, evaluation of risk is easier here than for other investment forms. Any regulatory change in permitted investments should be in keeping with the character of the typical organization rather than with the minority of larger, more sophisticated units.

This point is illustrated by the past experience of small commercial banks active in the bond field. Having been particularly heavy losers, during the Great Depression, from weaker classes of bonds—e.g., foreign governments and real estate mortgage bonds—the small commercial banks have, since then, confined most of their bond holdings to U.S. and municipal obligations. The former have provided liquidity and the latter tax exemption. Therefore, in view of the ample supply of federal obligations, it is doubtful whether most savings and loan associations would benefit from being allowed to go beyond that area of bond investment. Indeed, in recent years the extra yield from corporate over government bonds has been so narrow as to raise a question of whether it constitutes an adequate premium for risk.

Has not the specialization of the savings and loan association in the home mortgage field been advantageous to the community? Not only has this specialization done much to explain a high return to the small saver, but it has probably been an important factor in the record-breaking growth of home ownership. Except for the 1930's, savings and loan associations have had an excellent safety record. It is common knowledge that their depression troubles stemmed in part from unusual withdrawal demands during the banking crisis. Moreover, the price-level deflation of one third between 1929 and 1932—a monetary phenomenon beyond the control of these institutions—was so extreme as to mean inevitable losses for any system of property-secured debt investment. Even so, these associations might have fared better had unemployment not been so extreme.

The Commission's proposal to widen the permissible geographic area of lending for savings and loan associations is also likely to be questioned. Usually, risk increases when money travels farther from home. Historically, the wave of mortgage losses of the 1890's was attributed in part to the unfamiliarity of eastern lenders with midwestern property on which they had lent so heavily. The lender not only needs to be familiar with the borrower and his property, but also must be able to exercise loan supervision; both become more expensive as the distance increases. The requirement in the original law that federal savings and loan associations confine their lending to an area of 50 miles, with certain exceptions, was based on experience which showed that losses increase when lending goes beyond that distance.

It is significant to note that life insurance companies, which lend over a wide area, typically will not lend as much on an uninsured mortgage as will savings and loan associations. Clearly, local institutions are likely to enjoy an advantage in risk assumption and administration, for even a mortgage banker, who provides a valuable service to more distant lenders, cannot perform with quite the effectiveness of a responsible on-the-spot lender.

In short, before any of these Commission proposals can be accepted, certain questions need more complete answers. Specifically, will the proposed changes ensure increased economic efficiency? Or have the home mortgage sector and the thrift requirements of small savers been served less than adequately by existing institutions? A strong case for a negative answer to the latter question can be made from the remarkable growth of the savings and loan associations since 1945, as well as from their similar expansion during the 1920's. Whatever theoretical lack of investment mobility might seem to exist appears to have been met by:

1. The associations' promotional activities, often carried beyond state borders.

2. Their loan sharing.

3. The rise of the Federal Housing Administration and Veterans Administration systems of mortgage insurance and guarantee.

4. The nation-wide system of mortgage lending of our life insurance companies.

5. Competition for investments among different institutions.

These factors plus better communications and travel have made it easier for institutional funds to move into any areas of capital deficiency.

Commercial Banks

The Commission is tolerant of more concentration in commercial banking than now exists, and therefore recommends that national banks be permitted to establish branches throughout a "trading area," even when that area extends beyond the boundaries of a single state. While this power is recommended regardless of state laws, the Commission would have them revised to provide corresponding privileges to state-chartered banks. The Report notes that at present 16 states permit state-wide branching, 21 allow varying degrees of local branching, and 11 prohibit any branching.

However, the Commission does state that it is opposed to "concentration of financial power that discourages financial innovation, minimizes economies in operation of financial institutions, and prevents competitive sharing between borrowers, depositors, and shareholders of the benefits from innovation and operating economies." Yet it offers no evidence that further branching would not lead to such undesirable concentration. Moreover, the Commission would have regulatory bodies abandon any preferential treatment they now give to independent units or local banks when new charters are being sought. (Forthcoming studies which the Commission plans may supply evidence now lacking on this and other matters discussed here. The several planned volumes are expected to consist chiefly of the various financial trade associations' studies. Other studies were prepared by various economists and specialists.)

In evaluating the position on branching taken by the Commission readers of the Report should recognize that, of the twenty-five member Commission, six were drawn from commercial banking and one each from the life insurance and the savings bank fields. A ninth was an executive of a Federal Home Loan Bank, a federal agency that extends credit to home mortgage lending institutions and chiefly serves and supervises savings and loan associations. Of the first six, five were from branch or holding company bank systems and one was a vigorous advocate of branch banking in a unit banking state.

In this controversy at least three aspects need fuller analysis than is now available:

1. The comparative costs or economies that exist between unit and branch banking.

2. The bearing of unit versus branch banking on access to capital for small business and on competition generally.

3. An appraisal of developments of the last generation that may have made unit banking more effective or branch banking more necessary than formerly.

In some fields, such as automobile manufacturing and steel production, the advantages of large-scale operation are such that some concentration becomes economically inevitable. But in the field of banking, as in other service areas, no clear picture emerges of the advantages of size. For certain kinds of banking—viz., dealing in municipal and government obligations or serving corporate or personal trusts—some size is essential. But in deposit banking and lending, some authorities suggest that banks of relatively small size are just as efficient as larger ones in terms of cost and profitability.[3]

Much of the data will necessarily be subject to varying interpretation because of the substantial differences in these "department stores" of finance. A few have larger depositors, some have more savings deposits, others require more liquidity and invest more in Governments and prime paper, still others invest more heavily in real estate and personal loans, and some offer more ancillary services. But how should low return be appraised when it results from a zeal for growth which causes banks to open branches that offer only distant hopes of normal profit?

Some will prefer to place less emphasis on costs and profits and more emphasis on the question of whether a strong unit banking system should not be cultivated for its importance to small- and medium-size business borrowers and the consequences for general competition. A study by C. T. Arndt, for example, shows not only a higher proportion of loans to small business by small banks—as would be expected—but also an unusually large proportion of term loans to small business made by such lesser banks.[4] It is only natural for the smaller independent unit bank to feel the greater need to encourage and work with lesser business firms that are more important customers for it than they would be for a larger bank. A big bank, in turn, will be expected to cultivate a big business customer more assiduously, simply because the latter will contribute more to its volume.

Smaller businesses tend to rely more heavily on bank and trade credit. Unlike large corporations, they lack access to the capital market of stocks and bonds. When money tightens, the large business may shift its borrowing from bank loans to bonds. This shift has been illustrated in the past ten years by increased bond financing by various kinds of finance companies that have traditionally been heavy users of bank credit. Therefore, as easy money was succeeded by tight money, bonds became a relatively more economical source of funds, especially when weight was given to the balance requirements needed for bank credit. (Some bond financing had existed earlier for other reasons.)

---

[3] See Paul M. Horvitz, "Concentration and Competition in New England Banking," an unpublished dissertation at Massachusetts Institute of Technology, 1958, reported in the *Journal of Finance*, December 1959, pp. 567–568. The study concluded that branch banking is desirable but found that the cost advantages of a branch facility were small or nonexistent as compared with a unit bank, that unit banks charged less for unsecured loans to small business and made more such loans, and that branch managers were often not qualified or permitted to make commercial loans.

See also Eugene M. Lerner and Donald P. Jacobs, "Why We Need a Better Market for Bank Stocks," *Banking*, August 1960, pp. 43–45, September 1960, pp. 76–77. An inverse relation between asset size and return on capital was found for insured commercial banks for 1947–1958, although a reversal in the later years suggested the need for further analysis.

[4] "Member Bank Term Lending to Business, 1955–57," *Federal Reserve Bulletin*, May 1959, p. 362.

Thus, for small business, any major curtailment of bank credit could be fatal, rather than merely inconvenient. A good financial system should permit monetary controls to operate without disproportionate pressure on small business. But more evidence may be needed to make a wholly convincing case for those who hold that a minimum of banking concentration is of major importance for the maintenance of small business—and that such business, in turn, is desirable in order to maintain the kind of competition that is favorable to innovation, growth, and the better allocation of our resources.

However, more qualitative as well as quantitative analysis is needed in order to decide whether the Commission's recommendations are necessary for, or indeed consistent with, "adequate competition" among our financial institutions. It is suggested that the growing size of business borrowers will require bigger lending institutions, but nothing is said by the Commission of adaptive developments to meet that need, e.g., loan sharing where groups of banks lend as a syndicate to the large borrower, the commercial paper market, and small banks sharing larger loans with their correspondents.

It is also difficult to judge how far the Commission has recognized the degree to which increasing ease of communication and travel has widened the market area of the individual bank and consequently the amount of interbank competition. On the national scale, a large New York bank will find it easy to fly its representatives to solicit business from midwestern manufacturers. Locally, the businessman situated in the trading area around Chicago may borrow from a neighborhood bank, a major downtown bank, or even go to Peoria. The greater the number of banks and their availability, the greater the possibility of less well-rated borrowers finding one bank that has the means and the temperament to extend the desired credit. Today the automobile has enabled even the housewife to travel farther on her shopping and banking trips. She may, for example, use a bank which she visits rarely because of banking by mail and, increasingly, cashing of checks by stores.

Another recommendation of the Commission is that banks should be allowed to compete freely in the rates they pay for time deposits, with regulatory bodies having only stand-by authority to act. Such freedom for the several thrift institutions would facilitate the movement of funds to the areas of greatest need, which would allow commercial banks, for example, to bid more for savings should local needs—e.g., short and intermediate business loans—make it profitable to do so.

Even though rates were not freed from regulation for savings deposits, as the Commission recommends, one halfway step could be useful, namely, freedom in the rate paid on time certificates of deposit. Certificates issued in denominations like those of bonds or commercial paper would permit a bank to bid more effectively for funds to meet customer needs. Funds should be obtainable much more quickly by this device than by the slow building of thrift accounts. Such a rate could be raised more rapidly than on savings accounts already committed at lower rates to long-term loans and bonds.

In view of the unique position of the commercial bank as a supplier of short-term money, this flexibility in acquiring funds would give it the power to serve its borrowers in the same way that major corporate borrowers are served by the commercial paper market. It could tailor its certificates to fit its borrowers' demands. A different rate for certificates than for deposits would also permit recognition of differences between the cost of handling certificates and that of handling thrift accounts.

The Commission would also rely on thrift institutions themselves to determine their needs for cash reserves or other liquidity against their savings accounts. Until statutory reserve requirements are repealed, the Commission recommends, all should be subject to the same rules.

PERTINENT QUESTIONS

These, then, are the major Commission recommendations for our private financial institutions. But a review of these recommendations raises questions that need answering:

1. Have any important inadequacies in our present institutions been disclosed?

2. Have any weaknesses shown up in our credit standards as a result of the general prosperity of the United States since 1945?

3. How much risk should our financial institutions bear and how should they be protected against undue loss and failure?

Each of these questions is worthy of independent discussion.

Adequate Institutions?

Has any major inadequacy in our private financial institutions been disclosed? Certainly nothing like the gap found in our system by the Aldrich Commission, i.e., our lack of a central bank. Our private financial institutions are remarkable because of their variety and interinstitutional competition as suppliers of funds. But, in addition to those institutions discussed here, there are also the commercial finance (receivables finance and factoring), installment finance, and personal loan companies that suggest the power of innovation in our financial system. These companies grew to fill a need and drew the bulk of their funds from commercial banks, only to find the latter becoming competitive rivals. As a result, the younger institutions opened the door to these newer forms of lending for the commercial banks by providing them with a better basis for risk appraisal.

The market for business debt is shared chiefly by life insurance companies, commercial and savings banks, and pension funds; the mortgage market is shared by savings and loan associations, life insurance companies, and commercial and savings banks. These institutions have financed an extraordinary growth in debt in every field since the end of World War II. Many experts will doubt that they have supplied less than an adequate amount of credit for economic needs or shown any lack of mobility and competition in meeting these needs. Even small business has probably been served more handsomely than ever before. The experience of the Small Business Administration may well demonstrate, as did its predecessors—the Reconstruction Finance Corporation and the small business loan programs of the Federal Reserve banks and the Veterans Administration—that the number of credit-worthy small concerns which go unserved is small relative to the huge number that do obtain credit from existing private institutions.

The greatest change in the institutional capital market has occurred in the last decade with the opening of the door to common stock investment. The life insurance company and the savings bank—both institutions traditionally committed to debt investment—have been permitted limited investment in this field. But far more important to the stock market has been the expansion of holdings by investment companies, pension funds, trustees investing for individuals (chiefly trust departments of commercial banks) and for endowed institutions, and the various profit-sharing and other deferred-compensation plans of industry. Should the variable annuity group policy be launched on a large scale by life insurance companies, another accession of funds will flow into an already inflated stock market. (Or, thanks to this new institutional recognition, we may have to become accustomed to a higher level of stock prices relative to earnings and dividends.)

High stock prices for our leading corporations have served the smaller companies that seek equity capital. Such high prices have pushed investors seeking growth and better yield to the stocks of lesser companies. These prices have also created a favorable market for the new Small Business Investment Corporations. These SBIC's provide equity and near-equity capital for the companies which are not yet ready for direct financing in the securities market. In the last few years, the equity market has risen so high in relation to the debt market that it is now difficult to argue that our private credit institutions must buy stocks either to raise their own rate of return or to care for an unmet economic need.

The recent creation of real estate investment trusts (which have a tax position similar to that held by the investment companies) will close the last major gap in our institutional picture. Until their advent, the field of equity investment in large rental properties was the only major area which did not possess a suitable institutional market.

Credit Weakness?

In the absence of any outstanding inadequacies of credit supplies, of variety, of innovation, or of competition, the question arises: Should other weaknesses receive critical attention in any general survey on money and credit? Often periods of prosperity lull our economy into lowering credit standards and so provide overstimulation which leads to subsequent losses and instability. The willingness in this country to innovate often leads to defective risk appraisals in the new area.

Our financial institutions as a whole largely employ "other peoples' money" for which they have a fixed obligation—often payable on short notice. With only a small equity cushion to absorb losses, these institutions can find their position rapidly impaired by substantial losses. The consequent threat to confidence can have serious repercussions.

In general, institutional investments represent extensions of credit to government, to business, and on real estate. Little need be said concerning government credit. However, those who argue that depressions should be met by federal deficits ordinarily assume—mistakenly—that federal debt will be reduced during prosperity. But no such reduction has been made during the long period of prosperity since 1945, although about 40% of the national debt was retired during a similar period of prosperity that marked the decade of the 1920's. Since 1945, the burden of this national debt has been lightened by inflation and growth in real income, but rising interest rates have worked in the opposite direction. Failure to reduce this debt may have raised doubts in some European minds regarding our will to resist inflation and our ability to meet the developing gold crisis with firmness.

Between 1945 and 1960 state and municipal debt rose from $13.7 billion to $60.0 billion. The future needs of a burgeoning population will find communities less willing to incur additional debt and higher taxes—a factor for anyone to consider who counts on a continuation of recent growth rates in capital spending. Yet the overall credit picture is still regarded as sound, although financial problems may develop in major cities where higher income families and industry have migrated to the suburbs. In these cases, the real estate tax base has deteriorated and budgets bulge because of expanding social services and also, in some instances, lax political administration.

Business indebtedness is also regarded as generally sound, even though corporate long-term debt grew from $38 billion to $138 billion and short-term debt from $47 billion to $156 billion between 1945 and 1960.[5] At the end of World War II business was unusually liquid and debt was low. Consequently, corporate debt is relatively (as well as absolutely) heavier today than in 1945. Railroad debt is the only area where serious weakness is readily apparent, and here most of the trouble is in northern and eastern states (trunk-line territory).

[5] In general, figures are from the *Economic Report of the President*, January, 1961, and are mostly for June 30 of the given year.

In the last 15 years, nonfarm mortgages rose from $27 billion to $174 billion. About three fourths of the second total is home mortgage debt. Thus, the volume of mortgages makes them important for almost all of the institutional investors discussed here. At the end of 1960, home mortgage debt (one- to four-family houses) consisted of $85 billion of conventional, uninsured mortgages, $27 billion of FHA insured loans, and $30 billion of VA guaranteed mortgages. Periods of repayment have gradually been extended and down payments reduced for government-underwritten mortgages.

Recently, competition has led institutional lenders to move in the same direction for conventional loans. A sampling study of savings and loan associations, for example, showed that in 1950 only 26% of their conventional loans ran 20 years or longer as compared with 61% in 1959. Loans of 75% or more on property value increased from 16% to 46% during the same period. Government-underwritten mortgages have been on easier terms. In 1959, the median term for FHA insured mortgages on new one-family homes had risen to 28.8 years, and the median ratio of loan to property value had climbed to 93.5%.[6]

The possible effects of the longer repayment period on maintaining the loan-to-property ratio have been largely ignored. Rising interest rates also have reduced the amounts devoted to principal repayment during the early years. This point may be illustrated as in Table 26–1.

The extension of the repayment period from the conventional savings and loan association mortgages of the 1920's—11 years and 7 months—has made it a very different loan. (A 40-year term, such as can be used in public housing projects and even in some FHA loans, provides less than 1% reduction during the earliest years.) Sound finance would require that a debt should be reduced at least as rapidly as normal depreciation. The inadequacy of the longer term repayment plans has been made greater by including in the mortgage base the value of equipment—such as refrigeration or laundry equipment—that has a useful life which is shorter than that of the mortgage.

Because home maintenance expenses and replacements for things such as heating equipment, roofing, and plumbing tend to increase as property ages, the paradoxical effect of longer term mortgages is to create a pattern of increasing cash outlays as the house gets older and its rental value declines. For this reason, home ownership appears "cheaper than renting" in the early years, when the monthly charges fail to allocate real costs properly over the life of the property. (A separate discussion of these peculiarities in regard to mortgages on older houses would be desirable. Such mortgages are likely to be on stricter terms than for newer houses, but a shorter useful life expectancy makes suitable amortization even more necessary.)

[6] *Savings and Loan Fact Book* (Chicago, United States Savings and Loan League, 1961), p. 118.

TABLE 26–1

Percentage of Mortgage Reduction Over First Years Under Equal Monthly
Payment Plan

	One year	Three years	Five years
4½ % — 20 years	3.2%	9.9%	17.3%
4½ % — 25 years	2.2	7.0	12.2
6% — 25 years	1.8	5.7	10.1
6% — 11 years, 7 months	6.2	19.7	34.9

Inflation has concealed parts of this weakness. Moreover, easy credit may have inflated housing costs. Since 1947–1949, residential construction costs have risen faster than either wholesale commodity or consumer prices. Should analysis or growing foreclosures cause a reassessment of the situation and stiffer terms, the resulting deflation could lower the market values of houses more than general prices. Any such decline in market prices, however, would direct attention to the lowered down payments. Down payments for some mortgages today no longer cover the cost of restoring and selling foreclosed property, nor do they cover any accumulation of delinquent interest and taxes, or errors of appraisal, to say nothing of the hazard of lower real estate prices, whether from price deflation, improved technology, or changing styles.

How Much Risk?

There is one final and important question yet to be asked: How much risk should our financial institutions bear and how should they be protected against undue loss and failure? Because a great amount of their funds is from fixed obligations, they have generally been permitted to assume only minimal risks. Any other policy would be unsuitable for such high leverage institutions. Their cushion to absorb losses consists of their retained income, surplus, or "loss reserves" in the case of mutual institutions, plus the stockholders' contribution in the case of stock corporations.

Too often the limits for some type of more risky asset have been determined by law as a percentage of assets without regard to the size of this shock absorber for losses. Even when the legal limitation is set as some percentage of "surplus" or "equity," it ignores the adequacy of that cushion to absorb other portfolio risks. Thus, a life insurance company with a total surplus equal to 3% of total portfolio might be deemed to have no spare reserves to invest in common stocks. In the same way, a savings and loan association should not assume the risks of land development until its "surplus" is more than adequate to care for losses on its mortgage portfolio.

This general approach should serve as a policy guide for regulatory purposes for all financial institutions. Therefore, the first step to sensible risk administration would be a classification of assets with respect to risk. This procedure is employed by some bank examiners regarding different kinds of loans and investments. Here, a suitable percentage of risk cushion is computed for each class. If the equity is inadequate, the appropriate remedy may be a reduction of risk exposure, additional stockholder investment, or restrictions on dividends.

Admittedly, the classification problem is difficult and can never be completely resolved. Loss experience, naturally, will vary for the same type of investment with different managements and different locations. Thus, all we can seek is a regulatory principle that will provide for the best job possible. For this job the best thinking of the regulatory authorities and of the institutions should be enlisted to solve the problem of classification and risk management.

Risk can never be measured with any precision because it involves irregularly occurring future losses. Some of these are cyclical and depend on the severity of future depressions, others depend on local business conditions, and still others on changing technology. Prudence requires the most careful provision for losses that is possible.

This idea also has tax implications. Taxable income of financial institutions should be computed after a proper allowance is made for average losses over good and bad years. This principle is already accepted for commercial banks, which are allowed to make a loss reserve deduction based on their individual 20-year-average experience, until a ceiling figure has been accumulated. As valid as it is, this rule is defective since it makes no allowances for a change in investment policy either in the direction of greater or less conservatism. A better rule would be to base the allowance on the type of loans currently held and their probable risk. Certainly, a bank with assets which consist chiefly of cash, short-term Governments, and prime paper needs little in the way of loss reserves as compared with a bank heavily committed to business loans to less well-rated companies, personal loans, and mortgages on commercial and industrial real estate.

And how should the "equality of tax treatment" recommended by the Commission be applied to different kinds of institutions without some such unifying principle? Admittedly, the typical savings and loan association fully invested in conventional mortgages require more loss reserves than does the liquid bank just referred to. The present tax rule allowing associations to accumulate a tax-free "surplus" equal to 12% of its shareholders' or depositors' balances might not be too far from actual need for the generous types of conventional mortgages described above. But now the tax law makes no distinction between such an association and one fully invested in FHA insured mortgages.

If the existing kinds of financial institutions could accept the general principle advanced here, the present acrimonious controversy might at least be abated. However, we should be wary that interinstitutional combat may end with no group having the right to set up adequate tax-deductible loss reserves on its expanding mortgage portfolio.[7] Income taxes that take sums needed to meet future losses are, in effect, taxes on capital. Thus, they can imperil future solvency. Furthermore, the Commission's recommendation to abandon controls over the interest rates which are paid to savers would be more logical if some regulatory rule were in force that prevented the distribution of amounts needed for adequate loss reserves.

If attention were focused more forcibly on the risk problem by the regulatory process and by equitable taxation, enthusiasm for federal credit agencies and guarantees might be somewhat dampened. In normal times, the use of federal credit for private purposes is likely to push excessive risks on the government and the taxpayer. Therefore, inadequate premiums are likely to be charged for risk assumed. If the premium were deemed to be adequate, a private institution would be likely to make the loan. (With the recent rise in foreclosures, a comparison of losses on FHA, VA, and conventional mortgages would doubtless be instructive.)

Consequently, use of government credit in ordinary times tends to make for an uneconomic allocation of resources and to preserve weak situations that are best liquidated when prosperous conditions make reallocations possible with less hardship to labor. Government credit is more likely to be an effective stimulant if its use is reserved for depression, when it can aid in a restoration of confidence and when widespread pessimism causes an excessive estimate of risk. (Witness the successful operations of the Reconstruction Finance Corporation and the Home Owners' Loan Corporation.)

CONCLUSION

The section of the Commission Report devoted to a study of private financial institutions, Chapter 6, contains such a variety of recommendations that almost every reader will find something to endorse and something which he dislikes. The very breadth of the ground covered by the Commission leaves so little space for supporting evidence that the unconvinced will probably remain so. Consequently, the Report may find its chief purpose that of stimulating thinking about the functions and quality of our financial institutions.

[7] See John Lintner, *Mutual Savings Banks in the Savings and Mortgage Markets* (Cambridge, Harvard University Press, 1948). Even though mortgage debt presumably does not face the ordeal of the 1930's, the weaker amortization and down-payment terms of today make it more vulnerable; risk increases more than proportionately as loans rise above the two thirds level, which was the common institutional limit before 1930.

Because the Report centered on recommendations for change, it conveys an air of dissatisfaction with institutional performance. However, the predominant attitude of the Commission is actually one of general approval. Its recommendations are undoubtedly intended to be comparatively mild but desirable improvements. Moreover, the Commission on Money and Credit appears to have rejected the philosophy of the Gurley-Shaw school, which would impose stricter governmental controls throughout our financial system to achieve planned monetary policy and economic goals.

Nevertheless, in its effect, the Report seems to underrate the degree to which our institutions have provided a varied, inventive, adaptable, and competitive system. Comparisons with other countries reveal that our system allows an unusual degree of competition and willingness to assume risk —characteristics so ably espoused by the Commission. An outside observer might even feel that we have made the entry of the less competent into business too easy and created a situation in which cyclical instability is likely to be even more pronounced. Generally, however, we have been willing to pay the price for what we believe are important factors in our economic progress and growth.

The difficulty faced by the Commission is also inherent in the economy. How shall an optimum balance be achieved between safety and risk assumption? We have seen how ill-suited most of our financial institutions are for risk assumption because of their heavy obligations fixed in dollars and their small equity cushions. For such institutions, adequate safety must be a matter of paramount concern.

It follows that a fully satisfying study of money and credit should provide:

1. A broad examination into the quality and suitability of the investments of private financial institutions.

2. A desirable principle of regulation which would attempt to limit the risks assumed by the various institutions to their ability to bear loss. Conversely, it would permit freer investment and risk assumption whenever the equity cushion exceeded what was necessary for its basic portfolio of high-quality debt investment.

3. A discussion of risk appraisal which would appear essential to give reality to the Commission's recommendations for tax equality among these institutions. Only by defining taxable income as that which allows reserve deductions for cyclical losses can a proper balance be had between low-risk and high-risk portfolios. Tax policy that provides such a graduated allowance for risk assumption can be a strong and impelling force for the accumulation of adequate loss reserves. It should also reduce the insolvency hazard for financial institutions and reduce the need to rely on government support except in the gravest emergencies.

If the foregoing emphasis on risk analysis seems disproportionate, it may be regarded as a counterbalance to the Commission's heavy emphasis on permitting greater risk assumption to stimulate growth, production, and full employment. Certainly, regulatory rules and tax laws have often been defective in their neglect of, or failure to analyze, this factor. Fundamental economic analysis requires that risk assumption receive full attention in the area of finance where it is so important. A good deal of our economic instability can be traced to mistaken appraisals of risk in capital spending. But such investments seemed desirable to further growth and prosperity at the time they were made. Therefore, the greater the hazard, the more desirable it is that such hazards be borne outside the debt-oriented institutions discussed here.

V

RECENT STUDIES ON THE OPERATIONS OF INDIVIDUAL FINANCIAL INSTITUTIONS

Studies are constantly being made into the performance and problems of financial institutions. While an entire readings book could be filled with the studies about one type of institution, the purpose of Part V is to acquaint the student with studies of a variety of institutions. The eight following articles deal with specific areas of commercial banks, savings and loan associations, pension funds, sales finance companies, investment companies, common trust funds, and life insurance companies.

27.

Bank Debenture Financing:
A Comparison of Alternatives

STANLEY SILVERBERG

During the same week in June 1965, the second and third largest banks in the United States each offered bond issues that were substantially larger than any previously offered by commercial banks. These two bond issues—one a straight debenture, the other, convertible into common stock—have provoked wide discussion in recent financial literature. This paper explores the relative advantages and disadvantages of these alternative approaches to bank debt financing. The final section of the paper attempts to dispel the confusion about the effect of bank borrowing on bank deposits and money market conditions that has recently been evidenced in the financial press.

I. BANK BORROWING AND LEVERAGE

It will be convenient initially to set forth the relationships among bank operations, bank earnings, and bank leverage. "Leverage" refers to the practice whereby business firms finance the acquisition of assets through borrowing in order to increase the ratio of assets to equity investment. If the return on acquired assets exceeds the cost of borrowing, the firm is able (through leverage) to raise its rate of return on equity investment. Although many nonfinancial firms are primarily equity-financed, for commercial

Reprinted from *The National Banking Review*, Vol. III, No. 1, September 1964, pp. 45–33, by permission of the publisher.

banks, leverage—through deposits—necessarily plays a major role in operations. Earnings on bank assets typically are substantially less than the cost of bank capital.[1] However, the earnings margin on deposits (the difference between earnings on the investment of deposit funds and their cost of acquisition and retention) tends to raise the rate of return on equity investment to a level which equals or exceeds the cost of bank capital. As long as deposit-derived funds are invested profitably, the higher the ratio of deposits to capital, the higher will be the rate of return on bank capital, other factors held constant. However, there exist certain constraints on the extent to which banks may increase their deposit leverage.[2]

Borrowing through instruments that are subordinate to depositor claims enables banks to increase leverage without impairing the protective cushion afforded depositors. However, it is important that we distinguish two different situations whereby leverage is increased through borrowing. First, assume a bank has sufficient capital "to cover" its deposits. By selling debentures, it acquires additional funds and is able to increase further its ratio of earning assets to equity investment. As long as a bank can earn more on its investments than its cost of borrowing, it will raise its earnings and its rate of return on equity investment. A second possibility is that the bank has *insufficient* capital, however this insufficiency is determined, and sells debentures to make up the capital deficiency. This use of debentures as an alternative to increasing equity investment can provide a substantial addition to leverage (or, looked at differently, can forestall the reduction in leverage that would occur if common stock were sold).

To illustrate the difference between these two cases, assume that two banks each have deposits of $1 billion. The first bank has equity of $80 million (assumed to be the approximate minimum), and assets of $1,080 million. It chooses to sell $20 million in debentures, raising its asset total to $1.1 billion and its ratio of assets to equity from 13.50 to 13.75.[3] The second bank has equity of only $60 million and assets of $1,060 million. It sells $20 million in debentures to bring its total capital up to $80 million and its total assets to $1,080 million. Its ratio of assets to equity is now 18.0. Had the second bank raised the "necessary" $20 million by selling additional stock, its ratio of assets to equity would have fallen from 17.67 to 13.50. Thus, in this second case, where debentures were used as a substitute

---

[1] The term "cost of capital" in this article refers to the return that must be earned on stockholder investment to attract, maintain, or justify such investment. See Stanley Silverberg, "Bank Borrowing: An Analysis of Recent Experience," *The National Banking Review*, December 2, 1964, pp. 215–216.

[2] *Ibid.*, pp. 215–216.

[3] Financial writers have sometimes assumed that additions to capital would enable a bank to increase its earnings immediately by an amount equal to the capital increase times the bank's average return on capital (for example, see *American Banker*, May 19, 1965, p. 2). Other things equal, this would not be the case, unless the bank could maintain its degree of leverage.

for equity, their effect on bank leverage would be substantially greater than in the first example, where the "need" for capital did not exist.

II. STRAIGHT DEBENTURES

Most of the debenture issues sold by banks during the past two years have reflected some combination of the two situations cited in the preceding section. Where capital was "needed," most banks have sold more than they "had to." In the future, however, some of these banks may restrict retained earnings relative to deposit growth in order to lower their capital-deposit ratios to the minimum level, and thereby take advantage of increased leverage possibilities.[4]

Let us further examine the hypothetical bank with deposits of $1 billion, equity investment of $60 million, and $20 million in debenture liability. If the bank wishes to maintain its leverage, then, as deposits grow, the bank will have to add proportionately not enough to equity (say, through retained earnings), but also to its indebtedness. If deposits grow by an average of 4 percent per year, then the bank will have to increase its capital by an average of 4 percent a year to maintain its capital-deposit ratio. However, unless debt continues to account for 25 percent of the bank's capital (or more), the degree of leverage will decline—a dollar of equity will support fewer dollars of earning assets.

Suppose the debenture issue requires annual redemption payments, say, to retire the indebtedness in 20 years. In this case, barring any subsequent debt financing, increases in equity will have to be large enough to meet redemption payments and to match deposit growth—if the bank is to maintain its capital-deposit ratio. In this case, the reduction in the bank's leverage is accelerated.

One might pose the question, what can the bank gain through the *temporary* use of debentures? It might gain the use of borrowed funds at lower cost than the rate the bank is able to earn on these funds. It can temporarily substitute debt for equity and, in this sense, lower its capital cost, since it is cheaper to acquire $20 million of equity over a 20-year period in the future than to acquire $20 million of equity immediately. In addition, the debenture financing may enable a bank to substitute retained earnings for the sale of common stock as a means of adding to equity. The combination of a higher tax rate on dividend income than on capital gains, and the fact that the latter are taxed only when realized, makes "implicit financing" through retained earnings cheaper than the sale of common stock. Thus, even when debenture financing does not provide a vehicle for *permanently*

---

[4] This possibility is discussed by David Cates in "Bank Dividend Policy," *Bankers Monthly*, March 15, 1965, pp. 19–20.

increasing leverage, there are several reasons for its attractiveness vis-a-vis straight equity financing.[5]

The decision whether debentures are to play a permanent role in a bank's capital structure does not have to be made at the time of the bank's initial debt financing, as long as the bank confines itself to a straight (as opposed to a convertible) debenture. The presence or absence of a redemption provision in the bond indenture may be a reflection of state banking regulations, lender requirements, or standard financial practice, rather than any indication of the temporary or permanent nature of debt. A bank may choose to come back into the market periodically to replace its retired debt, to expand its debt in order to *maintain* its debt-equity ratio, or to expand debt in order to *raise* its debt-equity ratio.

III. CONVERTIBLE DEBENTURES

In the case of convertible debentures, the decision whether debt will ultimately be replaced by equity will be determined primarily by subsequent earnings performance of the bank and the market's response to this performance, although the precise timing of conversion may be determined by the bank's subsequent dividend policies.

Leverage is not the principal attraction of convertible bonds. By setting a conversion price above the current market, a bank is able to obtain an immediate addition to capital with less equity dilution than would occur through the sale of common stock. The equity dilution does not immediately occur and, under certain (unfavorable) circumstances, it may never occur. However, the basis for conversion is determined before the convertible bonds are sold, and thus, convertible bondholders can be said to share successful operations from the time the bonds are sold—assuming conversion ultimately will take place.

The value of the conversion feature enables banks to sell convertible bonds with a lower coupon than the market would require on straight debentures. Nevertheless, the coupon on the convertible bond typically provides a higher yield to the investor than a similar investment in the same bank's stock. Even though this is the case, the after-tax cost of interest payments to the bank may be *less* than the cash outlay of additional dividend payments if the bank had chosen to sell stock.[6] For example, if the First

[5] Of course, there is still a considerable difference between temporarily substituting debt for equity and thereby delaying the acquisition of equity funds, and using debt to acquire earning assets when the additional capital is *not* needed.

[6] In Table 27-1 are listed for several banks that have recently sold convertible debentures, the debenture coupon, conversion price, dividend, and the percentage increase in the dividend that will bring about conversion (assuming an accompanying increase in the stock price). It is apparent from these figures that the after-tax cost of the convertible debenture coupon in the case of Valley National Bank of Phoenix exceeded the dividend cost that would have been incurred initially by selling stock.

TABLE 27–1

Bank	Debenture Coupon	Conversion Price*	Dividend*	Dividend increase to induce conversion (in percent)
American Fletcher NB	3.625	70	2.00	26.9
FNB of Atlanta	3.50	75	1.60	64.1
FNB of San Jose	4.00	30⅝	1.00	22.5
FNCB of New York	4.00	66⅔	1.60	66.7
Valley National Bank	3.50	85	1.00	197.5
Wells Fargo Bank	3.25	60	1.00	94.6

* At time of debenture offering. These figures do not take account of stock dividends and changes in cash dividends since the debenture offering.

National City Bank in its recent financing had offered additional stock at $50 per share, the current $1.60 dividend would have represented a 3.2 percent yield—less than the 4 percent coupon on the convertible debenture actually offered. However, this would have entailed a greater cash expense to the bank than the *after-tax* interest payments of only about 2 percent. The conversion price set on this issue was $66⅔, about 25 percent above the market at the time of the offering. Thus, a $100 bond could be converted into 1.5 shares of common stock which would pay $2.40 at the bank's current $1.60 dividend. The bank's dividend per share would have to be raised to $2.67 (by about 67 percent) before the dividends on the 1.5 shares would equal the current bond coupon. If the bank's dividend payout and the market's valuation of the bank's earnings continue to approximate present relationships, then the bank's stock price would reach the conversion price long before the bank's dividend reaches $2.67. However, bondholders will not exercise their conversion option until potential dividends exceed the bond coupon, unless the issue matures or is called.

Thus, for a substantial period of time, a bank will continue to realize a tax saving by paying out bond interest instead of dividends. The potential tax saving is an important factor in deciding upon the debenture package, and may subsequently influence a bank's dividend policy. Insofar as there exists a trade-off between the conversion price and the coupon saving from a convertible debenture, the potential tax saving would encourage a package with a high coupon and a high conversion price. Too low a coupon may lead to early conversion, unless the bank chooses to restrict its dividend payout.

What happens if conversion has not occurred by the time the debentures mature? This would be true if the stock price is below the conversion at the time of maturity.[7] In this case, the convertible debenture acquires the same characteristics as a straight debenture with no required sinking fund.

[7] Even if conversion would lower the income of bondholders, they would, of course, convert prior to the bond maturity if the market value of the acquired stock exceeded the par value of the debenture.

IV. CONVERTIBLE VERSUS STRAIGHT DEBENTURES

The principal advantage of a convertible debenture vis-a-vis a straight debenture is the lower coupon that can be obtained on the former. Also, the convertible issues may present no refinancing problems and require no sinking fund payments. The fact that the conversion price is set above the market, and thus entails less dilution than straight equity financing, is no advantage compared with straight debenture financing. A bank could get virtually the same results (at a somewhat higher coupon cost) by selling a straight debenture and eventually replacing it with common stock, when, presumably, the price of the bank's stock will be higher. Straight debentures may also enable a bank to postpone the sale of equity to what it considers to be a desirable time, without having to make an advance commitment as to price. And, of course, the use of the straight debenture allows the option of replacing debentures with retained earnings, or with other debentures.

The cost of a convertible debenture will depend upon its coupon and conversion price, the bank's capital cost, and the number of years before conversion is effected. Assume the conversion price is set at 25 percent above the current market (approximately the situation in the recent First National City financing), and that the bank's cost of equity is 7 percent. Then, as a first approximation, the capital cost of the convertible debenture would be $\frac{1}{1.25}$ (.07) = .056 or 5.6 percent. However, it also is necessary to take account of the cash saving a bank will realize by paying interest instead of dividends until conversion is effected. The cost of the debenture coupon will be the same throughout its life (assuming tax rates remain constant), whereas the dividend saving will vary according to the bank's current dividend rate. In the case of First National City's convertible debenture, the dividend cost to the bank would be approximately $6.4 million if the entire issue were converted in the first year (4 million shares multiplied by the $1.60 dividend). However, the amount of potential dividend payments will increase in subsequent years if the dividend per share is increased. The cost of the interest payment on the debenture to the bank will remain approximately $5.33 million per year (assuming a 50 percent applicable tax rate) as long as the debenture remains outstanding. Let us assume that the dividend per share is increased by 4 percent per year, and that the bank's capital cost is 7 percent. If these assumptions prove correct, debenture holders will convert at the end of the 13th year. The cash saving to the bank will lower its capital cost by approximately 0.56 percent[8] to a level, given our assumptions, of approximately 5 percent, compared with a capital cost of about 7 percent for straight equity financing.

In the case of a straight debenture, the capital cost will vary according to subsequent replacement or refinancing. The cost of a perpetuity bond, presumably, would be the after-tax cost of the bond coupon. This would also be the case if a straight debenture were sold with no sinking fund and were periodically refinanced at the same coupon. Where debentures are replaced by equity—through retained earnings or common stock—the capital cost will range between the cost of straight debentures and the cost of retained earnings or equity financing. The longer equity financing is delayed, the closer the capital cost will be to the cost of perpetual debt financing.[9]

Thus far we have considered only the advantages of increased leverage; we have not taken account of the possible increased risk associated with it. It is generally conceded that, at some point, the risk associated with increased leverage raises the cost of equity. However, whether moderate amounts of leverage necessarily raise the cost of equity is an issue that has been debated in recent economic and financial literature. With respect to banks, there is little evidence that the cost of equity has been affected by leverage. However, when deposits afforded the only basis for bank leverage, supervisory authorities may have limited bank leverage to levels associated with very modest risk—given the nature of bank assets and operations. Borrowing may enable banks to attain a degree of leverage (consistent with supervisory standards) that will result in an increase in the cost of bank equity. To the extent that this occurs, at least part of the earnings advantage of permanent debt and increased leverage will be offset by less favorable valuation of expected earnings and dividends in the stock market. And, to the extent that this occurs, the ultimate advantage of straight debentures compared with convertible debentures will be correspondingly diminished.

V. DEBENTURES, BANK DEPOSITS, AND MONETARY POLICY

When banks sell debentures they receive as payment checks drawn on themselves or on other commercial banks. Initially, one kind of bank lia-

---

[9] If a bank sells bonds at an interest cost of 2.5 percent and replaces them with common stock after 10 years, assuming earnings and deposit growth of 4 percent and a 7 percent cost of equity, the bank's capital cost would be 5.20 percent. If the bonds were replaced after 25 years the cost would be 4.13 percent. The effect of alternative financing strategies on bank stock prices is examined in the Appendix.

[8] The present value of the cash saving to the bank would be:

$$\$6.4 \text{ million } \Sigma \frac{1}{1.07^2} + \frac{1.04}{(1.07)^2} + \frac{(1.04)^2}{(1.07)^3} \cdots + \frac{(1.04)^{n-1}}{(1.07)^n}$$

$$-\$5.33 \text{ million } \Sigma \frac{1}{1.07} + \frac{1}{(1.07)^2} + \ldots \frac{1}{(1.07)^n}$$

$$= \$21.4 \text{ million where } n = 13.$$

Multiplying $21.4 by .07 to convert cash saving into a *perpetual* flow yields approximately $1.5 million, or 0.56 percent of $266.6 million financing.

bility is exchanged for another. This has tended to cause some confusion among financial writers concerning the effects of debenture financing on bank deposits and reserves.[10]

When financing takes place outside of the banking system, payments are still made by checks drawn on the banking system. But such transactions do not directly affect the volume of member bank deposits or reserves. Checks are drawn on the accounts of nonbank lenders and deposited to the accounts of borrowers, with no appreciable effect on the volume of bank reserves, required reserves, or deposits.[11]

When banks sell debentures and reinvest acquired funds, there is no significant direct effect on bank reserves, although bank earning assets and liabilities are increased. One can conceive of the process as follows: Instead of insurance companies or pension funds lending to nonfinancial corporations (which in turn spend the acquired funds on goods and services), they lend to banks, which in turn lend to the same nonfinancial corporations, etc. Another layer of financial assets and debt is created, but the volume of ultimate spending by nonfinancial firms remains unaffected. Of course, it is possible that bankers prefer different kinds of borrowers or maturities than other institutional lenders. Some shifts may occur in the degree of ease or tightness existing in various sectors or geographic regions of financial markets. However, such effects are apt to be small and unlikely to negate the generalization that bank debenture financing has little effect on financial market conditions. The result would be different if those who purchase debentures use funds that would otherwise remain on deposit with commercial banks. If the latter is the case, then a given volume of bank reserves will support a greater volume of financing *and* spending. A lower volume of bank reserves and deposits will then be consistent with a given level of monetary ease or tightness.

The question, where do debenture purchases ultimately come from, relates not only to financial market conditions generally, but also to the financing strategy of the selling bank. It has been argued that some portion of bank debentures will be sold to the bank's own depositors, who will exchange one kind of liability for another of the same bank.[12] Presumably, this is more likely to be the case for a bank that sells its debentures locally, since the purchasers of the debentures are then more likely to be depositors of the selling bank. This may, indeed, be the case in a few instances. How-

---

[10] For example, see *The New York Times*, June 6, 1965, Section 3, pp. 1, 12.

[11] To the extent that a greater share of financing takes place outside the banking system (say, through nonbank intermediaries or through the corporate bond market), a lower volume of bank reserves, deposits, and credit will be consistent with any desired level of monetary ease or tightness.

[12] See Paul Nadler, "Can Debentures Save the Smaller Bank?" *Banking*, November 1964, p. 98; Morris A. Schapiro, "Taking Another Look at Long-Term Bank Financing," *The Commercial and Financial Chronicle*, May 28, 1964, p. 10.

ever, it is important to realize that this approach presupposes that the sale of debentures by the XYZ bank will persuade an individual or a financial institution to alter its asset portfolio by substituting bonds for demand or time deposits. This seems extremely unlikely in most cases, particularly where we are concerned with institutional investors (most bank debentures have been purchased by pension funds and insurance companies). After all, at any time there are outstanding bonds of comparable quality and yield. Why should the sale of *a* particular bond persuade a lender to make a switch from cash to bonds that he would not otherwise have made?

In the case of convertible bonds, many existing stockholders may exercise rights to acquire bonds in order to maintain their equity interest. However, even in this case, although bonds will be paid for by checks written on the selling bank, those who acquire the convertible bonds are likely to make other portfolio shifts, so that the ultimate source of funds used to pay for the bonds may be proceeds of other security sales. In those instances where convertible or straight debenture sales do result in a deposit reduction, such a reduction is more likely to be in time than in demand deposits.[13]

One final point should be noted with respect to debenture sales and bank deposits. A bank utilizing debenture proceeds for commercial loans may be in a stronger position to compete for commercial accounts. Also, a larger capital account and, possibly, a larger loan limit may increase the bank's ability to compete for larger commercial accounts. In this sense, debentures may indirectly enable a bank to acquire deposits at the expense of competing banks.

---

[13] To the extent that this occurs, the shift from time to demand deposits would result, other things equal, in an increase in required reserves and a decline in bank deposits, assuming no adjustment in member bank reserves.

28.

Bank Charge Cards—
A Step Toward
the "Checkless" Society

J. VAN FENSTERMAKER

Commercial banks throughout the nation are launching an innovation which will have far reaching effects on bank operations and competition, consumer borrowing and spending patterns, retail merchandising, and the nation's money supply—the bank charge card. Over 1,000 banks offer charge card plans and the number is growing daily. This movement is a major step toward the "checkless" society.

The charge card system is relatively simple. It is similar to the department store or travel and entertainment card. The bank gives an individual a line-of-credit up to a certain amount and issues a charge card which he uses to purchase goods and services at any participating establishment. The seller deposits the sales slip, and the bank credits the merchant's account, less a discount of 2½ to 7 percent.

The charge card holder has up to 25 days after billing to pay the account with no additional charge; however, after 25 days the unpaid part automatically becomes a loan with a finance charge of 1 to 1½ percent per month. The balance of the account can be paid in full at any time or in predetermined monthly payments. The card holder may also get a cash loan at any time from his bank.

Reprinted from *Business and Government Review*, Vol. IX, No. 1, January-February 1968, pp. 26–31, by permission of the publisher.

GROWTH OF THE CHARGE CARD PLAN

Several types of bank charge accounts were started in the early 1950's in the United States. The Franklin National Bank in Mineola, New York, however, began the first one which involved use of a card. At first the system did not spread rapidly. By January 1954 only 62 banks offered charge card plans and most of these were small banks in small communities.

In 1959 the idea began to spread. Several large banks joined with the smaller ones to offer charge card services. These included the Bank of America in California, the Chase Manhattan Bank in New York, the Citizens and Southern National Bank in Atlanta, and the Marine Midland Bank of Western New York. By 1964 over 200 commercial banks had tried charge card banking, and the majority of them discontinued their own charge plans. The degree of success varied widely.

The Bank of America system was a striking success. In 1964 its outstanding charge card credit was $144 million, and a conservative estimate indicated profits of $4.5 million.[1] At the other extreme the Chase Manhattan Bank experienced large losses, became disenchanted and sold its system, which became the profitable Unicard System in New York City.[2]

Growth Factors

A thorough analysis of several charge plans over a 7 year period, 1954–1960, indicated that in most cases banks discontinued the service as a result of failure to generate enough volume to reach the breakeven point. The average breakeven point for 36 banks was an annual volume of $1,030,000.[3]

A number of banks which survived the experimentation period made their operations profitable to such an extent that they attracted many others into the credit card business. While only 70 banks had charge card plans in 1965, over 1,000 banks were issuing cards in January 1967. There were over 10 million bank charge card holders at that time.[4] The breakthrough came as banks identified the necessary elements of successful operation. These involve:

> a substantial population size in the market area
> a large number and variety of types of retail businesses in the market area

[1] "The Charge-It Plan That Really Took Off," *Business Week*, February 27, 1965.

[2] "Throwing in the Sponge (Chase Manhattan Abandoning Credit Card Dream)," *Forbes*, February 1, 1962, p. 15. "The Charge-It Plan That Really Took Off," *Business Week*, February 27, 1965.

[3] Harlan R. Patterson, "What Spells Success for Bank Charge Plans," *Banking*, February 1964, pp. 53 and 98.

[4] "Stores Honor Many Banks' Credit Cards Under Midwest Plan," *The Wall Street Journal*, January 17, 1967, p. 1.

the ability to compete effectively with other credit facilities in the
market area

an aggressive and sound bank management[5]

Other reasons for growth are the greater use of computers, which cut
the administrative cost of charge card plans, increasing familiarity of consumers and stores with credit cards, and a growing acceptance of use of
instalment credit by consumers.[6]

Types of Card Plans

Several different charge card systems are developing throughout the
nation. The local plans came first and are the most numerous. The bank
operates a charge card plan within its surrounding community. Regional
plans operate in more than one community and often encompass several
counties. State wide plans range from a single bank with branches throughout the state, such as the Bank of America in California with 900 branches
or the Valley National Bank in Arizona, to an exchange system set up such
as the California Bankcard Association involving 60 banks.[7] Five major
New York City banks with combined assets of $26 billion and 400 branches
are currently studying a cooperative credit card operation.[8]

Interstate plans operate in more than one state. The Midwest Bank
Card system is the best known. It has 12 members and 700 participating
banks (on a correspondent relationship) with over 4 million card holders,
50,000 participating merchants who honor the cards of any bank in the
group, and an estimated volume of $120 million of charge card credit for
1967. The system spreads over Illinois, Michigan and Indiana. It has a particular advantage in that large banks make arrangements with smaller banks
in other areas of the state and/or county to use the cards, in many cases at
no cost. This increases the charge card credit volume of the correspondent
bank thus lowering per unit costs and at the same time permitting the
smaller bank to offer credit card services in an area which would not support such activity on its own. All members use a common symbol on their
cards for easy identification.

The Inter-bank plan operates nationally. For example, the Bank of
America issues charge cards through a franchise plan to banks around the
nation. Interbankard is the newest innovation. The organization represents
seven large banks throughout the nation who plan to honor each other's
cards thus making each card national in scope.

[5] Patterson, *op. cit.*

[6] "New Deal in Cards: Midwest Banks' Credit Cards Are Usable Regionally," *The Wall Street Journal*, January 17, 1967, p. 12.

[7] "California Bankcard Group Enlists 56 Additional Banks," *The Wall Street Journal*, January 19, 1967, p. 28.

[8] "Credit Card is Studied by Five New York Banks," *The Wall Street Journal*, March 27, 1967, p. 8.

BENEFITS OF THE CHARGE CARD

The benefits to banks, consumers, and merchants are large enough to spur the movement on. Many of the returns to commercial banks are obvious. Participating merchants must maintain demand deposit accounts with the bank sponsoring the charge plan. By signing up more merchants the bank gets more accounts. Each new merchant must pay an initiation fee and rent an imprinter. The bank earns income through discounting the sales tickets at between 2½ and 7 percent. But the largest income will ultimately be derived from the outstanding consumer loans. Typically, consumer loans are the most profitable of all bank loans. Although charge card holders do not have to maintain deposits with the card issuing bank, the credit card provides a tie for soliciting demand and time deposit accounts and for selling other bank services. A further incentive is that each bank is afraid that its competition will start a plan and draw away customers. Therefore, one bank initiates a plan first, forcing the competition to set up plans as a counter move to prevent loss of customers. The first bank to offer a card plan in a given community often has a competition advantage.

Merchant Benefits

Charge card benefits to the merchant are numerous. They deposit sales slips at their bank to credit their accounts. The discount rate varies among bank plans and with the size of the average purchase and the total merchant volume over a specific period. Thus, the merchant reduces capital tied up in credit. Banks generally discount the sales slips without recourse which removes the merchant's problem of collecting delinquent bills.

The charge plans reduce the overhead of merchants who carry their own charge accounts. Estimates are that bank charge plans cost 40 to 80 percent less than a private charge department.[9] Banks also make charge plans available to merchants who do not have their own. Merchants believe that credit cards tend to make consumers more susceptible to impulse buying, and banks advertise in such a way as to benefit the merchant in the plan. Advertisements encourage consumers to look for merchants who accept the credit cards.

The typical costs to the participating merchants are listed in Table 28–1. Banks often waive the initiation fee.

Consumer Benefits

Bank charge cards have several benefits for the consumer. They reduce the amount of cash he has to carry, the number of credit cards he must

[9] "Encouraging Report on Charge Credit," *Burroughs Clearing House*, March 1960, p. 40.

TABLE 28–1

Typical Merchant Participation Terms

Initiation fee	$20-25
Imprinter fee	$ 5-12 per year
Discount rate	2½-7%
Type of recourse	without recourse

TABLE 28–2

Typical Contract for Bank Credit Cards

Billing period with no service charge	25 days
Service charge	1 to 1½ % per month
Line of credit	$350-1,000
Amount of instant cash	up to line of credit
Payment schedule per month	$10 or 5-10% of loan, whichever is higher
Limit of any one purchase without permission	$50

keep, and the number of checks he has to write. They increase his ability to shop at numerous stores for the best prices. The ability to get immediate cash is a great convenience and increases the likelihood of borrowing from banks relative to other financial intermediaries or of using the instalment credit plans of department stores. The idea of a ready source of credit at his disposal appeals to the consumer. The automatic loan aspects eliminate the time consuming chore of filling out credit applications whenever time purchases are made. The consumer has 25 days to pay without a service charge. Table 28–2 presents the typical characteristics of credit card conditions applying to consumer use of bank credit cards.

THE FUTURE

The growth of charge card programs will continue and will take several directions. Many more banks will offer charge services either to expand their array of bank services or as a defensive measure to guard against customer loss to other banks.

The tendency will be for individual bank plans to join with others in clearing associations to gain wider acceptance of their cards. There will be a major effort to develop a personal identification number for every person to facilitate use of the cards. The American Bankers Association currently has a committee to examine this problem. Exchanges will develop to provide credit information for the various credit granting institutions on the local, regional and national levels. Ultimately, there could be a single credit card acceptable on a national level.

Checkless Banking

Properly developed the bank charge card system could lead to a "cashless" and "checkless" society. The groundwork has been laid and future steps involve:[10]

1. Interchange agreements and clearing arrangements among all major bank charge card systems so that a single card will be honored by all merchants. Perhaps the Federal Reserve System will clear sales slips through their check clearing mechanism.
2. Development of centers to provide credit information for large regions.
3. Development of a national electronic network for exchanging information among banks and regional centers.
4. Use of the electronic network to transfer funds between banks.
5. The adoption of common symbols on credit cards to make them readily identifiable.
6. Finally, installation of terminal devices in merchant establishments which will tie in directly with banks and credit centers. When this network is complete, the electronic transfer of balances will be practical.

Once these steps are completed, the "checkless" society will be a fact. The consumer will use a charge card (some prefer to call it a "money card" at this stage) for all but minor transactions. The sales clerk will insert the buyer's card into a transmittal device which connects with the bank. The device will dial the buyer's bank account, debit it, and then credit the store's account. If the account has insufficient funds the computer will check the buyer's line-of-credit and, if it is adequate, automatically make a loan. Neither checks nor cash will change hands in the transaction. Money will become the electronic movement of information.

The National Association for Bank Audit, Control and Operations is currently studying the feasibility of the electronic network or credit-transfer

---

[10] Roger J. Aboucher and Nicholas E. Magnis, "Bank Credit Cards—Implication for the Future," *Bankers Monthly Magazine*, January 15, 1967, pp. 22–27.

system and the steps necessary to establish "checkless banking."[11] As these progressions take place the bank charge card system will continue to reduce the amount of cash needed and the number of checks written per capita.

IMPLICATIONS OF THE MOVEMENT

The overall effect of bank charge cards on the economy cannot be defined at this point, but several possible effects can be speculated. With a continuous line-of-credit the consumer can expand his choice of goods and services and alter the mix. The plan is well suited to purchases of small durable goods, nondurable goods, vacations and a variety of other services. The consumer will have the advantage of shopping many more sellers, such as discount houses, who may not offer credit. The consumer, with a ready source of credit, may also change his preference between spending now and later.

Bank Operations

The impact on traditional commercial bank financing could be great if, as a result of the new credit, the consumer makes more purchases out of current income thus reducing the flow of personal savings into financial institutions. Commercial banks would then have to search for new sources of funds to finance business.

As "checkless banking" approaches, banks face another problem. Instantaneous transactions will remove the float, or checks in circulation which have not been presented for payment. The float amounts to billions of dollars daily and is an important source of funds for bank lending. The loss of the float can cut bank earnings and force them to search for new ways to earn profits.

Monetary Policy

The potential effects on monetary control are strong enough to warrant the Federal Reserve Board of Governors to set up a special committee to study the development of charge card plans. Monetary policy may have to be modified to effect stricter control over consumer credit. The handy credit of consumers may prompt an increase in total consumer borrowing. Whether or not this would contribute to inflationary tendencies or to an increase in output depends upon the level of employment at a particular time. It is possible that—if charge card purchases are used for nondurable

---

[11] "Taking the 'Bluesky' Out of 'Checkless Banking'," *Burroughs Clearing House*, April 1967, p. 35.

goods and services, which tend to be less income elastic than durables—charge card use might help moderate the business cycle. On the other hand, if used to expand credit during full employment, that will increase inflationary pressures.

The Federal Reserve must consider the possible effects of changes in the money supply which can result from changes in the secular velocity, or turnover, of demand deposits of individuals and businesses. It must evaluate the effects of a reduction in the per capita cash needed by the public. As the "checkless" society approaches, the Federal Reserve will have to consider ways to offset the decrease in the money supply resulting from elimination of the float.

Installment Credit and Retail Firms

The credit card can affect competition among suppliers of instalment credit, for their relative shares of the market may change. Certainly department stores, sales finance, and consumer finance company credit is vulnerable, for bank charge plans improve the relative competitive position of commercial banks.

The growth of bank charge systems could alter the current relationship between large and small retail firms. In an environment where the trend is toward increasingly larger firms, bank charge cards, by providing charge programs for small retailers, may provide a way for more small firms to survive through neutralizing the credit elements in the retail service mix.[12]

Commercial Bank Competition

The bank card could effect the extent of interbank competition. Large banks will be able to compete effectively among themselves, but smaller banks will be at a disadvantage. Customers of small banks may switch to larger banks which offer card plans. In an effort to regain or to hold customers, small banks may incur extraordinary heavy costs to set up their own programs. In an attempt to recover such costs the small bank may assume too much risk in its loan and investment portfolio, thereby increasing the chance of failure.

The majority of small banks will probably align with larger banks in order to use their card plans or will join other small banks to set up joint plans. In either case, individual banks will lose part of their independence. Large and/or ambitious banks could use card plans as a step toward eventual merger or acquisition. Charge card plans could thus be another factor in the trend toward fewer and larger commercial banks in the nation.

---

[12] For further discussion of this point see: Robert H. Cole, *Financing Retail Credit Sales Through Charge Account Bank Plates*, Business Management Survey No. 5, Bureau of Business Management, College of Commerce and Business Administration, University of Illinois.

CONCLUSION

Bank charge cards are ushering in a new era, and most of society will be affected. Changes will occur in retail merchandising, consumer borrowing and buying habits, commercial banking, and the character of the nation's money supply. Along with its blessings are many problems which, if solved now, can provide an orderly transition to the "checkless" society.

A major problem of who will own, operate, and maintain the electronic network or credit transfer system is yet unanswered. Commercial banks, communication companies, the Federal Reserve Banks, and credit bureaus are all candidates. The psychological problem of getting people to accept the new system will probably be the largest hurdle. Thus, educating the public on the advantages of the new money system will be the biggest challenge.

29.

Cyclical and Growth Problems Facing the Savings and Loan Industry— Policy Implications and Suggested Reforms

ARNOLD W. SAMETZ

Over the past fifteen years, there have occurred wide cyclical swings in housing starts. Residential construction expenditures have ranged between $20 billion and $25 billion annually (in constant dollars) and the period began and ended with a nearly constant level of $20 billion in annual expenditures. On the other hand, over the same fifteen-year period, consumer expenditures on durable goods, such as automobiles, refrigerators, and washing machines, rose from $35 billion to $65 billion in constant dollars, while gross business fixed investment increased from $41 billion to $65 billion. Over this fifteen-year period, real GNP has varied between peak and trough by less than five percent while residential expenditures have varied anywhere between twenty percent to thirty-five percent.

Many individuals and policy-makers, in noting the wide countercyclical swings in housing, have expressed sympathy with the industry's plight. At the same time, these expressions of concern have been offset, to a marked degree, by the feeling that such swings in the residential construction sector have been counterbalanced by more or less offsetting changes in expendi-

Reprinted from *The Bulletin* of the Institute of Finance of the Graduate School of Business Administration of New York University, No. 46–47, March 1968, pp. 6–14, by permission of the publisher and Arnold W. Sametz, editor.

tures in other sectors and, therefore, that such changes in the public's tastes and preferences merely represent the inevitable outcome of the operations of a free and efficient market economy. In such an economy, so the argument runs, households have the right to allocate their incomes in any way that they deem fit and, further, this applies not only to current consumption of goods and services but also to how much of their disposable incomes they will employ in the consumption of such goods and how much they will save. Given their savings decisions, real resources will be freed which can then be employed in the construction of homes, commercial buildings, industrial plant and equipment, and other capital goods. Presumably, those willing to pay the highest prices for such saving, i.e., the highest rates of interest, more or less in line with the expected rates of return from their investments, will procure the freed resources. In this manner, economic welfare will be maximized since not only will households be purchasing out of their disposable incomes those currently produced goods and services that yield them the greatest satisfaction relative to the prices of such goods and services, but they will also be receiving interest on their saving that will then be employed in the most productive or efficient types of investment. Thus, a free market economy, with its corollary, freedom of consumer choice, tends to result in the most efficient allocation of society's scarce resources and, therefore, to an optimization of economic welfare.

No one would wish to argue with the benefits associated with a free market economy, as outlined above. However, it must be pointed out that, contrary to the above assumptions with respect to the free-market model, the housing market and the financing of that market contain serious imperfections that distort the ideal resource allocation here pictured and so lead to a situation that falls far short of maximizing economic welfare. Two of the most flagrant imperfections tending to distort a more efficient resource allocation are to be found in actions undertaken in the public sector, namely, (a) the impact of a particular set of monetary and fiscal policies on housing expenditures and (b) a particular regulatory mix that markedly affects the financial capabilities of those depository institutions helping to service the residential sector, namely, savings and loan associations, mutual savings banks, and commercial banks. To the extent that the activities of the public sector have a *selective* impact on resource allocation, their actions tend to lead to a deviation from the postulates and results inherent in the free-market model, a model that implicitly assumes a neutral impact of governmental activity on the economy's allocation of resources.

To show the selective impact of governmental activity on the housing industry and the sources of its financing relative to other sectors of the economy, let us begin with a brief examination of our monetary-fiscal policy mix over the past fifteen years. This policy mix can rightfully be designated as one of tight money and easy fiscal measures over the course of the business cycle. Thus, during expansions and boom periods there has been no attempt through an increase in personal and corporate income tax rates to restrain overall aggregate demand from raising the general level of prices. As a result, during this phase of the cycle, the monetary authorities have had to bear or shoulder the brunt of an anti-inflationary policy. The result has been not only an increase in interest rates resulting from an overall rise in the level of credit demanded by all sectors of the economy, but an acceleration of the rate increases due to the deceleration of the rate of growth of the money supply induced by the tight money policy of the Federal Reserve System. Further evidence of monetary stringency during these periods has also been seen in the increasing use of credit rationing to meet the excess demand for borrowed funds. High and rising open-market rates have also led to disintermediation, as in the credit crunch of 1966, when depositors in savings and loan associations, mutual savings banks, and commercial banks withdrew deposits from these intermediaries to invest them, in turn, in open-market securities yielding higher rates of return.

On the other hand, during those periods of mild and relatively short-lived recessions that we have experienced in the last fifteen years, an easy fiscal policy has reacted vigorously through cuts in corporate and personal income tax rates, as in 1954 and again in 1964. As a result, monetary policy has not had to loosen appreciably during recessions, or a relatively easy monetary policy has been quickly reversed with the end of a short-lived recession. Consequently, over the course of the entire cycle interest rates on the average, have risen secularly with a subsequent concentration of spending restraints on private housing rather than on other private and public expenditures.

The reason why residential construction has absorbed the greatest restrictive impact of this special set of monetary-fiscal policies (with the possible exception of small business and the financing of state and local government expenditures) relative to other sectors can be stated as follows: (a) during the boom phase of the cycle, disposable real income tends to rise less than proportionately to the cost *and* availability of mortgage funds; (b) such income increases as occur may look relatively impermanent; and (c) large ticket items bought on credit, such as housing, are dependent on other terms besides mortgage rates. During booms and the subsequent squeeze on available funds employed by depository institutions, the mortgage maturity structure may be shortened and the loan-to-value ratio increased so that the demand for mortgage funds is curtailed not only by rising mortgage rates but also by higher monthly payments and larger down payments. On the other hand, business investment spending varies primarily with volatile profit expectations, which are exceedingly high during periods of boom. Also, interest is only a minor cost in many forms of business investment, whereas it is a major cost in long-term investments represented by housing expenditures. Further, large corporations have many alternative means of financing investment expenditures open to them besides recourse to bank loans, whereas prospective home buyers are strictly limited in their sources of mortgage finance. Finally, federal expenditures unlike housing expenditures are basically insensitive to financial terms.

Turning now to the question of how the current regulatory mix has had a selective impact on the financing of the housing industry, let us begin by noting that 85 percent of the assets of S & L's are held in the form of mortgages, compared to 75 percent for mutual savings banks and only roughly 15 percent for commercial banks. Therefore, to the extent that quasi-governmental controls over these institutions in the form of regulations by the Federal Home Loan Banks System and the Federal Reserve System tend to favor one set of institutions over another, the total volume of mortgage financing will be affected.

Prior to 1957, and the Federal Reserve's decision to lift the savings and time rate ceiling under Regulation Q, there would appear to have been a rough regulatory compromise existing between the Federal Reserve Board (Fed) and the Federal Home Loan Bank Board (FHLB). Commercial banks, as department stores of finance, were relatively free on the uses side of their portfolios, while savings and loan associations and, to a somewhat lesser extent, mutual savings banks were relatively restricted, through law and regulation, to the acquisition of mortgages. On the other hand, on the sources side, the latter were relatively free compared to the commercial banks in attracting thrift accounts since no rate ceilings were imposed on them.

1957 witnessed the beginning of the end of this rough regulatory compromise since, at that time, the balance was tilted in favor of commercial banks as the rate ceiling under Regulation Q was revised upward; this, in turn, was followed by many further upward revisions in subsequent years. Such revisions during periods of rapidly rising interest rates meant, in effect, that if the savings and loan associations and mutual savings banks were once again to redress the competitive balance, they had to be able (a) to borrow long in the open market, (b) if continuing to borrow short, to limit increased savings rates to *new* depositors only, given the relatively slow turnover of their mortgage portfolios, or (c) to lend short. Unfortunately, these options were not open to the S & L's and the mutual savings banks but only to the commercial banks, given the prevailing regulatory mix. If the S & L's and the mutual savings banks had been free to bid for funds in the open market (via debentures and common stock issues, for example) or had been allowed to make short-term loans, or had been able to raise nominal mortgage rates while continuing to hold down the size of monthly payments (via increases in the mortgage maturity structure), or had been allowed to raise loan-value ratios beyond the existing permissible limits, there is little doubt that some of the mortgage volume would have been restored during periods of tight money.

What have been the effects of these imperfections in the housing sector induced by a *particular set* of monetary-fiscal policies and regulatory mixes? For one thing, allocational efficiency has suffered since less resources have been devoted to housing than free consumer choice would dictate. Thus, given the prevailing regulatory mix, households have not been able to bid for mortgage funds by trading off higher mortgage rates against longer terms, or higher loan-to-value ratios. Also, given the existing tight-money, easy fiscal policy, interest rates, on the average, have been higher than they would have been with a different counter-cyclical policy mix, with the major burden of such a mix being borne by the housing sector in the form of sharply reduced demands for residential construction. Finally, both monetary-fiscal policy and the regulatory mix prevailing over the past fifteen years have led to disintermediation and a type of credit rationing whose incidence falls very heavily on nonbank depository intermediaries and, thus, on those households heavily dependent on these intermediaries for mortgage credit.

In addition to allocational inefficiency induced by prevailing public policies, the particular mixes employed have also given rise to operational inefficiencies. That is, not only has the volume of housing construction been less than it would have been in the presence of a freer housing sector, but even that amount constructed has been produced inefficiently since the resources actually employed produce less housing than they are capable of. This follows, among other things, from the fact that there are more idle resources, on the average, in a stop-and-go industry, such as residential construction, than in the less volatile sectors of the economy. Incidentally, the argument that cyclical unemployment in the housing sector is more or less counterbalanced by inverse movements of nonresidential private construction so that resources are not wasted cannot bear the weight of careful scrutiny. Although, over the last decade and a half, commercial and industrial construction has been positively correlated with *increases* in housing expenditures, they have reached a plateau, rather than declining with concurrent *deceases* in home purchases. As a result, there have been either labor shortages in the construction industry during the former periods or an excess of idle workers in the latter periods. Such allocational problems have been closely related to operational inefficiencies inasmuch as the threat of unemployment in the housing sector, even for those currently employed, has encouraged the continuance of restrictive work rules and featherbedding, with the result that productivity per worker in the industry is low. Also this threat, combined with the stop-and-go nature of the housing sector, has discouraged mechanization, innovations, and other managerial efficiencies, further contributing to the low productivity in the industry.

How can an alternative set of public measures increase economic welfare without, at the same time, decreasing the overall efficacy of stabilization policy? For one thing, a tight fiscal, easy monetary policy in place of the current mix will restrain aggregate demand during inflationary periods and encourage additional spending during recessions while at the same time yielding lower average interest rates and encourage greater credit availability. The result will be a diffusion of the impact of stabilization policy so that the brunt of it no longer falls primarily on the housing sector but also on other consumer durables and business fixed investment expenditures. The $5 billion decrease in housing expenditures brought on by the current mix of monetary-fiscal policies to combat inflation can be spread over many sectors by a changed mix with only marginal declines in expenditures for all sectors. Further, to the extent that higher interest rates were needed to prevent hot money flows abroad from increasing our balance of payments difficulties, this new mix can be somewhat amended so as to be designated a tighter fiscal, somewhat easier monetary policy. In either case, the housing sector will no longer be singled out to bear the brunt of stabilization policy.

Changes in the current regulatory mix on S & L's and mutual savings banks, relative to commercial banks, may redress the regulatory balance once again and ensure a more ample flow of funds into the housing market. On the sources side, S & L's and mutual savings banks may be empowered (a) to issue a varied assortment of consumer savings certificates to meet the savings preferences of households, much in the same manner that commercial banks have been able to do both for households and for business firms; (b) to issue debentures to raise funds in the same way that banks have recently done; (c) to issue mortgage participation certificates yielding some ¼ percent more than AAA corporate bonds, thereby attracting funds from large institutional investors such as pension funds; and (d) to convert freely from mutual to stock companies and to issue new equity offerings. Also, relevant regulatory agencies may reallocate savings funds by agreeing to adjust the interest rate differentials on these funds now almost obliterated by the maximum ceiling rates currently in force; by encouraging ease of entry and expansion of offices by S & L's and mutual savings banks *relative* to commercial banks; and by giving the Fed permanent authority to purchase and sell FHLB obligations, the proceeds of which may then be employed by the FHLB as advances to member S & L's and mutual savings banks when needed at penalty rates.

On the uses side, the FHLB should allow more flexible mortgage terms so that trade-offs between rates and maturity as well as loan-value ratios become easier for households wishing to purchase homes. Also, open-ended mortgages should be encouraged with outstanding mortgage loans increased at least back to par after several years of satisfactory mortgage experience. Obviously, such a line of credit can be applied with equal relevance to consumers and to business firms, which are granted just such credit lines by banks. It must also be remembered that the economic capacity of households to maintain such lines of credit improves with age. S & L's, as well as mutual savings banks, should have the option to make such consumer loans as are closely related to housing expenditures. The decision to purchase a home actually is enhanced by the knowledge that cheap and ample sources of supply are available to equip that home. Further, there should be some family financing package available to the small saver through S & L's and mutual savings banks that affords cheap and easy access to saving in the form of equities and life insurance. Neither mutual funds nor life insurance companies find it profitable to go out and solicit the few dollars a week or month that the typical wage earner can invest. A simple savings plan in which a monthly deposit in thrift institutions is allocated between a deposit, mutual fund, and life insurance should prove most attractive and relatively cheap to the small saver since no sales force is needed. Finally, S & L's and mutual savings banks should be empowered to purchase short-term securities, such as government agency issues and commercial paper, which may be substituted for direct governmental obligations as liquidity reserves while, at the same time, affording higher yields to these institutions.

In conclusion, it should always be kept in mind that the current status quo in public policy and regulatory mixes is in no way to be confused with the economic welfare attained when free market choice prevails. Furthermore, changes in these mixes not only will enhance freedom of consumer choice and economic welfare by widening the options available to households, but will also help cut down on the cyclical volatility of expenditures in the housing industry and the means for financing such expenditures, while resulting in only marginal changes in expenditures for the products of other sectors of the economy.

The above has been concerned with the cyclical problem of mortgage flows and a particular set of public policy and regulatory measures that distorts the allocation of resources. As a result of the analysis, changes in the mix of monetary-fiscal policy and regulatory activity were advocated that would go far toward stabilizing the housing sector and its financing, thereby extending the options available to households and enhancing economic welfare.

30.

Pension Fund Investments

FEDERAL RESERVE BANK OF CHICAGO

Pension funds have been playing an expanding role on the financial scene during the past 20 years. About 28 million workers in private employment, more than half of the total, are now covered by pension plans compared with 6 million in 1945. An additional 5 million government employes are covered by plans sponsored by state and local governments, more than twice as many as at the end of World War II.

Each year these private and state and local pension funds increase in size as income from contributions and investments exceeds payments of benefits and expenses. Last year net receipts of these funds amounted to more than 12 billion dollars. The great bulk of these funds was invested in corporate stocks and bonds. During the Sixties, the pension funds have been the most important buyers of both types of securities.

The total market value of private and state and local pension funds now exceeds 134 billion dollars—more than the total assets of savings and loan associations or life insurance companies (exclusive of reserves of insured pension plans). As a proportion of the assets of all savings-type, nonbank financial institutions and private and state and local pension funds have risen steadily from 9 percent in 1945 to 27 percent in 1965.[1]

Pension plans are provided for additional millions of workers under social security, railroad retirement and civil service funds. These funds,

Reprinted from *Business Conditions*, September 1966, pp. 6–20, by permission of the publisher, the Federal Reserve Bank of Chicago.

[1] Nonbank financial institutions include pension funds, life insurance companies, savings and loan associations, mutual savings banks, open-end investment companies (mutual funds) and credit unions.

however, are invested exclusively in U.S. Treasury obligations. To the extent that receipts exceed disbursements for these funds, the Treasury's needs for financing in the money and capital markets are reduced. Social security, Federal employe and railroad retirement funds do not directly influence the market for private stocks and bonds; the private and state and local funds do have an impact to an important degree.

SPURS TO DEVELOPMENT

Employe pensions have a long history in military service, governmental employment and in some industries, such as public utilities and financial institutions, where the work force is relatively stable. The absence of provisions for pension programs in most private industries until World War II was given as an important reason for support of social security legislation in the mid-Thirties.

The social security program (old age, survivors' and disability insurance—OASDI) continues to operate as the prime element in promoting the Government's policy of "assuring reasonably adequate retirement income to workers, their widows and dependents." Increasingly, however, OASDI has been supplemented by private plans, in part, because these have been encouraged by Federal legislation and court decisions.

The principal support given to private pensions by Government is in favorable tax treatment of both contributions to the funds and income earned on fund investments.

First, employer contributions to private pension funds conforming to statutory standards (mainly relating to equity for all classes of employes and standards of management) are deductible for purposes of determining taxable net income. This applies to lump-sum payments required to fund *past-service liabilities* to employes arising from service prior to the establishment of plans as well as to contributions covering liabilities currently accrued. Second, employes are not required to report employer contributions to pension funds in their behalf as current income. Third, investment income of funds, whether from interest and dividends or capital gains, is not taxable when earned.

In effect, the tax rules for pension funds permit employes to defer taxes on income earned currently until benefits are received in retirement years. Any postponement of taxes amounts to an indirect reduction of tax rates because of interest that is or could be earned in the interval. In addition, effective tax rates for individuals during retirement years almost invariably are lower than during working years because of reduced income and double personal exemptions allowed to those over age 65.

Initiation of pension plans was stimulated during World War II and the Korean War by higher than normal tax rates on both corporations and individuals and by the corporate excess profits tax. Once in effect, pension plans tend to be taken for granted as a condition of employment and are unlikely to be terminated except in the case of firms suffering severe financial setbacks.

Most of the private pension plans instituted prior to the late Forties were unilateral in the sense that they were established by managements motivated principally by a desire to reduce labor turnover. After World War II some of the largest industrial unions began to press for establishment of pensions for their members in labor-management negotiations.

The Supreme Court in 1949 confirmed a National Labor Relations Board ruling that pensions were a legitimate subject for collective bargaining. In subsequent years employe pension plans were started by firms in major unionized industries, such as auto, steel and rubber. Since then, plans have been expanded and liberalized periodically.

In industries (such as apparel, construction and trucking) which include many small firms with relatively high employe turnover, workers are covered by so-called multi-employer pension plans with contributions paid into a common fund controlled by both management and labor.

Tax advantages similar to those available to private pension plans were extended to the self-employed in 1962 after the passage of the Self-Employed Individual Tax Retirement Act. Little is known concerning the amounts of funds set aside under this legislation, but doubtless these are growing rapidly.

Public policy also has been directed toward maintaining confidence in the administration of pension funds, mainly by requiring public disclosure of pertinent financial data. To this end, the Welfare and Pension Plans Disclosure Act was passed in 1958 and strengthened through amendments in 1962,

Most unilateral pension plans initiated by employers are contributory —employes pay a portion of their income into the fund thereby supplementing employer contributions. Benefits of these plans usually vary with employe income. Most union-negotiated or bargained plans are noncontributory with all payments made by employers. Benefits of negotiated plans usually are uniform, varying with length of service but not with earnings.

FUNDING THE PRIVATE PLANS

Private pension plans are of two main types: insured and noninsured. The first group is administered by insurance companies which, until recently, mingled contributions for pensions with their total cash inflow when making investments. The noninsured funds administered by trustees can be subdivided into corporate funds and those of nonprofit organizations and multi-employer plans. (Some of the later are administered by insurance companies.)

The market value of all private pension plans at the end of 1965 was nearly 100 billion dollars.

Assets	Billion dollars	Percent
Insured pension reserves	27.3	28
Noninsured corporate funds	65.6	66
Other noninsured funds	5.9	6
Total private funds	98.8	100

The great bulk of the corporate funds are administered by the trust departments of about 20 banks headquartered in New York, Chicago and other large centers. Financial reports of funds covering 26 workers or more must be filed annually with the Department of Labor and are available for inspection. Also, the Securities and Exchange Commission (SEC) publishes estimates of the total assets of all private funds and all corporate funds with a breakdown of investments by major class and also purchases and sales of stock. (Since 1933 pension funds that invested in securities of the parent firm or its subsidiaries have been required to file reports with the SEC. Purchases of parent company stock have been confined largely to deferred profit sharing funds.)

Individual corporations that negotiate pension agreements with unions have almost complete discretion in the procedures followed in making contributions to funds and in the investment policies of these funds. In effect, the typical corporation undertakes to pay certain benefits to workers. These disbursements can be made directly out of current cash flow, but in most cases a reserve is established. The reserve may or may not be fully funded, that is, with assets sufficient to cover accrued liabilities to employes in the event the fund were to be liquidated.

No pension plan can be fully funded in a precise sense. Estimates of future disbursements are based upon actuarial assumptions regarding the average durations of employment of workers presently employed and their longevity (and in some cases that of their survivors) after retirement. These assumptions hardly ever will match future developments exactly. Employe turnover rates may change and affect the proportion acquiring vested interests in the employer's contributions. Moreover, when plans are liberalized, an additional past-service liability usually is created that may not be offset immediately by a lump sum payment by the employer. The basis of valuing fund assets on any given date for the purpose of comparisons with estimated future payments is a further question. Finally, it is unrealistic in the case of most funds to think seriously of liquidation. Short of bankruptcy of the contributing firm, most pension funds reasonably can be expected to increase in size for many years, if not indefinitely, because contributions and earnings are likely to continue to exceed disbursements. This prospect diminishes the significance of accurate and complete funding.

When the major industrial pension funds were established in the late Forties and early Fifties, there was widespread discussion of the desirability of funding the past-service liabilities created at a moment in time by the signing of a contract. From the standpoint of equity, it was reasonable that a fund should be set up separate from the corporation's own books in order to offer some assurance that accumulated liabilities to employes would be paid regardless of the fortunes of the firm agreeing to the plan. On the other hand, concern was voiced that accumulation of large sums—100 billion dollars was visualized as early as 1949—would threaten economic stability if sufficient productive investment opportunities did not develop concurrently.

Under Federal law, up to 10 percent of the estimated past-service liability incurred upon the commencement of a pension plan added to a fund annually can be deducted from taxable income. Managements of most large corporations seek to fund their plans fully and as soon as possible. They have, however, tended to vary annual contributions in response to variations in before-tax profits. (Total employer contributions to corporate pension funds declined in 1954 and 1958 and increased only slightly in 1961, all recession years.) Most corporate managements have decided, sooner or later, to attempt to speed the process of funding by purchases of common stocks expected, in time, to increase in market value.

TRUSTEED FUNDS PREFER STOCKS

Three-fourths of the assets of corporate pension funds in 1951 consisted of corporate bonds (45 percent) and Government securities (32 percent). Only 12 percent of total assets was in common stocks. Since benefits are fixed by contract, most administrators of pension funds believed that prudent investment practice required that pension funds be placed predominantly in bonds or mortgages—fixed-income obligations with definite maturity dates. This view is still held by a small and dwindling number of managers of large funds.

In the early Fifties, pension fund managers increasingly became interested in common stocks. Government security purchases were curtailed by most funds and some began to liquidate these assets, but corporate bonds continued to be the most important outlet for new money.

The proportion of new money placed in common stock by corporate pension funds rose from 25 percent of new investments in 1953 to more than 50 percent in 1959. Until the latter year, net bond purchases had exceeded net common stock purchases. The gap widened in subsequent years. Stocks accounted for 62 percent of new investments in 1965 compared with 23 percent for corporate bonds and 9 percent for mortgages—another type of investment that has gained favor in recent years.

At book value, common stocks first exceeded holdings of corporate bonds in corporate pension funds in 1964.[2] At the end of 1965, 44 percent of the book value of these funds was in common stocks compared to 39 percent in bonds.

The growing importance of common stock investments by pension funds is more striking when market values are considered. Market values of common stocks in pension portfolios at the end of 1965, because of the general rise in stock prices, was 59 percent *more* than book value. Reflecting the effects of rising interest rates in recent years, the market value of corporate bonds in pension portfolios at that time was 5 percent *less* than book value. As a result, common stock amounted to 56 percent of the market value of corporate pension fund portfolios compared with only 30 percent for corporate bonds. Entirely because of the rise in stock prices, the total market value of corporate pension funds exceeded total book value by 24 percent.

Substantial variations exist between the portfolios of different pension funds. In some cases, notably the Sears Roebuck Savings and Profit Sharing Pension Fund, virtually all of the fund is in common stock. At the other extreme are the funds of the Bell Telephone System which at the end of 1964 held less than 15 percent of their assets in common stocks. Many corporate funds follow a policy of investing about 50 percent of the net additions to assets in common stocks, obviously a rough rule of thumb. The number of firms with a policy of investing 60 or 70 percent of new money in stock has been rising.

Deferred profit sharing plans, like Sears, are included with the regular corporate pension funds in the total for the corporate sector. In most of these, retirement benefits to covered workers, perhaps in lump sums, are affected by gains or losses in market values of assets of the funds. In the other funds, this is not the case because benefits are set by contract. Favorable investment experience may result in reduction of payments into the fund, or it may cause corporate managements to agree more readily to liberalizations of benefits. Private studies indicate that a 1 percent increase in annual investment performance of a pension fund (interest, dividends and capital gains) permits corporations to either reduce pension costs or increase benefits by about 20 percent, depending upon certain assumptions.

Since assets of most pension funds are expected to continue to rise indefinitely and because payouts tend not to fluctuate but to rise gradually, fund managers do not need to give great attention to liquidity when selecting investments. Funds are unlikely to have to sell stocks when market conditions are unfavorable. For such investors, since common stocks are noncallable, highly marketable and have no maturity, stocks appear suitable

[2] Book value is the purchase price for stocks and amortized purchased price for bonds.

vehicles for long-term investment. Purchases of stock, moreover, are made on the tacit or explicit assumption that prices of these securities and the dividends paid on them will tend to move upward more or less in line with rising standards of living and typical pension benefits. Over the long run this has been true in the past, but periodic declines in the market and unfortunate selections of particular stocks can invalidate the theory in some cases.

Investment policies of the various corporate pension funds are determined by executives of the parent firms in discussions with trust officers and other investment counselors. The discretion allowed to trustees by corporate managements varies from case to case. Union officials have taken little direct part in investment decisions on the general make-up of fund portfolios and the particular securities to be purchased. Unions have urged, on occasion, that a portion of these funds be invested in low-income housing, slum clearance and other projects that might benefit workers. But the emphasis of those responsible for the funds has been on maximizing investment performance, both in income and in capital gains.

Multi-employer pension plans and those of nonprofit organizations in general follow investment practices similar to those of the corporate plans. Some large multi-employer plans, however, have made relatively large investments in mortgages and real estate.

IMPACT ON THE STOCK MARKET

The total market value of all stock of United States corporations was estimated at almost 780 billion dollars at the end of 1965. Individuals—including personal trust funds—owned the great bulk (86 percent) of this total. Next to individuals, the largest group of stockholders were the pension funds with almost 40 billion dollars or 5 percent of the total. Open-end investment companies (mutual funds) held 31 billion in stock, 4 percent of the total. Stock holdings of pension funds first exceeded those of open-end investment companies in 1959. The gap has widened each subsequent year.

Pension fund purchases of stock are much more important than indicated by the proportion of total stock they own. For one thing, the funds confine their purchases almost entirely to *blue chip* stocks of large, well-managed firms that typically are listed on the New York Stock Exchange (NYSE). These funds own about 7 percent of all the stock on the Big Board and much larger proportions of particular issues.

Several of the funds have assets of a billion dollars or more. Placing even a tiny proportion of their assets in the stock of a moderate-sized firm could influence the price of these shares substantially. Moreover, sizable holdings of stock of smaller firms could result in a pension fund gaining working control, a development frowned upon by Government and most fund managers alike.

Sales of stock on the NYSE totaled 73 billion dollars in 1965, less than 14 percent of the market value of all listed issues at year-end. Pension funds accounted for about 10 percent of the volume of the exchange either as buyers or sellers, compared with 16 percent for the open-end investment companies. Pension fund purchases of stock exceeded sales by 3 billion dollars, however, more than twice as much as the net purchases of open-end investment companies.

One of the remarkable financial developments of the Sixties is the small volume of new common stock issues. During the period 1960–65, net new issues of preferred and common stock (new issues less retirements) totaled only 6.5 billion dollars or 1.1 billion a year. (One-third of the six-year total was accounted for by two large issues by American Telephone & Telegraph Co.) During the last three years, the average was less than 0.5 billion dollars a year.

In short, the supply of common stock has been virtually stable. Under these circumstances, appreciable net acquisitions of stock by pension funds and other financial institutions have been possible only because of net liquidations by individuals. The total value of stocks held by individuals, of course, has continued to increase as market prices rose, but, nevertheless, individuals have been selling more stock than they purchased.[3]

Each year from 1955 (and probably earlier) through 1965, the private pension funds have been the largest net purchasers of common stock. Individuals, on the other hand, have sold more stock than they purchased each year since 1957. Since 1961, moreover, individuals' net purchases of open-end investment company shares have fallen far short of their net sales of corporate stock.

A question arises of what the trend of stock prices would have been in the past decade if the pension funds had not been buying stocks or had been buying them less heavily. At the end of 1965, Standard and Poor's 500 stock composite index was more than twice as high as 10 years earlier and 60 percent above its level at the end of 1960.

Unfortunately, stock prices sometimes move down. In late August, the Standard and Poor's composite stock index was 11 percent lower than at the end of December. This implies a decline in the market value of the stock held by private pension funds of about 4.3 billion dollars, an amount

[3] Doubtless, net sales of stock by individuals as a class reflects large sales by a relatively small group of wealthy individuals who acquired these shares when prices of the stock were much lower. The two largest secondary issues of this type in recent years were the 570 million dollar sale of TWA stock by Howard Hughes in the spring of 1966 and the 660 million dollar offering of Ford Motor Co. shares in 1956. It is likely that a considerable majority of individual stockholders have been net purchasers of stock in recent years.

substantially greater than their net receipts for the period. The Standard and Poor's index of prices of high-grade stocks, perhaps more representative of issues purchased by pension funds, was 14 percent lower in August than at the end of December.

Much has been written in recent years about the stabilizing influence of pension fund purchases on stock prices. For the most part the funds buy stocks to hold "for the long pull." Normally they do not move in and out of particular issues seeking speculative profits.

Sales of common stock by the pension funds in 1965 amounted to 46 percent of their purchases compared with 79 percent for open-end investment companies. But sales of stock by the funds have tended to rise relative to purchases since the mid-Fifties when purchases exceeded sales by more than five to one.

Stock trading activity of pension funds in the future may increase further. Fund managers, like other investors, presumably should wish to sell shares that seem to be overpriced and to reduce stock purchases when it appears the general market may be trending downward.

The incentive to adjust portfolios on the basis of market judgments is increasing because of the growing interest in investment performance—interest and dividends plus changes in market values as a percent of market value at the start of the year (allowing for net contributions to the fund). Corporations can shift from one trust company or investment adviser to another or threaten to do so if the performance of their fund seems inadequate. Revitalized competition from life insurance companies seeking pension fund accounts may also promote more active management of investments.

REBIRTH OF INSURED FUNDS

Life insurance companies from their earliest period have sold annuities to persons wishing to provide retirement income for themselves and to business firms doing so for their employes. The number of individual annuities in force at the end of 1965 was 1.1 million, somewhat less than in the early Fifties. Group annuities issued under insured pension plans, however, have grown steadily to cover a total of over 6.2 million workers at the end of 1965.

Pension reserves of life insurance companies amounted to 27.3 billion dollars in 1965 and accounted for 22 percent of all reserves of these institutions. Twenty years ago these pension reserves were only one-tenth their present size and only 7 percent of total life insurance company reserves.

Despite rapid growth, insured pension reserves have fallen far behind privately administered funds. Insured plans had 1.5 times the assets of noninsured private plans in 1945; this proportion had dropped to 64 percent by 1955 and to 39 percent by 1965. Insurance company executives have indicated that they now have the necessary authority to reverse this relative decline.

Insurance companies in recent years have overcome a number of legal obstacles that had hampered them in competing with bank trust departments in managing pension funds. A revenue code change in 1959 permitted insurance companies to separate earnings on pension fund investments from other income for tax purposes. An SEC ruling in 1963 exempted insurers from the need to file prospectuses on pension investment programs. Most important, the state of New York amended its law in 1962 to permit insurance companies headquartered in the state or doing business there to keep "separate accounts" for pension reserves and to invest these funds with the wide discretion permitted trust companies. Several other states had passed similar legislation in earlier years, but the action in New York was necessary to permit most major insurance companies to make substantial investments in common stock and to emulate the capital gains reported by noninsured plans.

Pension reserves prior to 1962 were mingled with other life insurance company funds. The New York law limited common stock to 5 percent of total assets, and most life insurance companies operating on a national scale held such investments to an even lower proportion. At the end of 1965, 37 percent of all life insurance company assets were in mortgages and an equal proportion was in corporate bonds. Stocks accounted for only 6 percent of total assets.

Life insurance companies had been relatively successful in retaining the pension business of smaller firms. Now portions of such funds can be invested in common stock if desired by the contributing firms. A number of smaller funds can be pooled to form a single account large enough to permit diversification of the investment portfolio. Large plans normally are handled individually.

The annuities purchased out of pension fund separate accounts when employes retire are conventional. Future benefits for each individual are determined at the time of retirement and are supported by all of the assets of the life insurance company administering the plan.

Major life insurance companies now are promoting separate accounts vigorously. Reserves for these accounts rose from 85 million to 260 million dollars during 1965. Still, only about 1 percent of all insured pension funds were of the new type at the end of last year. It is anticipated that the proportion of insured pension funds administered through separate accounts will grow rapidly in the next few years, partly as a result of amendments to existing insured plans. If so, net purchases of common stock by life insurance companies, only 400 million dollars in 1965,[4] will rise appreciably.

[4] Excludes stock acquired through conversions of bonds or preferred stock.

STATE AND LOCAL FUNDS

Employes of the states and their political subdivisions commonly were covered by pension plans long before the private plans burgeoned in the late Forties. State and local pension funds also have grown rapidly in the postwar period as payrolls have risen and benefits have been liberalized.

For the past 10 years, state and local pension funds have been growing at an average rate of 13 percent a year—about as fast as the total of private plans (insured and noninsured). Total assets of the state and local funds reached 35 billion dollars in 1965, up from only 2.5 billion in 1945. About 70 percent of the assets of these funds are administered by the states and the remainder by other governmental bodies.

State and local pension plans often are grouped with Federal programs and included in an aggregate of "public" plans. But state and local pension funds are more similar to private plans in their investment policies than to Federal programs. Like private plans, and in contrast to federally administered plans, state and local pension funds invest most of their excess of receipts over disbursements in corporate securities.

On the other hand, state and local plans differ from private plans in a number of ways. Forty percent of the contributions to these funds are made by employes as compared with only 12 percent for corporate pension funds. Other differences include the following: governmental bodies do not reduce or slow the rise in their contributions in recession years; state and local funds approximate full-funding of liabilities more closely, and administrators of most state and local funds are strictly circumscribed on their investment policies.

Investment rules for state and local government pension funds are far from uniform and even vary between separate funds in particular states. Some lists of eligible investments carry a prescribed order of preference; in other states, investments of funds for both state and local employes are covered by the same rules as life insurance companies. The tendency has been to broaden the discretion of fund managers to enable them to increase earnings. The investments of state administered pension funds in the states of the Seventh Federal Reserve District as of June 30, 1965 are shown below.

Investments	Illinois	Indiana	Iowa	Michigan	Wisconsin
			(percent)		
Governments	8	52	20	37	1
Municipals		4		7	
Mortgages	29	10		55	12
Corporate bonds	58	26	66		52
Corporate stocks	5	8			8
Other			14	1	27
Total	100	100	100	100	100

SOURCE: Investment Bankers Association of America.

Like corporate funds, differences in the makeup of state and local pension fund investments relate to local traditions and policies as well as legal restrictions. The time, effort and skill devoted to investment programs, of course, tends to vary also with the size of plans that range from those of small municipalities to the 3.7 billion dollar fund of the state of New York.

As late as 1955, 45 percent of all assets of state and local funds were invested in governments and 26 percent in municipals, often consisting of the securities of the state and local governments that operate the plan. (More than 60 percent of the state and local securities held by these funds in recent years were issues of the administering government.) Even then, 27 percent of the state and local funds were in corporate bonds, the largest outlet besides Governments.

State and local funds by mid-1965 had reduced the relative share of their investments in Governments to 23 percent and municipals to less than 9 percent. Since 1961 municipals have been liquidated on balance. Obviously, tax-exempt securities have greatest value to investors who pay taxes. Corporate bond holdings had increased to 48 percent of all assets of these funds in 1965 and mortgages to 11 percent. Common stock investments, although rising, accounted for only 5 percent of the total.

The proportion of corporate bonds, common stocks and mortgages in state and local pension portfolios is likely to continue to rise. Some state and local funds continue to purchase debt securities almost exclusively, and a few have as much as 98 percent of their funds in Governments. A few states (mainly in the South) have large investments, as much as 40 percent, in municipals. (Legal requirements or preferences usually are responsible for such investments.) On the other hand, several states have 75 percent or more of their funds in corporate bonds and a few have as much as 25 percent in common stocks.

During the period 1960–65, state and local pension funds increased their holdings of corporate bonds by 10 billion dollars. Private pension funds during the same six years acquired 12 billion dollars in bonds (allocating life insurance company holdings to pension plans on the basis of the proportion of total reserves). Together these institutions accounted for over 54 percent of the increase in outstanding bonds during this period.

PROBLEMS AND POLICIES

While pension funds are expected to grow in size for many years, the rate of growth probably will decline gradually. Virtually all major employers have been contributing to pension funds for the past decade. Many of these plans are nearing maturity. As more long service employes reach retirement age, disbursements rise. As relatively full funding is achieved, contributions are related more closely to liabilities incurred currently. Actually, the trend toward slower growth of pension funds has been under way for years as shown by the average annual rate of increase in market values.

Year	Total	Average increase in market value State and local	Total private
		(percent)	
1946-50	20	16	22
1951-55	18	15	20
1956-60	14	13	14
1961-65	12	12	12

These percentage gains are made, of course, on an increasing base. Increases, in dollar terms, of 14 billion dollars in each of the last two years in total market value of reserves of private and state and local pension funds combined, have been much larger than in any earlier period.

Pension funds will continue to increase as the number of covered workers rises and as wages and salaries increase. Payments into funds are growing, not only because basic pensions at normal retirement age have been increased but also because of a trend toward earlier eligibility of new workers for coverage under the plan, disability payments, early voluntary retirements and survivors' benefits. These factors also will increase payouts but not so fast as receipts.

The President's Committee on Retirement and Welfare Programs, reporting in January 1965, recommended that all plans be adequately funded to protect workers in case of the parent firm's insolvency and that workers should be granted "some reasonable measure of vesting," that is, a firm claim to the employer's contribution.

Many plans already meet these standards. Legislation relative to eligibility for tax purposes could induce additional plans to move toward these goals. The object of the Committee's recommendations is to increase worker security and to improve the mobility of older workers who might refuse to leave for better jobs because of a reluctance to lose pension rights. One important effect of both funding and vesting is to increase the size of pension funds.

The Committee's staff estimated that the book value of private pension plans would increase at a rate of about 8 percent a year for the 1965–75 period. If so, funds would more than double in the next 10 years.

Recent studies have concluded that pension funds do not cause most covered workers to reduce current savings in other forms, indicating that most, if not all, of the additions to pension reserves represent net additions to personal savings. One study concluded, on the basis of surveys, that workers with pension rights also save *more* in other ways than those who do not have such coverage. It also has been suggested that pension reserves represent a net increase in the supply of capital funds available for private investment.

Several imponderables hamper evaluations of the effect of pension plans on saving, spending and investment. Would regular incomes have increased more in the absence of the new pension plans? If pension accumulations had not been subsidized through tax incentives, would other taxes have been reduced?

Pension reserves are not available to individuals for spending on goods and services as are savings in other financial media. But this does not necessarily mean that many people, believing their retirement income assured, are not more willing to spend freely out of current cash income.

Even more perplexing is the relation of pensions to the old savings-investment controversies of the Thirties. If individuals attempt to save beyond the need for investments, the theory goes, income of others is reduced. If the process becomes cumulative, the economy as a whole is affected adversely.

In the late Fifties and early Sixties, it is generally agreed, the United States economy was operating below its potential. The sector lagging most noticeably, following the capital spending boom of 1955–57, was business investment. Nevertheless, additional spending by consumers based on higher current cash income or reduced saving might have simulated additional expenditures for new plant and equipment.

The President's Committee found no clear reason to recommend investment guidelines for private pension funds. It merely suggested that purchases of the securities and other obligations of the firm contributing to the fund be limited to 10 percent of new investments, a restriction that would affect very few plans. To help police investment practices, the Committee urged fuller disclosure of investments and operations and greater use of consulting actuaries and public auditors.

A number of questions arise concerning the growing common stock investments of private pension funds and the tendency of insured and state and local plans to follow a similar path. First is the question of control or lack of control over management of firms in whick stock is purchased. There is little evidence that pension fund managers have attempted to use their voting power to control operating managements. In fact, many trustees specifically avoid any participation in annual meetings or proxy fights. But here is a dilemma. These trustees are among the most knowledgeable of stockholders and presumably have a duty as well as a right to scrutinize and criticize the activities of firms in which they hold shares.

A broader question arises about the economic effects of pension fund stock purchases. Newly issued bonds or mortgages provide the funds for new investment. But common stock is purchased, almost invariably, in a "secondhand" market. Money is transferred from the funds to existing holders of stock certificates. No data is available on the use of funds by individuals who liquidate stocks.

Experience of pension funds with stock investments has been "favorable" in that capital gains have been achieved. But these are paper values that can be wiped out in a falling market while benefit obligations remain unchanged. Meanwhile, benefits are being paid out of a portion of the receipts from contributions, interest, dividends and realized capital gains. More important, the apparent success of the decision to invest in stocks has been validated, in large degree, by the purchases of those making the decision. Pension fund managers buy stocks expecting prices to rise, and it may be that prices have risen in large degree because pension funds have directed such a large portion of their net inflow to stock purchases.

PENSION FUND PROSPECTS

Because of the growth of private and state and local government pension funds since World War II, an increasing number of American families have dual assurance of retirement income—both from Federal old age insurance and employer-employe plans. Doubtless, the plans will be further liberalized in the future from the standpoint of benefits, minimum retirement age and ability of individuals, through vesting, to transfer claims resulting from past service to different jobs.

Pension fund accumulations have added a new dimension to the nation's financial structure. Resources of these funds now exceed in value personal holdings of any other single class of financial assets, other than common stocks. Pension funds are by far the most important net purchasers of common stocks. In addition, these funds in most recent years have purchased more than half of the net new issues of corporate bonds and are becoming a growing, although still minor, factor in the mortgage field. Channeling pension funds to uses best adapted both to requirements of the plans and to the needs of the economy places a heavy responsibility on those responsible for investment policies.

31.

Interest Rates, Liquidity,
and the Financing of
Captive Finance Companies

VICTOR L. ANDREWS

I. INTRODUCTION

Borrowing by the credit subsidiaries of nonfinancial corporations has mounted to impressively yearly rates, and by the end of 1963 had resulted in $4.4 billions of debt outstanding.[1] An overwhelming part of this debt issuance came in the last decade. Company policies with respect to liquidity-maintenance and cost-minimization, together with relative interest rates, have determined the pattern of the subsidiaries' demand for financing.

This article reports a study of the financing of the credit captives. It argues that the captives have fashioned the term structure of their outstanding debt so as to assure liquidity rather than take the gamble on the term structure of interest rates necessary for cost minimization. Within short-term financing, however, the captives have exploited interest rate differentials aggressively, constrained principally by supply conditions in the open money market and by costs of market access.

Reprinted from *The National Banking Review*, Vol. II, No. 4, June 1965, pp. 461–481, by permission of the publisher.

[1] Because of the distortions which would be introduced by its great size relative to the rest of the industry, all of the data and discussion in this article exclude General Motors Acceptance Corporation.

TABLE 31–1

Assets of a Sample of Captive Finance Companies, Excluding GMAC, 1955-1963

(Assets in Thousands of Dollars)

Year	Number of Companies Included	Cash and Securities	Wholesale Notes Receivable	Retail Notes Receivable	Miscellaneous Assets	Total Assets
1955	33	$ 78,444	$ 270,676	$ 715,598	$ 52,495	$1,117,213
1956	39	115,581	356,316	1,011,337	72,017	1,555,251
1957	48	148,262	496,057	1,312,095	91,921	2,048,335
1958	53	172,903	597,685	1,606,188	93,677	2,470,453
1959	53	189,460	801,747	2,065,068	114,726	3,171,001
1960	56	239,558	716,752	2,949,861	80,474	3,986,645
1961	63	301,123	755,501	3,560,377	92,428	4,709,429
1962	62	305,316	895,406	3,882,204	106,178	5,189,104
1963	60	282,423	1,017,039	4,262,492	191,137	5,759,690

II. AGGREGATE DEMAND OF THE CAPTIVES FOR FUNDS

The size of the credit captives' demands for financing is a result of their growth in numbers and of individual company assets.

A. Growth of Numbers and Assets

An earlier article[2] reported the identification, by industry classification and birth date, of 102 finance subsidiaries which operated actively for at least some time in the post-World War II period through 1960. Subsequent work turned up others, and with them new company originations during 1961–1963 combined to raise this total to 132. Births were heaviest during both periods in the same industrial classifications—the manufacture of electrical and nonelectrical machinery and transportation equipment, and retail trade.

Table 31–1 is a breakdown of the assets held by a progressively enlarged sample of finance subsidiaries for the period 1955–1963. Net growth of aggregate assets exceeded $4.6 billion. About $3.5 billion flowed into net credit extension through retail notes receivable, i.e., deferred payment sales contracts representing a mixture of consumer and business financing

[2] Victor L. Andrews, "Captive Finance Companies: Their Growth and Some Speculations on Their Significance," *Industrial Management Review*, II, Fall 1961, p. 31. Reference to this article should be made for points of detail, definitions, and an extensive description of sources of data and methods used. The definition of captives employed there and throughout this paper is: (a) financial subsidiaries of nonfinancial parent corporations dealing in greater than local markets with (b) assets composed predominantly of notes receivable. Virtually all of the subsidiaries of so-called shell home companies were excluded.

TABLE 31-2

Debt Issuance by a Sample of Captive Finance Companies, Excluding GMAC, 1947-1963

(Dollars in Millions)

Year	No. of Cos.	Net Change in Short-Term Borrowing			New Issues and Retirements of External † Long-Term Debt				Total Net Flota-tions ‡	Net Change Short-and Long-Term
		Bank Loans *	Comm'l Paper	Total	Senior		Subordinated			
					New Issues	Retire-ments	New Issues	Retire-ments		
1963	60	$160.9	$227.3	$388.3	$111.3	$18.4	$59.5	$3.0	$149.3	$537.6
1962	62	−309.5	645.3	335.8	113.3	38.1	78.8	1.9	152.0	487.8
1961	63	−28.0	185.3	157.3	349.9	10.0	71.0	8.5	402.4	559.7
1960	56	175.7	206.4	382.1	164.5	24.2	35.1	1.0	174.4	556.5
1959	53	88.6	166.7	255.3	109.4	30.2	11.5	9.8	80.9	336.2
1958	53	57.3	63.4	120.7	54.2	45.7	13.0	4.1	17.4	138.1
1957	48	283.7	25.4	309.1	159.4	11.2	33.0	3.0	178.2	487.3
1956	39	121.5	73.6	195.1	104.3	—	28.0	—	132.3	327.4
1955	33	85.4	70.3	155.7	43.8	8.5	20.0	2.0	53.3	209.0
1954	25	−41.5	12.7	−28.8	41.1	2.5	8.0	—	46.6	17.8
1953	19	175.0	49.1	224.1	.9	2.5	—	—	−1.6	222.5
1952	16	87.9	64.2	152.1	.7	2.5	—	—	−1.8	150.3
1951	15	23.0	28.2	51.2	26.3	2.5	—	—	23.8	75.0
1950	14	52.1	22.7	74.8	24.0	—	—	—	24.0	98.8
1949	14	51.2	2.7	53.9	14.0	—	2.0	—	16.0	69.9
1948	12	14.1	22.8	36.9	46.0	—	3.0	—	49.0	85.9
1947	9	10.2	19.4	29.6	—	—	—	—	—	29.6
Total		1,007.6	1,885.5	2,893.1	1,363.1	196.3	362.9	33.3	1,496.2	4,389.4

*Includes some borrowing from an independent finance company by one captive in the years 1957-1961.
†Debt issuance by the captive to lenders other than the parent company.
‡Net flotation figures shown here will not necessarily check with yearly balance sheet differences shown elsewhere in connection with this research. Flotation figures here are on a calendar year basis; elsewhere, they have been and will be shown in tabulations made from fiscal year closing dates for individual companies. Also, balance sheet tabulations are subject to some error in the classification of current maturities of long-term debt.

(mostly the latter). Net expansion of lending on inventory-secured (wholesale) notes receivable absorbed approximately $.75 billion.

With negligible exceptions, captive company assets are not included in tabulations of the FTC-SEC *Quarterly Financial Report for Manufacturing Corporations.* A comparison indicates that in 1963, receivables held by this sample of captives within their respective industries were equal to 22.5 percent of receivables aggregated by the *Quarterly Report* in nonelectrical machinery, 37 percent of those in electrical machinery, and 33 percent of those in transportation equipment.[3]

B. Demands for Funds by the Captives

Issuance of debt, by year, for a continually enlarging group of captive finance companies[4] is shown in Table 31-2 for the post-World War II period through 1963. Over the years 1947-1963, this sample of captives bor-

[3] Figures for earlier years are reported in Andrews, *op. cit.*
[4] For 1955-1963, the sample is the same as that covered by Table 31-1.

rowed in excess of $4.4 billion net, most of it between 1955 and 1963. The increase in bank debt outstanding equaled $1 billion, and the net growth of commercial paper outstanding was more than $1.9 billion. Gross long-term borrowing was about $1.7 billion, higher than net long-term flotations by the $.2 billion of retirements. About $3.70 gross of senior long-term debt was floated for each $1 gross of subordinated issues.

III. FINANCIAL PATTERNS

Discussions of the financial structures of independent finance companies often include distinctions by size of company.[5] Table 31–3 follows this lead in breaking down liabilities of the captives covered in the sample of Table 31–1 above, and indicates the number of companies tabulated in each of the size groupings.[6] Table 31–4 presents the same items as percentages of total liabilities.

The liabilities breakdowns show rough similarity in the proportional division of long- and short-term sources across size classes. This similarity is evident for 1963, for example, when negotiated short-term debt (bank loans plus commercial paper outstanding) comprised 45, 49, 50, 39, and 56 percent of total assets for the size groups from smallest to largest, respectively. Approximate uniformity between size classes holds at slightly different levels for other years. The long-short division of total financing was least stable for the aggregate of captives in the under $10 million asset category.

Parent company financing of an individual captive consists of the sum of equity, loss reserves, and loans.[7] Over the period shown, the average value of parent financing for captives under $10 million is clearly higher

---

[5] Many examples could be cited; a few will suffice. See *Consumer Installment Credit*, Board of Governors of the Federal Reserve System, Part I, Vol. II and Part II, Vol. I, Washington, D.C.: U.S.G.P.O., 1957; *Monograph on the Consumer Finance Industry for the Commission on Money and Credit*, National Consumer Finance Association, Englewood Cliffs, N.J.: Prentice-Hall, Inc., 1962; and Francis R. Pawley, "Survey of Finance Companies, Mid-1960," *Federal Reserve Bulletin*, 47, October 1961, pp. 1140–1160.

[6] The number of companies within each size bracket varies from year to year as the total number tabulated grows and as individual companies move between size classes. Except by coincidence, the composition of each size class is not constant from year to year.

[7] Parent loans are polyglot. Advances are nominally short-term, but are difficult to distinguish from accruals on many balance sheets. Some parent commitments are clearly long-term, especially subordinated indebtedness which serves as part of the foundation for senior debt. But this facet of short-term loans is not as easily distinguished. Some of the latter are noted on balance sheets as demand notes. Many times no such notation is made, but swift year-to-year fluctuation gives it the telltale mark of serving as a demand note in purpose, if not in name. Furthermore, some short-term debt to parent companies is subordinated.

than the corresponding average for the others. There is a suggestion in the same figures for other size classes that the total of parent company financing is inversely related to size of captive, but the relationship is irregular. However, the sum of equity and parent-supplied subordinated debt (most of the risk-bearing base) *is* inversely related to size,[8] as the next section shows.

A. The Debt/Equity Division of the Captives' Financing

Time after time it has been stated to the author, by both lenders and management of parents and captives, that heavy usage of debt financing has been the captives' prime *raison d'être*.

In contrast with the fractional debt/equity ratios typical of their non-financial parents, the captives can boast debt several times the size of their equity, or several times the size of their equity plus subordinated debt. This is readily observed in Tables 31–3 and 31–4. These multiple ratios are made feasible by the low "risk" in cash flows from the captives' receivables.[9] Low variance in cash flows, of course, derives from low loss rates, diversity of (uncorrelated) risks, and large numbers. If we assume the independence of probabilities, portfolio loss rates no worse than historic levels will make lender net losses virtually impossible in the ranges of debt/equity common to the independent finance companies and to captives, even if only modest numbers of receivables are held.[10]

Nonetheless, probabilities of loss on receivables are certainly not entirely independent, and the relative lack of industry diversity in the captives' assets may raise the covariance between cash flows from individual receivables and from the remainder of the portfolio above levels characteristic of the portfolios of independent finance companies. The embarrassment of a number of captives over the years is also a dramatic reminder that credit policies which allow extraordinary loss rates *can* result in equity loss, if not losses to creditors also. In addition, it has been pointed out elsewhere that characteristics of captive relationships with parent companies raise

[8] The rapidity of growth of individual companies made it impossible to provide a sample with constant identities within size classes which retained respectable numbers for a significant period. However, for the period 1957–1961, a constant identity sample of 31 companies was selected, and its balance sheets tabulated by years in the same size classes used in Tables 31–3 and 4. This presumably eliminated the effects of shifting company composition. Generalities made above regarding the similarities of short- and long-term financing and parent financing across size classes hold also for the constant company sample.

[9] A clean liability break between parent and captive usually exists. In most instances, receivables are sold by the parent to the captive without recourse or with only limited recourse. Parent companies seldom guarantee the debt of their captives. Thus, the subsidiaries' creditors have rather clear protection from the solidity of the receivables once the transfer is a fact.

[10] Fred Leonetti, "Risk and Return of a Financial Subsidiary," unpublished Masters degree thesis, School of Industrial Management, Massachusetts Institute of Technology, 1961. All this waives questions of outright mismanagement.

TABLE 31-3

Liabilities of a Sample of Captive Finance Companies, Excluding GMAC, by Size of Company, 1955-1963

(Dollars in Millions)

Asset Size Group by Year		No. of Cos.	Negotiated Short-Term Borrowing		Accruals	External Long-Term Debt		Borrowing from Parent			Loss Reserves	Equity
Size	Year		Bank Loans*	Comm'l Paper		Senior	Subdt.	Advcs. and Accruals	Long-Term Debt Senior	Subdt.		
Under $10	1963	11	$20.8	$1.7	$1.9	$2.5	$1.3	$1.7	$1.6	$3.8	$.7	$13.6
	1962	10	27.4	2.8	2.3	1.0	1.3	1.1	1.7	3.0	.5	8.7
	1961	15	41.3	—	1.6	6.0	1.0	4.4	—	6.6	.5	15.3
	1960	20	39.1	—	4.5	—	—	8.5	—	2.5	.4	17.2
	1959	22	22.8	—	2.6	4.7	—	5.1	—	2.2	.8	19.5
	1958	25	32.2	—	4.6	4.8	—	9.5	—	3.3	.9	17.9
	1957	26	31.7	—	4.3	11.7	—	9.0	—	4.3	1.2	14.5
	1956	24	20.8	—	4.5	17.9	—	17.2	—	.2	.5	17.5
	1955	24	23.8	—	4.2	10.0	—	19.4	—	9.1	.5	23.2
$10-$25	1963	17	110.0	31.9	10.3	34.8	4.6	18.0	—	19.8	3.3	72.3
	1962	23	167.4	31.0	10.6	49.7	10.6	12.1	—	25.9	4.9	81.5
	1961	15	106.7	24.0	3.1	26.5	—	9.7	—	14.3	2.2	37.8
	1960	11	67.8	8.7	3.1	47.6	—	5.7	—	13.4	3.0	22.9
	1959	10	56.3	3.6	4.6	39.8	—	4.4	—	9.0	1.6	20.8
	1958	10	75.6	2.1	2.6	29.0	—	4.6	—	9.8	.3	19.3
	1957	6	50.0	—	2.2	12.6	—	.8	—	17.0	—	16.2
	1956	6	35.9	2.2	3.8	—	—	17.4	—	13.5	.2	23.4
	1955	2	16.7	—	.1	—	—	4.4	—	—	.3	10.7
$25-$100	1963	15	240.0	115.6	12.5	162.8	26.6	34.5	6.3	12.4	8.1	93.6
	1962	15	239.9	143.3	15.3	197.3	36.6	62.9	3.0	17.6	9.4	126.7
	1961	19	317.8	66.4	20.5	160.3	28.1	123.6	—	47.5	16.0	128.5
	1960	14	404.8	39.1	19.3	29.5	20.6	70.1	—	46.3	12.6	158.3
	1959	12	403.8	16.7	13.9	40.7	4.0	49.7	—	52.3	7.7	82.3
	1958	12	391.3	21.6	29.0	37.9	16.0	72.1	—	54.5	7.4	77.2
	1957	11	323.9	5.8	15.8	26.8	12.0	5.8	—	57.5	5.7	40.0
	1956	5	132.1	—	8.4	26.1	12.0	26.6	—	15.9	4.1	7.5
	1955	3	72.0	—	6.6	23.8	6.0	2.1	—	—	2.1	10.0
$100-$250	1963	11	364.0	259.1	38.3	477.6	85.4	53.9	—	102.5	26.8	244.5
	1962	9	179.9	344.1	36.4	438.5	88.5	73.9	—	63.8	18.2	228.2
	1961	9	358.6	345.3	38.4	468.7	95.5	55.0	—	72.5	21.5	328.9
	1960	7	592.9	112.2	29.8	253.0	30.5	40.7	—	68.0	14.3	153.7
	1959	5	438.4	14.7	23.7	173.0	23.0	38.4	—	51.8	5.6	67.8
	1958	3	59.2	119.4	12.5	221.5	32.0	54.3	—	41.5	4.3	25.2
	1957	2	55.0	154.6	8.0	96.5	20.0	3.2	—	—	2.4	46.5
	1956	2	—	148.6	9.7	222.5	27.0	27.7	—	12.0	3.5	13.9
	1955	3	124.8	182.0	15.5	144.4	25.0	22.1	—	7.0	7.2	51.7
$250 and up	1963	6	272.9	1477.3	116.9	475.8	207.5	96.2	—	—	46.1	408.2
	1962	5	232.2	1137.1	93.8	374.2	132.0	61.2	—	9.2	35.6	314.1
	1961	4	331.9	577.0	80.0	364.8	62.5	22.3	—	39.0	31.6	206.2
	1960	4	212.9	662.7	78.1	326.6	82.5	4.9	26.0	33.0	22.5	203.2
	1959	4	216.2	582.4	67.7	258.6	72.5	24.0	26.0	18.5	18.9	180.3
	1958	3	190.6	306.5	53.3	146.0	50.0	8.2	36.0	21.0	15.7	153.8
	1957	3	231.0	225.8	53.0	233.0	32.0	38.7	37.5	38.0	15.4	90.8
	1956	2	219.0	210.0	52.3	16.0	20.0	2.6	50.0	31.0	11.2	70.7
	1955	1	50.0	105.3	37.7	—	—	—	50.0	26.0	4.2	21.1

*Includes borrowing from a finance company by one captive in the years 1957-1961.

TABLE 31–4

Liabilities of Captive Finance Companies, Excluding GMAC, by Size of Company, 1955-1963

(As Percent of Total Claims*)

Asset Size Group by Year — Size in Millions	Year	No. of Cos.	Negotiated Short-term Borrowing — Bank Loans	Comm'l Paper	Accruals	External Long-Term Debt — Senior	Subdt.	Borrowing from Parent — Advcs. and Accruals	Long-Term Debt — Senior	Subdt.	Loss Reserves	Equity
Under $10	1963	11	42%	3%	4%	5%	3%	3%	3%	8%	2%	16%
	1962	10	55	6	5	2	3	2	3	6	1	18
	1961	15	54	—	2	8	1	6	—	9	1	20
	1960	20	54	—	6	—	—	12	—	3	1	24
	1959	22	40	—	5	8	—	9	—	4	1	34
	1958	25	44	—	6	7	—	13	—	5	1	24
	1957	26	41	—	6	15	—	12	—	6	2	19
	1956	24	26	—	6	23	—	22	—	—	1	22
	1955	24	26	—	5	11	—	22	—	10	1	26
$10-$25	1963	17	38	11	4	12	2	6	—	7	1	25
	1962	23	44	8	3	13	3	3	—	7	1	22
	1961	15	48	11	1	12	—	4	—	6	1	17
	1960	11	39	5	2	28	—	3	—	8	2	13
	1959	10	40	3	3	28	—	3	—	6	1	15
	1958	10	53	1	2	20	—	3	—	7		13
	1957	6	51	—	2	13	—	1	—	17	—	16
	1956	6	37	2	4	—	—	18	—	14	—	24
	1955	2	52	—	—	—	—	14	—	—	1	33
$25-$100	1963	15	34	16	2	23	4	5	1	2	1	13
	1962	15	28	17	2	23	4	7	—	2	1	15
	1961	19	35	7	2	18	3	14	—	5	2	14
	1960	14	51	5	2	4	3	9	—	6	2	20
	1959	12	60	2	2	6	1	7	—	8	1	12
	1958	12	55	3	4	5	2	10	—	8	1	11
	1957	11	66	1	3	5	2	1	—	12	1	8
	1956	5	57	—	4	11	5	11	—	8	2	3
	1955	3	59	—	5	19	5	2	—	—	2	8
$100-$250	1963	11	23	16	2	30	5	3	—	6	2	15
	1962	9	12	23	3	30	6	5	—	4	1	15
	1961	9	20	19	3	26	5	3	—	4	1	18
	1960	7	46	9	2	20	2	3	—	5	1	12
	1959	5	52	2	3	21	2	5	—	6	1	8
	1958	3	10	21	2	39	6	10	—	7	1	4
	1957	2	14	40	2	25	5	1	—	—	1	12
	1956	2	—	32	2	47	6	6	—	3	1	3
	1955	3	22	31	3	25	4	4	—	1	1	9
$250 and up	1963	6	9	48	4	15	7	3	—	—	2	13
	1962	5	10	47	4	15	5	3	—	—	2	13
	1961	4	19	34	5	21	4	1	—	2	2	12
	1960	5	13	41	5	20	5	—	2	2	1	12
	1959	5	15	40	5	18	5	2	2	1	1	12
	1958	4	19	31	5	15	5	1	4	2	2	16
	1957	4	23	23	5	23	3	4	4	4	2	9
	1956	3	32	31	8	2	3	—	7	6	2	10
	1955	1	17	36	13	—	—	—	17	9	1	7

*Detail may not add to 100% due to rounding.

ambiguities for some creditors.[11] Despite these qualifications, however, it is true that the high liquidity of a captive finance company's assets makes it a shell of prime collateral value. The general creditors of such a company hold liquidation claims upon a nearly certain cash flow, and the certainty of the flow allows heavy proportions of debt in total financing.

[11] Victor L. Andrews, "Captive Finance Companies," *Harvard Business Review*, July-August 1964, pp. 80–92.

TABLE 31-5

Ratio of Senior Liabilities to Capital Base,* by Size of Captive Company

Asset Size of Company (in millions)	1963	1962	1961	1960	1959	1958	1957	1956	1955
$ 0 - 10	2.4	2.6	2.3	2.6	1.6	2.3	2.8	3.4	1.7
10 - 25	1.9	2.0	3.2	3.3	3.6	3.6	2.0	1.5	1.9
25 - 100	4.0	3.5	3.2	1.9	2.9	3.6	4.9	5.3	5.7
100 - 250	2.6	2.8	2.4	4.0	4.9	4.5	4.3	4.7	5.7
over - 250	3.5	4.6	5.4	4.0	4.3	3.0	4.6	4.3	4.9

*Includes equity, loss reserves, and all subordinated debt.

B. Quantitative Limitations on Creditor Risk: Debt/Equity Ratios

Quantitative limitation of senior debt relative to a risk-bearing base-capital, surplus, and subordinated indebtedness—is the principal device used for limiting risk exposure of the captives' creditors. The limits imposed are almost always ratios of 3 or 4 to 1. One occasionally encounters higher ratios when parent guarantees are attached.[12] The lower figure loosely applies to the subsidiaries with higher proportions of supposedly high-risk wholesale paper; the higher limit applies loosely where retail paper is in clear predominance. Also, consumer paper in a captive's assets tends to be associated with borrowing ratios of 5 to 1, or even higher.

Table 31-5 summarizes data from Table 31-3 of the debt/capital base ratios, by size of subsidiary.[13] With allowance for year-to-year variability, the ratios suggest a positive association between size of captive and borrowing limit. There are only five instances recorded in all the observations of companies with over $100 million of assets where the ratio dropped significantly below 4. Ratios in the lower size classes have been irregularly lower, and seem to have been persistently lower for the $0–$10 million group than for the intermediate size groups.

Section V below emphasizes that captives in the upper size ranges enjoy a significant measure of independence of the banking system because of their access to the commercial paper market. It is quite likely that this bargaining position enables the large subsidiaries to stretch their capital bases further.

Other risk limitation devices imposed by bankers are occasionally

[12] When there is enormous disparity between the sizes of parent and financing subsidiary, the attraction of a parent guarantee for a creditor is understandable and real. Otherwise, it seems superfluous. See Andrews, "Captive Finance Companies," *op. cit.*

[13] End-of-fiscal-year balance sheets are nearly always a seasonal low in assets and borrowing. Hence, the ratio between senior claims and the risk-bearing base will be at its low. The smallest captives tend somewhat more strongly than others to be lenders on wholesale paper where seasonality will exert its strongest influence.

knitted together with limitations on debt/equity ratios. For example, one credit line agreement which limits borrowing to a 4 to 1 debt/capital base ratio also reads in part:

> The Credit Agreement between [name withheld] and the banks requires, among other things, that the Corporation maintain working capital, as defined in the agreement, [current assets less current liabilities without reclassification of receivables with maturities in excess of one year] equal to at least 25 percent of the outstanding amount borrowed from banks under the credit agreement and imposes certain limitations on borrowing, acquiring capital assets, and paying the principal of the subordinated indebtedness.

IV. USE OF LONG-TERM DEBT

A. Asset Growth and Debt Issuance

It is imaginable that the issuance of long-term debt by the subsidiaries is induced simply by asset growth and adherence by management to a target proportion of long-term debt-to-total[14] financing. In Chart 31–1, annual asset growth and net yearly flotations of long-term debt are plotted on the same time scale. Loosely, peaks and valleys in the two series coincide. Sometimes, however, net flotations rose as the pace of asset growth fell sharply and *vice versa*, and the pace of asset expansion outran flotations for several years at a time. Because of the looseness of this association and, more significantly, because this interpretation ignores some fundamental roles played by long-term debt in the structuring of claims, other relationships must be explored.

B. Term Structure of Liabilities

Broadly, there are three options for the captives in the election of a term structure of financing. First, the term structure of debt could be managed so as to minimize interest costs.[15] This is feasible because there can be differences in short- and long-term interest rates at a moment in time, because these differences fluctuate through time, and because short- and long-term rates are rigidly related to each other mathematically. Such an attempt would necessarily involve captive-management in a series of successive moves substituting short- for long-term debt, and *vice versa*, since shifts in the term structure of interest rates require new structures of commitments in the futures markets for money. Second, the term structures of receivables and debt could be matched so as to freeze the difference between

---

[14] The great majority of these issues are long-term, of 15-years maturity or more. Few are term loans.

[15] For a recent interpretation of this old view of the term structure of interest rates, see David Meiselman, *The Term Strucure of Interest Rates*, Englewood Cliffs, N.J.: Prentice-Hall, 1962, Ch. 1 and Ch. 2, sections 2.2 & 2.4.

CHART 31–1

Expansion of Assets and Long-Term Debt Flotation by Captives Other
Than GMAC

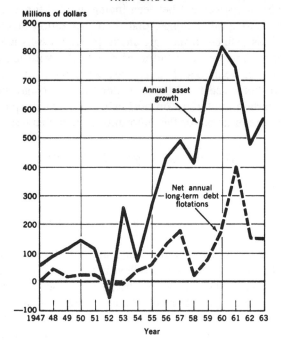

rates on each. Third, the term structure of debt could be employed to achieve a desired position of liquidity. It would only be coincidental if the structure chosen for this purpose also proved appropriate for cost minimization or hedging cash flows.

C. The Influence of Short- and Long-Term Rate Differentials

There seems to be no way to infer directly whether or how management has used the term structure of captive-company debt to minimize interest cost over rate cycles. Interviews of company officials revealed little evidence that the term structure of interest rates played a significant role in the planning of capital structure. Occasionally, it was asserted that long-term debt had been issued as a hedge to safeguard the earnings on outstanding receivables against fluctuating interest costs.[16] However, these policies are encountered infrequently.

---

[16] Matching of specific receivables with debt contracts is sometimes done in these instances, occasionally in collateral trusts. This is true of financing particularly long-lived, high-priced (relative to the borrower's resources) equipment with high collateral value.

With the lack of conclusive direct evidence, it is worthwhile to consider what may be learned indirectly of the subsidiaries' response to the term structure of rates. Through 1963, 118 separate new long-term debt issues by captive companies were tabulated. To eliminate the effect of a changing number of companies in the sample, a calculation was made, by year, of the number of long-term issues per company. This statistic is ranged in Chart 31–2 against the differential between yearly average yields on Aaa grade corporate bonds and four-to-six month commercial paper. The rate differential is employed here as a proxy of a yield curve. A positive differential, of course, implies an upward sloping yield curve, generally thought to be associated with market anticipations of rising interest rates, and conversely.[17] Presumably, if the flotations of the subsidiaries were sensitive to rate expectations *and* the captives' managers held anticipations implied in the term structure of interest rates, issues per company would be high in periods of a wide long-short rate differential and *vice versa*. The evidence of Chart 31–2 is equivocal. The years 1954 and 1961, for example, saw a relatively wide rate differential and the number of issues per company was relatively high in both years. However, the same is not true of 1958. Also, years of a low differential, such as 1956, 1957, and 1959, did not produce a particularly low value for issues per company. Numerical calculation shows a concentration of new issues in years of extreme rate differentials, for example, 1.2–1.4 percent, but short of that extreme there is no palpable sensitivity of new issues to rate structure.

D. A Test of the Influence of a Target Level of Long-Term Debt and Rate Differentials

Multiple regression and correlation analyses were used to test the effect on new issues per company of long-term debt as a fraction of total financing in the previous year, and of lagged and unlagged differentials between yearly average rates on Aaa bonds and four-to-six month commercial paper. If a target level of debt in total financing operates in captive financing policies, high levels in one year would tend to be followed by low rates of issuance in the next year, and *vice versa*. The influence of interest

---

[17] See Meiselman, *op. cit.*; and Roland Robinson, *The Management of Bank Funds*, 2nd Ed., New York: McGraw-Hill Book Company, 1962, Ch. 19. Clearly, the crudity of the measure employed here will not reflect refinements such as "humps" or "shoulders" in term structure of yields, but it does reflect adequately the slope in yield curves for corporate rates. Indeed, differentials shown here are generally consistent in their relative magnitudes with the slope of basic yield curves for corporate debt. Simple correlation of the yield differential between one-year and 30-year corporate bonds as shown in yearly basic yield curves with new issues per company produced a lower correlation than the same correlation employing the yield differential cited here. Use of a differential between annual averages conceals significant variation within years. Issues per company cannot be stated for time intervals finer than a year, however, and so it is necessary to work in corresponding time intervals in the rate histories.

CHART 31–2

New Long-Term Issues Per Company and Yield Differentials

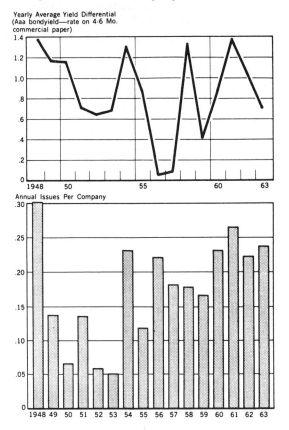

rate differentials would be as hypothesized above. Coefficients of determination derived from the analyses were not significantly different from zero.
The resulting net regression coefficients of the interest rate differential were
not statistically significant, and partial correlation coefficients were low
for both the lagged and unlagged associations. Similarly, for the relationship
between new issues per company and the previous year's level of long-term
debt, statistically insignificant regression and partial correlation coefficients
were obtained in company with lagged and unlagged interest rate differentials. Moreover, the sign of the coefficient for the previous level of long-
term debt did not indicate an inverse association with new issues.

We can tentatively[18] conclude that the captives have shunned prob-

---

[18] These data are not absolutely conclusive. The necessity to employ the difference
between yearly averages of short- and long-term rates introduces ambiguities about

lematic reduction of interest cost through manipulation of term structure, and that there is no statistical evidence of the influence of a target ratio of long-term debt-to-total financing in the captives' policies.

Other evidence also implies that management of the captives was willing to concede the freedom to play upon the term structure of rates. Many of the captive-company long-term note agreements examined by the author incorporate nonrefunding and/or redemption limitations eliminating or circumscribing the ability to refinance when (and if) rates fall in the future, thus redistributing some of the risk of rate fluctuation. Since there presumably is a higher interest rate which the captives could have paid to induce lenders to supply funds without these limitations, it follows that they preferred to forego freedom with respect to the term structure of debt and, by implication, the term structure of rates.

E. Long-Term Debt in the Maintenance of Liquidity

The preponderance of evidence points to the use of long-term debt by the captives principally as a determinant of liquidity. In this analysis, we start from the basic truth that parent and wholly-owned subsidiary comprise a single command center. The officership of parent and captive usually overlaps heavily, so that no question of conflicting policy arises. Given this, it would seem that term structure of debt must be viewed within a perspective of unified parent-captive liquidity. Unless the liquidity of the parent and captive *is* managed as a unit, there is a risk of incurring the cost of redundant financing; for example, the parent might have excess cash while the captive was borrowing from external creditors.

The means for joint liquidity control are readily at the hand of management. Deferral of payment of accrued expenses owed by subsidiary to parent, or the reverse, will effect near-term, small-scale transfers of liquidity. For companies with assets of less than $100 million, the behavior of accruals and advances owed to the parent, shown in Tables 31–3 and 31–4 rather strongly implies that they have been used for temporary liquidity transfers. Outright loans also transfer funds between the two, and the balance sheets of parents and captives contain many examples evidencing these kinds of liquidity transfers. But, more fundamentally, operating agreements typically commit a parent company to sell on variable terms to its financial

---

response to rate relationships within short periods. This ambiguity is compounded by lags in issuer response to rate developments introduced by negotiation procedures in connection with long-term debt issues. An additional perplexity is that the series on rate differentials plotted in Chart 2 has numerous turning points; if an issuer responds by adjusting term structure in the neighborhood of a turning point, the likelihood that he will respond again is probably reduced, and so a tabulation of issues per company through time cannot be perfectly representative of responses.

CHART 31–3

Captive Long-Term Debt as a Proportion of Total Assets and Consolidated Liquidity Ratios, 1960 & 1961

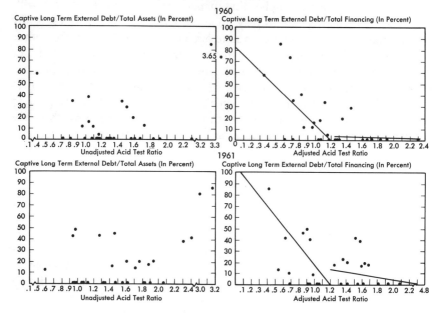

subsidiary some *variable part*[19] of its notes receivable generated by operations. Discretionary control of the fraction of receivables sold and of the terms of sale is all that is required for discretionary allocation of liquid assets and the burden of their financing between parent and captive. Since the means are available to a command center operating with the incentive to manage parent and captive as a unit, it must be concluded that consolidated figures are relevant in measures of liquidity.

The term structure of debt can be used to regulate the pressure of short-term liabilities against liquidity. With given assets, greater long-term debt diminishes the weight of short-term debt and *vice versa*. In the following, we shall consider the role of captive-company term structure in regulating the amount of short-term debt relative to the consolidated liquid assets of parents and captives. Since financing of the subsidiary by the parent does not affect consolidated liquidity,[20] it is permissible to work with

[19] In the case of the rare exceptions, this reasoning will not apply. Also, the reasoning with respect to the captive's earnings from the sale price of the receivables does not apply without qualification to companies which solicit outside business.

[20] Note that this is not inconsistent with viewing all or some part of parent financing as a permanent commitment, i.e., long-term financing."

captive company long-term debt exclusive of debt to the parent as an appropriate variable.

A positive policy of liquidity-risk avoidance would result in maintenance of short-term liabilities no larger than the stock of liquid assets.[21] A commonly employed balance sheet liquidity ratio will serve the purpose of testing behavior of the parent-captive liquidity units in this respect. The "acid-test" ratio relates cash and cash inflows scheduled in accounts receivable to current liabilities. Such a ratio computed from *consolidated* balance sheets will reflect the total of virtually sure liquidity available to parent and captive against possible near-term cash outflows. If an amount equal to a captive's long-term debt is added to consolidated current liabilities, the resulting acid-test ratio will show what consolidated liquidity *would have been* without the captive's long-term debt. The ratio with this adjustment will be referred to here as the "adjusted acid-test" ratio.[22]

A number of companies have either published or made enough information available to the author to permit computation of the adjusted ratio.[23] Scatter diagrams of the proportion of captive company external long-term debt in total financing against unadjusted acid-test ratios, and against adjusted ratios for a group of 31 companies, appear in Chart 31–3 for the years 1960 and 1961. No systematic association between the proportion of long-term debt in total financing and unadjusted ratios would be anticipated. Because this association is *ex post*, most of these ratios should lie upwards of a "solvency minimum" in the neighborhood of one. The left hand panels of Chart 31–3 bear out this supposition.

The effect on the adjusted ratios of adding the captive's long-term debt to short-term liabilities is shown in the contrast of the right hand panels, where the ratios affected are moved toward lower liquidity readings. The extreme lowness of some of the ratios on the liquidity scale is indicative of

---

[21] If the textbook-venerated "ideal formula" (See Bion B. Howard and Miller Upton, *Introduction to Business Finance*, New York: McGraw-Hill Book Company, 1953, Ch. 13, pp.. 310–314) and the rule oft repeated by practitioners that "short-term assets should be financed short-term and long-term should be financed long-term" were applied to the financing of cash plus receivables, the policy described here would result.

[22] The use here of these ratios as a quantitative expression of liquidity for correlation and regression is not meant to imply that the ratio itself is a focus of decision-making. The decision-focus is "liquidity."

[23] The most frequently encountered stumbling block is that the financial statements fail to disclose the volume of receivables held with life in excess of one year, or otherwise to divulge the information to permit a computation of quick assets. There is no discernible reason to suppose that a nonrandom sample of the companies discloses this information, however, and therefore there is no apparent reason why their data could not be employed in correlation analysis. At this point, it is worth noting that error in the estimation of these ratios will depress the coefficients derived later by employing them as independent variables in regression and correlation.

the quantitative importance of the long-term debt of the captives in their respective consolidated liquidity positions.[24]

A multiple regression employing the logarithm of company asset-size and adjusted acid-test ratios as independent variables explaining the proportion of external long-term debt in total captive company financing was fitted to the data for 1960 and 1961 above and below the solvency minimum.[25] We are concerned not only with the question whether long-term debt is used to structure liquidity, but also the question whether, for a given parent or captive, the *subsidiary's* capital structure has been employed this way. Of course, the *parent's* term structure could be manipulated to produce the desired limitation of short-term debt, and if this is generally true, no systematic relationship in a broad sample will exist between joint liquidity and subsidiary term structure. A third independent variable was added to overcome a problem of common elements in regression terms. Long-term debt of the captive appears both in the numerator of the dependent variable and in the denominator of the adjusted acid-test ratio. By incorporating it as a separate independent variable, we eliminate its effects in partial correlation.

Table 31–6 summarizes some of the results of the regressions and correlations based on 1960 and 1961 data.[26] First, consider the values for the functions fitted to data below the solvency minimum, i.e., adjusted acid-test ratios below 1.2. Regression coefficients and squares of the partial correlation coefficients for the size variable, X_2, indicate that it has only modest influence. Moreover, the regression coefficients are small relative to their standard errors. The neutrality of size in this sample is probably traceable to the fact that all the subsidiaries are large enough to float long-term issues in size ranges where cost of flotation exerts little impact. On the other hand, the size of the coefficients for the adjusted acid-test ratios, X_3, makes clear that through the cross-section small changes in consolidated parent-captive liquidity exert material influence over the term structure of captive company debt. The sign of the coefficients indicates inverse association, i.e., higher proportions of captive long-term debt are associated with low adjusted acid-test ratios (which imply illiquidity without the captive's longer debt maturities). The t-ratios of these coefficients are significant at the one percent and five percent levels for 1960 and 1961, respectively. Squares of the partial correlation coefficients for X_3 show that correlation with consolidated liquidity accounts for a reduction of about one-half of the unex-

---

[24] In general, ratios for 1961 below one will lie farther to the right, and ratios above one will lie farther to the left, than their 1960 counterparts. Recession in 1960 and revival in 1961 depressed and expanded receivables, respectively. Simultaneous corresponding movements of current liabilities will move the ratios below one upward. An opposite effect exists for the ratios above one.

[25] Fixed by inspection and experimentation at an adjusted ratio of 1.2.

[26] Observational error on the liquidity ratios (see above, fn. 22) undoubtedly has reduced the correlation and regression coefficients significantly.

TABLE 31–6

Summary of Regression Results: Term Structure of Captive Financing as a Function of Size and Parent-Captive Liquidity

(Figures in parentheses are standard errors)

Item	Adjusted acid-test ratios < 1.2		Adjusted acid-test ratios < 1.2	
	1960	1961	1960	1961
a	.853	1.21	.058	.179
$b_{12.34}$	−.076 (.099)	−.181 (.149)	−.008 (.029)	.055 (.063)
$b_{13.24}$	−.694 (.188)	−.886 (.286)	−.021 (.053)	−.112 (.142)
$b_{14.23}$	.004 (.000)	.004 (.000)	.002 (.000)	.001 (.000)
$r^3_{13.24}$	.053	.131	.016	.049
$r^3_{12.34}$	.509	.514	.026	.049
$r^3_{14.23}$	.359	.377	.620	.209

Test equation: $x_1 = a + b_{12.34} x_2 + b_{13.24} x_3 + b_{14.23}$
 x_1 = captive company external long-term debt as a fraction of total financing
 x_2 = log of captive company assets in millions of dollars
 x_3 = adjusted acid-test ratios
 x_4 = long-term external captive debt in millions

plained variance in term structure when size and the common element in terms, X_4, are eliminated.

Next, contrast these results with those derived from fitting the function to the data for both years in the region of adjusted acid-test ratios lying above 1.2. Coefficients for the size variable again signify no systematic effect of size. Low regression coefficients for the liquidity ratios are consistent with the anticipation that no long-term debt will be issued by subsidiaries having joint liquidity positions above the solvency minimum. Low squared coefficients of partial correlation are consistent with the anticipation that adjusted ratios above the solvency mimimum could lie to the right indefinitely (which implies no correlation) on the horizontal axis of the scatter diagram.

These data are convincing evidence that joint liquidity positions are systematically associated with term structure of captive company debt and exert a significant influence over it.[27]

[27] A coefficient of determination of a regression fitted without segmentation of adjusted acid-test ratios is lower for the functions, both for 1960 and 1961, than for the corresponding figures derived from the regression outlined here. It should be mentioned, too, that the same regressions described here were performed with the percentage of captive long-term debt-to-total external debt as the dependent variable. Lower correlations were obtained uniformly. The economic difference is that the proportion of long-term debt in total external debt ranged against adjusted acid-test ratios ignores the fact that consolidated receivables (in the numerator of the acid-test ratio) are in part equity financed. Hence, this comparison would ignore the liquidity support implicit in equity committed to captive receivables. Captive long-term debt as a proportion of its total financing, on the other hand, is commensurate with policy toward total financing of stocks of cash and receivables.

V. NEGOTIATED SHORT-TERM FINANCING

Captive short-term financing policies are responsive—depending on the scale of borrowing, its economies, and the cost of access to the open money market—to the pull of the usual differential between bank and open money market rates, to cyclical variations of the differential, and to structural differences of supply of funds to the dealer and direct placement segments of the open market. In short, a combination of micro- and macro-financial influences affects the captives' short-term debt policies.

A. Recent Growing Use of Commercial Paper by the Captives[28]

In Table 31–7, there is presented a summary of the captives' indebtedness on commercial paper, broken down by directly- and dealer-placed totals, and a comparison, at year end 1950–1963, with the volume of commercial paper outstanding as reported in the *Federal Reserve Bulletin*. The absolute volume outstanding attributable to the captives rose by twenty-five fold from $76 million in 1950 to almost $1.9 billion in 1963. After the late 50's, the great bulk of absolute growth was in directly-placed paper.[29] The share of this sample of subsidiaries in the total outstanding grew steadily from less than one-tenth in the early years to more than 28 percent in 1963.

After late 1957, the difference between the prime bank rate and the 90-day prime commercial paper dealer rate was substantial, and was in excess of a full percentage point for nearly all of the period from mid-1960 to mid-1963. Basically, it is this attraction that accounts for the burgeoning of commercial paper sales by the captives.

Inspection of annual net changes in bank loans and commercial paper outstanding, as shown in Table 31–2 for the entire sample, suggests that the distribution of captive debt between the bank and open loan markets has been sensitive over short periods to the relative interest rates in these markets. Regression and correlation was undertaken to test the sensitivity of the captives' policies. Ratios of bank loans outstanding in one year-to-bank loans in the previous year were divided by corresponding ratios of commercial paper. This variable was then regressed on, and correlated with, the annual averages of the monthly average differential between the bank prime rate and the 90-day dealer rate on commercial paper over the years 1948–1963. The constant of the resulting regression equation indicates that, with a zero rate differential, the ratio of yearly bank loan growth-to-

[28] The author is greatly indebted to Goldman, Sachs and Co., and to anonymous issuers of commercial paper for exceedingly generous cooperation in work on this phase of the captives' financing.

[29] Through 1963, a half dozen of the largest captives in addition to GMAC had undertaken direct placement. So far as the author knows, they were: Sears Roebuck Acceptance Corp., General Electric Credit Corp., Ford Motor Credit Co., International Harvester Credit Corp., Montgomery Ward Credit Co., and Westinghouse Credit Corp. In 1964, J. C. Penny Credit Corp. started direct sales.

TABLE 31–7

Captive Company* Commercial Paper Outstanding, 1950-1963

(Dollars in Millions)

Year	No. of Cos. Tabulated	Year-End Total Outstanding†	Absolute Totals of Captives Tabulated			As Percentages		
			Total‡	Directly Placed	Dealer Placed	Total	Directly Placed	Dealer Placed
1950	1	$ 920	$ 18	$ —	$ 18	100	—	100.0%
1951	1	1,331	31	2	29	100	6.5	93.5
1952	2	1,745	121	66	55	100	54.5	45.5
1953	2	1,966	176	109	67	100	61.9	38.1
1954	3	1,924	203	100	103	100	49.3	50.7
1955	3	2,008	220	120	100	100	54.5	45.5
1956	3	2,183	275	185	90	100	67.3	32.7
1957	4	2,672	306	191	115	100	62.4	37.6
1958	8	2,751	426	254	172	100	59.6	40.4
1959	10	3,202	602	420	182	100	69.8	30.2
1960	16	4,497	819	504	315	100	61.5	38.5
1961	23	4,686	1,056	755	301	100	71.5	28.5
1962	22	5,988	1,662	1,321	346	100	79.5	20.5
1963	26	6,747	1,887	1,456	431	100	77.2	22.8

*Data on captive company totals exclude GMAC.
†As reported by the *Federal Reserve Bulletin*.
‡These figures will differ somewhat from those shown elsewhere in this article because they were tabulated from a special mail confirmation of the figures shown. Minor corrections resulted from the confirmation. Comparison, however, will show that the differences are not material.

CHART 31–4

Total Assets and Commercial Paper Outstanding of Captives Selling Directly and Through Dealers

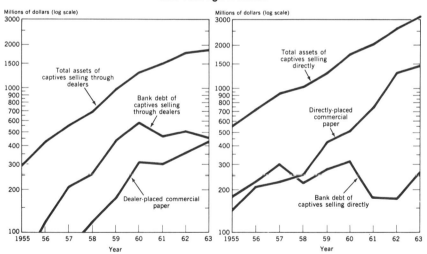

yearly commercial paper growth was 1.39, reflecting a secular reliance upon banks to finance growth in the absence of a rate superiority of commercial paper. The regression coefficient which resulted was −.499, indicating that an increase of a percentage point in the bank-commercial-paper rate differential was associated with a reduction of one-half in the ratio of yearly bank loan growth to the corresponding yearly commercial paper growth. However, the simple correlation coefficient was only $-.54$, reflecting a loose relationship, though the true correlation undoubtedly is stronger.[30]

Chart 31-4 illustrates a point vital to the reasoning in the sections below. Total assets of subsidiaries selling open market notes directly and of those selling through dealers are plotted, by year, 1955–1963,[31] together with the volume of commercial paper and bank loans outstanding from each group. If we may take total assets as an index of demand for financing, the fact that the demands of the direct sellers did not exceed that of the others until the very late 1950's or early 1960's is most noteworthy. Even then, the difference was not marked. The series on short-term indebtedness of the two groups show clearly that, ultimately, reliance by the direct sellers upon banks dwindled to proportionate insignificance, while for captives selling through dealers, bank debt remained the principal source of short-term financing. Moreover, directly-placed paper tended to outrun dealer-placed paper in volume outstanding and rate of growth well before any differences in demand between the two groups became evident. If demand differences are not responsible, supply conditions in the direct-sale and dealer-placement segments of the open market are the probable cause of differences in financing patterns.

B. Differentiation Among the Captives With Respect to Use of the Open Market

As one studies the captives, a picture emerges of some which limit their negotiated short-term financing to bank debt only, a significant number of intermediate-sized ones whose short-term borrowing is palpably influenced by money market rate differentials and availability of open market funds, and a small third group which finds the permanent differential between the bank and open market rates, together with an adequate quantity of funds available, to be a sufficiently potent attraction to warrant primary reliance upon direct sale of open market notes.

A factor which accounts for the mixing of open market notes and bank debt in the short-term debt of some captives is the choke-rein held by the banks. The banks seem able to exercise enough informal power to limit the fraction of commercial paper in the short-term borrowing of the captives that lack easy access to private placement. If the banks are able to limit use of the open market by some captives, they may be capable of stopping oth-

---

[30] Observational error on the dependent variable has depressed the value obtained for the correlation. Bank loan and commercial paper totals were taken from balance sheets at various company fiscal year closing dates during the calendar year, and are aggregated for yearly periods which incorporates error.

[31] Selling practices employed in 1963 were the basis of classification of subsidiaries. In one or two instances, there were brief periods during the years covered when companies selling directly in 1963 placed paper through dealers, but the amounts involved were negligible for purposes here, and the periods were brief.

ers altogether. Managerial lethargy may also be a factor in explaining why many captives rely solely on banks for short-term debt. Quality rationing also operates, but the primary test of the rating agency would exclude few of the captives discussed here.

The core of the cost superiority of commercial paper is the persistent differential between the prime bank rate and the prime commercial paper rate. There is also a saving on compensating balances. The usual agreement between a bank and a borrower specifies that a deposit balance equal to a given percent of a credit line will be maintained when lines are active, but that a lower percentage applies against idle lines. As given loan needs are met with open market notes, the accompanying reduction of bank borrowing also effects a reduction of required compensating balances.[32] Also, the balances are financed, in essence, at the lower open market rate.

These savings are open to all potential issuers of open market paper among the captives.[33] The costs of access and the availability of funds will

[32] Financing subsidiaries employing commercial paper limit the open market's risk of evanescent fund supplies by maintaining bank deposits to reserve unused lines of credit. At balance sheet dates in 1961, the six captives selling directly averaged a trifle more than dollar-for-dollar of commercial paper outstanding relative to idle bank lines. Fourteen companies selling through dealers averaged commercial paper outstanding equal to 51 percent of open lines. The excess of balances over transactions requirements is probably large for all but the largest captives, because when administrative services are supplied by the parent, as is nearly always true in the case of small- and intermediate-sized ones, transactions to be financed from cash balances are low in volume and number. The cost of borrowing deposits idled in excess of transactions requirements is a precautionary reserve cost which is an offset to the savings described above.

[33] Added minor savings, perhaps an eighth of a point, are sometimes in fact achieved in direct placement by beating the base-rate on comparable maturities of dealer-placed paper. Moreover, if the yield curve is upward sloping, the borrower profits from cultivation of the short-end of the market, and direct sellers are free to exploit maturity rate differences. In the range of maturities under 270 days (the uppermost commercial paper maturity) the yield curve almost always slopes upward. Perhaps the most obviously successful use of these flexibilities has been made by Sears Roebuck Acceptance Corporation (SRAC). Paper as short as five days has not been uncommon in private placement, but SRAC's experience indicated the existence of a market for very short (three-five day or even less) maturities in the form of "bumps" in cash flow of corporations difficult for their managers to invest otherwise, particularly for weekends. Consequently, in April of 1961, SRAC began offering notes written with maturities in this range, and this contributed further to a shortening of the maturities of its notes outstanding which had been underway previously. An article in a financial daily quoted the SRAC near-term rate at 2½ percent when 30-59 day notes were offered at 3 percent, with a trifle higher yield at discount. The average maturity of paper placed in 1957 was 133 days; in 1960, this had been somewhat more than halved, and in 1961 and 1962 average maturity fell to 36.4 and 33.9 days, respectively.

On the other hand, some captives have resorted to concessions, such as one-eighth point on rates across all maturities on million dollar deals, in the early phases of their direct placement as a means of rapid market penetration. Another author has pointed out, however, that there is a persistent differential of about one-half point between dealer rates and direct placement rates. This, however, is a comparison of dealer rates with rates obtained by only one direct seller. See Richard T. Selden, *Trends and Cycles in the Commercial Paper Market*, New York: National Bureau of Economic Research, 1963, p. 68.

determine whether these savings are sought through the dealer or the direct placement markets. The overhead cost of maintaining an apparatus for private sale must be netted against possible savings from circumventing the ¼ percent per annum dealer commission.[34] The incremental costs required to save this commission include fixed or semi-fixed salaries of field personnel, the costs of maintaining their activities and supporting office facilities, and variable money handling costs for each transaction.[35] It appears from data shown to the author that in direct placement approximately $700 of variable cost annually supports about $1 million of average daily balances outstanding (ADO). If gross savings of dealer commissions are $2500 per $1 million of ADO's (¼ percent x $1 million), the saving contributed toward the covering of overhead is about $1800 per $1 million of ADO. The smallest volume of commercial paper outstanding from a captive after a full year of active direct placement was $45 million, perhaps suggesting the size requisite for direct sale. Thus, in terms of possible savings, direct placement is favored only for the large issuer, but differences in cost of access are not as powerful a consideration as availability of funds.

C. Supply of Funds to the Dealer and Direct Placement Segments of the Open Market

The customary flexibility and convenience of direct placement afford the issuer the opportunity for exploitation of a market in which suppliers have cash flows not necessarily consonant with the rigid maturities offered in the dealer market.[36] However, other more powerful considerations also point to greater elasticity of supply in the direct-placement market.

One author recently argued to good effect that analysis of supply in the open money market must start with the observation that treasury bills, directly-placed open market paper, and dealer-placed paper are close substitutes for each other in competition for lenders' dollars.[37] *Ceteris paribus*, the elasticity of supply to each of these segments of the money market must be high because of the interchangeability of these instruments in lenders' portfolios.

However, differences between fund suppliers result in substantially different elasticities of supply to the direct placement and dealer markets. Although the dependence of commercial paper dealers upon the country

[34] The commission is higher to less powerful issuers, reaching as high as ½ percent in some instances.

[35] Surprisingly few salesmen are required; a few years ago the maximum maintained was eight by GMAC, and substantially fewer by the smaller finance companies.

[36] Moreover, private sales enable the issuer to put forward informal bail-out assurances in the event of unforeseen lender need. Most issuers do not promise such a contingency resort, but to the best of the author's knowledge accommodation has not been denied to embarrassed lenders.

[37] Selden, *op. cit.*, pp. 67–81.

banks as suppliers of funds is diminishing, the bulk of the dealers' placements is still made with them.[38] Direct placements, on the other hand, are made overwhelmingly with nonfinancial corporations.[39] Significant expansion of dealer placements would involve a change of market and marketing apparatus. In contrast, the direct sellers have many more choices available to them in setting terms, and they can push field selling more vigorously and with greater numbers of large investors than can the dealers.

Moreover, marginal opportunity costs do not behave alike for the country banks and the nonfinancial corporations. In order to draw increasing funds from the banks, open market dealers must bid these funds away from the banks' margin of indifference between the low rates, liquidity, and virtually unassailable quality of commercial paper, and the considerably higher rates, less liquidity, and (probably) greater risk on a wide spectrum of other loan options. Consequently, steep increases in offered rates would be required for dealers to raise significantly larger amounts at a given time. Nonfinancial corporations, on the other hand, have few options in investing cash reserves, since all of their investments, except for real assets, pay closely similar rates.[40] Hence, for sellers of directly-placed commercial paper to bid funds away from competing outlets, only relatively slight rate increases will be required. From the differences in marketing apparatus and in the marginal opportunity cost schedules of the suppliers, it seems fair to surmise that elasticity of supply is appreciably higher in the direct than in the dealer market.

The behavior of the captive companies with respect to the bank loan, direct-placement, and dealer-placement segments of the open market can be summarized as follows. After 1957, but particularly after mid-1960, increasing supplies of funds in the open market invited short-term financing by the subsidiaries at rates consistently and materially lower than bank loan rates. Intermediate-sized captives, confined by scale of requirements to the use of dealers, moderately expanded commercial paper in their financing, principally on the basis of increased dealer sales to country banks. Large subsidiaries can sustain the overhead and inconvenience costs of access to direct placement. Even though the aggregate demand of this group did not significantly exceed that of the companies selling through dealers, the greater elasticity and cyclically-induced movements of the supply curve to the direct-placement segment of the market resulted in an expansion of directly-placed open market notes outstanding to a level several times the size of outstanding dealer-placements.

[38] *Ibid.*, p. 29.

[39] *Ibid.*, Chart 3, p. 26.

[40] It is generally assumed that liquid and real assets are not really rival investments. If true, their comparative rates are not relevant here.

VI. SUMMARY AND CONCLUSIONS

The very briefest restatement of the principal findings will serve adequately as a summary. Broadly, with respect to the term structure of external debt, the financial managers of the captives have chosen safety in preference to a gamble on interest rates, behaving as liquidity-risk averters rather than as interest-rate speculators. However, within the short-term component of debt, the persistent differential in interest rates between the bank and open money markets, and the secularly increasing absorptive capacity of the latter, have induced substantially enlarged reliance upon commercial paper, particularly by direct sales.

Beyond this, it is appropriate to enlarge upon some implications of our findings. One can hardly help but speculate that policy toward term structure has been needlessly lopsided, even if it is granted that a penchant for liquidity-safety should dominate. In the face of a far shorter maturity range on an entire portfolio of receivables, the customary 15–25 year maturities on long-term debt of the captives entail risks of their own. A reduction of receivables would lead to redundancy of funds; commitments to long-term debt extending over periods of favorable rate developments may bind the firm to unnecessarily high costs.[41]

Instead, managers might consider financing a part of their portfolios through frequent flotation of term loans approximately matched in maturity with newly-acquired notes receivable. This would provide "hedged" cash flows, and would freeze-in the difference between lending and borrowing interest rates.[42] The borrower could combine this with a portion of short-term financing fashioned according to his desire to attempt interest-cost minimization versus liquidity-risk. It is curious, too, that stand-by arrangements with lenders have not been coupled in practice with the assumption of risk toward liquidity structure, term structure of rates, or extra-heavy reliance upon commercial paper.

Officers of both short- and long-term lenders argue that the segregation of receivables in a captive should enhance total borrowing capacity. While it is easy enough to see that individual creditors, or classes of creditors, may benefit[43] from collateral segregation, it is not easy to see that, if liquidity and cash flows are the protection of creditor rights, segregation of parts can enhance total borrowing capacity. Cash and earnings flows and

---

[41] To be sure, nonprice concessions from lenders in debt contracts can mitigate both these risks. But it would seem that employment of intermediate-term maturities would substantially eliminate the first risk and reduce the second without necessitating a trade-off between interest rate and nonprice terms. Incidentally, examples of materialization of both these risks for the captives can be cited.

[42] Red tape of repeated note issuance could be slashed, perhaps, by use of collateral trust agreements between a given borrower and lender which adapt the features of shorter-term receivables financing arrangements.

[43] Andrews, "Captive Finance Companies," *op. cit.*

liquidity stock can only be divided among parent and captive, not multiplied. The administration of liquidity of parent and captive as a unit, which we have found here, is evidence of the tacit recognition of this fact by company management. If debt capacity has been enhanced by the existence of a captive, it has been dependent upon market imperfections or the shifting of lender preferences between risk and income.

32.

Mutual Fund Portfolio Activity, Performance, and Market Impact

F. E. BROWN
and DOUGLAS VICKERS

The portfolio structure, activity, and performance of the financial institutions in the savings-investment process engage the economist's attention from two related standpoints.[1] The first concerns the internal criteria of portfolio performance, or the manner in which the results of portfolio management either vindicate or disappoint the expectations of individual shareholders or savers. The second concerns the ways in which institutional activity is affected by, and in turn influences, the external market environment, and the ways in which institutional activity is thereby a determinant of the decision-making constraints that investors in general confront. The two viewpoints are interdependent, and the consideration of portfolio turnover, given the characteristics and constraints of the securities markets, establishes a further relationship between them.

From the first of these standpoints, the extent to which performance results accord with shareholders' expectations is at least partially indicated by changes in the structure of the savings flow and the associated distribu-

Reprinted from *Journal of Finance*, Vol. XVIII, No. 2, May 1963, pp. 377–391, by permission of the publisher and the authors.

[1] This paper is a by-product of the larger *Study of Mutual Funds* recently completed at the Securities Research Unit of the Wharton School of Finance and Commerce, University of Pennsylvania. The results of that study, in the preparation of which the present authors collaborated with Professors Irwin Friend and Edward S. Herman, have been published as a Report of the Committee on Interstate and Foreign Commerce (House Rept. No. 2274 [August, 1962]).

tion of assets among the various financial institutions. Research findings are confounded, and firm conclusions are made difficult by the uncertainty that exists regarding the extent to which relative performance results measure shareholders' subjective preferences and their relative indifferences between such diverse investment objectives as income, capital security, income and/ or capital growth, etc.

Investor preferences and indifference with regard to investment objectives are not easily amenable to quantification, and further investigation of investor motivation is required before a readily usable theory or rationalization on this level can be advanced. But, while this is so, the hypothesis is testable that, at the margin, variations in performance results have been associated with changes in the structure of the savings flow to institutions. At the same time, shifts in the savings flow have no doubt occurred not only because some institutions have failed to realize investor expectations, but also because relative performance results have induced changes in investor preferences.

COMPARISONS MADE AND QUESTIONS EXAMINED

In our *Study of Mutual Funds*, two types of comparisons within the mutual fund industry were made in this regard: (1) among types of funds and (2) among individual funds within type. The common-stock funds received a higher share of mutual fund net inflow in each succeeding year between 1953 and 1958, rising from 47.8 percent in 1953 to 75.6 percent for the first nine months of 1958. Balanced funds, on the other hand, fell from 46.2 percent to 21.5 percent during the same period. As would be expected during this time period, the crude performance figures for common-stock funds were much better than those for balanced funds. Within the group of common-stock funds, those with an announced "growth" objective recorded the best performance and also experienced the largest increase in share of inflow, as well as the greatest absolute net inflow.

Comparing individual funds within the balanced sector of the industry and within the common-stock sector, a positive relation between fund performance and inflow was found within each of five subgroups. This relation appeared on a cumulative basis, taking the performance results and the new money inflow to each fund for the entire 5¾ years, but was not clearly observable in the annual figures (inflow lagged 1 year behind performance), although there was a slight suggestion of such a pattern.

The study noted the possible presence of a relationship between changes in market prices as measured by the Dow-Jones Industrial Average and the changes in net inflow to the funds. While the strength of this relationship varied from time to time, owing to the variety of causal and motivating factors associated with such new money flows, it is noteworthy that the relationship again appeared strongly following the sharp stock-market break in May, 1962. In the following month, June, 1962, the gross inflow, at $218.6 million, was 26 percent lower than the monthly average for the first 5 months of the year. The net inflow for June, 1962, owing to a higher rate of redemptions in that month compared with the early months of the year, was only 60 percent of its average for the preceding 5 months.

From the second of the standpoints referred to above, that of certain external criteria relating to the market environment within which the funds' portfolio activity is conducted, it is to be noted that certain features of the funds' operations which may also affect shareholders' positions via performance results, such as rapidity of portfolio turnovers, variations in portfolio structures, distributions of trading by market channels, timing of security transactions, etc., also affect, and are influenced by, the external environment and market constraints. In this connection, the current size of the mutual fund industry and its recent rate growth, and the large size and potential market power of certain individual funds, render the economist's model of competitive market activity only tenuously applicable. For the funds are conceivably price-makers in the security markets and not only price-takers.

It would seem, on the basis of our larger study, that the mutual funds as a whole may have to some extent the ability to fulfil their own market predictions, and, in particular, to validate their own appraisal of individual security issues. For these reasons, it is of some significance to examine closely, and to compare with appropriate external market standards, the issues to which this paper is principally directed: namely, the rates of fund portfolio turnovers, the measurement of performance results, and the impact of fund trading activity on price formation in the market.

Questions on these levels are finally significant for the economist's analysis of the savings-investment process, of course, for the light they can throw on the broader question of the efficiency with which the security and capital markets perform the economic function of allocating capital resources among competing economic uses. The question can be put in other words by asking to what extent the potential economic benefits of pooling investment funds in institutional hands are realized in actual fact; namely, to what extent is the opportunity of balancing investment risks and prospective returns at more profitable levels of investment actually realized?

The present paper will attempt to throw some light on questions such as these by examining the way in which certain analytical-methodological problems in portfolio turnover, performance, and market impact might best be handled and by making some intra-industry and intra-market comparisons where appropriate. A note will be added finally on some economic aspects of the mutual funds' predictive ability, by examining their success in channeling investment money into security issues which have subsequently had a favorable trend in earnings.

Performance measures are of significance principally to the fund shareholders, both as a group and individually, and attempt to appraise the success realized by the fund in its portfolio management, given its announced portfolio objective. Market impact has a broader social significance, and the study of it examines the extent to which mutual funds influence conditions in the securities markets. Portfolio turnover is not, in and of itself, either desirable or undesirable. But, as an indication of the extent of portfolio activity, it raises interesting questions concerning the results of such activity, either on performance and thereby on shareholder benefits, or on the funds' market impact.

PORTFOLIO TURNOVER RATE

Portfolio activity is generated by two forces: the need to invest new monies received from the sale of the fund's own shares (or to liquidate investments in the case of redemptions) and management decisions to change existing portfolio structures. Were it not for sales and repurchases of the fund's own shares, portfolio turnover rate might be calculated quite simply as the average of portfolio sales and purchases during a given time period divided by the average value of the portfolio at the beginning and end of that period (eq. [1]):

$$PTR = \frac{(P + S)/2}{(V_1 + V_2)/2} = \frac{P + S}{V_1 + V_2},$$
(1)

P = Total purchases of portfolio securities,
S = Total sales of portfolio securities,
V_1 = Value of portfolio at beginning of period,
V_2 = Value of portfolio at end of period.

If transactions were neatly tagged as "for portfolio changes," "investment of new monies," or "for repurchase of own shares," there would be no problem. In such a case, only items for the first purpose would be included in the numerator since our interest in portfolio turnover is directed toward an understanding of portfolio shifts which represent a conscious effort to alter the structure of the existing portfolio. It should be observed that portfolio structure can be shifted also by the direction of inflow into specific securities, or by a corresponding liquidation of securities, when cash is needed for repurchases of the fund's own shares. We shall not attempt to incorporate portfolio shifts accomplished in this manner in our measurements, but it should be obvious that a large inflow permits considerable shifts in portfolio without any switching from one security to another. Our turnover rates, which ignore structural changes accomplished by the direction of inflow or outflow, will therefore be somewhat lower than they would be if the concept of turnover were defined to include such changes.

During the 5¾ years covered by our data, the gross inflow of new money to the funds was approximately three and a half times as large as the gross outflow. Thus it is apparent that a considerable portion of the repurchases of the funds' own shares could have been financed by inflow rather than by liquidation of existing holdings. If all repurchases were financed by inflow, transactions to accomplish portfolio changes would be shown by portfolio purchases plus portfolio sales minus those purchases accomplished with the *net* inflow (eq. [2]):

$$PTR = \frac{P + S - NI}{V_1 + V_2}, \tag{2}$$

where NI = net inflow.

In the case of a net outflow, the same procedure would be followed, so that the formula would be better expressed by deducting in the numerator the absolute value of net inflow.

If repurchases of the fund's own shares were financed by portfolio liquidations, the appropriate reduction to $P + S$ would be gross inflow plus gross outflow, since every capital change would be accompanied by a portfolio transaction (eq. [3]):

$$PTR = \frac{P + S - I - O}{V_1 + V_2}, \tag{3}$$

where I = gross inflow and O = gross outflow. This is undoubtedly a quite unrealistic view. Only if cash and near-cash items are deemed to be a part of the portfolio would it have any justification.

In the absence of any data permitting the identification of portfolio transactions made for different purposes, it remains conjectural how much of outflow has been financed by inflow. A generalized formula permitting various assumptions is given in equation (4), where K is the portion of outflow assumed to be financed by inflow:

$$PTR = \frac{P + S - I - O(1 - 2K)}{V_1 + V_2}. \tag{4}$$

If all of the outflow is assumed to be financed by inflow, equation (4) reduces to equation (2). If one-half of outflow is assumed to be financed by inflow, equation (4) would become

$$PTR = \frac{P + S - I}{V_1 + V_2}. \tag{5}$$

The denominator of the ratio has been identified as the average value of the portfolio. Clearly, both numerator and denominator should refer to the same kind of securities. But one can move in either of two directions: (1) a very broad definition of portfolio with a resulting comprehensive measure of turnover, but so broad that intra-industry comparisons may not be justified; or (2) a compartmentalization of portfolio into rather homogeneous subgroups with a series of figures, but no single measure that reflects both turnover within subgroups and turnover among subgroups.

The first approach might expand the coverage to include all assets, although cash would not enter into the transactions of the numerator. The danger of this approach (the broad definition) is that the funds with the higher portions of their assets in short-term governments or other high-turnover items would appear as high-turnover funds regardless of the rate at which they turned over other assets.

The second approach of a series of turnover figures has the advantage of permitting more meaningful comparisons between funds, but it is not so comprehensive and encounters further difficulties in terms of inflow adjustments. For example, suppose we attempt to measure the rate at which the common-stock portfolio is turned over. Given that a decision has been made with respect to the proper offsetting of total inflow against total outflow, what portion of the result should be applied in an adjustment to common-stock transactions? Perhaps the distribution of assets among various asset types should be accepted as the appropriate distribution to employ in allocating the inflow-outflow adjustment among the same asset types. Or, alternatively, the distribution of actual portfolio purchases or sales (net or gross) might serve as the basis for the allocations.

A third possibility involves the abandonment of the attempt to allocate the inflow-outflow adjustment among portfolio asset types and uses as the numerator of the turnover-rate formula the lesser of portfolio purchases or sales of the particular securities under consideration. The use of such a procedure is justified by the fact that the numerator states the level of the security transactions at which purchases and sales are equal, thus indicating a completed portfolio turnover in that type of security—i.e., a portfolio liquidation followed by a reinvestment. The extent to which the purchases of that security type exceed the sales represents the purchases due either to the reinvestment in that type of security of the proceeds of other portfolio liquidations, or to the investment of part of the fund's net inflow proceeds. Similarly, if sales exceed purchases, the excess will represent either a partial financing of the fund's outflow or a liquidation to finance a reinvestment in some other section of the portfolio.

The calculation of the turnover rate for the total portfolio requires fewer assumptions, and the only part of the portfolio considered separately in our larger study was the equity section and a sample of equity securities. Our alternatives for the calculation of equity turnover were equation (4), with all terms defined as appropriate for equities (including the appropriate portion of inflow and outflow), and equation (6):

$$PTR = \frac{X}{(V_1 + V_2)/2},$$ (6)

where X = the lesser of total purchases or sales of equities, and V_1 and V_2 = the value of equity holdings at the beginning and end of the period.

Three principal conclusions concerning differences within the mutual fund industry emerged in both total portfolio turnover rates and equity turnover rates and also emerged regardless of the inflow-outflow assumptions. (1) Turnover rates were inversely related to fund size throughout the period. (2) The distribution of turnover rates was skewed to the right for every year studied, and there was a considerable amount of dispersion. (3) Turnover rates increased in 1954 and 1958, both years in which there was a pronounced upward price movement in the stock market.

The funds in the smallest size group had the highest turnover rates throughout the study period. The combined rate for the funds in the smallest size class (total portfolio using all of net inflow as the adjustment factor) did not fall below 32 percent for any year and rose to 47 percent in 1957. The largest size group, on the other hand, showed the lowest rates for each year: below 20 percent for every year and below 15 percent in 4 of the 6 years. A test was made to ascertain whether the high-turnover rates for the small funds were produced by newly formed funds which might be shifting from a temporary liquid position into permanent portfolio securities. This was not the case; the average small fund had higher rates regardless of whether it had been recently formed.

Average portfolio turnover figures for the industry and for subgroups of funds conceal the wide degree of dispersion and are somewhat distorted by the high positive skewness present in every year. This distortion is counteracted in weighted figures for the entire industry because of the size differences among funds but not within more narrowly defined subgroups. In any event, it should be noted that funds vary widely in the rate at which they engage in portfolio activity. The interquartile range, which ignores completely the funds with the more extreme rates, exceeded 20 percent (total portfolio turnover adjusted by total net inflow) in every year except 1954. Examining the extremes, over one-tenth of the funds had turnover rates in excess of 50 percent in every year except 1955, and, at the other extreme, over one-tenth had turnover rates below 10 percent in every year except 1954. This wide variability among funds raises interesting questions concerning the performance records of funds with such apparently different approaches to portfolio activity, and the possible relation between turnover and performance will be commented on below.

The third general conclusion, that turnover rates seemed to rise as the stock-market prices rose, was most pronounced in 1954 but was also observable within most subgroups during the first 9 months of 1958. It should be noted that the first of these years, 1954, was also a year with somewhat less dispersion among funds in portfolio turnover and the only year in which less than one-tenth of the funds had turnover rates below 10 percent. In 1958, however, the higher industry figure was accompanied by an increase in dispersion among funds. This conclusion raises questions concerning the role of the mutual funds in these rising markets, with particular emphasis on the way in which the funds changed their portfolio structures.

PERFORMANCE

The concept of investment fund performance, as used in our study, relates to the effectiveness or efficiency with which the assets of the fund are administered, or the degree of success achieved by the fund in investing the capital intrusted to it by its shareholders. It is not, therefore, coterminous with the concept of investor experience. For an appraisal of the latter it would be necessary to consider costs of entry to the fund (and exit if appropriate) and tax liabilities (both income and capital gains taxes).

It is clear from the variety of investment objectives announced by the funds, and from their announced intentions to maintain certain types of portfolio structures, that the assessment of performance for different types of funds demands different criteria. There are no necessary reasons, for example, why a balanced fund should record, or should be expected to record, changes in asset values in a given market environment similar to those of a common-stock fund. Despite this fact, the performance of a fund may be shown by some combination of income dividends, capital gains distributions, and unrealized capital appreciation, or it may be shown for certain purposes and in certain kinds of funds by dividend yields or by earnings yields on the fund's portfolio. Questions arise concerning the ways in which these performance characteristics might be combined to provide meaningful measures of performance and the ways in which appropriate standards for internal and external comparisons might be constructed.

A composite performance relative in which these characteristics are combined is given by equation (7). The main study discusses other combinations of the three terms and the theoretical justification for each.

$$Perf = \frac{NA_{t+1} + DI + DC}{NA_t}, \qquad (7)$$

NA_{t+1} = Net assets per share at close of period,
NA_t = Net assets per share at beginning of period,
DI = Dividends per share from investment income during period,
DC = Distribution per share from profits realized from sale of securities during period.

The distinction among the three components may be somewhat artificial, since they are all expressed in dollar values and, except for tax considerations, the dollar values are interchangeable. The distinction is even less important when funds of similar type are compared.

What is an appropriate standard to use in appraising the performance of mutual funds? The fund managers select specific securities for investment from among a large array of securities on the market. It is appropriate, therefore, to compare the performance of the securities selected with the performance of the total from which the selection is made. This is not to suggest that the funds should attempt to cover the entire market, but simply to ask what discernment the fund managers show in choosing from the total market.

Cogent arguments can be presented for almost any division of the total market into sectors as a basis for comparison between the fund's performance and the market's behavior. In our larger study such a division was carried to five sectors: common stocks, preferred stocks, corporate bonds, U.S. government bonds with more than 1 year until maturity, and all other assets; on the basis of this division a series of "Standardized Performance Relatives" was computed, in which each sectoral market index was weighted by the proportion of the funds' portfolios held in the corresponding securities.

Standard and Poor publishes indices for each of the first two components referred to, as well as several bond indices for various ratings and maturities. Their composite Common Stock Index, based on 500 stocks, represents approximately 90 percent of the market value of all stocks listed on the New York Stock Exchange (though prior to March, 1957, the Index was based on 90 stocks representing 50 percent of such market value). With this wide coverage, it comes fairly close to duplicating movements in the market. The further need for daily figures at various parts of the study and the need of indices for different types of securities as indicated above dictated the use of Standard and Poor indices, although others, such as the Securities and Exchange Commission stock index, are of equal theoretical soundness.

The fact that a limited number of issues account for a substantial portion of the Standard and Poor Composite Common Stock Index is as it should be, because these same issues account for a substantial portion of the total market value of all common stocks. The bond indices chosen represent the most typical rating and maturity for the holdings of the funds, and all indices were adjusted for dividend or interest payments.

Performance relatives were computed on an annual basis for each fund. Cumulative performance figures were obtained by chaining the annual values. This assumes that all distributions are held in cash until the end of the calendar year and then reinvested. Any bias resulting from the employment of this assumption rather than the alternative assumption that reinvestments are made on the dates of distribution is quite small. The average capital gains realization is only about 3½ percent per year, and the typical payment date is in the latter part of the year. This means that only a very minimal change in the performance variables would result from the alternative assumption. Offsetting, at least in direction, the possible bias in the present procedure are the somewhat higher dividend payments for the indices, which are also assumed to be reinvested only at the end of each year.

The determination of the appropriate division of the funds' portfolios among security types, for purposes of making comparisons between their performance relatives and the market's standardized relative as indicated above, was based on the actual portfolio structures for 11 subgroups of funds established on the basis of type and size classifications. Standards of performance were calculated for the funds within these subgroups, using changing portfolio weights over time, and with constant weights over time (based on subgroup averages). There were no significant differences in the two sets of standards.

The basic conclusion of the performance analysis was that the funds, on the average, performed no better and no worse than the composite markets from which they selected their securities. The cumulative performance relative, representing the average of all funds for the 5¾ years under study was 196.7, and the standardized cumulative relative for the market was 198.2. Full details of the comparisons for the type and size subgroups of funds are given in our larger report.

Since the market indices used are designed to measure the total market, the external standard represents a portfolio without changes in structure during the period or periods under review. For this reason, it is of interest to examine the relationship between the performance results and the turnover rates of the funds for possible indications of the way in which the funds' performance was affected by the extent of their movement from a static portfolio.

Before turning to that comparison, however, it should be noted that there was considerable variability of performance relatives among funds of a given subgroup both on an annual basis and on a cumulative basis.[2] Some funds, of course, performed substantially better than the relevant market standard for the 5¾ years (other funds performing substantially worse). However, there was not much statistical evidence of a consistent tendency toward superior or inferior performances on a year-to-year basis by particular funds, though the evidence does not permit definitive conclusions.

There was no persistent relationship between annual portfolio turnover rates and performance results of the same year or performance of the fol-

[2] It should be noted that variability of performance results among funds within a given type class may be due to the fact that, while their announced investment objectives are the same, the division of their portfolios among types of securities, or among grades of securities within a given type, may be different.

lowing year. The analysis was made for balanced funds and common-stock funds separately, each stratified into high- and low-inflow funds. The contingency tables employed suggested either a positive or a negative relationship for certain subgroups during specific years, but the relationship was not uniform either throughout the period within a particular subgroup or for all subgroups within a specific year. The high turnover figures of 1954 and 1958 likewise failed to show any consistent relation with performance. The implication of such an analysis is that increased "management," as shown by greater portfolio activity, has changed the portfolio but has worked neither to the advantage nor to the disadvantage of shareholders. This is true at two stages: comparisons among funds with different turnover figures and comparisons of average fund performance with that of a theoretically constructed static portfolio.

MARKET IMPACT

Portfolio activity and portfolio management can influence the market environment in a number of ways other than by its impact on the level and stability of market prices, but these are the only features of market impact that we shall consider in this paper. It is extremely difficult to isolate the impact of mutual funds from other influences, particularly when the long-run impact of the funds on stock prices as a whole is being considered.

For the 5¾ years studied, considering this time period as a whole, probably the most feasible approach is essentially qualitative: i.e., comparing broad market movements in the net inflow of money to mutual funds, and through them into the stock market, with the corresponding movements in common-stock prices. For shorter time periods, it was possible to make quantitative and somewhat more satisfactory regression or correlation tests relating average stock-market prices to the mutual fund net common-stock activity. For individual stock issues, an even more extensive analysis of fund impact on market price was possible. However, even if these interrelationships are high, there may be problems in establishing the direction of causation. Theoretical reasoning is one method at our disposal, and, at the empirical level, testing can be made in terms of leads and lags.

The regression analysis for individual securities possesses two inherent advantages not found in the aggregate data. The data can be adjusted for price changes in other securities, so that the factors affecting the general level of stock prices are kept constant to a considerable extent. Moreover, the number of observations is considerably increased, permitting more powerful analyses in terms of statistical tests.

In both the aggregate and the individual security regression equations, the introduction of an initial level for prices serves as a crude attempt to permit the separation of long-run and short-run effects. Both monthly data and daily data were examined, and both directions of causation were investigated by the lead-lag approach. Inflow was also introduced as an additional independent variable in the aggregate analysis. Linear, logarithmic, and difference equations were all used in the aggregate analysis, and as many as five different values of the independent variable were employed in some of the equations. Equations (8) and (9) are examples of two different approaches used with aggregate monthly data:

$$M_t = a + b_1 P_t + b_2 P_{t-1} + b_3 P_{t-2} + cM_{t-3} \qquad (8)$$

and

$$M_t = a + b \sum_{t-2}^{t} P_t + cM_{t-3} \qquad (9)$$

where M = Standard and Poor's Composite Index at close of month, and P = fund common-stock net purchases (in $100,000) during month.

The principal equation used for the analysis of individual securities is shown by equation (10):

$$\frac{M_{it}}{M_t} = a + b_1 P_{it} + b_2 P_{i(t-1)} + b_3 P_{i(t-2)} + c\frac{M_{i(t-3)}}{M_{t-3}} \qquad (10),$$

with the same definitions as before and the subscript i referring to the security of interest. Equations similar to (8)—(10) were also employed in the daily analyses, but typically with more values for the independent variables.

The results of the analyses show that fund net purchases have significantly affected price movements of individual stocks and, to a lesser extent, price movements of the market in general. Of the 30 mutual fund favorites,[3] the monthly price (relative to the Standard and Poor average) of 23 was positively correlated with fund net purchases of that security in the preceding month. The regression coefficient was larger than its own standard error for 13 of the securities and more than double the standard error for 6 of them. Fund net purchases with an additional month's lead were positively correlated with price for 22 of the issues. The evidence was somewhat less conclusive for day-to-day fluctuations but was again positive. The data for aggregate activity suggested that fund activity may have had a fairly substantial impact on daily prices, but, contrary to the results for individual issues, the evidence was not so strong in the case of monthly fluctuations.

Using an equation similar to (9) for daily data of the third quarter of 1958, the results suggest that if the funds' average 5-day net purchases were

---

[3] This refers to a sample of 30 common stocks used at numerous points of the *Study of Mutual Funds*. The sample included the 30 stocks which accounted for the largest aggregate value in the funds' portfolios in the years 1951 through 1957.

increased by about one-third, average market common-stock prices would be increased by about 3.3 percent of their average level for that 3-month period. It is possible that the funds foresaw the short-run price movements which did occur, though if they did, there is no indication that any such predictive ability resulted in superior long-run performance. The analyses for investigating the opposite direction of causation (the effect of market-price changes on fund net purchases) in short-run fluctuations failed to reveal any consistent relationship.

An examination of fund activity within cyclical movements was conducted by dividing the time span for which data were available into periods of major market movements and into three subperiods (of approximately equal duration) within each such movement. Fund activity, segregated into that portion that was assumed to reflect the inflow of new money to the funds and the portion more directly reflecting managerial discretion within these periods, was then examined. Sixty percent of inflow was arbitrarily taken as the portion of inflow that would normally be channeled into common-stock purchases, but the precise ratio does not influence the conclusions derived.

There is no evidence that the funds followed a different policy in channeling their inflow into common stocks in periods of market rise than in periods of decline. Within market movements, however, net inflow seemed to be decreasingly invested in common stocks during a market decline and to a lesser extent increasingly channeled into common stocks during a market rise. The high portfolio turnover rate of 1958 is a case in point, where the funds purchased common stocks very heavily as the market advance continued, although net purchases of common stocks represented less than 50 percent of net security purchases in the first 6 months of the year. The funds, therefore, may tend to accentuate certain stock-market movements, and this seems to reflect discretionary action rather than the automatic channeling of inflow into the stock market.

There was also evidence of somewhat destabilizing fund activity with respect to individual securities, particularly within market declines. On the other hand, fund activity in the 2 months preceding cyclical turning points of individual issues (established for each issue independently) seems to have contributed to these reversals. Analyzing price increases and price decreases separately, the funds had net purchase balances in 22 of 31 instances preceding price increases and in only 13 of 27 instances preceding price decreases. This difference between the funds' behavior preceding a downturn and an upturn is statistically significant, lending support to the hypothesis that the funds may have been partially responsible for (and may have partially forecast) the major turning points in these issues. Any adjustment for inflow would have reduced the number of net purchase balances preceding both kinds of reversals, but would leave the basic conclusions unaltered. The evidence with respect to total market activity was limited, but it suggested that discretionary action by the funds may have been stabilizing at the lows and destabilizing at the highs, using the criterion that a positive correlation between net purchases and price changes at turning points is stabilizing.

CONCLUSION

The analysis of interrelationships between fund portfolio activity and fund performance and between fund portfolio activity and market impact has led to two main conclusions. Variations in fund portfolio turnover rates have not been associated with variations in fund performance: i.e., high levels of portfolio activity have worked neither to the advantage nor to the disadvantage of the shareholder. Similarly, the shifting of portfolio structures by fund managers has, on the average, resulted in no better (and also no worse) performances than those that would have been achieved by a constant portfolio. The second main conclusion is that fund portfolio activity has influenced market prices. The short-run influence can be demonstrated quantitatively, at least for individual securities. Fund impact has not been uniformly stabilizing or destabilizing but has contributed both to the prolonging of market movements and to the reversals or turning points of these movements.

A related question concerns the success that funds have enjoyed in channeling investments into securities that have subsequently experienced a favorable trend in earnings per share. A few simple tests, using data for the 30 mutual fund favorite stocks, compared fund net purchases with (1) average increase in per share earnings and (2) the ratio of 1953 prices to 1958 earnings. None of the results showed statistically significant differences between the issues in which the funds invested more heavily and those in which the funds made smaller investments.

33.

The Investment Performance
of Common Stock
Common Trust Funds

EDWARD K. GILL
and EDWARD W. REED

The number of common trust funds and their total
market value have grown significantly in recent years. From the end of 1960
to the end of 1965, the number of such funds increased from 420 to 1016,
and the number of commercial banks and trust companies operating them
increased from 327 to 464. The total market value of these funds advanced
during the same period from $2.8 to $7.5 billion.[1] There has been little information publicly available concerning the performance of common trust
funds. The objective of this study is to provide some evidence of this performance.[2]

The elements of performance which we shall consider are: appreciation, yield, and stability. We shall first compare a composite of common

Reprinted from *The National Banking Review*, Vol. IV, No. 2, December 1966, pp.
159–166, by permission of the publisher.

[1] Stanley Silverberg, "Bank Trust Investments in 1965," *The National Banking
Review*, June 3, 1966, p. 492.

[2] When classified according to asset composition, common trust funds fall into
three broad categories: fixed income funds, equity or common stock funds, and diversified funds. The latter are composed of portfolios of common stocks and debt instruments combined, and are expected to provide some appreciation while yielding a more
stable income than is provided by common stock funds.

trust funds with Standard and Poor's 500 Stock Index and with several mutual fund indexes prepared by Arthur Wiesenberger and Company.[3] Then, we shall attempt an analysis of relative performance among common stock common trust funds. For this purpose, simple coefficients of correlation are developed between measures of appreciation, yield, and stability. The period covered is from the end of 1960 through the end of 1964, though some deviations were necessary.

I. SOURCE OF DATA

Data for this study were obtained through questionnaires sent to the 207 trust institutions which, according to a list provided by the Office of the Comptroller of the Currency, operated common stock funds as of late 1964. There were 146 respondents to the questionnaire, a 71 percent return. This is sufficiently high to permit analysis, but it should be kept in mind that bias might exist. For example, reluctance to return the questionnaires might have been greater among those institutions whose funds performed poorly. Possibilities such as this cannot be disproved.

II. COMMON TRUST FUND INDEXES

In order to make the comparisons with the Standard and Poor's 500 Stock Index, and the mutual fund indexes, the data for the common trust funds were combined into indexes. Because of the lack of correlation between the various funds' valuation dates, four indexes were prepared. Regulation 9 of the Comptroller of the Currency, which provides the ruling for the operation of common trust funds, requires only that they be valued once each quarter. Most funds hold to the quarterly valuation, though some are valued monthly. Fortunately for this study, most of the funds (124 of those which provided data, or 85 percent) use the last business day of their chosen month or quarter. Therefore, one index of monthly-valued funds, and three of quarterly-valued funds, were readily feasible.

The indexes were given a base of 100 on their first valuation date. Funds begun after this date were added to the indexes in the same manner that new issues are added to a common stock index. Values of the Standard and Poor's 500 Stock Index and the mutual fund indexes were converted to a base of 100 on the dates which make up the first valuation dates of the common trust fund indexes.

---

[3] Arthur Wiesenberger and Company, *Investment Companies*, New York: Arthur Wiesenberger and Company, 1965.

CHART 33–1

17 Common Trust Funds
(12/31/1960 = 100)

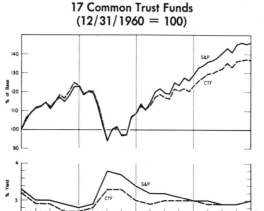

CHART 33–2

11 Common Trust Funds
(12/31/1960 = 100)

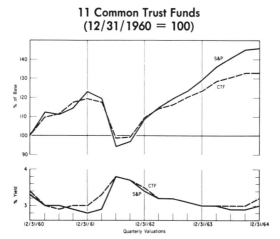

III. COMPARISON WITH STANDARD AND POOR'S
500 STOCK INDEX

The common trust funds are compared with Standard and Poor's 500 Stock Index in Charts 33–1 through 33–4, and with the mutual fund indexes in Charts 33–5 through 33–8. Since three different base dates are used, the charts can be compared to each other only to a limited extent.

The yields on the common trust fund indexes and the Standard and Poor's 500 Stock Index are compared in the lower part of each chart. Yield

CHART 33–3

75 Common Trust Funds
(1/31/1961 = 100)

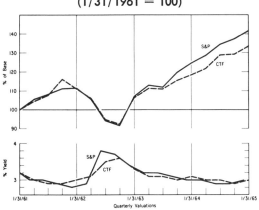

CHART 33–4

21 Common Trust Funds
(2/28/1961 = 100)

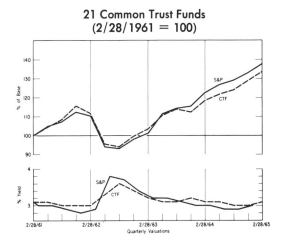

percentages for the Standard and Poor's Index were available only for quarters ending March 31, June 30, September 30, and December 31. As a result, the yield comparisons in Charts 33–3 and 34–4 are not for exactly corresponding quarters. However, the discrepancy is not considered to be sufficient to hide any significant variations in yields. All yield figures are rounded to the nearest tenth of a percent.

The composite performance of common trust funds was not greatly different from that of the Standard and Poor's 500 Stock Average during the first two and one-half years of the four-year period. As the 1963–1964 bull market continued, however, the price performance of the common trust funds was inferior to that of the general market. Yield performance was very similar, except during the low period of 1962. The yield on the Standard and Poor's Index increased about 33 percent during early 1962, as the value of the index declined roughly 25 percent.[4] Common trust funds lost almost as much value as did the Standard and Poor's Index, but the yields did not rise as sharply during the decline. It may be that some common trust fund managers were switching part of their stocks to short-term government securities during the latter part of the decline. This would have prevented the common trust funds from receiving the mid-year dividends on the stocks sold. The interest on any government bills acquired in the late phases of the decline would not have been received until well past the middle of the year, and this interest would not have fully offset the lost dividends. Yields on government bills were about 2.6 percent during the period, as compared with about 3.8 percent on the Standard and Poor's Index.

Stability performance, which can be judged from the graphs only by the size of the fluctuations from valuation date to valuation date, appears to be very similar for the common trust fund indexes and the Standard and Poor's 500 Stock Index. The yield performances are also very nearly equal, and price performance favors the Standard and Poor's Index only after mid-1963.

Common trust funds have several disadvantages, however. They must pay brokerage and other expenses. The temporarily idle cash which they hold will restrict their price performance in periods of rising stock prices. Moreover, the newer funds did not, in general, perform as well as the older funds in the indexes. Of the 75 funds in Chart 33–3, 40 were in operation at the beginning of the four years. The average annual appreciation of these was 8.6 percent, while that for the entire index was 7.3 percent.

Although some allowance should be made for these limitations, its exact value would be difficult to determine. We assume that such an allowance would make up the differences in price performance between the common trust fund indexes and the Standard and Poor's Index. This assumption is not unrealistic and does not greatly alter the conclusion to be drawn from this section. It allows us to state that: During the four-year period covered, the average performance of common stock common trust funds was equivalent to that of the general stock market as measured by the Standard and Poor's 500 Stock Index.

---

[4] This movement reflects the fact that dividend payout by corporations did not decline in 1962, even though stock prices dropped sharply. If a stock declined 25 percent in value, its yield would increase 33 percent with no change in dividend rate, for example.

IV. COMPARISON WITH MUTUAL FUND INDEXES

Two indexes of mutual fund performance for each of two categories of funds composed entirely of common stock—classified as "growth" and "growth-with-income"—are published in an annual survey by Arthur Wiesenberger and Company.[5] These four mutual fund indexes will be compared with the common trust fund indexes. Two of these mutual fund indexes are not designated as such by Wiesenberger's, but since they are averages of the performance of virtually every major mutual fund in each category, they are considered here to be general indexes of performance.

In computing the performance measure for each mutual fund in each of these general indexes, it is assumed that capital gains and income are reinvested. The value at the end of the period, and the start of the period is divided into the value at the end of the period, and the resulting percentage increase or decrease is the measure of that fund's performance. The common trust fund price and value indexes were constructed exclusive of income distributions, so in order to allow exact comparisons it was necessary to assume that income was not paid out but was held and reinvested. Two common trust fund indexes which are valued on December 31, were reconstructed on this basis. The valuation dates of the other two did not correspond exactly to the dates on which the mutual fund performance figures were computed.

The important results of these comparisons can be stated briefly. From the end of 1960 through the end of 1964, the growth mutual fund index appreciated 39 percent, and the corresponding growth-with-income index increased 47 percent. The two common trust fund indexes, with income assumed to be reinvested, grew by 51.1 percent and 49.8 percent. During 1962, a year of major decline, the growth mutual fund index dropped by 19 percent, the growth-with-income index declined 12 percent, and the common trust fund indexes as compared here declined 9.5 percent and 6.1 percent.

The second pair of mutual fund indexes is set forth in graphical comparison with the four common trust fund indexes in Charts 33–5 through 33–8. These mutual fund indexes are designated as Wiesenberger's Indexes in the annual investment company report of Wiesenberger and Company. Each index consists of the average values of five mutual funds, each fund selected for homogeneity of objective. Quarter-by-quarter values for these indexes were available only from the end of 1961 on; therefore, these charts cover three years rather than four. Yield comparisons on an annual basis are set forth in the lower right corner of Chart 33–5.

The charts indicate that the price performance of the common trust funds was quite similar to that of the growth-with-income index. Particular

[5] Arthur Wiesenberger and Company, *op. cit.*

CHART 33–5

17 Common Trust Funds
(12/31/1961 = 100)

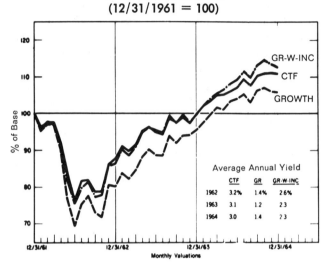

Monthly Valuations

CHART 33–6

11 Common Trust Funds
(12/31/1961 = 100)

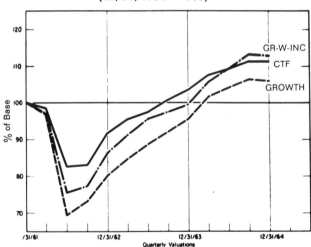

Quarterly Valuations

notice should be given to Chart 33–7 regarding this point, since it contains 60 percent of the common trust funds in all the common trust fund indexes. Common trust funds were somewhat more stable in the 1962 decline than was the growth-with-income mutual fund index, but they did not grow as rapidly after mid-1962. Common trust funds were clearly more stable and

CHART 33–7

75 Common Trust Funds
(1/31/1962 = 100)

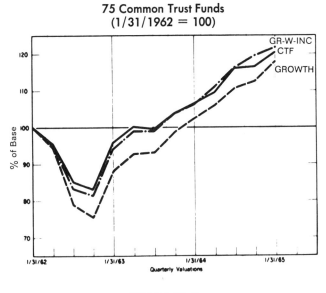

CHART 33–8

21 Common Trust Funds
(2/28/1962 = 100)

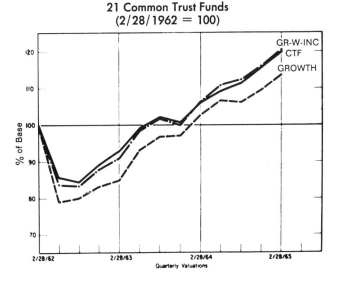

provided more appreciation during the three years than did the growth mutual fund index. Yield performance of common trust funds was vastly superior to that of either mutual fund index.

The comparisons in Charts 33–5 through 33–8 produce results similar to those of the earlier four-year comparisons with the general mutual fund

indexes. On this basis, it may be concluded that: The investment performance of common stock common trust funds was superior to that of common
stock mutual funds, as reflected by the Wiesenberger Indexes, for the four-
year period ended December 31, 1964, and for the three-year period ended
December 31, 1964.

V. SIMPLE CORRELATION ANALYSIS OF
COMMON TRUST FUND PERFORMANCE

In this section, we deal with the relative performance of the funds.
Forty funds, in operation throughout the four-year period ending January
31, 1965, are analyzed. Three measures of performance for each fund were
computed: one for appreciation, one for yield, and one for stability. The
appreciation, or growth, measure is the change in value from January 31,
1961 to January 31, 1965, expressed as a percent of the January 31, 1961
value. The yield measure is the mean quarterly yield. The quarterly yields
were computed by dividing the total past year's income for the fund by its
value at the end of each quarter. The stability measure is the July 31, 1962
value of the fund expressed as a percent of its January 31, 1962 value. This
is an arbitrary measure, but since the early 1962 market decline was very
sharp in its effect and encompassed the entire market for common stocks,
it was a good test of the stability of common stock portfolios.

Coefficients of correlation were computed for each pair of performance
measurement series and were found to be as follows:

Between growth and yield	.0680
Between growth and stability	.3778
Between yield and stability	.5271

The usual tests of the null hypothesis of no correlation (which assume normally distributed populations) indicate that the first coefficient is not significant, and the second and third coefficients are significant at the 2 percent
and .1 percent levels, respectively.

The nature of the relationship between the three pairs of series is
clearer in Charts 33–9 through 33–11. The various points of growth-yield,
growth-stability, and yield-stability are plotted, and the least squares line
of best fit has been computed for each. It must be pointed out that this
section is not based on regression analysis, even though the lines are computed by finding regression coefficients. Regression analysis assumes a
causal effect of one of the variables on the other, while correlation analysis
simply seeks a degree of association. The nature of any causal relationships
between the variables dealt with here would be very difficult to define, so
correlation analysis seems most appropriate.

The first coefficient of correlation indicates no significant relationship
between growth and yield. The funds which grew most produced yields at

least as high as did the slower growing funds. This result is important, since it would normally be expected that rapid growth would be accompanied by low yields and slow growth by higher yields. The low positive correlation between growth and yield indicates that the selection of stocks primarily for growth may not have been fruitful during the four-year period studied. This same lack of success in the case of mutual funds was apparent in the previous section. Those mutual funds with rapid growth objectives did not advance as much during the four years as did the growth-with-income funds which place more emphasis on providing reasonable yields.

The second coefficient of correlation indicates a strong positive relationship between growth and stability. By the measures used here, the funds which grew most over the four years declined least during early 1962. Of course, there is some built-in bias here, because those funds which fell least in 1962 did not have as far to go to reach new highs during the subsequent period. Nonetheless, the opposite result, that is, a negative correlation between growth and stability, would normally be expected, because lack of stability is characteristic of the so-called growth stocks.

The third coefficient reveals a high positive correlation between yield and stability. This meets with normal expectations. It means that the higher-yielding funds, which apparently seek reasonable income returns, were most stable. The most successful common trust funds during the four years, then, as well as the most successful mutual funds, appear to be those which sought reasonable yields and did not invest primarily in the so-called growth

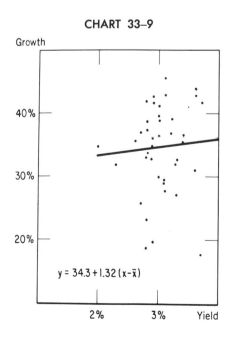

CHART 33–9

$$y = 34.3 + 1.32(x - \bar{x})$$

CHART 33–10

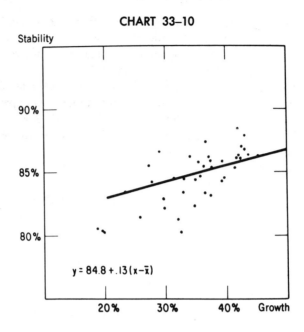

$$y = 84.8 + .13(x - \bar{x})$$

CHART 33–11

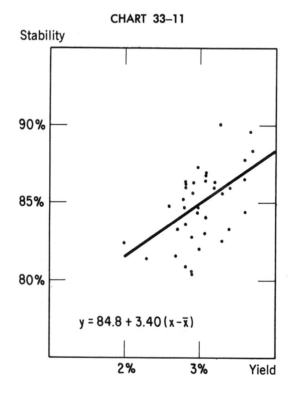

$$y = 84.8 + 3.40(x - \bar{x})$$

stocks. In fact, it may be that common trust fund managers would have been in error to invest primarily for growth, at the expense of income, at any time in the recent past. The general performance record of growth stocks in the 1940's and 1950's is slightly inferior to the performance of Standard and Poor's 500 Stock Index.[6] IBM was the outstanding exception to this record, but as the Wharton Study pointed out, IBM shares made up only about one-half of one percent of the value of common stock holdings of mutual funds just prior to the period of its rapid growth.[7]

VI. TWO FUNDS COMPARED

A number of trust institutions operate more than one common stock fund. An opportunity to compare a "growth" fund with a "growth-with-income" fund is provided in one situation where the two funds were started on the same date, by the same institution, with the same management for both funds. These funds were started near the market high of 1961. By the end of 1964, the growth fund had appreciated 3 percent, the growth-with-income fund 8 percent. During that period, the growth fund provided an average yield of 1.8 percent, the growth-with-income fund 3.8 percent. From February 28, 1962 to May 30, 1962, the growth fund declined 23 percent while the growth-with-income fund declined 14 percent.

VII. SUMMARY AND CONCLUSIONS

The objective of this study was to provide some evidence of the investment performance of common stock common trust funds. The following are our conclusions:

1. During the four-year period from the end of 1960 through the end of 1964, the average performance of common stock common trust funds was equivalent to that of the general market as measured by the Standard and Poor's 500 Stock Index.

2. During the four-year period through the end of 1964 and the three-year period through the end of 1964, the average performance of common stock common trust funds was superior to that of common stock mutual funds as measured by Wiesenberger's Indexes.

3. During the four-year period ending January 31, 1965, the common stock common trust funds which appreciated most were also the most stable and produced yields equal to those of the slower-growing, less-stable funds.

---

[6] Benjamin Graham, et al., Security Analysis, New York: McGraw-Hill, 1962, p. 535.

[7] U.S. Securities and Exchange Commission, A Study of Mutual Funds, Report of the Committee on Interstate and Foreign Commerce, 87th Congress, 2d Session, 1962.

34.

Trends in Life Insurance
Company Competition
for Pension Funds

RAYMOND G. SCHULTZ

At the present time individuals in the United States have an interest in nearly sixty-five billion dollars of pension reserves and funds which are held and administered by life insurance companies and corporate trustees. Two decades ago these reserves and funds amounted to about two billion dollars.

In 1940 life insurance companies administered most of the private pension funds whereas in 1961 they handled about one-third of the total invested funds. In 1940 life insurance companies accounted for two-fifths of individuals' savings, while in 1961 this industry's share of individuals' savings has declined to one-fourth, although in dollar amounts it has increased five times over this same period.

In short, the life insurance industry has been caught in a two-way squeeze during this period: (1) other savings media have greatly (and most effectively) increased their competition for individuals' savings, and (2) within the area of administering funds for group retirement insurance itself the life insurance industry has lost even more ground. Both of these situations are well recognized, but the extent of these trends and the recent de-

Reprinted from *The Journal of Risk and Insurance*, Vol. XXXI, No. 2, June 1964, pp. 193–205, by permission of the publisher. The author would like to express his gratitude for the cooperation and assistance that he received at Pacific Mutual Life Insurance Company while studying there under an A.R.I.A. Fellowship during the summer of 1963. The author, however, takes full responsibility for all views in this article and would like to emphasize that his views do not necessarily reflect those of the officers and management of Pacific Mutual Life Insurance Company.

velopments within the life insurance industry designed in part to counteract them do not appear to be fully appreciated in current literature.

TRENDS OVER THE LAST TEN YEARS

Savings in Institutions

Table 34-1 presents a summary of the growth in the major institutional savings media. The most spectacular rates of growth were realized by corporate pension funds and investment companies, both of which invest most heavily in equity securities. The corporate pension funds of course receive much of their growth impetus from such non-investment factors as labor union-management wage negotiations, income tax considerations, and personnel policy trends. Concern over inflationary price trends probably has stimulated pension fund growth too, but undoubtedly not to the extent that such trends have influenced mutual fund popularity.

The substantial percentage growth of credit unions can in part be explained by their relatively low base, but relatively high rates of return have been a major factor too. The savings and loan associations have also achieved their remarkable growth because of their high rates of return, which have stemmed from similar patterns of growth and yields in residential and commercial real estate.

Growth rates for life insurance companies and mutual savings banks are virtually identical, while savings accounts in commercial banks have grown somewhat more due to their great overall growth and size, convenience, and aggressiveness. It is interesting to note that while life insurance company reserves increased 65 percent over this ten-year period,

TABLE 34-1

Savings in Institutions

(Billions of Dollars)
(1952-61)

Year	Life Ins. Res.	Sav. & Loan Assoc.	Com. Banks	Mut. Sav. Banks	Invest. Co's.	U. S. Sav. Bonds	Cred. Un.	Postal Sav.	Pen. Funds
1952	$ 62.6	$19.1	$39.3	$22.6	$ 4.9	$49.2	$1.4	$2.7	n.a.
1953	66.7	22.8	42.0	24.3	5.1	49.4	1.7	2.5	n.a.
1954	70.9	27.2	44.7	26.3	7.3	50.0	2.0	2.2	n.a.
1955	75.4	32.1	46.3	28.1	9.0	50.2	2.4	2.0	$15.9
1956	79.7	37.1	48.5	30.0	10.3	50.1	2.9	1.7	17.6
1957	84.1	41.9	53.7	31.7	9.9	48.2	3.4	1.4	19.9
1958	88.6	47.9	60.0	34.0	14.8	47.7	3.9	1.2	24.6
1959	94.0	54.6	62.9	34.9	17.5	45.9	4.4	1.0	28.2
1960	98.5	62.1	67.1	36.3	18.2	45.7	5.0	.8	32.2
1961	103.3	70.8	75.9	38.3	24.9	46.5	5.7	.7	39.2

Notes: Commercial bank figures are savings deposits only; pension fund figures are at market value.

Sources: *Life Insurance Fact Book, Savings and Loan Fact Book, Federal Reserve Bulletin,* and the Securities and Exchange Commission *Statistical Bulletin;* by permission of the Institute of Life Insurance.

insurance in force increased by 127 percent. The differential between these two figures can be attributed to relatively greater sales of term insurance (particularly group insurance) beginning with World War II. Postal Savings are in a gradual process of liquidation while United States Government Savings Bonds have remained relatively stable.

Pension Operations

Table 34–2 presents a more detailed picture of the private pension area. The yields for the insured pension plans are those earned by the industry on all of its investments. Yields for corporate pension plans are calculated on both book value and market value since while the latter basis is more commonly used, the former probably affords a more similar basis of comparison with the life insurance industry figures (due to the existence of substantial unrealized gains in non-insured pension plan assets taken at market value). Regardless of which yields are used, however, it is obvious that the life insurance industry has realized at least as comparable yields on its investments as have the corporate pension funds.

On the other hand, the non-insured pension plans have an additional unrealized capital gain of $6.8 billion to date, which, if added to realized capital gains, dividends, and interest (as most mutual funds calculate their "yields"), would increase returns based on book value by nearly one percent and on market value by three-quarters of one percent, on the average, since 1940. It is of course true that life insurance companies could also calculate their returns in this manner for purposes of comparison, but since their

TABLE 34–2

Private Pension Funds

(Billions of Dollars)
(1952-61)

| Year | Insured Pension Reserves | | | Non-insured Pension Funds | | | | | Other |
	Reserves	Return	Unreal. Apprec.	Assets (B.V.)	Return (B.V.)	Assets (M.V.)	Return (M.V.)	Unreal. Apprec.	Funds
1952	$ 7.7	3.28%	.1	n.a.	n.a.	n.a.	n.a.	n.a.	n.a.
1953	8.8	3.36	.1	n.a.	n.a.	n.a.	n.a.	n.a.	n.a.
1954	10.0	3.46	.5	$12.2	n.a.	n.a.	n.a.	n.a.	$ .8
1955	11.3	3.51	.2	14.2	3.93%	$15.9	3.51%	n.a.	1.1
1956	12.5	3.63	—.2	16.6	3.62	17.6	3.39	—.7	1.3
1957	14.1	3.75	—.1	19.3	3.77	19.9	3.69	—.4	1.5
1958	15.6	3.85	.4	22.1	3.86	24.6	3.67	1.9	1.8
1959	17.6	3.96	.2	25.3	3.94	28.2	3.60	.4	2.0
1960	18.8	4.11	—	28.7	3.99	32.2	3.64	.6	2.3
1961	20.2	4.22	.9	32.4	4.00	39.2	3.48	3.4	2.7

Notes: The rates of return and unrealized appreciation figures indicated for insured pension reserves are those of the life insurance industry's entire investment portfolio. Unrealized appreciation figures are estimates based on available data for each industry. Other funds are multi-employer and union plans. B. V. refers to book value and M. V. to market value.

Sources: *Life Insurance Fact Book,* and Securities and Exchange Commission *Statistical Bulletin;* by permission of the Institute of Life Insurance.

TABLE 34–3

Investment Policies of Life Insurance Companies and Corporate Pension Funds,
1961

(Billions of Dollars)

Life Insurance Companies			Corporate Pension Funds			
				(Book Value)		(Market Value)
Bonds			Bonds				
U. S. Gov't	$ 6.1	4.9%	U. S. Gov't	$ 2.1	6.5%	$ 2.0	5.1%
Other Gov't	5.5	4.3	Corporate	15.1	46.6	14.2	36.2
Corporate	49.3	38.8	Stocks				
Stocks			Preferred	.6	1.8	.6	1.5
Preferred	2.1	1.6	Common	11.8	36.5	19.6	50.0
Common	4.2	3.3	Mortgages	.9	2.8	.9	2.3
Mortgages	44.2	34.9	Cash	.5	1.5	.5	1.3
Real Estate	4.0	3.2	Other	1.4	4.3	1.4	3.6
Policy Loans	5.7	4.5					
Other	5.7	4.5	Totals	$32.4	100.0%	$39.2	100.0%
Totals	$126.8	100.0%					

Sources: *Life Insurance Fact Book,* and Securities and Exchange Commission *Statistical Bulletin;* by permission of the Institute of Life Insurance.

equity investments (which would comprise most of the assets carried at market value) were substantially smaller (see Table 34–3), their approximate unrealized capital gains of $2 billion would not increase their results by more than .2 percent annually.

When these crude adjustments are taken into account, it can be seen that over the last six years the corporate pension funds would have had returns of 4.9 percent (on book value) or 4.4 percent (on market value) compared to the life insurance industry's 4.2 percent. When the extent of aggregate pensions is considered, these margins are most significant. It should be noted, however, that since the corporate pension funds have grown at a more rapid rate than life insurance funds during the past decade of generally rising interest rates, their aggregate rate of return could be expected to be higher solely from the different pattern of incidence of receipt of funds.

Table 34–3 indicates where the corporate pension funds have realized their main advantage over life insurance companies in their respective investment operations—viz., common stock investments. The corporate pension funds have allocated one-third of their resources to common stocks, yet these holdings represent half of their assets on a market value basis. Life insurance companies, on the other hand, are greatly restricted by most states (particularly New York) in their investment allocations and must, as a result, content themselves basically with holdings of high quality and fixed principal.[1]

[1] Robert E. Schultz and Raymond G. Schultz, "The Regulation of Life Insurance Company Investments," *Journal of Insurance,* December 1960, p. 58.

Since it is not unusual to find that most employers are more concerned with the scale of immediate pension fund contributions that are based in part on substantial amounts of assumed future capital gains rather than guaranteed investment results (plus additional dividends, if realized) derived from more conservative operations, the life insurance companies are competing for pension funds under a marked handicap. Indeed the growth of deposit administration and similar types of pension plans handled by life insurance companies relative to deferred group annuity plans reflects this tendency also (see Table 34–4). The typical employer seems to be far more interested in initial contributions than in long-run guarantees, and undoubtedly the so-called "profit squeeze" of recent years has added to this feeling.

This discussion of recent trends in pension fund competition would not be complete without the mention of the rise to prominence of firms that specialize (in varying degrees) in pension plan origination and administration. The life insurance industry has been rather slow in adjusting to the advent of extensive pension fund utilization. The typical agent in the field is not equipped to deal with pension plans, and as a result such agents have not put forth the same sales effort in this area as in ordinary life insurance. Much of the life insurance industry has not been aggressive in promoting pension plan business either, although this condition has been changing in recent years.

The consequence of these competitive weaknesses has been the formation of firms that in effect perform many of the functions of life insurance companies for the client. These firms actively solicit pension business, perform the necessary actuarial and legal service required, and in many cases administer or service the plans once they are in operation. These firms receive fees for their services and/or a brokerage commission when they place the plan with an insurance company. Many of these firms employ highly qualified actuaries and attorneys in their operations.

Once a pension consulting firm has handled a number of plans, it be-

TABLE 34–4

Insured Pension Plan Reserves

(Billions of Dollars)

	1950		1961		1962	
Deferred Group Ann.	$4.1	74%	$12.0	59%	$12.6	58%
Deposit Admin.	.2	4	4.2	21	4.8	22
Individual Policy	.7	12	2.3	11	2.3	11
Other	.6	10	1.8	9	1.9	9
Totals	$5.6	100%	$20.3	100%	$21.6	100%

Source: The Tally of Life Insurance Statistics, May 1963, Institute of Life Insurance; by permission of the Institute of Life Insurance.

comes quite proficient in its functions and usually is able to reduce the bulk of the process to a relatively standardized procedure. The need for full-time actuaries and attorneys tends to diminish, but unfortunately these specialists' salaries do not. On the other hand, once a life insurance company has decided to solicit pension business actively, organize its group department for the operation, and train enough field men to perform the initial steps in selling and establishing a pension plan, it has a cost advantage over the pension consulting firm in that it already has its actuaries and attorneys within its organization and may utilize these individuals' services without materially affecting its operating costs.

Insofar as the life insurance industry is concerned, the damage has already been done; the larger pension consulting firms will survive more intensive life insurance company competition and as a result they will always have a substantial portion of the private pension business under their control and administration.

RECENT DEVELOPMENTS IN THE PRIVATE PENSION FIELD

The preceding section has indicated the main competitive problem that life insurance companies face in the pension area today—the inability to match corporate pension fund investment results. There have been three recent and significant developments within the life insurance industry designed to eliminate this problem: (1) tax-exemption of insured pension plans, (2) investment year method of allocating investment income, and (3) segregated assets or accounts.

Tax-Exempt Status for Insured Pension Plans

One of the more significant competitive advantages that non-insured pension trusts have had over insured plans is their tax-exempt status. The fact that life insurance companies were forced to pay higher taxes on investment income under the 1959 revision of the *Internal Revenue Code* did not enhance their ability to attract pension funds and in fact continued the inequitable tax treatment as far as such pension operations were concerned. However, since 1961 such pension income is exempt from taxation since the reserves attributable to such funds are excluded from the composition of Adjusted Life Insurance Reserves (for tax purposes).[2] During the 1958–61 period, the tax code provided for a gradual transition from the fully-taxed status to the tax-exempt basis that these funds now enjoy.[3]

[2] *Internal Revenue Code*, Sec 805 (c) (1) and (d) (1).
[3] *Ibid.*, Sec. 805 (d) (2) Due to the mechanics of calculating the exemption for insured pension funds under this section, it may be more accurate to say that these funds are substantially tax exempt rather than entirely tax exempt.

Investment Year Method

While investment rates earned by the life insurance industry on its total portfolio have been increasing in recent years, they have not matched the increases achieved by other savings media (especially mutual funds and savings and loan associations). Indeed, the present rate level (4.22 percent in 1961) is not such that it permits the life insurance companies to bargain on even terms for pension funds, using the portfolio average rate. The steady increase in life insurance company investment rates indicates that the industry has been able to realize much higher earnings on new investments than on existing invested funds over the last decade. When the earnings from recent investments are averaged with the earnings from the older investments, however, the mean current rate will be lower than the rate on new investments.

While pension fund earnings are computed in the same manner, the greater emphasis on equity securities makes the pension funds' results much more responsive to current market rates and movements. When there is a sustained increase in stock market prices, pension fund investment rates will consistently lead life insurance company rates, and vice-versa. Since, however, there seems to be a long-run inflationary price trend in the American economy (approximately 2 percent per year since 1900), the pension funds will usually have a competitive advantage over the life insurance companies. Some life insurers are attempting to overcome this disadvantage, at least in the short run, by computing investment results in a different manner.

Regulation 33 of the *New York Insurance Laws*, for example, recognizes two separate and distinct methods of allocating net investment income:

(1) In proportion to total mean policy reserves and liabilities of each major line of business or in proportion to the total mean funds of each of the major lines of business; or

(2) ". . . by an investment year method if its use of such method complies with the rules stated in Section E."[4]

Section E provides a description of the investment year method as well as the restrictions applying to its use;

(f) Such method treats as a single period all years of investment prior to the year of investment as to which such method first became effective;

(g) Such method treats as a single and separate period each year of investment commencing with the year of investment as to which such method first became effective; provided, however, that an insurer may transfer any one or more years of investment on a first-in, first-out basis to the single period referred to in (f) after demonstra-

---

[4] *New York Insurance Laws*, Reg. 33, Sec. D.

tion to the satisfaction of the Superintendent that such transfer would be equitable; and (h) in computing investment yield rates for each of the periods referred to in (f) and (g), such method takes into account the incidence, by year of investment, of receipt of premiums and considerations and of payout of benefits and expenses, and also takes into account on an actual basis "fixed or frozen" assets, other invested funds, uninvested funds and funds made available for re-investment.[5]

If the investment year method is used, it must be applied to all major and secondary lines of business, and capital gains and losses must also be so distributed.[6]

The life insurance company, by treating each new year's investments as a separate fund, no longer must average the current year's results in with all other investment experience. A newly established deposit administration plan, for example, would receive the same investment income credit as all other plans or contracts written in that same year on the funds actually contributed to the life insurer for that year. This same rate of credit would apply to funds contributed in the same year by contracts written in prior years.

In each succeeding year, results are also kept separate for all new contributions under both existing and new contracts plus amortized funds, proceeds from a sale of assets, etc., reinvested in that year. Thus the longer such a plan continues in effect, the greater the process of averaging results realized by each separate investment year, but such a plan is not affected by investments made prior to its inception.

Under such an approach each plan or contract is credited with the results actually earned on the funds that were invested by the company according to the year of receipt under the provisions of the plan. Individuals or organizations acquiring coverage in more recent years do not "carry" the older plans or coverages, and vice-versa. The long run effect is to create a substantially greater degree of equity for all insureds. In the short run, with rising investment rates, the effect will be to make the life insurance industry far more competitive with corporate pension funds in soliciting new plans.

Had the entire life insurance industry been on the investment year method since 1952, pension plan funds received during this period would have had the benefit of considerably higher and more variable investment rates. Table 34–5 presents an estimate of such earnings rates for the year of investment based on an investment year method. Since data are not available on the actual annual amortization schedules of the industry over this ten-year period, such amortization was assumed at a constant factor of 6.5 percent of invested assets. The 6.5 percent figure was derived from amorti-

[5] *Ibid.*, Sec. E. Subsec. 1.
[6] *Ibid.*

TABLE 34-5

Estimated Investment Results on an Investment Year Basis

(Billions of Dollars)

Year	Net Inv. Return	Net Inv. Income	Average Total Invest.	Current Invest.	Return on Cur. Inv.
1952	3.28%	$2.2	$ 66	$ 9	$3.8%
1953	3.36	2.4	70	8	4.0
1954	3.46	2.6	75	10	4.2
1955	3.51	2.8	80	10	3.9
1956	3.63	3.1	84	9	4.6
1957	3.75	3.3	89	10	4.6
1958	3.85	3.5	91	8	4.9
1959	3.96	3.9	98	13	4.8
1960	4.11	4.3	105	13	5.5
1961	4.22	4.7	111	13	4.9

Note: The average annual rate of amortization of mortgages and securities was estimated at 6.5 per cent. This assumption was based on data presented in *Life Insurance Companies as Financial Institutions*, Life Insurance Association of America, pp. 180-185.

zation estimates for the industry in the 1958–59 period compiled by the Life Insurance Association of America.[7]

To the extent that actual amortization, prepayments, and asset sales varied from this factor, the estimated investment year rates will be inaccurate, but it is doubtful whether any of the rates are materially in error. At any rate, it can be seen from this table that investment year rates during this period would have been higher and much more erratic than average net investment income rates. The insureds of a company on the investment year method should be prepared for such fluctuations since they are inherent in it. However, it should be noted that the return on a contract under which funds have been paid in over a period of years would be the *weighted average* for the specific years brought up to date for reinvestment of amortization.

One last aspect of the investment year method that should be mentioned at this point is the fact that there seems to be considerable variation in the content of state laws and administrative procedures. Regulation 33, issued in accordance with the *New York Insurance Laws* is a good example of a formal enactment of the investment year method. In other states, such as California, the procedure is permitted by administrative directive. Apparently under some state enactments the investment year method of investment income allocation may be applied to some lines of the business but need not be applied to all lines of business, as the New York regulation requires.[8]

The insurer also has the ability to shift from one method of investment income allocation to the other under the various state enactments, but in

[7] Life Insurance Association of America, *Life Insurance Companies as Financial Institutions*, p. 184.

[8] *New York Insurance Laws, loc. cit.*

some jurisdictions the insurance commissioner must approve such changes, whereas under other approaches the entire decision is left to the discretion of the company. It would seem that on each of these points the New York regulation (as well as other states' requirements that are similar to it) provides the best approach—if a company decides to use the investment year method, it must do so consistently and equitably.

Segregated Assets or Accounts

NATURE OF THE STATE LAWS. While the investment year method of investment income allocation may provide a more equitable basis of distribution than the traditional industry approach of using relative reserves or funds, this method does not overcome the underlying problem that the life insurance industry faces in its competition with pension funds and certain other savings media—viz., its inability to invest more extensively in equity securities. For example, the American Bankers Association has made this statement:

> Trusteed plans have grown more rapidly than insured plans because of the greater flexibility which they afford and because of the greater scope permitted for investment management, notably in the liberal use of equity securities.[9]

The pension funds achieve their competitive investment advantage over life insurance companies because of materially less restrictive regulations governing their asset allocations. Nearly four-fifths of the states now follow the "prudent-man rule" either by statute or court decision. The essence of this approach is that

> . . . the trustee (unless restricted by the trust agreement) . . . (may) make such investments as a prudent man would make, having due regard for the preservation of principle and the regularity of income.[10]

Some of the states, such as New York (which requires that 65 percent of trust funds be invested in fixed income securities),[11] place certain statutory restrictions on the application of this doctrine.

The remaining states follow a "legal list" approach in which they prescribe by statute eligible investment categories for trust funds. The "legal list" investment restrictions are more similar to the usual life insurance company investment regulations than are the "prudent-man rules."

Since it is most unlikely that states such as New York would be willing to dilute their laws restricting the latitude of life insurance companies' investing in equity securities, the industry has come up with an alternative that

---

[9] American Bankers Association, *The Commercial Banking Industry*, p. 313.

[10] Robinson, Boehmler, Gane and Farwell, *Financial Institutions*, Third Edition, p. 429.

[11] *Ibid.*, p. 430.

has proved to be acceptable to approximately two-fifths of the states to date —segregated assets or accounts. There are four basic aspects to the majority of the segregated assets laws:

(1) Special funds are to be established for the contributions of each employer. These funds are to be kept separate from the general assets of the insurer and may either be kept separate for each employer or commingled with similar funds of other employers. Employees' contributions cannot be placed in these funds.

(2) These special funds are to be invested under greatly liberalized investment rules which would permit substantial equity securities investments.

(3) The life insurance company and the employer agree to accept whatever the investment results of the funds are—i.e., the insurer does not guarantee investment results and its liability consists only of the value of the fund when the assets (or a portion of them) are transferred to the insurer's general asset accounts. In effect these funds are immediate participation plans without guarantees of investment results.

(4) Ultimately the life insurance company will shift funds from the segregated funds to its general assets as employees become eligible for benefit payments. Annuity benefits would be purchased subject to the usual cost and interest guarantees now afforded by insurers under nonsegregated asset agreements.

There are of course variations in this general approach in different states. In some states, such as California, the investment restriction applied to such segregated accounts are the same as those applied to the investment of "excess funds,"[12] with certain minor modifications.

The New York approach is to modify the present investment regulation by exempting segregated accounts from some restrictions—e.g., the overall 5 percent limitation on stock investments[13]—and increasing other limitations—e.g., the 2 percent limit on investment in any one stock issue is raised to 10 percent[14]—but the overall regulatory structure still applies to these accounts.

Some state laws (e.g., New York's) permit the use of segregated accounts only for group pensions, while the proposed (as of fall 1963) Oregon segregated accounts law would permit its use for pension plans, variable annuities, proceeds of policies left with the insurer at interest, and dividends left with the company at interest as well as in other less obvious circumstances.[15] It is interesting to note that some life insurers doing business in Oregon are alarmed by this proposed law—they feel that it is too broad.

[12] Schultz, *op. cit.*, p. 58.
[13] *New York Insurance Laws*, Sec. 81(13).
[14] *Ibid.*, Sec. 81(15).
[15] *Senate Bill 257*, 1952 Legislative Assembly, State of Oregon.

Needless to say, the banking industry has exerted strong opposition to segregated asset laws. In California the law was held up several years by banking interests and might well have not passed even in 1963 except for the fact that these same interests saw that many foreign insurers had already been granted such powers and only the few large life insurance companies domiciled in California were being blocked from using them.

In California a life insurer must have assets of at least $50,000,000 before it may offer an employer a segregated investment account.[16] The principal objection raised by the banking industry against segregated assets is that the life insurance companies would be doing a trust business. In answer to this point, the *New York Insurance Laws* contain the following subsection:

> (1) Amounts allocated by the insurer to separate accounts shall be owned by the insurer, the assets therein shall be the property of the insurer and no insurer by reason of such accounts shall be or hold itself out to be a trustee.[17]

The other usual objection raised by the banking industry is that the bank trustee's investment performance in effect is guaranteed by its capital and surplus, whereas the life insurer's net worth is not involved in segregated asset investment operations. In the New York law there is a provision for the establishment and maintenance of a special contingency reserve for these separated funds, which must equal the minimum capital and surplus required of a life insurance company domiciled in New York. This special reserve is restricted to "defray a liability or expense incurred" in connection with segregated asset accounts.[18]

A problem of a slightly different nature also has been a source of concern for both banks and life insurance companies as a result of segregated assets laws—might insurance authorities at some future date seek supervisory jurisdiction over bank-administered pension plans and might banking authorities seek similar control over life insurers that have segregated asset accounts? At this time there do not seem to be any such problems developing, but such changes are not out of the realm of possibility in the future.

TAXATION AND SECURITIES AND EXCHANGE COMMISSION REGULATION. PUBLIC LAW 87-858, which was passed in 1962, specifically exempts life insurance companies from taxation on investment income and realized capital gains credited to segregated asset accounts where such funds represent qualified pension plans.[19] The committee report in explanation of this law reads in part as follows:

> . . . to provide tax equality for these segregated pension accounts with the tax-exempt pension trusts, it is necessary that the invest-

---

[16] *Assembly Bill 1869*, 1963 California Legislative Session.
[17] *New York Insurance Laws*, Sec. 227(1).
[18] *Ibid.*, Sec. 227(2).
[19] *Internal Revenue Code*, Sec. 801(g).

ment income and capital gains credited to policyholders in these segregated accounts be free of tax in the same manner as is already true in the case of non-insured pension trusts.[20]

This law of course merely extends the now tax-exempt status of insured pension plans in general to such plans with segregated assets and reserves.

Relative to the possible regulatory jurisdiction of the Securities and exchange Commission over segregated assets, this body has specifically waived any rights that it might have had to regulate such operations.[21] The SEC did so because only the contributions of employers will be held in such accounts (employee contributions will be part of the general assets of the life insurer at all times). Since the Investment Company Act of 1940 was not deemed to apply to non-insured pension plans, it would not be logical that the Act should apply to insured pension plans. However, if policyholders were to receive variable annuity-type benefits once they had become eligible for benefits under the segregated pension plan, the SEC would have a basis for requiring compliance with the provisions of the Act. Thus the proposed Oregon segregated assets law presents life insurers with potential regulatory problems as well as broad investment powers.

UTILIZATION OF SEGREGATED ASSET PROVISIONS. Unlike investment year allocation, which is being used by a number of companies, segregated assets have not been extensively used to date by the life insurance industry. Several of the large pension-writing companies have set up a few of these plans, but for the most part the industry is cautiously feeling its way through this period of development. The slowness of the industry to utilize segregated assets can be attributed in large part to the need for permissive legislation and interpretive rulings at both the federal and state levels. In utilizing segregated assets there are two basic administrative questions that each company must work out for itself:

(1) What eligibility criteria will be used in establishing these plans? There are three main factors involved in determining whether a pension plan should be set up on a segregated assets basis:

(a) *Cost of administration per plan.* This will involve an allocation of expenses for salaries, general overhead, brokerage charges, etc. per plan and should establish a minimum cost figure for any size of pension plan.

(b) *Relative size of the plan.* The greater the annual contribution and/ or aggregate assets involved, the more time and effort a life insurance company can afford to devote to the management of a given fund.

(c) *Competition for pension funds.* The operations and charges of commercial banks and other trust companies will provide the life insurers with both guidelines and keen competition. In addition, intraindustry competition, particularly between the larger insurers, will also have to be met by

---

[20] *Prentice-Hall Tax Service*, Para. 16,026 *et seq.*
[21] *Securities and Exchange Commission Regulations*, Para. 270. 3c—3.

individual companies if their programs are to be successful. Thus, in the final analysis, competitive forces may be the most important single factor in shaping pension plans.

(2) What methods of investment operation will be employed? Life insurers have two possible methods of investing segregated assets:

(a) *The individual fund approach.* This method would involve establishing a separate and distinct investment policy and program for each fund. Each fund's experience would be independent of other funds' results. A relatively high minimum size would have to be established for funds treated in this manner, and probably only the largest life insurers could afford to undertake very many of these plans.

(b) *The commingled or mutual fund approach.* This method would be similar to common trust fund operations. In effect a life insurer would establish a mutual fund and apportion shares in it to various pension funds. With a uniform investment policy as well as a broad base over which to allocate management costs, this method could be used for smaller pension funds, and the life insurer's ability to handle large numbers of such funds on this basis would be quite extensive.

Larger life insurance companies would probably use both methods— a commingled fund and individual investment funds for larger plans which desire separate funds. The larger plans might also entail certain unique investment requirements (such as considerable purchases of the employer's own securities) that could only be handled on an individual basis.

PROBABLE INVESTMENT POLICIES FOR SEGREGATED ASSET AC-COUNTS. Table 34–6 summarizes the investment results of eighteen large life insurance companies in bonds, preferred stocks, and common stocks over the 1952–61 period and the overall industry earnings on mortgage loan operations during this same period. The relative results that the industry has achieved in these investment areas together with its likely competitive

TABLE 34–6

Life Insurance Company Investment Results, 1952-61

Type of Investment	Rate of Int. or Div. Return	Rate of Total Return***
Bonds*	3.48%	3.44%
Preferred Stocks*	4.36	4.68
Common Stocks*	6.48	11.06
Mortgages**	3.65	3.65

Notes: *Results are for eighteen large life insurance companies. **Estimates are for the entire life insurance industry and the results are net of origination, servicing, and home office expense. ***Total return includes realized capital gains and losses as well as interest and dividends.

Source: *1962 Record of Life Insurance Investments,* Life Insurance Association of America; by permission of Life Insurance Association of America.

position vis à vis the banks and trust companies in the future will dictate investment policies for segregated accounts.

The life insurance industry should have operating advantages over commercial banks and trust companies in investing funds in bonds and mortgages. Relative to bond investments, life insurance companies invest more extensively than banks and trust companies do in these securities, and as a result they have much more experience in general and are more familiar and skilled in private placements in particular. In fact private placement operations might well be a most important competitive weapon for the life companies because such investments tend to have higher yields than marketed bond issues and do not involve fluctuations in market prices. At the present time three-fourths of life insurance company bond holdings originated from private placements, and annually the industry buys well over 90 percent of its new bonds in this manner.[22]

In mortgage loan operations life insurance companies should also have an advantage over banks and trust companies. The latter tend to be localized in their lending operations, do less lending in the aggregate, and have less well-developed loan operations than life insurers. A number of life insurance companies have their own regional mortgage loan offices and are able to save substantially on origination and servicing fees. Life insurers tend to loan on a nationwide basis, and are therefore able to allocate funds to areas where mortgage loan rates are higher. The only problem that the life industry may have in the area of mortgage lending in the future is that the intensive (as well as extensive) competition from other lenders (chiefly the savings and loan associations and more recently commercial banks in some areas) may drive yields down (this happened during the first six months of 1963).

The life insurance industry probably will face difficulties in increasing the scale of its equity investments. Mutual funds and noninsured pension plans have been investing extensively in equity securities for some time, and as a result they have had much more experience in such operations and probably have developed stronger financial channels with issuers and investment bankers. It may take the life insurance industry a while to overcome this disadvantage, but the problem does not seem insurmountable by any means.

Life insurance companies may have a significant investment advantage in deploying segregated account funds in their real estate operations. Well-conceived and administered sale-and-leasebacks, shopping centers, industrial parks, etc. could provide good yields, stability, and long-term capital gains for pension funds. Individual properties or units could be allocated

---

[22] Life Insurance Association of America, *Record of Life Insurance Investments* (1962, pp. 27–28).

to several accounts to achieve some degree of diversification. The amortization of principal over the life of the initial lease would afford both a strong degree of safety as well as a cash throw-off to add to liquidity of the entire fund.

The investment policies of life insurance companies in administering segregated asset accounts will depend in part on the wishes of employers but primarily on their own experience and judgment. Private placements of bonds and real estate investments will be major but somewhat irregular transactions. Due to their desirability, these investments will probably comprise somewhere between one-fourth and one-third of the typical large pension fund's assets after it has been in existence for a few years.

Mortgages will probably account for another 25–33 percent of the average pension fund since such assets are available in smaller units (than real estate or private placement investments), yield reasonably well, and are fairly liquid (the principal is amortized, prepayments are quite common, and payoffs take place frequently). Mortgage investments will provide a pension fund with both stability and flexibility.

The remaining portion of pension funds will be composed of equity securities, because of their yield, marketability (and flexibility), and potential capital gains—especially the last factor. If such a segregated pension fund had been in existence during the period covered by Table 34–6, it would have had an interest-dividend return in excess of 4 percent and a total-rate of return (capital gains included) greater than 6 percent. Admittedly this is a period of favorable stock market trends, but the point is that such returns compare quite favorably to non-insured pension plan investment results during this same period (see Table 34–2).

CONCLUSIONS

The life insurance industry has undergone three recent developments which should enable it to compete much more effectively for pension plans in the future. The tax-exemption of income earned by pension fund reserves has eliminated a source of inequity for life insurers. The investment year method of investment income allocation also will provide life insurance policyholders with more equitably determined earnings. In addition it presents the industry with a short-run competitive weapon to employ against non-insured pension trustees. Segregated assets or accounts enable the life insurance industry to avoid some of the present state (quantitative) restrictions on equity investments and in effect offer employers the same type of investment service as is now carried out by banks and trust companies.

The life insurance industry's investment operations are such that it should be able to compete on at least even terms with non-insured pension plans. The only question that remains to be answered is whether the life insurance industry will be aggressive in its utilization of these new investment developments by soliciting new pension business. The life insurance industry cannot complain about a lack of favorable opportunities or environment relative to its future efforts in the pension area.

VI

COMPETITION
IN FINANCIAL MARKETS

A great deal of discussion today centers around the competition among financial institutions. Part VI is concerned with two types of competition in the financial markets: among different types of institutions and among institutions of the same type. The first article examines the factors that have influenced the distribution of consumer savings between savings and loan associations and commercial banks. The two articles by the Federal Reserve Bank of Chicago present a thorough review of the literature on competition among commercial banks.

35.

Competition
for Savings Deposits:
The Recent Experience

JACK R. VERNON

During the first decade following World War II, the commercial bank share of total savings of households in commercial banks and savings and loan associations (S & Ls) declined sharply.[1] This decline, which continued during the first part of the second postwar decade at a somewhat diminished pace, halted recently. During 1962 through 1965, the share of commercial banks remained essentially constant.

This paper discusses the factors which contributed to this change in trend, and assesses the present comparative strengths of commercial banks and S & Ls in markets for savings. The role of mutual savings banks, which are less important in terms of total savings, and are geographically concentrated in the Northeast, is not considered.

Reprinted from *The National Banking Review*, Vol. IV, No. 2, December 1966, pp. 183-192, by permission of the publisher.

[1] Much attention was accorded this in the literature. See David and Charlotte Alhadeff, "The Struggle for Commercial Bank Savings," *Quarterly Journal of Economics*, LXXII, February 1958, pp. 1-22; Joseph Aschheim, "Commercial Banks and Financial Intermediaries: Fallacies and Policy Implications," *Journal of Political Economy*, LXVII, February 1959, pp. 59-71; Deane Carson, "Bank Earnings and the Competition for Savings Deposits," *Journal of Political Economy*, LXVII, December 1959, pp. 580-588; J. G. Gurley and E. S. Shaw, "Financial Aspects of Economic Development," *American Economic Review*, XLV, September 1955, pp. 515-538. Paul M. Horvitz comments on several of these articles and analyzes bank earnings on time deposits in Section V of his study paper for the Commission on Money and Credit, which appears in *Private Financial Institutions*, Englewood Cliffs, N.J.: Prentice-Hall, 1963.

I. THE PRICE FACTOR

Table 35–1 suggests that the decline in the spread between returns paid to savers by S & Ls and commercial banks was the principal factor accounting for the change in the trend of the bank share. During 1947 through 1955, when the bank share was declining sharply, this spread was relatively constant. During 1956 through 1961, when the spread narrowed, the rate of decline in the bank share diminished significantly. During 1962 through 1965, when the spread declined to less than one percentage point, the decline in the bank share halted.

A regression of the change in the commercial bank share (S) and the spread (P), using the annual observations for 1947 through 1964 from Table 35–1, tends to confirm this view. The result, equation (1), indicates that the variation in spread explains approximately three-quarters of the variation in the change in the bank share.

$$(1) \qquad S = .024575 - 3.14253 \, (P)$$
$$ (.00594) \quad (.44464)$$
$$\bar{R} = .8615$$
$$\bar{R}^2 = .7422$$
$$\text{F-value} = 49.9502$$
$$\text{Durbin-Watson coefficient} = 1.66125$$

The year 1946, the first postwar year, is excluded in these considerations. The data for this year appear to reflect the influence of nonprice factors, which caused a change in the trend of the bank share at the end of World War II. David and Charlotte Alhadeff have thoroughly examined this earlier change.[2] Noting that the bank share increased during World War II, though the spread between returns paid by S & Ls and banks was greater during the War than following it, they argued that savers, affected by rising incomes and accumulations of liquid assets, were more willing to bear risk in savings accounts after the War, and shifted toward the higher-yielding S & L shares, where risks were greater. The strong relative performance of banks during the War also may reflect the influence of the rapid expansion during those years of a newly-introduced, fixed-value redeemable claim, the U.S. savings bond, which possibly was more highly substitutible with S & L shares than with the bank savings deposits.

II. FACTORS IN THE MORE EFFECTIVE PRICE COMPETITION OF BANKS

The more effective price competition for savings by commercial banks during the second postwar decade was the product of several factors. Im-

---

[2] David and Charlotte Alhadeff, *op. cit.*

TABLE 35-1

Spread Between Returns to Savers by S & Ls and Commercial Banks, and Change in Percent of Savings of Households in Banks and S & Ls, 1946 Through 1964

	Savings of Households in Banks and S & Ls* (billions)	Percent in Banks	Change in Percent in Banks	Spread Between Returns to Savers in S & Ls and Banks	Returns to Savers in S & Ls †	Returns to Savers in Banks ‡
1945	34.5	78.55	—	—	—	—
1946	39.3	78.12	− .43	.0156	.0240	.0084
1947	41.7	76.50	−1.62	.0143	.0230	.0087
1948	43.2	74.54	−1.96	.0139	.0229	.0090
1949	44.8	72.10	−2.44	.0143	.0234	.0091
1950	46.3	69.76	−2.34	.0158	.0252	.0094
1951	49.8	67.67	−2.09	.0155	.0258	.0103
1952	55.6	65.47	−2.20	.0154	.0269	.0115
1953	61.7	63.05	−2.42	.0157	.0281	.0124
1954	68.7	60.26	−2.79	.0155	.0287	.0132
1955	75.2	57.31	−2.95	.0156	.0294	.0138
1956	82.4	54.98	−2.43	.0145	.0303	.0158
1957	92.4	54.65	− .33	.0118	.0326	.0208
1958	103.8	53.76	− .89	.0117	.0338	.0221
1959	114.0	52.11	−1.65	.0117	.0353	.0236
1960	124.3	50.04	−2.07	.0130	.0386	.0256
1961	139.3	49.10	− .94	.0119	.0390	.0271
1962	158.9	49.53	+ .43	.0090	.0408	.0318
1963	177.9	48.68	− .85	.0086	.0417	.0331
1964	196.6	48.22	− .46	.0077	.0419	.0342
1965	216.6	49.08	+ .86	—	—	—

° Board of Governors of the Federal Reserve System, Flow of Funds, Assets and Liabilities, 1945-65.

† Ratios of dividends to savers to average savings capital for members of the Federal Home Loan Bank System. Federal Home Loan Bank Board, Combined Financial Statements.

‡ Ratios of interest payments on time and savings deposits to average time and savings deposits, federally-insured commercial banks. Federal Deposit Insurance Corporation, Annual Report.

portant among them were changes in the regulatory environment, a relative decline in home mortgage interest rates, and acceptance of greater credit risks by banks on assets corresponding to savings deposit funds.

A. Regulatory Changes

Several changes in the regulatory environment, beneficial to the commercial bank competitive position, occurred during the second postwar decade. One very important change was significant reductions in reserve requirements against time and savings deposits for member banks of the Federal Reserve System. These banks accounted for 80 percent or more of time and savings deposits in all commercial banks throughout the postwar period. During the first postwar decade, the reserve requirements on savings deposits varied between 7½ percent and 5 percent. During the second postwar decade, these requirements were lowered to 4 percent, and, more important, beginning with late 1960, member banks were permitted to count all vault cash as reserves. S & Ls have been generally free of requirements as to nonearning-asset reserves throughout the postwar period.

We can estimate the effect of this change in reserve requirements on the spread between returns paid to savers by S & Ls and member banks from 1955 through 1964, by computing the amount by which returns to time and savings deposits would have been lowered for 1964 if member banks had been subject in that year to the reserve requirements of 1955. The change in the spread was .0086 for member banks, compared to .0079 for all commercial banks. Let us assume that nonearning-asset reserves for member banks had equaled 7.75 percent, rather than 4 percent, of time and savings deposits during 1964, that the additional reserves were secured through a reduction in holdings of U.S. securities, and that the reduced interest income was matched by reductions in interest payments on time and savings deposits. (The 7.75 percent represents 5 percent in reserve deposits at Federal Reserve banks plus 2.75 percent in vault cash, estimated from the "vault cash" holdings of S & Ls for 1964.) The change in reserve requirements accounts, on this basis, for approximately .0014 of the .0086 by which the spread between returns to savers paid by S & Ls and member banks declined from 1955 through 1964.

Commercial banks also benefited from a reduction in the preferential tax treatment accorded to S & Ls. Commercial banks have paid federal income taxes on the same basis as other firms throughout the postwar period, with the exception that since 1947 they have been permitted relatively modest tax-exempt allocations of net income to loss reserves. In addition, as financial firms, they have benefited from tax exemption of interest income earned on state and local government obligations. S & Ls, by contrast, paid only negligible amounts of federal income taxes prior to 1963. They first became subject to federal income taxes in 1951, but until 1963 they were permitted tax exemption on virtually all allocations to reserves and undivided profits. This meant that almost all net income was tax exempt, since most S & Ls were mutual rather than stock organizations.

Beginning with 1963, the amount of net income that mature S & Ls were able to transfer to reserves and undivided profits on a tax-exempt basis was significantly reduced. As a result, the ratio of federal income payments to net income for S & L members of the Federal Home Loan Bank System, which equaled .01525 for 1955 and .00400 for 1962, rose to .14177 for 1964.

We can estimate the effect of this tax change on the spread between returns to savers paid by S & Ls and banks from 1955 through 1964, as the amount by which returns to savers for 1964 could have been raised if S & Ls had paid federal income taxes in that year at the rate paid in 1955, and had placed the additional after-tax income in returns to savers. On this basis, the tax change accounts for about .0013 of the .0079 by which the spread declined from 1955 through 1964.

Commercial banks realized modest additional benefits from changes which occurred in 1954 and 1964 in the methods permitted for computing tax-exempt transfers of income to loss reserves.

The competitive position of commercial banks benefited also from liberalizations in restrictions on investments in conventional mortgage loans by national banks. Prior to late 1955, national banks were prohibited from investing in low-downpayment, long-term conventional mortgage loans, on which returns net of lending costs have been somewhat higher than those available in most of the investment categories available to commercial banks, including federally-supported mortgage loans. National banks were not permitted to invest in conventional mortgage loans with loan-to-value ratios exceeding 60 percent and terms exceeding 10 years, and even then the amount of such loans could not exceed 60 percent of time and savings deposits or the amount of capital, whichever was greater.

Since late 1964, the date of the most recent liberalization, national banks have been permitted to invest in conventional mortgage loans with loan-to-value ratios of no more than 80 percent and maturities of no more than 25 years. Such loans have been permitted to equal 70 percent of time and savings deposits. The effect of this factor on changes in the spread between 1955 and 1964, however, was probably small. The percentage of time and savings deposits in conventional mortgage loans for all banks has remained modest, declining from 15.1 at the end of 1955 to 14.8 at the end of 1964. The failure of this percentage to expand may be due as much to the relative decline in mortgage interest rates during recent years as to low preferences of national banks for such loans.

Average loan-to-value ratios and maturities on conventional mortgage loans by national banks probably have increased. Unfortunately, data availability does not permit analysis of this factor.

There have also been changes in the restrictions placed on the returns paid to savers by commercial banks and S & Ls. It appears, however, that any significant change was confined to the year 1965. It is true that ceilings on returns to savers by banks were raised on several occasions in the period 1956–1964. These increases, however, only matched the rise in interest rates in general, as is apparent from Table 35–2, where the yield on U.S. bonds serves as the indicator of the general level of interest rates. The conclusion that these increases contributed to a decline in the spread during this period would be justified only if the rates stood higher, relative to the U.S. bond yield, than during the period 1946–1955.

It does appear that changes in restrictions on returns to savers affected the decline in the spread during 1965. In that year, the Federal Home Loan Bank Board instituted a policy of denying loans for purposes of expansion to member institutions which raised returns to savers above levels prescribed by the Board. In addition, the Board placed ceilings on returns to savers paid by federally-chartered associations which participated in plans permit-

TABLE 35–2

Yield on U.S. Bonds, and Ceilings on Returns to Time and Savings Deposits by Commercial Banks

	Yield on U.S. Bonds (per cent)	Ceilings on Bank Returns to Time and Savings Deposits* (percent)						Date of Change
		Savings Deposits		Other Time Deposits				
		under one year	over one year	0 to 3 mo.	3 to 6 mo.	6 to 12 mo.	over 12 mo.	
1946	2.19	2½	2½	1	2	2½	2½	Jan. 1, 1946
1947	2.25	2½	2½	1	2	2½	2½	
1948	2.44	2½	2½	1	2	2½	2½	
1949	2.31	2½	2½	1	2	2½	2½	
1950	2.32	2½	2½	1	2	2½	2½	
1951	2.57	2½	2½	1	2	2½	2½	
1952	2.68	2½	2½	1	2	2½	2½	
1953	2.94	2½	2½	1	2	2½	2½	
1954	2.55	2½	2½	1	2	2½	2½	
1955	2.84	2½	2½	1	2	2½	2½	
1956	3.08	2½	2½	1	2	2½	2½	
1957	3.47	3	3	1	2½	3	3	Jan. 1, 1957
1958	3.43	3	3	1	2½	3	3	
1959	4.07	3	3	1	2½	3	3	
1960	4.01	3	3	1	2½	3	3	
1961	3.90	3	3	1	2½	3	3	
1962	3.95	3½	4	1	2½	3½	4	Jan. 1, 1962
1963	4.00	3½	4	1	4	4	4	July 17, 1963
1964	4.15	4	4	4	4½	4½	4½	Nov. 24, 1964
1965	4.21	4	4	5½	5½	5½	5½	Dec. 6, 1965

° Board of Governors of the Federal Reserve System, **Federal Reserve Bulletin, Supplement to Banking & Monetary Statistics.**

ting different returns on various accounts. Prior to 1965, S & Ls had been generally free from restrictions on returns to savers.

Moreover, in late November 1964, the Federal Reserve Board raised to 4½ percent the ceiling on the return which member banks were allowed to pay on time certificates of deposit with maturities of more than 90 days. This rate was appreciably higher, relative to the yield on U.S. bonds, than was the case at the end of the first postwar decade. In December 1965, this ceiling was raised to 5½ percent and extended to the shorter maturities. The ceiling on returns to regular savings deposits remained at 4 percent through the end of 1965, but certificates of deposit were issued in small denominations, and appear to have attracted significant amounts of savings from households by the end of 1965.

B. Relative Decline in Home Mortgage Interest Rates

As shown in Table 35–3, interest rates on home mortgage loans, especially conventional home mortgage loans, declined relative to interest rates in general during the second postwar decade. This was perhaps the most important factor in the more effective price competition for savings by banks.

TABLE 35–3

Yields on Selected Long-Term Securities, 1955 Through 1964

	Conventional Home Mortgage Loans*	FHA Insured Home Mortgage Loans	U.S. Bonds†	State and Local Government Bonds†	Corporate Bonds†
1955	.0516	.0464	.0284	.0218	.0306
1956	.0534	.0479	.0308	.0251	.0336
1957	.0583	.0542	.0347	.0310	.0389
1958	.0572	.0549	.0343	.0292	.0379
1959	.0593	.0571	.0407	.0335	.0438
1960	.0624	.0618	.0401	.0326	.0441
1961	.0599	.0581	.0390	.0327	.0435
1962	.0593	.0563	.0395	.0303	.0433
1963	.0582	.0547	.0400	.0306	.0426
1964	.0580	.0545	.0415	.0309	.0440
1965	.0581	.0545	.0421	.0316	.0449
1965 less 1955	.0065	.0081	.0137	.0098	.0143

* U.S. averages, based on FHA field office opinions. The data were provided by the Division of Research and Statistics, Federal Housing Administration.

† **Federal Reserve Bulletin.** The series for U.S. bonds are averages of daily figures for bonds maturing or callable in 10 years or more. The series for state and local government bonds and corporate bonds are Moody's Investors Service series for Aaa rated securities.

A rough approximation of the effect of this factor from 1955 through 1964 is the amount by which S & L rates for 1964 could have been higher if the yield on their mortgage portfolios had increased as much as did yields on long-term securities in general. As the estimator of the latter, we may use the yield on the U.S. securities portfolio of mutual savings banks. This portfolio was largely in long- and intermediate-term securities, with U.S. bills and certificates accounting for no more than 6.3 percent during the period. The yield on that portfolio rose by .0112, as contrasted with an increase of .0080 in the case of S & Ls. If S & Ls had earned the higher rate and passed it on to savers, returns for 1964 would have been higher by .0031. The .0031 figure actually understates the effect of the relative decline in home mortgage interest rates, since there was also, apparently, an accompanying increase in the average risk quality of mortgages held. Table 35–4 reveals a shift within the portfolio from federally-supported mortgages to conventional mortgages.

The relative decline in home mortgage interest rates during the second postwar decade seems to have been the result principally of changes in the demand for home mortgage funds. Demographic factors of a temporary nature appear to have been of major importance. The low birth rates during the 1930's adversely affected the demand for home mortgage funds in the decade 1955–1965. This effect has recently been reversed because of the higher birth rates which occurred during the 1940's.

C. Acceptance of Increased Credit Risk

The remainder of the decline in the spread between returns to savers

TABLE 35–4

Percent of Financial Assets of Commercial Banks and S & Ls in Major Asset
Categories at Year End, Selected Years

	1955	1958	1961	1964
Commercial Banks*				
Member bank reserves, including vault cash	10.8	9.4	8.1	6.9
Interbank deposits	8.2	7.9	7.0	5.8
U.S. Government securities	31.5	30.1	26.4	20.5
State and local government bonds	6.3	7.2	7.8	10.3
Corporate bonds	.8	.6	.3	.3
Loans	38.9	41.4	46.3	51.8
Bank loans, n.e.c.	21.0	22.4	24.8	27.4
Mortgage loans	10.3	11.0	11.6	13.4
Federally-supported mortgages	6.5	6.7	6.8	7.6
Conventional mortgages	3.8	4.3	4.8	5.8
Consumer credit loans	6.5	6.9	8.2	9.0
Other loans	1.1	1.1	1.7	2.0
Security credit	2.5	2.0	2.4	2.6
Miscellaneous financial assets	.9	1.2	1.7	1.7
Savings and Loan Associations*				
Demand deposits and currency	3.7	3.3	2.6	2.3
U. S. Government securities	6.6	7.6	6.9	6.4
Loans	84.6	84.1	85.1	86.0
Mortgage loans	83.3	82.7	83.8	84.9
Federally-supported mortgages	19.9	16.7	13.7	9.6
Conventional mortgages	63.4	66.0	70.1	75.3
Consumer credit loans	1.3	1.4	1.3	1.1
Miscellaneous financial assets	5.0	5.1	5.4	5.2

° Board of Governors of the Federal Reserve System, **Flow of Funds, Assets and Liabilities, 1945-65.**

paid by S & Ls and commercial banks appears to be the result primarily of
the acceptance of greater credit risks by commercial banks. This acceptance
is reflected in Table 35–4. The percentage of assets in loans, where credit
risk generally is higher than for other bank assets, increased in the period
1955–1964, from 38.9 percent to 51.8 percent. The comparable change in
the case of S & Ls was from 84.6 percent to 86.0 percent.

III. COMPETITIVE STRENGTHS OF COMMERCIAL BANKS AND S & Ls

The competitive strength of commercial banks relative to S & Ls in
markets for savings is the product primarily of three factors: an advantage
possessed by banks as to returns to savers, a possible disadvantage of banks
as to earnings net of lending costs on savings, and a disadvantage of banks
as to capital costs.

The advantage of banks as to returns to savers can be estimated by
substituting zero for (S) in equation (1) and solving the equation for (P).
This yields an estimate of the spread between returns paid by S & Ls and
banks at which the latter would just maintain their share of savings of

households in the two types of institutions. The result is .00782, or just above three-quarters of a point.

This advantage may reflect in small measure a difference in the manner in which interest and dividend payments are made to savers by banks and S & Ls. Commercial banks ordinarily have paid interest for the full period that funds are on deposit. S & Ls most often have not paid returns to savings withdrawn prior to quarterly or semi-annual payment dates.[3] As a result, there has been a financial penalty for instant liquidity in S & L shares, except at payment dates.

It also may reflect in small measure the fact that the terms on which savings may be withdrawn are not identical for banks and S & Ls. Federally-insured, commercial-bank savings deposits can be obtained within 30 days, or slightly longer, in all eventualities. S & Ls, in most states, can delay redemption of federally-insured savings for extended periods, in cases of illiquidity. In the event of a serious financial crisis such as that of the early 1930's, savers in S & Ls might have to wait for considerable periods for their funds. It is doubtful, however, whether most savers have been aware of this difference in the insurance arrangements.

Primarily, the advantage held by banks probably reflects the premium assigned by savers for the convenience of one-stop banking. This is an advantage which S & Ls cannot duplicate, or materially reduce. Because the convenience premium is presumably independent of the level of return, the linear arithmetic form was used in estimating the return-to-saver advantage.

The disadvantage of banks as to earnings on savings now need not be of great consequence. Banks may earn yields net of lending costs on assets corresponding to savings accounts which approach those earned by S & Ls. Although the relative earnings position of banks has benefited greatly during recent years from the relative decline in home mortgage interest rates, recovery in these rates, and consequent lagged recovery in yields on mortgage portfolios, will probably not restore to S & Ls the earnings advantage they enjoyed during the first postwar decade. As a result of the legislative changes of the past decade, banks now may achieve a substantial specialization of their own in the profitable low-downpayment, long-term conventional home mortgage loans. They cannot equal the specialization of S & Ls in this respect, but they may approach it.

Moreover, banks are not restricted as to investments in federally-supported home mortgage loans, where interest rates have averaged less than one-third of a point below those available in conventionals during the first postwar decade. Banks also possess the option, not available to most

[3] The Federal Home Loan Bank Board recently instituted a regulation permitting federally-chartered S & Ls to pay, at their discretion, returns on all savings withdrawn prior to regular payment dates. See Federal Home Loan Bank Board, *Digest*, VIII, March 1966, p. 2. Prior to this, these institutions could pay returns only on those savings which had been on deposit for six months or more.

S & Ls, of diversifying their investments over a wide range of debt securities. Most important, they may invest without restriction in consumer credit loans, where yields net of lending costs traditionally have significantly exceeded those available even in mortgages. The Federal Reserve Bank of Boston estimates that yields net of lending expenses were 5.67 percent for consumer credit loans during 1962 for 24 New England banks reporting to the Bank's Functional Cost Project, compared with 4.64 percent for mortgage loans and 4.12 percent for other loans.[4]

Member banks retain a small disadvantage as to the portion of savings accounts which must be held in nonearning assets, but, at the end of 1965, this was of small consequence. If member bank requirements as to nonearning-asset reserves against time and savings deposits had been .0263 during 1965, which was the ratio of demand deposits plus currency to savings accounts for S & Ls at the end of 1965, rather than .0400, and the difference had been placed in U.S. securities, with the earnings on these securities added to interest payments on time and savings deposits, returns on these deposits would have been higher by only .0005, or one-twentieth of a point.

The advantage of S & Ls as to capital costs is of two sorts. First, the preferential treatment of S & Ls with respect to income taxes, while greatly reduced, remains substantial. The ratio of income taxes to net earnings after returns to savers for all S & L members of the Federal Home Loan Bank System for 1964 was 14.6 percent, which reflects the effects of the most recent tax change. The effective income tax rate for insured commercial banks for 1965, by contrast, was 35.7 percent, including an approximate adjustment for the effects of investments in tax-exempt securities.[5]

Second, most S & Ls follow the mutual form of organization. Mutual institutions do not have capital costs, in the sense of an obligation to produce returns to stockholders, as do banks and capital stock S & Ls. Their "capital costs" arise instead from their practice of maintaining approximately constant ratios of capital accounts (reserves and undivided profits)

---

[4] Federal Reserve Bank of Boston, "Time Deposit Operating Results, 1962," *New England Business Review*, June, p. 3.

[5] Where N_a is actual net income before taxes, T_a is actual income taxes, N_b is an estimate of the income before taxes which would have been realized if investments in tax-exempt securities had been placed instead in U.S. securities, and T_b is an estimate of the income taxes which would have been paid on N_b, assuming an income tax rate R_n, which equals the ratio of T_a to estimated nontax exempt income, the estimated effective income tax rate for insured commercial banks, adjusted for the effects of tax-exempt income, is computed as:

$$\frac{T_b}{N_b + [(N_a - T_a) - N_b - T_b)]}$$

In effect, it is T_b divided by the sum of N_b and the gain in net income realized as a result of the investments in tax-exempt securities.

to assets and savings. Since they do not issue capital stock, they accomplish this solely by allocations of net income to capital. Their total capital costs —that is, their nontax capital costs plus their tax capital costs, with the latter a positive function of the former—therefore depend on their growth rates of assets and savings, and vary directly with them.

Should savings of households in banks and S & Ls grow at the rate which has prevailed for the United States as a whole during recent years, the mutual S & Ls would have significant capital cost advantages relative to banks. The ratio of capital costs per year to average capital accounts for banks, estimated as the average of annual observations of ratios of the sum of retained earnings and cash dividends to average capital amounts for insured commercial banks during 1956 through 1965, is .1584. This figure is inflated by the estimated effective income tax rate for insured banks for 1965, of 35.7 percent. If federally-chartered S & Ls, all of which are mutuals, had incurred capital costs at this rate during 1964, and had possessed a ratio of average capital accounts to average assets in that year equal to the 1965 figure for insured commercial banks, with the increase in payments to capital subtracted from dividends to savers, and the increase in average capital accounts subtracted from average savings accounts, returns to savers would have been lower by .0052, or about one-half of a point. This is an approximation of the capital-cost advantage which accrues to mutuals just maintaining their share when savings of households in banks and S & Ls grow at rates typical of recent years. Savings in the federally-chartered associations grew at about 10.3 percent during 1964, which is slightly below the average growth (11.09 percent) of savings of households in the two types of institutions during 1956 through 1965.[6] The advantage to the mutuals is much greater in areas where deposit-type savings of households grow at less rapid rates—much smaller, and even negative, where the reverse situation prevails.

Capital stock S & Ls would seem to be at a disadvantage relative to both commercial banks and mutual S & Ls at the growth rates of deposit-type savings which have prevailed in the United States during recent years. They share the return-to-saver disadvantage of the mutuals, but only the tax advantage. In fact, from 1955 through 1964, savings in these institutions grew more rapidly than savings in either the mutuals or banks. They accounted for 21.96 percent of all association assets at the end of 1964, compared to 10.54 percent at the end of 1955. The apparent explanation for this is the concentration of capital stock association growth in areas where demand for funds was such that interest rates on loans, and consequently rates of growth of deposit-type savings, were significantly greater than the

----

[6] In addition, the ratio of capital to savings declined slightly during 1964, from .08097 to .08064. If the capital to savings ratio had been maintained exactly at .08097, returns to savers would have been lower by .00474, still about one-half of a point.

national average. The rapid growth rates for savings cancelled the capital cost advantages of the mutuals in these areas, while Regulation Q rates, which were uniform nationally, and attuned to national averages for interest rates on loans, cancelled the advantages of banks. Significantly, the savings flows of the S & Ls of these areas were most adversely affected during early 1966 by the sharp increase in Regulation Q rates relative to the U.S. bond rate of late 1965, and the banks of these areas were the most aggressive in raising returns to savers to the new maximums.

It appears that the possibilities for significant advantages and disadvantages of banks relative to S & Ls are confined to the three factors: returns to savers, yields net of lending costs on assets corresponding to savings, and capital costs. There is little reason for supposing that there are significant differences in processing costs for savings accounts between the two types of institutions. Further, it may be assumed that, for the individual bank, the amount of demand deposits outstanding is independent of the return to savers.

IV. CONCLUSIONS

The decline of the share of commercial banks in savings of households in commercial banks and S & Ls, which proceeded at a rapid pace throughout most of the first postwar decade, and at a diminished pace into the second, halted during the past several years. Most effective price competition by banks has been the primary factor in this change of trend. Regulatory changes favorable to banks, a relative decline in home mortgage interest rates, and acceptance of increased credit risks by banks in the investment of savings deposit funds have been important elements affecting the ability of banks to compete more effectively for savings on a price basis. The primary source of competitive strength of banks is the advantage they possess concerning returns to savers. This advantage appears to at least equal, for most areas, any disadvantage banks may have with respect to capital costs and yields net of lending costs on assets corresponding to savings.

36.

Competition in Banking:
The Issues

FEDERAL RESERVE BANK OF CHICAGO

In an economy characterized by private property and production for profit, competition among buyers and sellers has long been considered a prime prerequisite of economic efficiency—efficiency in this context being construed to include both the maximizing of output for any given resource used and the allocation of resources among all possible uses such that total production is maximized.

So strong has been the American belief in impersonal market forces to set prices and guide production, as opposed to joint decisions among producers or the decrees of government boards, that our country early put on the books the strictest and most comprehensive antitrust legislation in the world. The basic statutes are the Sherman Act of 1890 and the Clayton and Federal Trade Commission Acts of 1914.

To be sure, it has long been recognized that the technologies of some industries preclude primary reliance upon competition to guide investment, production and pricing. In these so-called "natural monopolies," such as the production and distribution of electric power and other "public utilities," the discipline of the marketplace has been replaced by the deliberations of public regulatory agencies.

Still other industries, although not considered natural monopolies, have been acknowledged as greatly affecting the public interest and have been partially shielded from the impact of unrestrained competition. Put another

Reprinted from *Business Conditions*, January 1967, pp. 8–16, by permission of the publisher, the Federal Reserve Bank of Chicago.

[421]

way, the failure or other malfunctioning of an individual establishment in these industries has been deemed to have adverse effects on the economy over and beyond the injury accruing to the firm's stockholders. Consequently, public regulation has been imposed in order to assure that certain minimal operating and fiduciary standards are met. Of the industries accorded such treatment, commercial banking is probably the most prominent.

WHY BANKS ARE REGULATED

Demand deposits of commercial banks provide the primary means of payment and, hence, are the major component of the money supply. Widespread failures of banks and sharp declines in the money supply have been associated with economic crises in past years. Furthermore, banks, while presumed by the public to be safe depositories, typically have liabilities that are very large in proportion to their capital and consequently could provide an attractive temptation to gambling by reckless entrepreneurs. These conditions alone would suggest the desirability of regulation to assure the liquidity and solvency of commercial banks. In addition historical experience lends support to the view that permitting banks to engage in unrestrained competition may lead to disastrous results. The evils of the past—specifically, the chaos and instability that attended the era of "free banking" between 1837 and 1863, the large numbers of bank failures in the 1920's and the banking collapse and economic depression of the early 1930's—have sufficed to convince most people that some measure of Government intervention is not only desirable but an absolute necessity.

The Federal and state governments have responded to the apparent need by constructing over the years a highly detailed and extensive system of commercial bank regulation that includes specific lending and borrowing restrictions, usury laws, ceilings on rates that banks may pay on time deposits, the prohibition of interest on demand deposits, capital and management requirements for the establishment of new banks, geographical restrictions on branching, requirements for periodic publication of statements of condition and examinations by public officials.

WHY COMPETITION IN BANKING?

Since official regulation imposes numerous limitations on the activities of banks, vigorous competition among banks may appear both superfluous and inconsistent. After all, one may ask, is not the public's interest in having quality services provided at reasonable prices protected in banking through public regulation, as it supposedly is for electric utilities and transportation? The answer, clearly, is in the negative.

Although commercial banks are subject to a great number of specific regulations limiting the scope of their activities, a broad range of discretion still remains open to them. As far as their lending and investment activities are concerned, banks retain the prerogative of emphasizing particular kinds of loans (for example, business, consumer, agriculture and mortgage loans) and of setting prices for these loans at whatever levels they choose, subject only to the ceilings on some types of loans established by state usury laws. Thus, there is ample room for the play of competitive forces to establish the actual levels of charges.

The scope for nonprice competition in banking is even wider. The services provided in conjunction with the bank's lending and deposit business provide a variety of opportunities for nonprice maneuvers designed to win new customers and retain old ones. It is the incomplete nature of regulation which, while imposing definite constraints on each bank's choice of alternative policies, nevertheless permits a wide latitude for the exercise of individual discretion that provides a meaningful role for competition in banking. This is the consideration that lay behind the Supreme Court's dictim in *U.S. vs. Philadelphia National Bank* that the regulated character of banking "makes the play of competition not less important but more so."

CHANGING VIEWS ON COMPETITION

Interest in banking competition has intensified in recent years. After virtually ignoring the commercial banking industry for many years, the Justice Department brought suit in the late 1950's in a number of cases involving clearinghouse agreements to set uniform service charges. In more recent years, despite a long and widely held belief to the contrary, the courts have ruled that the antitrust laws apply to acquisitions and mergers in banking as well as in other areas.

It may appear rather anomalous that the Federal Government, having established a superstructure of regulation designed at least in part for the purpose of limiting competition in banking, now undertakes to restrict banks' actions which might tend to reduce competition. The issue is further confused by the fact that the Office of the Comptroller of the Currency and the Department of Justice—two agencies of the Federal Government—have been on occasion cast in the roles of opposing parties in recent bank merger cases. It would be inaccurate to portray these events as reflecting merely a jurisdictional dispute between Federal agencies. Instead there appears to be a growing conviction on the part of public officials and bankers alike that a reevaluation and revision of policy may now be in order—though there is little agreement on specific issues.

Until recently students of banking were generally agreed that competition was not only less essential in banking than in most other industries but in many circumstances inherently destructive. However, new evidence and reexamination of old arguments now suggest that competition in banking may not have been the culprit it has been painted to be in bringing about the financial crises of earlier days. The banking troubles of the era before 1863 are now considered to have been the result of the absence of a uniform national currency as well as excessive competition and the lack of detailed controls over banking. This deficiency was remedied in part by the passage of the National Banking Act of 1863, which substituted national bank notes for the bewildering variety of state bank issues then in circulation.

Similarly, the periodic epidemics of bank failures of the late nineteenth and early twentieth centuries, as well as the striking and unprecedented attrition of banks in the decade following World War I, appear to have had their roots more in cyclical factors and secular changes in transportation and agriculture than in any inherent tendency toward destructive competition in banking. Even the banking debacle of the early 1930's is no longer uncritically viewed as the inevitable result of imprudent banking practices attributable largely to excessive competition for deposits. On the contrary, all of these instances of injury to the banking system—and in most cases, to the economy as well—are now generally agreed to have had their major cause in developments much broader than local competition and often far removed from the sphere of individual bank management.

Moreover, today there exist numerous safeguards against any widespread and self-reinforcing epidemic of bank failures. To the extent that violent cyclical fluctuations in aggregate economic activity may have been responsible for the waves of bank failures in the past, the announced readiness of the Federal Government and the Federal Reserve System to take whatever fiscal and monetary measures are required to maintain a high and growing level of income and employment serves as protection against similar future disturbances. To the extent that bank failures were the result of "runs" on banks occasioned by general fears on the part of the public of the inability by banks to redeem their deposits for currency, Federal Deposit Insurance and the readiness of the Federal Reserve to act as the lender of last resort appear to afford a sufficient remedy. These safeguards suggest that competition can play a more important role in banking than it has until recently without leading to undesirable consequences.

Regulation frequently has been unsuccessful in suppressing competition even where it has undertaken to do so. For example, the attempt to reduce interbank competition by erecting strict legal barriers to entry has been at least a major contributing cause to the rapid and continuing growth of such nonbank financial intermediaries as savings and loan associations, a growth that has brought with it increased interindustry competition.

The attempt to relieve effects of unduly severe competition among banks by prohibiting them from paying interest on demand deposits has been only partially successful at best. Far from eliminating competition, the prohibition simply caused banks to substitute less overt but nonetheless vigorous nonprice rivalry for the rate competition that previously existed. In effect, "interest" on demand deposits continues to be paid through an earnings credit offset to deposit service charges and numerous "free" services, all dependent largely on the size of the average balance and the number of transactions associated with each account. On the other hand, the depositor has been deprived of the option of being paid in cash.

CHANGES IN NUMBER OF BANKS

While much of the recent interest in competition in banking has been focused on the system of bank regulation as presently constituted, expressions of concern have also been voiced concerning the merging and branching activities of the banks themselves. Despite virtually uninterrupted prosperity and population growth in the postwar period, the number of commercial banks in the United States has been declining until very recently.

After a small immediate postwar rise from 14,011 in 1945 to 14,181 in 1947, the number declined steadily, reaching a low of 13,427 at the end of 1962. Since then the number of banks has increased slightly to 13,784 in November 1966. The net decrease of 227 banks since World War II— an average of about 10 a year—is small compared to the rate that prevailed throughout the generally prosperous 1920's when the average net annual attrition exceeded 700. However, in contrast to the earlier period when a significant part of the attrition resulted from bank failures and voluntary liquidations, virtually all the recent decline has been the result of mergers and acquisitions that have absorbed formerly independent banks.

NUMBERS AND COMPETITION

To many observers this decrease in the number of banks provides evidence that the availability of alternative sources of supply of banking services, and hence the vigor of competition, is undergoing a decline. This conclusion is based on the theory that the chances of collusion are less and the likelihood of independent rivalry greater when sellers are many than when they are few.

However, in evaluating the effect of the decline in the number of banks, it must be noted that all of the more than 13,000 banks in the United States do not compete in a single, nationwide market. A relatively few giant banks do operate in what is loosely referred to as the "national banking market"—the market for the loans and deposits of the largest corporations that have banking connections throughout the country.

But it is a widely acknowledged fact that, for most bank customers, the national market is segmented by the real and psychic cost of distance into relatively narrow regional and local submarkets. For this less mobile majority of customers, the most relevant consideration is the number of independent banks within the confined area in which their reputations are known and in which they find it practicable to seek accommodation. This number of banks, however, is not deducible from a knowledge of how many banks there are in some broader area, such as the state. Given the ability of banks to have branch offices in approximately two-thirds of the states, it is possible for the average number of individual banks competing in each local market to increase even though the number of banks in these states or in the nation overall is declining.

Although states which permit branch banking have experienced wide declines in the number of banks, it does not necessarily follow that significantly fewer different banks are represented in individual communities in these states than in those that prohibit branch banking. This apparent contradiction is explained by the great expansion in the number of branch offices during the past several decades. Similarly, even when mergers have decreased the total number of banks in the country and the number of alternatives available to customers in particular local markets, they may have added to the number of effective competitors in the markets serving large- and medium-sized corporate customers by permitting the merging banks to attain the minimum size required to operate in these markets.

Concomitant with the decline in the number of banks, the average size of bank and the percentage of banking resources concentrated in the hands of a relatively few large banks have increased in many broad areas of the country. Concentration in this sense is often considered to have a potentially adverse effect on competition because, however large the total number of banks in a market, if one or a few of them control most of the total supply, they will be able to influence prices strongly.

Available data on concentration of deposits in major metropolitan areas indicate that concentration levels were generally higher in the early 1960's than a decade earlier. On the other hand, they appear to have been lower than in the prewar year of 1939. Inasmuch as concentration and changes in concentration have significance for competition only in relation to specific product markets and particular groups of customers, it is necessary to take account of important interarea differences. For the period 1960–64 increases in concentration have been typical in metropolitan areas in states where statewide branching is prevalent. In metropolitan areas where restricted branch banking is the rule, increases and decreases were about equally frequent. Decreases predominated in these areas where unit banking was the most common form of bank organization.

Some would interpret these figures as demonstrating that unit banking is more conducive to competition than branch banking. However, such a conclusion follows only if certain conditions are satisfied. Among these is the rather crucial assumption that metropolitan areas serve equally well as approximations to local banking markets under both branch and unit banking. To the extent that locational convenience serves to restrict the practicable range of alternatives of some customers to an area smaller than the whole metropolitan area, concentration in unit banking areas is understated by the measure used here. A more important qualification is that competition has not been shown to depend in any simple and reliable way on the degree of concentration in bank markets.

PUBLIC POLICY TOWARD BANK MERGERS

In deciding whether to approve or disapprove a particular application to merge, the appropriate regulatory agency must arrive at a judgment concerning the probable effect of the merger on the public interest. The fundamental questions that must be answered include the justification of the consolidation in terms of economies of scale or the ability of a larger bank to render better, cheaper and more complete banking services and its effect, via changes in the number and size distribution of banks, on the competitive relations among the remaining firms. It is over answers to these questions that much of the interagency conflict has arisen.

For example, advantages in the form of lower operating costs have often been advanced as a major factor in bank mergers. Yet, available empirical studies tend to indicate that such economies may be quite modest —at least when the differences in output mix between large and small banks are taken into consideration, as they must be.

A second argument in support of mergers emphasizes the ability of a bank with greater resources to hire better management and to utilize more fully the services of a large number of specialists. This argument appears to have fairly general validity as indicated by both casual observation and a number of recent studies. Large banks generally do offer a broader variety of services than is obtainable at small banks in the same locality. However, whether this constitutes a net advantage is not immediately obvious. It must be determined whether a decrease in the number of alternative sources of banking services is adequately compensated by the availability of a number of special, but infrequently utilized, services that only large banks can supply.

BRANCH BANKING

Any discussion of the relative merits of large and small banks must include consideration of the arguments in support of and opposition to branch banking. One of the major advantages claimed for branching is that it is often the quickest way a bank can grow to large size. Also, since the full resources and facilities of the bank can be made available to the customers of each branch, branch banking provides a means of bringing a fuller range of banking services and larger lending capacity to individual communities.

The advantages and disadvantages of branch banking constitute one of the oldest and most vitriolic controversies in American banking. The arguments involve questions both political and economic in character. Without evaluating the merits of the arguments, it may be noted that the unit-branch issue is an inseparable part of the larger public debate over competition in banking reviewed above.

The precise relationship between the branch banking and banking competition is a matter of dispute. A number of economists, bankers and public officials maintain that branching is an essentially procompetitive form of banking that facilitates the penetration of additional banking markets and brings to bear the force of potential competition on even the smallest and most isolated banking markets. On the other hand, many students of banking hold that branching is a monopolistic device whose prime purpose is the attenuation of competition. Which characterization is the more accurate may depend as much on what one understands by competition as on the objectively determinable facts of the case.

It is hardly open to serious doubt, for example, that some portion of the criticism of branch banking is of a protectionist nature, more concerned with preserving locally owned unit banks than with fostering vigorous interbank rivalry. Independent bankers frequently feel themselves threatened by the presence of a nearby office of a large branch bank.

On the other hand, it is not always easy to distinguish in practice between the protection of competitors and the preservation of competition. One reason is related to the difference between the incentives required to induce merger and those required to induce *de novo* establishment of a new bank or branch. It appears easier for two existing banks to come to terms on a merger agreement which has as one of its "fringe benefits" the elimination of competition than it is for a potential entrant into the banking field to obtain financing and run the regulatory gauntlet required to obtain a charter for a new bank. As was indicated above, it is in these areas where the possibility of operating an acquired bank as a branch maximizes the incentive to merge that the disappearance of banks and the concentration of banking have proceeded most rapidly. This pronounced assymmetry between merger and entry is the primary reason why branching via merger, which *ipso facto* involves the elimination of an independent source of supply, may have adverse and irreversible effects on competition. It is also one of the considerations that prompted Congress in 1950 to strengthen the Clayton Act and to pass the Bank Merger Acts of 1960 and 1966.

It might still be maintained, on the other hand, that *de novo* branching could have nothing but beneficial effects on competition. Its immediate effect is always to introduce a new competitive force into a banking market or submarket. When, for example, a branch bank sees a potentially profitable location for a banking office and opens a branch there—perhaps years in advance of the time when it would have been profitable to organize a new unit bank—it benefits the community to have banking facilities where none existed before or would otherwise have existed for a considerable period of time. Whether this is a net gain in the long term depends on the potential benefit to the local populace of having an independent source of supply of banking services when it would become feasible to open a new unit bank.

Where banks find it easy to establish branches within a local banking market they may—and often do—anticipate profitable locations and saturate entire areas with branches, thereby largely foreclosing future entry by competitors. In this they may be inadvertently aided and abetted by the regulatory agencies, which are frequently reluctant to grant a new charter that could conceivably result in "overbanking." Overbanking typically implies a situation in which insufficient banking business is considered to exist to support all of the banking institutions in the area and which must eventually result in the forced exit of one or more of them.

At a theoretical level a good case can be made for removing all geographic restrictions on branching, while simultaneously discouraging concentration in particular local banking markets. However, this would require a uniform national policy with respect to branching and the chartering of new banks, a development not now on the horizon. Legislation regarding branching traditionally has been left to the states. Nevertheless, the competitive environment created by state branching restrictions is clearly one of the many factors that must be taken into account in Federal Agency decisions governing mergers.

CONCLUSION

There exists a great deal of uncertainty at the present time as to what public policy would promote optimum competition in banking. Ideally, policy should undertake to attain a degree of interbank rivalry that assures that consumers will be provided bank services of high quality at minimum cost, without sacrificing the private and public benefits of large-scale production or the regulatory aim of ensuring the liquidity and solvency of the banking system. The extent to which these goals can be realized simultaneously and even the direction in which policy should move to approach them as closely as possible is still imperfectly understood. However, a start toward collecting and interpreting the data that would permit a more objective basis for deciding these issues has been made. In a subsequent article the limited but growing body of empirical knowledge of the relationship between banking structure and performance will be reviewed. This information, limited and inconclusive as it is, constitutes the hard-won fruit of numerous past and current research studies.

37.

Competition in Banking:
What Is Known?
What is the Evidence?

FEDERAL RESERVE BANK OF CHICAGO

Certain aspects of recent controversy over the role of competition in banking were discussed in general terms in the January issue of this review. In banking as in baking, however, the proof of the pudding is in the eating. This second instalment, therefore, undertakes to describe the actual results achieved in the marketplace, as gauged by prices charged and paid and services rendered, under alternative banking structures.

Studies of structure and performance in banking markets have been handicapped both by data difficulties and by the impossibility of holding "all other things equal" when seeking to measure the effects of specific factors present in different market situations. Nevertheless, by cross classification of the data and the use of multiple regression analysis, it often has been possible to isolate the more important and consistent relationships which shed light on certain of the issues.

Summarized here are the major results of a generous sample of research efforts that have been undertaken in the past two decades. These are listed on the following pages together with their reference numbers.

It deserves stress that the conclusions indicated by these studies are suggestive rather than final. In some instances, clear inconsistencies are

Reprinted from *Business Conditions*, February 1967, pp. 7–16, by permission of the publisher, the Federal Reserve Bank of Chicago.

revealed in the results. Complete consistency in the findings could scarcely be expected simply because of the widely diverse samples of banks and bank markets studied and the possibilities that some of these were not representative of all banks. Where all but one or two of several investigators report similar findings, the relationship found by the majority may still be a valid one, but it should be studied further before being accepted as conclusive and providing a basis for generalization.

THE EFFECTS OF BANKING CONCENTRATION

With these reservations in mind, we proceed to present the available evidence. Among the structural characteristics of banking markets most frequently alleged to have an effect on performance are the number and size distribution of banks and other financial institutions. There is a presumption—partly based on experience in other industries and partly derived from economic theory—that the smaller the number of independent sellers in a particular market or the greater the concentration of business in the hands of a few, the lower is likely to be the quality of the product or service and the higher the price.

Several analysts have attempted to determine the relationships, if any, between concentration—generally measured as the percentage of total deposits in a given banking market accounted for by some small number of banks—and various measures of banking performance. On this basis, and other things equal, it would be expected that interest rates on loans should be higher, interest rates on time deposits lower, the ratio of time to total deposits lower and pretax earnings on assets higher in markets where concentration is high than in those with greater diffusion of "market power."

In addition, it has been suggested that concentration would be likely to result in less activity in the form of direct lending and more in purchases of securities, which would be reflected in a lower loan to deposit ratio than would otherwise prevail. The number of banks in the market, on the other hand, would be expected to be related to measures of performance in a manner opposite to that premised for concentration.

Results of four published studies [5, 6, 7, 13] and two preliminary studies that examined the relationships between concentration and performance are generally consistent with expectations. The inconsistencies are so few and tentative as to be attributed reasonably to chance characteristics of the data. The one exception concerns the relationship between interest rates on business loans and concentration.

Although three of the four studies [5, 6, 13]—including a major research effort that utilized extensive data from the Federal Reserve's 1955 and 1957 surveys of business loans [5]—found a direct relationship, another study [7] utilizing many of the same data came to the conclusion that "no easily identifiable relationship exists between concentration ratios and the level of interest rates charged by commercial banks on business loans."

According to the author of this research paper [7], intercity variation in loan rates is better explained by regional differences in such factors as the rate of change of employment, bank operating expenses and competition from nonbank financial institutions. He further contends that the direct or positive relationship between concentration and loan rates found by the earlier studies is a spurious result ascribable to the pronounced but misleading correlation between concentration and the true explanatory factors.

The technical nature of these questions precludes any attempt to demonstrate which of the conflicting results seems more acceptable. Suffice it that competent scholars have been unable to reach agreement on this issue on the basis of the data currently available. Nevertheless, this still unresolved controversy serves to illustrate the dangers of accepting the results of any one study as conclusive, especially in the absence of thorough familiarity with the data and methods employed in the analysis. But with the possible exception of interest rates on business loans, the evidence so far available is consistent with the view that differences in the degree of banking concentration may be responsible for at least a part of any differences observed in performance in banking markets.

The results of two published studies [12, 13] and two preliminary studies that examined the effects on performance of the number of banks in the market are also generally in accord with theoretical expectations. As with concentration, the most important inconsistencies concerned interest rates on loans. Two of the studies found a positive relationship between number of banks and loan rates—that is, the greater the number of banks the *higher* the level of loan rates—and two found the "expected" negative relationship. In all four studies, average loan rate was measured as the ratio of interest received on loans during the year to total loans outstanding.

Such a gross measure is, of course, open to many objections, particularly that it glosses over differences in the makeup of credit demand and resulting bank-to-bank variations in loan composition. The distortion caused by the use of such a measure of the interest rate on loans would tend to be smaller for large samples and for samples consisting of banks that are alike in as many characteristics as possible. For this reason, the negative relationship between the number of banks in individual market areas and average interest rates on loans found in a study [13] of 672 banks in Iowa is more persuasive than the contrary result reported on the strength of an analysis [12] of 106 one- and two-bank towns throughout the country. At the same time, the highly localized character of the Iowa sample makes any generalization to conditions elsewhere hazardous; a preliminary study at the Chicago Federal Reserve Bank of 413 Indiana banks under somewhat less uniform conditions yielded generally inconclusive results.

A second unpublished paper, which examines the relationship between loan rates and changes in the number of banks in Indianapolis in the post-war period, lends further support to the view that interest rates on loans tend to vary inversely with the number of competing banks. As for the relation-ships between the number of banks and other performance variables—spe-cifically, interest rates on time deposits, ratios of loans to assets, time to total deposits and pretax earnings to assets, and service charges on demand deposits—none of the four studies contradicts the conjectures made above although in a few cases the data also fail to give them positive support. Im-portantly, however, of the four foregoing studies only the one for Iowa reported relationships that were "significant" in the statistical sense that the results might not reasonably have occurred by chance.

Additional evidence is offered in two other bank studies, one in New York state [15] and the other in the Chicago area [19]. The former found some tendency for rates on new car loans, conventional mortgage loans and small business loans to be higher and rates paid on savings deposits to be lower in upstate New York towns with only one banking office than in towns with two or more offices. On the other hand, service charges on checking accounts were generally lower in the one-bank towns. The Chicago study found that interest rates on automobile loans tended to be lower in suburbs having larger numbers of banks. The samples in both of these studies, however, were relatively small and the results are therefore only tentative.

The findings reviewed thus far generally conform with expectations. This is not true, however, of the results of a number of other studies that have been made. An example is furnished by investigations of the effects on bank behavior ascribable to the presence of nonbank financial institutions.

COMPETITION FROM THRIFT INSTITUTIONS

Students of banking and bankers alike are aware that, although com-mercial banks offer checking deposit services that are unique, they face strong "outside" competition in the supply of other financial services. This is particularly true for savings. The savings and time deposits offered by commercial banks compete with mutual savings bank deposits, savings and loan association and credit union shares and other highly liquid financial assets.

The intensity of such competition has been in sharp focus during the recent "rate war" between the banks and savings and loan associations and had been evident in the earlier dramatic rise in commercial bank time and savings deposits following the revision of Regulation Q in 1962. Neverthe-less, evidence so far examined indicates that the presence of a thrift insti-tution in a community has no systematic influence on the rates paid by commercial banks on time deposits.

Of three studies that examined this question [12, 13, 18], only one—which looked at unit banks in Minnesota—supports what would be expected on a priori grounds, namely that the additional competition afforded by the presence of a nonbank financial institution would raise the interest rates on time deposits paid by commercial banks. The Iowa study [13] found no such relationship and the previously mentioned study of 106 unit banks [12] showed results precisely opposite to what would appear plausible.

The evidence regarding the effect that the presence of a thrift institution has on the ratio of commercial bank time deposits to total deposits and total local savings (savings held in local institutions) relative to population or income is somewhat more helpful. Both the study of Iowa banks [13] and that of the 106 unit banks located throughout the country [12] found that the ratio of commercial bank time deposits to total deposits tends to be lower in those communities where a nonbank thrift institution is present, indicating that to some degree commercial bank and other savings are substitutes.

A related finding is the conclusion of a follow-up study [14] of the same Iowa counties included in study [12]. This study was supplemented by an analysis of data for 48 states and showed that the volume of local savings at banks and thrift institutions combined—both in the aggregate and per capita—is larger, the greater is the proportion of local "deposits" held by the nonbank institutions. Similarly, a study of large metropolitan areas found that savings are greater relative to income in areas with mutual savings banks [19]. On balance, this evidence, if not that relating to time deposit interest rates, confirms the existence of considerable inter-industry competition between commercial banks and thrift institutions.

BRANCH BANKING AND PERFORMANCE

Perhaps the most controversial issue in American banking history and one on which feelings have been stronger than any other concerns branch banking. While much of the emotion surrounding discussion of this subject is undoubtedly attributable to aspects of a noneconomic nature, much of the writing and debate have focused upon purely economic considerations. Certain of the claims and counterclaims made over the years regarding the economic effects of branch banking have recently been subjected to the impersonal assessment of statistical analysis.

Seven studies [2, 6, 10, 12, 16, 19, 20] comparing bank performance in unit and branch areas reveal only one clear-cut contradiction: one [12] found interest rates on time deposits to be higher in branching areas while another [6] found them to be lower.

Of 12 other measures of performance, six were observed to be generally more favorable to bank customers in branch banking areas than in unit banking areas. The ratios of time to total deposits and loans to assets were higher under branch banking as were personal savings relative to income and the number of banking offices relative to population. At the same time, interest rates on mortgage and unsecured instalment loans were lower.

The six remaining measures of performance, on the other hand, were more favorable in unit banking areas. Interest rates on business and new car loans, the average return on all loans, the ratio of net current earnings both to assets and to capital and service charges on checking accounts were all lower in unit banking areas. However, the lower earnings to assets and earnings to capital ratios of unit banks are to be viewed as advantageous to consumers only insofar as they reflect competitive pricing in the market, which is already partially taken into account in the measures of time deposits and loan interest rates. If the lower earnings rates of unit banks are the result of inefficiency—that is, higher unit costs for a given package of services—they may actually be detrimental to the interests of consumers in the long run by leading to a deterioration in the quality of service.

The observed relationships may be due to factors other than the prevalent form of banking organization. In particular, branch and unit banking follow fairly definite geographic patterns in the United States, suggesting that regional differences in demand or in the character of state bank regulation could have pronounced effects on bank performance that may not properly be attributed to organizational characteristics. It may be useful, then, to look at the results of seven studies [1, 2, 6, 12, 15, 19, 21] that have compared the performance of unit and branch banks *within* branch banking states.

A comparison of these findings again illustrates the extent to which the results of individual studies have occasionally differed on particular questions. The only results not contradicted by at least one of the seven studies are that branch banks generally have higher net current earnings relative to capital and higher loan to asset ratios than unit banks in the same state. The latter findings has been reported with unvarying regularity.

Inasmuch as loans bear greater risks than Government securities, the reduction in risks attributable to the geographic and industrial diversification of lending enabled by branch banking would be expected to result in higher ratios of loans to deposits and loans to assets; competition may or may not be an important factor in accounting for them. These ratios, in turn, are important in accounting for the higher earnings rates of branch banks.

Somewhat less thoroughly documented, but still worthy of consideration is the finding reported in two recent contributions [6, 12] that ratios of time to total deposits are lower for branch banks than for unit banks in the same states. Also receiving support from two studies [15, 21] is a tendency for service charges on checking accounts to be higher at branch banks. But while the latter finding simply confirms what was learned in the comparisons between branch banking and unit banking areas, the former flatly contradicts the reported results of the inter-area comparisons.

What at first glance seem to be inconsistent conclusions are in fact two valid aspects of the relationship between branch banking and the ratio of time to total deposits. Although branch banking areas typically have higher time deposit ratios than unit banking areas, unit banks within the branch banking areas surpass branch banks in their proportion of time to total deposits. If, as has been tacitly assumed here, the time to total deposit ratio reflects competitive forces—in the sense that vigorous competition for deposits will result in some demand deposits being bid away to the interest paying time deposit categories—then the inter-area comparisons suggest that deposit competition is keener in branch banking areas.

This interpretation, however, may attribute to branching laws the influence of regional differences in saving habits or other factors. Similarly, the generally higher interest rates paid on time deposits and higher ratios of time to total deposits of unit banks within branch banking areas lend themselves to various interpretations. They might mean, among other things, that unit banks in branch banking areas must resort to rate competition to make up for the greater locational convenience offered by branch systems.

ENTRY BY BRANCHING

A distinctive type of comparison between branch and unit banking was the before-and-after study carried out in Nassau County, New York [17]. This examined the effects of New York state's Omnibus Banking Act of 1960, which opened suburban counties to branches of the New York City banks. The findings for Nassau County were as follows: Somewhat surprisingly, the aggregate rate of return to capital in banking did not fall in the years immediately following entry, possibly because of the strong and growing demand for banking services during the period in question. On the other hand, there was a "significant increase in number of offices and number of banks per submarket," a reduction in instalment loan interest rates and a gradual increase in interest rates on time and savings deposits.

But although these results strongly suggest that benefits are to be derived from liberalization of branching laws and subsequent entry by branching, the study deals only with the immediate, short-run effects of such a move. It tells nothing about the potential long-term influence of big city branches on competition in the suburbs, nor does it adequately isolate the influence of liberalizing the branching law from that of the extraordinary growth and economic change in Nassau County in affecting the measures of bank performance used. Nevertheless, the figures presented are sufficiently impressive to make a strong *prima facie* case that the change in banking law favorably affected the price and quality of banking services in Nassau County.

BRANCHING BY MERGER

A final type of study bearing on the merits of branch and unit banking looks at the changes in lending behavior and pricing policy that occur when a unit bank becomes, through merger, a branch of a larger bank. Two studies [12, 15]—which utilized similar questionnaires—purport to shed some light on this area of banking controversy.

The results of the two studies are striking in their agreement. In only one of 17 measures of performance is any inconsistency evident; this disagreement concerns service charges on regular checking accounts. Whereas the New York state study [15] found that mergers generally led to reduced service charges, the other study [12]—which surveyed all national banks that acquired other banks through merger in 1962—reported that service charges were usually raised. With respect to every measure but two—service charges on special checking accounts under two alternative assumptions regarding activity and average balances—the effects of mergers were generally favorable to consumers. After merger, interest rates on savings deposits were higher; interest rates on 24-month new car loans, 15-year conventional mortgages and unsecured small business loans were lower; secured and unsecured lending authority of the chief lending officer was greater; maturities on car loans and conventional, FHA- and VA-mortgage loans were longer, and maximum amounts on car loans and all three types of mortgage loans were greater. Thus, the quantitative measures of bank performance relied on in these two surveys failed to discern any of the noncompetitive results that opponents of branch banking and mergers often allege to be inherent in multiple office banking.

Closer examination, however, reveals that the results reported are at best misleading and at worst potentially dangerous. It would be absurd, for example, to use them as a guide to future policy, for the favorable effects found to accompany most of the mergers are themselves partly the result of the discretion exercised by regulatory authorities in the past in deciding which mergers to permit. This is less true of the New York study [15], which examined mergers that occurred from 1951 to 1961 when little public control was exercised over bank mergers. Nevertheless, the bias imparted by the selected nature of the samples studied cannot safely be ignored.

Even if it is the case that mergers are, on balance, beneficial to consumers, this would not be grounds for giving blanket approval to all branching by merger. Both studies found some mergers to be detrimental to the public interest. The emphasis must continue to be on strengthening the ability to identify in advance, for purposes of prevention, those mergers that would be likely to have adverse effects on bank customers.

BRANCH LENDING POLICIES

Certain other charges against branch banking receive support from the studies cited. The New York state study [15] found that the out-of-town branches of branch banks were less willing to make small (less than $25,000) unsecured loans than were unit banks. This was evidenced by the greater volume, whether measured by number or dollar amount, of unsecured loans relative to deposits at unit banks. The same observation was made several years earlier in a study of New England banking [10].

Often voiced in conjunction with the charge that branches tend to have much more impersonal lending policies than unit banks is the argument that branch banking is undesirable because it drains some localities of funds and lends them elsewhere. The charge receives support from the New York finding that branches showed a much greater dispersion of loan to deposit ratios than did unit banks, clearly indicating that some branches were primarily deposit collecting agencies, whereas others were primarily loan outlets.

Although the evidence apparently bears out the factual basis of these two charges, it has nothing to say about their logic. Their underlying premise—the notion that deposit funds generated locally should stay at home—has little to recommend it, either as banking practice or public policy. It amounts to a contention that the interests of bank borrowers and depositors perfectly coincide, which is not generally true.

Any attempt to limit the lending activities of banks to a specified geographic area or otherwise to favor local borrowers would be almost certain to divert bank credit into less profitable channels. This, in turn, would reduce the earnings from which depositors can be paid for the use of their funds and introduce a distortion in the allocation of society's resources.

BANK SIZE AND PERFORMANCE

An additional characteristic of banks that may be systematically related to bank performance is absolute size, measured in terms of assets or deposits. The studies that have been made of the influence of this factor fall into two broad categories: first, studies of economies of scale [1, 3, 8, 9, 11, 19] and, second, studies of the price, quality and availability of banking services at banks of different sizes [2, 4, 6, 12, 19, 21].

Studies in the first category are concerned with finding which size of bank is most "efficient"—that is, which scale of production results in minimal costs per unit of output. Although several of these studies are the products of imaginative and laborious research, none of them satisfactorily comes to grips with a major conceptual problem—namely, the specification of just what it is that banks "produce."

Banks of different size and location offer diverse combinations of services that cannot readily be measured with a common yardstick. The failure to solve this problem in an adequate manner—a failing of which most investigators in the field are fully aware—robs their quantitative findings of much significance. In fact, since most studies arbitrarily measure bank output in terms of the dollar value of assets and since it is well established both that larger banks in general make larger loans than small banks and that costs per dollar are regularly lower for large than for small loans, these studies embody a systematic bias in the direction of overstating the relative efficiency of large banks.

Despite this, a finding common to almost all of the studies was that the greatest part of the potential savings due to size may be realized by banks with no more than 10 million dollars in deposits. When output is measured by the number of loans or deposit accounts rather than the dollar volume, as in a recent study of the costs of a sample of New England banks [3], the results are even less favorable to large size. Extremely moderate economies of scale were reported for each of six separate bank activities for which cost to output relationships were estimated.

Another interesting attempt to measure economies of scale defined bank output as the yield weighted sum of 16 earning asset categories [9]. The study found that average costs of banks in the Kansas City Federal Reserve District decreased up to a deposit size of about 300 million dollars, then began to increase. In sharp contrast to the conclusion reached in a study of all member banks in 1959 [11] that branch offices were more expensive to operate than unit banks of the same size, it was reported by the Kansas City study that merging unit banks into a branch system would reduce costs even if the output of each office remained unchanged.

At the present time—given the conflicting results, inadequate data and imperfect methodology of extant studies—there is no firm basis for judgment on which size of bank is most efficient. In all probability this will depend on the composition of the services rendered so that at best there may be only an optimal distribution of sizes of banks, rather than a single optimal size for all banks.

The influence of size on other banking performance variables has been the subject of several studies [2, 4, 6, 12, 19, 21]. At first glance, the results seem to be entirely in favor of size. Not only do larger banks pay higher average rates on savings, but they charge lower average rates on loans, have higher ratios of time to total deposits and—despite this price situation, which would appear to be unfavorable to bank profits—they end up with higher net current earnings relative to both assets and capital. The problem, similar to that encountered in studies of economies of scale, is that the effective rates of interest were computed as the ratios of total interest income on loans to total loans and total deposit interest paid to total time deposits (except for the Chicago area study [19], which gives the quoted rates on specific types of loans).

It is well known, however, that large banks have a larger share of their assets in large, low-cost, low-risk loans to major corporations on which interest rates charged are relatively low. Similarly, large banks normally have a much larger share of their time deposits in large denomination certificates of deposits, which entail little administrative expense and generally command higher interest rates than are paid on regular savings accounts. For this reason the findings presented contain a pronounced bias and must be regarded as possessing only limited validity.

Some additional insight into the relationship of size to banking performance is shed by a recent questionnaire survey of 2,650 commercial banks [21]. Using cross-classification tables to sort the separate influences of bank structure (branch versus unit), size and location (city versus other), the authors concluded that "size is what matters in the provision of banking services, not location, and not structure."

Thus, larger banks more frequently made automatic allocations from depositors' demand deposits to their savings accounts; maintained Christmas Club programs, and provided trust services, parking facilities, drive-in windows, special checking accounts, data processing, payroll and locked box services, foreign exchange, revolving credit and safe deposit boxes. On the other hand, charges on regular checking accounts were found to be generally lower at small banks than at large banks.

But although the authors concluded that "banking services definitely increase with bank size," they hastened to add that "where small banks are less apt to provide the service than large ones . . . usually it is because there is little demand for this service by the customers of the smaller banks."

POLICY IMPLICATIONS

No attempt has been made in this article either to present every detail of each study or to survey more than a small sample of recent research in the general area of banking markets. Nevertheless, most of the major empirical studies that deal directly with banking competition have been included so that the results presented are biased to only a minimal degree by selective omission. If the findings are taken at their face value—which, as has repeatedly been indicated, is very hazardous—they would seem to suggest the desirability of a public policy toward banking structure that discouraged concentration, encouraged new entry, liberalized branching and permitted banks to grow to large size.

That these immediate goals in many market situations would be mutually contradictory follows as a matter of arithmetical necessity. These contradictions—apparently inherent in a society where technological advantages of size exist side by side with an economic system that relies on competition to prevent exploitation of consumers and the stagnation of industry—are the essence of the problem faced by the public agencies entrusted with channeling the evolution of the banking system along those lines most conducive to the public interest.

Valuable as they are as a start toward providing a factual basis for decisions bearing a crucial impact on the quality and prices of banking services today and in the future, empirical studies like those summarized above can provide only part of the answers to questions involving fundamental value judgments. There is the possibility that particular changes in the banking structure may have much more pronounced effects on some classes of bank customers than on others. There is also the fact that bank performance is far from being uniquely determined by bank size or structure or even the intensity of external rivalry but that it does depend heavily on the qualities of individual bank managements and personnel—factors that are not easily reducible to terms suitable for statistical investigation.

Imperfect knowledge, nevertheless, is greatly to be preferred to total ignorance. If the great amount of effort currently being expended on research in the field of banking markets and banking competition yields nothing else, it will have been worthwhile if it dispels some of the prejudices and preconceptions that have marked discussion of these subjects in the past.

REFERENCES

1. Alhadeff, David A. *Monopoly and Composition in Banking.* Berkeley: University of California Press, 1954.
2. Anderson, Bernard Eric. "An Investigation into the Effects of Banking Structure on Aspects of Bank Behavior." Unpublished Ph.D. dissertation, Ohio State University, 1964.
3. Benston, George J. "Economies of Scale and Marginal Costs in Banking Operations," *National Banking Review*, II (June, 1965), 507–49.
4. Carson, Deane and Cootner, Paul H. "The Structure of Competition in Commercial Banking in the United States." *Private Financial Institutions.* (Commission on Money and Credit, Research Studies.) Englewood Cliffs: Prentice-Hall, 1963, pp. 55–155.
5. Edwards, Franklin R. *Concentration and Competition in Commercial Banking: A Statistical Study.* Research Report No. 26, Federal Reserve Bank of Boston, 1964.
6. Edwards, Franklin R. "The Banking Competition Controversey," *National Banking Review*, III (September, 1965), 1–34.
7. Flechsig, Theodore G. *Banking Market Structure & Performance in Metropolitan Areas.* Washington: U.S. Board of Governors of the Federal Reserve System, 1965.
8. Gramley, Lyle E. *A Study of Scale Economies in Banking.* Kansas City, Missouri: Federal Reserve Bank of Kansas City, 1962.
9. Greenbaum, Stuart I. "Banking Structure and Costs: A Statistical Study of the Cost-Output Relationship in Commercial Banking." Unpublished Ph. D. dissertation, Johns Hopkins University, 1964.
10. Horvitz, Paul M. *Concentration and Competition in New England Banking.* Research Report No. 2. Boston: Federal Reserve Bank of Boston, 1958.
11. Horvitz, Paul M. "Economies of Scale in Banking." *Private Financial Institutions.* (Commission on Money and Credit, Research Studies.) Englewood Cliffs: Prentice-Hall, 1963, pp. 1–54.

12. Horvitz, Paul M. and Shull, Bernard. "The Impact of Branch Banking on Bank Performance," *National Banking Review*, II (December, 1964), 143–88.
13. Kaufman, George G. "Bank Market Structure and Performance: The Evidence from Iowa," *Southern Economic Journal*, XXXII (April, 1966), 429–39.
14. Kaufman, George G. and Latta, Synthia M. "Near Banks and Local Savings," *National Banking Review*, III (June, 1966), 539–42.
15. Kohn, Ernest. *Branch Banking, Bank Mergers and the Public Interest.* Albany: New York State Banking Department, 1964.
16. Kreps, Clifton H. Jr. "Character and Competitiveness of Local Banking: A Summary." Unpublished paper, Federal Reserve Bank of Richmond, 1965.
17. Motter, David C. and Carson, Deane. "Bank Entry and the Public Interest: A Case Study," *National Banking Review*, I (June, 1964), 469–512.
18. Phillips, Almarin. "Competition, Confusion, and Commercial Banking," *Journal of Finance*, XIX (March, 1964), 32–45.
19. Schweiger, Irving and McGee, John S. *Chicago Banking, The Structure and Performance of Banks and Related Financial Institutions in Chicago and Other Areas.* Chicago: University of Chicago, Graduate School of Business, 1961.
20. Wallace, Richard S. "Banking Structure and Bank Performance: A Case Study of Three Small Market Areas." Unpublished Ph.D. dissertation, University of Virginia, 1965.
21. Weintraub, Robert and Jessup, Paul. *A Study of Selected Banking Services by Bank Size, Structure, and Location.* U.S. Congress, House Committee on Banking and Currency, 88th Cong., 2d Sess., 1964.

VII

INTERNATIONAL
FINANCIAL MARKETS

The international money and capital markets are used to lend and borrow U.S. dollars and major European currencies outside their countries of origin. In recent years the size and structure of these markets have changed rapidly. The flow of funds through international markets now has a major impact on the capital formation and the monetary policies of many nations. The following article examines the sources and uses of short-term funds in the international money market.

38.

The International Money Market:
Structure, Scope
and Instruments

FRED H. KLOPSTOCK

During the past five years, the magnitude and institutional pattern of international financial transactions have undergone far-reaching changes. The changes have been so varied and rapid that the monetary analyst finds it difficult to keep posted on all their facets and to familiarize himself with their theoretical and policy implications. This observation applies with particular force to one of the most significant developments in the evolving international financial scene—the rapid emergence of broad international money markets, notably the so-called Euro-currency markets, and the growing inter-linkage of major national money markets. The actual and potential flow of funds into and out of international money markets has assumed major importance for domestic and foreign monetary policy formation of several countries. Funds moving across national borders for profitable short-term employment have increased sharply and their deployment and ultimate use has become quite different from the pattern of the past. For all these reasons, a new look at the scope and supply-and-demand structure of international money markets appears timely.

This is the purpose of the present paper. It will identify and assess the determinants of the supply of funds to international money markets. Draw-

Reprinted from *Journal of Finance*, Vol. XX, No. 2, May 1965, pp. 182–208, by permission of the author and the publisher. The views expressed in this article do not necessarily reflect those of the Federal Reserve Bank of New York.

ing on statistics of very diverse origins, it will attempt to trace both the major suppliers of funds and the ownership structure and magnitude of funds in individual market sectors. The paper will survey the factors bearing on the suppliers' choice among the various investment media available to them in international money markets, and will consider the implications for the international economy of the rise to prominence of Euro-currency deposit markets. In the concluding section, the paper will examine the interconnections of the various sectors of these international deposit markets and their links to other money markets.

I. A BIRD'S EYE VIEW OF INTERNATIONAL MONEY MARKETS

At the outset, a quick survey of the existing international money markets may help to provide perspective. They fall into two distinct groupings. First, there are several major national money markets in which nonresidents have traditionally sought outlets for temporarily unemployed funds, either making use of the major short-term securities or placing time deposits with the banking institutions that are part of these markets. Second, and of more recent origin, are foreign-currency deposit markets for a variety of currencies, notably United States dollars. In these, often referred to as Euro-currency deposit markets, nonresidents (and in some countries residents) place short-term balances with banks in currencies other than that of the country in which the accepting bank is located—for example, dollar deposits in banks in London, Toronto, or Milan, or sterling deposits in banks in Paris or Zurich. Much of recent international money market history relates to the rapid growth of these international deposit markets.

The two major markets of the first and more traditional type, our own and the London market, continue to receive foreign funds that in the aggregate greatly exceed those placed in foreign-currency deposit markets. The reason is solely that under the operation of the gold exchange standard a great many foreign central banks place very sizable portions of their monetary reserves in New York and London money market assets and time deposits. This is not to say that use of these two markets by private foreign interests—primarily commercial banks and corporations—is insignificant. In the United States such holdings run into the respectable sum of $4 billion —more or less, depending on the classification of various assets, as will be explained below. Sterling assets held by private nonresidents are much smaller, particularly in the marketable security category. But these holdings are dwarfed by the stake of commercial banks and corporations in the foreign-currency deposit markets.

Other national money markets in which foreign funds are employed include that of Canada, in which United States investors have long been active. United States and some European investors also hold, in an indeterminate amount, short-term paper issued by Mexican companies and to a lesser extent paper issued by South American banks and commercial companies. Foreigners own considerable amounts of local currency deposits in several European countries and in Japan in the form of so-called free yen deposits.

Foreign-currency deposit markets, in contrast, are multi-centered. Canada's chartered banks and London's foreign, British overseas, and merchant banks are the most important participants, but many European banks, notably in Paris, Rome, Milan, Amsterdam, and Zurich, stand ready to quote rates and to accept and offer deposits in several European currencies for maturities ranging from overnight to more than a year. Rates quoted reflect the credit standing of banks as well as the international financial position of their country. Thus rates are not uniform and their differentials have given rise to a large volume of arbitrage operations, as banks of relatively superior credit standing pass on funds at a small turn to banks that must pay somewhat higher rates to obtain funds.

Largely because there are very sizable interbank deposits, statistical measurement of this market is a complex task and its over-all size remains conjectural. But there is no doubt that for commercial banks and corporations the Euro-currency deposit markets have become the most important segment of the international money market.

II. INVESTOR BEHAVIOR CHARACTERISTICS

The many diverse participants in international money markets respond to quite different factors, and few generalizations regarding their behavior are safe from contradiction. An attempt must be made, however, to single out certain broad characteristics, since the supply of funds in these markets depends largely on the aggregate motivations and predilections of potential investors.

Monetary Authorities

Among the suppliers of funds to international money markets, monetary authorities stand at the top of the list. Several central banks in Europe, Latin America, and the Far East—some of them flush with funds—find it attractive to invest a large part of their monetary reserves in interest-earning assets, rather than holding gold. Quite a number of central banks, to be self-supporting, need the earnings they can obtain from their international reserves. This consideration has played an important role especially among central banks in some of the developing countries. In these areas, several monetary authorities have shown little interest in gold also for the reason that it has been their tradition—or that of their predecessors when their countries were colonies—to use dollars, sterling, or French francs, rather than gold, as the "backing" of their currencies. Central banks in several countries, in order to obtain credit facilities, habitually hold a sizable proportion of their monetary reserves in United States banks.

Monetary authorities have very few options as to where to invest their exchange reserves. Their primary investment considerations are liquidity, safety, and the breadth and resiliency of trading facilities—requirements that can be satisfied by no more than a handful of markets. The United States, because of its unrivaled role as an international financial center, the wide range and breadth of its investment and banking facilities, and the intrinsic strength and usefulness of the dollar, remains the preferred repository for foreign monetary reserves not held in the form of gold. No other market, except perhaps that of London, has the same ability to absorb the large transactions typically undertaken by central banks. In recent years some central banks outside the sterling area that have close financial ties to London have been holding varying portions of their reserves in sterling assets, but it is only the monetary authorities of the overseas sterling countries that hold very large sterling balances. The new central banks of the French franc area keep most of their reserves in Paris.

For some central banks, rate levels play a fairly important role in decisions regarding their portfolio composition; thus some monetary authorities place funds in time deposits rather than Treasury securities. Moreover, several central banks interested in maximizing their earnings place funds in Euro-currency markets. On the whole, however, monetary authorities are not specifically motivated by relative interest rate considerations in selecting the currency in which to place their reserves. They rarely shift funds from one market to another. For instance, the decision whether to put funds into dollar or sterling assets is typically a matter of basic policy rather than interest rates.

Banks and Corporations

It is particularly hazardous to venture generalizations on the attitudes of banks and corporations regarding the placement of short-term balances in international money markets. The differences in their investment behavior are hardly surprising, since they operate in very different environments and are subject to a great variety of considerations in seeking investment outlets.

One not uncommon characteristic of this category of suppliers is a relatively small emphasis on profit maximization. It would be unrealistic to picture them as surveying investment opportunities in many markets and selecting those that provide the highest net yields. These institutions are not in the business of deriving major parts of their earnings from money market investments: profitable employment of liquidity reserves, albeit important, is simply a sideline of their operations. The liquidity and safety of the funds to be invested, the peace of mind of the investor, and a host of related constraints plays a major part in determining their choice of investment outlets and in many countries also the magnitude of funds to be invested in international money markets. The top management officials of many important suppliers, whether banks or nonfinancial corporations, are often primarily risk averters willing to make substantial yield sacrifices in order to sleep well. Indeed, the student of market imperfections, of non-response to profit opportunities and similar seemingly irrational attitudes, finds ample material for analytical treatment in the behavior of operators in international money markets.

Because of the emphasis on liquidity, some banks and corporations hesitate to enter foreign money markets at all. Even sophisticated and mobile investors, who might be tempted to respond to covered arbitrage incentives frequently refrain from doing so because they thereby incur a liquidity loss. Should the invested funds be required before maturity, the reversibility of the swap transaction without a rate penalty is uncertain: The spreads between spot and forward rates may have moved against the investor in which case he would suffer a loss that might wipe out all or part of his earnings in the interim. This hazard is particularly real to banks that must take into account the fact that they may become subject to a liquidity squeeze during the life of the hedged investment. Of course, to banks and corporations that are certain to retain their investment until maturity, the liquidity loss is unimportant. Others are willing to make use of a covered investment vehicle if the interest differential provides adequate compensation for their loss of liquidity. (Conversely, alert investors who put a premium on liquidity may be quite ready to accept a corresponding yield loss in moving from a covered investment vehicle to one in their domestic money market or in another market where they need not cover forward because of commitments in the same currency.)

Since safety considerations are so predominant an influence, virtually all suppliers who do place funds abroad operate with fixed limits on currency, country, and borrower exposures. This is true of investors in foreign marketable securities as well as of those operating solely in foreign-currency deposit markets. Whatever the interest rate differential between comparable investment opportunities in their own market and in foreign markets, or among various foreign markets, potential suppliers of funds will ignore rate incentives once the exposure limits are reached. As a result, certain classes of borrowers, or borrowers in particular countries, can obtain funds only at relatively high rates. In foreign-currency deposit markets, some banks place funds only with banking friends whose operations and credit status they know intimately. Others refuse to place funds with arbitragers, confining their placements to banks that employ these solely for customer loans. Still others confine their placements to prime banks that give them reciprocal business or credit lines and other valuable services.

Among corporations, there are several further, less rational, attitudes that serve to reduce or even prevent participation in foreign money markets. Here, too, broad generalizations are hazardous, because circumstances vary widely. On the whole, even large companies often hesitate to move into unfamiliar surroundings in their search for short-term investment outlets. Their boards of directors and their senior management are frequently not well acquainted with political and financial conditions in remote places where money markets offer attractive rates. Opportunities are simply ignored, because of paucity of information on the foreign institutions involved, an only rudimentary knowledge of the foreign exchange transaction techniques required, and vague fears of the risks associated with foreign currency investments. The small yield advantage of placements abroad relative to deposits in local banks or domestic money market investments, particularly in comparison with the overall profit level of the corporation that has cash to invest, operates in the same direction. Thus the advice of financial officers and foreign exchange traders is often ignored when they attempt to obtain senior management sanction for taking advantage of foreign short-term investment opportunities.

As a result, inertia is a typical attribute of many corporate investors in their response to the lure of relatively high rates abroad. This inertia tends to direct corporate funds to domestic money markets or to local banking institutions (which then may pass them on to international money markets). The need of corporations for local credit facilities and for a broad variety of other local banking services also tends to make large amounts of corporate funds the captive of domestic banking institutions, at least in countries where strong local banks operate.

True enough, there have been important changes in this area. Many international corporations in North America and Europe, including some of the more affluent foreign subsidiaries of United States, Canadian and British companies, have become major suppliers in international money markets. As has been frequently observed, the sophistication of corporate treasurers, notably in the United States, has greatly increased. The margin of indifference—the rate differential required to impel them to place funds abroad—has diminished significantly in recent years. Several banking institutions and money brokers stand ready to help the actively interested investor in his search for profitable short-term investment outlets abroad. The growing integration of the world economy works in the same direction—notably the fact that not only large international organizations but also many smaller companies are now engaged in manufacturing and trading operations in many countries of the world and have become more familiar with financial markets in distant areas. The greater ease of international communication, particularly the ability of financial executives to move quickly to foreign countries to make on-the-spot decisions, has also added to the willingness of potential suppliers of funds to go abroad if rates are attractive.

The importance that banks and corporations attach to safety and liquidity considerations is one of several reasons for the often observed phenomenon of non-response of potential investors to the incentives offered by arbitrage transactions. If investors were always ready to take advantage of such incentives, forward exchange margins should quickly adjust themselves to their interest parity level; that is, the cost of exchange protection would soon offset the interest rate differential and international money market investments would tend to be self-limiting.[1] In the international money markets of the more traditional type disparities between forward margins and interest rate differentials have often persisted for relatively lengthy periods. In the newer foreign currency deposit markets, however, obstacles and hesitations which would limit the flow of covered arbitrage funds appear to apply with much less force. Covered yields in these markets are hardly ever long out of alignment. It is quite evident that some banks that are prominent participants in deposit markets are quick to take advantage of covered arbitrage possibilities neglected by the more conservative segment of the banking community. None of the major European banks will give their foreign exchange traders carte blanche for exploiting rate disparities, but those that are relatively speculative-minded tend to be quite liberal with respect to exposure limits and to use fewer safeguards in their choice of acceptors. Some of the banks, inasmuch as they continuously receive inquiries regarding exchange deals in several currencies, find themselves in a position to engage in two or three swaps consecutively involving different currencies in order to create funds for ultimate use at minimum cost. However, in some of the smaller segments of the Euro-currency market, banks eager to take advantage of profitable arbitrage opportunities find it impossible to do so because there are no partners for the required forward transactions. Although forward markets for foreign exchange have been broadening significantly in recent years, for some currencies they remain too thin and discontinuous to permit banks to respond to yield incentives for money market investments.

---

[1] As has been pointed out in several recent contributions to the literature, interest parity may fail to be established because of the emergence of a speculative demand for forward exchange on the part of commercial firms and other interests as the forward rate in response to arbitrage operations moves to the lower support point of the spot rate. As Mr. Auten has pointed out, such stabilizing speculation might cause a larger discrepancy from interest parity than otherwise would obtain and thereby augment the flow of arbitrage funds. See John H. Auten, "Forward Exchange Rates and Interest Rate Differentials," *Journal of Finance*, March 1963; and also William H. White, "Interest Rate Differences, Forward Exchange Mechanism, and Scope for Short-term Capital Movements," *IMF Staff Papers*, Vol. X, No. 3, November 1963, p. 485. (Of course, speculation has often had the opposite effect. It has repeatedly driven forward dollar and sterling rates to a point where outward arbitrage by habitual investors in dollar or sterling assets became unprofitable.) It should also be noted that at any one time there will exist a range of money market rates in each financial center. Accordingly there will be a range of interest parities which may provide different arbitrage incentives.

·

One of the most important sources of funds placed in time deposits abroad and in foreign markets for short-term securities is banks and other investors in countries that have no money market large enough to absorb available surplus funds; owners of liquid funds in these countries have no choice between placing funds at home and abroad. This is true of many developing countries. Some industrial countries, too, lack a broad money market of their own—particularly Switzerland, whose banking system has large balances to invest because it is the preferred repository for the liquid assets of foreigners in many parts of the world. In several other countries whose banks dispose of very sizable liquid funds, notably during periods of monetary ease, there are neither Treasury nor commercial bill markets of sufficient size to absorb these balances, and therefore they must seek a resting place abroad. International money markets can count on very large amounts of funds from these various sources.

For a full understanding of investor motivations and of the dimensions of international money markets, it is important to note that these markets obtain a very large variety of funds that for good and valid reasons are not covered. This is true, first of all, of central bank investments. Then there are very large uncovered balances that banks, business firms and wealthy individuals in the lesser-developed countries place abroad because of lack of faith in their own currencies and/or because they habitually use these foreign currencies as a store of value or for settlement purposes. Altogether, funds of this sort account for a very sizable proportion of the aggregate amount placed in international money markets, as is quite evident from an examination of the dollar and sterling liabilities to foreigners of major banking systems.

Foreign money market investments that do not call for an exchange hedge are often made by corporations that have commitments or anticipate payment needs in foreign currency. In the light of prevailing constellations of spot, forward, and interest rates, such corporations may find it attractive to make an interim investment in the money market for that currency, rather than employing the requisite funds at home and acquiring forward exchange to cover their prospective foreign currency needs. And suppliers to international money markets frequently place their own currencies abroad: United States corporations, for example, may put dollar balances in foreign banks, or Swiss banks may place Swiss francs in Milan. Virtually all banks active in interest-arbitrage operations obtain balances from these various sources and then may place these funds abroad in the same currency, thereby avoiding the need to obtain cover.

In addition, some uncovered investments are doubtless made in currencies whose spot rates are close to their lower support point and whose devaluation does not appear to be in the cards. While the degree of speculation by international money market investors is not known, it is probably true that quite a number of suppliers are willing to go out on a limb in acquiring high-yield assets in currencies that are not suspect. In Europe, reportedly, even banks do not always cover call money placed abroad if the rate differential between the domestic and the foreign money market provides what appears to be adequate compensation for the exchange risk.

III. FURTHER FACTORS AFFECTING THE SUPPLY OF FUNDS

In addition to the general behavioral characteristics of the suppliers, certain special factors importantly affect the supply of funds in international money markets. Chief among these are policy actions of monetary authorities and various influences that affect the operations of commercial banks.

Monetary Policy

Several interesting innovations in the area of international monetary policy have affected the participation of various European investor groups in foreign money markets, and on a few occasions that of some United States investors as well. Perhaps no other factor has so affected the growth of these markets as the various measures taken by central banks with a view to inducing foreign money market investments of an equilibrating type and curtailing undesired inflows of a disequilibrating type.

The best known of these devices are the swap facilities extended by the monetary authorities of Germany and Italy during the early 1960's,[2] and reestablished by the German authorities in 1964 for United States Treasury bill investments. These operations involved the sale of spot dollars to commercial banks and the simultaneous forward purchase of dollars at rates more favorable than those quoted in the foreign exchange market. The objectives were manifold, and differed for the two monetary authorities involved. But one of their common purposes was to make it profitable for commercial banks to add to their investments in foreign money markets. The Swiss National Bank has on occasion engaged in similar operations.

A different type of operation has involved direct central bank intervention in the forward exchange market to assure the availability of forward cover at rates that would either discourage banks from repatriating funds held abroad or encourage them to make additional placements in foreign money markets. The United States monetary authorities have been closely involved in such operations. At various times since 1961 they have sold foreign currencies forward in order to induce foreign investors to acquire or retain money market assets denominated in dollars. In a few cases, the operations were also intended to discourage United States investors from

[2] For an authoritative exposition of these and similar measures see Arthur I. Bloomfield, "Official Intervention in the Forward Exchange Market: Some Recent Experience," Banca Nazionale del Lavoro, *Quarterly Review*, March 1964.

shifting their funds into foreign money markets. In the absence of these preventive actions, the flow of United States corporate balances into foreign money markets would probably have been much larger.

Yet another way in which the supply of funds has been affected by central banks is through reserve requirements. In Germany and Switzerland, specified types of foreign-source deposits must be wholly or partly redeposited in the central bank unless they are re-exported. This has made it attractive for the banks involved to shift such funds into foreign money markets. Consequently, new offerings automatically come forward from banks in these two countries as specified types of their liabilities to foreigners increase. German banks affected by these provisions engage in money market investments abroad even at rates below domestic rates for comparable market instruments, since the adverse differential is offset by earnings on funds that otherwise would have to be sterilized in the central bank. As a result of these reserve requirements, large amounts of "hot money" have on occasion been diverted to foreign money markets. Comparable regulations have been adopted in other countries: For instance, in Italy, banks were at time required not to have any net foreign exchange liability to foreigners. The purpose of these provisions has been to fence off domestic money markets from foreign-currency deposit markets.

Certain measures adopted to impede the inflow of funds into countries threatened by inflation have indirectly stimulated foreign deposit markets. These measures include, in particular, officially sponsored agreements under which foreign deposits denominated in the currency of the recipient country, or in any other currency, do not bear interest, or governmental prohibition of such interest payments. Holders of balances on which interest can no longer be earned have tended to offer their holdings to foreign banks that can employ these funds for customer loans. Such offerings have given added impetus to the growth of a market for Euro-Swiss francs and for some other Euro-currencies. The Euro-sterling market, on the other hand, received its stimulus from British exchange controls that restrict lending to nonresidents (as well as from relatively low rates paid on deposits by the clearing banks).

Through these various measures central banks have considerably affected the amount of funds that banking systems—and, in the United States, some corporate investors—supply to foreign money markets. By modifying their regulations or the terms and conditions of their market interventions, they have been able to vary the liquidity of their banks, curtail or bolster their monetary reserves, and alter their balance of payments.

Commercial Bank Operations

Banks of several countries have at times suddenly shifted substantial amounts of funds to or from international money markets in response to changes in their liquidity positions that stemmed from major shifts in the monetary policy of their countries.

Quite apart from the effects of such policy changes, the amounts of funds that commercial banks place in international money markets are for several reasons subject to frequent and sharp changes. One reason is that in many countries, banks are exposed to fairly severe pressures for funds at month-end, mid-year, and particularly end-of-year dates—the major settlement dates for bills and debts. To take care of their liquidity needs, many suppliers are compelled at such times to withdraw funds from foreign money markets. Tax dates cause similar pressures.

But the most pervasive market disturbances arise from the window-dressing of balance sheets, notably at mid-year and year-end. In some countries this involves merely offering relatively high interest rates to foreign depositors for brief periods thereby permitting the recipient bank to make a good showing in the race for deposits. More typically it involves a build-up, as of balance-sheet publication dates, of unusual and atypical amounts of domestic liquidity, notably cash balances held with the central bank and trade bills eligible for discount by the central bank. As banks withdraw funds for this purpose from international deposit markets, the banks deprived of the funds follow suit to safeguard their own liquidity or to maintain domestic cash balances at their usual level. Banks caught in a squeeze —that is, those unable to withdraw funds from the relevant foreign-currency deposit markets because they placed their balances at more distant maturity dates—may have to sell assets denominated in other currencies, including that of their own country, in order to obtain the requisite funds, or they may have to borrow the currency involved at relatively high rates. The resulting exchange and interest rate gyrations typically set in motion new foreign money market investments, as banks with cash reserves at their disposal attempt to exploit the concomitant earning opportunities. Foreign currency deposit markets and to a lesser extent other international money markets are subjected to further drains as some banks in countries where the rest of the banking system is starved for funds pull back their foreign balances in order to take advantage of high short-term rates at home. The Euro-currency markets have repeatedly been exposed to these types of disturbances.

IV. GEOGRAPHICAL ORIGIN OF FUNDS

Statistical information as to who invests how much in international money markets is very sparse, especially in regard to central banks, the most important foreign suppliers in the United States and British market. With few exceptions, monetary authorities have been unwilling to publish information on the currency or asset composition of their investment portfolios.

The problem of tracing the origin of funds is almost equally difficult in regard to the private investors in international money markets. Some information is available, however, on investments by the commercial banks and corporations of certain countries in certain sectors of the market, and by tying this to observations of experienced market observers and to a great variety of statistics published by several central banks certain qualified conclusions may be presented regarding the geographical origin of private funds in this market.

United States Participation

It is probably safe to say that by far the biggest private supplier of resident funds to international money markets is a relatively small number of United States corporations. Their preferred investment medium is time deposits in the Canadian chartered banks. These, being free of the fetters of Federal Reserve Board regulation of interest rates, have been able and willing to offer corporate investors in the United States rates for time balances denominated in United States dollars in excess of those offered by United States banks on negotiable certificates of deposit. Moreover, the Canadian banks are in a position to pay interest on short-dated deposits. The total amount of United States resident deposits in Canadian banks during the last year or two appears to have remained subsequently in excess of $1 billion.

Apart from the rate advantage, several factors have contributed to the flow of United States funds to Canada—among them the proximity of the country, and the fact that so many American companies have subsidiaries in Canada and are therefore in close touch with Canadian banks. The negotiation of time deposit arrangements has of course been facilitated by the fact that the Canadian banks are well represented in the United States by agencies and affiliates and employ representatives in several centers. Many United States corporations, because they place deposits through the agencies, mistakenly regard these funds as being held in the United States. The agencies, on behalf of their head offices, invest in New York varying parts and at times virtually all of any new deposits of United States resident funds in Canadian banks.

In view of this interrelationship, the question is sometimes raised whether the full amount of United States resident dollar deposits in Canada should be regarded as international money market investments. It is not an easy question to answer. Canadian banks obtain a large pool of United States dollar balances of diverse origin and it is difficult to tie these funds to particular uses in various money and loan markets. Canadian banks employ sizable dollar balances obtained in the United States in foreign deposit markets. At the same time, dollar balances obtained from Canadian and other non-United States depositors are invested in our money market. But a sufficiently close relationship exists between United States time deposits in

Canada and the use of the underlying funds in our money market to cast some doubt on the appropriateness of regarding all United States dollar assets in Canadian banks as international money market investments.

United States corporate and commercial bank deposits in the European segment of foreign currency deposit markets are of much more modest proportions. A very rough estimate would put them at $700 million, with the bulk of the funds placed in the United Kingdom and smaller amounts in Italy and Switzerland. Additional balances have been placed by some United States corporations directly with major corporations in Europe and in local currency time deposits in European banks. However, even very yield-conscious corporations in the United States hesitate to put large amounts of deposits with individual institutions in Europe.

Statistics on United States residents' short-term foreign investments do not include the large balances in foreign banks placed there by the more affluent affiliates of United States corporations; some of these balances may be of United States origin. Nor do they include the very sizable funds placed in foreign deposit markets by the branches of United States banks; with relatively few exceptions, these represent funds obtained abroad rather than from the head offices. United States residents hold substantial amounts of deposits in Mexican banks. Despite the high rates they pay, Japanese banks do not appear to have attracted large dollar amounts from United States residents. But there are indications that so-called free-yen deposits by United States companies now run into relatively sizable amounts, but for the most part these are related to the desire of United States companies to obtain bank financing facilities for their affiliates in Japan.

To turn from bank deposits to operations in short-term securities, here too Canada has in recent years been the preferred foreign short-term investment outlet for United States corporations. Whenever the covered interest arbitrage incentive is sufficiently favorable, the flow of United States corporate funds into the Canadian market, notably the commercial paper market, tends to rise rapidly. The appeal lies primarily in the availability of paper that is issued by Canadian subsidiaries of leading United States finance companies and carries the unconditional guarantee of the parent. Rate differentials relative to similar United States paper are particularly attractive for the more distant maturities.

Not very many United States companies have been willing to place sizable amounts of cash in the London money market, though in recent years an increasing number of firms and even individuals have shown some interest in relatively high-yielding outlets for short-term funds in London. The British money market has excited the interest of United States corporations mainly when the covered interest arbitrage incentive has been exceptionally favorable, as was the case, for instance, in 1960 and 1961 and temporarily in 1964. Among the large companies that have taken the plunge are several well known names whose operations are typically of such magnitude that they leave a noticeable mark on United States capital flows. On some recent occasions, however, the United States monetary authorities, in cooperation with foreign monetary authorities, have intervened in the forward exchange market when rate incentives to place funds in the Canadian and London money markets became exceptionally attractive, and consequently these outflows have rarely been very large during the past year.

Mexican commercial paper issued by agencies of the Mexican Government, by Mexican industrial companies and by American-owned companies has also been sold in the United States in fairly substantial amounts. Several commercial finance companies and wealthy private investors have acquired high-interest notes issued by Latin American companies, notably in Columbia, Argentina, and Peru. These notes are ordinarily guaranteed by prime banks in Latin American countries and payable at United States banks.

United States banks have generally not participated much in foreign money market operations for their own account, though there have been exceptions. Some corporations have been unable to place funds abroad because their corporate by-laws prohibit such investments. But perhaps the most important constraint has stemmed from the general reluctance of corporate managements to commit large amounts of funds to unfamiliar markets, and from the liquidity and safety considerations discussed previously. Reluctance to add to this country's balance-of-payments problems has also played a role, at least in the case of banks and financial corporations.

Thus, the total stake of United States residents in foreign money markets remains small relative to domestic short-term placements. Nevertheless, in the aggregate it has reached very substantial proportions. Adding the interest-bearing short-term balances in Canadian, European, Japanese, and Mexican banks to various money market investments in Canada and elsewhere, we arrive at an aggregate United States short-term commitment of approximately $3.3 billion, excluding, of course, commercial bank loans of an even larger magnitude. Most of the outflow has occurred in recent years in response to interest rate differentials between United States and foreign money markets. The monetary policy and balance-of-payments implications of these developments are self-evident.

Other Suppliers

Apart from United States corporations, the major suppliers to international money markets are the banking systems of Switzerland, Britain, and Canada. They act essentially as intermediaries, however, in that most, if not all, of the resources they employ abroad are obtained from banks, business firms, and individuals in many other parts of the world. A substantial portion of the funds reaching international money markets through some of these banks originates in the Middle East, in Central and South

America, and in other less developed areas where short-term funds cannot be employed domestically and where political and financial conditions make it desirable for individuals and companies to seek a safe haven for their liquidity. In addition, many of the banks here under discussion engage in large-scale arbitrage operations by bidding for balances offered by European and other banks, which they then employ for arbitrage operations.

Switzerland's banking system is one of the most important repositories of private foreign balances. An authoritative estimate puts the short-term foreign liabilities of the Swiss banks at about $2.6 billion as of the end of 1963. These balances are of various sorts. Some of them represent the savings of wealthy families in various part of the world and of residents of inflation-ridden countries, while others consist of liquidity reserves of international business firms and of companies in various overseas countries. But there are also large amounts of speculative funds and other balances of the "hot money" variety, some of them originating in Continental Europe. All these funds are subject to rapid withdrawal if financial or political conditions change in various parts of the world. The Swiss banks have felt constrained from employing them to any considerable extent in their loan operations. Since Switzerland has no substantial money market of its own, the banks must seek outlets for virtually all of these funds abroad.

Altogether, the international money market investments of Swiss banks are about equal to these banks' short-term liabilities to foreigners, with roughly two-thirds of their foreign short-term assets placed in the Euro-currency markets and the remaining third in the United States. In addition, Swiss corporations hold directly sizable amounts in various money markets. The preferred money market instrument of Swiss investors in the United States is commercial paper and also bankers acceptances which—unlike other marketable securities—are not subject to the Swiss stamp tax. But at various times major Swiss commercial banks have acquired both British and United States Treasury bills in response to attractive swap rates provided by the Swiss National Bank. The export of short-term capital from Switzerland has been given further impetus by a regulation under which additional deposits acquired from abroad by the Swiss banks since January 1, 1964 must be placed either with the central bank in blocked accounts that bear no interest or in foreign markets in a foreign currency.

Banks in Britain are major suppliers to foreign-currency deposit markets, their short-term foreign-currency assets held abroad amounting to over $4.0 billion on September 30, 1964. But a large proportion of these funds is held for account of the London branches of foreign banks. The head offices of these branches have used the Euro-currency market—of which London has become the center—as a source of funds with which to supplement their domestic deposit resources, a practice followed particularly by United States and Japanese banks in London. Perhaps one-quarter of the so-called external foreign-currency assets of British banks actually represent funds thus bid for under general or specific instructions of head offices and deposited at home. This type of operation is essentially different from the foreign short-term investments surveyed here.

Another important segment of the external assets of United Kingdom banks consists of short-term commercial loans to foreign banks and corporations. The emergence of London as the dominant center of the foreign-currency deposit market has added significantly to the opportunities of banks in Britain to add to their foreign loan business. Many of the merchant, overseas, and foreign banks in London have used funds obtained in the international deposit market to broaden substantially their participation in the financing of international trade transactions and to add to their books important accounts in foreign countries.

International interest arbitrage operations, in the narrower sense of the term, account for another large portion of British banks' foreign currency operations. They involve the re-depositing of United States dollar deposits in European banks. Relatively modest amounts of United States dollar deposits have been swapped into other currencies and then placed in Continental Europe. Moreover, varying portions of foreign deposits—depending on covered rate incentives—have at times been placed in the British money market, notably in local authority deposits.

The United States money market proper has not excited the interest of British banks, except during the period of exceptionally high interest rates here in late 1959 and early 1960. British investors other than banks, however, now hold more than $300 million of marketable short-term securities other than Treasury paper. In fact, British interests operating in the United States are among the most important single nonbank sources of foreign funds in the United States.

An analysis of Canadian bank participation in international money market operations runs into complex classification problems. As pointed out previously, the question has been raised whether all of the United States corporate deposits in Canadian banks should be classified as investments in a foreign deposit market. If one accepts the argument that some of them are international deposits only in a formal sense, it follows that Canadian investments in the United States money market, to the extent that they involve United States resident funds, should also not be regarded as foreign. How to resolve this tangled issue is not self-evident.

The great bulk of Canadian investments in our money market consists of call loans to securities dealers and brokers. These so-called Street loans are extended by the New York agencies of the Canadian banks out of head office funds that are held by the agencies in United States banks. The agencies have become specialists in this loan business, offering rates somewhat below those quoted by United States banks, primarily because, unlike the latter, they cannot offer securities business to the borrowers and, therefore, have to grant concessions in terms of lower rates. The aggregate amount of their Street loans amounted to more than $1 billion at the end of August 1964.[3] In addition, the agencies hold sizable amounts of United States securities as a liquidity reserve for the U.S. dollar-denominated liabilities of their head offices. They are also suppliers of Federal funds. The Canadian banks are important factors in the London sector of the Euro-dollar market, as is indicated by the fact that their United States dollar deposits in their London branches and in other banks in the United Kingdom amounted to $540 million on September 30, 1964.[4] But they are also known to have sizable dollar deposits in other sectors of the international deposit market. Their involvement as suppliers and takers of funds in several markets for United States dollar balances has meant that the Canadian banks play an important integrating role in the international money market,[5] a role that will be discussed in the concluding section of this paper.

German banks, early in 1962, had committed almost $1 billion to foreign money markets (excluding sight balances). By June 1964 their placements had dropped to $610 million, including approximately $150 million of United States Treasury bills. In the early 1960's, as was mentioned above, favorable swap rates provided by the German Bundesbank, and more recently the very high reserve requirements for foreign deposits that are not offset by short-term capital exports, were major factors in the role of German banks in international deposit markets. Although German banks have been active in all major sectors of Europe's foreign-currency deposit markets, in mid-1964 their Euro-dollar market placements were no longer significant and had actually dropped below their D-mark deposits with foreign banks.[6] Unlike many other banks in Europe, German banks do not generally operate on both sides of the market in the sense of accepting funds from abroad for the purpose of placing them in foreign countries at a somewhat higher rate of return.

Such transactions are largely responsible for the role of Italian banks as suppliers in international deposit markets. In March 1964 their total foreign currency assets abroad, including working balances and loans, amounted to more than $1.1 billion.[7] However, a major part of the foreign currency balances obtained by Italian banks both from domestic and foreign sources is employed for foreign currency loans to Italian business firms.

French banks are also major factors in Euro-currency markets. Their aggregate dollar deposits in the United Kingdom and in Italy amounted to approximately $235 million at the end of March 1964.

[3] Estimate based on statistics published in Supplement to the *Canada Gazette*, September 3, 1964.

[4] See Bank of England *Quarterly Bulletin*, December 1964, p. 329.

[5] For a description of these operations, see Report of the Royal Commission on Banking and Finance, Ottawa, 1964, pp. 137–139.

[6] See Deutsche Bundesbank, *Monthly Report*, August 1964.

[7] For statistical information on Italian foreign-currency assets, see Banca d'Italia, *Report for the Year 1963* (Rome, 1964).

At times Eastern European central and foreign-trade banks have placed sizable dollar balances in European banks, though at other times they have been large takers in the market. Actually, the foreign-currency deposit market owed much of its early growth to the fact that its anonymity and earning opportunities had strong appeal to the financial institutions of the Iron Curtain countries.

As mentioned previously, some of the developing countries of the world are important sources of foreign-currency deposits in European banks. It is noteworthy that Middle Eastern countries' foreign-currency deposits in banks in Britain, presumably consisting largely of balances owned by recipients of oil royalties,[8] amounted to almost $400 million on September 30, 1964. The developing areas are also important sources of sterling time deposits in British banks and dollar time deposits in the United States. There are important policy implications in these facts inasmuch as both in investment motivation and in response to changes in market conditions, suppliers of funds in less developed countries tend to differ significantly from those in industrial nations.

V. INVESTMENT MEDIA

Investors in international money markets make use of a broad range of money market instruments, since their portfolio preferences and their needs for the employment of cash surpluses are so different. Within groups of investors, however, certain similarities in portfolio policies are discernible, and at least in the foreign-currency deposit markets these similarities are reflected in the spectrum of interest rates.

Monetary authorities place the great bulk of their foreign exchange assets in Treasury securities in New York and London. The breadth and depth of the United States and British government securities markets and the narrow spread between bid and asked prices assure central banks that at a moment's notice they can acquire or liquidate very large amounts of such securities without giving up anything to the market. The fact that the credit of the two countries' governments is superior to that of any private obligor, and in fact is free of default risk, has made their securities the preferred investment medium of central banks.

For a variety of reasons, monetary authorities also hold substantial time deposit accounts in the United States and Britain, and have become fairly important investors in negotiable time certificates issued by United States banks. Some of them, as has been mentioned, place large amounts of deposits denominated in dollars with European commercial banks. The

---

[8] See on this also Paul Einzig, "Recent Changes in the Euro-dollar System," *Journal of Finance*, September 1964, p. 443.

only other market instrument of significance in the portfolio of central banks is dollar bankers acceptances.

Commercial banks and corporations throughout the world have shown unmistakably that bank deposits, notably of the Euro-currency variety, are their preferred investment medium in the international money market. One important reason for the popularity of deposits is, of course, the fact that the rates offered for them by banks are substantially higher than those quoted for marketable securities issued by governments. Investors have come to the conclusion that the difference in credit quality and liquidity between deposits with prime banks and Treasury securities does not warrant the rate sacrifice involved in purchasing the latter. Proper maturity spacing serves to make up for the lack of liquidity of deposits with a fixed term of repayment.

The ease and convenience of placing funds in commercial banks is another important factor that has made for this dominant role of deposits. There is little paper work involved in these transactions, no transfer of securities or certificates to custody accounts, and no stamp taxes to be paid—a consideration of particular significance to the Swiss banking community. In addition, deposits offer suppliers the opportunity to put funds to work for very brief periods. Banks in London accept overnight money either in sterling or in foreign currencies. Many banks in Western Europe and elsewhere stand ready to offer facilities for placements at two-day, seven-day, or thirty-day notice, as well as the more distant maturities. The close contact of market participants is also an important factor. Foreign exchange traders, who are intimately involved in the placement of funds with banks because of the requisite spot and forward exchange transactions, are in constant touch with one another by telephone and telex. They become quickly aware of needs of individual banks for placements or borrowings, and stand ready to make firm offers and bids.

It may be worth mentioning a special consideration that often affect European investors who contemplate acquiring money market assets in the United States—whether in the form of bank deposits or in marketable securities traded in New York. Financial institutions in this country open for business only after European financial executives and their foreign exchange traders have returned from lunch. Quotations can then be obtained, but it is much simpler to lay off funds with a few banks in Europe that are continuously in the market.

In placing bank deposits, especially of the Euro-currency type, suppliers of funds can choose among a variety of bank obligors of widely different credit standing. Most bank suppliers, as a matter of principle, are unwilling to tamper with the quality of their short-term portfolios, and place funds only with prime banks. But institutions wishing to earn better rates may find outlets for their funds in banks whose credit ratings are somewhat less than prime, or with banks in countries whose exchange positions are not entirely satisfactory. Thus, the rate structure in international money markets has acquired considerable diversity with a broad range of rates for each maturity now available to suppliers. The traditional investment media in national money markets are characterized by more homogeneous credit quality and a much narrower range of rates than are found in the international deposit markets.

Of course, commercial banks and corporations that participate in international money markets make use of many investment vehicles other than bank deposits. Bankers acceptances and to a lesser extent United States and Canadian finance paper are fairly important parts of the asset portfolios of important suppliers of funds, notably those who do not consider it wise to place their liquidity entirely in a currency other than that of the country where the head office of the recipient bank is located. Sizable funds obtained in the Euro-dollar market are employed by European banks in the United States Federal Funds market over the week end. A few foreign investors hold large amounts of United States federal agency paper. But investment media that are popular in the United States, such as negotiable certificates of deposit issued by United States banks, repurchase agreements, or short-term obligations of municipalities, are not employed to any important extent by foreign private investors.

Treasury bills, the most important money market instrument in New York and London, no longer play an important role in the asset portfolios of foreign commercial banks and corporations. A notable exception, however, is the Treasury bill holdings acquired by German and Swiss commercial banks in response to the special swap facilities provided by their central banks. Thus, favorable forward rates provided by central banks have at times not only affected the aggregate of international money market investments, as pointed out previously, but also the investment media employed by the important suppliers of funds to the market.

Tax considerations have been an important factor governing the portfolio preferences of foreign investors in the United States money market. All foreign residents are tax exempt with respect to their income from time deposits and bankers' acceptances but only foreign monetary authorities are exempt with respect to their income from Treasury securities in which they place their monetary reserves.

VI. PROFILES OF THREE MAJOR MARKETS

Though data on international money markets are far from adequate, enough is known to permit rough surveys of who holds what assets in each of the two major markets of the traditional type—the United States and Britain. In addition, some information is available on the magnitude and uses of the funds that enter Euro-currency markets.

United States

As is evident from Table 38–1, banks in the United States had short-term liabilities to foreigners (excluding those to international and regional institutions) totaling $22.2 billion on September 30, 1964. The bulk of these nonresident assets, approximately 55 percent, was held by foreign monetary authorities and governments, mostly in the form of United States Treasury securities, with a small portion—$200 million—in nonmarketable certificates of indebtedness, in which foreign central banks have invested various types of funds, including balances obtained under swap agreements.

In the holdings of foreign official institutions, time deposits are second in importance. These rose at a fast clip after Congress, in 1962, exempted them for three years from Regulation Q restraints on interest rates. Actually, official time deposits are even larger than shown in the table, since negotiable time certificates of deposit are included not under time balances but under "other holdings," where they constitute a substantial proportion. The emergence of a broad secondary market for certificates of deposit has done a great deal to attract the interest of monetary authorities in this instrument. On the other hand, it should be noted that foreign monetary authorities often place time deposits with United States banks not because

TABLE 38–1

Foreign Short-Term Holdings in Banks in the United States, September 30, 1964[a]

(In Millions of Dollars)

	Demand Deposits	Time Deposits	Government Securities	Other Holdings[b]	Total
Foreign official institutions	1,427	2,671[c]	7,012	1,207	12,317
Foreign banks	4,719[d]	855[d]	132	916[e]	6,622
Other foreigners	1,478	1,174	101	480	3,233
Total	7,624	4,700	7,245	2,603	22,172

[a] Holdings of international and interregional institutions are not included, nor are several hundred million dollars worth of Treasury notes and bonds maturing within less than one year after the reporting date.

[b] Mostly acceptances, federal agency paper, and negotiable certificates of deposit.

[c] Excluding large amounts represented by negotiable certificates of deposit, which are included under "other holdings."

[d] Approximately $3 billion of these demand and time balances represented deposits not in United States banks but liabilities of the New York agencies of foreign banks to their head offices; the agencies had employed approximately $1 billion of these balances in loans to securities dealers and brokers, and also held large balances in the form of money market and other securities. (For detailed statistics on the position of agencies, see the State of New York's *Annual Report of the Superintendent of Banks*.) Another sizable proportion of foreign banks' deposit balances consisted of funds that the foreign branches of United States banks deposited in their head offices in this country, which employed them for loans and investments. Thus the asset distribution of foreign banks' holdings in the United States would look quite different if the classification were made according to their ultimate use.

[e] Including a substantial amount of bills held by United States banks for collection on behalf of their foreign bank correspondents.

of yield considerations but in order to obtain loan, acceptance credit, and letter-of-credit facilities, either for themselves or for the commercial banks of their countries.

The "other holdings" of foreign official institutions consist, apart from negotiable certificates of deposits, mainly of bankers acceptances. In the 1920's these were the major investment medium of foreign central banks in the United States money market. After World War II, as the supply of acceptances broadened, they again became popular and accounted for a large fraction of the asset holdings of a number of foreign central banks. One important reason for this was that the discount on acceptances has long been tax-exempt for central banks of issue, while until 1961 several foreign central banks were subject to our withholding tax with respect to their earnings on Treasury securities. Acceptances lost this tax advantage in May 1961, when an amendment to the Internal Revenue Code exempted from the withholding tax any income from obligations of the United States in which the money reserves of central banks are invested. Since then, the interest of foreign official institutions in bankers' acceptances has greatly diminished.

As regards the holdings of foreign commercial banks, the data in the table must be interpreted with great caution, and with full consideration of the table footnotes. It is clear, however, that foreign banks have been fairly important investors in our money market; in some instances their investments here reflect a desire—for precautionary reasons—not to place all of their dollar balances in the European dollar market. Under the classification used in the table, their investments consist largely of "other holdings"; for the most part, these are made up of bankers' acceptances, but they also include substantial amounts of commercial and finance paper. Treasury bill holdings of foreign banks, which have been quite small for many years, have recently shown sizable increases in response to the special incentives provided by foreign central banks.

Foreign corporations and individuals make substantial use of the United States money market. This is true particularly of foreign corporations that need a high degree of liquidity in order to cover unexpected drains on their dollar balances, and of insurance companies that must conform with the liquidity requirements of insurance codes; wealthy individuals in inflation-ridden countries, particularly in Latin America, are also attracted by the tax-exemption feature of foreign-owned time deposits in the United States.

As of September 30, 1964, the interest-earning assets held in this country by nonbank private foreigners amounted to the respectable sum of $1.7 billion, of which more than $1 billion was held in time deposits, mostly for Latin American account. The group's "other holdings," amounting to almost $500 million in mid-1964, are mostly in various types of market-

TABLE 38–2

Foreign Short-Term Sterling Holdings in the British Money Market, September 30, 1964ª

(In Millions of Pounds Sterling)

	Bank Depositsᵇ	U.K. Treasury Bills	Commercial Bills & Promissory Notes	Total
Central Monetary Institutions				
Overseas sterling countries	169	839	—	1,008
Non-sterling countries	110	301	—	411
Total	279	1,140	—	1,419
Other Foreigners				
Overseas sterling countries	862	32	29	903
Non-sterling countries	791	24	50	845
Total	1,653	56	79	1,748
Grand Total	1,932	1,196	79	3,107

ª From Bank of England Quarterly Bulletin, December 1964. Holdings of British government and government-guaranteed stocks and investments of international organizations are excluded.

ᵇ Demand plus time deposits, designated respectively as current and deposit accounts.

able securities held by companies with important financial interests in the United States.

United Kingdom

Nonresident sterling holdings of a money market nature are summarized in Table 38–2.

As can be seen from Table 38–2, the central banks and currency boards of the overseas sterling countries, where sterling has always been a reserve currency, account for one-third of the total foreign holdings in the British money market. In the colonial period, the note issues of the countries now constituting the overseas Commonwealth were usually linked to sterling by statutory provisions, which required that the currency be covered by an equivalent amount of sterling holdings.[9] The new central banks of the Commonwealth countries are in general free to place their reserves in assets other than sterling. Nevertheless, past practice and a continuation of intimate political, business, and financial connections with London have caused the overseas sterling countries to place all or large parts of their monetary reserves in sterling instruments. It may be noted, incidentally, that a large part of their holdings is in longer-term government securities; as of September 30, 1964, as much as £998 million of such securities, some of them with very distant maturity dates, were held by banks in the United

[9] See "Overseas Sterling Holdings," *Bank of England Quarterly Bulletin*, December 1963, pp. 264 ff.

Kingdom for account of the central monetary institutions of these countries.

The table also shows that banks and commercial firms—both of overseas sterling and of non-sterling countries—continue to maintain very impressive amounts of demand and time deposits in London. What proportion of these holdings is in time deposits is not known, but it is believed to be large. The fact that many London banks offer relatively high yields for overnight and other short-dated funds has attracted sizable amounts not only of foreign-currency but also of sterling time deposits; these represent an important outlet for the temporarily unemployed balances of countless banks and corporations. Among the City institutions that offer short-term deposit facilities to foreign banks are the discount houses, which in recent years have made efforts to solicit day-to-day and seven-day money from European banks.

Foreign non-official investments in United Kingdom Treasury bills have been quite small in recent years, amounting to no more than £56 million in September 1964. Thus the British Treasury bill has almost lost the role it formerly played as the most important medium for short-term interest arbitrage between foreign financial centers and London.

Two types of London money market assets not covered in the table are deposits in hire-purchase finance houses and deposit receipts of the so-called local authorities, consisting mostly of the British metropolitan municipalities, county boroughs, and county councils. Deposits of overseas residents in hire-purchase finance houses, excluding those held through British bank nominees, totaled as much as £72 million at the end of December 1963. Since 1958, several British banks have taken an interest in hire-purchase companies, and now own some of them, and this has added to the companies' credit standing in the eyes of foreign depositors. Placements have also been facilitated by the fact that some banks act as brokers in placing foreign funds with the hire-purchase companies.

Local authorities arrange time deposits against receipts for fixed periods but also borrow money subject to withdrawal on two-day or seven-day notice, or after more extended periods. At times, fairly substantial amounts are placed with the authorities by nonresidents, either directly or through intermediaries. At the end of 1962 such foreign deposits came to £71 million, but they are believed to be substantially lower today. In addition, the local authorities have obtained varying amounts of foreign-source money from British overseas and merchant banks when these institutions have found it profitable to swap foreign-currency deposits into sterling.

The Euro-Currency Market

Much remains to be done to obtain a full statistical picture of the dimentions of the Euro-currency market. Impressive progress has been made in this direction, notably by the Bank for International Settlements, but the market still defies precise statistical measurement. As has been pointed out before, a sizable number of its participants are primarily arbitragers, in the sense that they pass on to other banks, at a small turn, most of the deposits they hold, rather than employing them for loans to "end-users," such as nonbank borrowers, or for investments in domestic financial markets. And some of the second-generation, perhaps even some of the third-generation, banks may do the same. The inclusion of such interbank deposits in the Euro-currency market statistics yields totals that are not particularly meaningful. Therefore the Bank for International Settlements has made an attempt to estimate a total deposit figure net of interbank deposits in Western Europe and Canada, the areas where most interbank dealings of this type occur. It arrived at a figure of $7 billion for the net volume of Euro-currencies at the end of September 1963, of which some $5 billion represented placements in the Euro-dollar market.

Where are these balances ultimately employed? It would appear that in 1963 and 1964 by far the largest end-users of Euro-currency deposits have been Italian importers and exporters. As of the end of March 1964, foreign-currency credits of Italian banks to Italian commercial firms were close to $1.6 billion—though some of the underlying balances were of domestic origin. No other single banking system has relied to the same extent on funds obtained in international deposit markets for foreign-currency credits to domestic customers.

Perhaps the second largest end-users of such funds are a few United States banks with branches in London and Continental Europe. Through their European branches, these banks have acquired very large foreign balances which they could not obtain directly because of rate ceilings established by the Federal Reserve Board. These funds are then mingled with balances obtained from many other sources, domestic and foreign. As money market conditions in the United States became less easy during 1964, the aggregate balances transferred for head-office use increased considerably. However, the branches retain a substantial proportion of their aggregate takings from the Euro-dollar markets, employing them in deposit and loan operations in Europe. Altogether the dollar balances placed in the European branches of United States banks account for a substantial proportion of Euro-dollar deposits.

German corporations are also major end-users and at times their aggregate indebtedness to German and foreign banks that had obtained the requisite balances in the foreign-currency deposit market may have exceeded the amounts transmitted by the branches of United States banks to their head offices. Next in importance are Japanese companies. Japanese banks ordinarily derive between $400 and $500 million from foreign-currency markets, but these funds are only a fraction of the balances made available to Japan by United States banks through acceptance credits and loans. In Scandinavia, Eastern Europe, and many other countries, banks and commercial firms have drawn on Euro-currency deposits in connection with a large variety of commercial operations, but primarily to obtain financing of international trade transactions. In addition, the British overseas, merchant and foreign banks have at times employed sizable amounts of foreign-currency deposits, after appropriate swaps, for sterling loans and money market investments in the United Kingdom. Similarly, Japanese banks have converted sizable dollar deposits into yen balances for employment in domestic loan markets.

VII. IMPLICATIONS OF EURO-CURRENCY MARKETS

A fairly large literature is now at hand on many aspects of foreign-currency deposit markets, much of it prepared by members of this panel.[10] Therefore, little purpose would be served by providing here another summary of the genesis, development, dimensions, merits, and risks of these markets. Nevertheless, several of the markets' characteristics deserve special attention within the framework of this paper.

In the first place, the rise of Euro-currency deposits to prominence has meant that for investors other than central banks, the major medium for international money market operations is now obligations of commercial banks denominated in currencies other than their own. These obligations are not negotiable, do not call for collateral, and rest on contractual evidence consisting solely of a letter confirming a telephone or telex message. Actually some of the methods and procedures in vogue in domestic interbank call-loan markets are now being used on a much broader and liberal scale in the far more intricate international deposit markets. Yet, these international markets stretch across the borders of many countries, often call for maturities much more distant than those in domestic markets, and deal in currencies other than those of the depositor and acceptor. The practice of borrowing short and lending long is reported to be not uncommon. These observations are intended not to cast doubt on the strength of international deposit markets, but to emphasize that the quality of credit in these markets is of quite a different order from that of markets in which the major obligors are governments, governmental corporations, or leading finance companies. While the Euro-currency market has given rise to only minimal losses and

---

[10] Oscar Altman, "Foreign Markets for Dollars, Sterling and Other Currencies," *International Monetary Fund Staff Papers*, Vol VIII, 1960–61, pp. 313–352; "Recent Developments in Foreign Markets for Dollars and Other Currencies," *ibid.*, Vol. X, March 1963, p. 48; Alan R. Holmes and Fred H. Klopstock, "The Market for Dollar Deposits in Europe," *Monthly Review* of the Federal Reserve Bank of New York, Vol. 42, No. 11, November 1960; Noris O. Johnson, *Euro-dollars in the New International Money Market*, New York, 1964; and Roy L. Reierson, *The Euro-dollar Market, Bankers Trust Company*, New York, 1964. See also Paul Einzig, *The Euro-Dollar System*, New York, 1964.

has repeatedly proved its resilience, it remains to be seen how shock-resistant it will be in periods of severe stress and strain.

Another aspect of this market not to be neglected in an appraisal of its structure and stature is the close linkage between what on the surface looks like anonymous money market transactions and loans to commercial firms. Such links have recently become more intimate as nonbank borrowers have entered the market on their own initiative. Large international corporations demand and obtain rates quite close to those quoted for placements in the interbank sector of the market. Major commercial borrowers have acquired the habit of shopping around among banks in foreign countries for balances with which to supplement or replace local sources of credit supply. In some countries, where corporate borrowing from foreign banks is not permitted or made difficult, foreign affiliates are often instructed to obtain the requisite funds either from local or foreign banks. Less well known companies in need of foreign-currency credits arrange with their local banking connections a guarantee of payment for funds obtained in the international deposit market, and are thus able to arrange for loan accommodation at relatively attractive rates.

The market has undoubtedly performed highly useful functions. Above all, it has tapped and mobilized large amounts of liquid reserves of various sorts and origins, primarily for the financing of international trade but in some countries also for the financing of domestic operations. The market has become the funnel through which temporarily unemployed funds in many parts of the world are quickly and efficiently transmitted to borrowers in need of loan accommodation. As a result, interest charges on foreign-trade loans have come under pressure in many countries and differences in local credit conditions throughout Europe have been significantly reduced.

It is impossible to say for sure where the balances placed in the market would have been lodged if the market had not developed. Some balances would probably have remained idle or have been invested in domestic money markets. Others would have been employed in various other foreign investment media for short-term funds, including time deposits in United States and British banks. But a large part of these balances would probably have been placed in Treasury and other negotiable paper in the United States and some other countries, including the United Kingdom. The existence of the market has doubtless caused several billion dollars worth of liquid balances that might have been placed primarily in various short-dated government and other negotiable securities to be shifted to the international departments of commercial banks in need of additional resources. Thus, by making it possible for banks in several countries to offer loan facilities at advantageous rates, the market has added immensely to the bank's ability to provide financing of their customers and to seek out new customers—with concomitant benefits to the international economy. It has contributed to the emergence of an international loan market in which some banks en-

croach on the domain of banks in other countries with favorable consequences for the cost of credit to commercial borrowers in Europe and
elsewhere.

Many commercial borrowers that draw on funds originating in Euro-
currency deposit markets show a preference for loans denominated in currencies whose interest rates are relatively low. These are primarily
currencies of low interest rate countries whose banks engage heavily in
international money market operations, i.e., banks that swap large portions
of their surplus funds into dollars and other foreign currencies or offer
directly deposits denominated in their own currencies to foreign deposit
markets. But such currencies also include at times those whose forward
rates reflect heavy "speculative" buying. These forward rates are then no
longer determined to any important extent by the demand of domestic arbitragers. As banks swap into currencies whose forward rates are at an intrinsic
premium they can offer loans in such currencies to commercial borrowers
at very attractive interest rates. Or they can offer low-cost deposits in such
currencies to banks abroad that will pass them on to their own commercial
customers. Actually, the Euro-currency market mechanism has thus performed the function of transferring to commercial borrowers some part of
the forward exchange rate premium paid by financial and commercial firms
for currencies that have attracted speculative interest.

For commercial borrowers to reap the advantage of the low interest
rate, they must be willing to carry the exchange rate risk. If they were to
cover forward their foreign-currency commitments, they would lose all, or
more than, the savings obtained from low-rate foreign-currency loans. In
actual practice, commercial borrowers typically do not cover forward liabilities arising from Euro-currency loans, including those denominated in
United States dollars. In fact, they frequently borrow various low-cost currencies, though they are in need of other currencies, which the lending bank
then acquire with the loan proceeds for the account of the borrower. A case
in point is the Italian banks, which at least until 1963 have swapped large
amounts of dollars into Swiss francs, Dutch guilders, and German marks
in order to extend low interest loans to domestic customers who used these
funds to acquire the currencies needed for the discharge of foreign trade
indebtedness. There is no doubt that the interest rate savings of "trader
speculators" on such foreign-currency borrowing have run into very impressive amounts. At the same time these operations have had a stabilizing
impact on forward exchange markets as the supply of forward dollars by
banks investing local currencies in the Euro-dollar market met the demand
for forward dollars of banks swapping dollars into foreign currencies which
are then employed for relatively low interest rate loans.

The emergence of foreign-currency deposit markets has contributed
materially to the interlinkage of national money markets. Ease or stringency in these national money and loan markets is now fairly quickly re-

flected in changes in the supply of, and demand for, funds in Euro-currency markets. Conversely, interest rate changes in Euro-currency markets as well as changes in forward exchange margins whether attributable to such interest rate changes or to other factors set into motion capital flows into and out of these markets. Actually, the Euro-currency deposit markets have become a medium through which in varying degree changing conditions in one national money market are transmitted to other national money markets. The foreign-currency deposit markets themselves are fully integrated. After allowance has been made for forward rates of the currencies involved, net yields of deposits with prime banks in the various sectors of the Euro-currency market exhibit very close co-variation, as one should expect in view of the lively arbitrage operations of major market participants. In these markets, interest and forward exchange rates react powerfully upon each other.

A significant relationship has at times been observed between United States Treasury bill rates and Euro-dollar rates. Recently the response of the Euro-dollar market to money market conditions in the United States appears to have become distinctly weaker—probably because credit conditions in several European countries now exert a stronger pull on Euro-dollar rates than in the past. Still, the co-movement of United States money market and Euro-dollar rates remains substantial. It is true that the degree of substitutability and interchangeability of funds between the United States money market and the Euro-dollar markets is relatively low; that is, a great many suppliers and users are unable or unwilling to switch placements or sources of funds in response to changes in rate differentials. But it is also true that a growing number of institutions are operating on a large scale simultaneously in the United States money market and the Euro-dollar markets, thereby increasing the confluence of rates and the fluidity between the two markets.

Among such market transactors, perhaps the most important are the Canadian chartered banks. They obtain balances denominated in United States dollars amounting to probably more than $3 billion from four distinct groups: (1) United States corporations and banks, (2) Canadian companies, including the Canadian affiliates of United States companies, (3) banks in London and on the Continent, and (4) customers and correspondent banks in the Caribbean and other Latin American countries, where some Canadian banks occupy an important role in local banking activities.

At the same time, as pointed out before, the Canadian banks place United States dollar balances in several diverse markets, notably the Street loan market in New York and the dollar-deposit markets in Europe. The Canadian banks have thus a foot in several sectors of the international money market. Their head offices, which control the far-flung international operations of their branches abroad, appear to operate with considerable flexibility as acceptors and suppliers. There are indications that they carefully scan rates in the various markets from which they draw and in which they place funds, and are ready to expand or curtail operations in different sectors as rate differentials change. Consequently, their operations appear to induce without much delay sizable equilibrating shifts of funds. This means that the Canadian banks exert an integrating effect on various markets for United States dollars and thus make a substantial contribution to the observed sympathetic movement of rates.

A similar function is performed by several United States banks through operations of their branches in European deposit markets. When rates for funds offered in London and various continental centers hover close to deposit rates quoted in the United States money market, at least some United States banks will instruct their branches to accept additional balances. Head-office decisions as to whether or not to draw on European markets depend primarily, of course, on the rates at which significant balances with convenient maturity dates can be obtained abroad relative to rates quoted here for various maturities of similar types of balances. Even if current rates in the Euro-dollar market are somewhat above New York rates, it may be profitable to draw on European centers, because balances placed by the branch in its head office are not subject to reserve requirements and Federal Deposit Insurance Corporation fees. Any widening of the differential, on the other hand, may induce the head offices to instruct their branches to place a larger proportion of newly accepted funds abroad and perhaps to curtail total takings in the market.

The Canadian and several major United States banks thus provide contact points between the United States and Euro-currency markets. So do a substantial number of United States and other international corporations that tend to increase or decrease their deposits in Canadian and on occasion in European banks in response to changing rate differentials between negotiable certificates of deposit and other United States money rates on the one hand and rates quoted in the dollar-deposit market on the other. Among investor groups showing some measure of rate sensitivity are also a few central banks. For instance, it has been observed that as rates in United States money markets reached levels that provided what these central banks considered a "reasonable" or "decent" return, they reduced their placements in the Euro-dollar market. There are also several foreign commercial banks that disburse their resources over a wide area and make marginal portfolio adjustments between holdings in the United States money and foreign-currency deposit markets.

It is thus apparent that there are quite a number of interlocking points between the United States money and European deposit markets. Taken together, they provide a satisfactory explanation for the measure of co-variation that exists between rates in these two markets.

More important perhaps are the monetary policy implications of the capital flows to which the co-variation must be attributed. These flows may be sizable enough to affect the position of the dollar in international exchange markets and to produce important changes in our balance-of-payments position. They provide additional evidence of a high degree of responsiveness of capital movements to interest rate variations. Monetary policy makers cannot afford to disregard this evidence.